Musicians
& Composers
of the 20th Century

Musicians & Composers
of the 20th Century

Volume 4

Gram Parsons—Igor Stravinsky

Editor

Alfred W. Cramer

Pomona College

SALEM PRESS

Pasadena, California   Hackensack, New Jersey

Editorial Director: Christina J. Moose
Developmental Editor: Jeffry Jensen
Acquisitions Editor: Mark Rehn
Manuscript Editor: Constance Pollock
Research Assistant: Keli Trousdale

Photograph Editor: Cynthia Breslin Beres
Production Editor: Andrea E. Miller
Page Design: James Hutson
Layout: William Zimmerman

Cover photo: Dolly Parton (Tom Hill/WireImage/Getty Images)

Library of Congress Cataloging-in-Publication Data

Musicians and composers of the 20th century / editor Alfred W. Cramer.
    p. cm.
Includes bibliographical references and index.
    ISBN 978-1-58765-512-8 (set : alk. paper) — ISBN 978-1-58765-513-5 (vol. 1 : alk. paper) —
ISBN 978-1-58765-514-2 (vol. 2 : alk. paper) — ISBN 978-1-58765-515-9 (vol. 3 : alk. paper) —
ISBN 978-1-58765-516-6 (vol. 4 : alk. paper) — ISBN 978-1-58765-517-3 (vol. 5 : alk. paper) —
1. Music—20th century—Bio-bibliography—Dictionaries. I. Cramer, Alfred William.
    ML105.M883 2009
    780.92′2—dc22
    [B]
                                               2009002980

First Printing

Contents

Key to Pronunciation. lxxiii
Complete List of Contents lxxv

Gram Parsons 1075
Arvo Pärt. 1077
Harry Partch. 1080
Dolly Parton 1082
Charley Patton. 1086
Les Paul 1088
Luciano Pavarotti 1091
Tom Paxton 1093
Carl Perkins 1095
Itzhak Perlman 1097
Oscar Peterson. 1100
Tom Petty 1103
Édith Piaf. 1105
Astor Piazzolla. 1109
Wilson Pickett 1112
Robert Plant 1114
Cole Porter 1118
Francis Poulenc 1121
Bud Powell. 1125
Pérez Prado 1129
Elvis Presley 1131
Sir André Previn. 1134
Leontyne Price. 1138
Charley Pride 1140
Prince. 1143
John Prine 1145
Professor Longhair 1147
Sergei Prokofiev 1149
Giacomo Puccini. 1153
Tito Puente 1157

Sergei Rachmaninoff 1161
Ma Rainey 1164
Bonnie Raitt 1166
Joey Ramone. 1169
Jean-Pierre Rampal 1172
Maurice Ravel 1174
Otis Redding. 1178
Jimmy Reed 1180
Lou Reed 1182
Steve Reich. 1185
Django Reinhardt 1188

Ottorino Respighi 1191
Silvestre Revueltas 1193
Sir Tim Rice 1196
Keith Richards. 1197
Jean Ritchie 1200
Tex Ritter. 1202
Max Roach 1205
Robbie Robertson 1209
Paul Robeson 1211
Smokey Robinson 1213
Jimmie Rodgers 1216
Richard Rodgers. 1220
Sonny Rollins 1225
Sigmund Romberg 1228
Linda Ronstadt 1231
Diana Ross 1233
Mstislav Rostropovich 1236
Nino Rota 1240
Miklós Rózsa. 1244
Artur Rubinstein 1248
Otis Rush. 1251
Tom Rush 1253
John Rutter. 1255
Frederic Rzewski 1258

Buffy Sainte-Marie 1261
Esa-Pekka Salonen 1263
Salt and Pepa 1266
Carl Sandburg. 1267
Pharoah Sanders 1270
Carlos Santana. 1272
Erik Satie. 1275
Pierre Schaeffer 1278
Artur Schnabel. 1281
Alfred Schnittke. 1284
Arnold Schoenberg 1287
Franz Schreker. 1291
Albert Schweitzer 1294
Gil Scott-Heron 1296
Aleksandr Scriabin 1298
Earl Scruggs 1301
Charles Seeger. 1303
Mike Seeger 1307
Peggy Seeger. 1309
Pete Seeger. 1311

Ruth Crawford Seeger 1315
Bob Seger. 1318
Andrés Segovia 1320
Rudolf Serkin 1323
Joseph Shabalala 1326
Tupac Shakur 1328
Ravi Shankar. 1331
Artie Shaw 1335
Wayne Shorter. 1337
Dmitri Shostakovich 1340
Jean Sibelius 1344
Beverly Sills 1348
Joseph "Run" Simmons 1351
Carly Simon 1353
Paul Simon. 1355
Nina Simone 1358
Frank Sinatra 1361
Grace Slick 1364
Bessie Smith 1366
Kate Smith 1369
Mamie Smith 1371
Michael W. Smith 1374
Patti Smith 1375

Snoop Dogg 1377
Sir Georg Solti 1379
Stephen Sondheim 1382
John Philip Sousa 1385
Phil Spector 1389
Bruce Springsteen 1391
Ralph Stanley 1394
Pops Staples 1396
Max Steiner 1398
Isaac Stern 1401
Cat Stevens. 1405
Rod Stewart 1407
William Grant Still 1409
Stephen Stills 1412
Sting 1415
Karlheinz Stockhausen 1418
Leopold Stokowski 1420
Mike Stoller 1423
Sly Stone 1426
George Strait. 1428
Richard Strauss 1430
Igor Stravinsky 1435

Key to Pronunciation

Many of the names of personages covered in *Musicians and Composers of the 20th Century* may be unfamiliar to students and general readers. For these unfamiliar names, guides to pronunciation have been provided upon first mention of the names in the text. These guidelines do not purport to achieve the subtleties of the languages in question but will offer readers a rough equivalent of how English speakers may approximate the proper pronunciation.

Vowel Sounds

Symbol	Spelled (Pronounced)
a	answer (AN-suhr), laugh (laf), sample (SAM-puhl), that (that)
ah	father (FAH-thur), hospital (HAHS-pih-tuhl)
aw	awful (AW-fuhl), caught (kawt)
ay	blaze (blayz), fade (fayd), waiter (WAYT-ur), weigh (way)
eh	bed (behd), head (hehd), said (sehd)
ee	believe (bee-LEEV), cedar (SEE-dur), leader (LEED-ur), liter (LEE-tur)
ew	boot (bewt), lose (lewz)
i	buy (bi), height (hit), lie (li), surprise (sur-PRIZ)
ih	bitter (BIH-tur), pill (pihl)
o	cotton (KO-tuhn), hot (hot)
oh	below (bee-LOH), coat (koht), note (noht), wholesome (HOHL-suhm)
oo	good (good), look (look)
ow	couch (kowch), how (how)
oy	boy (boy), coin (koyn)
uh	about (uh-BOWT), butter (BUH-tuhr), enough (ee-NUHF), other (UH-thur)

Consonant Sounds

Symbol	Spelled (Pronounced)
ch	beach (beech), chimp (chihmp)
g	beg (behg), disguise (dihs-GIZ), get (geht)
j	digit (DIH-juht), edge (ehj), jet (jeht)
k	cat (kat), kitten (KIH-tuhn), hex (hehks)
s	cellar (SEHL-ur), save (sayv), scent (sehnt)
sh	champagne (sham-PAYN), issue (IH-shew), shop (shop)
ur	birth (burth), disturb (dihs-TURB), earth (urth), letter (LEH-tur)
y	useful (YEWS-fuhl), young (yuhng)
z	business (BIHZ-nehs), zest (zehst)
zh	vision (VIH-zhuhn)

Complete List of Contents

Volume 1

Contents v
Publisher's Note vii
Editor's Introduction ix
Contributors xiii
Key to Pronunciation xix
Complete List of Contents xxi

Will Ackerman 1
Roy Acuff 2
John Adams 5
Cannonball Adderley 8
Toshiko Akiyoshi 11
Herb Alpert 13
Trey Anastasio 16
Laurie Anderson 18
Leroy Anderson 21
Marian Anderson 24
Dame Julie Andrews 28
Martha Argerich 32
Harold Arlen 34
Louis Armstrong 38
Eddy Arnold 42
Vladimir Ashkenazy 44
Chet Atkins 46
Hoyt Axton 49
Charles Aznavour 51

Milton Babbitt 54
Babyface 57
Burt Bacharach 60
Erykah Badu 63
Joan Baez 65
Samuel Barber 67
Daniel Barenboim 70
Ray Barretto 72
Béla Bartók 74
Count Basie 79
Amy Beach 83
Sidney Bechet 85
Beck 89
Jeff Beck 91
Sir Thomas Beecham 93
Bix Beiderbecke 96

Harry Belafonte 98
Tony Bennett 101
Alban Berg 104
Alan Bergman 107
Luciano Berio 109
Irving Berlin 114
Elmer Bernstein 118
Leonard Bernstein 120
Chuck Berry 123
Jussi Björling 126
Otis Blackwell 128
Rubén Blades 130
Eubie Blake 134
Art Blakey 136
Mary J. Blige 139
Kurtis Blow 141
Bono 142
Nadia Boulanger 145
Pierre Boulez 147
David Bowie 151
Jacques Brel 153
Benjamin Britten 155
Garth Brooks 159
Clifford Brown 161
James Brown 163
Roy Brown 166
Jackson Browne 168
Dave Brubeck 170
Jimmy Buffett 173
Johnny Burke 175
Solomon Burke 178
Gary Burton 180
Adolf Busch 182
Ferruccio Busoni 184
Paul Butterfield 188
David Byrne 190

John Cage 193
Sammy Cahn 196
Maria Callas 198
Glen Campbell 202
Mariah Carey 204
Wendy Carlos 206

Karen Carpenter 208
Benny Carter 210
Elliott Carter 213
Maybelle Carter. 216
Enrico Caruso. 219
Henri Casadesus 221
Pablo Casals. 223
Johnny Cash. 226
Ray Charles 230
Carlos Chávez 233
Maurice Chevalier 237
Charlie Christian 239
Chuck D 240
Kyung-Wha Chung. 242
Eric Clapton. 245
James Cleveland 248
Van Cliburn 251
Jimmy Cliff 253
Patsy Cline 255
Kurt Cobain 257
George M. Cohan. 260
Leonard Cohen 264
Nat King Cole. 267
Cy Coleman. 270
Ornette Coleman 272
Judy Collins 276
Phil Collins 278

Willie Colón. 281
John Coltrane 283
Sean Combs 287
Harry Connick, Jr. 290
Sam Cooke 292
Aaron Copland 294
Chick Corea 298
Elvis Costello 302
James Cotton 305
Sir Noël Coward 307
Henry Cowell 311
Bing Crosby 314
David Crosby 317
Andraé Crouch 320
George Crumb 322
Celia Cruz 325
Xavier Cugat 328

D. M. C. 332
Roger Daltrey 334
Hal David 336
Ray Davies 338
Miles Davis 341
Sammy Davis, Jr. 344
Claude Debussy 346
Sandy Denny 350
John Denver. 352

Volume 2

Contents xxxv
Key to Pronunciation xxxvii
Complete List of Contents. xxxix

Paul Desmond 355
Neil Diamond. 357
Bo Diddley 359
Marlene Dietrich 361
Willie Dixon. 363
Dr. Dre. 365
Charles Dodge 368
Arnold Dolmetsch 370
Eric Dolphy 372
Plácido Domingo 374
Fats Domino. 378
Thomas A. Dorsey 380
Lamont Dozier 383

Jacqueline du Pré 386
Bob Dylan 388

Steve Earle. 393
Fred Ebb 395
Duane Eddy 397
Danny Elfman. 399
Sir Edward Elgar 402
Duke Ellington 405
Cass Elliot 408
Missy Elliott. 410
Eminem 413
Brian Eno 416
Enya 419
Melissa Etheridge. 421
Bill Evans 423
Don and Phil Everly 426

Sammy Fain 430
Morton Feldman 432
Freddy Fender 434
Arthur Fiedler 437
Dorothy Fields 439
50 Cent 441
Dietrich Fischer-Dieskau 443
Ella Fitzgerald 446
Kirsten Flagstad 450
Lester Flatt 452
Béla Fleck 454
John Fogerty 456
Aretha Franklin 459
Lefty Frizzell 462
Blind Boy Fuller 464

Peter Gabriel 467
Sir James Galway 470
Jerry Garcia 472
Art Garfunkel 475
Judy Garland 477
Erroll Garner 481
Marvin Gaye 483
George Gershwin 486
Ira Gershwin 490
Stan Getz 492
Barry, Maurice, and Robin Gibb 495
Gilberto Gil 498
João Gilberto 501
Dizzy Gillespie 502
Philip Glass 507
Gerry Goffin 511
Jerry Goldsmith 513
Osvaldo Golijov 515
Benny Goodman 518
Dexter Gordon 521
Glenn Gould 524
Percy Aldridge Grainger 528
Grandmaster Flash 531
Amy Grant 533
Stéphane Grappelli 535
Adolph Green and Betty Comden 538
Al Green 541
Dave Grusin 543
Sofia Gubaidulina 546
Arlo Guthrie 550
Woody Guthrie 552
Buddy Guy 556

Merle Haggard 559
Bill Haley 562
Marvin Hamlisch 565
M. C. Hammer 567
Oscar Hammerstein II 569
Lionel Hampton 573
Herbie Hancock 577
W. C. Handy 580
Nikolaus Harnoncourt 583
Emmylou Harris 585
George Harrison 589
Lou Harrison 591
Deborah Harry 596
Lorenz Hart 598
Coleman Hawkins 600
Isaac Hayes 604
Jascha Heifetz 606
Fletcher Henderson 610
Jimi Hendrix 613
Victor Herbert 616
Bernard Herrmann 620
Paul Hindemith 624
Christopher Hogwood 628
Billie Holiday 630
Eddie and Brian Holland 634
Buddy Holly 637
Gustav Holst 639
Arthur Honegger 642
John Lee Hooker 645
Lightnin' Hopkins 648
Lena Horne 649
James Horner 652
Vladimir Horowitz 654
Son House 657
Howlin' Wolf 660
Alberta Hunter 663
Mississippi John Hurt 665
Chrissie Hynde 667

Ice Cube 670
Ice-T 672
Julio Iglesias 674
Burl Ives 677
Charles Ives 679

Janet Jackson 683
Mahalia Jackson 685
Michael Jackson 688
Sir Mick Jagger 691

James Jamerson 695
Elmore James 697
Etta James 700
Leoš Janáček 703
Bert Jansch 707

Keith Jarrett 708
Jay-Z 711
Blind Lemon Jefferson 713
Waylon Jennings 715
Joan Jett 718

Volume 3

Contents liii
Key to Pronunciation lv
Complete List of Contents lvii

Antônio Carlos Jobim 721
Billy Joel 723
Sir Elton John 727
Lonnie Johnson 729
Robert Johnson 732
Elvin Jones 735
George Jones 737
Hank Jones 740
Quincy Jones 744
Janis Joplin 747
Scott Joplin 749
Louis Jordan 752

John Kander 756
Herbert von Karajan 758
Jerome Kern 761
Aram Khachaturian 765
Ali Akbar Khan 768
Nusrat Fateh Ali Khan 770
Albert King 772
B. B. King 774
Carole King 777
Rahsaan Roland Kirk 780
Kitarō 782
Otto Klemperer 784
Zoltán Kodály 788
Kool DJ Herc 791
Erich Wolfgang Korngold 793
Serge Koussevitzky 796
Alison Krauss 798
Fritz Kreisler 800
Kris Kristofferson 803
Fela Kuti 805

Patti LaBelle 809
Wanda Landowska 811

K. D. Lang 814
Queen Latifah 817
Leadbelly 820
Peggy Lee 823
Michel Legrand 826
Lotte Lehmann 829
Tom Lehrer 831
Jerry Leiber 834
John Lennon 836
Gustav Leonhardt 840
Alan Jay Lerner 843
James Levine 846
Jerry Lee Lewis 848
John Lewis 851
György Ligeti 855
Gordon Lightfoot 859
Little Richard 861
LL Cool J 864
Sir Andrew Lloyd Webber 866
Frank Loesser 869
Frederick Loewe 872
Alan Lomax 875
Lyle Lovett 879
Alvin Lucier 881
Witold Lutosławski 884
Loretta Lynn 887

Yo-Yo Ma 891
Sir Paul McCartney 894
Bobby McFerrin 898
Roger McGuinn 901
Marian McPartland 903
Madonna 905
Gustav Mahler 907
Miriam Makeba 911
Henry Mancini 913
Bob Marley 917
Wynton Marsalis 920
Frank Martin 923
Sir George Martin 925

Bohuslav Martinů	927
Hugh Masekela	929
Johnny Mathis	932
Dave Matthews	934
Curtis Mayfield	936
Dame Nellie Melba	938
Lauritz Melchior	940
Memphis Minnie	943
Gian Carlo Menotti	945
Sir Yehudi Menuhin	948
Johnny Mercer	951
Ethel Merman	953
Robert Merrill	956
Olivier Messiaen	958
Pat Metheny	962
Darius Milhaud	964
Glenn Miller	967
Roger Miller	969
Ronnie Milsap	971
Charles Mingus	973
Joni Mitchell	977
Thelonious Monk	980
Bill Monroe	984
Wes Montgomery	987
Ennio Morricone	989
Jim Morrison	991
Van Morrison	994
Morrissey	997
Jelly Roll Morton	999
Anne-Sophie Mutter	1002

Conlon Nancarrow	1006
Milton Nascimento	1008
Fats Navarro	1011
Ricky Nelson	1013
Willie Nelson	1015
Aaron Neville	1019
Anthony Newley	1021
Alfred Newman	1023
Randy Newman	1026
Red Nichols	1029
Stevie Nicks	1031
Carl Nielsen	1033
Luigi Nono	1037
Jessye Norman	1039
Notorious B.I.G.	1041
Odetta	1044
David Oistrakh	1047
Mike Oldfield	1049
Pauline Oliveros	1052
Roy Orbison	1054
Carl Orff	1058
Johnny Otis	1060
Ignace Jan Paderewski	1063
Jimmy Page	1065
Eddie Palmieri	1067
Charlie Parker	1071

Volume 4

Contents	lxxi
Key to Pronunciation	lxxiii
Complete List of Contents	lxxv
Gram Parsons	1075
Arvo Pärt	1077
Harry Partch	1080
Dolly Parton	1082
Charley Patton	1086
Les Paul	1088
Luciano Pavarotti	1091
Tom Paxton	1093
Carl Perkins	1095
Itzhak Perlman	1097

Oscar Peterson	1100
Tom Petty	1103
Édith Piaf	1105
Astor Piazzolla	1109
Wilson Pickett	1112
Robert Plant	1114
Cole Porter	1118
Francis Poulenc	1121
Bud Powell	1125
Pérez Prado	1129
Elvis Presley	1131
Sir André Previn	1134
Leontyne Price	1138
Charley Pride	1140

Prince 1143	Erik Satie 1275
John Prine 1145	Pierre Schaeffer 1278
Professor Longhair 1147	Artur Schnabel. 1281
Sergei Prokofiev 1149	Alfred Schnittke 1284
Giacomo Puccini. 1153	Arnold Schoenberg 1287
Tito Puente 1157	Franz Schreker. 1291
	Albert Schweitzer 1294
Sergei Rachmaninoff 1161	Gil Scott-Heron 1296
Ma Rainey 1164	Aleksandr Scriabin 1298
Bonnie Raitt 1166	Earl Scruggs 1301
Joey Ramone 1169	Charles Seeger 1303
Jean-Pierre Rampal 1172	Mike Seeger 1307
Maurice Ravel 1174	Peggy Seeger 1309
Otis Redding 1178	Pete Seeger 1311
Jimmy Reed 1180	Ruth Crawford Seeger 1315
Lou Reed 1182	Bob Seger. 1318
Steve Reich 1185	Andrés Segovia 1320
Django Reinhardt 1188	Rudolf Serkin 1323
Ottorino Respighi 1191	Joseph Shabalala 1326
Silvestre Revueltas 1193	Tupac Shakur 1328
Sir Tim Rice 1196	Ravi Shankar. 1331
Keith Richards 1197	Artie Shaw 1335
Jean Ritchie 1200	Wayne Shorter 1337
Tex Ritter 1202	Dmitri Shostakovich 1340
Max Roach 1205	Jean Sibelius 1344
Robbie Robertson 1209	Beverly Sills 1348
Paul Robeson 1211	Joseph "Run" Simmons 1351
Smokey Robinson 1213	Carly Simon 1353
Jimmie Rodgers 1216	Paul Simon. 1355
Richard Rodgers 1220	Nina Simone 1358
Sonny Rollins 1225	Frank Sinatra 1361
Sigmund Romberg 1228	Grace Slick 1364
Linda Ronstadt 1231	Bessie Smith 1366
Diana Ross 1233	Kate Smith 1369
Mstislav Rostropovich 1236	Mamie Smith 1371
Nino Rota 1240	Michael W. Smith 1374
Miklós Rózsa. 1244	Patti Smith 1375
Artur Rubinstein 1248	Snoop Dogg 1377
Otis Rush. 1251	Sir Georg Solti 1379
Tom Rush 1253	Stephen Sondheim 1382
John Rutter 1255	John Philip Sousa 1385
Frederic Rzewski 1258	Phil Spector 1389
	Bruce Springsteen 1391
Buffy Sainte-Marie 1261	Ralph Stanley 1394
Esa-Pekka Salonen 1263	Pops Staples 1396
Salt and Pepa 1266	Max Steiner 1398
Carl Sandburg 1267	Isaac Stern 1401
Pharoah Sanders 1270	Cat Stevens. 1405
Carlos Santana. 1272	Rod Stewart 1407

William Grant Still 1409
Stephen Stills 1412
Sting 1415
Karlheinz Stockhausen 1418
Leopold Stokowski 1420

Mike Stoller 1423
Sly Stone 1426
George Strait 1428
Richard Strauss 1430
Igor Stravinsky 1435

Volume 5

Contents lxxxix
Key to Pronunciation xci
Complete List of Contents xciii

Billy Strayhorn. 1439
Barbra Streisand. 1441
Joe Strummer 1445
Jule Styne. 1446
Donna Summer 1449
Sun Ra 1451
Dame Joan Sutherland 1453
Shin'ichi Suzuki 1456
George Szell 1458
Joseph Szigeti 1461
Karol Szymanowski. 1463

Tōru Takemitsu 1467
Tan Dun 1471
Art Tatum 1473
Sir John Tavener. 1475
Cecil Taylor 1478
James Taylor. 1481
Renata Tebaldi. 1483
Sonny Terry 1486
Léon Theremin 1488
Michael Tilson Thomas. 1490
Virgil Thomson 1493
Dimitri Tiomkin 1496
Sir Michael Tippett 1499
Mel Tormé 1501
Arturo Toscanini 1503
Peter Tosh 1507
Pete Townshend. 1510
Merle Travis 1513
Ernest Tubb 1515
Big Joe Turner 1517
Tina Turner 1519
Jeff Tweedy 1522
Conway Twitty 1525
McCoy Tyner 1528

Umm Kulthum 1531

Ritchie Valens 1534
Vangelis 1536
Eddie Van Halen 1538
Jimmy Van Heusen 1541
Dave Van Ronk 1543
Townes Van Zandt 1545
Edgard Varèse. 1547
Sarah Vaughan 1551
Stevie Ray Vaughan. 1554
Ralph Vaughan Williams. 1556
Suzanne Vega 1560
Heitor Villa-Lobos 1562
Gene Vincent 1566

Tom Waits 1569
T-Bone Walker. 1571
Fats Waller 1573
Bruno Walter 1575
Sir William Walton 1578
Clara Ward. 1580
Dionne Warwick 1583
Dinah Washington 1585
Muddy Waters. 1587
Roger Waters 1591
Doc Watson 1593
André Watts 1597
Franz Waxman 1599
Jimmy Webb. 1601
Anton von Webern 1603
Ben Webster 1607
Kurt Weill 1609
August Wenzinger 1613
Paul Whiteman 1615
Hank Williams. 1618
John Williams 1620
Lucinda Williams 1624
Mary Lou Williams 1626
Sonny Boy Williamson I 1628

Sonny Boy Williamson II 1630
Meredith Willson 1633
Brian Wilson 1636
Jackie Wilson 1638
Julia Wolfe 1641
Stevie Wonder 1643
Tammy Wynette 1646

Iannis Xenakis 1649

Yanni 1653
Lester Young 1655
Neil Young 1658

Frank Zappa 1661
Hans Zimmer 1665

Appendixes
General Bibliography 1671
Glossary 1696
Chronological List of Musicians 1725
Electronic Resources 1733

Indexes
Category Index 1743
Geographical Index 1759
Personages and Groups Index 1767
Works Index 1779

Musicians
& Composers
of the 20th Century

Gram Parsons

American rock singer, guitarist, and songwriter

With his band the Flying Burrito Brothers, Parsons was a major figure in the emergence of country-rock.

Born: November 5, 1946; Winter Haven, Florida
Died: September 19, 1973; Yucca Valley, California
Also known as: Ingram Cecil Connor III (birth name)
Member of: International Submarine Band; the Byrds; the Flying Burrito Brothers

Principal recordings

ALBUMS (solo): *GP*, 1973; *Gram Parsons and the Shilos: The Early Years, 1963-1965*, 1979; *Live 1973*, 1981; *Another Side of This Life: The Lost Recordings of Gram Parsons, 1965-1966*, 2000; *Gram Parsons Archive, Vol. 1: Live at the Avalon Ballroom 1969*, 2007.

ALBUMS (with the Byrds): *Sweetheart of the Rodeo*, 1968.

ALBUMS (with Emmylou Harris): *Grievous Angel*, 1974.

ALBUMS (with the Flying Burrito Brothers): *The Gilded Palace of Sin*, 1969; *Burrito Deluxe*, 1970; *Sleepless Nights*, 1976.

ALBUMS (with the International Submarine Band): *Safe at Home*, 1967.

The Life

Ingram Cecil Connor III was born in Winter Haven, Florida, to a mother who was heir to a wealthy citrus grower and a father who suffered severe mood swings and later committed suicide. Parsons took the last name of his stepfather and even changed his name on his birth certificate. After seeing Elvis Presley in 1957, Parsons devoted himself to music and played in various bands. He went to Harvard, spending only a semester studying theology before he left to form the International Submarine Band.

After relocating to Los Angeles, Parsons was recruited by Chris Hillman to play with the Byrds, and Parsons strongly influenced the creation of what became the band's first country-influenced album, *Sweetheart of the Rodeo*. A disagreement over a concert in South Africa led to his departure from the band, though later he and Hillman reunited and launched the Flying Burrito Brothers. After two albums, Parsons departed again, developed a close relationship with Keith Richards of the Rolling Stones, and then embarked on a solo career that produced a pair of superlative albums.

Parsons's early death from an overdose and the grisly cremation of his body in the Joshua Tree National Monument by his road manager often overshadowed his considerable contribution to modern music.

The Music

Although *Safe at Home*, the International Submarine Band's only recording, includes "Luxury Liner," a Parsons song popularized by Emmylou Harris, Parsons did not come to any real public attention until he appeared with the Byrds on *Sweetheart of the Rodeo*, taking lead vocals on a few of the songs and contributing the standout cut "Hickory Wind" (which he recorded on a solo album six years later). Hired originally as a piano player, Parsons became the guiding force on the record.

The Gilded Palace of Sin. The debut of the Flying Burrito Brothers, *The Gilded Palace of Sin*, represented a heady fusion of rock, country, and soul. It featured inspired songwriting by Hillman and Parsons, audacious, beautiful arrangements, and original steel guitar playing by "Sneaky" Pete Kleinow, complete with swooping fills and fuzz-distorted solos. The band had no lead guitarist, so Kleinow assumed those duties and produced a sound never before heard in either traditional country or rock music. Songs such as "Christine's Tune," "Sin City," "Hot Burrito #1," and "Do You Know How It Feels?" reveal a rare depth of perception. Startling, yet surprisingly effective, are two cover versions of the soul classics "Do Right Woman" and "Dark End of the Street," which retain their soul roots but in the band's hands become neocountry in style.

Parsons and the Rolling Stones. During this period Parsons developed a near-symbiotic relationship with Keith Richards that resulted in the Flying Burrito Brothers' appearance at the Altamont Speedway Free Festival (a 1969 concert in

Gram Parsons. (Reuters/Landov)

California notorious for its disorganization and violent incidents) along with the Rolling Stones. Parsons inspired such countrified Rolling Stones tracks as "Country Honk," and it is rumored that Parsons did background vocals on "Sweet Virginia."

Parsons's consumption of alcohol and drugs escalated and led to erratic behavior and poor stage performances. By the time the band recorded its second album, *Burrito Deluxe*, Parsons was contributing little, and his distinct lack of energy and inspiration is palpably evident, though most remember the album for the cover of the Rolling Stones' "Wild Horses." The band immediately went back into the studio with plans to record a more traditional country album, and nine of those tracks can be found on *Sleepless Nights*.

GP. Discouraged by poor sales, a critical drubbing, and tensions in the band, Parsons embarked on a solo career and released *GP*, backed by a host of seasoned veterans from Presley's crack stage band. The album also features the debut of Emmylou Harris, whose duets with Parsons are inspired. Gone are the soul covers and the rock influ-

ences; Parsons gives himself over to pure country in six original compositions and covers of various country songs, one of the best of which is "Streets of Baltimore." While the arrangements are lively, the lyrics are often rueful, even dolorous, on songs such as "We'll Sweep Out the Ashes in the Morning" and "A Song for You." The most memorable tracks are "She," a song recorded by various other artists, and "The New Soft Shoe."

Grievous Angel. His second and last studio album was the posthumous *Grievous Angel*, another beautiful collaboration with Harris and members of the Presley band. Once again the disc combines original material with country standards, and tracks such as "Brass Buttons," "$1000 Wedding," "Ooh Las Vegas," and "In My Hour of Darkness" further confirm his reputation for brilliant songwriting. The result was another critical success.

After Parsons died, a few more recordings, of disparate quality, surfaced. *Gram Parsons and the Shilos: The Early Years, 1963-1965* features folk interpretations with his first band, the Shilos; *Another Side of This Life: The Lost Recordings of Gram Parsons, 1965-1966* presents demos and early acoustic versions of many songs. Two live recordings reveal his work with the Flying Burrito Brothers, *Gram Parsons Archive, Vol. 1: Live at the Avalon Ballroom 1969*, and his solo band, *Live 1973*.

Musical Legacy

Those who knew Parsons well have commented on the range of his musical tastes and his extraordinary knowledge of musical history. While many today regard him as a musical innovator and prescient in recognizing the viability of country music among rock aficionados, Parsons always referred to his work as Cosmic American Music.

Although his vocal range was limited, his singing was overwhelmingly evocative, often characterized by an aching, throbbing eloquence. His best songs offer a sense of brutal honesty, deeply felt emotion, and thorough conviction. Friends and bandmates were often appalled by his sloppy, unprofessional behavior, but many remarked on his fundamental decency and kindness. Parsons's influence on other artists is staggering, and an adequate testament to that influence can be seen in the various interpretations of his songs on the superb *Return of the Grievous Angel: A Tribute to Gram Parsons* (1999), with contributions from Harris, David Crosby, Sheryl Crow, Lucinda Williams, and others.

David W. Madden

Further Reading

Fong-Torres, Ben. *Hickory Wind: The Life and Times of Gram Parsons*. New York: Pocket Books, 1991. An early biography chronicles Parsons's background of privilege and family dysfunction and relies on interviews with key figures in the singer's life and career.

Hundley, Jessica, and Polly Parsons. *Grievous Angel: An Intimate Biography of Gram Parsons*. New York: Thunder's Mouth Press, 2005. A biography by a rock journalist and Parsons's daughter emphasizes his early Southern upbringing and features personal photographs, unpublished letters, and detailed interviews with friends and associates.

Kaufman, Phil, with Colin White. *Road Mangler Deluxe*. Glendale, Calif.: White-Boucke, 2005. Kaufman gives a detailed, if irreverent, account of his association with Parsons, paying particular attention to his fulfilling the singer's last wish that he be cremated in his favorite spot.

Meyer, Kevin N. *Twenty Thousand Roads: The Ballad of Gram Parsons and His Cosmic American Music*. New York: Villard Books, 2007. A comprehensive biography, with meticulous research and carefully documented interviews with all the major figures in Parsons's life and career.

See also: Everly, Don and Phil; Harris, Emmylou; McGuinn, Roger; Presley, Elvis; Richards, Keith.

Arvo Pärt

Estonian classical composer

Pärt's music, with its spiritual aspects and overt references to earlier styles, is classified as mystic minimalism.

Born: September 11, 1935; Paide, Estonia

Principal works

CHAMBER WORKS: *Collage über B-A-C-H*, 1964 (for oboe, strings, harpsichord, and piano); Wind Quintet, 1964; *Arbos*, 1977 (for seven flutes and three triangles); *Fratres*, 1977; *Spiegel im Spiegel*, 1978 (for violin or cello and piano); *Pari intervallo*, 1980 (for four flutes or organ); *Arbos*, 1986 (for brass and percussion; arrangement of flute work); *Psalom*, 1991 (for string quartet); *Summa*, 1991 (for string quartet; arrangement of choral work); *Mozart-Adagio*, 1992 (for violin, cello, and piano); *Passacaglia*, 2003 (for violin and piano).

CHORAL WORKS: *Meie Aed*, Op. 3, 1959 (*Our Garden*; cantata for children's chorus and orchestra); *Solfeggio*, 1964 (for chorus and string quartet); *Credo*, 1968 (for chorus, orchestra, and piano solo); *Cantate Domino Canticum Novum*, 1977 (for chorus and organ); *Missa Syllabica*, 1977 (for chorus and organ); *Sarah Was Ninety Years Old*, 1977 (for three voices, percussion, and organ); *Summa*, 1977; *De Profundis*, 1980 (for male chorus, percussion, and organ); *Passio Domini Nostri Jesu Christi Secundum Joannem*, 1982 (for soloists, chorus, ensemble, and organ); *An den Wassern zu Babel sassen wir und weinten*, 1984 (for chorus and organ or ensemble); *Stabat Mater*, 1985 (for chorus and string trio); *Te Deum*, 1985 (for three choruses, piano, strings, and tape); *Magnificat*, 1989; *Miserere*, 1989 (for soloists, chorus, ensemble, and organ); *The Beatitudes*, 1990 (for chorus and organ); *Beatus Petronius*, 1990 (for two choruses and two organs); *Bogoróditse Dyévo*, 1990 (*Hail Mary*); *Statuit ei Dominus*, 1990 (for two choruses and two organs); *And One of the Pharisees . . .*, 1992 (for three voices); *Berlin Mass*, 1992 (for chorus and organ or string orchestra); *Litany: Prayers of Saint John Chrysostom for Each Hour of the Day and Night*, 1994 (for soloists, chorus, and orchestra); *Dopo la vittoria*, 1997; *Kanon Pokajanen*, 1997; *Triodion*, 1998; *Cantique des degrés*, 1999 (for chorus and orchestra); *Cecilia, Vergine Romana*, 1999 (for chorus and orchestra); *Which Was the Son of . . .*, 2000; *Como anhela la cierva*, 2001 (for female chorus and orchestra; arrangement of vocal work); *Littlemore Tractus*, 2001 (for chorus and organ); *Nunc Dimittis*, 2001; *Anthem*, 2005.

ORCHESTRAL WORKS: *Nekrolog*, Op. 5, 1960; *Perpetuum Mobile*, Op. 10, 1963; Symphony No. 1, Op. 9, 1963; *Concerto Piccolo über B-A-C-H*, 1964 (for trumpet, string orchestra, harpsichord, and piano); *Pro et Contra*, 1966 (concerto for cello and orchestra); Symphony No. 2, 1966; Symphony No. 3, 1971; *Cantus in Memory of Benjamin Britten*, 1977 (for strings and bell); *Tabula Rasa*, 1977 (double concerto for strings and prepared piano); *Wenn Bach Bienen gezüchtet hätte*, 1984 (for piano, wind quintet, string orchestra, and percussion); *Festina Lente*, 1988 (for strings and harp); *Silouan's Song: My Soul Yearns After the Lord . . .*, 1991 (for strings); *Trisagion*, 1992 (for strings); *Darf ich . . .*, 1995 (for violin, tubular bells, and string orchestra); *Mein Weg hat Gipfel und Wellentäler*, 1998 (for strings and percussion; arrangement of organ work); *Orient and Occident*, 2000 (for strings); *Lamentate*, 2002 (for piano and orchestra).

ORGAN WORKS: *Trivium*, 1976; *Annum per Annum*, 1980; *Mein Weg hat Gipfel und Wellentäler*, 1989.

PIANO WORKS: Partita, Op. 2, 1959; *Two Sonatinas*, Op. 1, No. 1, 1959; *Für Alina*, 1976; *Variationen zur Gesundung von Arinuschka*, 1977; *Hymn to a Great City*, 1984 (for two pianos).

VOCAL WORKS: *Ein Wallfahrtslied*, 1984 (*Psalm 121*; for tenor or baritone and string quartet); *Es sang vor langen Jahren*, 1984 (for alto, violin, and viola); *Como anhela la cierva*, 1999 (for soprano and orchestra); *My Heart's in the Highlands*, 2000 (for voice and organ; based on Robert Burns's poem).

The Life

Arvo Pärt (AHR-voh pehrt) was born and grew up in Paide, Estonia, when the Soviet Union controlled the country. His parents separated when he was young, and he moved with his mother to the town of Rakvere, where he received his early musical training. In 1954 Pärt moved to Tallinn, the capital, to study at the Music Middle School (the equivalent of undergraduate work). After serving in the military for two years, he completed his course of study, and he was admitted to the Tallinn Conservatory in 1957.

Once he entered the conservatory, his curriculum expanded beyond music courses to include

such Soviet-mandated subjects as atheism and Communist history. Pärt worked as a recording engineer for Estonian radio during his student years. He also received commissions for film and theater music, and thus he had amassed a significant body of professional work by the time he completed his education.

While Estonia is more influenced by the West than other former Soviet states because of its location, Pärt grew up in the musical and political shadow of Moscow. In the 1970's, as he began to display a new and internationally acclaimed style, life in the Soviet Union became more difficult. Because his wife was Jewish, and the family was thus eligible for exit visas, Pärt and his family left Tallinn in 1980, ostensibly for Israel. They ended up in Vienna, where the composer Alfred Schnittke had arranged assistance for them. The following year, the family settled in Berlin.

The Music

Pärt's oeuvre traces many of the twentieth century's musical styles, including early works in a neoclassical idiom and later works in a serial style. In the 1970's, he developed a personal style based on the concept he called tintinnabuli—the ringing of bells. Fundamentally a two-voice style, tintinnabuli uses a melodic voice, which moves around a central pitch, and the tintinnabuli voice, which outlines the tonic triad. The tintinnabuli works, whose structure is predetermined by number or by textual outline, are rhythmically simple and do not change tempo.

Tintinnabuli developed out of a period of intense study after Pärt's piece *Credo* from 1968. *Credo*, with its overtly religious title and content, was a popular success and a lightning rod for the Soviet censors, and it was banned in the Soviet Union for ten years following its premiere (which was conducted by Neeme Järvi). After immersing himself in a study of early vocal music, Pärt exhibited the beginnings of a new style in Symphony No. 3. However, it was not until 1976 that Pärt's concept of tintinnabuli truly emerged in his music. Works from this period include *Cantus in Memory of Benjamin Britten, Fratres, Summa,* and *Tabula Rasa.*

Works from the 1980's on are mostly choral or chamber pieces, often with a religious or spiritual aspect. Notable is the *Passio Domini Nostri Jesu*

Christi Secundum Joannem, based on the gospel of John, a piece of enormous scale and drama, which is considered the pinnacle of the tintinnabuli style. In 1994 Pärt wrote *Litany: Prayers of Saint John Chrysostom for Each Hour of the Day and Night*, which uses a full orchestra for the first time since Symphony No. 3.

Credo. This work, for piano solo, chorus, and orchestra, is not the traditional liturgical Credo. The opening words are "Credo in Jesum Christum"; the rest of the text comes from the gospel of Matthew and sets two lines: "You have heard it said: an eye for an eye and a tooth for a tooth" and "But I say unto you: do not resist evil." The dialectic of the text—violence opposed to passive resistance, Old Testament and New—is reflected in the music, which moves from tonality to twelve-tone structure and back. The work is complex and shifts easily between styles. Notably, the tonal portions of the piece are represented by Johann Sebastian Bach, whose Prelude in C Major from *The Well-Tempered Clavier* (1722) is quoted and reworked.

This quotation frames the piece. While the middle section uses twelve-tone techniques, its row is built of perfect fifths. In spite of the serial techniques Pärt used, the work's essential harmonic movement is a familiar path from C to G, which is reinforced in the work's conclusion and which further echoes Bach's prelude.

Spiegel im Spiegel. This piece, whose title translates as "mirror in the mirror," follows the group of works that were collectively titled "tintinnabuli," and it offers a clear example of the techniques used in this style. For the first thirty-two measures, the piano (the tintinnabuli voice) outlines an F major triad in second inversion with occasional variations. The violin part is centered around A, and it creates a melody around that center by a simple process of adding notes. The tintinnabuli voice changes to accommodate the violin, echoing its adding pitches. The additive process of creating a melody, combined with the unchanging rhythm and tempo, make this work typical of tintinnabuli. *Spiegel im Spiegel* also exists in versions for cello, viola, clarinet, and horn.

Litany. In *Litany: Prayers of Saint John Chrysostom for Each Hour of the Day and Night*,

which is divided into two large sections of twelve prayers, each setting has a similar structure, though they vary greatly in length. While the tintinnabuli techniques are still in use, they are obscured in this work, partly by the size of the ensemble and partly by the stylistic moderations made by Pärt. While the work still uses the instrumental forces to highlight text or echo the melodic voices, the alternation between strings and winds blurs those distinctions.

Musical Legacy

Although Pärt has done little film scoring, his music has been used successfully in commercial films and documentaries around the world. *Cantus in Memory of Benjamin Britten* was used by Michael Moore in the film *Fahrenheit 9/11*. Pärt's music has also been extensively set by choreographers, in-

Arvo Pärt. (Belinsky Yuri/Itar-Tass/Landov)

cluding John Neumeier and the Pilobolus Dance Company.

Pärt's music is some of the most performed internationally. His work was featured in the Los Angeles Philharmonic's Minimalist Jukebox festival in 2006, and it was celebrated at the RTÉ Living Music Festival in Dublin in 2008. The relative simplicity of his music and its spiritual content make it popular with audiences.

Andrea Moore

Further Reading

Fisk, Josiah. "The New Simplicity: The Music of Górecki, Tavener, and Pärt." *Hudson Review* 47, no. 3 (Autumn, 1994): 394-412. This article places Pärt's work in historical context, linking it to New Age philosophy and to religious fundamentalism.

Hillier, Paul. *Arvo Pärt*. New York: Oxford University Press, 1997. This is an in-depth study of Pärt's work by conductor Hillier, who has been a champion of Pärt for many years.

Quinn, Peter. "Out with the Old and in with the New: Arvo Pärt's *Credo*." *Tempo*, New Series, no. 211 (January, 2000): 16-20. This is a sophisticated analysis of Pärt's transformative work, *Credo*.

Smith, Geoff. "An Interview with Arvo Pärt." *The Musical Times* 140, no. 1868 (Autumn, 1999): 19-22, 24-25. In this article, the composer discusses his compositional process from a personal perspective, with additional commentary from his wife, Nora Pärt.

See also: Britten, Benjamin; Schnittke, Alfred; Tavener, Sir John.

Harry Partch

American classical composer

Partch was notable for composing almost exclusively for instruments he designed and built and for employing unique melodic and harmonic ideas based upon the subdivision of the musical octave into microtonal intervals.

Born: June 24, 1901; Oakland, California
Died: September 3, 1974; San Diego, California

Principal works

CHAMBER WORK: *Castor and Pollux*, 1952.

ORCHESTRAL WORK: *And on the Seventh Day Petals Fell in Petaluma*, 1966.

PERFORMANCE WORKS (music, choreography, and libretto): *Oedipus*, 1952 (text by William Butler Yeats; based on the play by Sophocles); *The Bewitched*, 1957; *Windsong*, 1958 (revised as *Daphne of the Dunes*, 1967); *Revelation in the Courthouse Park*, 1961; *Delusion of the Fury: A Ritual Dream and Delusion*, 1969.

VOCAL WORKS: *Potion Scene from "Romeo and Juliet*," 1932, revised 1955 (text by William Shakespeare); *Seventeen Lyrics by Li Po*, 1932; *The Letter: A Depression Message from a Hobo Friend*, 1943; *Barstow: Eight Hitchhiker Inscriptions from a Highway Railing at Barstow, California*, 1944; *San Francisco: A Setting of the Cries of Two Newsboys on a Foggy Night in the Twenties*, 1944; *U.S. Highball: A Musical Account of a Transcontinental Hobo Trip*, 1944; *Yankee Doodle Fantasy*, 1944; *"I'm Very Happy to Be Able to Tell You About This . . .,"* 1945; *Two Settings from "Finnegan's Wake,"* 1945 (text by James Joyce); *Sonata Dementia*, 1949 (revised as *Ring Around the Moon*, 1950); *Even Wild Horses (Dance Music for an Absent Drama)*, 1953 (text from Arthur Rimbaud's *A Season in Hell*); *Water! Water!*, 1962.

WRITINGS OF INTEREST: *Bitter Music: Collected Journals, Essays, Introductions, and Librettos*, 1936; *Genesis of a Music: An Account of a Creative Work, Its Roots, and Its Fulfillment*, 1949.

The Life

Born in California to parents who had been missionaries in China, Harry Partch spent formative years in Arizona and New Mexico. As a teenager, he took an interest in music and theater, and while in high school he worked as an organist and pianist in a film theater in Albuquerque. After the death of his father in 1919, Partch moved with his mother to Los Angeles, where he briefly studied music at the University of Southern California. While performing and teaching piano in the following years, Partch often found work as a copy editor.

Partch moved frequently in his twenties and thirties while pursuing varied music projects. The award of a grant in 1934 allowed him to study in

Europe for six months. Returning to the United States, he worked as a transient laborer in the West for eight months, and then he settled in California. Beginning in 1941, Partch lived in several cities in the Eastern United States, supported by research grants and fees from his lectures and performances.

In the 1950's and early 1960's, Partch was associated with the University of Wisconsin and the University of Illinois, where most of his efforts were directed toward instrument-building and the creation of music to be performed at the schools. A series of recordings and documentary and experimental films were made during these years and later in California, where he lived from 1962 until his death in 1974.

The Music

Partch's career was in many respects unorthodox, largely because of the novelty of his ideas and the uncompromising ways he advanced them during a career lasting nearly half a century. His early training, though not extensive, seems to have made him a promising pianist. However, in 1923, his reading of *On the Sensations of Tone* (1863) by the German physicist Hermann von Helmholtz sparked his interest in the role of acoustics in music, and it led him to abandon the dominant tonal framework of equal temperament. Partch was convinced that this system of dividing the musical octave into twelve equal steps was a fundamental mistake for European music, one that had led to a loss of musical integrity.

Over the next three decades, Partch experimented in his compositions with alternative scales with varying numbers of notes, later settling on a scale of forty-three notes to the octave. His intonation schemes belong to the category known as just intonation, which, though hardly unknown, was little used in Western music. Partch also created the means of performing works composed in just intonation, and through the years he adapted existing instruments, he developed and built new instruments, and he trained musical collaborators in their use.

Seventeen Lyrics by Li Po. Among the composer's early works making use of an altered instrument—in this case, an adapted viola—are settings of verses by Li Po, a Chinese poet of the eighth cen-

tury. Like other Partch compositions, this was written over a period of years. The chronology of the composer's body of work is complex, with some compositions evolving over ten years or more and others being revised long after they were initially completed. Moreover, many works were not performed until years after their completion, with fewer still being recorded until Partch was much better established in the musical scene.

Barstow: Eight Hitchhiker Inscriptions from a Highway Railing in Barstow, California. A new phase of Partch's work began with this composition for baritone and adapted guitar. While hitchhiking in California's Mojave Desert in 1940, Partch had written down the humorous and wistful inscriptions he discovered on a highway railing, and the following year he composed the work over a period of five weeks. *Barstow: Eight Hitchhiker Inscriptions from a Highway Railing in Barstow, California* is among Partch's most accessible works, and it is cited as an excellent example of the composer's grasp of a specifically American cultural sensibility.

Oedipus. In 1934 Partch's wish to take up the theme of King Oedipus led him to visit the Irish poet William Butler Yeats to discuss the ancient Greek tragedy and to visually notate Yeats's voice reciting his translation of Sophocles' work. After many years of gestation, Partch's *Oedipus* was presented to sold-out audiences at Mills College in Oakland, California, in March, 1952. This opera-scaled work is a fusion of the composer's musical and theoretical ideas, and it also marks the full integration of his instrument-building activities with his theatrical ambitions.

Delusion of the Fury. A major work of Partch's final years, *Delusion of the Fury: A Ritual Dream and Delusion* was conceived in late 1964 as a two-act theater work, and it was composed during the next fifteen months. The scenario deals with human anger and reconciliation, with the first act being, in Partch's words, "intensely serious," and the second "highly farcical." The work's subtitle suggests Partch's goal of creating an intense form of ritual theater that bridges individual technical disciplines and his need to address profound issues of life, with its conflicts, ironies, and aspirations. *Delusion of the Fury* premiered with great critical success in early 1969 at the University of California, Los Angeles, and it was commercially recorded, bringing Partch a growing national and international audience.

Musical Legacy

Partch's approach to the fusion of music and theater is recognized as original and visionary, but his strictly musical influence has been constrained by the difficulty of authentically reproducing his work in performance, as Partch's original instruments are difficult to access and few reproductions have been made.

The acoustic, vocal, and compositional elements of Partch's musical style are so closely bound to his approach to intonation and microtonality that his work is likely to remain of limited appeal to most listeners. Nevertheless, successful performances of his work continue, and the integrity of Partch's artistic vision attracts interest in him as a cultural figure as well as a musician.

Clyde S. McConnell

Further Reading

Blackburn, Philip. *Enclosure 3: Harry Partch*. St. Paul, Minn.: American Composers Forum, 1997. This book is a compilation of material from the Harry Partch Archive, including manuscripts, concert programs, photographs, and notes by the composer.

Gilmore, Bob. *Harry Partch: A Biography*. New Haven, Conn.: Yale University Press, 1998. Comprehensive and readable, this biography is a scholarly work and also a kind of elegy for Partch's difficult life. A well-chosen selection of photographs provides essential impressions of Partch's instruments and environments.

McGeary, Thomas. *The Music of Harry Partch: A Descriptive Catalog*. Brooklyn, N.Y.: Institute for Studies in American Music, 1991. This documentary volume serves as an anthology and a guide, and it has several brief essays aimed at the nonspecialist reader.

Partch, Harry. *Genesis of a Music*. New York: Da Capo Press, 1972. This volume first appeared in 1949, the result of the composer's musical investigations and experiments dating back to the 1920's. Photographs, drawings, and diagrams reveal the depth and complexity of Partch's musical thought.

Ross, Alex. "Off the Rails: A Rare Performance of Harry Partch's *Oedipus.*" *The New Yorker* 81, no. 9 (April 18, 2005): 199-201. Ross, a sympathetic critic, writes that Partch's opera "is staggeringly strange, but also achingly beautiful."

See also: Berio, Luciano; Harrison, Lou; Ligeti, György; Milhaud, Darius; Oliveros, Pauline.

Dolly Parton
American country singer and songwriter

Parton helped to establish the popularity of the female singer-songwriter in country music, and she was instrumental in bridging the gap between country and pop music. Her gift for storytelling and the bluegrass and country folk elements she infuses into her music have created some of country music's classics.

Born: January 19, 1946; Rural Locust Ridge, Sevier County, Tennessee
Also known as: Dolly Rebecca Parton (full name)

Principal recordings

ALBUMS: *Hello, I'm Dolly*, 1967; *Just Because I'm a Woman*, 1968; *Just Between You and Me*, 1968 (with Porter Wagoner); *Always, Always*, 1969 (with Wagoner); *In the Good Old Days (When Times Were Bad)*, 1969; *Just Between the Two of Us*, 1969 (with Wagoner); *My Blue Ridge Mountain Boy*, 1969; *As Long as I Live*, 1970; *The Fairest of Them All*, 1970; *Once More*, 1970 (with Wagoner); *Coat of Many Colors*, 1971; *Golden Streets of Glory*, 1971; *Joshua*, 1971; *My Favorite Songwriter: Porter Wagoner*, 1972; *The Right Combination; Burning the Midnight Oil*, 1972 (with Wagoner); *Together Always*, 1972; *Touch Your Woman*, 1972; *Bubbling Over*, 1973; *Just the Way I Am*, 1973; *Love and Music*, 1973 (with Wagoner); *Mine*, 1973; *We Found It*, 1973 (with Wagoner); *Jolene*, 1974; *Porter 'n' Dolly*, 1974 (with Wagoner); *The Bargain Store*, 1975; *Love Is Like a Butterfly*, 1975; *My Tennessee Mountain Home*, 1975; *Say Forever You'll Be Mine*, 1975 (with Wagoner); *The Seeker; We Used To*, 1975;

All I Can Do, 1976; *Here You Come Again*, 1977; *New Harvest . . . First Gathering*, 1977; *Heartbreaker*, 1978; *Great Balls of Fire*, 1979; *Dolly Dolly Dolly*, 1980; *Nine to Five (and Other Odd Jobs)*, 1980; *The Best Little Whorehouse in Texas*, 1982; *Heartbreak Express*, 1982; *Kris, Willie, Dolly, and Brenda: The Winning Hand*, 1982 (with Kris Kristofferson, Willie Nelson, and Brenda Lee); *Burlap and Satin*, 1983; *The Great Pretender*, 1984; *Once upon a Christmas*, 1984 (with Kenny Rogers); *Real Love*, 1985; *Portrait*, 1986; *Think About Love*, 1986; *Trio*, 1987 (with Emmylou Harris and Linda Ronstadt); *Rainbow*, 1988; *White Limozeen*, 1989; *Home for Christmas*, 1990; *Eagle When She Flies*, 1991; *Straight Talk*, 1992; *Honky Tonk Angels*, 1993 (with Tammy Wynette and Loretta Lynn); *Slow Dancing with the Moon*, 1993; *I Will Always Love You*, 1996; *Treasures*, 1996; *Hungry Again*, 1998; *The Grass Is Blue*, 1999; *Trio II*, 1999 (with Harris and Ronstadt); *Little Sparrow*, 2001; *Halos and Horns*, 2002; *For God and Country*, 2003; *Those Were the Days*, 2005.

WRITINGS OF INTEREST: *Dolly: My Life and Other Unfinished Business*, 1994 (autobiography).

The Life

Dolly Rebecca Parton was the fourth of twelve children born to Robert Lee Parton and Avie Lee Owens. She was raised in a one-room cabin in Locust Ridge, Tennessee, located in the Great Smoky Mountains. Her family was poor, but music was a big part of her life from the beginning. Her mother played the guitar, and her grandfather was a fiddler and songwriter. She was also exposed to music at the Assembly of God church, where her grandfather was a preacher. When she was seven, Parton's uncle gave her a guitar, and within three years she was a regular on *The Cas Walker Farm and Home Hour* on WIVK television in Knoxville. When she was ten, she made her debut at the Grand Ole Opry, and in 1960 she recorded her first single, "Puppy Love," for Goldband Records.

After graduating from high school, where she played the snare drums in the marching band, Parton moved to Nashville to pursue a career as a singer and songwriter. At the Wishy Washy Laundromat in Nashville, she met Carl Dean, who ran an asphalt paving business. The two married on May 30, 1966, and they are still together, although they live separate lives. They have no children, although they helped raise several of Parton's younger siblings. The details of their marriage remain private, and little is known about their life together.

Parton's considerable success as a singer and a songwriter in both country and pop music was accompanied by a thriving career as an actress. She made numerous appearances on television variety and talk shows during the 1970's, and she had her own show, "Dolly," in 1976. She made her film debut in *Nine to Five* (1980) with Jane Fonda and Lily Tomlin. The film was a huge success, and it established her reputation as a major film star. She starred in other films, such as *The Best Little Whorehouse in Texas* (1982), *Rhinestone* (1984), and *Steel Magnolias* (1989) with Julia Roberts.

Along with her career as a singer, songwriter, and actress, Parton became a successful businesswoman. She founded a theme park, Dollywood, in Pigeon Forge, Tennessee, which helped to revive the area's economy. She also owns her own film and television production company, which has produced television shows such as *Buffy the Vampire Slayer* and films such as the popular *Father of the Bride* (1991, 1995) motion pictures.

Parton has shrewdly created and nurtured a public image that is immediately recognizable, with her tiny frame, large breasts, outsize blond wigs, exaggerated make-up, and flashy outfits. In spite of her penchant for publicity, she has managed to keep her private life out of the spotlight.

The Music

When Parton was fourteen years old, she signed with Mercury Records, but her first record, "It's Sure Gonna Hurt," was not a success, and she was dropped from the label. When she moved to Nashville after graduating from high school, she worked for a time with songwriter Bill Owens, and the two signed a contract with the publishing house Columbine Music. She also signed a contract with Monument Records, and she recorded several pop songs, which were not well received. Her first success as a songwriter came in 1966, when two songs she wrote with Owens, "Put It off Until Tomorrow" and "The Company You Keep," became Top 10 hits for Bill Phillips. In 1967 Parton had her own hit single, "Dumb Blonde," which attacked traditional female stereotypes, and it reached number twenty-four on the charts, followed by "Something Fishy," which reached number seventeen. Her first album, *Hello, I'm Dolly*, was released in 1967 on the Monument label.

These early hits brought Parton to the attention of established country star Porter Wagoner. He hired Parton to replace Norma Jean, his television partner, who left their show to get married. The show's fans at first were reluctant to approve of Parton, but soon they accepted her. Parton signed with Wagoner's label, RCA, and the two began a successful career as a duo, which lasted several years. Their first hit was Tom Paxton's "The Last Thing on My Mind" in 1968, and that same year they were named Vocal Group of the Year by the Country Music Association. Parton also recorded her first solo single with RCA that year, "Just Because I'm a Woman," which was a minor success.

Dolly Parton. (National Archives)

Early Hits. During this period, women had trouble establishing solo careers in country music, and Parton was no exception. Despite her success with Wagoner, she had difficulty finding an audience as a single act, and both Parton and Wagoner (because he had a large financial stake in her career) were frustrated by her lack of success. Finally, in 1970 Parton had her first solo hit with her version of "Mule Skinner Blues." Other solo hits followed, many of which have become American classics, such as "Joshua" (1971), the autobiographical "Coat of Many Colors," (1971), based on her childhood experience of coming to school with a homemade, patchwork coat, and "Jolene" (1974).

Tennessee Mountain Home. Parton stopped touring with Wagoner in 1974, but she appeared on his television show until 1976. This period, from the early to mid-1970's, was Parton's most creative musically. She was voted the Country Music Association's Female Vocalist of the Year in 1975 and 1976. In 1975 she recorded the album *My Tennessee Mountain Home*, containing perhaps her best and most personal work, a tribute to her childhood and a way of life that was fast disappearing.

After leaving Wagoner, Parton branched out from her country roots, writing and recording ballads such as "I Will Always Love You" (1974), which was about her breakup with Wagoner, pop songs such as "Here You Come Again" (1977), and even disco, with "Baby I'm Burning" (1978). Between 1974 and 1980, she had eight number-one records on the country charts.

New Harvest . . . First Gathering: The 1980's. Parton's first album after leaving Wagoner, *New Harvest . . . First Gathering*, featured "Light of a Clear Blue Morning," which reached number eleven on the charts. She followed it with *Here You Come Again*, a million-selling country-pop crossover effort. In 1978 she was named the Country Music Association's Entertainer of the Year, and by the early 1980's Parton was a superstar of both country and pop music.

Parton's career in the 1980's concentrated on commercial music, often in conjunction with her films, such as "Nine to Five" from the film of the same name. Between 1981 and 1985,

Parton had twelve Top 10 hits on the country charts and a number-one hit on the pop charts with her duet with Kenny Rogers, "Islands in the Stream." However, in 1986 Parton failed to have a Top 10 hit, and RCA did not renew her contract.

In 1987 Parton signed with Columbia Records, and she released a collaboration with Emmylou Harris and Linda Ronstadt, *Trio*, which met with great critical and popular success. The album was number one on the *Billboard* country albums chart for five weeks, it sold several million copies, and it won a Grammy Award for Best Country Vocal Performance—Duo or Group.

"I Will Always Love You": The 1990's. In 1992 Whitney Houston recorded Parton's "I Will Always Love You," as part of the sound track of the 1992 film *The Bodyguard*, and it became one of the most lucrative hits of her career, spending fourteen weeks at number one. Parton also recorded another collaboration album in 1993, with Loretta Lynn and Tammy Wynette, called *Honky Tonk Angels*.

By the mid-1990's, popular country music had welcomed a new generation of performers, and Parton had difficulty receiving radio air time. She took this opportunity to return to her musical roots, and she began writing and recording bluegrass music, which had always been close to her heart. In 1999 she released the album *The Grass Is Blue*, which was named Album of the Year by the International Bluegrass Music Association, and it won the Grammy Award for Best Bluegrass Album. She also recorded two more bluegrass albums, *Little Sparrow* and *Halos and Horns*.

Those Were the Days: The 2000's. In 2003 the tribute album *Just Because I'm a Woman: Songs of Dolly Parton* was released by Sugar Hill Records, featuring singers such as Norah Jones, Alison Kraus, and Shania Twain performing Parton's songs. At that time, Parton released *For God and Country*, a collection of patriotic and religious songs. In 2005 she released *Those Were the Days*, her interpretation of hits from the folk-rock era of the 1960's and 1970's, containing such iconic songs as "Imagine," "Where Do the Children Play?," and "Where Have All the Flowers Gone?"

Musical Legacy

Parton has had a powerful influence on country music, not only as one of the first female country su-

perstars but also as a pioneer in bringing country music into the mainstream of popular music. When she began her career, women in country music were rarely accepted in any role other than partner of a male singer in a duo. Although she began her career in partnership with Wagoner, she eventually established a career as a solo artist, and she became a successful female country artist, a successful pop singer, and one of the most recognized figures in the entertainment industry.

A shrewd businesswoman, Parton was one of the first artists to cross over from country to pop, and she was in large part responsible for the huge popularity of country music in the 1980's. She broke down the boundaries between the genres, and, with her poetic lyrics and distinctively expressive soprano voice, she introduced a new audience to country music.

Although best known for her pop hits, such as the hugely successful "I Will Always Love You," "Here You Come Again," and "Islands in the Stream," Parton's lasting musical legacy will surely rest with her reputation as one of America's best songwriters, and her traditional country songs, such as "Jolene" and "Coat of Many Colors," hold a place of honor in American musical heritage.

Mary Virginia Davis

Further Reading

James, Otis. *Dolly Parton: A Photo-Bio*. New York: Jove Books, 1983. Good biography with numerous black and white photographs.

Mahoney, Judith Pasternak. *Dolly Parton*. New York: Friedman-Fairfax, 1998. A book of photographs of Parton, with some biographical information.

Nash, Alanna. *Dolly, Updated Edition: The Biography*. New York: Cooper Square Press, 2002. This is a comprehensive biography of Parton (an updated version of Nash's 1978 biography, *Dolly Parton: The Early Years*).

Parton, Dolly. *Dolly: My Life and Other Unfinished Business*. New York: HarperCollins, 1994. Parton's autobiography chronicles her rags-to-riches life, but it does not offer any previously unrevealed details about her notoriously private life.

Parton, Willadeene. *Smoky Mountain Memories: Stories from the Hearts of the Parton Family*. Nashville, Tenn.: Thomas Nelson, 1996. A collection of stories about the Parton family by Parton's oldest sister, including rare family photographs.

See also: Atkins, Chet; Blackwell, Otis; Burke, Solomon; Cline, Patsy; Harris, Emmylou; Iglesias, Julio; Kristofferson, Kris; Lynn, Loretta; Nelson, Willie; Paxton, Tom; Perkins, Carl; Ritchie, Jean; Ronstadt, Linda; Stevens, Cat; Summer, Donna; Wynette, Tammy.

Charley Patton

American blues singer, guitarist, and songwriter

Patton is generally regarded as the father of the Mississippi Delta blues. His raspy, hollering vocal style, his unique and varied repertoire of songs, and his innovative percussive guitar playing influenced blues artists who followed.

Born: April, 1891; Edwards, Mississippi
Died: April 28, 1934; Indianola, Mississippi
Also known as: Elder J. J. Hadley; Masked Marvel; Reverend J. M. Gates

Principal recordings

ALBUMS: *King of the Delta Blues: The Music of Charley Patton*, 1991; *Founder of the Delta Blues: 1929-1934*, 1992.

SINGLES: "Banty Rooster Blues," 1929; "Down the Dirt Road Blues," 1929; "I'm Going Home," 1929; "It Won't Be Long," 1929; "Lord I'm Discouraged," 1929; "Mississippi Boweavil Blues," 1929; "Pea Vine Blues," 1929; "Pony Blues," 1929; "Prayer of Death," 1929 (as Elder J. J. Hadley); "Screamin' and Hollerin' the Blues," 1929 (as the Masked Marvel); "Shake It and Break It, but Don't Let It Fall," 1929; "A Spoonful Blues," 1929; "Tom Rushen Blues," 1929; "Elder Greene Blues," 1930; "Going to Move to Alabama," 1930; "Green River Blues," 1930; "Hammer Blues," 1930; "Heart like Railroad Steel," 1930; "High Water Everywhere, Parts I and II," 1930; "I Shall Not Be Moved," 1930; "Jesus Is a Dying-Bed Maker," 1930; "Magnolia Blues," 1930; "Mean Black Cat Blues," 1930; "Mean Black Moan," 1930; "Moon Going Down," 1930; "When Your Way Gets Dark," 1930; "Bird Nest Bound," 1931; "Circle Round the Moon," 1931; "Devil Sent the Rain," 1931; "Dry Well Blues," 1931; "Frankie and Albert," 1931; "Jim Lee Blues, Part I," 1931; "Some Happy Day," 1931; "Some of These Days I'll Be Gone," 1931; "Some Summer Day, Part I," 1931; "You're Going to Need Somebody When You Die," 1931; "Jim Lee Blues, Part II," 1932; "Joe Kirby," 1932; "High Sheriff Blues," 1934; "Jersey Bull Blues," 1934; "Love My Stuff," 1934; "Oh Death," 1934 (with Bertha Lee); "Poor Me," 1934; "Stone Pony Blues," 1934; "Thirty-four Blues," 1934; "Troubled 'bout My Mother," 1934 (with Bertha Lee); "Hang It on the Wall," 1935; "Revenue Man Blues," 1935.

The Life

Charley Patton fit the stereotype of the colorful, itinerant, rakish blues musician of the 1920's. Though married at least six or eight times, and famous for his hot temper and heavy drinking, Patton was a natural, self-taught musical genius. He was a master of many styles of music, and he was also the ultimate entertainer. Nevertheless, Patton was an elusive and mysterious figure. There is only one known Patton photograph. His recording career spanned just five years and fifty-two songs. On those, his lyrics are often illogical or slurred. Patton knew almost every blues musician of his day, and he inexorably influenced all with whom he came in contact.

Patton was a small man, about five feet five inches, and 135 pounds. Though labeled Negro by the classification of the Jim Crow South, he had one Caucasian grandfather and one Native American grandmother. Patton's father moved his large family to work on the Dockey cotton plantation, a large tract of forty square miles that was almost its own self-contained town, and Patton would often return to the area between jaunts for much of his life. The family was not typically poor, however, and Patton likely started learning guitar when he was seven years old. He was talented, and by his early teens he was playing professionally. By the 1920's he was making a good living as a traveling musician of some notoriety.

Patton had no opportunity to record until 1929, when he met H. C. Speir, a record store owner in Jackson, Mississippi, and talent scout for labels looking for artists for "race" records targeted at African American audiences. His first songs sold well—within a year he became the largest-selling blues artist—and twenty-six more were recorded in Grafton, Wisconsin, for Paramount, which specialized in jazz and blues in the 1930's. These songs established Patton's reputation as a recording artist rather than just a live performer. However, the Depression, personal demons, and at least one stint in jail kept Patton from recording again until 1934. These later ten recordings for Vocation/Brunswick in New York betrayed a tired and ill Patton, his singing suffering from having his throat cut during a bar fight in 1933 in Holly Ridge, Mississippi (some say by his wife at the time, Bertha Lee). He died a few months later from heart disease.

The Music

"Pony Blues." Patton recorded his first sides in Richmond, Indiana, on June 14, 1929, for Paramont, and this session was his best work. "Pony Blues," his first recorded song, became a signature piece and the most frequently requested number at live performances. It was also his best-selling record. The most outstanding characteristic of this song was the irrationality of the text. The first and third stanzas talk about horses, but other lyrics deal with such varied themes as trains, depression, and marriage. Such disconnects, while hardly uncommon in the blues, are often elevated to a fine art in Patton's music.

"Down the Dirt Road Blues." A second tune from this session, "Down the Dirt Road Blues," is perhaps Patton's masterpiece. It tells of his frustration with life in the South on the plantation. This song also shows the difficulty of interpreting the Patton canon. Researchers have long debated the contents of the first line of the song. Many say it is "I'm going away to a world unknown," reflecting the doubt and uncertainty of life for African Americans in the rural South. Others say it is "I'm going away to Illinois," reflecting the exodus of African Americans to Chicago during the Depression. Regardless, Patton revived the tune as "Thirty-four Blues" during his last recording session, making it

more personal, by mocking a foreman on the Dockey plantation who fired him after Patton stole another man's wife.

"Screamin' and Hollerin' the Blues." Paramont decided that releasing thirteen songs from the same artist at once was not a prudent marketing strategy, so it attributed this song to the Masked Marvel and offered a prize to anyone who could identify the singer. This newspaper campaign apparently was successful. The song, another trademark piece, was played in Patton's favored Spanish tuning (the guitar tuned to an open G-chord, making certain patterns easier to play and allowing for some strings to drone in the background). The song is noted for Patton's typical rhythmic complexity, surprising variations, and shifting accent patterns.

"High Water Everywhere, Parts I and II." In April and May of 1927 was the worst flooding of the Mississippi River in modern history. Perhaps as many as five hundred people died as the waters ravaged seven states. Unlike the dozens of other blues artists who sang about the flood, Patton sang from personal experience. As a witness, Patton painted pictures with his voice of lost property and lost hopes in poignant and vivid terms.

Musical Legacy

Patton had an inestimable impact on the development of the blues. He directly influenced such blues icons as Robert Johnson, Howlin' Wolf, Son House, and Lightin' Hopkins. It was not that other musicians covered his songs or imitated his style (an almost impossible task). Rather, Patton offered fresh instrumental and vocal ideas. A seminal showman, Patton was a source of inspiration to other blues artists who sought his popularity, his success, and his lifestyle. Generations later, Bob Dylan sang "High Water (For Charley Patton)" on his 2001 album *Love and Theft*.

James Stanlaw

Further Reading

Calt, Stephen, and Gayle Dean Wardlow. *King of the Delta Blues: The Life and Music of Charlie Patton.* Newton, N.J.: Rock Chapel Press, 1988. A detailed biography by authors who state that Patton was solely responsible for the birth of the Delta blues.

Davis, Francis. *The History of the Blues: The Roots, the Music, the People, from Charley Patton to Robert Cray*. New York: Hyperion, 1995. Overview of blues history, with discussion of Patton's life, times, and music.

Evans, David. *Big Road Blues: Tradition and Creativity in the Folk Blues*. New York: Da Capo Press, 1988. Covers dozens of early blues artists, placing Patton and his music in a broader context.

Fahey, John. *Charley Patton*. London: Studio Vista, 1970. An in-depth musicological analysis of Patton's songs by the late, famous American guitarist.

Shadwick, Keith. *The Encyclopedia of Jazz and Blues*. London: Quantum, 2007. A reference work on more than three hundred blues artists, with a two-page sidebar on Patton.

Titon, Jeff Todd. *Early Downhome Blues: A Musical and Cultural Analysis*. 2d ed. Chapel Hill: University of North Carolina Press, 1994. A detailed social, cultural, and musical commentary on early blues, with a discussion of how blues changed African American society when commercial recordings became available.

See also: Dylan, Bob; Hooker, John Lee; Hopkins, Lightnin'; House, Son; Howlin' Wolf; Johnson, Robert; Staples, Pops; Turner, Big Joe.

Les Paul

American jazz and swing songwriter and guitarist

Paul invented one of the earliest solid-body electric guitars in 1941, and the Gibson Les Paul remains one of the most played and copied electric guitars. He is widely credited as the inventor of multitrack recording and of such recording techniques as overdubbing, reverb effects, sound-on-sound recording, close miking, and echo and delay sound effects.

Born: June 9, 1915; Waukesha, Wisconsin
Also known as: Lester William Polfus (birth name); Red Hot Red; Rhubarb Red
Member of: Les Paul and His Trio

Principal recordings

ALBUMS (solo): *Les Paul Now!*, 1968; *The Guitar Artistry of Les Paul*, 1971; *Chester and Lester*, 1977 (with Chet Atkins); *Guitar Monsters*, 1978 (with Atkins); *Multi Trackin'*, 1979; *California Melodies*, 2003 (Les Paul and His Trio); *Les Paul and Friends: American Made World Played*, 2005 (with others).

ALBUMS (with Mary Ford): *Hawaiian Paradise*, 1949; *The New Sound*, 1950; *Les Paul's New Sound, Vol. 2*, 1951; *Bye Bye Blues!*, 1952; *The Hit Makers!*, 1953; *Les and Mary*, 1955; *Time to Dream*, 1957; *Lover's Luau*, 1959; *Bouquet of Roses*, 1962; *Warm and Wonderful*, 1962; *Swingin' South*, 1963; *Fabulous Les Paul and Mary Ford*, 1965.

The Life

Les Paul was born Lester William Polfus on June 9, 1915, in Waukesha, Wisconsin. Paul's interest in music began when he took up the harmonica at age eight, but he received little formal music training. He learned to play the guitar and harmonica by listening to Pie Plant Pete on Chicago's WLS radio broadcasts. Appearing as Red Hot Red, Paul performed around his hometown. At age seventeen, Paul played guitar with Rube Tronson's Cowboys and then dropped out of high school to join Wolverton's Radio Band in St. Louis on KMOX with his friend and fellow guitarist Sunny Joe.

Sunny Joe and Paul appeared briefly on KWTO radio in Springfield, Missouri, before moving to Chicago's WBBM radio in 1934. Paul continued playing country music as Rhubarb Red (a name given to him by Sunny Joe) on WJJD radio and playing jazz as Les Paul on WIND radio. Paul's first records in 1936 were issued on the Montgomery Ward label, with him performing as Rhubarb Red.

In 1937 Paul married Virginia Webb, and he formed a trio with Jimmy Atkins and Ernie Newton. In 1938 the trio moved to New York and landed a featured spot with Fred Waring's Pennsylvanians, which gave Paul nationwide exposure on its broadcasts. In 1941 Paul built his first solid-body electric guitar, and he continued to make refinements to his prototype throughout the 1940's. His job with Fred Waring's Pennsylvanians ended in 1941, shortly after he was nearly electrocuted in an accident during a jam session in his basement. After a long recovery period, Paul moved to Hollywood in 1943, and he took a job as a staff musician at NBC. Later in 1943, Paul was drafted into the Army, and he served in Hollywood as a regular player on the Armed Forces Radio Service. In 1944 Paul was discharged for medical reasons.

Paul's career as a musician nearly came to an end in 1948, when a near-fatal car accident in Oklahoma shattered his right arm and elbow. However, he instructed the surgeons to set his arm at an angle that would allow him to cradle and pick the guitar. After his recovery, Paul and singer and guitarist Colleen Summers (also known as Mary Ford) recorded many hits together, which are among the earliest multitracked pop songs. After Paul's divorce from Webb, he and Ford married; they later had a son and adopted a daughter. In 1952 Paul and Ford performed for the Queen of England. Between 1953 and 1960, Paul and Ford produced their own hit television show, *The Les Paul and Mary Ford at Home Show*.

Although the hits stopped coming suddenly in the mid-1950's, Paul and Ford continued recording for Columbia Records from 1958 to 1963. Paul and Ford divorced in 1964, and Paul went into semiretirement in the mid-1960's.

Paul returned to performing in 1974, recording a Grammy Award-winning album called *Chester and Lester* with Chet Atkins that was released in 1976. A television documentary in 1980, *The Wizard of Waukesha*, charted his life and revived interest in his career. Between 1984 and 1995, he played weekly at Fat Tuesday's in New York City, and he began giving weekly performances at New York's Iridium Jazz Club in 1996.

The Music

Paul's output includes numerous recordings as a brilliant guitarist in country, jazz, and popular styles, and he was exposed to a wide audience through national radio programs. While his most famous recordings were multilayered hits for the popular music market during the 1950's, his overall recorded output shows his mixture of country and jazz styles with a fluid technique. Paul's musical

Les Paul. (CBS/Landov)

language and personality includes a hard-swinging jazz style, extremely rapid runs, humorous effects, fluttered and repeated single notes, and sensitive rhythm accompaniments. His contribution to popular music often is centered upon his pioneering work on multitracking and solid-bodied guitars. His equally impressive abilities as a performer and arranger are evident in his numerous recordings.

Blues. Paul's performance at the inaugural Jazz at the Philharmonic concert in Los Angeles on July 2, 1944, is recorded on Verve's *Jazz at the Philharmonic: The First Concert*. In this performance, Paul's witty chase sequence with Cole on "Blues" and his solo playing demonstrate his imaginative melodies and fluid technique. This performance from 1944 shows his early prowess as a jazz player.

"It's Been a Long, Long Time." Paul's association with Bing Crosby at NBC led to this recording on Decca Records, featuring Crosby and Les Paul and His Trio. Paul and Crosby's new arrangement of "It's Been a Long, Long Time" was a number-one hit in the United States and a popular recording with Americans returning from the war overseas. Paul's sensitive accompaniment to Crosby's singing and his extended solo on this recording foreshadow his style in many of the hits Paul would later have with Ford.

The New Sound. With Crosby's encouragement, Paul began extensive work on creating new recording equipment and techniques. *The New Sound* showcases the new close miking and sound-on-sound disc recording techniques. Paul performed all the parts on this recording, and he acted as arranger, recording engineer, and producer at the same time. *The New Sound* included two big hits for Paul. "Lover" featured eight guitar parts, several parts recorded at half-speed, then played at normal speed to produce fast lines. "Brazil" includes six guitar parts, all played by Paul. The sound-on-sound techniques used in this recording led to Paul's experiments with multitrack tape recordings. Later, in 1957, Ampex built the revolutionary eight-track tape recorders designed by Paul.

"How High the Moon." Paul and Ford had their first number-one hit single with "How High the Moon" in March of 1951. Paul created the recording using twelve overdubbed tracks of Ford's voice and his guitar. The resulting sound included Ford harmonizing with herself and a driving rhythm guitar accompaniment. "How High the Moon" was the first of twenty-eight hit recordings for Les Paul and Mary Ford from 1950 to 1957. Although Paul and Ford continued to record during the late 1950's and early 1960's, popular music became dominated by the new rock-and-roll sound.

Chester and Lester. *Chester and Lester* is among Paul's most successful recordings since his semiretirement in the mid-1960's, and in it Paul and country-great Atkins blend country and jazz improvisation styles. The individual musical personalities of Atkins and Paul are complementary in their performances of jazz standards and of several of Paul's previous hit tunes, including "It's Been a Long, Long Time." Atkins and Paul were given a Grammy Award in 1977 for *Chester and Lester*.

Les Paul and Friends: American Made World Played. This album was recorded in honor of Paul's ninetieth birthday, and it is a musical celebration of his life and of the Gibson Les Paul guitar. This recording features performances by many well-known guitarists, including Sting, Eric Clapton, Peter Frampton, Jeff Beck, and Steve Miller. Paul received two Grammy Award nominations for *Les Paul and Friends: American Made World Played*.

Musical Legacy

In 2003 *Rolling Stone* named Paul the forty-sixth best guitarist of all time. He was inducted into the Rock and Roll Hall of Fame in 1988, and he received the Emmy Lifetime Achievement award in 2004. In 2005 he was inducted into the National Inventors Hall of Fame for his development of electric guitars, and in 2006 he was inducted into National Broadcasters Hall of Fame. He was nominated for two Grammy Awards for his album *Les Paul and Friends: American Made World Played*, and he has received five Grammy Awards (three for instrumental albums, one technical award, and one for lifetime achievement). In 2007 he was awarded the National Medal of Arts.

Paul's musical contribution is apparent in modern recording techniques and modern electric guitars. Revered guitarists in country music (Chet Atkins), in jazz (George Benson, Stanley Jordan), in blues (B. B. King), and in rock styles (Keith Richards, Paul McCartney, Eric Clapton, Jeff Beck) cite Paul as a major influence on their playing and their equipment. While recording equipment has changed since his inventions, Paul's multitrack recording concept paved the way for modern recording technology.

David Steffens

Further Reading

Bacon, Tony. *Fifty Years of the Gibson Les Paul*. San Francisco: Backbeat Books, 2002. This book includes a detailed history of the Les Paul electric guitar, from 1952 to 2002. The reference section includes model identification charts, model chronology, and a dating methods guide.

Bacon, Tony, Les Paul, and Paul Day. *The Gibson Les Paul Book: A Complete History of Les Paul Guitars*. San Francisco: GPI Books, 1993. This book presents a detailed history of the designs of the many different models of Gibson Les Paul guitars produced. The reference section includes model identification charts, model chronology, and a dating methods guide.

Lawrence, Robb. *The Early Years of the Les Paul Legacy, 1915-1963*. New York: Hal Leonard, 2008. Chapter one includes a detailed description of Paul's contributions to recording and performance. Chapters two through nine provide a detailed description of the many Gibson early solid-body electric guitars and the Les Paul model guitars produced between 1952 and 1963.

Ratliff, Ben. "Celebrating a Birthday on His Own Terms." *The New York Times*, June 21, 2005. This is a brief review of Paul's Carnegie Hall performance during the 2005 JVC Jazz Festival.

Shaughnessy, Mary Alice. *Les Paul: An American Original*. New York: William Morrow, 1993. This detailed biography of Paul includes an extensive bibliography and a discography.

Waksman, Steve. *Instruments of Desire: The Electric Guitar and the Shaping of Musical Experience*. Cambridge, Mass.: Harvard University Press, 1999. This book chronicles the history and the development of the electric guitar and how its use shaped the course of popular music. The author traces two competing sound ideals: one with a focus on tonal purity (favored by Paul, Atkins, and Wes Montgomery) and the other centering on a distorted sound (used by Jimi Hendrix and Jimmy Page). Chapter two, "Pure Tones and Solid Bodies: Les Paul's New Sound," includes a detailed discussion of Paul's place in the development of the electric guitar.

See also: Atkins, Chet; Beck, Jeff; Clapton, Eric; King, B. B.; Loesser, Frank; Page, Jimmy; Sting; Van Halen, Eddie; Watson, Doc.

Luciano Pavarotti

Italian classical and opera singer

A celebrated tenor, Pavarotti had leading roles in Italian operas. With his wide-ranging appeal, he introduced opera, through recordings and live television performances, to millions of people with little previous exposure to opera.

Born: October 12, 1935; Modena, Italy
Died: September 6, 2007; Modena, Italy

Also known as: King of the High C's
Member of: Three Tenors

Principal works

OPERATIC ROLES: Rodolfo in Giacomo Puccini's *La Bohème*, 1961; Edgardo in Gaetano Donizetti's *Lucia di Lammermoor*, 1965; Tebaldo in Vincenzo Bellini's *I Capuleti e I Montecchi*, 1966; Tonio in Donizetti's *La Fille du Régiment*, 1966; Duke of Mantua in Giuseppe Verdi's *Rigoletto*, 1971; Arturo in Bellini's *I puritani*, 1973 (*The Puritan*); Alfredo in Verdi's *La Traviata*, 1978; Rodolfo in Verdi's *Luisa Miller*, 1978; Mario Cavaradossi in Puccini's *Tosca*, 1978; Gustavus III in Verdi's *Un ballo in maschera*, 1982 (*A Masked Ball*); Ernani in Verdi's *Ernani*, 1983; Italian Singer in Richard Strauss's *Der Rosenkavalier*, 1986; Manrico in Verdi's *Il trovatore*, 1988; Radames in Verdi's *Aida*, 1989; Nemorino in Donizetti's *L'elisir d'amore*, 1990; Rodolfo in Verdi's *Luisa Miller*, 1991; Des Grieux in Jules Massenet's *Manon*, 1993; Calàf in Puccini's *Turnadot*, 1997.

Principal recordings

ALBUMS (solo): *Arias*, 1990; *Luciano Pavarotti*, 1990; *Amore: Romantic Italian Love Songs*, 1992; *Ti Amo: Puccini's Greatest Love Songs*, 1993; *Luciano Pavarotti—Nessun Dorma (Arias and Duets)*, 2001; *Ti Adoro*, 2003.

ALBUMS (with the Three Tenors): *Carreras, Domingo, Pavarotti: The Three Tenors in Concert*, 1990; *The Three Tenors*, 1997; *The Three Tenors Christmas*, 2000; *Romantic Arias*, 2002; *Romantic Tenors*, 2002.

The Life

Luciano Pavarotti (lew-CHYAH-noh pah-vah-ROHT-tee) was born to Fernando and Adele Pavarotti. Fernando was a baker in his native Modena and an accomplished tenor. Well into his eighties, Fernando was still hired by locals to sing at weddings, funerals, and other milestone events. Adele was fully supportive of her son's development as an operatic tenor. Nevertheless, his parents, realizing the uncertainties of pursuing an operatic career, encouraged their son, following his graduation from secondary school, to enter Modena's teacher-training institution to earn a teaching license. At age twenty, teaching license in hand, he taught for two years in a local elementary school. Pavarotti's ability to acquaint audiences new to opera about the medium was perhaps attributable to his early training as a teacher.

Despite his meteoric rise to prominence, the genial Pavarotti was unfailingly patient and polite throughout his career. It was his personality as well as his extraordinary voice that drew people, even those with little previous exposure to opera, to his concerts. When he lost his battle with pancreatic cancer in 2007, the world mourned his death.

The Music

Teaching in a Modena elementary school from 1955 until 1957, Pavarotti continued the voice training that he had pursued since he was four, commuting regularly to nearby Mantua for instruction in singing. This training helped him to learn operatic roles and to develop and preserve his voice. Many

Luciano Pavarotti. (AP/Wide World Photos)

tenors strain their voices so that their careers are shortened, but Pavarotti's voice remained strong from the 1960's through the 1980's, although his high notes began to waver in the 1990's. Illness forced his retirement in 2004. His upper range won him the nickname the King of the High C's.

La Bohème. Pavarotti's operatic career began in earnest when, as a result of his winning the Concorso Internationale in 1961, he was cast as Rodolfo in Giacomo Puccini's *La Bohème* at the Teatro Municipale in Reggio, Emilia. He again performed this role in his operatic debut at London's Covent Garden two years later, then in his debuts at the San Francisco Opera Company in 1967 and at the Metropolitan Opera in New York the following year.

Bringing Opera to the Masses. Some critics have complained that Pavarotti confined his operatic singing to roles in Italian opera and to bel canto pieces in Italian, suggesting that he was somewhat indolent. Such reservations do not diminish Pavarotti's wide-ranging appeal and his ability to educate people about opera, especially those who had had little exposure to it.

Opera worldwide had a much smaller following before Pavarotti became an international operatic figure in the 1960's and 1970's. Not only did he perform to huge audiences throughout the world, but also he produced recordings of twenty-two operas between 1966 and 1980, ten of them with the Australian coloratura soprano Joan Sutherland.

Pavarotti's participation in some of the early live television performances of operas made him a pioneer in performing opera in this medium. For the first of these live performances in 1977, Pavarotti returned to the role that marked his earlier operatic debuts, that of Rodolfo in *La Bohème*.

Through his television performances and recordings, Pavarotti reached audiences approaching a billion people. With his magnetic appeal, often his personal appearances had to be staged in huge stadiums rather than in such theaters as the Metropolitan Opera House, with its seating capacity of about four thousand.

The Three Tenors. In the 1980's, Pavarotti helped conceive of the Three Tenors project, in which he and two other renowned tenors,

Plácido Domingo and José Carreras, toured the world, bringing opera to the masses. The first of these concerts was part of the activities associated with soccer's World Cup, but the performances proved to be so popular that the three principals continued them for several years and also produced recordings and videos that sold millions of copies.

Popular Concerts. After having played the role of a sexy opera singer in the feature film *Yes, Giorgio* (1982), Pavarotti began staging popular concerts with such rock stars as Elton John, Sting, and Bono for the benefit of Pavarotti and Friends, a charitable foundation that he had established. His last performances at the Metropolitan Opera, where he had sung in 379 performances, were in 2004, when he sang the leading tenor role in several successive performances of Giacomo Puccini's *Tosca*.

Musical Legacy

Pavarotti's greatest legacy was bringing opera to millions of people who had not been exposed to it previously or who, having been exposed to it, did not like or appreciate it. It was the force of his personality—warm, genial, and sincere—that won over the audiences for whom he sang.

R. Baird Shuman

Further Reading

Breslin, Herbert and Anne Midgette. *The King and I: The Uncensored Tale of Luciano Pavarotti's Rise to Fame by His Manager, Friend, and Sometime Adversary.* New York: Doubleday, 2004. An account, sometimes short on objectivity and professional detachment, of Breslin's thirty-six year professional and personal relationship with Pavarotti.

Kesting, Jürgen. *Luciano Pavarotti: The Myth of the Tenor.* Translated by Susan H. Ray. Boston: Northeastern University Press, 1996. Kesting examines Pavarotti's career in the light of the adulation of the tenor by audiences with whom Pavarotti quickly and consistently established an easy rapport.

Pavarotti, Adua, with Wendy Dallas. *Pavarotti: My Life with Luciano.* New York: Rizzoli, 1992. This revealing, if at times uncritical, view of Pavarotti by his first wife is enhanced with more than two hundred photographs. Writing in a style that appeals to the general reader, Adua notes her hus-

band's love of food and of cooking for the hordes of guests who frequented their palatial summer home at Presaro.

Pavarotti, Luciano, with William Wright. *Pavarotti: My Life.* New York: Random House, 1995. A well-written and thoroughly interesting presentation of Pavarotti's life and career. An essential source for anyone interested in the tenor's career and background.

Rudas, Tibor. *Three Tenors in Concert, 1994.* San Francisco: Collins, 1994. An account of the performances by the three tenors and of the sites of their concerts by the man who helped create the Three Tenors phenomenon and arranged the sites for their presentations.

See also: Bono; Caruso, Enrico; Domingo, Plácido; John, Sir Elton; Puccini, Giacomo; Sinatra, Frank; Sting; Sutherland, Dame Joan.

Tom Paxton

American folksinger, guitarist, and songwriter

Known for his topical and satiric songs that have retained their relevance, Paxton was a major contributor to the development of the folk-music scene in the 1960's.

Born: October 31, 1937; Chicago, Illinois
Also known as: Thomas Richard Paxton (full name)
Member of: Chad Mitchell Trio

Principal recordings

ALBUMS: *Ramblin' Boy*, 1964; *Ain't That News*, 1965; *Outward Bound*, 1966; *Morning Again*, 1968; *The Things I Notice Now*, 1969; *Number Six*, 1970; *How Come the Sun*, 1971; *Peace Will Come*, 1972; *New Songs for Old Friends*, 1973; *Children's Song Book*, 1974; *Something in My Life*, 1975; *Saturday Night*, 1976; *New Songs from the Briarpatch*, 1977; *Heroes*, 1978; *Up and Up*, 1979; *The Paxton Report*, 1980; *Bulletin*, 1983; *Even a Gray Day*, 1983; *The Marvelous Toy and Other Gallimaufry*, 1984; *One Million Lawyers . . . and Other*

Disasters, 1985; *And Loving You*, 1986; *Balloon-Aloon-Aloon*, 1987; *Politics Live*, 1988; *It Ain't Easy*, 1991; *A Child's Christmas*, 1992; *Peanut Butter Pie*, 1992; *Suzy Is a Rocker*, 1992; *Wearing the Time*, 1994; *A Car Full of Songs*, 1997; *Goin' to the Zoo*, 1997; *I've Got a Yo-Yo*, 1997; *A Car Full of Fun Songs*, 1999; *Fun Animal Songs*, 1999; *Fun Food Songs*, 1999; *Under American Skies*, 2001; *Looking for the Moon*, 2002; *Your Shoes, My Shoes*, 2002; *Best of Friends*, 2004.

The Life

Thomas Richard Paxton was born to Burt and Esther Paxton on October 31, 1937, in Chicago, Illinois. The family moved to Arizona and then to Bristow, Oklahoma, in 1948, where his father soon died of a stroke. He was young when he discovered his love of music, and he was first given a ukulele and then a guitar while still in his teens.

Paxton studied drama at the University of Oklahoma. While in college, he became interested in folk music, listening to songs by Woody Guthrie and the Weavers. He sang in a folk group during his college years. Paxton graduated from the University of Oklahoma in 1959, and soon after he joined the Army. He was stationed at Fort Dix, in New Jersey, and while there he had the opportunity to explore New York City's Greenwich Village and its growing folk-music scene. After his honorable discharge from the Army, he remained in New York City, performing at such places as the Gaslight Café and the Bitter End. He met his wife, Midge, in 1963 at the Gaslight, and they were married the same year.

Throughout the 1960's and 1970's, Paxton performed across the United States and England, in coffeehouses and on college campuses. His songs were widely covered by other artists, including Judy Collins, John Denver, and Peter, Paul, and Mary.

During the 1980's and 1990's, Paxton began writing children's music, recording nine albums for children, and writing children's books, publishing sixteen children's books.

In 2000 Paxton returned to writing political and topical music. He was nominated for a Grammy Award in 2002 for his children's album *Your Shoes, My Shoes* and in 2003 for *Looking for the Moon* in the Best Contemporary Folk Album category. He received a Lifetime Achievement Award from the American Society of Composers, Artists, and Publishers (ASCAP), and he was honored by the British Parliament on January 22, 2007. Paxton and his wife, who have two daughters and three grandsons, settled in Alexandria, Virginia.

The Music

Although Paxton played in the musical group called the Travelers while still in college, his musical career began when he was in the Army, stationed at Fort Dix. He began traveling regularly to Greenwich Village, where he became acquainted with some of the emerging talents of the folk revival, including Bob Dylan and Phil Ochs. Paxton was briefly a member of the Chad Mitchell Trio, and he was the first songwriter for folk music producer Milt Okun's company, Cherry Lane Music Publishing. Paxton's songs range from singalong standards such as "Bottle of Wine" and "Rambling Boy," to war-protest songs such as "Jimmy Newman" and "My Son John," to satiric songs such as "What Did You Learn in School Today?," to serious topical songs such as "On the Road to Srebrenica" and "The Bravest."

"Ramblin' Boy." In the early 1960's, while working at the Gaslight, Paxton wrote three songs between sets one night. By his admission, the first and the third of the songs were not good. However, the one in the middle was "Ramblin' Boy," a song he recorded first in 1964 for Electra Records. In 1964 Paxton sang "Ramblin' Boy" with Pete Seeger on Seeger's television show, *Rainbow Quest*. This is perhaps Paxton's best-known song.

"Last Thing on My Mind." Paxton included this song on his first album for Elektra Records, and it was popular with performers and with audiences. After his first recording of "Last Thing on My Mind" in 1964, it was recorded more than thirty times by other artists, including Judy Collins in 1964; the Kingston Trio and Peter, Paul, and Mary in 1965; the Seekers in 1966; Porter Wagoner and Dolly Parton in 1967; and José Feliciano in 1968. Shortly after this song was released, Paxton embarked on his first tour of England, where he achieved a great deal of popularity. Over the years, he toured England some forty times to enthusiastic audiences.

Short Shelf-Life Songs. Paxton has written and performed what he terms "short shelf-life songs."

These are topical pieces, written in response to events of the day. These songs tend to be humorous but pointed: for example, in 1965, during the Vietnam War, he wrote and performed "Lyndon Johnson Told the Nation," a song that satirized the U.S. policy in Vietnam. In 2006 Paxton rewrote this song as "George W. Told the Nation" to mock George W. Bush as the instigator of the war in Iraq. Another such song was "The Ballad of Spiro Agnew," written to satirize Richard Nixon's vice president, and it was covered by John Denver in 1969. Like Seeger, Paxton used such topical songs to call attention to what he perceived as social injustice and to demonstrate the absurdity of modern life.

Musical Legacy

Paxton was a founding member of the folk-rock movement of the 1960's. He continued to perform acoustic music long after others in the genre had turned to electric instruments. Paxton was influenced by such singers as Seeger, Woody Guthrie, Burl Ives, and John Hurt; his influence on his fellow musicians extends across generations. John Denver, Judy Collins, Ani DeFranco, and Holly Near are just a few artists who have found expression in Paxton's music. Perhaps his greatest contribution to his genre was his demonstration that folk music could embrace newly written music as well as traditional songs.

Diane Andrews Henningfeld

Further Reading

Alarik, Scott, and Robert Corwin. *Deep Community: Adventures in the Modern Folk Underground.* Cambridge, Mass.: Black Wolf Press, 2003. For this collection, *Boston Globe* journalist Alarik compiled 120 of his articles on the contemporary folk scene, including interviews and stories about Paxton.

Hood, Phil. *Artists of American Folk Music: The Legends of Traditional Folk, the Stars of the Sixties, the Virtuosi of New Acoustic Music.* New York: Quill, 1986. Hood profiles the major American folksingers from 1950 through 1986, and he includes a chapter on Paxton.

LaBland, Michael. "Tom Paxton." In *Contemporary Musicians: Profiles of the People in Music.* Detroit, Mich.: Gale Research, 1991. This chapter includes a biographical sketch as well as a consideration of Paxton's music and influence.

Paxton, Tom. *The Honor of Your Company.* New York: Cherry Lane Publishing, 2000. This idiosyncratic autobiography is filled with anecdotes, and it includes photographs and lyrics to many of Paxton's songs.

_____. *Wearing the Time.* New York: Cherry Lane Publishing, 1994. This book is a companion to Paxton's album of the same name. It includes words, music, and guitar arrangements to twelve of Paxton's songs as well as his own commentary about the music.

See also: Collins, Judy; Copland, Aaron; Denny, Sandy; Denver, John; Dylan, Bob; Guthrie, Woody; Parton, Dolly; Seeger, Pete; Watson, Doc.

Carl Perkins

American rockabilly singer, guitarist, and songwriter

Perkins was one of the first to link country and western, rhythm and blues, hillbilly, and rock and roll into the rockabilly style.

Born: April 9, 1932; Tiptonville, Tennessee
Died: January 19, 1998; Jackson, Tennessee
Also known as: Carl Lee Perkins (full name)

Principal recordings

ALBUMS: *Dance Album*, 1957; *Whole Lotta Shakin'*, 1958; *On Top*, 1969; *Boppin' the Blues*, 1970; *Brown Eyed Handsome Man*, 1972; *My Kind of Country*, 1973; *From Jackson Tennessee*, 1977; *Country Soul*, 1979; *Disciple in Blue Suede Shoes*, 1984; *Sweeter than Candy*, 1984; *Born to Rock*, 1990; *Carl Perkins and Sons*, 1993; *Take Me Back*, 1993; *King of Rockabilly*, 1995; *Go Cat Go*, 1996; *All Shook Up*, 1996; *Turn Around*, 1998.

SINGLES: "Gone Gone Gone," 1955; "Blue Suede Shoes," 1956; "Boppin' the Blues," 1956; "Honey Don't," 1956; "Everybody's Tryin' to Be My Baby," 1957; "Glad All Over," 1958.

The Life

Carl Lee Perkins was one of three sons, along with Jay and Clayton, of poor sharecroppers Fonie "Buck" Perkins and Louise Brantley. Perkins picked cotton as a youngster, and he was influenced by the gospel and blues music sung by the black workers. When he was seven years old, his father built him a guitar out of a cigar box, and Perkins became proficient at playing. As a teen, Perkins formed a band with his brothers, and they performed at local clubs, even though the Perkins family continued to sharecrop. As an adult, Perkins worked as a baker. He married Valda Crider in 1953, and they had three sons and a daughter.

In 1955 Perkins signed a recording contract with Sun Records and toured with Elvis Presley and Johnny Cash. Perkins's song "Blue Suede Shoes," released in 1956, became a hit, and Perkins was invited to New York to perform on national television shows. On the drive north, he was seriously injured in an automobile accident that incapacitated him for months.

Carl Perkins. (Hulton Archive/Getty Images)

Perkins began to drink heavily, and though he had some minor hits, his career never regained momentum. He toured and recorded with Cash for ten years and eventually recovered from his alcoholism. In the mid-1970's he formed C. P. Express with two of his sons and started his own record label, Suede. He also owned two restaurants and established a child-abuse-prevention center. A throat cancer survivor in the early 1990's, Perkins died following a succession of strokes in 1998.

The Music

A performer from the mid-1940's until his death, Perkins was known for his dynamic guitar playing and for his ability to write simple, catchy tunes. Most of his best-known songs, however, were bigger hits for other artists. Though an important figure as the first white musician to cross over from pure country to rhythm and blues and pop rock with a style known as rockabilly, Perkins was more widely admired in England than in the United States. Unlike more famous artists (such as Presley, Cash, Roy Orbison, and Jerry Lee Lewis) who were able to capitalize on a switch to rock and roll as the rockabilly trend died, Perkins never really outgrew his country roots.

"Blue Suede Shoes." Featuring a rock-oriented opening salvo, this was Perkins's first and only Top 40 hit. The song in 1956 reached number two on the *Billboard* jukebox chart, hit number one on the country chart, and became Sun Records' first million-seller. Based on an incident Perkins witnessed while performing at a honky-tonk bar, it became his signature tune (he afterward sported blue suede shoes onstage) and gave its name to Perkins's Tennessee restaurants and his record label (both called Suede). Presley had a hit with his cover of the song while Perkins was recovering from his near-fatal traffic accident.

"Glad All Over." This was one of the last recordings Perkins cut for Sun Records, along with "Right String Baby (But the Wrong Yo-Yo)," before moving to Columbia Records. A minor hit for the rockabilly star, it was one of a number of Perkins songs performed by his longtime admirers the Beatles during their 1963 live appearances on the BBC (although not the song with the identical title that became a hit for the Dave Clark Five). During a 1964 British tour, Perkins met the Beatles and was present at sessions when they recorded five of his songs. Capable of vocally duplicating the rockabilly sound, George Harrison was a particular fan of Perkins's work, and Paul McCartney once claimed Perkins was the Beatles' greatest influence.

"Daddy Sang Bass." This autobiographical tune mentions Perkins's hardscrabble upbringing as a sharecropper, when hard times were relieved by family musical get-togethers. Cash recorded the song on his 1968 album *Hello, I'm Johnny Cash*. As a single, "Daddy Sang Bass" rose to number one on the country charts and did well on popular charts. Other artists, including Lewis, the Statler Brothers, and Flatt and Scruggs also covered the tune.

"Let Me Tell You About Love." A rockabilly-flavored tune extolling the virtues of love by comparing a current love to famous lovers of history (Adam and Eve, Samson and Delilah, Bonaparte and Josephine, Romeo and Juliet), this was co-written by Perkins and Wynona Judd. Perkins was featured on guitar on the song, which appeared on the Judds' 1989 *River of Time* album. The single of "Let Me Tell You About Love" made it to number one on country charts.

"Silver and Gold." Cowritten by Perkins and his sons, Greg and Stan, this song has religious undertones woven among themes that stress the importance of true love and making each moment count. Recorded by Dolly Parton on her 1991 number-one country album *Eagle When She Flies*, the single of "Silver and Gold" reached number fifteen on country charts. It was also reprised on Parton's 1996 compilation album, *I Will Always Love You, and Other Greatest Hits*.

Musical Legacy

Of incalculable influence on songwriters, singers, and guitarists, Perkins had an impact on the early style of the Beatles, the Rolling Stones, and other groups in England. Through his example as songwriter and performer, he also contributed to the development of such domestic stars as Presley, Orbison, Cash, and Lewis, all of whom surpassed Perkins in popularity. He was inducted into the Rock and Roll Hall of Fame in 1987. Perkins left an important nonmusical legacy: the Carl Perkins Center for the Prevention of Child Abuse.

Jack Ewing

Further Reading

Clayson, Alan. *George Harrison*. London: Sanctuary, 2001. In this biography of the late Beatle, Harrison discusses Perkins as a major influence on his music.

McNutt, Randy. *We Wanna Boogie: An Illustrated History of the American Rockabilly Movement*. Hamilton, Ohio: HHP Books, 1989. Features interviews with and many photographs of early rockabilly pioneers, including Perkins.

Naylor, Jerry, and Steve Halliday. *The Rockabilly Legends: They Called It Rockabilly Long Before It was Called Rock 'n' Roll*. Milwaukee, Wis.: Hal Leonard, 2007. A tribute and a biography, this contains hundreds of photographs of Presley, Orbison, Cash, Perkins, Buddy Holly, and others.

Perkins, Carl, and David McGee. *Go, Cat, Go! The Life and Times of Carl Perkins, the King of Rockabilly*. New York: Hyperion, 1996. An autobiography of the rockabilly star, illustrated with photographs and with a complete discography.

Poore, Billy. *Rockabilly: A Forty-Year Journey*. Milwaukee, Wis.: Hal Leonard, 1998. Poore was a personal friend of many 1950's rockabilly artists, and he shows their influence on later generations of musicians. Profusely illustrated with tour and chart information.

See also: Cash, Johnny; Harrison, George; Jefferson, Blind Lemon; Lewis, Jerry Lee; Monroe, Bill; Orbison, Roy; Presley, Elvis; Twitty, Conway; Vincent, Gene.

Itzhak Perlman

Israeli classical violinist

A leading violin virtuoso, Perlman is noted for his dedication to teaching, his active promotion of the Jewish klezmer music tradition, and his support for the rights of the disabled.

Born: August 31, 1945; Tel Aviv, Palestine (now Israel)

Principal recordings

ALBUMS: *Paganini: Caprices for Violin*, 1965; *Paul Hindemith: Sonata for Violin and Piano in E-flat*

Major, Op. 11, 1965; *Bach: Concerto for Violin No. 1 in A Minor*, 1974; *Beethoven: Sonata for Violin and Piano No. 4 in A Minor, Op. 23*, 1974; *Beethoven: Violin Concerto in D Major, Op. 61*, 1980; *Sir Edward Elgar: Concerto for Violin in B Minor, Op. 61*, 1981; *Brahms: Sonata for Violin and Piano No. 2 in A Major, Op. 100*, 1983; *Mozart: Concerto for Violin No. 2 in D Major*, 1985; *Sergei Prokofiev: Love for Three Oranges, March in B Minor, Op. 33*, 1990; *Tchaikovsky: Violin Concerto in D Major, Op. 35*, 1990; *Debussy: Petite Suite for Piano, No. 3, Four Hands*, 1992; *Mendelssohn: Songs Without Words*, 1992; *Dvořák: Romance for Violin and Orchestra in F Minor, Op. 11*, 1993; *Felix Mendelssohn: Violin Concerto in E Minor, Op. 64*, 1993; *Bits and Pieces*, 1994; *Beethoven: Kreutzer Sonata/Franck: Violin Sonata*, 1999; *Brahms: Violin Sonatas*, 1999; *Bach: Violin Concertos*, 2002; *Classic Perlman: Rhapsody*, 2002; *Dvořák: Violin Concertos*, 2003.

The Life

Itzhak Perlman (IHT-zahk PURL-mahn) was born on August 31, 1945, to barber Chaim Perlman and his wife Shoshana. Permanently paralyzed by polio at the age of four, Perlman developed his musical inclinations in the violin studio of Ryvka Goldgart at the Schulamit Conservatory in Tel Aviv. In 1958 he was the winner of a talent-search competition, which led to an appearance in the United States on the televised *Ed Sullivan Show*. After emigrating to New York in the same year, Perlman enrolled in the pre-college program at the Juilliard School, working with Ivan Galamian and Dorothy DeLay.

Perlman had his Carnegie Hall debut in 1963, performing Henryk Wieniawski's Violin Concerto No. 1 (1853). In 1964 he won first prize in the Levintritt Competition, marking the start of an international career as violinist, conductor, and teacher. Since that time, he has performed with every major orchestra throughout the world, returning for soloist appearances in tours with his homeland orchestra, the Israel Philharmonic, in 1987, 1990, and 1994. He has collaborated with performers and conductors, such as Vladimir Ashkenazy, Martha Argerich, Pinchas Zukerman, Isaac Stern, John Williams, Daniel Barenboim, Seiji Ozawa, and Zubin Mehta.

In recognition of his recordings, Perlman received fifteen Grammy Awards, for Best Classical Performance, Instrumental Soloist or Soloists (with Orchestra) in 1977, two in 1980, 1981, 1982, 1987, 1990, and 1995; Best Classical Performance, Instrumental Soloist or Soloists (without Orchestra) in 1980; Best Chamber Music Performance in 1978, 1980, 1981, and 1987; Best Chamber Music or Other Small Ensemble Performance in 1990; and Best Classical Album in 1978. In 1995, in celebration of Perlman's fiftieth birthday, EMI released a set of twenty compact discs entitled *The Itzhak Perlman Collection*.

Perlman has been recognized with a range of awards and honors throughout his career. In 1981 he was named Musician of the Year by Musical America. In 1986 and 2000 he was honored with a Medal of Liberty from President Ronald Reagan and a National Medal of Arts from President Bill Clinton. His fiftieth birthday was celebrated with a festival in London entitled The Definitive Perlman Experience, during which Perlman performed four concerts at the Royal Festival Hall. In 2003 he received a Kennedy Center Honor; and in 2005 the Juilliard School presented him an honorary doctorate and a centennial medal at the school's hundredth commencement ceremony. Perlman also holds honorary doctorates from Harvard University, Yale University, Brandeis University, Roosevelt University, Yeshiva University, Hebrew University, Brown University, and Columbia University. Perlman, his wife Toby, and their five children settled in New York.

The Music

Repertoire and Recordings. Perlman has performed or recorded the majority of sonatas and concerti within the standard violin repertoire; chamber works such as the trios of Johann Sebastian Bach, Ludwig van Beethoven, and Peter Ilich Tchaikovsky; traditional Jewish klezmer melodies; and other collaborative projects, such as the violin solos for John Williams's Academy Award-winning film *Schindler's List* (1994). Highlights of his recorded repertoire include the complete violin sonatas of Bach (a collaboration with Zukerman and Barenboim) and Johannes Brahms (a collaboration with Ashkenazy), and a collaboration with Argerich featuring Beethoven's *Kreutzer* sonata

(1802) and César Franck's Sonata in A Major (1886).

Perlman has recorded solo, concerto, and chamber music primarily for EMI Music, but he has also recorded for Deutsche Grammophon, Sony Classical, Angel Records, and RCA Victor Records. In 1995 he was named EMI Artist of the Year.

Conducting. As a conductor, Perlman has collaborated with orchestras such as the Berlin Philharmonic, the London Philharmonic, the Concertgebuow Orchestra, the Israel Philharmonic Orchestra, the Chicago Symphony, the New York Philharmonic, the Los Angeles Philharmonic, the San Francisco Symphony, the New World Symphony, the Toronto Symphony, the Philadelphia Orchestra, the

Itzhak Perlman. (AP/Wide World Photos)

National Symphony Orchestra, the Houston Symphony, the Pittsburgh Symphony, and the English Chamber Orchestra. From 2001 to 2005, he appeared regularly as principal guest conductor of the Detroit Symphony Orchestra, and from 2002 to 2004 he served as music adviser to the St. Louis Symphony.

Teaching. Perlman has placed a heavy emphasis on teaching as an integral part of his career. For fifteen years (1975-1990), he taught at the Brooklyn College Conservatory of Music. In 1999 he joined the strings faculty of the Juilliard School, teaching violin performance and coaching chamber music. In 2003 he was appointed to the Dorothy Richard Starling Chair of Violin Studies at the Juilliard School. Perlman has also taught and conducted as artist-in-residence at the Perlman Music Program since its inception in 1995. Founded by his wife and based in Shelter Island, New York, the six-week summer program attracts pre-college applicants from around the United States.

Musical Legacy

Perlman will perhaps best be remembered for his love of the violin and in performance transmitting that joy to nonspecialist audiences. He has established a connection with popular culture through television appearances on *The Late Show with David Letterman, Sesame Street, The Tonight Show with Jay Leno,* and *Live from Lincoln Center.* He also received four Emmy Awards for special programs produced in conjunction with the Public Broadcasting System (PBS): *Perlman in Russia* (Outstanding Classical Program in the Performing Arts, 1992), *The Dvořák Concert from Prague: A Celebration* (Outstanding Individual Achievement in Cultural Programming, 1994), *Itzhak Perlman: In the Fiddler's House* (Outstanding Cultural Music-Dance Program, 1996), and *Itzhak Perlman: Fiddling for the Future* (Outstanding Classical Music-Dance Program, 1999).

Perlman's active promotion of the tradition of klezmer music, a Yiddish musical style based on Jewish spiritual, dance, and folk melodies, is another legacy. He has helped preserve this tradition by performing and recording with some of the leading klezmer groups in the United States, including the Klezmatics, the Klezmer Conservatory Band, the Andy Statman Klezmer Orchestra, and Brave Old World. Finally, Perlman has become an effective role model for persons with disabilities in achieving excellence despite, or perhaps even because of, his confinement to a wheelchair.

Siu-Yin Mak

Further Reading

Katims, Milton, and Virginia Katims. *The Pleasure Was Ours: Personal Encounters with the Greats, the Near-Greats, and the Ingrates.* Mill Valley, Calif.: Vision Books, 2004. A series of personal interviews with musical artists (among them violinist Jascha Heifetz, composer Igor Stravinsky, and cellist Pablo Casals) includes a profile of Perlman.

Roth, Henry. *Violin Virtuosos: From Paganini to the Twenty-first Century.* Los Angeles: California Classics Books, 1997. This resource contains biographical information about violin virtuosos, including Perlman. It also includes performance and recording evaluations made by the author.

Swan, Annalyn. "Itzhak Perlman: Top Fiddle." *Newsweek* 95, no. 15 (1980): 62-72. In a wide-ranging interview with Perlman, the violinist offers insights into his career and offers his opinion on the work of other violinists.

See also: Argerich, Martha; Ashkenazy, Vladimir; Barenboim, Daniel; Chung, Kyung-Wha; Debussy, Claude; Heifetz, Jascha; Hindemith, Paul; Previn, Sir André; Prokofiev, Sergei; Stern, Isaac; Williams, John.

Oscar Peterson

Canadian jazz composer, pianist, and singer

Peterson's pianistic style was characterized by its hard-driving swing and by its virtuosity, as he transferred techniques of his classical training to the jazz idiom.

Born: August 15, 1925; Montreal, Quebec, Canada
Died: December 23, 2007; Mississauga, Ontario, Canada
Also known as: Oscar Emmanuel Peterson (full name)

Principal recordings

ALBUMS: *Evening with Oscar Peterson*, 1950; *Oscar Peterson Plays Pretty*, 1950; *Oscar Peterson Piano Solos*, 1950; *Oscar Peterson Plays Cole Porter*, 1951; *Oscar Peterson Quartet*, 1952; *Oscar Peterson Plays Count Basie*, 1955; *The Oscar Peterson Trio*, 1956; *The Oscar Peterson Trio at the Stratford Shakespearean Festival*, 1956; *Ben Webster Meets Oscar Peterson*, 1959; *The Jazz Soul of Oscar Peterson*, 1959; *Oscar Peterson Plays the Cole Porter Song Book*, 1959; *Oscar Peterson Plays the Duke Ellington Song Book*, 1959; *Very Tall*, 1961 (with Milt Jackson); *Affinity*, 1962; *Night Train*, 1962; *Canadiana Suite*, 1964; *Blues Étude*, 1965; *With Respect to Nat*, 1965; *On a Clear Day (You Can See Forever)*, 1967; *My Favorite Instrument*, 1968; *Hello, Herbie*, 1969 (with Herbie Ellis); *Motions and Emotions*, 1969; *Oscar's Choice*, 1970; *Great Connection*, 1971 (with Niels-Henning Ørsted Pedersen); *Reunion Blues*, 1971 (with Jackson); *The Trio*, 1973; *Oscar Peterson and Dizzy Gillespie*, 1974; *Oscar Peterson and Roy Eldridge*, 1974; *The Personal Touch*, 1980; *Tribute to My Friends*, 1983; *Two of the Few*, 1983 (with Jackson); *Time After Time*, 1986; *The More I See You*, 1995; *Oscar and Benny*, 1998 (with Benny Green).

WRITINGS OF INTEREST: *A Jazz Odyssey: My Life in Jazz*, 2002 (autobiography).

The Life

Oscar Emmanuel Peterson was born in Montreal, one of five children of Daniel and Olivia John Peterson, both of whom had immigrated to Canada from the West Indies. Like his other siblings, Peterson began classical piano lessons with his father at an early age. He went on to study piano with Lou Hooper and then with Hungarian pianist Paul Alexander de Marky. At age fourteen, Peterson won an amateur competition sponsored by the Canadian Broadcasting Company, and soon afterward he began playing for a weekly radio show. In his late teens, he became the only black member of the Johnny Holmes Orchestra, an immensely popular group that toured both Canada and the United States. By 1945 he was also leading a trio of his own at Montreal's Alberta Lounge.

In September, 1949, Peterson debuted at Carnegie Hall with Norman Granz's Jazz at the Philharmonic. He joined Jazz at the Philharmonic the next year, and at that time Granz managed Peterson's career, organizing concert dates and producing albums on his Verve and Pablo labels. Beginning in

1950, Peterson toured extensively with Jazz at the Philharmonic, visiting locations across the United States as well as in Europe and Japan. He first appeared in a duo with bassist Ray Brown, then he formed the Oscar Peterson Trio in 1952 with the addition of guitarist Irving Ashby. Ashby was succeeded on guitar first by Barney Kessel (1952-1953) and then by Herb Ellis (1953-1958). The trio continued to play and tour with Jazz at the Philharmonic, appearing with such leading musicians as Ella Fitzgerald, Dizzy Gillespie, and Roy Eldridge. They also recorded regularly on Granz's Verve label. When Ellis left the trio in 1958, Peterson and Brown altered the composition of the group by adding drummer Ed Thigpen (1959-1965). During this time, Peterson, Brown, and Thigpen also ran the Advanced School of Contemporary Music in Toronto (1960-1964), established for the purpose of teaching jazz to young people. After Thigpen left the trio in 1965 and Brown in 1966, Peterson performed with various personnel before turning his focus to solo performance in the early 1970's. From the mid-1970's until his death in 2007, Peterson continued to perform and record, appearing with symphony orchestras, with small combos, or unaccompanied.

The Music

While Peterson was influenced by pianists such as Art Tatum and Nat King Cole, he developed an individual style rooted equally in the blues and in his complete mastery of the instrument. While his amazing speed and his wealth of thematic invention sometimes overwhelmed critics, he remained a popular jazz pianist with audiences. Peterson was praised for his melodic ideas, his virtuosity, his rhythmic drive, and his control. His playing was both subtle and technically superb, whether he was performing as accompanist, with his trio, or as a soloist. Peterson also composed several large-scale works, the most famous of which is his *Canadiana Suite* (1964).

The Oscar Peterson Trio at the Stratford Shakespearean Festival. Peterson made this live recording on August 8, 1956, at the Stratford Shakespearean Festival with Brown on bass and Ellis on guitar. One of Peterson's most popular albums, *The Oscar Peterson Trio at the Stratford Shakespearean Festival* documents an exciting live performance before an attentive and enthusiastic crowd. Ellis referred to

the album as one of the best recorded representations of the trio in performance. The album includes exquisite arrangements, such as "Noreen's Nocturne" and "Fifty-second Street Theme." The latter tune presents an artful arrangement of the Thelonious Monk standard at an exceedingly fast tempo, with scorching solos by Ellis and Peterson. Another highlight of the album is "How High the Moon," which features Brown and includes masterful solos by Ellis and Peterson. Also notable are the renditions "Swinging on a Star," "Love You Madly," and "How About You?"

Ben Webster Meets Oscar Peterson. This album is one in a series of Peterson's masterful collaborations with leading jazz artists, including Louis Armstrong, Count Basie, Ella Fitzgerald, Stan Getz, and Lionel Hampton. The recording is the fourth the tenor saxophonist and Peterson made together on Verve. While the earlier recordings included guitar, this one features Peterson's new trio configuration with Thigpen on drums joining Brown on bass. *Ben Webster Meets Oscar Peterson* features slow tempi in swinging rhythms, more in keeping with Webster's typical style than with Peterson's lightning-fast playing. Note, for example, the opening track, "The Touch of Your Lips," a beautiful ballad that is a perfect vehicle for Webster's rich sound and elegant solos. However, Peterson and his trio are at home in slow tempi as well as fast, and "The Touch of Your Lips" demonstrates their perfect accompaniment to Webster, as well as engaging solos by both Peterson and Brown. The subtlety and beauty of Webster's playing comes through on the album's other ballads, including swinging versions of "Bye-bye Blackbird" and "This Can't Be Love."

Oscar Peterson Plays the Cole Porter Song Book. This recording is one of nine song book albums Peterson made with Brown and Thigpen in 1959 (among the others are those of George Gershwin, Duke Ellington, Irving Berlin, and Harold Arlen), and it recalls Peterson's earlier projects recording albums of these and other popular songwriters (including *Oscar Peterson Plays Cole Porter* in 1951). For the song book albums, Granz requested that Peterson play in a simpler, more accessible style aimed at a general audience rather than at jazz aficionados. While Peterson was at times criticized for employing popular song so frequently in jazz, he remained true to his jazz ideals

Oscar Peterson. (AP/Wide World Photos)

and swinging rhythms while seeking to bring jazz to a wider audience. *Oscar Peterson Plays the Cole Porter Song Book* features both hard-swinging performances such as "It's All Right with Me," masterful versions of such ballads as "In the Still of the Night," and funky versions of "Love for Sale" and "Just One of Those Things."

Night Train. One of the finest recordings of the Oscar Peterson Trio, this features Brown on bass and Thigpen on drums. It includes a wonderful variety of tunes, including several Ellington standards, Milt Jackson's "Bags's Groove," and Hoagy Carmichael's "Georgia on My Mind," with Peterson and the trio at their swinging best throughout. Highlights of the album include Brown's melodic, bluesy solo on Ellington's "Night Train," accompanied first by Peterson and then Thigpen, before the entire trio comes together for a blues-based chorus, and the trio's funky and virtuosic rendition of the rhythm-and-blues hit "The Honeydripper." The album concludes with a rare Peterson composition,

the gospel-inspired "Hymn to Freedom" (known variously as "The Prayer (A Jazz Hymn)" and "My Prayer").

My Favorite Instrument. In this solo album, Peterson's virtuosity and musicality are strikingly evident. In fact, Peterson's friend and biographer Gene Lees considers this one of the greatest jazz piano albums ever made. *My Favorite Instrument* features a wide variety of tunes and styles, from Gershwin's "Someone to Watch over Me" to Billy Strayhorn's "Take the A-Train" to Juan Tizol's bop standard "Perdido." Peterson is equally at home in each of these different tunes, and he stamps each with his distinctive solo style. Those who think of Peterson exclusively in relation to his lightning-fast streams of notes may be surprised at the tenderness of his ballad playing in such tunes as "Who Can I Turn To?" and "Little Girl Blue." In addition, Peterson's dazzling swing is evident throughout the album, as in the opening ballad "Someone to Watch over Me" and his vibrant renditions of "Lulu's Back in Town" and "Take the A-Train."

The Trio. This album, recorded live at Chicago's London House with Joe Pass, guitar, and Niels-Henning Ørsted Pedersen, bass, is Peterson's tribute to the blues. It opens with Peterson's own "Blues Étude," which features the pianist at his swinging best. After the opening chorus and a scorching solo by Pass, Peterson's improvisation ranges from hard bop to boogie-woogie to stride, all indelibly stamped with his own individual style. "Blues Étude" is followed by another Peterson composition, "Chicago Blues," an earthy and expansive version of the blues that opens with an extensive and far-ranging piano solo before the guitar and bass join to back Peterson's improvisation. The track also features funky and virtuosic solos by Pass and Pedersen and a second solo by Peterson. This outstanding album, which also includes "Easy Listening Blues," "Come Sunday," and "Secret Love," was awarded a Grammy Award for Best Jazz Performance by a Group in 1974.

Musical Legacy

Peterson was one of the most decorated jazz pianists of the twentieth century. While sometimes negatively reviewed by critics, he remained one of the most consistently popular jazz pianists with the general public, as evidenced by the fourteen *Down Beat* Readers' Polls for Best Jazz Pianist he won between 1950 and 1972 and the ten *Playboy* All-Star Jazz Polls for Best Jazz Pianist he won between 1959 and 1975. In addition, Peterson won eight Grammy Awards, including the Instrumental Soloist Lifetime Achievement Award in 1997. He was appointed Companion of the Order of Canada in 1984, and he received thirteen honorary doctorates (1973-1999). Furthermore, Peterson has been inducted into the *Down Beat* Jazz Hall of Fame (1984), the American Jazz Hall of Fame (1989), the International Jazz Hall of Fame (1997), and the Canadian Jazz and Blues Hall of Fame (2001).

While Peterson has been widely celebrated and admired, he has not been imitated. Because his approach to piano playing was so distinctive, younger players have not sought to emulate his style. His influence, though, has been felt in small-combo jazz performance, for which the Oscar Peterson Trio provided a superb model over the course of several decades. The trio particularly set the mold for virtuosic jazz performance in the absence of traditional front-line instruments such as trumpet or saxophone. Peterson's enormous discography documents the outstanding contributions he made to the jazz repertoire, as well as his many collaborations with other leading jazz musicians.

Mark A. Peters

Further Reading

Feather, Leonard. "Oscar." In *From Satchmo to Miles.* New York: Da Capo Press, 1972. The story of Peterson's life and music by leading jazz critic Feather. This is a firsthand account of Peterson from a fan, enhanced by quotes from Peterson and others.

Lees, Gene. *Oscar Peterson: The Will To Swing.* New York: Cooper Square Press, 2000. A fascinating account of Peterson's life and music by his longtime friend, Lees. The narrative is enlivened by Lees' personal reminiscences and by many stories and quotes from interviews he conducted with Peterson and others. Lees not only details Peterson's life and music but also presents a compelling picture of the pianist as a man and an artist.

Lyons, Len. "Oscar Peterson." In *The Great Jazz Pianists Speaking of Their Lives and Music.* New York: William Morrow, 1983. Short biographical sketch followed by interview with Peterson. Addresses Peterson's early training and influences, his various trio members, his beliefs about jazz, the technical details of his approach to jazz piano, and young players he admired.

Palmer, Richard. *Oscar Peterson.* New York: Hippocrene Books, 1984. Short biographical sketch followed by account of Peterson's music making from its beginnings up to the 1980's. Concludes with a consideration of Peterson's style and its importance for jazz. Selected discography.

Peterson, Oscar. *A Jazz Odyssey: My Life in Jazz.* New York: Continuum, 2002. Peterson's autobiography, detailing his life and music, as well as his many relationships in the world of jazz. Complete picture of Peterson as man and musician.

See also: Akiyoshi, Toshiko; Armstrong, Louis; Basie, Count; Carter, Benny; Cole, Nat King; Fitzgerald, Ella; Getz, Stan; Gillespie, Dizzy; Grappelli, Stéphane; Hampton, Lionel; Hancock, Herbie; Lewis, John; Monk, Thelonious; Previn, Sir André; Tatum, Art; Webster, Ben; Young, Lester.

Tom Petty
American rock guitarist, singer, and songwriter

Fusing country, rhythm and blues, and 1950's-era rock, Petty has created popular rock-and-roll anthems, in his early, aggressive new wave approach and in his later twelve-string-guitar-dominated acoustic sound.

Born: October 20, 1950; Gainesville, Florida
Also known as: Thomas Earl Petty (full name)
Member of: The Heartbreakers; the Traveling Wilburys; Mudcrutch

Principal recordings

ALBUMS (solo): *Full Moon Fever*, 1989; *Wildflowers*, 1994; *Highway Companion*, 2006.

ALBUMS (with the Heartbreakers): *Tom Petty and the Heartbreakers*, 1976; *You're Gonna Get It!*, 1978; *Damn the Torpedoes*, 1979; *Hard Promises*, 1981; *Long After Dark*, 1982; *Southern Accents*, 1985; *Let Me Up (I've Had Enough)*, 1987; *Into the Great Wide Open*, 1991; *Echo*, 1999; *The Last DJ*, 2002.

ALBUMS (with Mudcrutch): *Mudcrutch*, 2008.

ALBUMS (with the Traveling Wilburys): *Traveling Wilburys, Vol. 1*, 1988; *Traveling Wilburys, Vol. 3*, 1990.

The Life

Thomas Earl Petty was born on October 20, 1950, in Gainesville, Florida. Described by Petty as abusive, his father, an insurance salesman, did not appreciate Petty's artistic nature. However, his mother and his brother, Bruce, were supportive of Petty's early musical interests. Fortunately, Petty found his musical counterparts in Gainesville. His longtime band, the Heartbreakers, was formed when Mike Campbell (guitar), Benmont Tench (keyboards), and Petty (guitar and vocals), all formerly of the local band Mudcrutch, joined forces with the local Gainesville rhythm section of Ron Blair (bass) and Stan Lynch (drums) in 1976. The original Mudcrutch members of the Heartbreakers continued to record and tour with Petty.

As soon as Petty and the Heartbreakers began releasing successful records, Petty began to confront record companies about maintaining creative, legal, and financial control over his music. In 1979 Petty set a precedent in the music industry when he refused to be sold to MCA Records when it purchased ABC Records. Petty declared bankruptcy, which voided his record contract, and he then resigned to an MCA subsidiary with the rights to his music in hand. In 1981 Petty refused to allow MCA to hike the price of his *Hard Promises* album from $8.98 to $9.98.

Petty was married to Jane Benyo, and they had two daughters, Adria and Anna Kim. Petty and Benyo divorced in 1996, and in 2001 Petty married Dana York.

The Music

Tom Petty and the Heartbreakers, the band's 1976 debut album, was received with lukewarm reviews and sales. In 1977, however, Shelter Records released one of the tracks, "Breakdown," which placed on the *Billboard* Top 50. The final track on the debut album, "American Girl," has since become a national rock anthem. The Heartbreakers' second record, *You're Gonna Get It!*, was the band's first gold record, and it featured the hit "Listen to Her Heart." The band hit its creative stride with its third record, *Damn the Torpedoes*, produced by Tommy Iovine, and it is recalled today as setting the standard for pristine 1980's rock-and-roll production. The record contained such hits as "Refugee," "Here Comes My Girl" and "Don't Do Me Like That." *Hard Promises*, the band's fourth record, was also produced by Iovine, and it opened with "The Waiting" and featured "Insider," a duet with Fleetwood Mac front-woman Stevie Nicks. After *Hard Promises*, bassist Blair left the group, and he was replaced by Howie Epstein, who was working as Del Shannon's musical director at the time. He lent his bass playing and high harmony vocal talents to the Heartbreakers' next three records, *Long After Dark*, *Southern Accents*, and *Let Me Up (I've Had Enough)*.

The Traveling Wilburys *and* Full Moon Fever. In 1988, after ten years of near-constant touring and studio work with the Heartbreakers (including a world tour in 1986 as Bob Dylan's backing band), the band went on hiatus while Petty joined up with Roy Orbison, George Harrison, Bob Dylan, and Jeff Lynne to form a songwriting supergroup known as the Traveling Wilburys. When it came time for Petty to record his next album, he enlisted fellow Wilbury Jeff Lynne and Heartbreakers' guitarist Campbell as producers for the non-Heartbreakers' effort *Full Moon Fever*. The acoustic-based album featured some of Petty's biggest hits, from "Free Fallin'" to "I Won't Back Down" and "Runnin' Down a Dream." In 1993 Petty and Heartbreakers released a greatest-hits album (featuring a new hit single, "Mary Jane's Last Dance") that remains one of their best-selling records, reaching diamond record status.

Wildflowers. In 1994 Petty released *Wildflowers*, another non-Heartbreakers' project (even though most of the Heartbreakers participate), and it was produced by Rick Rubin, Petty, and Campbell for Warner Bros. Records. This album was the first to feature Steve Ferrone on drums, and he became a permanent member of the Heartbreakers. Once again, the album featured multiple hit songs, from "You Don't Know How It Feels" to "You Wreck Me" and "It's Good to Be King."

Later Works. After *Wildflowers*, Petty and the Heartbreakers released *Echo* and *The Last DJ*. The Heartbreakers celebrated their thirtieth anniversary as a band with a concert in Gainesville, Florida, with Campbell, Tench, Blair (who rejoined the band after Epstein's death in 2003), Ferrone, and Scott Thurston (a multi-instrumentalist who began touring and recording with the Heartbreakers in 1991). Petty released *Highway Companion* in 2006, reuniting with the production team of Lynne and Campbell.

Musical Legacy

Petty releases consistently revered rock music with a profoundly American point of view. Through his combination of intelligent yet accessible lyrics and the infusion of various genres of American music, Petty has amassed a massive collection of hit records since the 1970's. He has won two Grammy Awards (one as a member of the Traveling Wilburys and one for "You Don't Know How It Feels" from *Wildflowers*). He has also received the George and Ira Gershwin Award for Lifetime Musical Achievement (University of California, Los Angeles, 1996), the Golden Note Award (American Society of Composers, Authors, and Publishers, 1996), a star on the Hollywood Walk of Fame (with the Heartbreakers in 1999), and induction into the Rock and Roll Hall of Fame (with the Heartbreakers in 2002).

Eric Novod

Further Reading

Block, Debbie Galante, with Melinda Newman and Craig Rosen. "Getting at the Essence of the Heartbreakers." *Billboard* 118, no. 12 (March 25, 2006): 46-48. A brief article with several musicians discussing what makes the Heartbreakers an exemplary live band.

Petty, Tom. *Running Down a Dream: Tom Petty and the Heartbreakers*. San Francisco: Chronicle Books, 2007. A voluminous book version of the coinciding 2007 documentary film of the same name. This book contains a biography of the band and numerous photographs of the band in action.

Waterman, Douglas J. *Song: The World's Best Songwriters on Creating the Music that Moves Us*. Cincinnati, Ohio: Writer's Digest Books, 2007. The interview with Petty contains a detailed history of the beginnings of the Heartbreakers and Petty's thoughts on the songwriter's craft.

Wixen, Randall. *The Plain and Simple Guide to Music Publishing*. Milwaukee, Wis.: Hal Leonard, 2005. Petty wrote the foreword to this book, in which he discusses his experiences in retaining the publishing rights to his music.

Zollo, Paul. *Conversations with Tom Petty*. London: Omnibus Press, 2005. More than three hundred pages of in-depth interviews with Petty, covering his entire musical career.

See also: Burke, Solomon; Domino, Fats; Dylan, Bob; Eno, Brian; Harrison, George; Nicks, Stevie; Orbison, Roy; Prine, John; Reed, Jimmy; Stills, Stephen; Williams, Lucinda.

Édith Piaf

French singer

One of France's most celebrated singers, Piaf rose from poverty to international fame. She became a French cultural and artistic icon with her dynamic, soulful, and emotional performances of French ballads and love songs.

Born: December 19, 1915; Paris, France
Died: October 11, 1963; Paris, France
Also known as: Édith Giovanna Gassion

Principal recordings

ALBUMS: *Live at Carnegie Hall*, 1957; *Inedits et documents*, 1973; *But Not Forgotten*, 1977; *The Very Best of Édith Piaf*, 1977.

SINGLES: "L'Étranger," 1936; "Mon Légionnaire," 1937; "C'est lui que mon cœur a choisi" (he is what my heart has chosen), 1938; "L'Accordéoniste," 1940; "La Vie en rose," 1946; "Les Trois Cloches," 1946 (with Les Compagnons de la Chanson); "Hymne à l'amour," 1949; "L'Orgue des amoureux," 1949; "Milord," 1959; "La Belle Histoire d'amour,"

1960; "Non, je ne regrette rien," 1960; "L'Homme de Berlin," 1963.

WRITINGS OF INTEREST: *The Wheel of Fortune: The Autobiography of Édith Piaf*, 1958; *My Life*, 2000.

The Life

Born Édith Giovanna Gassion, Édith Piaf (AY-diht pyahf) had an impoverished childhood. Her father, Louis-Alphonse Gassion, was a traveling circus acrobat, while her mother, Annetta Giovanna Maillard, was a singer. When her father joined the French army in 1916, Piaf was left with her maternal grandmother, who neglected her. Piaf was then left with her paternal grandmother in a brothel in Normandy. Later, Piaf toured France and Belgium with her father's circus caravan.

Édith Piaf. (AP/Wide World Photos)

At fifteen she sang for money in the streets of Paris with her half sister Simone "Momone" Berteaut; they were often homeless and hungry. She then lived in poverty with Louis Dupont, and in 1933 they had a daughter. Piaf left Dupont, and their child died before the age of two.

In 1935 Louis Leplée, the owner of a popular Parisian nightclub, heard Piaf sing. He named her "La Môme Piaf" (Kid Sparrow) because she was under five feet tall. From then on, she used the name Piaf. In her trademark black dress, she made her professional debut at the nightclub and was soon heard on Parisian radio. In early 1936 she released her first recording, "L'Étranger" (the stranger), for Polydor Records. In April, 1936, Leplée was murdered, possibly by gangsters.

In 1937 Piaf began a successful collaboration with songwriter Raymond Asso. Composer Marguerite Monnot and Asso wrote Piaf's first hit, "Mon Légionnaire" (my legionnaire). Asso was also her mentor and lover for several years.

During the war years, Piaf's career continued to grow. In 1940 she appeared in Jean Cocteau's play *Le Bel indifférent*, and in 1941 she acted in and wrote songs for Georges Lacombe's film *Montmartre-sur-Seine*. She also secretly helped forge photo identification cards that enabled French prisoners of war to escape.

In 1946 Piaf became internationally known when "La Vie en Rose" was a best-selling recording in the United States. In 1947 she went to America, where she became a star after performing at the elegant supper club Versailles. She also had a turbulent two-year affair with Marcel Cerdan, the world middleweight boxing champion. She was devastated when he died in a plane crash on his way back to New York.

During the 1950's, Piaf continued her successful film, concert, and recording career, but she also suffered from alcoholism and major illnesses. Car accidents resulted in a dependence on morphine. Her marriage to the singer Jacques Pills in 1952 ended in divorce in 1956. However, "Milord" and "Non, je ne regrette rien" were huge hits, and she made a comeback appearance at Paris's Olympia Theater on December 29, 1960. Although in deteriorating health, in 1962 she married Théo Sarapo, a twenty-six-year-old French singer, who cared for Piaf until her death.

The Music

Piaf began her career in the tradition of the Parisian *chanson*, or French popular song. Primarily a cabaret or music hall performer, she favored the realistic songs of Marie-Louise Damien, known as Damia, "La Tragedienne de la Chanson." These were popular songs of the 1920's with morbid lyrics and usually tragic endings. Soon Piaf's powerful but tender voice and her soulful and passionate performances firmly established her reputation in the most famous Parisian music halls and cafés, such as Moulin Rouge and ABC. Composers and songwriters wrote songs specifically for her style, and she herself wrote many hit songs. She transformed Parisian cabaret singing into an international phenomenon for film, television, and large concert halls, with huge orchestras and audiences.

Early Successes. Her first hit recording, "Mon Légionnaire," was a sad, romantic song of a woman longing for a legionnaire she had loved for one night and who was later found dead in the desert. Another song by Raymond Asso, "C'est lui que mon cœeur a choisi" (he is what my heart has chosen), was a hit in 1938. In 1940 she met the composer Michel Emer and recorded his "L'Accordéoniste" (the accordionist), which sold more than a million copies and was her biggest seller thus far.

"La Vie en rose." During World War II, Piaf wrote the words for "La Vie en rose" (life in pink), and the melody was composed by Louis Gugliemi, who wrote under the pen name of Louiguy. Recorded in 1946, the song was an immediate international hit and became Piaf's signature song. The lyrics speak of a woman who sees life in rosy hues because a man has spoken words of romance to her and promised her lifelong love. The song was so popular that Piaf included it in most of her later albums. Her friend Marlene Dietrich sang it in the film *Stage Fright* (1950).

"Les Trois Cloches." In 1941 in Lyons, the singing ensemble Compagnons de la Musique (companions of music) was started, consisting of nine young men born into the Compagnons de France (a craftsman's guild). This group of harmony singers featured three tenor, three bass, and three baritone voices. They specialized in folk repertoire with controlled technique. In 1944 Piaf was impressed by their performance at a benefit event, and she became their patron and mentor.

By 1946 they had changed their name to Les Compagnons de la Chanson (the companions of the song). Piaf felt they should also change their repertoire, so she and the group recorded "Les Trois Cloches" (The Three Bells), a song written in 1945 by the Swiss composer and actor Jean Villard-Gilles. This haunting song tells of Jean-François Nicot, who was born, married, and died in a village in the valley, with bells ringing each time. The recording sold more than a million copies and the group accompanied Piaf on her first trip to New York in October, 1947. They often toured together and made more hit recordings, including "Céline," "Dans les prisons de Nantes," and "C'est pour ça." "Les Trois Cloches" was later translated into English and was a number-one hit on both popular and country-music charts in 1959 for the Browns, an American country-music group.

"Hymne à l'amour." When in 1949 the boxer Cerdan died in a plane crash en route to visit her in New York, Piaf was stricken with grief and guilt. She called Cerdan her one true love and wrote "Hymne à l'amour" (hymn to love) as a tribute. Monnot wrote the music. The lyrics express a love that survives the sun falling from the sky or the seas running dry. It is a love that will last through eternity, after life on earth. On May 2, 1950, Piaf recorded "Hymne à l'amour," and it became one of her most popular songs, selling several million copies. Geoffrey Parsons later wrote an English version, "If You Love Me (Really Love Me)." The song was recorded by many singers, including Vera Lynn in 1952, Kay Starr in 1954, and Shirley Bassey in 1959.

"Milord (Ombre de la rue)." Monnot wrote the music and Piaf's lover Georges Moustaki wrote the lyrics for this song. Recorded in 1959, "Milord," or "Ombre de la Rue" (shadow of the street), immediately topped European music charts. In this song the singer is a lower-class French girl who feels she is only a "shadow of the street" in love with a "milord" or upper-class English traveler.

"Non, je ne regrette rien." Charles Dumont wrote the music and Michel Vaucaire wrote the lyrics for this classic, which Piaf recorded in 1960. Often considered Piaf's epitaph, "Non, je ne regrette rien" (no, I regret nothing) became one of the most famous songs of all time. The song expresses a total renunciation of the past, because life and happiness have been reborn with a new love.

"L'Homme de Berlin." In early 1963, Piaf recorded her final song, "L'Homme de Berlin" (man in Berlin), with lyrics by Michèle Vendôme and music by Francis Lai.

Musical Legacy

Piaf was one of most beloved and highest paid artists ever. During her lifetime, Piaf wrote thirty songs and performed more than two hundred. She had many devoted friends, and she generously supported and mentored young artists such as Yves Montand and Charles Aznavour. Her collaborators and friends included Charlie Chaplin, Maurice Chevalier, and Dietrich. When he heard that Piaf had died, Cocteau planned to deliver her eulogy, but he died later that same day. Piaf was buried in the famous Père Lachaise Cemetery in Paris. Hundreds of thousands of people marched in her funeral procession, and more than forty thousand fans attended the ceremony at the grave.

After her death Piaf's music and legend continued to inspire and fascinate new generations of artists and fans through film, television, recordings, and other media. She had transformed the old music hall Parisian *chanson* into a style of song enjoyed worldwide. Stars such as Josh Groban and Patti LaBelle recorded her "Hymne à l'amour."

Piaf's signature song, "La Vie en rose," became a standard in the popular-song repertoire and was recorded by more than fifty famous artists, including Grace Jones, Louis Armstrong, Julio Iglesias, Celine Dion, and Plácido Domingo. Piaf's 1950 Columbia recording of "La Vie en rose" received a 1998 Grammy Hall of Fame Award. Since it was first sung by Dietrich in the film *Stage Fright*, the song has been featured in more than twenty movies.

Pam Gems wrote a Tony Award-winning play entitled *Piaf*. In 2007, a highly acclaimed French feature movie called *La Môme* (the kid) or *La Vie en Rose* (for English-speaking audiences) was released.

Alice Myers

Further Reading

Berteaut, Simone. *Piaf*. New York: Harper & Row, 1972. Vivid, detailed, and fascinating biography by Piaf's half sister, who sang in the streets with Piaf when they were young and poor. Piaf's lifelong companion, Berteaut has written an intimate and revealing account. Illustrated. Index.

Bret, David. *Piaf: A Passionate Life*. London: JR Books, 2007. Written by Britain's leading authority on French music halls, this is a definitive biography of Piaf. This paperback version coincided with the release of the film *La Vie en Rose*. Illustrated. Bibliography, index, discography, and filmography.

Crosland, Margaret, and Ralph Harvey. *A Cry from the Heart: A Biography of Édith Piaf*. London: Arcadia, 2002. Well-researched and objective biography covering Piaf's entire life, including her drug addictions, love affairs, marriages, and friendships. Illustrated. Bibliography, discography, filmography, and index.

Grimault, Dominique, and Patrick Mahé. *Piaf and Cerdan: A Hymn to Love*. London: W. H. Allen, 1984. Translated by Barbara Mitchell. Readable account of the relationship between Piaf and Cerdan, the boxing champion Piaf called her greatest love. Illustrated. Bibliography.

Jones, Stacy. *Torch Singing: Performing Resistance and Desire from Billie Holiday to Édith Piaf*. Lanham, Md.: AltaMira Press, 2007. An innovative perspective and cultural critique on torch songs, sentimental love songs about unrequited love. The author sees torch singers as not only expressing desire and victimization but also seeking to resist and change. Bibliography and index.

Piaf, Édith. *The Wheel of Fortune: The Autobiography of Édith Piaf*. London: Peter Owen, 2004. Written in 1958, five years before her death, this autobiography consists of Piaf's reminiscences about her life and career. Although not comprehensive and not in chronological order, this volume reveals many of Piaf's thoughts, experiences, and relationships. Illustrated.

Piaf, Édith, and Jean Noli. *My Life*. London: Peter Owen, 2000. Dictating from her hospital bed before her death, Piaf speaks in detail about her childhood, love affairs, drugs, alcoholism, the money she earned, and stardom. Piaf attempts to set the record straight and to show that—in the words of her song, "Non, je ne regrette rien"— she did not regret anything. Illustrated.

See also: Armstrong, Louis; Domingo, Plácido; LaBelle, Patti.

Astor Piazzolla

Argentine Latin accordion and bandoneón player and composer

Piazzolla extracted the tango from the streets of Buenos Aires and brought it to the finest music halls of the world. By highlighting its lyricism and subduing its sentimentality, he transformed tango into a contemporary musical form that showed the classical influences of Maurice Ravel, Claude Debussy, Giacomo Puccini, and Olivier Messiaen and the jazz influences of Gerry Mulligan and Lennie Tristano.

Born: March 11, 1921; Mar del Plata, Argentina
Died: July 4, 1992; Buenos Aires, Argentina
Also known as: Astor Pantaleón Piazzolla (full name)

Principal recordings

ALBUMS: *Adios nonino*, 1960; *Tiempo nuevo*, 1962; *La guardia vieja*, 1966; *Libertango*, 1975; *Il pleut sur Santiago*, 1976; *Suite punta del este*, 1982; *Tangos: The Exile of Gardel*, 1985; *Astor Piazzolla Plays Astor Piazzolla*, 1986; *Tango: Zero Hour*, 1986; *The Rough Dancer and the Cyclical Night*, 1987; *The New Tango*, 1988 (with Gary Burton); *La camorra: La soledad de la provocación apasionada*, 1990; *Lumiere*, 1990; *Five Tango Sensations*, 1991; *Los grandes exitos*, 1991; *Ballet Tango*, 1992; *Sur*, 1992; *A intrusa, Vol. 3*, 1994; *Armaguedon, Vol. 2*, 1994; *Otoño porteño, Vol. 2*, 1994; *El porteño*, 1994 (with David Tanenbaum); *Histoire du Tango: Five Pieces*, 1995 (for flute and guitar); *Pulsación*, 1995; *Cincuenta y siete minutos con la realidad*, 1996; *Original Tangos from Argentina*, 1996; *Songs from a Heavy Heart*, 1996; *Balada para un loco*, 1997; *Le Grand Tango: Music of Latin America*, 1997 (with others); *Muerto del ángel*, 1997; *Quinteto*, 1997; *Spirit of Buenos Aires*, 1997; *El tango*, 1997; *Tangos and Milongas*, 1997 (with Jorge Luis Borges); *Tanguedia de amor*, 1997; *Tres minutos con la realidad*, 1997; *Astor Piazzolla and Amelita Baltar*, 1998.

The Life

In the 1920's the Piazzolla family moved from a poor region in southern Italy to Argentina, then among the richest countries in the world. Born with a badly twisted and shorter right leg, Astor Pantaleón Piazzolla (pih-aht-SOL-lah) had from his childhood a feeling of being an outsider. When he was two his family moved to Greenwich Village in New York, where for fourteen years he had a fairly strict upbringing. He grew up listening to his father's tango records and to jazz singer Cab Calloway at a Harlem nightclub. At age eight he received a bandoneón (a type of large accordion) from his father, an amateur musician with aspirations of a musical career for his son. Piazzolla played the button squeeze box for a couple of years until he came to a true discovery of music when he heard his Hungarian neighbor, Béla Wilda, play Johann Sebastian Bach. Wilda became Piazzolla's piano teacher, and soon Andrés d'Aquila, an Argentine musician living in New York, became his bandoneón teacher.

Piazzolla's return to Argentina at age sixteen marked the beginning of his immersion in the tango culture of Buenos Aires, where tango had emerged in the 1880's as a synthesis of such dance forms as zarzuelas, habaneras, polkas, waltzes, and milongas. Initially considered indecent music, its reputation improved after it gained approval in Paris and Hollywood in the late 1890's. By the time Piazzolla arrived in Buenos Aires, tango was a strong enough genre to instill in him a desire to push it forward, redefining its style and voice. This vision of refined tango music playing in great music halls propelled his professional career and life passion.

Both as a businessman of great humor (his friends called him "a machine gun of jokes") and a family man with his wife Dedé and his two children, Diana and Daniel, Piazzolla led a fruitful life. His family provided continuous support throughout the years of scarcity, incessant moving, extensive traveling, touring, and resistance to the so-called traditionalists or "anti-piazzollistas" who objected to his imaginative and innovative ideas. His musical life—composed of late nights, billiard sessions, smoking, and cabaret and dance halls—along with his difficult character and recurrent fighting with his friends culminated in a heart attack in 1973 and a subsequent stroke in 1990. He died two years later, still a workingman.

The Music

Filming some scenes with Carlos Gardel in 1935's *El día que me quieras* (the day you will love me) and serving as his accompanist several times on the bandoneón opened the door to Piazzolla's professional career. He had met Gardel in 1933, when the Latin American music superstar, known as El Zorzal Criollo, the Creole Thrush, made his appearance in New York, singing tangos and making movies and radio programs. Gardel was a strong influence on the aspiring bandoneón player. Further exposure came years after his return to Buenos Aires, when Piazzolla met such leading musicians as Pedro Laurentz, Pedro Maffia, Ciriaco Ortiz, and Aníbal Troilo, all of whom supported tango evolution and opposed the tango traditionalists who resented any attempt to modernize it. During these years, Piazzolla, a disciplined young man, spent his daytime hours listening to two of his favorite composers, Igor Stravinsky and Béla Bartók, and analyzing their scores while at nighttime he explored the streets of Buenos Aires, seeking the musical secrets of tango. On radio stations and in cabarets and bars, tango had a pervasive presence. In 1939 Piazzolla got a chance to make his debut as bandoneón player on Radio El Mundo.

Piazzolla had three influential teachers: the city of Buenos Aires, Nadia Boulanger, and composer Alberto Ginastera. The opportunity to study with Boulanger came as a prize for his *Buenos Aires Symphony*, which, after scandalizing some members of the audience, won the Fabien Sevitzky competition and premiered in 1953 with Sevitzky as conductor. This opened the door to France and to Boulanger, a composition teacher who helped Piazzolla. Later Ginastera gave him the musical foundation he needed: orchestration.

The 1946 Band. The day Piazzolla founded the Orquesta Típica de Astor Piazzolla was the most important of his life. His first recording for Odeon Records was with Roberto di Filippo, who exerted a significant influence on Piazzolla's bandoneón style and the sound track to 1947's *El Hombre del sábado* (the Saturday

man) directed by Leopoldo Torres Ríos. The band also played for numerous radio stations and in concert halls, cafés, and tango bars. The bandoneón variations, counterpoint, and violin solos won Piazzolla's band a revolutionary reputation, but its moderate popularity under Juan Perón's first presidency (1946-1952) began to wane as Piazzolla felt the pressure that eventually led him to dissolve the band. He was expected to play *ad honorem* for government-sponsored events and felt obliged to compose "Hymn to Perón," which he later destroyed. Ironically, after the band's dissolution, during the 1950's Piazzolla was forced to compose for films that were subsidized by the government.

Tango and Ballet. In 1960 Piazzolla began collaboration with a number of ballet companies and choreographers, including Ana Itelman, for whom he composed music for a ballet based on Jorge Luis Borges's short story "Hombre de la esquina rosada" (man on the rose corner). Later that year he collaborated with Juan Carlos Copes and María Nieves in *Tango Argentino*, which would become a

Astor Piazzolla. (Hulton Archive/Getty Images)

hit show in the 1980's. He toured with Copes's company Compañía Argentina Tangolandia, and, later, in 1968-1969, he wrote the three-movement *Tangazo* for the choreographer Oscar Araiz's documentary on tango, which was never released. Throughout the rest of his career his music attracted prestigious choreographers, and today Piazzolla's music forms part of the repertoire of all major ballet companies in the world.

Jazz Tango. Two extremely fruitful periods stand out in Piazzolla's life. The first was after his return from France, when a synthesis of his major influences—Troilo, Alfredo Gobbi, Ginastera, and Boulanger—consolidated his style imbued with new rhythms, sound effects, string counterpoint, percussive violin, cello, bass, and electric guitar. He formed his Octet, whose objective was to push forward Piazzolla's musical revolution. This audacious group played in bordellos as well as New York's Philharmonic Hall. Unfortunately, it lasted only eighteen months, after facing much resistance to its innovations and the sabotage of radio personalities who refused to play the Octet's records.

The First Quintet. The avant-garde of the 1960's saw the birth of Piazzolla's first Quintet, including bandoneón, electric guitar, piano, contrabass, and violin. With the Quintet he approached the pinnacle of his career. His "operita de tango" *Maria de Buenos Aires*, played by a ten-piece orchestra, almost bankrupted him, but it did not deter him. It also marked the beginning of his collaboration with singer Maria Amelia Baltar, known as Amelita, with whom he would later have a love affair.

Piazzolla's other fruitful period began in 1968, his most prolific as a composer. At that time, among other works, he composed, in collaboration with lyricist Horacio Ferrer, the acclaimed "Balada para un loco" (ballad for a madman), an icon in the history of tango. In the 1970's, during the Argentine dictatorship, Piazzolla moved to Italy, where, in collaboration with his Italian agent Aldo Pagani, he released his famous *Libertango, Summit*, and *Suite troileana* that earned him worldwide recognition.

The Nonet. The Nonet, an ensemble of nine members, marked the summit of Piazzolla's composing and performing career. *Concierto de nácar para nueve tanguistas y orquesta* (mother-of-pearl concert for nine tango players and orchestra) was inspired by the events of August 22, 1972, when the military regime massacred a group of alleged guerrilla fighters trying to escape. The Nonet was followed by the second Quintet and the Sextet, along with additional compositions and arrangements.

Musical Legacy

With the polyrhythmic complexities, counterpoint, fugues, and harmonies that Piazzolla infused in the genre, tango emerged in the twentieth century as music that is triumphant and romantic, bohemian and delicate. The strong-willed composer not only uprooted the essence of tango but also refined it with compelling classical and jazz rhythms and jazz-style improvisation. Bringing the bandoneón to its greatest height, Piazzolla made a quintet sound like a twenty-piece orchestra. The newspaper *Marcha* described him as a man who defied a traditional establishment greater than the state, greater than the gaucho, greater than soccer: He dared to challenge the tango. Piazzolla's musical revolution paralleled his country's political revolution. He enraged the tango traditionalists and resisted the "cheap tango" *empresarios*. Although it was not until the end of his life that he received a respected place in classical music, he stands today as a composer of magnitude.

Sylvia P. Baeza

Further Reading

Azzi, María Susana, and Simon Collier. *Le Grand Tango: The Life and Music of Astor Piazzolla*. New York: Oxford University Press, 2000. With a foreword by Yo-Yo Ma in an interview with Azzi, this text exposes Piazzolla the man and the musician in all his vulnerable aspects as artist, husband, and cultural icon. Arranged chronologically, the chapters open with quotations from the composer, shedding light on his artistic vision. Includes a glossary of South American terms and an appendix on Piazzolla on compact disc.

Baim, Jo. *Tango: Creation of a Cultural Icon*. Bloomington: Indiana University Press, 2007. This history of tango covers its origins and its evolution in Europe and the United States. Two chapters relate to Piazzolla: "Argentina Claims Its Native Dance" and "Tango in the World of Art Music."

Croppa, Carlos G. *The Tango in the United States*. Jefferson, N.C.: McFarland, 2004. Two chapters discuss Piazzolla within the context of the ascendance of tango in America; other chapters cover Argentine influence on the New York tango scene.

Gorin, Natalio. *Astor Piazzolla: A Memoire*. Translated, annotated, and expanded by Fernando Gonzalez. Portland, Oreg.: Amadeus Press, 2001. Succinct account of the composer's life as told to the journalist Gorin in a series of interviews held two years before the composer's death. Documents his rise in the music world and his contribution to music. Includes a separate chapter on the bandoneón, a discography of recordings, a chronology, and a bibliography. Illustrated with photographs, handwritten scores, fully annotated.

Prieto, Carlos. *The Adventures of a Cello*. Austin: University of Texas Press, 2006. Includes information on Piazzolla as one of the preeminent composers for the cello.

See also: Boulanger, Nadia; Burton, Gary; Copland, Aaron; Debussy, Claude; Golijov, Osvaldo; Ma, Yo-Yo; Messiaen, Olivier; Puccini, Giacomo; Ravel, Maurice.

Wilson Pickett

American rhythm-and-blues singer and songwriter

Pickett's unique sound, combining elements of rhythm and blues, blues, rock, jazz, and gospel, paved the way for soul.

Born: March 18, 1941; Prattville, Alabama
Died: January 19, 2006; Reston, Virginia
Member of: The Violinaires; the Falcons

Principal recordings

ALBUMS: *It's Too Late*, 1963; *In the Midnight Hour*, 1965; *The Exciting Wilson Pickett*, 1966; *The Wicked Pickett*, 1966; *The Sound of Wilson Pickett*, 1967; *I'm in Love*, 1968; *The Midnight Mover*, 1968; *Hey Jude*, 1969; *Right On*, 1970; *Wilson Pickett in Philadelphia*, 1970; *Don't Knock My Love*, 1971; *Engine No. 9*, 1971; *Miz Lena's Boy*, 1973; *Mr. Magic Man*, 1973; *Pickett in My Pocket*,

1974; *A Funky Situation*, 1978; *I Want You*, 1979; *Right Track*, 1981; *American Soul Man*, 1987; *It's Harder Now*, 1999.

The Life

One of eleven children, Wilson Pickett was born March 18, 1941, in Prattville, Alabama. After his parents separated, the family moved to Louisville, Kentucky, and when he was fourteen Pickett went to Detroit to live with his father. Pickett discovered music at church, and he made his first recording, for Chess Records, in 1957 as part of the gospel quartet the Violinaires. In 1961 he replaced Joe Stubbs as lead singer for the Detroit group the Falcons, whose members included Eddie Floyd and Mack Rice, who both became famous as singer-songwriters. In 1962 Pickett wrote and sang lead on the Falcons' second hit, "I Found a Love," after which he left to begin his solo career.

After the solo hits "If You Need Me" and "It's Too Late," Pickett signed a contract in 1964 with Atlantic Records, a pioneer in recording rhythm-and-blues performers. Disappointed with Pickett's initial sessions in New York, legendary producer Jerry Wexler wanted Pickett to work with Atlantic subsidiary Stax Records in Memphis, Tennessee, suggesting that working with Southern musicians would better suit Pickett's gospel-influenced style.

The resulting Stax sessions with members of the label's house band—Booker T. and the MGs, including guitarists Steve Cropper and Donald "Duck" Dunn, drummer Al Jackson, and the Memphis Horns—produced four hits in 1965: "In the Midnight Hour," "Don't Fight It," "634-5789 (Soulsville, U.S.A.)," and "Ninety-nine-and-a-half (Won't Do)."

When Stax banned outside productions, Wexler transferred Pickett's recording sessions to the soulful Muscle Shoals, Alabama, studio of Fame Records, where he continued to flourish. By the mid-1970's, he had more than forty songs on the rhythm-and-blues and pop charts, but no hits after "Fire and Water" in 1972. Pickett told interviewers that labels such as RCA did not know how to market the songs of African American artists.

Pickett was inducted into the Rock and Roll Hall of Fame in 1991, the same year his music was prominently used in Alan Parker's film *The Commitments* (1991). The plot involved young Irish musicians hoping to meet Pickett while he is performing in Dublin, but they just miss him. (Pickett is unseen in the film.)

In the 1990's, "Wicked" Pickett, a nickname bestowed by Wexler, had several altercations with the law while living in Teaneck, New Jersey. He was charged with assaulting his girlfriend, convicted of drunk driving after hitting a pedestrian, and arrested while driving his car over the mayor's front lawn.

Pickett made a comeback with *It's Harder Now*, nominated for a Grammy Award for Best Traditional Rhythm and Blues Performance. In 2003 he appeared in Chris Hegedus and D. A. Pennebaker's tribute to Stax Records, *Only the Strong Survive*. He stopped performing because of poor health at the end of 2004, and he died of a heart attack at a hospital in Reston, Virginia, near his home in Ashburn, on January 19, 2006. Little Richard presented the eulogy at his funeral in Louisville.

The Music

Pickett frequently sang in a gospel style, employing a shout of indefinite pitch. This type of shouting contributes to the rhythmic complexity of his singing, as he shifts back and forth between high and low notes. While some have described Pickett's voice as harsh, it has, beyond the shouting, considerable range, with soft, tender, and quite melodic qualities.

"In the Midnight Hour." Pickett cowrote several songs with Cropper, including "In the Midnight Hour," which became a number-one rhythm-and-blues hit and reached number twenty-one on the pop charts. The song's combination of an impassioned vocal with loping beats has been credited with helping rhythm and blues make the transition to soul. The pulsating horns opening this and other tunes sung by Pickett helped create a template for soul extended by Stax's arrangements for Otis Redding, whose voice had a plaintive quality missing from Pickett's.

Danceable Soul. Pickett's signature style—soulful and seemingly effortless—stood out in an era dominated by the Motown sound of the Supremes and the British Invasion sound inspired by 1950's American blues and rock. The Stax arrangements stood out as well for emphasizing the versatility of horn sections at a time when the guitar was

Wilson Pickett. (AP/Wide World Photos)

the dominant pop instrument. The music achieved a perfect balance among Pickett's voice, the guitars of Cropper and Dunn, and the Memphis Horns. While Redding and Aretha Franklin sang of the pains of love, Pickett showed that soul could be danceable as well.

"Mustang Sally." Pickett had a huge hit in 1966 with "Mustang Sally," which Rice had written and recorded a year earlier. It has remained one of the most popular and frequently recorded songs from the 1960's. "Land of One Thousand Dances," previously recorded by Cannibal and the Headhunters, became Pickett's biggest pop hit, reaching number six on the charts. Moving to American Studios in Memphis in 1967 and working with legendary recording engineer Tom Dowd, Pickett recorded several hits written by Bobby Womack. Pickett's success continued after he left Stax and Atlantic for other labels, where he released "Don't Knock My Love" and "Engine No. 9."

Ballads by Womack. After a period of hard-driving songs, Pickett returned to his original style with ballads written by Womack: "I Found a Love,"

"I'm in Love," and "Jealous Love." He alternated between ballads and funky songs for the rest of his career. His 1971 rhythm-and-blues hit "Don't Let the Green Grass Fool You" was also a hit on the country charts.

Versatility. Pickett further showed his versatility by recording a mournful version of the Beatles' "Hey Jude," and he brought a soulful bounce to the Archies' hit "Sugar, Sugar." During the late 1960's and early 1970's, Pickett frequently recorded songs originated by others, including Randy Newman's "Momma Told Me Not to Come," the Supremes' "You Keep Me Hangin' On," and Jimi Hendrix's "Hey, Joe," bringing his distinctive rhythms to each.

Musical Legacy

Pickett performed with many musicians who became famous later. Isaac Hayes played piano on some of his Stax recordings, and Duane Allman played guitar on "Hey Jude," a song he had recommended to the soul singer. Songs written by Pickett have been recorded by Aerosmith, Creedence Clearwater Revival, the Grateful Dead, Led Zeppelin, Los Lobos, the Rolling Stones, Bruce Springsteen, and Van Halen.

Pickett's vocal style had a notable impact. He clearly learned from Hank Ballard, James Brown, Ray Charles, Sam Cooke, and Little Richard, and just as obviously he influenced numerous others, including Redding, Franklin, Al Green, Etta James, and Tina Turner. Pickett arguably recorded the most energetic and danceable type of soul, and he was instrumental in making it a major force in American popular music.

Michael Adams

Further Reading

Bowman, Rob. *Soulsville, U.S.A.: The Story of Stax Records*. New York: Schirmer Books, 1997. This history of the label includes comments from those who worked with Pickett about his difficult personality.

Guralnick, Peter. *Sweet Soul Music: Rhythm and Blues and the Southern Dream of Freedom*. New York: Harper & Row, 1986. This outstanding musical history includes interviews with Pickett.

Hirshey, Gerri. "Wilson Pickett, 1941-2006." *Rolling Stone* (February 9, 2006): 17-18. In this article, Hirshey recalls her often tempestuous interviews with the singer.

Wexler, Jerry, and David Ritz. *Rhythm and the Blues: A Life in American Music*. New York: Knopf, 1993. The producer's autobiography includes anecdotes about Pickett.

See also: Burke, Solomon; Charles, Ray; Cooke, Sam; Franklin, Aretha; Hayes, Isaac; Little Richard; Newman, Randy; Redding, Otis; Seger, Bob; Springsteen, Bruce.

Robert Plant

English rock singer and songwriter

As a lead singer for Led Zeppelin, Plant is known for his wide-ranging vocal style, his stage bravado, and his mystical lyrics.

Born: August 20, 1948; Birmingham, England
Also known as: Robert Anthony Plant (full name)
Member of: Led Zeppelin; the Honeydrippers; Page and Plant

Principal recordings

ALBUMS (solo): *Pictures at Eleven*, 1982; *The Principle of Moments*, 1983; *Shaken 'n' Stirred*, 1985; *Now and Zen*, 1988; *Manic Nirvana*, 1990; *Fate of Nations*, 1993; *Dreamland*, 2002; *Enchanter*, 2005; *Mighty Rearranger*, 2005; *Raising Sand*, 2007 (with Alison Krauss).

ALBUM (with the Honeydrippers): *The Honeydrippers, Vol. 1*, 1984.

ALBUMS (with Led Zeppelin): *Led Zeppelin*, 1969; *Led Zeppelin II*, 1969; *Led Zeppelin III*, 1970; *Led Zeppelin IV*, 1971; *Houses of the Holy*, 1973; *Physical Graffiti*, 1975; *Presence*, 1976; *The Song Remains the Same*, 1976; *In Through the Out Door*, 1979; *Jukebox*, 2006.

ALBUMS (with Page and Plant) *No Quarter: Robert Plant and Jimmy Page Unledded*, 1994; *Walking into Clarksdale*, 1998.

The Life

Robert Anthony Plant developed a strong passion for the blues at an early age, mainly through his admiration for Elvis Presley. Other influences included Robert Johnson, Otis Rush, Bukka White, Muddy Waters, Skip James, Jerry Miller, and Sleepy John Estes. In 1966 Plant left home to establish himself as a professional musician. His early career was spent in several Midlands-based rhythm-and-blues bands. By 1967 Plant had recorded six sides for CBS, had formed Band of Joy with drummer John Bonham, and had created crucial working relationships with Terry Reid and veteran blues bandleader Alexis Korner. Although Plant's early career met with little commercial success, he developed a formidable reputation as a vocalist, lyricist, and front man.

In 1968 guitarist Jimmy Page was in search of a new lead singer. Page and his manager Peter Grant heard Plant performing in a local act called Hobbstweedle, and the singer was invited to join the New Yardbirds. Shortly thereafter, Plant and Page commenced their collaboration by writing new versions of classic blues songs. Led Zeppelin was formed in 1968, and their self-titled debut album hit the charts in 1969. They quickly became known as one of England's most talented and exciting musical acts. The band's emphasis on familiar blues-rock forms embellished with exotic flavors resonated with audiences of the 1970's. Within a few short years, Led Zeppelin was shattering album sales and box-office records. By 1972 Plant was fronting one of the most successful bands in rock history.

In the middle and late 1970's, Led Zeppelin endured a series of tragedies that ultimately ended the legendary alliance. Two events in Plant's personal life significantly disrupted the band's artistic momentum, casting a shadow over its success. In 1975 Plant and his wife Maureen were seriously injured in an automobile accident in Rhodes, Greece. This incident sidelined him (and the band) for two years. In 1977 Karac, his oldest son, tragically died of a viral infection while Plant was on a concert tour of the United States. Led Zep-

pelin suffered a final debilitating blow on September 25, 1980. While rehearsing for an upcoming American tour, drummer John Bonham was found dead of asphyxiation following excessive alcohol consumption. Led Zeppelin was disbanded shortly thereafter, the members believing that Bonham was irreplaceable.

Plant began contemplating a solo career, and the project entitled *Pictures at Eleven* demonstrated the eclectic singer's interest in new musical avenues. A second successful album, *The Principle of Moments*, followed in dramatic fashion. The singer then acknowledged his Presley infatuation and rhythm-and-blues roots through his participation in an all-star group called the Honeydrippers. Plant moved in the direction of less-conventional music in his solo album *Shaken 'n' Stirred*, and he resumed recording in 1987 with a group of innovative young musicians. *Now and Zen* was hailed by many critics as a striking return to form, and the singer's rejuvenation continued on *Manic Nirvana* and *Fate of Nations*.

In 1994 Plant collaborated with Page on *No Quarter: Robert Plant and Jimmy Page Unledded*, featuring a mixture of Egyptian, North African, and folk sounds, and in 1998 the duo released an album of

Robert Plant. (AP/Wide World Photos)

original material titled *Walking into Clarksdale*. At the close of 1999, Plant performed in several small venues with his folk-rock band Priory of Brion. Plant's wide-ranging appetite for exotic sounds collided with his lifelong appreciation of psychedelic rock in a new band known as Strange Sensation. Its first album, *Dreamland*, received critical acclaim and two Grammy Award nominations. The group's second album, *Mighty Rearranger*, contained eclectic original material, and it also received favorable reviews and two Grammy Award nominations.

In 2007 Plant and bluegrass star Alison Krauss released the album *Raising Sand*. This remarkable partnership showcased lesser-known material from rhythm-and-blues, country, and folk songwriters.

Led Zeppelin officially reunited to perform at the Ahmet Ertegün charity concert in London on December 10, 2007. Jason Bonham, the son of deceased Zeppelin member John Bonham, sat in as drummer.

The Music

Plant's finest works are characterized by a successful blending of disparate influences. His eclectic body of repertoire represents a career of musical experimentation marked by an interest in exotic musical materials. As a performer, he is noted for his ability to sing a wide range of songs in a refined and cultivated manner.

Early Years. Plant's early musical career was spent in several rhythm-and-blues bands, including the New Memphis Bluesbreakers and the Crawling King Snakes (with drummer John Bonham). He joined Listen in 1965, a Motown-influenced act, which later signed a contract with CBS Records. Plant prepared for a solo career with the release of two singles in 1967, "Laughing, Crying, Laughing" and "Long Time Coming." After returning to Birmingham, the singer formed Band of Joy, in which his fascination with psychedelic music flourished. This promising group disbanded in 1968, and then Plant was briefly associated with Alexis Korner, a legend in the British blues and rhythm-and-blues circuit. Plant worked as harmonica player and covocalist in various Korner ventures.

"Dazed and Confused." The initial collaboration between Plant and Page resulted in the elon-gation of blues forms with extended solos and psychedelic effects. The band worked tirelessly to establish Led Zeppelin's reputation in 1968, and the agonizing blues classic "Dazed and Confused" provided widespread exposure. Recorded at Olympic Studios in London, the song was included on Led Zeppelin's 1969 self-titled debut album. An expanded arrangement had been performed by the Yardbirds, and the version developed by Led Zeppelin featured different lyrics. The recording highlighted tour de force vocals by Plant, supported by menacing instrumental performances. The work became an early highlight of live concerts, frequently lasting up to forty-five minutes.

"Stairway to Heaven." Plant's vocal contribution to this memorable song is among his most significant achievements with Led Zeppelin. The group's untitled fourth album, also known as *Led Zeppelin IV*, remains an enduring milestone, and "Stairway to Heaven" represents a fully realized hybrid of the folk and hard-rock genres that the band embraced. The eight-minute epic draws influences from folk, blues, and Celtic traditional music. Most of the lyrics were written spontaneously by Plant in 1970 at Headley Grange; he created genuine poetry with his numinous images and words. It showcases a carefully constructed arrangement, the effective use of dynamics, and an impressive climax. The song achieves a palpable intimacy, and it consequently became the centerpiece of live concerts.

"Kashmir." This intriguing song appeared on Led Zeppelin's *Physical Graffiti*. Its Eastern flavor, with allusions to Moroccan, Indian, and Middle Eastern music, and its orchestral sound launched Led Zeppelin into a new direction. The song was originally titled "Driving to Kashmir." The lyrics were composed by Plant during a holiday in southern Morocco, and they were inspired by the long drive from Goulimine to Tantan. The deeper meaning of the song lies in the intersection of the mystical powers of Arabian music and the communicative powers of rock.

"Sea of Love." Plant formed the Honeydrippers in 1981 to satisfy his desire of creating a rock band with vintage rhythm-and-blues origins. In addition to Plant, the band comprised Page, Jeff Beck, Nile Rodgers, and other well-known studio musicians. The group released an album of five classic songs,

The Honeydrippers: Vol. 1, on November 12, 1984. The inclusion of "Sea of Love" recalls Plant's infatuation with Presley and his rhythm-and-blues roots. It was written by John Phillip Baptiste (Phil Phillips) and George Khoury. The Honeydrippers' cover version reached number three on the *Billboard Hot 100* chart in 1984.

"Big Log." This mysterious ballad appears on Plant's second solo album, *The Principle of Moments*. In this project, he renewed his partnership with guitarist Robbie Blunt, bassist Paul Martinez, keyboardist Jezz Woodroffe, and drummer Phil Collins. The song features a vague Latin ambiance and a discreet synthesizer accompaniment that complements Blunt's guitar. Plant achieves an effective subtle tension in his bluesy vocals. He demonstrates his penchant for experimenting with ethnic materials and blending them with softer acoustic sounds. The title is likely meaningless, because the phrase does not appear in the lyrics. As the album's first single, "Big Log" reached the Top 20 in the United States and in England, and it was Plant's first hit as a solo artist. The song's introspective aura recalls the mystery of Led Zeppelin's finest work, and it helped establish Plant as an engaging solo artist.

Musical Legacy

Plant's unique approach to songwriting has influenced scores of musicians. His lyrics are frequently mystical, philosophical, and spiritual, featuring allusions to classical and Norse mythology. He also draws upon Welsh mythology. Growing up in Kidderminster, close to the Welsh border, he often took summer trips to the Snowdonia Mountains. Plant has been influenced by the works of J. R. R. Tolkien, resulting in overt references in some early Led Zeppelin classics such as "The Battle of Evermore," "Misty Mountain Hop," and "Ramble On." Conversely, Plant often used blues-based lyrics dealing primarily with sexual innuendo, such as found in "The Lemon Song," "Black Dog," and "Trampled Under Foot."

Plant enjoyed great success with Led Zeppelin, developing an image of the charismatic front man, such as Roger Daltrey and Jim Morrison. His distinctive vocal technique is a defining characteristic of Led Zeppelin's music. Plant possesses a high tenor voice with a remarkable range, and he is recognized for his lyrical improvisation in live performances, often singing verses not found on studio recordings. One of Plant's vocal trademarks is the mimicking of Page's guitar effects. This notable characteristic can be heard in Led Zeppelin songs such as "Dazed and Confused," "How Many More Times," and "The Lemon Song." As one of the most significant rock singers of recent generations, Plant influenced the vocal style of many of his contemporaries.

Christopher W. Cary

Further Reading

Clayson, Alan. *Led Zeppelin: The Origin of the Species*. Surrey, England: Chrome Dreams, 2006. This source recounts the musical influences and the early careers of band members, including Plant, and it chronicles the formation of Led Zeppelin. Tracing recordings and live sessions, it contains a family tree of musical colleagues, a discography, and a list of live performances.

Daniels, Neil, and Paul Stenning. *Robert Plant: Led Zeppelin, Jimmy Page, and the Solo Years*. Shropshire, England: Independent Music Press, 2008. The first biography to cover Plant's solo years, his collaborations with Page, and his numerous guest appearances. His later work is placed in a context of both Led Zeppelin's legacy and the broader history of modern music.

Shadwick, Keith. *Led Zeppelin: The Story of a Band and Their Music 1968-1980*. San Francisco: Backbeat Books, 2005. Offers an in-depth history of Led Zeppelin and reviews of its music. Chronicles the evolution of members as they emerged from the Yardbirds until the death of drummer Bonham.

Welch, Chris. *Led Zeppelin: Dazed and Confused*. New York: Thunder's Mouth Press, 1998. Reveals the origins of songs on all studio albums, together with stories behind post-Led Zeppelin material, such as *No Quarter: Robert Plant and Jimmy Page Unledded*.

See also: Beck, Jeff; Domino, Fats; Johnson, Robert; Krauss, Alison; Morrison, Jim; Page, Jimmy; Presley, Elvis.

Cole Porter

American musical-theater composer and lyricist

Breaking with the simple and sentimental style of Tin Pan Alley that dominated American popular music in the early part of the twentieth century, Porter introduced complicated musical composition, intense emotions, and clever rhymes and lyrics filled with sly sexual innuendos in his popular songs and musical comedies.

Born: June 9, 1891; Peru, Indiana
Died: October 15, 1964; Santa Monica, California
Also known as: Cole Albert Porter (full name)

Principal works

BALLET: *Within the Quota*, 1923 (libretto by Gerald Murphy).

MUSICAL THEATER (music and lyrics): *See America First*, 1916 (libretto by Thomas Lawrason Riggs and Porter); *Hitchy-Koo of 1919*, 1919 (revue; libretto by George V. Hobart); *Hitchy-Koo of 1922*, 1922 (revue; libretto by Harold Atteridge); *Greenwich Village Follies of 1924*, 1924 (revue; lyrics with Irving Caesar and John Murray Anderson); *Paris*, 1928 (libretto by M. Brown); *La Revue des ambassadeurs*, 1928; *Fifty Million Frenchmen*, 1929 (libretto by Herbert Fields); *Wake Up and Dream*, 1929 (revue; libretto by John Hastings Turner); *The New Yorkers*, 1930 (libretto by H. Fields; based on a story by E. Ray Goetz and Peter Arno); *Gay Divorce*, 1932 (libretto by Dwight Taylor); *Nymph Errant*, 1933 (libretto by Romney Brent; based on James Laver's novel); *Anything Goes*, 1934 (libretto by Guy Bolton, P. G. Wodehouse, Howard Lindsay, and Russel Crouse); *Jubilee*, 1935 (libretto by Moss Hart); *Red, Hot, and Blue*, 1936 (libretto by Lindsay and Crouse); *Leave It to Me*, 1938 (libretto by Bella Spewack and Sam Spewack); *You Never Know*, 1938 (libretto by Rowland Leigh); *Du Barry Was a Lady*, 1939 (libretto by Fields and Buddy G. DeSylva); *The Man Who Came to Dinner*, 1939 (libretto by Hart and George S. Kaufman); *Panama Hattie*, 1940 (libretto by H. Fields and DeSylva); *Let's Face It!*, 1941 (libretto by H. Fields and Dorothy Fields); *Something for the Boys*, 1943 (libretto by H. Fields and D. Fields); *Mexican Hayride*, 1944 (libretto by H. Fields and D. Fields); *Seven Lively Arts*, 1944 (revue; libretto by Hart, Kaufman, and Ben Hecht); *Around the World in Eighty Days*, 1946 (libretto by Orson Welles; based on Jules Verne's novel); *Kiss Me, Kate*, 1948 (libretto by B. and S. Spewack; based on William Shakespeare's play *The Taming of the Shrew*); *Out of This World*, 1950 (libretto by Taylor and Reginald Lawrence); *Can-Can*, 1953 (libretto by Abe Burrows); *Silk Stockings*, 1955 (libretto by Kaufman, Leueen MacGrath, and Burrows); *High Society*, 1998 (libretto by Arthur Kopit).

SONGS (music and lyrics): "Easy to Love," 1936; "I've Got You Under My Skin," 1936; "Rosalie," 1936; "Between You and Me," 1939; "I Concentrate on You," 1939; "I've Got My Eyes on You," 1939; "Please Don't Monkey with Broadway," 1939; "Dream Dancing," 1941; "Since I Kissed My Baby Goodbye," 1941; "So Near and Yet So Far," 1941; "Something to Shout About," 1942; "You'd Be So Nice to Come Home To," 1942; "Don't Fence Me In," 1944; "Be a Clown" 1948; "The Pirate Ballet," 1948; "True Love," 1955.

The Life

Cole Albert Porter had a musical gift. He began playing the violin at six, and when he was nine he took up the piano. At ten he and his mother composed an operetta. Porter's wealthy grandfather sent him to Yale in 1909.

His grandfather insisted that Porter, after graduating from Yale, attend Harvard Law School, but Porter soon transferred to the Harvard School of Music to learn music theory. Later, he studied music in New York City with Pietro Yon and Vincent d'Indy. In 1916 came Porter's first Broadway show, *See America First*. The show failed, and Porter retreated to Paris, where he lived on a generous allowance from his grandfather.

During World War I, Porter worked for the Duryea Relief Fund, and after the war, in 1919, he married Linda Lee Thomas, a wealthy divorcé eight years his senior. They remained married for thirty-four years. His marriage to Thomas allowed Porter to maintain a high social status throughout his life.

In Paris the Porters often brought groups such as the Monte Carlo Ballet to their home to entertain guests such as Igor Stravinsky, Irving Berlin, and Fanny Brice. Despite his long marriage, Porter led a sexually ambiguous life and had several male lovers.

Porter's first musical hit was *Paris*, and from there he went on to become one of America's most celebrated musical-theater composers. Life was good to Porter until he had a horseback-riding accident in 1937 that broke both his legs. After months in the hospital and more than thirty surgeries, Porter never walked again. This unfortunate event did not dim his energy, and he continued to compose with great success.

In the early 1950's two major influences in his life, his mother and his wife, died. These deaths were followed by increasing complications in his injured legs, and in 1958 he had to have his right leg amputated. Porter never wrote another song. His health continued to decline, and he died in 1964.

The Music

Early Works. Porter began composing songs and lyrics while studying at Yale, writing student musical shows, and his two football fight songs, "Yale Bulldog" and "Bingo Eli Yale," are still played today. In 1924 he wrote for the *Greenwich Village Follies*, but his attempts throughout the 1920's to write a successful Broadway musical failed.

Paris. Porter's first major Broadway success was *Paris*, a production created by a team of writers and composers. His song, "Let's Do It," was the outstanding composition of the show and became popular throughout the English-speaking world. In the 1950's Noël Coward wrote his own variations on the original lyrics for his performances in Las Vegas and New York. Porter had now introduced to a wide audience his unique musical composition and clever language.

Fifty Million Frenchmen. Porter composed all the music and lyrics for the musical *Fifty Million Frenchmen*, which contained another highly popular song, "You Do Something to Me." It became widely known through the film of the musical made in 1931.

The 1930's. The success of *Wake Up and Dream*, which featured the song "What Is This Thing Called Love?," proved that Porter was an important figure in American musical theater and a composer of highly popular songs. In 1932 *Gay Divorce* opened, featuring the song "Night and Day."

In 1934 came the major hit *Anything Goes*, starring Ethel Merman, who would go on to star in several more Porter works. In addition to the title song, *Anything Goes* introduced "I Get a Kick Out of You," "You're the Top," and "Blow, Gabriel, Blow." Two film versions were made of the musical, and it is still revived.

Building on the success of *Anything Goes*, Porter joined with Moss Hart in 1935 to create *Jubilee*, featuring "Begin the Beguine" and "Just One of Those Things." In the following year came *Red, Hot, and Blue*, starring Merman, Bob Hope, and Jimmy Durante and featuring "It's De-Lovely," a song still popular, especially with the 2004 release of the film *De-Lovely*.

Cole Porter. (Library of Congress)

In 1936-1937 Porter went to Hollywood to do film scores for the movies *Born to Dance* and *Rosalie*. The former featured the song "I've Got You Under My Skin," and the latter was enriched by the lovely ballad "In the Still of the Night," another song of enduring popularity. To close out the decade Porter returned to Broadway in 1938 with *Leave It to Me*, featuring Mary Martin singing "My Heart Belongs to Daddy." In 1939 came *Du Barry Was a Lady* with the song "Do I Love You?"

The 1940's. In the first half of the 1940's Porter composed for four successful Broadway musicals: *Panama Hattie, Let's Face It!, Something for the Boys,* and *Mexican Hayride*. *Let's Face It!* featured the song "A Little Rumba Numba," which demonstrated how interested Porter had become in Latin music. With the exception of "Hey, Good Lookin'" in *Something for the Boys*, there was little of musical significance to be found in Porter's shows of the early 1940's. He did compose "You'd Be So Nice to Come Home To" for the film *Something to Shout About* (1943). Nevertheless, some feared Porter's career as a lyricist and composer was over. In 1948, however, he wrote the words and music for one of the most significant theatrical musicals of the twentieth century: *Kiss Me, Kate*.

Kiss Me, Kate. With a book by Sam and Bella Spewack, *Kiss Me, Kate* is a musical adaptation of Shakespeare's *The Taming of the Shrew*. The book is excellent, but the words and music are superb, and each song fits comfortably into the script. First is the rousing "Another Op'nin', Another Show." After that are the rollicking "Wunderbar," "So in Love," "We Open in Venice," "Too Darn Hot," "We've Come to Wife It Weathily in Padua," "Always True to You (in My Fashion)," and "Brush Up Your Shakespeare." It is rare for a Broadway musical to have so many showstopping tunes.

Kiss Me, Kate won five Tony Awards, including for Best Musical and Best Composer and Lyricist. Indeed, it was the first musical ever to win a Tony Award. The production ran for a record 1,077 Broadway performances. In 1951 *Kiss Me, Kate* opened in London's West End, where it ran for 400 performances. In 1953 a successful film version was released. In 1999 another Broadway outing won a Tony Award for Best Revival of a Musical, and it was also revived on London's West End in 2001. In addition, there have been four major television pro-

ductions, as well as productions every year in professional theaters throughout the United States and Canada.

Later Works. Porter wrote several more musicals, including *Out of This World, Can-Can,* and *Silk Stockings*. *Out of This World* featured the number "I Am Loved." "I Love Paris" was the prominent song in *Can-Can*, and "All of You" was the feature of *Silk Stockings*. However, none of them would have the impact of *Kiss Me, Kate*. Porter was also busy in his later years composing scores for several films, including *High Society*, starring Bing Crosby, Frank Sinatra, and Grace Kelly.

Musical Legacy

Almost every aspect of popular music of the first half of the twentieth century reflects Porter's influence. He brought a new sense of urbanity and detached sophistication to both his music and his lyrics. Writing usually in minor keys with pleasingly unexpected interior rhymes, Porter mixed high culture with pop culture. Moreover, he was unafraid to approach taboo subjects with his sophisticated wit or to present intense human emotions in his songs. For example, his fearless ribald humor in "Love for Sale" forced the song to be banned on radio.

Porter created or helped to create more than twenty major Broadway musicals, many of which continue to be revived. There were films made of several of his shows, and more than eighty films used Porter songs or music. Roy Rogers recorded a country version of Porter's "Don't Fence Me In," and the Four Seasons recorded a rock version of "I've Got You Under My Skin." In 1955 a hard-rock version of "Let's Do It" was used in the film *Tank Girl*. Porter and his songs were the subject of two biographical films: *Night and Day* (1946), starring Cary Grant and Alexis Smith, and *De-Lovely* (2004), starring Kevin Kline and Ashley Judd.

August W. Staub

Further Reading

Bloom, Ken. *American Song: The Complete Musical Theatre Companion, 1877-1995*. 2 vols. New York: Gale Group, 1996. Discussion of songs that have been featured in more than one hundred years of American musical theater. Particular attention is paid to the different melodic and lyric approaches of the major composers, with a thorough discussion of Porter's special contributions.

Bloom, Ken, and Frank Vlastnik. *Broadway Musicals: The 101 Greatest Shows of All Time.* New York: Blackdog & Leventhal, 2004. Discusses in considerable detail the creation and production history of major Broadway musicals. Each musical is set in historical context with photographs and synopses. Useful work for understanding how some of Porter's musicals were assembled.

Gänzl, Kurt. *The Encyclopedia of Musical Theatre.* New York: Schirmer Books, 2001. A thorough presentation of musical theater since its inception. Porter's works are given considerable attention, especially how Porter's innovations influenced musical productions.

Suskin, Stephen. *Show Tunes: The Songs, Shows, and Careers of Broadway's Major Composers.* 3d ed. New York: Oxford University Press, 2000. Porter's musical career, songs, and shows are analyzed and discussed in detail.

Wilmeth, Don, and Christopher Bigsby, eds. *Post-World War II to the 1990's.* Vol. 3 in *The Cambridge History of American Theatre.* New York: Cambridge University Press, 2000. Thorough discussion of all aspects of American theater of the period, with Porter anchored in the total picture.

Wilmeth, Don, and Tice L. Miller, eds. *Cambridge Guide to American Theatre.* New York: Cambridge University Press, 1993. Contains a long entry on the American musical and Porter's place in its history, and a separate entry on Porter and his most important musicals.

See also: Brubeck, Dave; Chevalier, Maurice; Cohan, George M.; Coward, Sir Noël; Crosby, Bing; Dietrich, Marlene; Fields, Dorothy; Fitzgerald, Ella; Horne, Lena; Iglesias, Julio; Jordan, Louis; Lang, K. D.; Lee, Peggy; Ma, Yo-Yo; Mathis, Johnny; Mercer, Johnny; Merman, Ethel; Parker, Charlie; Peterson, Oscar; Shaw, Artie; Sinatra, Frank; Stravinsky, Igor; Taylor, Cecil; Tormé, Mel; Warwick, Dionne.

Francis Poulenc
French classical composer

An important French composer of art songs, Poulenc is noted for his religious music, his secular choral and chamber music, his piano and orchestral works, and his operas.

Born: January 7, 1899; Paris, France
Died: January 30, 1963; Paris, France
Also known as: Francis Jean Marcel Poulenc (full name)

Principal works

BALLETS (music and libretto): *Le Biches*, 1924; *Aubade*, 1929 (choreography by George Balanchine); *Les Animaux modèles*, 1942 (*The Model Animals*; choreography by Serge Lifar; based on the fables of Jean de La Fontaine).

CHAMBER WORKS: Trio for Oboe, Bassoon, and Piano, 1926; *Suite française*, 1935 (for wind instruments, percussion, and harpsichord); Sextet in C Major, 1940 (for wind quintet and piano); Sonata for Violin and Piano, 1943 (revised 1949); Cello Sonata, 1948; Flute Sonata, 1958; Clarinet Sonata, 1962; Oboe Sonata, 1962; Sonata for Clarinet and Piano, 1963.

CHORAL WORKS: *Litanies è la vierge noire*, 1936; Mass in G Major, 1937; *Quatre motets pour un temps de pénitence*, 1939 (*Four Motets for a Time of Penitence*); *Exultate Deo*, 1941 (*Sing Aloud Unto God*); *Salve regina*, 1941; *Un Soir de neige*, 1945 (*Night of Snow*); *Quatre motets pour le temps de Noël*, 1952 (*Four Motets for Christmastime*); *Stabat mater*, 1951; *Gloria*, 1961.

OPERAS (music and libretto): *Les Mammelles de Tirésias*, 1947 (*The Breasts of Tirésias*; based on the play by Guillaume Apollinaire); *Dialogues des Carmélites*, 1957 (based on the play by Georges Bernanos); *La Voix humaine*, 1959 (*The Human Voice*; based on the play by Jean Cocteau).

ORCHESTRAL WORKS: *Concert champêtre*, 1928 (for harpsichord and orchestra); Concerto in D Minor, 1932 (for two pianos and orchestra); Concerto in G Minor, 1938 (for organ, strings, and timpani).

PIANO WORKS: *Le Bestiaire*, 1919 (*The Zoo*; lyrics by Guillaume Apollinaire; for voice and piano); *Chansons gaillardes*, 1926 (for voice and piano); *Airs chantés*, 1928 (lyrics by Jean Moréas; for voice and piano); *Deux novelettes*, 1928; *Cinq poèmes de Paul Eluard*, 1935 (lyrics by Paul Eluard; for voice and piano); *Le Soirées des Nazelles*, 1936; *Tel jour, telle nuit*, 1937 (*As Is the Night, So Is the Day*; lyrics by Eluard; for voice and piano); *Fiançailles pour rire*, 1939 (lyrics by Louise Leveque de Vilmorin; for voice and piano); *Banalités*, 1940 (lyrics by Apollinaire; for voice and piano); *L'Historie de Babar, le petit éléphant*, 1945 (*The Story of Babar, the Little Elephant*); *Trois mouvements perpétuels*, 1946; *Capriccio*, 1952; Sonata for Two Pianos, 1953.

VOCAL WORKS: *Rapsodie nègre*, 1917 (text by Makoko Kangourou).

The Life

Francis Jean Marcel Poulenc (PEW-lehnk) was the son of Emile and Jenny (Royer) Poulenc, a wealthy Parisian family. His father, Aveyronais by descent, was the director of a successful pharmaceutical business. His mother's family, with its long line of visual artists and craftsmen, was from Paris. His father was a devout Catholic, but his mother was not particularly religious. Poulenc believed that his diverse heritage manifested itself in his compositions: He was capable of writing expansive, deeply religious works as well as brief, frivolous, and vulgar trifles.

Poulenc began studying the piano at the age of five, immediately showing considerable talent for music. However, his father discouraged him from pursuing a musical career at too young an age, and he persuaded Poulenc to first complete a traditional education at the Lycée Concorcet. Poulenc's parents died when he was a teenager, and when they did, Poulenc abandoned the Lycée Concorcet in 1914, and he began studying composition with Ricardo Viñes. Through Viñes, Poulenc established relationships with other composers, such as Georges Auric, Erik Satie, and Manuel da Falla. He also frequented Adrienne Monnier's Rue de l'Odéon bookshop, where he met the poets Guillaume Apollinaire, Paul Eluard, and other important literary figures. Poulenc's infatuation with

French poetry fueled his desire to focus on songwriting for much of his career.

Poulenc's early works were often performed at concerts given at the studio of the painter Emile Lejeune, and these programs also included the works of Georges Auric, Darius Milhaud, Arthur Honegger, Germaine Taillefaire, and Louis Durey. A review of the concert by Henri Collet dubbed the group Les Six in 1920, and the name stuck. The six composers were more unified by their friendship than their compositional style. In 1922 Poulenc met Arnold Schoenberg, Alban Berg, and Anton von Webern, and in 1924 he met Sergei Diaghilev, who soon commissioned the ballet *Les Biches*. In 1926 Poulenc met singer Pierre Bernac, who would become his lifetime partner and significant interpreter of his songs.

Beginning in 1927, Poulenc divided his life between Paris and his country house in Noizay at Touraine, where he composed the majority of his works. He became increasingly devoted to and influenced by the writings of Eluard and Apollinaire, setting many of these poems in his songs and choral works. He also began a rediscovery of his Catholic faith, increasingly devoting himself to religious choral works and dramatic music with religious themes.

Poulenc composed consistently throughout his career, save a brief stint in the military in World War II and several concert tours with Bernac to the United States and elsewhere. He died of a heart attack in his Paris apartment on January 30, 1963.

The Music

Poulenc's music falls into several broad categories. He is a composer of melodies, piano works, chamber music, orchestral music, operas and other dramatic music, and choral music (sacred and secular). Poulenc was greatly influenced by the French poets of his day and by Claude Debussy and Maurice Ravel. His four favorite composers were Johann Sebastian Bach, Wolfgang Amadeus Mozart, Satie, and Igor Stravinsky, whose stylistic elements can be found in Poulenc's works. His musical style remained remarkably consistent, and though it was out of fashion by the end of his career, he remained a respected and well-known composer.

Early Works. Poulenc destroyed most of his student compositions, so few works survive from his student days as a pupil of Viñes. Poulenc's first composition, the *Rapsodie nègre*, was performed at the Théâtre du Vieux Colombier. With the help of Stravinsky, who admired his work, Poulenc's first works were published by Chester Music in London. Poulenc served in the military from 1918 through 1921, and during this time he composed *Trois mouvements perpétuels* for piano and *Le Bestiaire*, a cycle of melodies for voice and piano on poems by Apollinaire. He also contributed a waltz to the famous publication of six piano pieces by the members of Les Six.

Les Biches. *Les Biches* was the first work for which Poulenc won major acclaim, and it is one of his most beloved works. A one-act ballet with singing, it was premiered at Monte Carlo on January 6, 1924, by Diaghilev's Ballets Russes. The art direction and costumes were by Marie Laurencin, the choreography by Bronislava Nijinska, and the orchestra was conducted by Edouard Flament. While many ballets before *Les Biches* were attached to a specific narrative, Poulenc's work revels in a complete fantasy world, a place where nothing tangible ever occurs. Compositionally, it is a suite of dances, and the work contains some of Poulenc's most melodic writing. Milhaud, Poulenc's friend and fellow member of Les Six, particularly admired Poulenc's orchestration of *Les Biches*, complimenting the tasteful doublings and use of brass textures. The brass writing and the harmony evoked are somewhat ironic, poking fun at the orchestrations of Richard Wagner, whom Poulenc detested. Poulenc later reorchestrated the score in 1939 and 1940.

Concerto in D Minor. The Concerto in D Minor for two pianos premiered on September 5, 1932. Poulenc was one of the pianists who performed, under the baton of Désiré Defauw and the Orchestra of La Scala; the other pianist was Jacques Février. Its Paris premiere occurred on March 21, 1933, at the Salle Pleyel with the same pianists under the direction of Roger Désormière. In the first movement, Poulenc makes use of cello harmonics while the two pianos simultaneously arpeggiate, creating an atmosphere of impressionistic sonority. The entire work is light and playful, specifically alluding to Mozart in the second movement.

Francis Poulenc. (Hulton Archive/Getty Images)

Les Soirées des Nazelles. *Les Soirées des Nazelles* is a suite of eight variations for piano, enclosed by a Préamble and Final. A Cadenza immediately precedes the Final. Throughout the suite, Poulenc frequently makes use of the dominant thirteenth chord and intervals of perfect fourths in the bass. He layers several keys on top of one another, creating a complex harmonic sonority. Although compositionally the work is distinctly in the style of Poulenc, the titles of each movement pay homage to the keyboard suites of François Couperin. Some of these titles include "Le Combe de la distinction" (Variation I), "Le Cœeur sur la main" (Variation II), and "Le Charme Enjoleur" (Variation V). Other allusions abound, and Poulenc specifically references other musical figures, such as Franz Schubert and Edith Piaf. Interestingly, Poulenc never cared much for this piece, though it is widely regarded as his greatest piano work.

As Is the Night, So Is the Day. Although Poulenc's song output is vast, it can be argued that *As Is the Night, So Is the Day* is his most significant song cycle. The work sets nine poems of Eluard, taken from his 1936 collection *Les yeux fertiles*. (The alternate title of the song cycle was chosen by Eluard, related in correspondence with Poulenc.) Eluard, along with Apollinaire, was an important poetic influence on Poulenc's compositional career. This cycle contains many of Poulenc's innovations: some songs contain more than one tempo; voice and piano parts have different dynamic levels; some of the songs (Nos. 3, 5, and 8) serve as musical and poetic transitions between more substantial songs. While the poems do not form a successive narrative, the songs are musically linked through motivic structure and key relationships. The ninth song, "Nous avons fait la nuit," recalls the same key and tempo as the first song, "Bonne journée," bringing unity to the cycle. The first performance of *As Is the Night, So Is the Day* was on February 3, 1937. This song cycle is a masterpiece of the genre, standing alongside Schubert's *Winterreise* (1828), Robert Schumann's *Dichterliebe* (1840), and Gabriel Fauré's *La Bonne Chanson* (1896).

Stabat mater. *Stabat mater* represents the culmination of Poulenc's lifelong journey toward the rediscovery of his Catholic faith. In his early studies, Poulenc harmonized Bach chorale tunes with Charles Koechlin, and he studied Claudio Monteverdi's motets with Nadia Boulanger; this training is reflected in his harmonic writing in the *Stabat mater*. The work is structured in twelve movements, representing the twelve Stations of the Cross. In typical Poulenc fashion, mood shifts abruptly between movements, ranging from pious simplicity to dancelike revelry. The first performance occurred on June 13, 1951, at the Strasbourg Music Festival.

Dialogues des Carmélites. Poulenc's most famous opera, *Dialogues des Carmélites*, was commissioned by La Scala, where it was premiered on January 26, 1957. This opera beautifully dovetails several key features of Poulenc's mature style, depicting his deep Catholic faith, his flair for the dramatic, and his penchant for the depiction of terror and fear in his music. *Dialogues des Carmélites* is more about emotion than plot: a group of nuns await their certain doom over the course of the opera's three acts.

Poulenc dedicated the score to Giuseppe Verdi, Monteverdi, Debussy, and Modest Mussorgsky. The influence of these composers is reflected in various aspects of the opera. Poulenc's alternation of accompanied recitatives and arias is modeled after Verdi's mature style, but the melodic quality of the recitatives owes much to Monteverdi's *L'Incoronazione di Poppea* (1643) and Debussy's *Pelléas et Mélisande* (1902). The brooding sense of danger and menace beneath the surface of the opera matches the tone of Mussorgsky's *Boris Godunov* (1869).

As is the case in many of his works, Poulenc makes frequent allusions to the works of other composers. In the case of *Dialogues des Carmélites*, Poulenc models his principal characters after those from other grand operas: Verdi's Amneris (from *Aida*, 1929) serves as the prototype for Mother Marie, and Desdemona (from *Otello*, 1887) becomes the New Prioress; Wagner's Kundry (from *Parsifal*, 1882) becomes the Prioress; Jules Massenet's Thaïs (from *Thaïs*, 1894) becomes Blanche; and Mozart's Zerlina (from *Don Giovanni*, 1787) becomes Constance. Also in homage to Wagner, each of these five principal characters is attached to a leitmotif, representing the character and her emotions. Mother Marie's C major music, for instance, embodies loyalty and strength.

Musical Legacy

Poulenc claimed that he had no guiding principles to his compositions, rejecting the idea of music as an intellectual activity. Although more well schooled than he often chose to admit, it is perhaps his freedom from formal structure and counterpoint that gave his music its aura of spontaneity and freshness. A lifelong devotee of the philosophy of Cocteau and Satie, Poulenc favored simplicity to complexity, offering his music as an expression of the French spirit.

Poulenc's reputation has increased steadily since his death in 1963. He has emerged as the most enduring member of Les Six, and he is considered a master composer in some genres. His works for solo voice are particularly revered, and he is among the most respected song cycle composers.

Unlike most major composers of the twentieth century, Poulenc was not harmonically innovative. Rather, he used the existing tonal and—perhaps more important—modal languages to create inventive melodic ideas. In his writings, Poulenc directly compares himself to Schubert as opposed to Debussy and Ravel. Certainly in the realm of vocal music, Poulenc is an heir to Schubert.

Matthew Ryan Hoch

Further Reading

Bernac, Pierre. *Francis Poulenc: The Man and His Songs*. 2d ed. Translated by Winifred Radford. London: Kahn & Averill, 2002. More than ninety of Poulenc's songs were written specifically for Bernac, and this book provides an essay and two-column translation for every song in Poulenc's oeuvre.

Mellers, Wilfrid Howard. *Francis Poulenc*. New York: Oxford University Press, 1995. This is an excellent resource for placing Poulenc in the context of his time, and it includes musical analysis of many of Poulenc's significant works.

Poulenc, Francis. *Diary of My Songs*. 2d ed. Translated by Winifred Radford. London: Kahn & Averill, 2007. Originally a diary, this is the only full-length book by Poulenc. It offers insights into Poulenc's songs, describing his relationship with French poets and offering insight into his compositional process.

Schmidt, Carl B. *Entrancing Muse: A Documented Biography of Francis Poulenc*. Hillsdale, N.Y.: Pendragon Press, 2001. A useful biography of Poulenc, based on his letters, his interviews, and his writings.

_____. *The Music of Francis Poulenc: A Catalogue*. New York: Oxford University Press, 1995. At more than six hundred pages, this reference work is a comprehensive research tool for Poulenc scholars, although it is accessible to students of any level. A wealth of information is provided for every work in Poulenc's oeuvre.

See also: Anderson, Marian; Berg, Alban; Boulanger, Nadia; Copland, Aaron; Debussy, Claude; Honegger, Arthur; Landowska, Wanda; Milhaud, Darius; Piaf, Édith; Price, Leontyne; Rampal, Jean-Pierre; Ravel, Maurice; Satie, Erik; Schoenberg, Arnold; Shaw, Artie; Stravinsky, Igor; Sutherland, Dame Joan; Watts, André; Webern, Anton von.

Bud Powell

American jazz pianist and composer

Powell was a pianist of astonishing dexterity and inventiveness whose distinctive style translated the linear developments of the legendary founders of bebop—saxophonist Charlie Parker and trumpeter Dizzy Gillespie—to the piano.

Born: September 27, 1924; New York, New York
Died: July 31, 1966; New York, New York
Also known as: Earl Rudolph "Bud" Powell (full name)

Principal recordings

ALBUMS: *Bud Powell Trio Plays*, 1947; *My Devotion*, 1947; *The Amazing Bud Powell, Vol. 1*, 1949; *The Genius of Bud Powell, Vol. 1*, 1949; *Bud Powell's Moods*, 1950; *Bud Powell Piano*, 1950; *Bud Powell Trio*, 1950; *The Amazing Bud Powell, Vol. 2*, 1951; *Autumn Sessions*, 1953; *Charles Mingus Trio*, 1953 (with the Charles Mingus Trio); *In March with Mingus*, 1953 (with Charles Mingus); *Inner Fires*, 1953; *The Genius of Bud Powell, Vol. 2*, 1954; *Jazz Original*, 1955; *The Lonely One*, 1955; *Piano Interpretations by Bud Powell*, 1955; *Blues in the Closet*, 1956; *Strictly Powell*, 1956; *Time Was*, 1956; *The Amazing Bud Powell, Vol. 3*, 1957; *The Amazing Bud Powell, Vol. 4*, 1957; *Blue Pearl*, 1957; *Bud Plays Bird*, 1957; *Bud Powell*, 1957; *Swingin' with Bud*, 1957; *The Amazing Bud Powell, Vol. 5*, 1958; *Time Waits: The Amazing Bud Powell*, 1958; *Bud in Paris*, 1959; *A Tribute to Cannonball*, 1961; *Budism*, 1962; *The Invisible Cage*, 1964; *The Return of Bud Powell*, 1964; *Salt Peanuts*, 1964; *Ups and Downs*, 1964.

The Life

Earl Rudolph "Bud" Powell was born into a musical family in New York City in 1924. His father and grandfather were musicians, and so were his brothers Richie and William, Jr. Richie had a solid reputation as a jazz musician, and he played in the Clifford Brown-Max Roach band. (He was killed in the same car accident that killed Brown in 1956.) Powell's father, a stride pianist, supported his son's interest in music, and he encouraged Powell to study classical piano. Powell showed tremendous promise as a child, absorbing the influences of the popular pianists of the time, especially Earl "Fatha" Hines, Fats Waller, Art Tatum, and Teddy Wilson.

When Powell was fifteen, he quit high school and started playing in New York. When he was seventeen, he went frequently to Minton's Playhouse, where legend has it that Kenny Clarke, Thelonious Monk, Charlie Christian, Dizzy Gillespie, and later Charlie Parker invented bebop. Several years younger than Parker and Gillespie, Powell occasionally sat in to play, but mostly he listened. Monk befriended the younger pianist and mentored his musical development.

Powell was just nineteen years old when he got his first important gig, playing with trumpeter Cootie Williams. In 1945 Powell's mental health began to decline, worsened by his alcoholism. According to Williams, when Powell was twenty-one, he was arrested after a performance in Philadelphia. When his mother came to pick him up at the

jail, she found that he had been badly beaten and had sustained a severe head injury. He was institutionalized several times in the late 1940's, and he received electroshock therapy as well as other treatments that left him emotionally and mentally damaged and unstable.

Though struggling personally, Powell made a series of groundbreaking recordings during a six-year period beginning in 1947 that established him as the leading jazz pianist of the time. In 1953, after a period of relative mental stability, his mental health began to deteriorate, making his playing extremely erratic. After another series of stays in mental institutions, he moved to Paris in 1959.

Powell lived in Paris for five years. He was drinking heavily, and his playing was negatively affected. Until he contracted tuberculosis in 1962, he performed extensively in clubs in Paris, and he played concerts and festivals in France and Germany. He made a number of recordings there with both American and European musicians. While living in Paris, he met Francis Paudras, a commercial artist and amateur musician who later wrote a book about Powell that served as the basis for the 1986 film *'Round Midnight*. He lived with Paudras briefly while convalescing. In 1964, when he had recuperated sufficiently, he came to the United States for a visit, to play an extended gig at Birdland, but he never returned to Europe. He died in 1966 from alcoholism, tuberculosis, and malnutrition.

The Music

Like many jazz musicians, Powell first worked as a sideman for well-known musicians before leading his own groups. His performances and recordings with Williams in 1943 and 1944 established him as an up-and-coming pianist. In 1946, after he recovered from his first extended period of unstable mental health, Powell recorded extensively with a number of musicians and singers. Then, beginning in 1947, he began recording and performing as the leader of his own groups, mostly trios with bass and drums. The recordings he made during the six-year period beginning when he was twenty-three are considered his finest and most influential work. Aside from several important recordings with Parker and Gillespie in the early 1950's, Powell worked mostly in his own trios and small groups for the rest of his career.

Bud Powell. (Hulton Archive/Getty Images)

Early Career. In 1944 Powell recorded several albums with groups led by Williams. While Williams's group played more in the swing school than the emerging bebop style, Powell's playing on these early recordings, such as on "Floogie Bop" (a reworking of "Sweet Lorraine"), is notably modern in conception and execution.

In 1947, after his first hiatus from the music scene for medical reasons, he performed and recorded prolifically, appearing with Dexter Gordon and J. J. Johnson, among others. He also cut several records with the players from Minton's Playhouse: saxophonist Sonny Stitt, drummer Clarke, and trumpeters Kenny Dorham and Fats Navarro. Powell's first album as a leader, *Bud Powell Trio Plays*, has many of the tunes that became staples in his repertoire: "Indiana," "I'll Remember April," "I Should Care," and "Everything Happens to Me."

The Verve and Blue Note Recordings. Between May of 1949 and August of 1953, Powell made his most influential recordings. Mostly with Powell leading a trio, they capture his playing at the height of its inventiveness and energy. Powell recorded four sessions for Verve, of which three are trio recordings. These are arguably the best of his career, including definitive versions of his compositions "Tempus Fugit," "Celia," "I'll Keep Loving You" (performed solo), and "Strictly Confidential." The other trio recordings include Powell's idiosyncratic renditions of standards such as "Cherokee," "Sweet Georgia Brown," "Yesterdays," "April in Paris," and "Body and Soul." Throughout these recordings, Powell's right-hand eighth-note lines are authoritative and solid, whether on the up-tempo "All God's Chillin' Got Rhythm" or the medium-tempo "Celia."

The final Verve session, in February of 1951, contains solo piano performances that represent Powell at his most creative and fluent, including a brisk version of "Parisian Thoroughfare." Although Powell was strongly influenced by Tatum, these recordings show a mature solo piano conception quite different from Tatum's. While Powell employs many of Tatum's harmonic devices, particularly in the statements of the main themes, his focus remains the right-hand line. His rendition of "Parisian Thoroughfare" is essentially a solo version of what he might play with a trio. There is no stride piano here: His left hand plays the same stark, rhythmic harmonic shells he used in his trio playing. Not only is the harmony more oblique, but the rhythm is more syncopated. This deconstruction of the role of the left hand in solo playing modernized the conception of solo piano, allowing the same focus on the right-hand line as when the pianist is supported by a rhythm section.

Powell recorded three sessions for Blue Note, the first in August of 1949 and the last in August of 1953. Like the Verve recordings, these sessions capture Powell playing at his best. Most of these tracks are trio recordings, though Powell added Navarro and Rollins to the trio for several of the tracks recorded in 1949. Powell's right-hand lines are confident and secure. His solo on the extended vamp of "Un Poco Loco" foreshadows the fluid harmonic superimposition McCoy Tyner would pioneer on the piano more than ten years later. Powell records "Parisian Thoroughfare" here with the trio, and a comparison between this and the solo recording from the Verve session in 1951 reveals a strikingly similar approach.

Recordings with Parker and Gillespie. Powell made a number of important recordings with Parker between 1950 and 1953, most often with Gillespie on trumpet. By this time, Powell's style and reputation were well established. The sessions in May of 1950, March of 1951, and several in May of 1953 are now considered bebop classics. The group's repertoire included all the bebop classics: "Moose the Mooche," "Lullaby of Birdland," "All the Things You Are," "Woody 'n' You," "Salt Peanuts," "A Night in Tunisia," and "Anthropology." The 1953 recordings with Parker and Gillespie, along with the Blue Note recordings made the same year, mark the end of Powell's watershed years: He would never match the quality and quantity of the recordings and performances made during this period.

European Work and American Coda. Powell moved to Paris in 1959, and until he contracted tuberculosis in 1962, he recorded and performed frequently. His old friend, drummer Clarke, also lived in Paris, and they were frequent collaborators. Powell played with both European and American musicians. He made a number of recordings at clubs and festivals in France, Germany, Denmark, Sweden, and Switzerland, with Coleman Hawkins, Charles Mingus, Eric Dolphy, Zoot Sims, Cannonball Adderely, and Don Byas.

Many critics consider that, by this time, Powell had passed his prime, and he never played with the virtuosity and flair he displayed before he left the United States. In fact, Powell's playing on these recordings is extremely erratic. On some tracks, such as the version of "Just One of Those Things" made with Byas in 1961, he played with the same authority and clarity as he had in New York in the early 1950's. His solo on "Cherokee" from the same session, on the other hand, is tentative and frequently falters (though he never loses the beat or the changes).

When the jazz community heard Powell perform at the memorial concert for Parker at Carnegie Hall in 1964, they acknowledged that they had lost an important voice. While he had intended to return to Paris with his friend Paudras after his gig at Birdland (which was marred by extremely erratic performances as well), Powell remained in the United States, living in semiseclusion until his death in 1966.

Musical Legacy

Powell completely changed the nature of jazz piano. Before him, the two-handed piano style so powerfully embodied in the playing of Tatum or so elegantly shaped in the playing of Wilson was the principal model. While Tatum's style remained influential in solo piano, Powell redefined the role of the pianist in a jazz small group. His right-hand lines defined both the rhythm and the harmony, but more obliquely than pianists before him, allowing the drummer greater freedom to shade and shape the rhythmic subdivisions of the pulse. His stark, terse left-hand comping ceded greater linear freedom to the bass player. Bill Evans and Red Garland would later codify the voicing language of modern jazz piano, but Powell's deconstruction of the role of the pianist in a jazz group was an essential contribution to the development of the modern rhythm section.

Powell's lines were a ferocious, intimidating display of technical skill and musical invention. The emotional intensity and intellectual weight of these lines more than compensated for the de-emphasis of the left hand. More than just a transferal of Parker or Gillespie's horn lines to the piano, Powell's improvisations were intrinsically pianistic while still embodying the bebop vocabulary. The linear flu-

ency Powell pioneered has become a required component of contemporary jazz piano.

Matthew Nicholl

Further Reading

Collier, James Lincoln. *The Making of Jazz: A Comprehensive History*. New York: Dell, 1978. Contains an excellent chapter about the development of modern jazz, including an analysis of the origins of Powell's style and his influence on the development of modern jazz piano. Also contains extensive biographical information.

Groves, Allen, and Alyn Shipton. *The Glass Enclosure: The Life of Bud Powell*. New York: Continuum, 2001. Provides extensive biographical information and an excellent discography of Powell's recordings, both as a leader and a sideman. Exhaustively researched and well-indexed.

Lyons, Len. *The Great Jazz Pianists: Speaking of Their Lives and Music*. New York: Morrow, 1983. While it does not include an interview with Powell, the introduction presents a cogent and accurate history of jazz, placing Powell's contribution to the development of jazz piano in perspective. Many of the interviews refer to Powell and his influence.

Paudras, Francis. *Dance of Infidels: A Portrait of Bud Powell*. New York: Da Capo Press, 1998. This is written by an amateur musician and devoted fan who became Powell's friend and spent a great deal of time with him. This account of their time together is heavily colored by Paudras's obvious affection for the pianist. Still, it provides a useful look at Powell's day-to-day life from a unique perspective.

Smith, Carl. *Bouncing with Bud: All the Recordings of Bud Powell*. Brunswick, Maine: Biddle, 1997. A chronological overview of Powell's recordings written by a jazz fan. Contains useful discographical information.

See also: Akiyoshi, Toshiko; Corea, Chick; Gillespie, Dizzy; Gordon, Dexter; Jones, Elvin; Jones, Hank; Mingus, Charles; Monk, Thelonious; Navarro, Fats; Parker, Charlie; Roach, Max; Tatum, Art; Tyner, McCoy; Waller, Fats; Williams, Mary Lou; Young, Lester.

Pérez Prado

Cuban Latin music composer and pianist

One of the first to combine Latin musical elements with big band jazz, Prado was responsible for the mambo's widespread popularity and commercial success in Europe and the United States during the 1950's.

Born: December 11, 1916; Mantanzas, Cuba
Died: September 14, 1989; Mexico City, Mexico
Also known as: Dámaso Pérez Prado (full name); Mambo King; Rey del Mambo
Member of: The Pérez Prado Orchestra

Principal recordings

ALBUMS (solo): *Pérez Prado*, 1950; *Pérez Prado Plays Mucho Mambo for Dancing*, 1951; *Mambo Mania*, 1955; *Voodoo Suite Plus Six All-Time Greats*, 1955 (with Shorty Rogers); *Havana 3 A.M.*, 1956; *Prez*, 1958; *Latino!*, 1959; *Pérez*, 1959; *A Touch of Tabasco*, 1960 (with Rosemary Clooney); *La chunga*, 1961; *Exotic Suite of the Americas*, 1962; *Lights! Action! Prado!*, 1964; *Dance Latino*, 1965; *El unico*, 1972; *Salsa ala Pérez Prado*, 1972.

ALBUMS (with the Pérez Prado Orchestra): *Mambo by the King*, 1956; *Latin Satin*, 1957; *Mambo Happy!*, 1957; *Dilo (Ugh!)*, 1958; *Pops and Prado*, 1959; *Rockambo*, 1961; *The Twist Goes Latin*, 1962; *Our Man in Latin America*, 1963.

The Life

Dámaso Pérez Prado's mother was a schoolteacher, and his father worked for a newspaper. He began playing classical piano in his early childhood, and as a teenager he played professionally, expanding his repertory while working in nightclubs and motion picture theaters. The Afro-Cuban city of Matanzas was musically rich with African and traditional Cuban music. In 1942 Prado moved to Havana, where he arranged music for musical groups and orchestras, including the famous Sonora Matancera and Orquesta Casino de la Playa. He experimented with traditional Cuban rhythms, combining jazz and traditional music, and thus he angered musical purists. In 1948 he moved to Mexico City to form his own orchestra and to record for

RCA Victor. He adapted the mambo (a fast version of the Cuban danzón) using his big band sound. Prado and his orchestra recorded numerous singles in Mexico City.

In 1954, during a second tour to the United States, their performances at New York nightclubs sparked a fascination with the mambo. In 1955 Prado made his American breakthrough with his arrangement of "Cherry Pink and Apple Blossom White," by Louiguy (Louis Gugliemi), as the theme from the 1955 film *Underwater!* (starring Jane Russell). It topped the *Billboard* hits chart and remained there for months. In 1958 he had another hit with the cha-cha-cha "Patricia," which he composed. His compositions and arrangements enjoyed much commercial success worldwide. Prado also composed large, serious works. He is remembered for adding percussive shouts and grunts (usually indicating song breaks). Prado was at the height of his career in the 1950's and 1960's, but he continued working, releasing records and making appearances on television into the 1980's. In 1989 he died of a stroke in Mexico City.

The Music

Prado's upbeat big band flashy music combined elements of classical music, jazz, traditional Cuban, and newly composed music based on traditional Afro-Cuban dance rhythms. Brass, saxophone, and rhythm sections frequently shared the foreground, though trumpet solos were often featured. The hit song "Patricia" is unusual for featuring Prado on organ in the foreground. His music initiated the mambo craze in the United States. Sound engineers were not nearly as innovative with Prado's recordings as they were with those of Esquivel's Orchestra. However, Prado recorded during a period in which people enjoyed listening to music at home on their stereos as much as they would at nightclubs.

Mambo Mania. A compilation of Prado's Mexican singles released in 1955, this album contains the hit song "Cherry Pink and Apple Blossom White." The song is characterized by its slurred trumpet solo, portamento pitch glides, and bent notes. The purpose of this collection was to make this highly requested song and other songs accessible to listeners in North America. Prado's homage to Stan Kenton, "Mambo a la Kenton" (composed by Prado

Pérez Prado. (AP/Wide World Photos)

and Armando Romeu), and a cover of the popular standard "Skokiaan" (composed by August Msarurgwa) are also included.

Voodoo Suite Plus Six All-Time Greats. The serious composition, *Voodoo Suite*, was performed and recorded in 1955, just at the time Prado was enjoying the success of "Cherry Pink and Apple Blossom White." Venturing into the exotic around the same time as Les Baxter and Martin Denny, this recording paired Prado with Shorty Rogers, a creator of West Coast jazz. Prado and his orchestra perform Latin versions of the Dixieland standard "St. James Infirmary" and "Stompin' at the Savoy." The latter, composed by Chick Webb, exemplifies Prado's shouts and grunts, which suggest his sensitive hearing of the musical form.

Havana 3 A.M. This 1956 recording contains two famous songs, "The Freeway Mambo" (composed by Prado) and "The Peanut Vendor (El monicero)"

(composed by Moises Simon), and it concludes with Prado's impressionist composition "Mosaico Cubano" (Cuban sketch). The saxophone section opens "The Freeway Mambo" with a catchy melody accompanied by drums and shouts; saxophone sections in unison alternate with the familiar sound of a blaring trumpet chorus. "The Peanut Vendor" features a guitar solo followed by a meandering, blaring trumpet.

Exotic Suite of the Americas. The title song of this 1962 recording was another serious work by Prado that has many similarities to his *Voodoo Suite*. Its instrumental impressions of the exotic employ strings and drums more often than the earlier *Voodoo Suite*. Other songs included were his musical salute to the ladies in President John Kennedy's life, "Jacqueline and Caroline," and his mambo-inspired arrangement of Alan Jay Lerner's "I Could Have Danced All Night" from *My Fair Lady* (1956).

Musical Legacy

Prado stimulated interest in Latin music long before the Latin Grammy Awards existed. His style of conducting, arranging, and composing influenced the music of Latin contemporaries Esquivel, Tito Puente, and Xavier Cugat (who covered many of the same songs with their orchestras) as well as the jazz of Duke Ellington and Charlie Parker. His music is frequently used in films and commercials. Examples include "Patricia" in Federico Fellini's *La dolce vita* (1961) and Billy Kent's *The Oh in Ohio* (2006); "Cherry Pink and Apple Blossom White" in an episode of the television series *The Sopranos* (2004); and "Guaglione" and "Mambo No. 5" in television commercials for Guinness draught stout (1994 and 1999). In 1999 Lou Bega's vocal version of "Mambo No. 5" revived interest in Prado.

Melissa Ursula Dawn Goldsmith

Further Reading

Fernandez, Raul A. *From Afro-Cuban Rhythms to Latin Jazz.* Berkeley: University of California Press, 2006. The author discusses Prado's work with Latin musicians and his impact on jazz in the United States.

Gerard, Charley. *Music from Cuba: Mongo Santamaría, Chocolate Armenteros, and Cuban Musicians in the United States.* Westport, Conn.: Praeger, 2001. This describes Prado's adaptation and transmission of the charanga mambo and the cha-cha-cha.

Moore, Robin D. *Music and Revolution: Cultural Change in Socialist Cuba.* Berkeley: University of California Press, 2006. This covers Prado's use of big band mambo from the late 1940's and his success with recordings.

Roberts, John Storm. *Latin Jazz: The First of the Fusions, 1880's to Today.* New York: Schirmer Books, 1999. In this Latin jazz survey, musicologist Roberts provides details about Prado's Victor recordings, his musical sound, and other artists with whom he worked.

_____. *The Latin Tinge: The Impact of Latin American Music on the United States.* New York: Oxford University Press, 1999. This explores Prado, along with other Latin bandleaders in New York, and how he introduced the mambo and Latin jazz to the United States.

Sublette, Ned. *Cuba and Its Music: From the First Drums to the Mambo.* Chicago: Chicago Review Press, 2004. This history covers Prado's arrival in Havana and life in Cuba during the mambo's formative years.

See also: Cugat, Xavier; Lerner, Alan Jay; Professor Longhair; Puente, Tito.

Elvis Presley

American rock/pop singer

As the King of Rock and Roll, Presley bridged the gap between so-called white music and black music, and his intense performances were imitated by many artists who followed.

Born: January 8, 1935; Tupelo, Mississippi
Died: August 16, 1977; Memphis, Tennessee
Also known as: Elvis Aaron Presley (full name); King of Rock and Roll; Elvis the Pelvis

Principal recordings

ALBUMS: *Elvis,* 1956; *Elvis Presley,* 1956; *Elvis' Christmas Album,* 1957; *King Creole,* 1958; *Fifty Thousand Fans Can't Be Wrong,* 1959; *Elvis Is Back!,* 1960; *G.I. Blues,* 1960; *His Hand in Mine,* 1960; *Blue Hawaii,* 1961; *Something for Everybody,* 1961; *Girls, Girls, Girls!,* 1962; *Pot Luck,* 1962; *Fun in Acapulco,* 1963; *It Happened at the World's Fair,* 1963; *Kissin' Cousins,* 1964; *Roustabout,* 1964; *Girl Happy,* 1965; *Harum Scarum,* 1965; *Frankie and Johnny,* 1966; *Paradise Hawaiian Style,* 1966; *Spinout,* 1966; *Double Trouble,* 1967; *How Great Thou Art,* 1967; *Speedway,* 1968; *From Elvis in Memphis,* 1969; *Almost in Love,* 1970; *Elvis: Back in Memphis,* 1970; *Elvis: That's the Way It Is,* 1970; *Elvis Country,* 1971; *Elvis Sings the Wonderful World of Christmas,* 1971; *Love Letters from Elvis,* 1971; *Elvis Now,* 1972; *He Touched Me,* 1972; *Elvis,* 1973; *Raised on Rock,* 1973; *Elvis Forever,* 1974; *Good Times,* 1974; *Elvis Today,* 1975; *Promised Land,* 1975; *Elvis in Hollywood,* 1976; *From Elvis Presley Boulevard, Memphis, Tennessee,* 1976; *Moody Blue,* 1977; *Welcome to My World,* 1977.

SINGLES: "Blue Moon of Kentucky," 1954; "Good Rockin' Tonight," 1954; "That's All Right Mama," 1954; "You're a Heartbreaker," 1954; "Baby, Let's Play House," 1955; "I Forgot to Remember to Forget," 1955; "I'm Left, You're Right, She's Gone," 1955; "Mystery Train," 1955; "Heartbreak Hotel," 1956.

The Life

Elvis Aaron Presley was born to Vernon Presley and Gladys Love Smith in Tupelo, Mississippi. His family was poor, and he was often bullied at school, but his parents were regular churchgoers, and in church Presley found solace. At the age of eleven, he received his first guitar, and he quickly picked up popular songs. In 1948 the Presley family moved to Memphis, Tennessee, so that Vernon could find a job. After high school, Presley began driving a truck to help support the family, but he never gave up on music.

In 1953 Presley recorded a song for his mother at Sun Studios in Memphis. The studio owner, who auditioned him, eventually began to produce Presley's records. After recording with the studio, Presley's music career began to take off. Between 1953 and 1956, he became recognized regionally in the South for mixing so-called black and white music. In 1955 Colonel Tom Parker became Presley's manager, and he moved the singer to RCA Records. When Presley began making television appearances that year, his popularity skyrocketed. Conservative critics attacked the racial background of his music and his provocative stage performances; which were famous for his sexually suggestive pelvis thrusts.

However, the critics had little impact on Presley's career. Beginning with *Love Me Tender* (1956), Presley began to regularly star in films. Fans flocked to his concerts, and by 1957 his need for privacy prompted the singer to buy his famous homestead in Memphis, Graceland. In 1957 Presley was drafted into the armed services. Although irking his producers and his record company, the singer joined the armed forces after a short deferment, and he spent two years in Germany.

Upon returning home, Presley moved his career more toward filmmaking, starring in twenty-seven films in the 1960's. In 1967 Presley married Priscilla Ann Wagner, and the next year they had their only child, Lisa Marie Presley. By the end of the decade, his popularity was fading, and he blamed the poor quality of his film scripts and his films' songs. Depressed, he began to gain weight and abuse prescription drugs.

To support his film career, Presley had taken a hiatus from touring when he left the Army in 1960. In 1968 he began to tour again, concentrating more on his music than on his motion pictures. Arguably, during this period he produced many of his best works, mostly in the genre of gospel music. Although his songs were better, they did not stay long on the *Billboard* chart. Nevertheless, his concerts were always sold out.

Presley divorced Priscilla in 1973, after which he became depressed, gained a large amount of weight, and continued to overuse prescription drugs. By 1977 he rarely left his hotel room while he was on tour, other than to go on stage and give a truncated performance. On August 16, 1977, Presley died of a heart attack at Graceland. He was forty-two years old.

The Music

Presley's musical career was extremely potent—with 31 films, 101 singles, and 77 albums, Presley was likely the most productive singer of his time. He had seventeen chart-topping singles and

Elvis Presley. (AP/Wide World Photos)

seventy-two Top 40 singles on the *Billboard* pop singles chart. He was a powerhouse of popular music.

Sun Studios. Presley's first recordings were with Sun Studios in Memphis. He achieved a popular following in the American South because of his style of music. By the first time he appeared on television in 1955, he had already developed his sound and style. Influenced by gospel, rhythm and blues, bluegrass, and country and western, Presley had a unique sound for the time. His hip gyrations and pelvic thrusts attracted female fans, and, for most postwar youth, his image provided an expression of rebellion.

His Sun Studios recordings were raw with passion and experimental music. He produced the most successful hybrid sound to bridge the races, even though many white artists had covered black music. In addition, these recordings were the first rock-and-roll records ever made, starting with the single "That's All Right Mama." These original sessions were produced by Scott Phillips, and Presley was accompanied by Scotty Moore on lead guitar and Bill Black on bass; later Dominic Joseph Fontana was added on drums. These sessions also created such classics as "I Forgot to Remember to Forget" and "Mystery Train."

RCA Years. When Presley's contract was bought by RCA Records for thirty-five thousand dollars in 1955, he had more resources at his disposal. In 1956 he released his smash single "Heartbreak Hotel." His first album also debuted that year. *Elvis Presley* hit number one on the *Billboard* pop albums chart, and it stayed there for ten weeks. This work, which was the transition album between Sun Studios and RCA, helped cement Presley's rock-and-roll sound, and it was the album that made him a national sensation. It would launch his film career and begin to sustain his popularity.

Presley recorded the bulk of his mainstay repertoire during the 1950's; a good deal of this was recorded in the early months of 1958, before he went into the military. Many of his most famous songs also came out of his early years in films. "Love Me Tender" was the title track for Presley's first movie in 1956. *Loving You* was just as popular in 1957, and this time Presley had a number-one record and a starring role in a film. His music of the late 1950's was emulated by many artists, and by the time he returned from the Army in 1960, rock and roll was the most popular form of music in the United States. His early recordings also set the standard for many artists to come. His films set a new trend for musicals: Combining popular music and the film industry into a crossover product was largely successful.

Film Appearances. Most of Presley's career in the 1960's revolved around films. He refused to tour until the end of the decade, and much of his new material came from the films that he starred in. He made twenty-seven films in the 1960's, although he had little control over the songs he sang in the films. Perhaps the most famous of his films were *Blue Hawaii* (1961) and *Viva Las Vegas!* (1964). The former contained such songs as "Blue Hawaii" and "Can't Help Falling in Love," although the rest of the sound track had little merit. *Viva Las Vegas!* included some of Presley's best work—as an actor and as an on-screen singer. Although RCA decided not to release the sound track, the songs from *Viva Las Vegas* are some of Presley's most famous work;

most notable was the title track. During the 1960's, RCA frequently released compilations of Presley's earlier work and his film songs to make up for the lack of studio albums.

Final Years. Following his last film in 1969, Presley returned to touring, and he expanded his sound. He had already won his first Grammy Award in 1967 for his gospel album *How Great Thou Art*. This would be the only genre in which he would capture the coveted award, and he did so two more times—in 1972 and in 1974. With such achievements, Presley showed his range as a musician and a performer.

Presley tried to regain his prestige during the 1970's; however, depression sapped his talent. Many of his albums of the 1970's were recordings of live performances, leaving his fan base aging rather than increasing.

Musical Legacy

When Presley rose to stardom, there was no other act like him. He brought together various musical cultures to create a sound that became immensely popular among the young. He was one of the first and one of the most popular singers to be lambasted by the press and conservative critics for his music. He opened doors for other artists to emulate black musicians in white America. In addition, his music was a steppingstone for black musicians to take a place in mainstream popular music.

Presley was one of the most commercially viable personalities of all time. He shifted the population's ear to rock and roll, bringing further commercial value to the industry. More than just the inventor of a genre, he was the inventor of the music industry as it exists today.

Presley is often overlooked as a musician, although he was a talented singer and guitarist. What he lacked in songwriting ability, he made up for in delivery. He was influential in any genre he tried, from country to gospel. He helped make music on television successful, and he moved from the stage to television to motion pictures flawlessly.

Daniel R. Vogel

Further Reading

Esposito, Joe. *Remember Elvis*. Las Vegas, Nev.: TCB JOE, 2006. This book is filled with hundreds of interviews with Presley and his confidants throughout his career. It covers the creation of Presley as a rock-and-roll icon to his unfortunate demise.

Guralnick, Peter. *Careless Love: The Unmaking of Elvis Presley*. Boston: Little, Brown, 1999. The author's second book on Presley covers the artist's return to the United States in 1960 after his military service until his death. This volume delves into Presley's life and influences on his later music.

_____. *Last Train to Memphis: The Rise of Elvis Presley*. Boston: Little, Brown, 1994. The author's first book on Presley covers his roots until his time in the Army. A detailed look at the singer's early career.

Jorgensen, Ernst, and Peter Guralnick. *Elvis Presley: A Life in Music—The Complete Recording Sessions*. New York: St. Martin's Griffin, 2000. This book has a complete listing of Presley's recording career, from studio albums to bootleg versions of hotel recordings, giving a sense of how dedicated Presley was to producing music.

Presley, Priscilla Beaulieu, and Sandra Harmon. *Elvis and Me*. New York: Putnam, 1985. This book covers Pricilla's time with Presley, and it illuminates what it was like for Presley during some of his roughest years, during the middle to end of his career.

See also: Acuff, Roy; Arnold, Eddy; Atkins, Chet; Axton, Hoyt; Blackwell, Otis; Brown, Roy; Carter, Maybelle; Dylan, Bob; Eddy, Duane; Fender, Freddy; Haley, Bill; Holly, Buddy; Howlin' Wolf; Leiber, Jerry; Lennon, John; Lewis, Jerry Lee; Little Richard; McGuinn, Roger; Miller, Glenn; Milsap, Ronnie; Monroe, Bill; Nelson, Ricky; Orbison, Roy; Otis, Johnny; Page, Jimmy; Parsons, Gram; Perkins, Carl; Pride, Charley; Reed, Jimmy; Stanley, Ralph; Stoller, Mike; Twitty, Conway; Vincent, Gene; Wilson, Jackie.

Sir André Previn

American classical conductor, pianist, and film-score composer

A remarkably adaptive musician, Previn enjoyed multiple roles as a Hollywood composer and arranger, jazz pianist, orchestral conductor, classical pianist, and serious composer.

Born: April 6, 1929; Berlin, Germany
Also known as: Andreas Ludwig Previn (full name); André George Previn

Principal works

CHAMBER WORK: Concerto, 1968 (for cello).

FILM SCORES: *The Secret Garden*, 1949; *Three Little Words*, 1950; *Kiss Me, Kate*, 1953; *Bad Day at Black Rock*, 1954; *It's Always Fair Weather*, 1955; *Silk Stockings*, 1957; *Gigi*, 1958; *Porgy and Bess*, 1959; *Bells Are Ringing*, 1960; *Elmer Gantry*, 1960; *Four Horsemen of the Apocalypse*, 1961; *Two for the Seesaw*, 1962; *Inside Daisy Clover*, 1965; *Paint Your Wagon*, 1969; *The Music Lovers*, 1970.

MUSICAL THEATER (music): *Coco*, 1969 (lyrics and libretto by Alan Jay Lerner); *The Good Companions*, 1974 (lyrics by Johnny Mercer; libretto by J. B. Priestly); *Every Good Boy Deserves Favour*, 1977 (libretto by Tom Stoppard).

OPERA: *A Streetcar Named Desire*, 1998 (libretto by Philip Littell; based on Tennessee Williams's play).

ORCHESTRAL WORKS: Symphony, 1962 (for strings); *The Four Outings*, 1974; *Principals*, 1980.

VOCAL WORKS: *Honey and Rue*, 1992; "Sally Chisum Remembers Billy the Kid," 1994.

Principal recordings

ALBUMS (as composer and pianist): *André Previn All Stars*, 1946; *André Previn*, 1947; *Double Play!*, 1957; *André Previn Plays Vernon Duke*, 1958; *Like Previn!*, 1960; *André Previn Plays Harold Arlen*, 1960; *A Different Kind of Blues*, 1980; *After Hours*, 1989; *Old Friends*, 1991; *What Headphones?*, 1993; *Alone*, 2007.

ALBUMS (as conductor): *Aaron Copland: The Red Pony; Benjamin Britten: Sinfonia da Requiem,*

1963; *Lambert: The Rio Grande, Concerto for Solo Piano and Nine Players, Elegiac Blues, Elegy; Walton: Symphony No. 2*, 2005.

ALBUMS (as pianist): *My Fair Lady*, 1956; *Li'l Abner*, 1957; *Pal Joey*, 1957.

WRITINGS OF INTEREST: *No Minor Chords: My Days in Hollywood*, 1991.

The Life

Born in Berlin, Andreas Ludwig Previn (PREH-vihn) fled Adolf Hitler's Germany with his parents and found a safe haven in Hollywood, where his uncle had found a position as a film studio musician. Like other European Jews, such as Albert Einstein and Arnold Schoenberg, Previn was a creative gift to America. While a student at Hollywood High School, Previn found employment at Metro-Goldwyn-Mayer, starting in 1946, as an arranger of film scores; there he became friends with such film stars as Deanna Durbin, Judy Garland, and Mickey Rooney. Eventually he won Academy Awards for his arrangements and orchestrations for the film versions of the musical *Gigi* (1958) and the opera *Porgy and Bess* (1959), for which he expanded the size of the orchestra from George Gershwin's original thirty musicians to one hundred.

Drafted into the Army in 1950, Previn returned to Hollywood and had a succession of marriages, usually to well-known creative figures, including the jazz singer Betty Bennett, the lyricist Dory Langdon, the film star Mia Farrow, and the concert violinist Anne-Sophie Mutter. Previn's involvement with and marriage to Farrow, who had been married to Frank Sinatra, was front-page news; in addition to having twins, the couple adopted four children.

Although Previn has modestly described himself as "only a guest" at the banquet of jazz, he began a second career as a jazz pianist. An admirer of such jazz pianists as Art Tatum and Oscar Peterson, he recorded with jazz regulars such as drummer Shelley Manne on a succession of popular albums of jazz renditions of Broadway musicals. His album *My Fair Lady* was the first jazz album devoted to jazz versions of a single Broadway musical.

To the bewilderment of his Hollywood friends, Previn sought a third career as a serious orchestral conductor, and he was the surprise choice as music director of the Houston Symphony in 1967. Having revealed an unexpected enthusiasm for British music, Previn was the controversial choice as director of the London Symphony Orchestra in 1968, despite the efforts of some British critics to dismiss him as "Hollywood Previn." His involvement in the Farrow-Sinatra publicity hastened his exit from Houston after only two years, but his successful tenure with the London Symphony lasted for a decade.

In 1978 he was hired to succeed William Steinberg as the music director of the Pittsburgh Symphony. Although Previn eventually left the Pittsburgh Symphony abruptly under controversial circumstances, he established himself as a solid conductor of the late Romantic European repertory, with large doses of British and American music. Oddly, he avoided some corners of the standard repertory, programming little music by Richard Wagner or Anton Bruckner. He frequently conducted Wolfgang Amadeus Mozart's piano concerti from the keyboard. His occasional forays into the modern repertory were marked with some controversy, such as when conservative Pittsburgh audience members walked out of his performance of Olivier Messiaen's *Turangalîla-Symphonie* (1948).

During his Pittsburgh years and later, Previn became more active in his fourth career, as a serious classical composer. He collaborated with the English playwright Tom Stoppard on an amusing comedy about a man who imagines that he hears a symphony orchestra playing, *Every Good Boy Deserves Favour* (1977). More ambitiously, he wrote a full-length operatic version of Tennessee Williams's classic American play, *A Streetcar Named Desire* (1947), specifically for soprano Renée Fleming. His name invariably came up for consideration for the position of music director at top American orchestras, such as the New York Philharmonic and the Chicago Symphony. He continues to compose and to conduct in the international orchestral circuit.

The Music

Hollywood and Broadway. Previn's skill at creating the lush orchestral sound of 1950's Hollywood musicals is clear from his scoring of Frederic Loewe's *Gigi* (1958) and George Gershwin's *Porgy and Bess* (1935), for which he won his first two Academy Awards. As a film composer, Previn showed a flair for musical characterization. A good example is his score for *Inside Daisy Clover*, for which he provided music and a hit single, "You're Gonna Hear from Me," to depict the free-spirited title character, played by Natalie Wood. In 1969 he made his debut as a Broadway composer with the musical *Coco*, based on the life of Coco Chanel; despite the star quality of its headliner, Katharine Hepburn, the show achieved only lukewarm reviews and closed quickly.

Jazz Pianist. Although cool jazz albums of the 1950's can seem tepid today, Previn's albums of jazz stylings of Broadway musicals still seem accessible and intelligent. *My Fair Lady* was the first jazz album devoted exclusively to one show, and it was Previn's best-selling album, succeeded by versions of such shows as *Pal Joey* and *Li'l Abner*. Previn and his group were clearly inspired by Leonard Bernstein's *West Side Story* (1961), which became the basis for his best jazz album. Previn and his sidemen reworked the melodies and the rhythmic components in original ways. For example, "Cool" was reconceived as a blues number, while a rousing version of "America," taken out of sequence from its place in the show, provides the album with a vigorous climax. Previn's two later jazz albums with the classical violinist Itzhak Perlman are pleasant but now seem more polite and genteel than genuinely jazzy. Previn's skills as both a jazz and classical pianist are evident in his early recording of the piano solo parts in George Gershwin's *Rhapsody in Blue* (1924) and Concerto in F (1925), conducted by André Kostelanetz.

Orchestral Conductor. Previn's first recording as an orchestral conductor was with the St. Louis Symphony, and they played Benjamin Britten's *Sinfonia da Requiem* (1941) and Aaron Copland's *The Red Pony Suite* (1948). The album helped to silence the critics who patronized Previn as merely a Hollywood musician. The choice of this pair reveals two of Previn's passions: for serious British music and for a Hollywood film score that is far more memorable than the motion picture for which it was written. Previn's conducting of *The Red Pony Suite* has energy, rhythmic incisiveness, and real affection for an undervalued score.

In Pittsburgh, Previn replaced a great exponent of the standard European repertory, Steinberg, whose mastery of this tradition was evident but whose tempi became reflective of his advancing age. Previn's appearance seemed like a new beginning, and indeed it marked a revitalization of a fine orchestra. Previn's fondness for British music shone through in some of his most powerful performances with the Pittsburgh Symphony, as when he accompanied the cellist Yo-Yo Ma in Edward Elgar's Cello Concerto (1919). Previn's insight into the British styles of such late Romantic composers as Elgar, Ralph Vaughan Williams, William Walton, and their younger contemporary Benjamin Britten is clear from the recordings he made with the London Symphony. Previn made a fine, idiomatic recording of Constant Lambert's eccentric 1929 collaboration with Dame Edith Sitwell, *The Rio Grande*, which should be better known in America as the British answer to Gershwin's *Rhapsody in Blue*. Under the echoes of

Sir André Previn. (Hulton Archive/Getty Images)

1920's American jazz, Previn locates the characteristic Elgar-like tone of nostalgia and regret that make the Lambert score so endearing.

In Mozartean fashion, Previn often conducted Mozart's piano concerti from the keyboard (with his back to the audience) with incisiveness but with a restraint that could seem insufficiently energized. Frustratingly, his conducting often seemed more efficient than inspired, but there was never any doubt about his proficiency and the skill of his technique. Distinctive among his many recordings with the Pittsburgh Symphony is his version of Jean Sibelius's Symphony No. 5 (1919), for which Previn finds the right note of Nordic energy and determination. Previn also shows an unexpected sympathy for the second-tier German Romantic composer Karl Goldmark, reflected in Previn's genial approach to Goldmark's *Rustic Wedding Symphony* (1876) and his Violin Concerto (1877), with Itzhak Perlman (a frequent visitor to Pittsburgh in those days) as a warm and engaging soloist.

Range and Diversity. Previn's series for public television, *Previn and the Pittsburgh*, showed the range of his talents, as a popular spokesman for serious music and as a collaborator with such disparate figures as the jazz singer Ella Fitzgerald, the operatic soprano Leontyne Price, and the violinist Itzhak Perlman. In addition, it introduced the Pittsburgh Symphony, which Previn brought up to international standards, to wide public attention.

Serious Composer. Previn skillfully chose texts and subjects that played to the strengths of the singers for whom he composed. He wrote the extended narrative song "Sally Chisum Remembers Billy the Kid" for the fine American soprano Barbara Bonney. The song cycle *Honey and Rue* was commissioned for the American novelist Toni Morrison and Previn by the soprano Kathleen Battle. *Honey and Rue* reveals Previn's affection for jazz, blues, and spirituals. Fleming was an ideal choice to portray the demented, delusional Blanche du Bois in Previn's operatic setting of *A Streetcar Named Desire*; one aria in particular, "I Want Magic," is strong enough to find a life of its own in soprano recitals, although the opera itself is hard pressed to find a musical idiom to reflect the complexity of Blanche's character. Previn's sharply witty incidental music for Stoppard's *Every Good Boy Deserves Favour* suc-

cessfully complements Stoppard's fantasy of a political dissident in Eastern Europe who imagines that he hears the sounds of a major symphony orchestra—and, thanks to Previn, he does.

Musical Legacy

Previn's success rested in his ability to combine a remarkable variety of roles: as a Hollywood composer and arranger, as a jazz pianist, as an orchestral conductor, as a classical pianist, and as a serious composer of orchestral works, song cycles, and an opera. As a child refugee from Hitler's Germany, he had an affinity for European musical tradition, but he quickly absorbed American idioms: the Hollywood film score, jazz, and the American melding of pop music, jazz, spirituals, and blues with European art music. One model for Previn's career was provided by Bernstein, who combined a facility for jazz and Broadway show tunes with a passionate devotion to the European classical tradition. In addition, both were major orchestral conductors. Previn won serious critical attention during his tenure as the music director of the Houston Symphony, the London Symphony, and the Pittsburgh Symphony. On a regular basis, he conducted the world's major orchestras.

Previn showed a youthful mastery of the lush Hollywood sound of the 1950's, and he won two Academy Awards before the age of thirty. Previn carved out a distinctive career as a jazz pianist, even though he claimed only a modest role as a jazz performer. His jazz albums revealed his taste, his solid technique, and his clear ability to swing. As a serious composer, he did not achieve the prestige of Bernstein or Aaron Copland, but the song cycles he wrote for American singers demonstrated his sharp instinct for adapting to the strengths of his performers. His opera *A Streetcar Named Desire*, written for the soprano Fleming, was an audacious attempt to find a musical equivalent for a steamy classic American play. Previn's remarkable career was an "only-in-America" success story.

Byron Nelson

Further Reading

Bookspan, Martin, and Ross Yockey. *André Previn: A Biography.* Garden City, N.Y.: Doubleday, 1981. A popular biography, though at times overly effusive and lacking in objectivity.

Davis, Peter G. "Captain of Industry." *New York Magazine* (June 10, 1996): 51-52. Commends Previn for his astonishing variety of musical skills.

Holland, Bernard. "Pursuing the Soul of *Streetcar* in Opera." *The New York Times*, September 20, 1998. A journalist finds much to admire in the first production of Previn's opera, but he notes the difficulty of setting Williams's classic play in operatic terms.

Nelson, Byron. "Previn's Preference." *Pittsburgh Magazine* (March, 1980): 70. Assesses Previn's first five seasons with the Pittsburgh Symphony and questions the conservative nature of his programming.

Previn, André. *No Minor Chords: My Days in Hollywood*. New York: Doubleday, 1993. Previn fondly recounts his early days as a Hollywood composer, arranger, and orchestrator of film musicals at Metro-Goldwyn-Mayer.

Ruttencutter, Helen Drees. *Previn*. New York: St. Martin's Press, 1987. This biography appeared shortly after Previn's Pittsburgh years.

See also: Ashkenazy, Vladimir; Bernstein, Leonard; Chung, Kyung-Wha; Fitzgerald, Ella; Green, Adolph, and Betty Comden; Lerner, Alan Jay; Loewe, Frederick; Mercer, Johnny; Mutter, Anne-Sophie; Perlman, Itzhak; Price, Leontyne; Rózsa, Miklós; Schoenberg, Arnold; Shankar, Ravi; Tatum, Art.

Leontyne Price

American classical and opera singer

With her elegant voice and extraordinary vocal range, Price captivated the world with her powerful operatic performances.

Born: February 10, 1927; Laurel, Mississippi
Also known as: Mary Violet Leontyne Price (full name)

Principal works

OPERATIC ROLES: Mistress Ford in Giuseppe Verdi's *Falstaff*, 1952; Saint Cecelia in Virgil Thomson's *Four Saints in Three Acts*, 1952; Bess in George Gershwin's *Porgy and Bess*, 1952; Tosca in Giacomo Puccini's *Tosca*, 1955; Aida in Giuseppe Verdi's *Aida*, 1957; Madame Lidoine in Francis Poulenc's *Dialogues des Carmélites*, 1957; Pamina in Wolfgang Amadeus Mozart's *Die Zauberflöte*, 1958 (*The Magic Flute*); Donna Anna in Mozart's *Don Giovanni*, 1960; Minnie in Puccini's *La fanciulla del west*, 1961 (*The Girl of the Golden West*); Butterfly in Puccini's *Madama Butterfly*, 1961; Elvira in Verdi's *Ernani*, 1962; Leonora in Verdi's *Il trovatore*, 1962; Lenora in Verdi's *La forza del destino*, 1963 (*The Force of Destiny*); Fiordiligi in Mozart's *Così fan tutte*, 1964; Tatyana in Peter Ilich Tchaikovsky's *Eugene Onegin*, 1965; Cleopatra in Samuel Barber's *Antony and Cleopatra*, 1966; Liù in Puccini's *Turandot*, 1966; Amelia in Verdi's *Un ballo in maschera*, 1969 (*A Masked Ball*); Ariadne in Richard Strauss's *Ariadne auf Naxos*, 1970; Giorgetta in Puccini's *Il tabarro*, 1970; Manon in Puccini's *Manon Lescaut*, 1970.

The Life

Mary Violet Leontyne (lee-AHN-teen *or* LEE-ahn-teen) Price is the daughter of a carpenter, James Anthony Price, and a midwife, Kathrine Baker. She was exposed to music while she was a toddler. While her mother attended rehearsals and sung in the choir at the local church, Price sat next to her and heard her mother's beautiful soprano voice. Price had her first music lesson with a music teacher from the Negro Oak Park Vocational High School at the age of three. Her mother had high hopes of her daughter pursuing a career in music. Her father was not supportive of Price's music interest until he heard her perform her first piano recital at the age of five. From that point on, her parents did everything they could to ensure that Price had a future in music.

Price had a normal childhood, enjoying her toys and girlfriends. Before she was allowed to play, however, she had to practice. During her teen years, Price played piano and sang at funerals, weddings, and other events. She was well compensated for her performances.

Education was important to Price and her parents, and she graduated cum laude from high school. Soon after, she attended Wilberforce College in Wilberforce, Ohio, on a full scholarship. At first she majored in music education, but she decided to pursue a concentration in voice after a recommendation from one of her voice teachers. She was even more confident that she wanted a career in opera after hearing Giacomo Puccini's *Turandot* (1926). At this time Price focused on a career in opera, one that lasted until she retired in 1985. She remains active in the music world, presenting recitals and teaching voice to talented sopranos.

The Music

Price possesses an extraordinary lyric soprano voice. During her first operatic world premiere in 1952, she was an immediate success. Her musical style is superb, and her voice is moving.

Porgy and Bess. Price first performed George Gershwin's *Porgy and Bess* (1935) in 1952, when the opera was set for an all-black cast. *Porgy and Bess* transforms jazz and blues idioms into an operatic classical art form. The opera was highly regarded, but not all African Americans were willing to accept its negative depiction of blacks. Price played the role of Bess, and William Warfield, who later became her husband for two years, played Porgy. Each time Price performed the role of Bess, critics commented on her remarkable vocal power and purity. They believed Price sung the most electrifying and breathtaking Bess ever heard.

Tosca. Price premiered in Puccini's *Tosca* (1900) in 1955 on NBC-Television's *Opera Workshop* production. She was the first African American opera singer to premiere in a televised opera. Several stations in the South threatened not to televise the opera because of its interracial aspects. However, the opera was aired, and it was a success. Critics believed Price's performance as Floria Tosca was astonishing.

Aida. Price felt a personal connection to the role of Aida in Giuseppe Verdi's *Aida* (1871). The opera is a love story set in ancient times when Ethiopia and Egypt were at war. Princess Aida of Ethiopia is abducted with other Ethiopians and forced into slavery in Egypt. While a servant to Pharaoh's daughter, she initiates contact with the captain of the Egyptian army, and they fall in love. Price first premiered in *Aida* at the San Francisco Opera House in 1957. She portrayed Aida with charm.

Leontyne Price. (Library of Congress)

Some critics believed Price was born for this role and that the composer would have found Price was the ideal soprano for the role of Aida.

Il Trovatore. Price made history when she played the leading role, Leonora, in Verdi's *Il trovatore* (1853) at the Metropolitan Opera in 1961. *Il trovatore* is a love story about Leonora, the queen of Spain, who is in love with a nomadic poet and musician. However, his brother, the count, also loves her. Price's performance was so astonishing that the audience gave a standing ovation for forty-two minutes at the conclusion of the opera. Price believed that she had reached the peak of her success with this performance.

Antony and Cleopatra. In 1966, Price gave the world premiere of Samuel Barber's *Antony and Cleopatra* at the Lincoln Center, for the opening of the Metropolitan Opera House. Cleopatra's role was customized specifically for Price.

Musical Legacy

Price captivated the world with her extraordinary lyric soprano voice, using its power to integrate audiences in Laurel, Mississippi, for the first time in history. Known as the first lady of opera, Price has been honored with numerous awards. She was the first opera singer to be given the Presidential Medal of Freedom. Italy honored her with the Order of Merit. She has collected three Emmy Awards and twenty Grammy Awards. Price also received the Kennedy Center Honors Award and the National Medal of Arts.

Monica T. Tripp

Further Reading

Bolden, Tonya. *And Not Afraid to Dare: The Stories of Ten African-American Women.* New York: Scholastic Press, 1998. This book recounts the lives and major accomplishments of ten extraordinary African American women, including a brief biography of Price and details on her opera debuts.

Gates, Henry Louis, Jr., and Cornel West. *The African-American Century: How Black Americans Have Shaped Our Country.* New York: Simon & Schuster, 2000. A brief overview of the achievements of the leading African Americans, including Price, who have helped transform America.

Lyon, Hugh Lee. *Leontyne Price: Highlights of a Prima Donna.* New York: Authors Choice Press, 2007. This book offers a candid view of Price's personal life based on interviews with her teachers, family members, and friends.

Price, Leontyne. *Aida.* San Diego, Calif.: Voyager Books, 2007. Details about the opera *Aida* through the eyes of the performer.

Sargeant, Winthrop. *Divas.* New York: Coward, McCann & Geoghegan, 1973. This book examines the life and major works of leading female opera singers, including Price.

See also: Anderson, Marian; Barber, Samuel; Björling, Jussi; Harrison, Lou; Norman, Jessye; Previn, Sir André; Puccini, Giacomo.

Charley Pride

American country singer, songwriter, and guitarist

Pride was the first commercially successful African American in country music.

Born: March 18, 1938; Sledge, Mississippi
Also known as: Charley Frank Pride (full name)

Principal recordings

ALBUMS: *Country Charley Pride,* 1966; *The Country Way,* 1967; *The Pride of Country Music,* 1967; *Make Mine Country,* 1968; *Songs of Pride . . . Charley, That Is,* 1968; *The Sensational Charley Pride,* 1969; *Charley Pride's Tenth Album,* 1970; *Christmas in My Home Town,* 1970; *Just Plain Charley,* 1970; *Charley Pride Sings Heart Songs,* 1971; *Did You Think to Pray?,* 1971; *From Me to You,* 1971; *I'm Just Me,* 1971; *A Sunshine Day with Charley Pride,* 1972; *Amazing Love,* 1973; *Songs of Love by Charley Pride,* 1973; *Sweet Country,* 1973; *Country Feelin',* 1974; *Pride of America,* 1974; *Charley,* 1975; *The Happiness of Having You,* 1975; *Sunday Morning with Charley Pride,* 1976; *She's Just an Old Love Turned Memory,* 1977; *Burgers and Fries,* 1978; *Someone Loves You Honey,* 1978; *You're My Jamaica,* 1979; *There's a Little Bit of Hank in Me,* 1980; *Roll on Mississippi,* 1981; *Charley Sings Everybody's Choice,* 1982; *Country Classics,* 1983; *Night Games,* 1983; *Power of Love,* 1984; *Collector's Series,* 1985; *Best There Is,* 1986; *After All This Time,* 1987; *I'm Gonna Love Her on the Radio,* 1988; *Moody Woman,* 1989; *Country in My Soul,* 1991; *My Six Latest and Six Greatest,* 1994; *Classics with Pride,* 1996; *A Tribute to Jim Reeves,* 2001; *Comfort of Her Wings,* 2003; *Happy Christmas,* 2004.

The Life

Charley Frank Pride was born on a cotton farm in Sledge, Mississippi. Pride's early exposure to country music came from listening to Grand Ole Opry radio broadcasts with his father. At age fourteen, Pride bought his first guitar from Sears, Roebuck, and he began learning to play by ear. Baseball was Pride's real passion, however, and at fifteen he left home to pursue it as a career.

Pride played in the Negro and minor leagues before being drafted by the Army. After his discharge, Pride moved to Montana, and he worked at a smelting plant, singing in bars at night. Pride tried repeatedly to break into baseball's major leagues, but he was unsuccessful.

Pride was urged by Red Foley and Red Sovine to go to Nashville, Tennessee, where he signed a management deal with Jack Johnson. In 1966 Pride caught the attention of the influential musician Chet Atkins, and he signed a contract with RCA. The record company withheld publicity photographs for his first two singles in order to hide the fact that Pride was African American.

After winning a Grammy in 1966, Pride became a fixture on country music's Top 10 lists. His recording career slowed considerably after he departed RCA in 1986, but Pride remains an active performer.

The Music

Pride's music is solidly in the "countrypolitan" tradition. Also known as the Nashville sound, countrypolitan music replaced the rougher edges of honky-tonk (with its fiddles and nasal vocals) with smoother-sounding lead vocals, polished instrumental arrangements, backing choruses, and other elements—including song structure—taken from 1950's pop music. In contrast to the down-home sound of honky-tonk records, countrypolitan music boasted a pristine production quality. When combined with a gentle, mannered voice such as Pride's, the result was a new type of country, aimed at (and reaching) a much wider audience.

"Snakes Crawl at Night." "Snakes Crawl at Night" was Pride's debut single in 1966, released on his album *Country Charley Pride*. The midtempo lilt of the song and its good-natured melody seem incongruous with the lyrics, which tell the story of a husband's murderous revenge for his wife's infidelity. The harmonic vocabulary is straightforward, but the placement of the chord changes is often surprising, highlighting key words in the lyrics and often at odds with the poetic structure.

"Just Between You and Me." While "Snakes Crawl at Night" and his second single, "Before I Met You," gained Pride a small following, his commercial success began with the release of his third single, "Just Between You and Me." This song, about love and heartbreak, earned Pride a Grammy Award in 1966. Audiences were captivated by Pride's smooth baritone voice, backed by clever writing for the steel guitar. "Just Between You and Me" was a perfect example of the up-and-coming Nashville sound: laid-back lead vocals, thoughtful instrumental writing, backing singers, and clean production quality. These factors, combined with its universal lyric sentiment, made it ripe for mass consumption.

"Is Anybody Goin' to San Antone." "Is Anybody Goin' to San Antone" was a number-one hit for Pride in 1970, and it is a good example of the flexibility of Pride's style and appeal. The instrumental arrangement is appropriate to the Tex-Mex

Charley Pride. (AP/Wide World Photos)

style alluded to in the title (complete with mariachi fiddles). Pride was a country and not a Western singer, and the musical and lyrical references to the Southwest in this song are unusual for him.

"Kiss an Angel Good Mornin'." After six straight number-one singles from 1969 to 1971, the song "Let Me Live," from Pride's gospel album, *Did You Think to Pray?*, broke his streak of number-one singles, but it won a Grammy Award that year for Best Gospel Performance. Pride recovered momentum quickly, however, and, upon returning to the countrypolitan sound, he released two of his most commercially successful songs: "I'm Just Me" and "Kiss an Angel Good Mornin'."

"Kiss an Angel Good Mornin'," from *Charley Pride Sings Heart Songs*, is a celebration of happiness in love. Pride's smiling, velvety delivery provides an atmosphere of authentically felt emotion, which is balanced by sophisticated touches such as the recurring motto in the steel guitar and piano and rich harmonies in the background vocals. Besides reaching number one on the *Billboard* country charts, "Kiss an Angel Good Mornin'" also became a crossover hit, reaching number twenty-one on the *Billboard* pop chart and number seven on the adult contemporary chart.

"You're So Good When You're Bad." Pride remained in the upper country charts throughout the 1970's, with six more number-one singles between 1972 and 1977. In the first half of the 1980's, Pride produced four more number-one hits, among them "You're So Good When You're Bad," from *Charley Sings Everybody's Choice*.

This record contains soulful singing, betraying Charley's roots in the Deep South much more than in previous albums. Nevertheless, the vocals for the down-tempo song "You're So Good When You're Bad" are accompanied by a tightly arranged array of strings, electric piano, and electric guitar, making it equally at home on country and adult contemporary radio stations.

Musical Legacy

Pride was the first African American to obtain commercial success in country music, earning this honor despite substantial difficulties. As the highest-selling act for RCA since Elvis Presley, Pride released twelve gold albums in the United States and thirty gold and four platinum albums internation-

ally. He topped the *Billboard* country charts twenty-nine times in the course of his career. In 1971 Pride was named the Country Music Association's Entertainer of the Year, and in 1971 and 1972 was also the Country Music Association's Male Vocalist of the Year. He was given the Academy of Country Music's Pioneer Award in 1994, and he was inducted to the Country Music Hall of Fame in 2000.

When the novelty of an African American singing country music wore off over time, Pride's success in forging the Nashville sound could be viewed on its own terms. The music made by Pride and others in the 1960's and 1970's brought country music to mainstream audiences.

Carey L. Campbell

Further Reading

Kelley, Brent P. "Charley Pride." In *"I Will Never Forget": Interviews with Thirty-nine Former Negro League Players*. Jefferson, N.C.: McFarland, 2003. This chapter in a book about the Negro League is a refreshing reversal of Pride's habit of talking about baseball in music interviews.

Malone, Ann. "Charley Pride." In *Stars of Country Music: Uncle Dave Macon to Johnny Rodriguez*, edited by Bill C. Malone and Judith McCulloh. Urbana: University of Illinois Press, 1975. In this interview, Pride discusses the influences on his music.

Nash, Alanna. "Charley Pride." In *Behind Closed Doors: Talking With the Legends of Country Music*. New York: Cooper Square Press, 2002. In this chapter, Pride discusses his early days in the recording business.

Pride, Charley, with Jim Henderson. *Pride: The Charley Pride Story*. New York: William Morrow, 1994. This autobiography details Pride's early life and baseball career, and it provides vivid accounts of his difficulties breaking into the country-music scene.

Streissguth, Michael. "Charley Pride: American." In *Voices of the Country: Interviews with Classic Country Performers*. New York: Routledge, 2004. This chapter provides information on Pride's personal and professional life.

See also: Atkins, Chet; Fender, Freddy; Presley, Elvis.

Prince

American pop and soul/funk singer, guitarist, and songwriter

As an artist in the studio, Prince blended pop, rock, soul, funk, and rhythm and blues in his memorable songs. As a performer onstage, he entertained with sexually provocative imagery and complex productions that shaped the concert landscape throughout the 1980's.

Born: June 7, 1958; Minneapolis, Minnesota
Also known as: Prince Rogers Nelson (birth name); Artist Formerly Known as Prince
Member of: The Revolution; New Power Generation

Principal works

FILM SCORE: *Under the Cherry Moon*, 1986.

Principal recordings

ALBUMS (solo): *For You*, 1978; *Prince*, 1979; *Dirty Mind*, 1980; *Controversy*, 1981; *1999*, 1982; *The Black Album*, 1987; *Sign o' the Times*, 1987; *Lovesexy*, 1988; *Batman*, 1989; *Come*, 1994; *Gold Experience*, 1995; *Chaos and Disorder*, 1996; *Emancipation*, 1996; *The Truth*, 1997; *Rave Un2 the Joy Fantastic*, 1999; *The Rainbow Children*, 2001; *N.E.W.S.*, 2003; *Musicology*, 2004; *3121*, 2006.

ALBUMS (with New Power Generation): *Graffiti Bridge*, 1990 (all songs written by Prince); *Diamonds and Pearls*, 1991; *The Love Symbol*, 1992; *New Power Soul*, 1998; *Planet Earth*, 2007.

ALBUMS (with the Revolution): *Purple Rain*, 1984; *Around the World in a Day*, 1985; *Parade*, 1986.

The Life

Though he eventually dropped his middle and last names, the entertainer was born Prince Rogers Nelson on June 7, 1958, to John L. Nelson (a pianist and songwriter) and Mattie Shaw (a singer). As a result of his parents' musical background, he instantly developed an affinity for artistry while growing up in Minneapolis, Minnesota. His childhood became troubled, however, when his parents divorced. After his mother remarried,

Prince clashed with his stepfather and left home. He spent some time living in his father's home (where he learned to play the guitar), and then he moved in with family friends, the Andersons, when he was in junior high.

Prince struck up a friendship with their son Andre (who was renamed André Cymone for the stage), and the pair joined the local band Grand Central. Though starting as a guitarist for the entirely instrumental band, he soon produced the band's material before stepping up to the microphone in high school (when the players evolved into a new entity called Champagne). His experience on the local scene inspired Prince to cut a demo record in 1976, which quickly got attention and generated record-label interest. Warner Bros. Records signed him, releasing his debut project two years later and launching his incredibly successful career.

Prince was especially flamboyant during his early performances, leading some to speculate about his sexual orientation. Soon, however, he began a series of high-profile romantic relationships in the 1980's and 1990's, with such celebrities as Vanity, Madonna, Sheila E., Anna Fantastic, and Carmen Electra. His personal life calmed down during the 1990's, when he began investigating the Jehovah's Witnesses, under the direction of mentor Larry Graham (of Sly and the Family Stone fame). Prince officially joined the faith in 2001, and as a result he became increasingly vocal about his beliefs in his albums and in his live performances, replacing sexually suggestive songs with biblically inspired material. With little fanfare, he married Manuela Testolini in 2001; she filed for divorce in 2006. Undaunted by that personal setback, Prince maintained his prominent career presence and devotion to his spiritual beliefs.

The Music

Early Works. Upon signing with Warner Bros. Records, Prince saw his career slowly begin its ascent to international fame. His 1978 album *For You* did not produce any major hits, though it did introduce listeners to his inventive union of pop, rock, funk, soul, and rhythm and blues. In addition, *For You* showed the newcomer to be an incredibly talented force, whose credits included producing, arranging, composing, and performing the entire project. The following year's self-titled effort forced a wider audience to take notice, thanks in part to the funky single "I Wanna Be Your Lover" and the soulful "I Feel for You" (which was later covered by Chaka Khan). Certain notoriety came from 1980's *Dirty Mind*, though it was focused mostly on the suggestive album cover (which included Prince provocatively posed in a pair of black briefs) and the sexually charged lyrics behind the title cut and "Do It All Night." Prince accepted the public scrutiny over what was generally deemed to be scandalous material and continued in the same vein with 1981's new wave-flavored *Controversy*, known for the racy "Sexuality" and "Jack U Off."

1999. Prince sanitized his songs' lyrics a bit and featured a refined synthesizer sound on *1999* (ironically released in 1982), made with his newly named backing band the Revolution. With those elements, plus the infectious sounds on singles "Little Red Corvette" and "1999," Prince became a household name and an early example of an African American artist expanding into the mainstream during the MTV era.

Purple Rain. In 1984 Prince and the Revolution had tremendous success with *Purple Rain*, which served as the sound track to the singer's film of the same name. The project spawned an astounding five singles ("When Doves Cry," "Let's Go Crazy," "Purple Rain," "I Would Die 4 U" and "Take Me with U"), incorporating contemporary pop elements with old school funk and soul. With the popular album and motion picture combination, Prince's reputation soared, and he took home Grammy Awards for Best Rock Vocal Performance by a Duo or Group and Best Album of Original Score Written for a Motion Picture or TV Special and an Academy Award for Best Original Song Score.

Around the World in a Day. After the great response to the blockbuster *Purple Rain* (with sales reaching almost twenty million copies), 1985's *Around the World in a Day* was somewhat overlooked, though it still sold more than two million copies and featured the smash hit "Raspberry Beret." The next year Prince attempted to reclaim the *Purple Rain* success with a motion picture and sound track for *Under the Cherry Moon*, although the music had a European sound and lacked mainstream appeal (outside the single "Kiss").

Sign o' the Times. In the fading limelight, Prince reinvented himself and attracted additional audiences with 1987's epic *Sign o' the Times*. The double album was a solo affair, without backing by the Revolution, and featured reexaminations of tracks from previously shelved projects. The concept collection was packed with sixteen songs of varied sounds: experimental, jazz, electronic rock, and ballad. Though it failed to match Prince's peak, *Sign o' the Times* yielded the highest number of hits since *Purple Rain*, including the title cut, "If I Was Your Girlfriend," "U Got the Look," and "I Could Never Take the Place of Your Man."

The Love Symbol. After working on several sound tracks and making acting appearances, Prince returned with 1991's *Diamonds and Pearls* (with the New Power Generation backing band). However, he became increasingly disgruntled with Warner Bros. for not allowing him to explore unusual creative visions, which began surfacing on 1992's *The Love Symbol* (structured as a rock-and-roll soap opera). Tensions between the artist and label increased as he sought additional independence, resulting in 1994's *Come*, which was announced as his last recording under the Prince moniker. As promised, that stage name was officially dropped on 1995's *Gold Experience* in favor of the unpronounceable icon depicted on *The Love Symbol* cover. Though the project retained his familiar sound with the New Power Generation, it was a media sensation, focused more on the clash between Prince and the record label than the quality of the music.

Emancipation. The Artist Formerly Known as Prince and Warner Bros. officially parted company after 1996's *Chaos and Disorder*. That same year, the entertainer released a triple album set of new material called *Emancipation* on his label, NPG Records. The title was a direct reference to his squabbles with Warner Bros. and symbolized a new freedom in producing his music. Although Prince continued making music on his own terms for the rest of that decade and into the 2000's, the name change confused some listeners and, as a result, several albums earned little attention.

Musicology. In 2001 *The Rainbow Children* was credited to Prince, who justified the return to that name because his publishing contract with Warner/Chappell Music finally expired. Prince released a few more independent albums, but in 2004 he allowed Columbia Records to distribute *Musicology*. As a result of wider availability, it sold more than two million copies, bolstered by a tour that featured new songs and old hits. The momentum started an upward trend that culminated in 2006's *3121* debuting at number one on the *Billboard* Top 200 album charts. In 2007 Prince's Super Bowl halftime performance built anticipation for *Planet Earth*.

Musical Legacy

Prince sold millions of records and had a steady stream of hit singles throughout the 1980's, and he was a dominant crossover force. He was one of the first African American artists to appear regularly on MTV, and his songs seamlessly combined the worlds of rock, pop, soul, rhythm and blues, funk, and jazz. Whether recording on his own or with the Revolution or New Power Generation, Prince consistently crossed the boundaries between accessibility and experimentation. He nurtured other artists as diverse as funk band the Time, all-girl pop group Vanity 6, and soul siren Sheila E. He influenced such performers as Lenny Kravitz, Seal, and Beyoncé.

During his tenure as an unpronounceable symbol, the star was among the first to rebuff a major record company and emancipate himself from its demands. Though the period following his departure from Warner Bros. met with little commercial success, the artist worked under his own terms and presented several projects that showcased diversity and excellence in his singing, writing, producing, performing, and arranging capabilities. Because of his perseverance, Prince regained his position under his original stage name.

Andy Argyrakis

Further Reading

Carcieri, Matthew. *Prince: A Life in Music*. Lincoln, Nebr.: iUniverse, 2004. Billed as a playlist history, this book provides analysis of and insight into fifty of Prince's most popular songs.

Hoskyns, Barney. *Prince: Imp of the Perverse*. London: Virgin, 1988. Discussion of Prince's sexually charged stage presence, his mysterious personality, and his life behind the scenes.

Jones, Liz. *Purple Reign: The Artist Formerly Known as Prince*. New York: Citadel Press, 1999. Culls Prince quotes from other sources and includes interviews with former band members and those close to the singer.

Matos, Michaelangelo. *Sign o' the Times*. New York: Continuum, 2004. An exhaustive study of the songs and messages contained in Prince's classic *Sign o' the Times*.

Morton, Brian. *Prince: A Thief in the Temple*. Edinburgh, Scotland: Canongate, 2007. The biography includes information on Prince's early career, his hit-making years, his occasional missteps, and his return to the public eye.

Nilsen, Per. *Dance Music Sex Romance: Prince, the First Decade*. London: SAF Publishing, 2004. The longtime editor of Prince's fan magazine *Uptown* covers Prince throughout the 1980's, including his artistic innovations and his commercial peak.

See also: Stone, Sly; Brown, James; Davis, Miles; Hendrix, Jimi.

John Prine

American folksinger, guitarist, and songwriter

With his unusual voice, his deadpan humor, and his idiosyncratic wordplay, singer-songwriter Prine defined the Americana music movement of the 1970's.

Born: October 10, 1946; Maywood, Illinois

Principal recordings

ALBUMS: *John Prine*, 1971; *Diamonds in the Rough*, 1972; *Sweet Revenge*, 1973; *Common Sense*, 1975; *Bruised Orange*, 1978; *Pink Cadillac*, 1979; *Storm Windows*, 1980; *Aimless Love*, 1984; *German Afternoons*, 1986; *The Missing Years*, 1991; *A John Prine Christmas*, 1994; *Lost Dogs and Mixed Blessings*, 1995; *In Spite of Ourselves*, 1999; *Souvenirs*, 2000; *Fair and Square*, 2005; *Standard Songs for Average People*, 2007 (with Mac Wiseman).

The Life

John Prine (prin) is the third of four sons born to Bill and Verna Prine, who migrated from rural western Kentucky to Maywood, Illinois, a working-class suburb of Chicago. His father was a machinist by trade. The family frequently visited Kentucky, and its music, language and lore made a lasting impression on Prine.

An indifferent student, Prine joined the U.S. Army and then got a job with the U.S. Postal Service. Though his older brother Dave had taught him rudimentary guitar fingerpicking at age fourteen, Prine later refined his guitar playing and songwriting in classes at Chicago's Old Town School of Folk Music. Here he befriended fellow songwriter Steve Goodman, who introduced Prine to Kris Kristofferson. Kristofferson helped Prine secure a recording contract with Atlantic Records.

The debut album *John Prine* contains a number of songs that remain his most popular: "Hello in There," "Sam Stone," "Paradise," "Illegal Smile," and "Angel from Montgomery." The album was lauded by critics, especially those seeking a "new Dylan" (at a time when Bob Dylan to have lost his musical edge). Prine toured extensively, and he made several more albums for Atlantic Records. In 1978 Prine signed with David Geffen's fledgling Asylum Records. With Goodman at the production helm Prine released *Bruised Orange*, perhaps his most highly regarded album. His follow-ups for Asylum were not as critically or commercially successful, and in 1980 Prine no longer had a recording label.

With the help of longtime manager Al Bunetta, Prine established his own recording label, Oh Boy Records. Though located in Nashville, Tennessee, Prine's company did not operate like a mainstream corporate music label. Working with songwriter Roger Cook as producer, Prine released a series of albums in the 1980's that won general acclaim and helped reestablish his importance as a songwriter and as a performer to a new generation of alternative country musicians who seeking were an audience and selling a product outside the mainstream music industry.

Prine's sound and his critical and commercial popularity improved when Howie Epstein, bass player for Tom Petty and the Heartbreakers, took over the role of producer for the Grammy Award-winning Folk Album of the Year *The Missing Years*. The Americana radio format, arising out of the college and alternative-radio movement of the 1980's,

was ideally suited to Prine, since his musical catalog ran the gamut from folk and blues to rock and country. Prine earned his second Grammy Award for Folk Album of the Year for *Fair and Square*. In the meantime, he had won a battle with throat cancer. He married for the third time, and he had three children.

The Music

Prine's songwriting is a deceptive blend of simplicity and complexity. His melodies and chord progressions can be remarkably simple, in a folk or traditional manner. However, his unusual vocal phrasing (modeled on Dylan, blues singers, and other folk artists) compensate for what a song might lack in melody. His lyrics are the basis for the acclaim of his songwriting. Prine operates lyrically in two modes: as a keen-eyed documentarian of the margins of society and as a social critic capable of mixing the personal and the populist, with surreal imagery and absurd wordplay.

Documentarian. Prine the documentarian was evident from his first album. "Hello in There" takes as its subject an aged couple who have drifted into uselessness at the end of life. In a single stanza, Prine's narrator provides a family history that reveals its disconnectedness: One son is married and living in Omaha, another is a wanderer, and son Davy was killed senselessly in the Korean War. Similarly, on his second album, *Diamonds in the Rough*, "The Torch Singer" captures the ambiance of a dive bar, with its catwalk that creaks when the bartender walks on it and the smoke "too heavy to rise."

Social Critic. Prine the social critic found his voice in the much-covered "Paradise," in which a coal company destroys the western Kentucky ecosystem. However, unlike the apocalyptic critical voice of Dylan (who indicts "Masters of War" and other powers), Prine takes a down-to-earth, even fatalistic, position in which the coal companies of the world always end up destroying the paradises. A sense of tragic loss predominates over a sense of indignation. Similarly, in "Picture Show" from *The Missing Years*, Prine lambastes American culture's preoccupation with its own image: the song contrasts the young James Dean dreaming of being a film star with the Native American belief that taking one's photograph steals a piece of one's soul.

"Bruised Orange." These two modes come together beautifully in the classic "Bruised Orange (Chain of Sorrow)" from *Bruised Orange*. The song's narrator is haunted by an accidental death he witnesses as a youth (an anonymous altar boy run over by a commuter train). The details are masterly— from the train's naked "howl" to the optical illusion of the speeding train seeming to approach slowly before hitting the boy. However, the narrator then broadens the scope of the song from an individual to a universal tragedy, in which the human heart becomes imprisoned in its own "chain of sorrow."

Musical Legacy

Prine's musical legacy is twofold. First, he helped to establish the role of the Americana singer-songwriter as quirky, personal, and accessible (as opposed to the distance between the artist and the audience typified by Dylan). Second, he established the artist as entrepreneur, creating his own label and using Americana radio as a means of connecting with an alternative music audience.

Luke A. Powers

Further Reading

Fanning, Charles. "John Prine's Lyrics." *American Music* 5, no. 1 (Spring, 1987): 48-73. A discussion of the development in Prine's lyrics from a traditional folk-revival style to increasingly bizarre surrealism.

Fricke, David. *Great Days: The John Prine Anthology*. Rhino, 1993. Fricke, who also served as compilation producer to this retrospective of Prine's recording career from 1971 to 1991, wrote the fifty-page booklet (with numerous illustrations) that accompanies the album. It provides ample biographical information as well as Prine's comments on the inspirations for various songs.

Kibby, Marjorie. "Home on the Page: A Virtual Place of Music Community." *Popular Music* 19, no. 1 (January, 2000): 91-100. A review and analysis of the chat room on Prine's Oh Boy Records' Web site and its ability to create "virtual community" between artist and fans similar to that of a traditional folk musician and his or her community.

Poston, Frances, et al. "Our Readers Write: Who Is an Artist or Musician Whose Works Can Be Used Successfully in English Class?" *The English Journal* 74, no. 7 (November, 1985): 75-82. A group of secondary and college English professors share notes on popular culture figures for classroom study. Prine is included in a section with Steve Goodman.

See also: Carter, Maybelle; Dylan, Bob; Kristofferson, Kris; Petty, Tom; Travis, Merle.

Professor Longhair
American rhythm-and-blues pianist, singer, and songwriter

Professor Longhair, although little recorded, was significant in jazz piano-based rock and New Orleans music.

Born: December 19, 1918; Bogalusa, Louisiana
Died: January 30, 1980; New Orleans, Louisiana
Also known as: Henry Roeland Byrd (birth name); Fess

Principal recordings

ALBUMS: *Rock 'n' Roll Gumbo*, 1977; *Live on the Queen Mary*, 1978; *Crawfish Fiesta*, 1980; *Mardi Gras in New Orleans*, 1981; *The Last Mardi Gras*, 1982; *House Party New Orleans Style*, 1987.

The Life

Professor Longhair was born Henry Roeland Byrd on December 19, 1918, in Bogalusa, Louisiana, to musicians Ella Mae and James Byrd. Because of racist threats, Ella Mae, Byrd, and his brother Robert relocated to New Orleans. She became a jazz combo piano player, while Byrd was a sidekick for a Hadacol (snake oil) salesman and later a street tap dancer. From there, he gravitated toward working in French Quarter clubs as a guitarist, a drummer, and finally as a self-taught piano player. As a young man, he worked construction, was a cook, had a brief stint in the Army, entered a short-lived marriage, and became a gambler. Ultimately he became Professor Longhair, and he toured locally in the 1940's and nationally in the 1950's. He played on only one recording, with Earl King, in 1965. He disappeared until 1970, when Allison Miner, Parker Dinkins, and Quint Davis set out to find him for the first New Orleans Jazz and Heritage Festival. Davis found him in 1971, at the One Stop record store, working as a janitor and delivery boy. At the 1972 festival, when Longhair took the stage, everyone, including the other musicians playing at the time, walked over to watch and listen. In 1977 the owners of a New Orleans music club named it Tipitina's, after his song. Longhair toured worldwide in 1979, and his album *Crawfish Fiesta* was released one day after he died in his sleep. He was a subject of the posthumously released documentary *Piano Players Rarely Ever Play Together* (1982).

The Music

Piano mentor Tuts Washington noticed that Byrd was entranced with the boogie-woogie sound, which had a rolling bass line (rolling left hand). Byrd combined this style with a percussive technique (he would also kick the piano to mark beats), along with influences from various musical styles—blues, jazz, New Orleans's second line, Jelly Roll Morton's riffs and breaks, and the newly emerging sound of rock—to create a style few could re-create. His rollicking piano playing was accentuated by a rough-sounding yodeling or wailing vocal technique, which often featured extreme changes in volume and pitch. The songs themselves are blues influenced (standard eight and twelve bar) in structure, with a superimposition of fast triplets played by the right hand.

Early Years. Byrd developed his piano style by using his left hand for percussive effect. His idiosyncratic style of playing and singing contained elements of what we now call rock, rhythm and blues, funk and Afro-Cuban rumba. While still a teenager, he was approached by Champion Jack Dupree, Sullivan Rock, and Washington, and Dupree gave Byrd piano lessons. By 1947 Byrd called himself Little Lovin' Henry, fronting the Midriffs, which in 1948 landed a prestigious ongoing gig at the Caledonia Inn in New Orleans. Owner Mike Tessitore referred to Byrd as Professor Longhair, and the band became known as Professor Longhair and His Four Hairs Combo: Professors Longhair, Shorthair, Mohair, and Need Some Hair. As leader of Professor Longhair and the Shuffling Hungarians, Byrd recorded the Mercury version of

"Baldhead," and by 1953 he could be heard on the singles "East St. Louis Rag," "Baby Let Me Hold Your Hand," "Her Mind Is Gone," "Hey Now Baby," and "Professor Longhair's Boogie."

New Orleans Piano. This album collects Professor Longhair's Atlantic recordings from the 1940's and 1950's. It contains his signature piece, "Tipitina," which showcases his ubiquitous rolling piano lines, his use of polyrhythm (perhaps influenced by his admiration of Pérez Prado), and his unique tessitura, especially in his vocal use of pitches that suddenly rise and fall, combined with a high instance of switching from high to low notes, often to the point of briefly wandering off key. The album also includes the rhythm-and-blues hit "Ball the Wall" and the influential "Mardi Gras in New Orleans" (based on his earlier "East St. Louis Rag"). In "Mardi Gras in New Orleans," Professor Longhair whistles nearly an entire verse in the introduction and fadeout.

Rock 'n' Roll Gumbo. In this 1974 album, Professor Longhair works with Clarence "Gatemouth" Brown (guitar, violin), to produce higher quality versions of his best-known songs. The album is notable for the chemistry between the two performers. Songs collected on the album include "Stag O Lee," "How Long Has This Train Been Gone," "Rum and Coke," and "Junco Partner." The album was remixed in 1985 so that the piano would be more prominent, and horns could be added.

Crawfish Fiesta. Released in 1980, this album sold out within one week of its release. It features Professor Longhair collaborating with Dr. John (Mack Rebennack) on guitar and saxophonist Andy Kaslow, and it included "Big Chief," "Her Mind Is Gone," "Bald Head," and "Whole Lotta Loving."

Musical Legacy

Longhair's influence can be heard as early as 1955 in the music of Little Richard, Fats Domino, and Jerry Lee Lewis. In his later recording years, he mentored young pianists such as Dr. John and Allen Toussaint. He was inducted into the Rock and Roll Hall of Fame in 1992, and he won a posthumous Grammy Award in 1987. His image is prominent at Tipitina's, and it appears on two banners for the annual New Orleans Jazz and Heritage Festival.

Anthony J. Fonseca

Further Reading

Giddins, Gary. *Riding on a Blue Note: Jazz and American Pop.* New York: Da Capo Press, 2000. This discusses the incorporation of Latin rhythms in music.

Lichtenstein, Grace, and Laura Danker. *Musical Gumbo: The Music of New Orleans.* New York: W. W. Norton, 1993. This corrects biographical inconsistencies about Longhair in other sources, and it gives detailed descriptions of his music and his performances.

Welding, Pete, and Toby Byron. *Bluesland: Portraits of Twelve Major American Blues Masters.* New York: Dutton, 1991. This book discusses the artist as a player of Deep South piano and the barrelhouse blues.

See also: Domino, Fats; Lewis, Jerry Lee; Little Richard; Morton, Jelly Roll; Prado, Pérez.

Sergei Prokofiev

Russian classical composer

A leading composer of the twentieth century, Prokofiev dedicated much of his career to continuing the Russian tradition of the nineteenth century, producing music in every major genre, including opera, ballet, symphony, concerto, piano music, and film scores.

Born: April 23, 1891; Sontsovka, Ukraine, Russian Empire (now in Ukraine)
Died: March 5, 1953; Moscow, Soviet Union (now in Russia)
Also known as: Sergei Sergeyevich Prokofiev (full name)

Principal works

BALLETS (music and libretto): *Chout*, 1921 (*The Tale of the Buffoon*; based on Alexander Afanasyev's folktales); *Romeo i Dzhuletta*, 1938 (*Romeo and Juliet*; based on William Shakespeare's play); *Zolushka*, 1945 (*Cinderella*; based on the fairy tale); *Skaz o kammenom tsvetke*, 1954 (*The Tale of the Stone Flower*).

CHAMBER WORKS: *Overture on Hebrew Themes, Op. 34*, 1920 (for clarinet, string quartet, and piano); *Five Melodies*, Op. 35, 1925 (for violin and piano); Violin Concerto No. 2 in G Minor, Op. 63, 1935; String Quartet No. 2 in F Major, Op. 92, 1941; Flute Sonata in D Major, Op. 94, 1943; Violin Sonata No. 2 in D Major, Op. 94A, 1944; Violin Sonata No. 1 in F Minor, Op. 80, 1946; Cello Sonata in C Major, Op. 119, 1950.

FILM SCORES: *Lieutenant Kizhe*, 1934; *Poruchik Kizhe*, 1934 (*The Czar Wants to Sleep*); *Queen of Spades*, 1936; *Aleksandr Nevskiy*, 1938 (*Alexander Nevsky*); *The Partisans in the Ukrainian Steppes*, 1942; *Tonya*, 1942; *Kotovskiy*, 1943; *Ivan Groznyy I*, 1944 (*Ivan the Terrible, Part 1*); *Lermontov*, 1944; *Les Adventures extraordinaires de Jules Verne*, 1952; *Ivan Groznyy II: Boyarsky zagovor*, 1958 (*Ivan the Terrible*, Part 2).

OPERAS (music and libretto): *Lyubov k tryom apelsinam*, 1921 (*The Love for Three Oranges*; based on Carlo Gozzi's play *L'Amore delle tre melarance*); *Semyon Kotko*, 1940 (based on Valentin Katayev's novel *I Am the Son of Working People*); *Ognenny angel*, 1954 (*The Fiery Angel*; based on Valery Bryusov's novel); *Voyna i mir*, 1955 (*War and Peace*; based on Leo Tolstoy's novel).

ORCHESTRAL WORKS: *Scythian Suite, Op. 20*, 1916 (from Prokofiev's ballet *Ala I Lolli*); Symphony No. 1 in D Major, Op. 25, 1918 (*Classical*); *Petya i volk*, 1936 (*Peter and the Wolf*); Symphony No. 5 in B-Flat, Op. 100, 1945; Symphony No. 6 in E Minor, Op. 111, 1947.

PIANO WORKS: Piano Concerto No. 1 in D-Flat, Op. 10, 1912; Piano Concerto No. 2 in G Minor, Op. 16, 1913 (revised 1924); *Sarkazmi*, 1915 (*Sarcasms*); Toccata in D Minor, Op. 11, 1916; Piano Sonata No. 3 in A Minor, Op. 28, 1917; Piano Sonata No. 4 in C Minor, Op. 29, 1918; *Skazki staroy babushki*, 1918 (*Tales of an Old Grandmother*); *Visions Fugitives*, 1918; Piano Concerto No. 3 in C Major, Op. 26, 1921; Piano Concerto No. 5 in G Major, Op. 55, 1932; *Music for Children, Twelve Easy Pieces, Op. 65*, 1935; Piano Sonata No. 9 in C Major, Op. 103, 1948.

VOCAL WORKS: *Semero ikh*, 1924 (*Seven, They Are Seven*; text by Konstantin Balmont); *Rastsvetay, moguchiy kray*, 1947 (*Flourish, Mighty Land*; text by Yevgeni Dolmatovsky).

The Life

Sergei Sergeyevich Prokofiev (SEHR-gay sehr-GAY-yeh-vitch proh-KOHF-yehv) was born to Maria Grigorevna and Sergei Alekseevich, an agronomist and agricultural engineer, in the village of Sontsovka in central Ukraine. After studying piano and music notation with his mother, Prokofiev began formal composition study with Reinhold Gliere during the summer of 1902. Two years later, Prokofiev and his mother moved to St. Petersburg so he could enroll as a student at the conservatory. The youngest student ever admitted, he studied theory and composition with Anatoly Lyadov and Alexander Glazunov, conducting with Nikolay Tcherepnin, and orchestration with Nikolay Rimsky-Korsakov. Prokofiev, however, felt the conservatory's pedagogy stifled his creativity, and he wanted to develop a distinct voice as a composer. His modernistic innovations as a composer often left his teachers outraged.

After five years of study, Prokofiev graduated from the St. Petersburg Conservatory in 1909 with the title "free artist." With this title came the compositional freedom he had so long desired. He returned to the conservatory, however, the following fall to pursue graduate study in music. During this time, Prokofiev focused attention on his skills as a pianist, and he established professional relationships with music publishers and promoted his music through concerts. In 1914 Prokofiev finished his graduate studies, receiving the Anton Rubinstein Prize for piano by performing his Piano Concerto No. 1 in D-Flat. That same year, Prokofiev met Sergei Diaghilev, the impresario of the Ballets Russes in Paris, and Prokofiev was commissioned to write the ballet *Ala I Lolli*. The ballet was ultimately rejected, but Prokofiev recycled much of its music for *Scythian Suite*.

In 1917 Russia experienced a revolution that left the country in a state of chaos. In April of the following year, Prokofiev conducted the premiere of his Symphony No. 1 in D Major. Later that year, he decided to leave the upheaval of the revolution behind and visit the United States. Although he intended to stay abroad only a few months, he did not return to Russia for more than a decade.

His first two years in the United States proved to be important for Prokofiev. He started composing *The Love for Three Oranges* for the Chicago Opera; he

Sergei Prokofiev. (Library of Congress)

performed two concerts at Carnegie Hall; and he met a young woman named Carolina Cordina, who would eventually become his wife. In 1920 Prokofiev traveled to Paris, reconnecting with Diaghilev. The following year, he conducted the premiere of *The Tale of the Buffoon* with the Ballets Russes. The well-received performance put Prokofiev into the Paris spotlight, which he would enjoy for the next fifteen years. In December, 1921, *The Love for Three Oranges* premiered in Chicago.

After returning to the Soviet Union for the first time in 1927, Prokofiev permanently relocated to the Soviet Union in December, 1935; his family joined him the following spring. Prokofiev's renewed relationship with his homeland proved productive, particularly in the beginning. He was asked to provide music for the film *Lieutenant Kizhe* (1934), and he was commissioned to compose his first Soviet ballet, *Romeo and Juliet*. The official denunciation of Dmitri Shostakovich's opera *Lady*

Macbeth of the Mtsensk District (1932) in the name of Socialist Realism, however, changed the political climate for musicians. Suddenly, Prokofiev's compositions were performed less frequently, and some were criticized for not meeting the demands of Soviet aesthetics.

Troubles mounted for Prokofiev in 1948. Although he was married to his second wife, Prokofiev was dismayed when his first wife was arrested on spurious charges of espionage and sent to a prison camp. Prokofiev's music was attacked by Andrei Zhdanov, who was the Soviet leader in charge of cultural policy, with the composer being accused of formalism, the creative antithesis of the Soviet aesthetic of Socialist Realism. As a result, Prokofiev's music was targeted for discussion at the 1948 Congress of Composers, which was designed to make Russian composers adhere to the cultural standards set by the Soviet government. Left emotionally crippled and in failing health, Prokofiev spent the next few years of his life attempting to compose music that would appease the demands of Soviet officials; he would, however, have little success. On March 5, 1953, after spending the day working on his music, Prokofiev died—less than an hour before Joseph Stalin.

The Music

Prokofiev's musical style is easily described as eclectic, exhibiting considerable change over the course of his career. In his autobiography, the composer identified five distinct compositional trends or lines: a lyrical line, a classical line, a toccata line, a modernistic line, and a grotesque line, which Prokofiev thought was more accurately described as "scherzo-ish." His eclecticism as a composer is informed by the variety of his musical influences, which include Franz Josef Haydn, Wolfgang Amadeus Mozart, Ludwig van Beethoven, Robert Schumann, Edvard Grieg, Richard Wagner, and Aleksandr Scriabin. Most important, however, were those composers of the nineteenth century Russian classical tradition: Mikhail Glinka, Modest Mussorgsky, Alexander Borodin, Alexander Dargomyzhsky, Rimsky-Korsakov, and Peter Ilich Tchaikovsky. Although Prokofiev's early compositions indicate an interest in novelty and innovation, many of his later works demonstrate a respect for traditional forms and genres. These works are generally characterized by clear textures in which the melody predominates, rhythmic vitality, and triadic (though not always functional) harmonies. Prokofiev also possessed a gift for melodic inventiveness, a trait most clearly displayed in his film scores and stage works.

Piano Concerto No. 1 in D-Flat. As Prokofiev prepared to finish his graduate studies at the St. Petersburg Conservatory, he earned the opportunity to compete for the Anton Rubinstein Prize for Piano, an honor given to only the best students. While his four competitors elected to play classical concerti, Prokofiev performed his Piano Concerto No. 1 in D-Flat, much to the dismay of conservative teachers such as Glazunov. In the end, Prokofiev was selected as the winner of the competition, earning the votes of the younger and more progressive faculty members. This concerto is the shortest Prokofiev produced in the genre, consisting of a single movement in three sections; the main melodic material recurs throughout, imparting a pseudo-rondo structure. Composed to fit Prokofiev's strengths as a performer, this concerto requires displays of dazzling virtuosic technique. The opening octave passages reflect the influence of Tchaikovsky's Piano Concerto No. 1 in B-flat Minor (1875) and Grieg's Piano Concerto in A Minor (1869).

Symphony No. 1 in D Major. According to his autobiography, Prokofiev believed that "if Haydn had lived in our era . . . he would have retained his compositional style but would also have absorbed something from what was new." He also wanted to try to compose a symphonic work without the use of piano. The resulting work was his Symphony No. 1 in D Major. For this textbook example of early twentieth century neoclassicism, Prokofiev required a small Haydn-esque orchestra, with pairs of winds, horns, trumpets, timpani, and strings. He retained the standard four-movement structure of the eighteenth century; however, in place of the traditional minuet and trio, Prokofiev wrote a gavotte. His twentieth century touches also included oddly juxtaposed harmonies; in the final movement alone, he attempted to remove all the minor chords.

Seven, They Are Seven. Prokofiev claimed later in life that the events of the Russian Revolution deeply affected him as a composer and that he felt compelled to express these revolutionary events in music. A radical Prokofiev composition from the

1920's is the little-known *Seven, They Are Seven*, a mystical incantation (cantata) for large orchestra, chorus, and dramatic tenor soloist. The text is a free translation by the Russian Symbolist poet Constantine Balmont of an exorcism chant intended to repel seven great demons threatening to destroy the world; the cuneiform text had been discovered by a German archaeologist in an ancient Accadian temple. Drawing from Scythian music aesthetics heard in such works as Igor Stravinsky's *The Rite of Spring* (1913), *Seven, They Are Seven* is characterized by the use of ostinato figurations (frequently in multiple layers), highly dissonant polyharmonies, and passages of composed heterophony.

Peter and the Wolf. *Peter and the Wolf* is the product of the Soviet interest in children's music and Prokofiev's childlike imagination. Often used as a tool for introducing children to the instruments of the orchestra, *Peter and the Wolf* was commissioned by Natalia Satz, director of the Moscow Children's Musical Theater. In collaboration with Satz, Prokofiev developed a scenario for the work involving a combination of animal and human characters. His aim was to exploit the diversity of the orchestra's instrumental timbres as a means of communicating the various characters of the drama. The piece was composed in less than two weeks during April, 1936, and Prokofiev did not consider the work to be of any musical significance; nevertheless, *Peter and the Wolf* is by far his most well-known and frequently recorded composition, having been narrated by such individuals as Patrick Stewart, David Bowie, and U2 front man, Bono.

Composed for orchestra and narrator, *Peter and the Wolf* illustrates Prokofiev's excellent skills as an orchestrator and the influence of his interactions with his orchestration teacher, Rimsky-Korsakov. Prokofiev effectively represents the characters of *Peter and the Wolf* by association with an instrument: solo flute to represent the bird, solo oboe for the duck, solo clarinet to signify the cat, solo bassoon to characterize Peter's grandfather, and a trio of horns to represent the wolf. The music of the string section corresponds to the character of Peter. In addition to the timbral associations given to the various characters, Prokofiev associates a distinct melody and orchestral effect with each character, and they function as leitmotifs that recur throughout the work.

War and Peace. Based on Leo Tolstoy's 1864 novel, Prokofiev considered *War and Peace* (composed from 1941 to 1943 and revised 1946 to 1952) to be his finest achievement in opera, even though the work was never performed in its entirety during the composer's lifetime. Despite what the title suggests, the opera, like the novel, does not focus on Napoleon Bonaparte's invasion of Russia and the War of 1812; rather, the opera explores the impact of war on the lives of a group of Russian aristocrats. Written during the German occupation of Russia during World War II, *War and Peace* was revised several times throughout the composer's career, resulting in five different versions. Consisting of thirteen tableaux plus an overture and choral epigraph, the opera was initially produced in two parts—the "Peace" scenes and the "War" scenes. Part 1, the "Peace" portion of the opera, premiered in 1946 in the Maly Theater under the direction of Samuil Samosud. The second part, the "War" portion, was scheduled to premiere the following year; however, the production was canceled because party officials were dissatisfied with Prokofiev's musical style.

War and Peace clearly demonstrates the influence of nineteenth century Russian opera on Prokofiev's Soviet opera aesthetic. Prokofiev subtitled the work *Lyrical-Dramatic Scenes*, thus identifying two distinct sets of influences on the work. The "lyrical" element corresponds with part 1 of the opera and reveals a strong influence from the music of Tchaikovsky, particularly his opera *Eugene Onegin* (1879). These scenes are characterized by an emphasis on lyrical arioso writing and a predominance of dance music, such as the waltz, the mazurka, the polonaise, and the ecossaise. In contrast, the "dramatic" scenes are those of part 2; these scenes reveal influences from Glinka, Borodin, Mussorgsky, and Rimsky-Korsakov through Prokofiev's use of large choral episodes.

Musical Legacy

The sheer volume of music that he contributed to the standard repertoires for orchestra, ballet, opera, and various solo instruments marks Prokofiev as one of the leading composers of the twentieth century. He was dedicated to his art, believing that his music served a greater purpose. Prokofiev worked diligently to develop a compositional style that was accessible to all audiences. More than anything, however, he was dedicated to promoting Russian music and to continuing the tradition of Russian music from the nineteenth century, especially nineteenth century Russian opera.

To Prokofiev, opera was of singular importance. As a child, he developed a lifelong love for opera, and he devoted much of his professional career to writing it, even when Diaghilev and Stravinsky advised him that opera was antiquated and that he should instead turn to ballet. He refused to believe so, spending more than a decade each on *The Fiery Angel* and *War and Peace* with the hope that they would one day reach the stage. Although Prokofiev is often overshadowed in the West by other Russian composers, such as Shostakovich, through the educational and promotional efforts of the Serge Prokofiev Foundation and the Serge Prokofiev Archive in London, the composer is receiving the recognition he has so long deserved.

Terry L. Dean

Further Reading

Blok, Vladimir. *Sergei Prokofiev: Materials, Articles, Interviews*. Moscow: Progress Publishers, 1978. This work is a translation of documents by Prokofiev as well as recollections of the composer by his friends and colleagues. Contains illustrations.

Prokofiev, Sergei. *Prokofiev by Prokofiev: A Composer's Memoir*. Edited by David Appel and translated by Guy Daniels. Garden City, N.Y.: Doubleday, 1979. A detailed account of Prokofiev's life through 1909, this work provides insights to his experiences at the St. Petersburg Conservatory.

_____. *Selected Letters of Prokofiev*. Edited by Harlow Robinson. Boston: Northeastern University Press, 1998. This collection of letters to and from Prokofiev provides a candid look at the composer's personal and professional interactions.

_____. *Soviet Diary 1927 and Other Writings*. Edited and translated by Oleg Prokofiev. Boston: Northeastern University Press, 1992. A short, yet revealing diary Prokofiev kept during a tour of the Soviet Union. This translation also contains short stories by the composer as well as a brief autobiographical article.

Robinson, Harlow. *Sergei Prokofiev: A Biography*. Boston: Northeastern University Press, 2002. A well-researched biography of Prokofiev, which contains a substantial bibliography, a list of compositions, and illustrations of the composer.

See also: Argerich, Martha; Ashkenazy, Vladimir; Barenboim, Daniel; Berio, Luciano; Bono; Bowie, David; Cliburn, Van; Gould, Glenn; Heifetz, Jascha; Horowitz, Vladimir; Koussevitzky, Serge; Oistrakh, David; Perlman, Itzhak; Rostropovich, Mstislav; Scriabin, Aleksandr; Shostakovich, Dmitri; Stern, Isaac; Szigeti, Joseph; Tiomkin, Dimitri; Watts, André.

Giacomo Puccini
Italian classical composer

With the appealing melodies and sentimental characters of his operas, Puccini was considered the successor of Giuseppe Verdi.

Born: December 22, 1858; Lucca, Italy
Died: November 29, 1924; Brussels, Belgium
Also known as: Giacomo Antonio Domenico Michele Secondo Maria Puccini (full name)

Principal works

OPERAS (music): *Edgar, Ferdinando Fontana*, 1889 (based on Alfred de Musset's play *La Coupe et les lèvres*); *Manon Lescaut*, 1893 (based on Antoine François Prévost's novel); *La Bohème*, 1896 (libretto by Giuseppe Giacosa and Luigi Illica; based on Henri Mürger's novel *Scènes de la vie de bohème Turin*); *Tosca*, 1900 (libretto by Giacosa and Illica; based on Victorien Sardou's play); *Madama Butterfly*, 1904 (libretto by Giacosa and Illica; based on David Belasco's stage version of John Luther Long's story); *La fanciulla del West*, 1910 (libretto by Guelfo Civinini and Carlo Zangarini; based on Belasco's play *The Girl of the Golden West*); *La rondine*, 1917 (*The Swallow*; comedic opera; libretto by Giuseppe Adami; based on a German libretto by Alfred Maria Willner and

Heinrich Reichert); *Il trittico 1: Il tabarro*, 1918 (*The Cloak*; libretto by Adami; based on Didier Gold's play *La Houppelande*); *Il trittico 2: Suor Angelica*, 1918 (*Sister Angelica*; libretto by Giovacchino Forzano); *Il trittico 3: Gianni Schicchi*, 1918 (libretto by Forzano; based on text from Dante's *Inferno*); *Turandot*, 1926 (libretto by Adami and Renato Simoni; based on Friedrich Schiller's adaptation of Carlo Gozzi's play; completed by Franco Alfano).

The Life

Born Giacomo Antonio Domenico Michele Secondo Maria Puccini to a musical family in the Tuscan hill town of Lucca, Giacomo Puccini (JYAH-koh-moh pew-CHEE-nee) wrote a dozen operas that exemplify the late Romantic Italian operatic style. When Giuseppe Verdi died in 1901, Puccini was widely viewed as his heir and successor. Puccini was a choirboy at age ten, and by fourteen he was playing the organ at the cathedral church of San Martino in his hometown. For most of his adult life, he lived at a nearby country estate, Torre del Lago, although he traveled extensively. In 1880 he entered the Milan Conservatory, and he evoked the experience of his poverty during his student years in Milan in *La Bohème*. Puccini came to the attention of the music publisher Giulio Ricordi, who greatly assisted his career, and he achieved international success with the production of his opera *Manon Lescaut*, which premiered in Turin in 1893.

Puccini scandalized society by having an affair with and fathering the child of Elvira Gemignani, the wife of a merchant. Puccini could not marry Elvira until the death of her husband in 1904. In 1909, when the jealous Elvira accused Puccini of conducting an adulterous relationship with Doria Manfredi, a maid at the Torre del Lago estate, the woman swallowed poison and died. Elvira subsequently was brought to trial and convicted of slander. The scandal of the trial and the bad publicity sent Puccini into a creative decline for several years.

Puccini was fond of boating and racing in fast motor cars, and a serious accident in 1903 nearly killed him. He was a longtime chain-smoker (which eventually resulted in the throat cancer that killed him at age sixty-five), and he was discovered to be diabetic at the time of his car accident. Puccini decided to leave his Torre del Lago in 1921, when an

industrial plant was built nearby. He died unexpectedly in 1924 after an operation for his throat cancer by a specialist in Belgium. He and Elvira are buried in a mausoleum at Torre del Lago.

The Music

Early Operas. There are clear signs of the mature compositional style of Puccini in his early opera *Edgar, Ferdinando Fontana*. He achieved popular success with the production of *Manon Lescaut*. Not daunted by the success of two earlier operas based on the popular French novel, *Manon Lescaut* (1731), by Antoine François Prevost, Puccini selected four scenes from the novel and created a set of snapshots, from the first meeting of the flirtatious Manon with her earnest lover, the Chevalier des Grieux. Puccini's astonishing melodic gift is fully evident in the first of his operas to remain in the standard operatic repertory.

La Bohème. Like *Manon Lescaut*, Puccini's next opera, *La Bohème*, is a reduction of a novel into four vivid scenes. The source, Henri Mürger's *Scènes de la vie de bohème* (1851), began life as newspaper sketches about life among impoverished students in the Latin Quarter of Paris early in the nineteenth century. The young lovers, Mimi and Rodolfo, and their companions are so immediately appealing that few opera goers have worried about the lack of smooth transitions in the plot. *La Bohème* has delighted audiences since its premiere, conducted by Arturo Toscanini, in Turin in December, 1896. *La Bohème* is episodic, conversational, and impressionistic in its depiction in a group of likable and unpretentious students. Rodolfo's first-act aria, "Che gelida manina," epitomizes Puccini's skill in using the aria as a means of self-revelation; like all of the composer's arias and duets, it arises spontaneously and appropriately out of the dramatic situation.

Tosca. For his next opera, Puccini turned away from the episodic quality of his previous two operas in favor a tightly organized melodrama. He chose Victorien Sardou's melodrama, *La Tosca* (1887), which had been a star vehicle for the French actress Sarah Bernhardt. The result was one of Puccini's most popular operas. Of all Puccini's operas, *Tosca* is most indebted to the verismo operas of the 1890's for its shocking scenes of violence. As *La Bohème* evokes the Latin Quarter of Paris, *Tosca* vividly creates the flavor of specific locales in Rome.

Successful in its attempts to shock, *Tosca* is nonetheless limited by the contrived nature of Sardou's play: a too-melodramatic villain in Scarpia and scenes of sadistic violence. Nevertheless, the heroine, Floria Tosca, is fascinating and compelling.

The Belasco Operas. While visiting New York, Puccini was taken to see a play by the Broadway playwright David Belasco, called *Madame Butterfly* (1900), and while he scarcely understood a word of English, Puccini recognized the play's potential as an opera. Puccini based his next two operas, *Madama Butterfly* and *The Girl of the Golden West*, on plays by Belasco. While they are arguably his two musical masterpieces, the operas are somewhat limited by the sentimentality of Belasco's melodramatic plots. The fragile and vulnerable heroine of *Madama Butterfly*, Cio-Cio-San, is one of the most endearing of Puccini's characters. She waits, in poverty and social isolation, for the return of her faithless American husband, the naval officer with the unmistakably American name of Benjamin Franklin Pinkerton. When he finally returns—in the company of an American wife and hoping to reclaim the child he had fathered by Cio-Cio-San— "Butterfly," unwilling to live in shame, commits suicide.

The premiere of the opera, at La Scala in Milan in February, 1904, was a notorious failure. However, Puccini's faith in his score, which remained his personal favorite, was restored when the opera became an international triumph after its revision into a three-act format at its second production, in Brescia, in May, 1904.

Following the depression that resulted from the Manfredi scandal, Puccini after long delay settled on *The Girl of the Golden West*, which featured Enrico Caruso in its cast at its world premiere at the Metropolitan Opera in 1910. This cowboy melodrama seems remote from the traditional subjects of the Italian operatic tradition, but musically the opera is as sophisticated and inventive as anything that Puccini ever wrote. Minnie, the innocent saloon-keeper in a world of lonely goldminers during the Gold Rush, is a two-dimensional figure of virtue, while the villain, Sheriff Jack Rance, is a feebler version of Scarpia in *Tosca*. There are moments of gratuitous and sadistic violence, as when the hero, Dick Johnson (otherwise known as "Ramirrez" the bandit) is threatened with hanging. Although it is

the least performed of the operas from Puccini's middle period, *The Girl of the Golden West* is, despite its flaws, in many ways the most impressive.

La Rondine. Although *La Rondine* (premiered in 1917), Puccini's attempt to re-create the spirit of Viennese operetta, has occasionally been cited as proof of the exhaustion of the composer's imagination, in performance it exudes much charm.

Il Trittico. Eager to try something new, Puccini decided to assemble three one-act operas, with widely differing moods, into a single evening's entertainment, as *Il trittico*. First performed at the Metropolitan Opera in 1918, each opera shows distinctive strengths. The first in the series, *The Cloak*, is a grim study of jealousy and adultery among barge workers in Paris. The second, *Sister Angelica*, dramatizes the plight of an innocent woman who had been sent to live in a cloistered convent for having given birth out of wedlock. While *The Cloak* ends with a violent murder, *Sister Angelica* ends with a heavenly vision, as the nun's dead child seems to descend from heaven with a message of redemp-

Giacomo Puccini. (Library of Congress)

tion for his mother, who in her despair has poisoned herself. The third opera, *Gianni Schicchi*, is the composer's only attempt at a comic opera, and it is an amusing look at human greed and duplicity. Puccini's skill at sustaining comedy in music has made some critics wish that the composer had pursued comedy more frequently.

Turandot. For his final opera, *Turandot*, Puccini returned to the vein of orientalism that he had mined so successfully in *Madama Butterfly*. The story of the cold Chinese princess who forces her suitors to answer three riddles to win her hand—and to lose their heads if they answer incorrectly—has disturbed critics such as Joseph Kerman who find the plot psychologically offensive. Nevertheless, the score and its orchestration are remarkable for melodic inventiveness, stylistic variety, and sheer energy. Puccini made effective use of the chorus, which comments on the action and forces the dramatic crisis.

Ill with his terminal disease, Puccini left the score unfinished halfway through the third act. Upon the death of the composer in 1924, another composer, Franco Alfano, was commissioned to write a conclusion based on Puccini's sketches. This ending shows a clear falling-off in quality, but it is theatrically effective. *Turandot* premiered, with Alfano's ending, at La Scala in Milan in 1926.

Musical Legacy

Although he had a narrower range and produced a much smaller body of work, Puccini retains his status among the most frequently performed opera composers, in the company of Wolfgang Amadeus Mozart, Verdi, and Richard Wagner, More of his operas hold their place in the regular operatic repertory than those of such eminent Italian operatic forebears as Giacchino Rossini, Vincenzo Bellini, and Gaetano Donizetti. Puccini seldom wrote for any other forum than the operatic stage. His reputation among opera audiences seems secure, although critical opinion about his music remains divided.

Puccini's musical style is melodic and highly accessible. His characters are identified not so much by Wagnerian leitmotifs as by "reminiscences" or brief melodic tags. His arias are grounded firmly in the drama, although they are highly popular when sung separately. Often the melodies of the arias are

first stated by the orchestra, which then doubles the singer's vocal line to emphasize the emotional urgency of the situation. Puccini's recitatives are conversational and help to push the dramatic action along. His heroines tend to be innocent (such as Mimi and Cio-Cio-San) or to be conflicted (such as Tosca and Turandot); his tenors tend to be sympathetic but not particularly insightful. The villains, who are invariably baritones, are often overly melodramatic (such as Scarpia and Jack Rance). The chorus often acts like a Greek chorus in commenting on the action, and it can add a distinctive stylistic touch, as in the famous "humming" chorus in *Madama Butterfly*.

Puccini's musical style shows the influence of the Italian operatic tradition, Wagner, the French musical Impressionist composers such as Debussy and Massenet, and (in his later operas) the musical moderns, such as Igor Stravinsky and Arnold Schoenberg (in his harsh dissonances). Puccini used the orchestra in a sophisticated manner; the orchestra sometimes pushes forward the dramatic action and often comments on it. He made distinctive use of orchestral color, especially in the "exotic" operas (*Madama Butterfly*, *The Girl of the Golden West*, and *Turandot*), and he liked to add realistic touches, such as the musical depiction of snowflakes in *La Bohème* and the bird calls in *Madama Butterfly*. Unlike Verdi, who was inspired by political ideals, or Wagner, who posed philosophical questions, Puccini seems to avoided challenge, by turning to sensuality, excessive violence, and sentimentality. However, audiences continue to savor his operatic characters, who find themselves in emotionally painful situations. The great Italian operatic tradition, which began in the late sixteenth century and reached its greatest peak in the operas of Verdi, effectively came to an end with the death of Puccini.

Byron Nelson

Further Reading

Ashbrook, William, and Harold Powers. *Puccini's "Turandot": The End of the Great Tradition*. Princeton, N.J.: Princeton University Press, 1991. This resource describes Puccini's unfinished final opera as the "last flowering" of the Italian operatic tradition that had begun with Francesco Cavalli and Claudio Monteverdi at the turn of the seventeenth century. The authors suggest that a psychological block, rather than his terminal illness, prevented Puccini from completing the opera.

Carner, Mosco. *Puccini: A Critical Biography*. 2d ed. London: Duckworth, 1974. A valuable book-length study of the life and works of Puccini, heavily detailed and passionately argued, although now dated by its Freudian perspective.

_____, ed. *Letters of Puccini*. Rev. ed. London: Harrop, 1974. This resource provides a useful assortment of the composer's letters, with minimal context or commentary.

Hughes, Patrick. *Famous Puccini Operas: A Complete Guide to Puccini's Operas*. New York: Citadel Press, 1959. The book provides helpful analyses of the operas (although it inexplicably omits *La Rondine* from discussion).

Phillips-Matz, Mary Jane. *Puccini: A Biography*. Boston: Northeastern University Press, 2002. Thoroughly researched, this biography unearths new details from the often-chaotic private life of the composer.

See also: Björling, Jussi; Busoni, Ferruccio; Callas, Maria; Caruso, Enrico; Debussy, Claude; Domingo, Plácido; Flagstad, Kirsten; Janáček, Leoš; Lehmann, Lotte; Levine, James; Melba, Dame Nellie ; Merrill, Robert; Pavarotti, Luciano; Piazzolla, Astor; Price, Leontyne; Rota, Nino; Schoenberg, Arnold; Stravinsky, Igor; Tebaldi, Renata; Toscanini, Arturo; Whiteman, Paul.

Tito Puente

American Latin jazz and mambo percussionist and composer

An influential proponent of Latin American music in the United States, Puente popularized Cuban-based dance music, in Latin styles ranging from bossa nova to salsa.

Born: April 20, 1923; New York, New York
Died: May 31, 2000; New York, New York
Also known as: Ernest Antonio Puente, Jr. (full name); El Rey

Member of: Tito Puente Orchestra; Latin Percussion Jazz Ensemble; Golden Latin Jazz All Stars

Principal recordings

ALBUMS: *Mambos with Puente*, 1949; *Mambo on Broadway*, 1951; *Puente Goes Jazz*, 1956; *Dance Mania*, 1958; *Dance Mania II*, 1963; *Bossa Nova by Puente*, 1965; *My Fair Lady Goes Latin*, 1968; *Tito Puente and His Concert Orchestra*, 1973; *Homenaje a Beny Moré*, 1978; *On Broadway*, 1983; *Mambo Diablo*, 1985; *Salsa Meets Jazz*, 1988; *Goza mi timbal*, 1989; *The Mambo King*, 1991; *Navidad en las Americas*, 1994; *Jazzin'*, 1997.

The Life

Ernest Antonio "Tito" Puente, Jr. (TEE-toh PWEHN-tay) was born in New York City and grew up in Spanish Harlem. Puente's parents, Ernesto and Ercilla, who emigrated from Puerto Rico after the Spanish-American War in 1898, encouraged Puente and his sister Anna to become music and dance performers. He studied piano at the New York School of Music and studied drums, learning snare-drum technique, chart figures, and how to accompany shows. He and his sister danced together, and in 1935 they became members of the Stars of the Future, a group of talented children who met at the Puentes' parish church, La Milagros. Each year the most talented children, based on their artistic ability and popularity, were crowned king and queen; Puente was king four times.

At the age of sixteen, Puente dropped out of school to become a full-time musician. He spent three months in Miami as a drummer for the Cuban pianist José Curbelo. In June, 1942, Puente joined the Machito Orchestra, which was led by the Cuban bandleader Machito (Frank Grillo). Puente briefly left the orchestra to join the Jack Cole dancers, but he later returned to the Machito Orchestra. Soon after his return, Puente was drafted into the U.S. Navy, and he was assigned to the *USS Santee*, a converted aircraft carrier that escorted supply and passenger ships during World War II. His duties at sea included loading ammunition into the artillery and playing the alto saxophone and the drums in the ship's band. During his tour Puente learned to arrange music from a pilot who played the tenor saxophone and arranged music for Charlie

Tito Puente. (AP/Wide World Photos)

Spivak's big band. Puente was involved in nine battles, in the Atlantic and Pacific Oceans, before he was discharged in 1945 with a presidential commendation.

Immediately after the war, Puente studied conducting, orchestration, and theory at the Juilliard School of Music with the help of the G.I. Bill, a benefit awarded to military personnel after World War II to go to college or take vocational training. At that time, he worked with Frank Marti's Copacabana band, the José Curbelo Orchestra, and a Brazilian band led by Fernando Alvarez. In September, 1947, Puente became the drummer, the contractor who hired the orchestra's members, and the musical director for Pupi Campo's orchestra. In March, 1949, Puente formed his own musical group, the Picadillo Boys, later called the Tito Puente Orchestra.

In the 1950's and 1960's, the Tito Puente Orchestra produced albums for Tico Records, RCA Records, SMC Records, and Verne Records. In 1967 Puente presented his music in a live performance at New York City's Metropolitan Opera and hosted his own television program, *El Mundo de Tito Puente*, on the Spanish-language network. During the 1960's Puente recorded with the two most important Latin female vocalists, Celia Cruz and La Lupe. In the 1980's he established his Latin Percus-

sion Jazz Ensemble, and in the 1990's he formed the Golden Latin Jazz All Stars.

Over the years Puente received numerous awards. In 1957 the Cuban government formally recognized Puente in a ceremony honoring great Cuban musicians of the past fifty years, and Puente was the only non-Cuban recognized. In 1968 he was grand marshal of New York's Puerto Rican Day Parade, and in 1969 Mayor John Lindsay awarded Puente the key to New York City. Puente won his first Grammy Award in 1978 for the album *Homenaje a Beny Moré*, and he went on to win five more Grammy Awards, in 1983, 1985, 1990, 1999, and 2000. In 1987 he was voted the top percussionist in the *Down Beat* readers' poll. That same year, the National Academy of Recording Arts and Sciences honored Puente with a Eubie Award, and on August 4, 1990, Puente was given a star on the Hollywood Walk of Fame. In May, 2000, Puente died during heart surgery.

The Music

Puente's music emphasized the rhythms of Latin dance, encompassing all Latin styles from the mambo to cha-cha, salsa, and Latin jazz. His early music was influenced by the big band styles of Benny Goodman, Artie Shaw, and Duke Ellington, as well as Latin bands such as the Machito Orchestra and the music of Arsenio Rodríguez and Beny Moré. During the Palladium era (when Latin dance music was popularized at the Palladium nightclub in New York City), Puente became an independent bandleader and began his integration of jazz and Latin music. With albums spanning almost fifty years, from 1950 to 1999, Puente demonstrated his skill at adapting to cultural and musical change.

Early Works. Puente's early recordings reflect the Cuban style of the Machito Orchestra, Mario Bauzá, and the earlier Cuban tradition of Arsenio Rodríguez and Beny Moré. Songs that typify this early sound include "Picadillo" and "Abanquito."

With these works, Puente introduced a new sound, using the entire orchestra as a percussive device. His music is rhythmic, often using syncopation, tumbao patterns, and mambo riffs. Puente performed typical mambos of the day, but he also experimented with the infusion of jazz elements. For example, Puente was the first Latin music bandleader to use the vibraphone, an instrument that had been incorporated into jazz writing by Lionel Hampton and Milt Jackson.

"El cayuco." "El cayuco" is the first track for the album *Dance Mania*, which was recorded in November and December of 1957 and released in 1958. Considered a watershed album for Puente, *Dance Mania* is characterized by the use of innovative sounds, a wide range of arrangements and musicians, and the integration of musical styles. The album differs from Puente's previous works; it is his first record with vocalist Santitos Colón. Colón was not Cuban and did not follow the traditional Cuban style of singing in terms of tonal inflection and improvisation. In "El cayuco," Puente emphasizes vocals and instrumental ensembles, as the piece lacks instrumental solos. The song opens with syncopated riffs and breaks in the saxophone and brass sections followed by a *coro* (chorus) and a short *soneos* (improvisation) by Colón. In this composition, Puente combines a *son montuno* (Afro-Cuban) rhythmic bass with the style of cha-cha.

"Mambo gozón." Part of *Dance Mania*, "Mambo gozón" is a standard in the Latin dance repertory. This highly energetic piece opens with orchestral breaks and solo-piano *guajeo* (repeated chords). Puente continues the introduction with the entrance of the saxophone section in a *guajeo* and the entrance of the trumpets and trombones eight bars later. Immediately after the introduction, we hear the *coro* "a gozar este rico mambo, a gozar" ("to enjoy this rich mambo, to enjoy") and Colón's *inspiraciones* (phrases). The *coro* is followed by a bridge and then repeated as a shortened version of the original. "Mambo gozón" is typical of the 1950's mambo of Latin dance bands, but Puente tests the boundaries of the genre with unique harmonic practices, instrumentation, and percussive style.

"El rey del timbale." The major hit associated with the album *Tito Puente and His Concert Orchestra* is "El rey del timbale," in which Puente shows off his virtuosic skill on the timbales. The work begins with a percussion introduction, and then the full orchestra enters with the main theme, followed by the *coro* and main verse. Puente's timbale solo, which occurs in the second part of the arrangement, became a marker for mastery of the instrument. Additional tracks include Puente's performance on the kintos (small timbales), vibraphone, marimba, melodica, timpani, and other percussion instruments.

On Broadway. In the 1980's the majority of Puente's albums belonged to the Latin jazz idiom, in which Puente adapted jazz, popular standards, and traditional tunes to Latin rhythms and forms. *On Broadway* was the first recording released by Puente's Latin Ensemble, and the title track is an arrangement of the rhythm-and-blues hit originally recorded by the Drifters and rerecorded by George Benson. Puente made "On Broadway" with a blend of jazz, rhythm-and-blues, and Latin sounds. The melodic and harmonic schemes are constructed over a cha-cha rhythm, while the main theme is sung by the electric guitar. After the guitar solo, the music shifts to a *guajira* (Cuban song), which features a Puerto Rican acoustic *cuatro* (guitarlike instrument). The latter part of the work features flute accompaniment and a return to the cha-cha rhythm of the main theme.

The Mambo King. Puente's hundredth album, titled *The Mambo King* after his recent work on the motion picture *The Mambo Kings* (1992), features composition and arrangements that Puente popularized throughout his career in an updated, contemporary style. Puente is featured on timbales, vibraphone, and synthesizer. Vocalists who had worked with Puente throughout his career also appear on the record. These include Ismael Miranda, Oscar d'León, Colón, and Cruz, who sings and improvises with Puente on "Celia and Tito."

Musical Legacy

Puente popularized the traditional Latin music of his day, and he shaped the new direction of Latin music with his percussive sound and his infusion of jazz. Puente embraced Latin jazz in the 1980's, and he is known for his performance on the timbales and vibraphone in this genre. During his sixty-year career, he worked with nearly every major Latin and jazz artist, including Cruz, La Lupe, jazz trumpeter and bandleader Doc Severinsen, and clarinetist and bandleader Woody Herman. Puente's music was popularized by artists such as Carlos Santana, who recorded a cover of "Oye como va." In addition to his regular concert appearances and recordings, Puente's music was heard on numerous film sound tracks, including *The Mambo Kings*, for which he acted as the musical coordinator, recorded sound tracks, and portrayed a major bandleader in the Palladium era. Although Puente died in 2000, his legacy lives on through his albums, through his motion-picture recordings, and through the Tito Puente Scholarship Fund, established in 1980 to aid young musicians.

Sandra J. Fallon

Further Reading

Loza, Steven. *Tito Puente and the Making of Latin Music*. Chicago: University of Illinois Press, 1999. A major biographical study features interviews with Puente as well as with his fellow musicians and music journalist Max Salazar. Includes a thorough discussion of Puente's music, with musical examples, and his cultural impact on the Latin world. With discography and illustrations.

Olmstead, Mary. *Tito Puente*. Chicago: Raintree, 2005. A short biography of Puente geared toward young readers.

Powell, Josephine. *Tito Puente: When the Drums Are Dreaming*. Bloomington, Ind.: AuthorHouse, 2007. A friend and colleague of Puente provides a comprehensive biographical study.

Salazar, Max. *Mambo Kingdom: Latin Music in New York*. New York: Schirmer Books, 2002. A renowned Latin music journalist and historian discusses the development of Latin music in New York City, with details on the Palladium, the origins of salsa, and such artists as Puente, Curbelo, Colón, Cruz, La Lupe, Rodriguez, and Charlie Palmieri.

Schnabel, Tom. *Rhythm Planet: The Great World Music Makers*. New York: Universe, 1998. National Public Radio's Schnabel provides a career overview of Puente and discusses his radio interviews with the artist. Includes discography and illustrations.

Varela, Jesse. "Tito Puente: El Rey Del Timbale!" *Jazz Times* 30, no. 4 (2000): 56-64. A profile of the Latin music star who helped set the standard for modern-day salsa and Latin jazz.

See also: Cruz, Celia; Ellington, Duke; Goodman, Benny; Hampton, Lionel; Palmieri, Eddie; Prado, Pérez; Santana, Carlos; Shaw, Artie.

R

Sergei Rachmaninoff

Russian American classical composer, pianist, and conductor

Rachmaninoff was a composer, conductor, and pianist known primarily for his contribution to piano literature and his impeccable pianistic technique. He began composing in a late nineteenth century Romantic idiom, but his later works are characterized by leaner textures and occasional jazz influences. His piano concerti are revered for their haunting lyricism and their staggering technical difficulty.

Born: April 1, 1873; Semyonovo, Novgorod District, Russia
Died: March 28, 1943; Beverly Hills, California
Also known as: Sergei Vasilyevich Rachmaninoff (full name)

Principal works

CHAMBER WORKS: *Trio Elégiaque in G Minor*, Op. 9, No. 1, 1892 (for piano trio); *Trio Elégiaque in D Minor*, Op. 9, No. 2, 1893 (for piano trio).

CHORAL WORKS: *Two Pieces*, Op. 6, 1893 (for violin and piano); *Liturgiya svyatovo Ioanna Zlatousta*, Op. 31, 1910 (*Liturgy of Saint John Chrysostom*; for unaccompanied choir); *Vsenoshchnoye bdeniye*, Op. 37, 1915 (*The All-Night Vigil*; for unaccompanied choir); *Three Russian Songs*, Op. 41, 1927 (for chorus and orchestra).

OPERAS (music): *Francesca da Rimini*, Op. 25, 1906 (based on Dante's *Inferno*); *Skupoy ritsar'*, Op. 24, 1906 (*The Miserly Knight*; based on Alexander Pushkin's drama).

ORCHESTRAL WORKS: *Knyaz' Rostislav*, 1891 (*Prince Rostislav*; symphonic poem based on Aleksey Konstantinovich Tolstoy's poem for orchestra); Piano Concerto in F-sharp Minor, Op. 1, No. 1, 1891; *Utyos*, Op. 7, 1893 (*The Rock*; symphonic poem based on Anton Chekhov's short story "Na puti"); *Kaprichchio na tsiganskiye temi*, Op. 12, 1894 (*Caprice bohémien*; *Capriccio on Gypsy Themes*); Symphony No. 1 in D Minor, Op. 13, 1896; Cello Sonata in G Minor, Op. 19, 1901; Piano Concerto No. 2, Op. 18, 1901; Symphony No. 2 in E Minor, Op. 27, 1908; *Ostrov myortvikh*, Op. 29, 1909 (*The Isle of the Dead*); Piano Concerto No. 3 in D Minor, Op. 30, 1909; Piano Concerto No. 4 in G Minor, Op. 40, 1926; *Rhapsody on a Theme of Paganini in A Minor*, Op. 43, 1934 (for piano and orchestra); Symphony No. 3 in A Minor, Op. 44, 1936; *Three Symphonic Dances*, Op. 45, 1940.

PIANO WORKS: *Russian Rhapsody in E*, 1891 (for two pianos); *Morceaux de fantaisie*, Op. 3, 1892 (for solo piano); *Morceaux de salon*, Op. 10, 1894 (for solo piano); Suite No. 2, Op. 17, 1901 (for two pianos); Ten Preludes, Op. 23, 1903 (for solo piano); *Variations on a Theme of Chopin in C Minor*, Op. 22, 1903 (for solo piano); Piano Sonata No. 1 in D Minor, Op. 28, 1908; Thirteen Preludes, Op. 32, 1910 (for solo piano); *Études-Tableaux*, Op. 33, 1911 (for solo piano); Piano Sonata No. 2 in B-flat Minor, Op. 36, 1913; *Variations on a Theme of Corelli in D Minor*, Op. 42, 1931 (for solo piano).

VOCAL WORK: *Danse hongroise*, Op. 8, 1893 (six songs for voice and piano).

The Life

On April 1, 1873, Sergei Vasilyevich Rachmaninoff (SEHR-gay rahk-MAH-nih-nahf) was born to Vasily and Lubov Petrovna Rachmaninoff. One of six children, Rachmaninoff exhibited musical talent at an early age, and he was sent to the St. Petersburg Conservatory. (He later graduated from the Moscow Conservatory in 1892.) Despite what seemed to be an advantageous beginning, the premiere of his Symphony No. 1 in D Minor, Op. 13 was a complete failure, and Rachmaninoff plummeted into depression. Through the efforts of Nikolai Dahl, a hypnotist, Rachmaninoff rallied and emerged from his despondency to write his Piano Concerto No. 2, dedicating the work to Dahl, who had restored Rachmaninoff's ever-faltering confidence.

Rachmaninoff married his first cousin, Natalia

Skalon, in April of 1902. Living in Moscow and then Dresden, the family, which came to include two daughters, Tatiana and Irina, spent their summer holidays at Ivanovka, Natalia's Russian country estate. At Ivanovka, Rachmaninoff completed or started most of his Russian-period compositions, including *Variations on a Theme of Chopin in C Minor*, Ten Preludes, Symphony No. 2 in E Minor, Piano Concerto No. 3 in D Minor, Thirteen Preludes, *Liturgy of Saint John Chrysostom*, and the *Études-Tableaux*. Meanwhile, the Russian Revolution, which began in February, 1917, with the abdication of Czar Nicholas II, marked the end of the Romanov dynasty, and by October the Bolsheviks had risen to power. The revolution arrived when Rachmaninoff was at the zenith of his three musical careers, as composer, pianist, and conductor.

On December 23, 1917, the Rachmaninoff family left Russia permanently, under the auspices of a Swedish concert tour. To help his increasingly dire financial situation, Rachmaninoff decided to relocate to the United States and to make performing, rather than composition or conducting, his main focus. At the age of forty-five, he began learning a massive new keyboard repertory. Within a month of his arrival in the United States, Rachmaninoff signed contracts with Thomas Edison's gramophone company, the Ampico reproducing piano company, and the Steinway and Sons piano manufacturer. He also embarked on his first extensive North American concert tour, and while he came to loathe the strenuous schedule of concertizing, he also recognized performing as a necessary evil. His new role as a touring artist left little time for composition. He died extremely successful at the age of sixty-nine, at his home in Beverly Hills, California.

The Music

By the early twentieth century, Rachmaninoff's music was among the last bastions of Romanticism for many contemporary audiences. His writing for piano, reminiscent of Peter Ilich Tchaikovsky, Franz Liszt, and Frédéric Chopin, prioritized beautiful melodies embedded in a complex framework, generally supported by a strong left-hand bass. As a child, he had visited many country churches with his grandmother, and these experiences influenced his later writing not only through his use of church modes and interest in church music but also, as musicologist Glen Carruthers notes, for the "bell-like" gestures in his piano writing.

Piano Concerto No. 2. This opens with a bell-like alternation between forceful octaves and chords, cementing what was to become a standard trait in Rachmaninoff's music. Opening with the piano and flute in a sonorous exchange, the concerto's second movement is one of the composer's most beloved. Rachmaninoff's concerti are known for their pianistic lyricism and for their technical demands.

Preludes. Rachmaninoff's preludes bear many of the stylistic hallmarks seen consistently throughout his entire compositional output. His use of bell-like sonorities is evident, and so is his use of embedded melodies, a technique frequently associated with another virtuoso composer, Liszt. His Op. 32 preludes are more tonally adventurous and reflect his greater interest in harmonic experimentation in this period. As musicologist Christoph Flamm notes, Rachmaninoff's works composed from 1910 to 1917 are more daring in their dissonance and har-

Sergei Rachmaninoff. (Library of Congress)

monies, although they still remain well within a tonal framework and within Rachmaninoff's compositional idiom.

The All-Night Vigil. Although Rachmaninoff's choral compositions have often been overlooked, *The All-Night Vigil* is considered by some to be among the finest examples of Russian Orthodox Church music ever composed and also among the finest liturgical pieces of the twentieth century. He wrote the work in an attempt to outdo his setting of the *Liturgy of Saint John Chrysostom*. *The All-Night Vigil*'s fifteen numbers are for unaccompanied soprano, alto, tenor, and bass (SATB) choir, and the text is Old Church Slavonic.

Musically speaking, Rachmaninoff based No. 2 and No. 15 on Greek chants ("Praise the Lord, O My Soul" and "To the Mother of God"), while No. 4 and No. 5 ("Gladsome Radiance" and "Nunc Dimittis") were based on Kiev chants, and *znamenny* (Russian Orthodox) chant formed the basis for No. 9 ("Blessed Be the Lord"), No. 8 ("Praise the Name of the Lord"), No. 12 ("The Great Doxology"), No. 13 ("The Day of Salvation"), and No. 14 ("Christ Is Risen from the Tomb"). The other numbers employ Rachmaninoff's own settings of motives characteristic of Russian church music. His ingenuity in manipulating the chant material to suit his musical purposes reveals, once again, his masterful talent for melody.

Variations on a Theme of Corelli. The *Variations on a Theme of Corelli in D Minor* for solo piano are based on the la folia theme, which was first mentioned in Portuguese texts of the fifteenth century. Rachmaninoff incorrectly attributed its origin to Arcangelo Corelli, who had used la folia in his Sonata for Violin and Harpsichord, Op. 5, No. 12.

There are twenty variations and a coda, written primarily in D minor, the only exception being variations XIV and XV, which are in D-flat major. As musicologist Barrie Martyn notes, most variations emphasize thematic transformation and harmonic exploration, as well as pointed rhythmic attack. Overall, the work is wholly unlike anything else in Rachmaninoff's piano idiom. The piece was his final work for solo piano.

Rhapsody on a Theme of Paganini. For what many consider his fifth piano concerto, Rachmaninoff used Niccolò Paganini's twenty-fourth caprice from *Twenty-four Caprices in A Minor* (1805) for solo

violin as his thematic material, composing twenty-four variations around this melody. Having served as a judge at the 1924 Paul Whiteman concert that launched George Gershwin's massively successful *Rhapsody in Blue*, Rachmaninoff noticed the public's penchant for rhapsodies. Hence, he titled the work *Rhapsody on a Theme of Paganini*. Rachmaninoff opened the work with a brief introduction, followed immediately by the first variation, preceding the theme itself, which enters in the strings at measure thirty-four. Originally, Rachmaninoff did not plan to withhold the theme, as is evidenced by the pen-knife scratches that do not completely conceal the former variation numbers on the manuscript. A possible reason for this musical decision lies in the twenty-fourth variation. Here, too, as in the first variation, the orchestra merely outlines the theme. At both the end and the beginning of the work, Rachmaninoff made a conscious choice to reduce thematic complexity, a characteristic of much of his later, post-Russian-period writing.

The famous eighteenth variation is an inversion of the original thematic material. Of the countless composers who used this Paganini theme before him, Rachmaninoff was apparently the only one to incorporate melodic inversion in his work. The Latin chant *Dies irae* also features prominently in variations seven, ten, fourteen, and twenty-two. As musicologist Glen Carruthers notes, Rachmaninoff incorporated *Dies irae* in many works throughout his career, such as his Symphony No. 1 in D Minor, Symphony No. 2 in E Minor, Piano Sonata No. 1 in D Minor, *The Isle of the Dead*, *Rhapsody on a Theme of Paganini in A Minor*, Symphony No. 3 in A Minor, and *Three Symphonic Dances*.

In his *Rhapsody on a Theme of Paganini*, Rachmaninoff uses elements of jazz and programmatic elements in conjunction with thematic inversion and linear piano writing. Possibly his most popular and critically acclaimed work, *Rhapsody on a Theme of Paganini* is a staple in the concert repertoire.

Musical Legacy

Rachmaninoff's music, in many ways, marked the end of Romanticism, surviving as it did well into the twentieth century. While many contemporary critics dismissed his music as merely a nineteenth century leftover, his music had a loyal following in his lifetime, and today Rachmaninoff's music enjoys immense success. Undoubtedly, the musical element for which he is most remembered is melody. In his songs for solo voice and piano, his symphonies, and his piano works, lyricism is the hallmark of his stylistic idiom.

His music was scored in countless films, and the reverence accorded to his piano concerti grew to almost mythic proportions, as best seen in the film *Shine* (1997). Additionally, Rachmaninoff was regarded as one of the finest pianists of the twentieth century, and although he always preferred to be thought of as a composer first and pianist second, his legendary hand size and flawless technique placed him squarely alongside Vladimir Horowitz and Joseph Hoffmann as a premier pianist of his era. Nevertheless, when Rachmaninoff died in 1943, the "usual occupation" section on his death certificate listed only one word: composer.

Abby Anderton

Further Reading

Bertensson, Sergei, and Jay Leyda. *Sergei Rachmaninoff: A Lifetime in Music.* Bloomington: Indiana University Press, 2001. A complete account of Rachmaninoff's life, written with the aid of Sophia Satina, Rachmaninoff's sister-in-law.

Cannata, David. *Rachmaninoff and the Symphony.* Innsbruck: Studien Verlag, 1994. A fascinating look at Rachmaninoff's compositional process throughout his career, especially in regard to his late works: Symphony No. 3 and *Rhapsody on a Theme of Paganini.*

Carruthers, Glen. "The (Re)appraisal of Rachmaninov's Music: Contradictions and Fallacies." *The Musical Times* 147, no. 1896 (Autumn, 2006): 44-50. This article argues that the popularity of Rachmaninoff's music has become a liability in understanding its strengths and weaknesses.

Harrison, Max. *Rachmaninoff: Life, Works, Recordings.* New York: Continuum, 2005. A biographical and musical overview of Rachmaninoff's career, with musical excerpts located at the end of the book.

Martyn, Barrie. *Rachmaninoff: Composer, Pianist, Conductor.* Aldershot, England: Scolar Press, 1990. Thoroughly outlines all three of Rachmaninoff's careers and does an excellent job contextualizing his music within the framework of his life circumstances. Impeccable attention to detail in

this in-depth look at Rachmaninoff's total musical output.

Norris, Geoffrey. *Rachmaninoff.* New York: Oxford University Press, 2001. Rachmaninoff's life and his music are examined in this clear and concise volume for musicians and nonmusicians alike. Norris does not use the chronological approach in this work, but he groups Rachmaninoff's compositions into categories by genre.

See also: Argerich, Martha; Ashkenazy, Vladimir; Burton, Gary; Cliburn, Van; Gershwin, George; Heifetz, Jascha; Horowitz, Vladimir; Koussevitzky, Serge; Scriabin, Aleksandr; Watts, André.

Ma Rainey
American blues

Rainey was one of the last celebrated minstrel performers and a major influence on the development of the classic blues style.

Born: April 26, 1886; Columbus, Georgia
Died: December 22, 1939; Columbus, Georgia
Also known as: Gertrude Malissa Nix Pridgett (birth name); Gertrude Rainey; Mother of the Blues

Principal recordings

ALBUMS: *Night Time Blues*, 1924 (with Memphis Minnie).

SINGLES: "Bo Weavil Blues," 1923; "C. C. Rider," 1923; "Moonshine Blues," 1923; "Yonder Comes the Blues," 1923 (with Louis Armstrong); "Jelly Bean Blues," 1924; "Ma Rainey's Black Bottom," 1927; "Prove It on Me Blues," 1928.

The Life

Ma Rainey (RAY-nee) was born Gertrude Pridgett to Thomas Pridgett and Ella Allen, both from Alabama. The second of five children, Rainey was perhaps the most ambitious to take after a grandmother who had been on the stage after emancipation of African Americans after the Civil

War. In 1900 Rainey made her stage debut in a local show called the Bunch of Blackberries. Shortly after, she joined the minstrel circuit, and she traveled throughout the South. In 1902, while performing in Missouri, a local girl approached the tents and performed a poignant blues song about the man who had left her. Greatly struck by the song, Pridgett learned the song from the girl and included the blues in her act from that time on.

On February 2, 1904, she married fellow performer William Pa Rainey, and they formed a comedy team, traveling with the Rabbit Foot Minstrels. They were billed as Rainey and Rainey, Assassinators of the Blues. Famous for her stage persona, Rainey was well known for donning a necklace and earrings of gold pieces and other extravagant jewelry. A brilliant performer, Rainey was noted for her ability to captivate an audience. Although she and Pa Rainey split after a few years of marriage, Ma never lacked for lovers, male or female, as was the fashion at the time.

After the success of vaudeville singer Mamie Smith as a recording artist, Paramount recorded Rainey singing eight songs in Chicago in December, 1923. Unfortunately, Paramount at the time did not have the best technology, and the majority of Rainey's recordings were done acoustically with her singing directly into the horn. Throughout her recording career, she worked with such artists as Louis Armstrong, Jelly Roll Morton, and Fletcher Henderson. After the success of her early recordings, Rainey toured under the Theater Owners' Booking Agency with her Wildcats Jazz Band, which included the legendary Thomas Dorsey. Rainey continued to record until 1928, when listeners' taste started to favor swing. After she had recorded ninety-two songs, Rainey's down-home style was no longer in fashion.

In 1930, because of the Great Depression, her touring on the vaudeville circuit stopped, and Rainey toured with a carnival until the death of her sister, followed shortly by the death of her mother, in 1935. She returned to Columbus, Georgia, and lived with her brother, Thomas Pridgett, Jr., man-

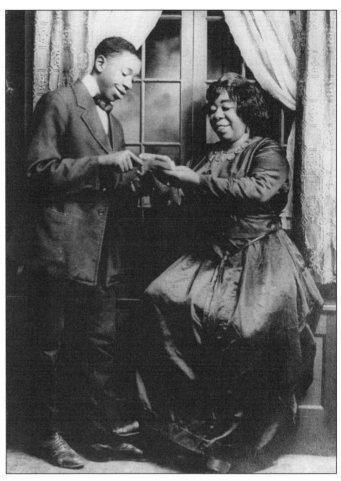

Ma Rainey. (AP/Wide World Photos)

aging two theaters she owned, the Airdrome and the Lyric, until her death from heart disease at the age of fifty-three.

The Music

Rainey did not sing the blues, she moaned them. With a style seeped in the Southern minstrel tradition, Rainey in her performances echoed the male singers of the rural blues. Her music enumerates the hardships, the joys, and the sorrows experienced by blacks who lived in the Southern states. Many of her songs are autobiographical, such as "Prove It on Me Blues." Rainey's voice displays a rough, rural sound, in contrast to the manicured vocals of New York-based singers. She was typically backed by jazz ensembles until late in her career, when she was viewed as too rural and downgraded to jug-band accompaniment.

"Bo Weavil Blues." One of her earliest recorded works, in December, 1923, "Bo Weavil Blues" was among her most popular. Representative of Rainey's down-home topics and style, this song was connected her to her fans.

"C. C. Rider." Rainey was the first performer to record this traditional blues. A twelve-bar blues, "C. C. Rider" features Henderson on piano, Armstrong on cornet, Charlie Dixon on banjo, Charlie Green on tuba, and Buster Bailey on clarinet. Rainey's voice evokes the blues sung in the rural South.

"Moonshine Blues." Perhaps one of Rainey's biggest hits, "Moonshine Blues" was later covered by Bessie Smith. One rendition contains spoken word as well as her striking vocals. The song is heavily swung, uses stop time, and the listener can easily sympathize with the heartbroken and drunk-sounding Rainey.

"Prove It on Me Blues." This song, about her arrest in Chicago for throwing an indecent party with young chorus girls, is highly autobiographical. Although recorded late in Rainey's career, this traditional style twelve-bar song utilizes a jug band, complete with jug bass and kazoo. Many of Rainey's songs displayed this type of sexual appetite, a part of her persona on and off stage.

Musical Legacy

Rainey influenced a younger generation of blues singers, who learned from her a dynamic stage presence, a strong delivery, and a way of handling a crowd. Her strong influence on Smith and many other blues singers is evident in the infusion of rural, Southern blues style and minstrel antics into the classic blues.

Amanda M. Pence

Further Reading

Bourgeois, Anna Stong. *Blueswomen: Profiles and Lyrics, 1920-1945*. Jefferson, N.C.: McFarland, 1996. The work contains a brief profile of Rainey and the lyrics of a few of her recorded songs.

Jackson, Buzzy. *A Bad Woman Feeling Good: Blues and the Women Who Sing Them*. New York: W. W. Norton, 2005. This book is a study of African American women in popular music. The opening chapter contains a discussion of Rainey's first recordings and of her contribution to the genre of blues.

Jones, Hettie. *Big Star Fallin' Mama: Five Women in Black Music*. New York: Viking Press, 1974. Rainey is the first singer covered in this book, with a look at her life, legacy, and music. Includes photographs and bibliography.

Lieb, Sandra R. *Mother of the Blues: A Study of Ma Rainey*. Amherst: University of Massachusetts Press, 1981. This work is an intensive study of the life, singing style, and music of Rainey. Includes photographs and bibliography.

Stewart-Baxter, Derrick. *Ma Rainey and the Classic Blues Singers*. London: Studio Vista, 1970. This book contains a chapter on Rainey and Smith, focusing on their styles, relationship, and biographies. Includes photographs and bibliography.

See also: Armstrong, Louis; Dorsey, Thomas A.; Henderson, Fletcher; Hunter, Alberta; Jackson, Mahalia; Jefferson, Blind Lemon; Memphis Minnie; Morton, Jelly Roll; Smith, Bessie; Smith, Mamie.

Bonnie Raitt

American country and rock singer, songwriter, and guitarist

Raitt revitalized interest in blues and American folk through her "blue-eyed soul" ballads during the 1980's and early 1990's.

Born: November 8, 1949; Burbank, California
Also known as: Bonnie Lynn Raitt (full name)

Principal recordings

ALBUMS: *Bonnie Raitt*, 1971; *Give It Up*, 1972; *Takin' My Time*, 1973; *Streetlights*, 1974; *Home Plate*, 1975; *Sweet Forgiveness*, 1977; *The Glow*, 1979; *Green Light*, 1982; *Nine Lives*, 1986; *Nick of Time*, 1989; *Luck of the Draw*, 1991; *Longing in Their Hearts*, 1994; *Fundamental*, 1998; *Silver Lining*, 2002; *Souls Alike*, 2005; *Bonnie Raitt and Friends*, 2006 (with others).

The Life

Bonnie Lynn Raitt (rayt) was born to Broadway musical singing legend John Raitt and pianist-singer Marge Goddard in Burbank, California, and she was raised in Los Angeles. Though she came from a musical family and grew up singing and playing guitar, her main interest was social activism in Africa. Her Quaker upbringing likely led to her early desire to help reverse the destruction of colonialism and mercantilism found in African countries such as Tanzania and to work toward democracy and socialist-based programs. She majored in African studies and social relations at Harvard's Radcliffe College.

Greatly impressed by the 1963 sound recording *Blues at Newport*, Raitt played and sang American folk songs and blues while in high school. During her first two years in Cambridge, Massachusetts, Raitt became increasingly interested in the folksong resurgence of the late 1960's and the activism of local musicians. She met blues promoter Dick Waterman during an interview for Harvard's radio station WHRB her freshman year, and they became close friends. When Waterman moved to Philadelphia, Pennsylvania, Raitt visited him often, eventually taking a semester off to study and play rhythm and blues under Waterman's mentorship. Her coffeehouse gigs helped her hone her talents and learn more about blues and African American music; so did her experience working directly with traditional blues legends.

Through Waterman, Raitt was introduced to and later opened for John Lee Hooker, Howlin' Wolf, Mississippi Fred McDowell, Sippie Wallace, Son House, and Muddy Waters. Working with these musicians at gigs and on the road encouraged Raitt to make the decision to leave Radcliffe to become a professional blues musician. By 1971 performances at the Gaslight Café in New York City led to her signing a contract with Warner Bros. Although her first albums received critical acclaim, they were not commercially successful.

Raitt's recording career meant increased touring and media attention. Though she was active in music scenes in the 1970's, recording seven of her own albums and working as a guest musician on others' albums (for example, *Warren Zevon*, which was released in 1976), Raitt appeared to favor performing in small, intimate venues rather than large concert arenas (with the exception of working for fundraisers). With the 1977 success of her rhythm-and-blues cover of Del Shannon's "Runaway," Warner Bros. was persistent about keeping her signed to its label, countering an offer from Columbia Records. In 1979 she was a key organizer of the MUSE (Musicians United for Safe Energy) concerts at Madison Square Garden. These concerts were so successful that Warner Bros. produced the documentary film *No Nukes* (1980), and the sound recording achieved a gold album status three times over. By the early 1980's, however, Raitt's studio recordings were viewed by Warner Bros. as commercial failures, and she was dropped from the label in 1983.

Although Raitt had struggled with drugs and alcohol, at this time she ended the abuse. She participated as a backup for the special television show *Roy Orbison and Friends: A Black and White Night* in 1987. During her recording of "Baby Mine" (from the 1941 motion picture *Dumbo*) on the Disney music tribute album produced by A&M Records, Raitt worked with Don Was of Capital Records.

Her tenth album, *Nick of Time*, with Was, initiated Raitt's great commercial success. Raitt won three Grammy Awards in 1989 and a fourth Grammy Award for her duet "In the Mood" on her friend John Lee Hooker's album *The Healer*.

In the mid-1990's, she won five more Grammy Awards, for *Luck of the Draw* and *Longing in Their Hearts*, which both achieved multiple platinum status. In 1998 she recorded with producers Mitchell Froom and Tchad Blake. Raitt married actor Michael O'Keefe in 1991; they divorced in 1999. Always the social and political activist, Raitt received attention for her anti-George W. Bush stance. In the 2004 election year, she appeared at the Stockholm Jazz Festival, promising to continue singing her song "Your Good Thing (Is About to End)" until the president leaves office. Along with performing and recording, she encourages children to learn to play instruments by funding organizations that support free programs and access to musical instruments.

The Music

Raitt's voice resembles her father's in its clarity, strength, and delivery. In second soprano range, her voice has a resonant and slightly raspy quality. She makes smooth vocal transitions from low to high register, adding slides, scoops, and blues notes. Raitt's guitar interpretations—whether on acoustic or slide—received critical acclaim at a time when women guitarists very rarely received attention. Her guitar playing also includes some bottleneck technique and combines folk, country, and blues.

Sweet Forgiveness. Raitt's sixth solo studio album features her hit cover of Del Shannon's "Runaway." Though some critics disliked her slow version, dismissing it as being too inspired by Al Green's rhythm-and-blues style, "Runaway" was ranked number twenty-five on the Top 40 hits charts. It was produced by Paul Rothchild (who produced for Elektra most of the Doors' albums). This was a great commercial success for Warner Bros., and it represents how Raitt maintains a unifying sound, most often referred to as "blue-eyed soul, while recording a diverse repertoire. Her title song, "Sweet Surrender," demonstrates gospel influence, while "Two Lives" and "Takin' My Time" sound like rock-country ballads, in the same vein as the Eagles' ballads. On "My Opening Farewell," which was originally written and performed by Jackson Browne, Raitt's vocal delivery and use of expressive range could be compared to Carole King's. The same vocal sound is accompanied beautifully by Raitt's dulcimer-like solo acoustic guitar work in "Louise."

Green Light. The last completed album before Raitt was dropped from Warner Bros. in 1983, *Green Light* employs the Bump Band, her on-the-road accompanying band during the 1970's. Her opening song, Fred Marrone and Stephen Holsapple's "Keep This Heart in Mind," a mixture of country and rock, reached number thirty-eight on the U.S. Top 40 chart. This is Raitt's most upbeat album, with songs such as Eddie Grant's "Baby Come Back" and her New Rhythm and Blues Quintet (also known as NRBQ) covers "Me and the Boys" and "Green Light," and Robbie Williams's "Talk to Me." All could have easily crossed over successfully into 1980's mainstream pop. Noticeably absent in these tracks is the intimacy of Raitt's ballads; however, these songs demonstrate that Raitt and her band were having fun performing and recording. It also features Raitt's convincing blues-rock version of Bob Dylan's "Let's Keep It Between Us." Generally, of all her albums, *Green Light* has caused the most controversy. Some argue that she "sold out" to the current new wave vocal style while others counter that the album reveals that she can master upbeat rock songs, adding her own personal style.

Nick of Time. In 1989 Raitt returned with strong songs on this album that showcased her at her stylistic best. The title song was ranked number one, and the album was nominated for four Grammy Awards, and it won three, including Album of the Year. "Have a Heart" and "Thing Called Love" also made their way onto hits charts, while "Love Letter" and "Too Soon to Tell" received much radio airtime. *Nick of Time* appeared to be a welcome return to Raitt's original intimate, soulful sound, with songs (Raitt's own and others) that fuse rock, country, blues, and what has become known as adult contemporary. Mature topics about love are a main focus. This same formula was used in her subsequent album, *Luck of the Draw*, which also won three Grammy Awards.

Luck of the Draw. A ballad-heavy album, *Luck of the Draw* contains of Raitt's best and most memorable ballad, "I Can't Make You Love Me." The song (written by Michael Reid and Allen Shamblin) focuses on the pain of unrequited love felt in a mature relationship. Raitt's resonant vocal and expressive ranges are exemplified here, accompanied by Bruce Hornsby on piano. The song's protagonist asks for one more night together before she goes; the final chord represents her departure. It reached number two on *Billboard*'s North America hits chart. The album also features several songs by Irish songwriter Paul Brady: "Not the Only One" and "Luck of the Draw." This album contained Raitt's largest string of hits, including "I Can't Make You Love Me," "Not the Only One," "Something to Talk About," "Slow Ride," "Come to Me," and "All at Once." It also features well-known musicians of mainstream rock and roll and country, such as Hornsby, Kris Kristofferson, Billy Vera, and Richard Thompson.

Longing in Their Hearts. Raitt received two more Grammy Awards for *Longing in Their Hearts*, which features the upbeat hit song "Love Sneakin' Up on You" as the first track. The title song, curiously not the first track, has a strong country influence, while "Feeling of Falling" is a combination of blues and rock. "You" is a ballad written in the same vein as those that appear on Raitt's previous albums.

Silver Lining. Raitt returns to a pop sound for this album, but she also includes blues, rock, and boogie-woogie in this album's set of songs. Hits include the title song (composed by David Gray), a ballad, and "Time of Our Lives" (composed by Teron Beal and Tommy Sims). Raitt and slide guitarist Roy Rogers composed "Gnawin' on It," a duel more than a duet between man and woman on slide guitar. Her slide work on this album foreshadows *Souls Alike*.

Musical Legacy

Raitt is known best for her masterful vocals and performances on both slide and acoustic guitars. Well-versed and studied in traditional blues (especially Delta blues) and a seasoned rock, country, and folk musician, Raitt exemplifies how popular musical genres can be combined into well-crafted songs. She cofounded the Rhythm and Blues Foundation in 1988, and she established the Bonnie Raitt Guitar Project in 1996 at Boys and Girls Clubs in the United States. Her expertise on guitar and her charitable work to help children with their first steps in musicianship have opened doors for other female guitarists.

Melissa Ursula Dawn Goldsmith

Further Reading

Bego, Mark. *Bonnie Raitt: Still in the Nick of Time.* Lanham, Md.: Cooper Square Press, 2003. This biography (updated from the original, published in 1995) is a thorough recounting of Raitt's life on and off the stage.

Gaar, Gillian G. "Smile for the Camera." In *She's a Rebel: The History of Women in Rock and Roll.* Seattle, Wash.: Seal Press, 1992. Gaar covers briefly the slow time in Raitt's career between the late 1970's and early 1980's, during which Warner Bros. dropped her from the label and she funded her tours with her own money. She also describes Raitt's recovery from drug addiction and alcoholism, her successful turning point with her 1989 album *Nick of Time*, and her charitable work with the Rhythm and Blues Foundation.

Mellers, Wilfred Howard. "Women and the Country Music Industry." In *Angels of the Night: Popular Female Singers of Our Time.* New York: Blackwell, 1986. Mellers, a musicologist, offers a brief biography of Raitt and others, including Loretta Lynn and Dolly Parton.

Raitt, Bonnie. "Manna from Heaven." In *A Hand to Guide Me*, edited by Denzel Washington and Daniel Paisner. Des Moines, Iowa: Meredith

Books, 2001. In this chapter, Raitt describes her rapport with Waterman and other musicians who guided her in music and in show business.

See also: Baez, Joan; Browne, Jackson; Charles, Ray; Cotton, James; Domino, Fats; Dylan, Bob; Hooker, John Lee; House, Son; Howlin' Wolf; James, Etta; King, Carole; Kristofferson, Kris; Staples, Pops; Waters, Muddy.

Joey Ramone
American rock singer, guitarist, and songwriter

Ramone's harsh vocals and hard lyrics symbolize punk rock.

Born: May 19, 1951; Forest Hills, New York
Died: April 15, 2001; New York, New York
Also known as: Jeffrey Hyman (birth name)
Member of: The Ramones

Principal recordings

ALBUM (solo): *Don't Worry About Me*, 2002.
ALBUMS (with the Ramones): *The Ramones*, 1976; *Leave Home*, 1977; *Rocket to Russia*, 1977; *Road to Ruin*, 1978; *It's Alive*, 1979; *Rock 'n' Roll High School*, 1979 (with others); *End of the Century*, 1980; *Pleasant Dreams*, 1981; *Subterranean Jungle*, 1983; *Too Tough to Die*, 1985; *Animal Boy*, 1986; *Halfway to Sanity*, 1987; *Brain Drain*, 1989; *Pet Semetary*, 1990; *Mondo Bizarro*, 1992; *Acid Eaters*, 1993; *¡Adios Amigos!*, 1995.

The Life

Joey Ramone (rah-MOHN) was born Jeffrey Hyman, and he was raised in New York City. He attended Forest Hills High School, which most of the other Ramones also attended. He turned to rock music and drumming during his teen years to escape his rough home life. Like his future bandmates, Joey Ramone never finished high school, and he began experimenting with drugs early in life. In 1974 he joined John Cummings (Johnny Ramone) and Douglas Colvin (Dee Dee Ramone) to form the Ramones, all taking Ramone as a stage name. Originally Joey Ramone was the drummer for the group, but he quickly turned to vocals. The group became regulars at New York's famous CBGB club, which helped it gain its legendary status as the home of punk rock.

Joey Ramone—six-foot-six with an untamed mass of black hair—was an imposing front man for the Ramones. His voice was rough, providing something different for the underground scene of New York. He never married, and he never had children. In 1980 his girlfriend left him for Johnny; this strained the relationship between the two men for the rest of Joey Ramone's life. Despite the fact that he would not talk to the other leading member of the band, the Ramones would carry on for sixteen more years.

The Ramones of the 1970's had a signature look and an innovative sound, but the constant touring and addictions to drugs and alcohol took a toll on the group, including Joey Ramone. During the 1980's, although the band members changed, Johnny and Joey remained. Eventually

the Ramones disbanded, and Joey Ramone began to work on a solo project. Although he was diagnosed with lymphatic cancer in 1995, he had a brief stint as a disc jockey, and he helped produce new punk bands. He never finished his solo album, succumbing to cancer on April 15, 2001.

The Music

Joey Ramone began his musical career as a drummer. Initially, he played the drums for the Ramones, while Johnny played the guitar and Dee Dee played bass. When they realized the sound was not working, Joey Ramone moved to vocals, and the band's manager, Thomas Erdelyi (Tommy Ramone), took over on drums.

The Ramones' style became recognizable as they began playing shows in 1974. The music was fast, and it included a heavily distorted guitar and scratchy vocals. Most of the songs were less than two minutes in length. In the 1970's, the lyrics were considered shocking. Many songs were sarcastic, silly, or dark and sardonic, although somehow the group's music was always upbeat at the same time.

The Ramones. At one of the CBGB shows, the Ramones attracted the attention of Sire Records head Seymour Stein. In 1975 Sire released their first album, *The Ramones*. Considered by some as the first punk album, *The Ramones* featured the notable lead vocals of Joey Ramone, and it included some of the group's most well-known songs, among them "Blitzkrieg Bop" (with its chant "Hey ho! Let's go!"), "Beat on the Brat," and "Now I Wanna Sniff Some Glue." Although many of the songs were credited to Dee Dee, Joey Ramone did write a few of them. The album cost less than seven thousand dollars to make, but with its success, the Ramones began a world tour.

The Ramones' next two albums were an assortment of their early songs. Notable songs include "Pinhead" on *Leave Home* and "Sheena Is a Punk Rocker" and "Rockaway Beach" on *Rocket to Russia*. Both albums had moderate success, but they did not

Joey Ramone. (Hulton Archive/Getty Images)

give the Ramones the star status they sought. In 1978 they moved in another direction. Tommy left the band, and Marc Bell (Marky Ramone) became the drummer. They also recorded the album *Road to Ruin*, which included what became another Ramones classic: "I Wanna Be Sedated."

End of the Century. The Ramones teamed with Phil Spector to produce their next album, *End of the Century*. Although Spector came to the Ramones with excellent credentials in the music industry, he altered the band's sound, producing a record that did not sound the Ramones. The trademark driving guitar was missing, and Spector included a pronounced instrumental background unfamiliar to the Ramones. Because of recording complications, Joey Ramone was the only member of the band to appear on every track of the release. Although the album was loved by critics, fans seemed to regard *End of the Century* as the low point of the Ramones' career.

Pleasant Dreams. The band continued to experiment with its sound, recording *Pleasant Dreams* in 1981. It was before this album that Ramone and Cummings became estranged, which may have produced the most famous song on the album: "The KKK Took My Baby Away." Reportedly the song is about the more conservative Johnny stealing Joey Ramone's girlfriend.

In 1983 Marky was kicked out of the band during the recording of *Subterranean Jungle*. Richard Reinhardt (Richie Ramone) replaced him on drums. In 1984's *Too Tough to Die*, the band tried to get back to the hard-punk scene of the 1980's. Notably, there were fewer songs by Joey Ramone on this album; he was more famous for the balladic songs than for the hard-hitting tracks.

Animal Boy. On 1986's *Animal Boy*, Joey Ramone cowrote a protest song about President Ronald Reagan. "My Brain Is Hanging Upside Down (Bonzo Goes to Bitburg)" castigates Reagan for visiting a cemetery in which Nazi war criminals were buried. Ramone, who was Jewish, was sickened when he saw television coverage of the event. The song's unusually serious nature made it one of the album's more memorable tracks.

Brain Drain. *Brain Drain* was an important album for the group. It marked the return of Marky, and it was the last album for Dee Dee. To replace Dee Dee, Christopher Joseph Ward—C. J.

Ramone—was added. A single written for the film of the same name, *Pet Sematary* (1989), based on the Stephen King novel, became another popular Ramones song. *Brain Drain* was the last album the Ramones recorded for Sire Records.

Mondo Bizarro. In 1992 Joey Ramone received most of the writing credits on *Mondo Bizarro*, something that had not happened since the beginning of the band's career. The lead track, "Censorshit," is an attack on censorship of the mid-1990's. It is addressed to Tipper Gore, wife of Vice President Al Gore, who actively promoted labeling albums that had songs with sexually explicit lyrics.

¡Adios Amigos! The Ramones' final studio album, *¡Adios Amigos!*, was released in 1995. The songs on this album are noticeably slower, a result of Joey Ramone's deteriorating singing abilities. As the title suggests, the band knew it would most likely be their last recording.

Don't Worry About Me. Joey Ramone went on be the producer for other bands. Between the breaking up of the Ramones and his death, he was working on a solo project, *Don't Worry About Me*, which was released posthumously in 2002. The album included a cover of "What a Wonderful World," and the title track was a breakup song, but hidden beneath the lyrics was a metaphoric good-bye to the world.

Musical Legacy

Joey Ramone was the godfather of punk, and his sound was emulated by vocalists who followed the punk style. The Ramones helped define the punk genre, and mainstream rock artists, such as U2, have acknowledged that the Ramones were a significant influence on their work. With their outlandish lyrics, the Ramones opened the door for other artists to be daring with lyrics. From songs about sniffing glue to songs about male prostitution, the members of the group always spoke their mind.

The Ramones set an example in showmanship, engaging their audience, encouraging sing-along vocals, and providing catchy, memorable lyrics. The pop punk of the 1990's and 2000's was built on the groundwork laid by the Ramones. The Ramones were inducted into the Rock and Roll Hall of Fame in 2002.

Daniel R. Vogel

Further Reading

Bessman, Jim. *Ramones: An American Band*. New York: St. Martin's Griffin, 1993. This resource was written with the authorization of the Ramones, while they were still a touring band, and it presents a personal history of each member.

Laitio-Ramone, Jari-Pekka. *Heaven Needed a Lead Singer: Friends Remember Joey Ramone*. Kauhajoki, Finland: Ramoniac, 2002. The author, an expert on the Ramones, spent time with the band toward the end of its career. This book includes a series of interviews with Ramone and articles written by fans.

_____. *Rock in Peace: Dee Dee and Joey Ramone*. Kauhajoki, Finland: Ramoniac, 2004. This book is a tribute, with fan articles and analysis, to the two Ramones who died of cancer. It chronicles the influence the band, and particularly Ramone, had on fans and on other bands.

Meyer, Monte A., and Frank Melnick. *On the Road with the Ramones*. London: Sanctuary, 2003. Because Melnick was the band's tour manager, this book is full of inside stories and personal views on the Ramones.

Porter, Dick. *Ramones: The Complete Twisted History*. London: Plexus, 2004. A good starting point for information on the Ramones, this book provides analysis of the band members and of the people connected to their career.

See also: Bono; Spector, Phil; Strummer, Joe.

Jean-Pierre Rampal

French classical flutist

Regarded as one of the most influential flutists of the twentieth century, Rampal was responsible for establishing the flute as a solo instrument on the international concert scene, attracting worldwide audiences comparable to those attracted by virtuoso pianists, violinists, and singers.

Born: January 7, 1922; Marseilles, France
Died: May 20, 2000; Paris, France
Also known as: Jean-Pierre-Louis Rampal (full name); Man with the Golden Flute

Principal recordings

ALBUMS: *Mozart: Concertos No. 1 and 2*, 1953; *Vivaldi: Concerto for Five Instruments in F Major*, 1954; *Baroque Sonatas for Flute and Harpsichord*, 1958; *Four Eighteenth Century Flute Quartets*, 1960; *Bach: Orchestral Suites 1 and 2*, 1962; *Récital Hean-Pierre Rampal*, 1963; *Flute Concertos—Flotenkonzerte*, 1964; *Hoffmeister: Flute Concerto in G Major*, 1967; *Handel: The Complete Flute Sonatas*, 1973; *Rampal Plays Bach*, 1974; *Bach: Complete Works for Solo Flute*, 1975; *Claude Bolling: Suite for Flute and Jazz Piano*, 1975; *Telemann: Suite in A Minor for Flute and Strings*, 1978; *Picnic Suite*, 1980 (with Claude Bolling); *Haydn: "London" Trios, Nos. 1-4/ Divertiments, Op. 100, Nos. 2 and 6*, 1982 (with Isaac Stern and Mstislav Rostropovich); *Suite No. 2 for Flute and Jazz Piano*, 1987 (with Bolling); *Bach: Brandenburg Concertos 1-6*, 1980; *The Romantic Flute*, 1981; *The Genius of Jean-Pierre Rampal*, 1983; *Rampal Plays Mozart*, 1984; *Haydn: Concerto for Flute, Oboe, and Orchestra*, 1985; *Mozart: Sonatas and Variations*, 1986; *Music for Flute and Guitar*, 1988; *Beethoven: Complete Chamber Music for Flute*, 1990; *Vivaldi: Six Double Concertos for Flute, Violin, Strings, and Harpsichord*, 1990; *Bach: Three Concertos for Flute*, 1991; *Twentieth Century Flute Master Pieces*, 1992; *Jean-Pierre Rampal: Master of the Flute*, 1996; *Boccherini: Flute Quintets*, 1997.

The Life

Born in Marseilles in 1922, Jean-Pierre-Louis Rampal (zhahn pyehr lwee rahm-PAHL) was born into a musical family. His father Joseph was principal flutist of the Orchestre des Concerts Classiques de Marseilles and professor of flute at the conservatory there. Jean-Pierre began playing the flute with his father at the age of twelve and won a first prize at the conservatory in 1937. Nevertheless, he was not encouraged by his parents to become a professional flutist; he was steered by his mother, Andree Roggero, toward a career in medicine instead. In 1943, World War II was at its height, and France was headed by the Nazi-installed Vichy government. While in his third year at the medical school of the University of Marseilles, Rampal was drafted for compulsory labor. Instead of reporting for duty, he went underground and escaped to Paris. In 1944, after only five months in the class of flutist Gaston Crunelle, he won a first prize at the Paris Conservatory.

Rampal was solo flutist at the Vichy Opéra Orchestra from 1946 to 1950 and principal flutist at the Paris Opéra from 1956 to 1962. His concert tours from 1947 led him through Europe, North and South America, Africa, and the Far East. He founded the Quintette à Vent Française (1946) and the Ensemble Baroque de Paris (1952), and his collaboration with the pianist and harpsichordist Robert Veyron-Lacroix lasted for thirty-five years (1946-1981). Appointed professor at the Paris Conservatory (1969-1981), he was also a founder of the Summer Nice Academy and taught master classes throughout the world. As the owner of a solid-gold flute made in 1869 by Louis Lot (which he rescued from an antiques dealer who wanted to melt it down for profit), Rampal earned the sobriquet Man with the Golden Flute.

Having married Françoise Bacqueyrisse (the daughter of the harpist Odette Le Dentu) in 1947, Rampal made his home in Paris. The couple would have two children. In his later years he maintained a rigorous schedule of international performances, both playing and conducting, and he reached beyond the classical repertoire to record folk music from all parts of the world, as well as American jazz. He even made television appearances on such popular programs as *The Muppet Show*, thus becoming a well-known ambassador of music to the American public. Rampal died of heart failure in Paris on May 20, 2000; he was seventy-eight years old.

The Music

"For me," Rampal once said, "the flute is really the sound of humanity," of a man "completely free from his body almost without an intermediary." Rampal gave renewed voice to the instrument in the years following World War II, reintroducing it to the modern repertoire and enthusiastically expanding its appeal to a broad, worldwide audience.

Rampal's repertoire spanned works from the early Baroque period to contemporary music. His extensive recordings include flute works by such major composers as Georg Philipp Telemann, Johann Sebastian Bach, Antonio Vivaldi, Franz Joseph Hadyn, Wolfgang Amadeus Mozart, Ludwig van Beethoven, Franz Schubert, and Robert Schu-

mann, as well as by such lesser-known composers as Domenico Cimarosa, Carl Reinecke, and Saverio Mercadante. Among the many composers who dedicated works to Rampal were Jean Françaix, André Jolivet, Jean Martinon, Francis Poulenc, and Pierre Boulez, and Rampal premiered numerous works by contemporary composers such as Leonard Bernstein, Aaron Copland, and Krzysztof Penderecki. Besides performing Western classical music, he performed in recordings of jazz music and English folk song, as well as Japanese, Chinese, and Indian classical music.

Rampal appeared in many of the world's major musical venues, including London's Royal Albert Hall, Paris's Théâtre de Champs-Elysées, Carnegie Hall and Avery Fisher Hall in New York City, the Hollywood Bowl in Los Angeles, the symphony halls in Boston and Chicago, and the Kennedy Center in Washington, D.C. He played with all the most important orchestras worldwide, and among the many major festivals in which he performed were the Mostly Mozart, Ravinia, Tanglewood, Saratoga, and Meadowbrook Festivals.

Rampal Plays Bach. Beginning with their first flute-piano recital in Paris's Salle Gaveau in 1949 and their first international tour in 1953, Rampal and Veyron-Lacroix made regular duo appearances and produced many award-winning recordings together, including *Rampal Plays Bach*, released by RCA in 1974. The three-record set contains the complete works for solo flute by Bach, including sonatas identified in the Bach-Werke-Verzeichnis (Bach Works Catalog) as BWV 1020 and 1030-35, Sonata for Two Flutes and Continuo (BWV 1039), and Sonata for Flute, Violin, and Continuo (BWV 1038). Rampal's thirty-five-year partnership with Veyron-Lacroix came to an end in 1981, when Veyron-Lacroix retired because of ill health. In the last twenty years of his own career, Rampal collaborated with American pianist John Steele Ritter.

Claude Bolling: Suite for Flute and Jazz Piano. Written in 1975 by French jazz musician Claude Bolling, the *Suite for Flute and Jazz Piano Trio* is a revolutionary work that mixes Baroque and jazz styles. Containing seven movements, titled "Baroque and Blue," "Sentimentale," "Javanaise," "Fugace," "Irlandaise," "Versatile," and "Veloce," the work was recorded and released in 1975. The album enjoyed a big success, hitting the top of the *Billboard* charts for two years and remaining there for ten years. Bolling and Rampal later collaborated on *Picnic Suite* (1980) and *Suite No. 2 for Flute and Jazz Piano* (1987).

Haydn: "London Trios" and Divertimenti. Active as a chamber musician, Rampal collaborated with numerous soloists, including two of his closest friends, violinist Isaac Stern and cellist Mstislav Rostropovich. Containing the four "London Trios" and two divertimenti (Op. 100, Nos. 2 and 6) by Franz Joseph Haydn, the album illustrates a good example of the three virtuosos' common approach to playing music. Their other collaborations included concerts celebrating Rampal's sixtieth and seventieth birthdays.

Twentieth Century Flute Master Pieces. Released by Erato in 1992, the two-compact-disc set contains contemporary flute works recorded by Rampal from the 1950's through the 1970's. Many of the pieces were dedicated to or commissioned by Rampal himself, such as Jolivet's Concerto for Flute and Orchestra and Poulenc's Sonata for Flute and Piano. Originally written for the violin and orchestra in 1940, Aram Khachaturian's famous concerto was transcribed for flute by Rampal with the composer's endorsement in 1967. Rampal's version of the concerto became a standard part in the flute repertoire.

Musical Legacy

Rampal's legacy was to popularize the flute for a broad audience in the second half of the twentieth century, to resurrect Baroque music for the modern repertoire, and to encourage new composers, such as Francis Poulenc, whose works have become standards of the modern classical repertoire.

Rampal also left a legacy of more than four hundred recordings—more, it is believed, than any other performer of classical works. Many were issued by such major labels as L'Oiseau-Lyre, Erato, Philips, Denon, Sony Classical, RCA, and CBS. Not only was he heard on radios worldwide, but also he was seen on many television programs, especially in France, the United States, and Japan. His editions of hundreds of flute pieces from the Baroque to the twentieth century were published by Georges Billaudot in Paris and the International Music Company in New York.

Among the hundreds of awards and honors Rampal received throughout his career are the Grand Prix du Président de la République (1976), the Léonie Sonning Music Prize (1978), and the Prix d'Honneur of the Thirteenth Montreux World Recording awards (1980). In France he was made an Officer of the French Legion of Honor (1979), a Commander of the National Order of Merit (1982), and a Commander of the Order of Arts and Letters (1989), and in the United States he was the first person to receive the National Flute Association's Lifetime Achievement Award (1991). Beginning in 1980, the Jean-Pierre Rampal International Flute Competition has been held in his honor by the City of Paris.

Sonia Lee

Further Reading

Andrews, Christina. "Jean-Pierre Rampal: Looking Back a Year After His Death." *Flutist Quarterly* 26, no. 4 (Summer, 2001): 42-46. A brief biography of Rampal.

Rampal, Jean-Pierre, with Deborah Wise. *Music, My Love: An Autobiography.* New York: Random House, 1989. In this autobiography, which he wrote in his sixties, Rampal offers anecdotes about his life, family, friends, and career.

Verroust, Denis. "Still Passionate About Music: An Interview with Jean-Pierre Rampal." *Flute Talk* 18, no. 5 (January, 1999): 8-13. Presents an interview with Rampal in which the flutist discusses his musical influences, his opinions about the quality of contemporary flute playing, and his comments on developing technique.

See also: Galway, Sir James; Mancini, Henry.

Maurice Ravel

French classical composer

Ravel explored new areas of harmony and tone color in his meticulously crafted compositions. His music is often a fusion of Baroque or classical idioms with Impressionism and jazz.

Born: March 7, 1875; Ciboure, France
Died: December 28, 1937; Paris, France
Also known as: Joseph Maurice Ravel (full name)

Principal works

BALLETS: *Daphnis et Chloé*, 1912 (choreography by Michael Fokine and Maurice Ravel); *Ma Mère l'oye*, 1912 (*Mother Goose*; choreography by Jeanne Hugard); *La Valse*, composed 1920, first performed 1929 (choreography by Bronislava Nizhinska); *Le Tombeau de Couperin*, 1920 (*Tombeau for Couperin*; choreography by Jean Börlin and Rolf de Maré); *Boléro*, 1928.

OPERAS (music): *L'Heure espagnole*, 1911 (*The Spanish Hour*; comedic opera; libretto by Franc-Nohain); *L'Enfant et les sortilèges*, 1925 (*The Bewitched Child*; lyric fantasy; libretto by Colette).

ORCHESTRAL WORKS: *Shéhérazade: Ouverture de féerie*, 1898; *Une Barque sur l'océan*, 1906; *Rapsodie espagnole*, 1908 (*Spanish Rhapsody*); *Fragments symphoniques*, 1911 (Suite No. 1); *Alborada del gracioso*, 1918; *Tzigane*, 1924 (rhapsody for violin and orchestra).

PIANO WORKS: *Pavane pour une infante défunte*, 1899 (*Pavane for a Dead Infanta*); *Jeux d'eau*, 1902; *Miroirs*, 1906; *Gaspard de la nuit*, 1908 (*Demons of the Night*); *Valses nobles et sentimentales*, 1911 (*Noble and Sentimental Waltzes*); *Menuet antique*, 1929; Piano Concerto for the Left Hand in D, 1930; Piano Concerto in G, 1931.

VOCAL WORKS: *Shéhérazade*, 1903 (orchestral song cycle; based on Tristan Klingsor's poetry); *Don Quichotte à Dulcinée*, 1933 (*Serenade of Don Quixote to Dulcinea*; for voice and piano).

The Life

Joseph Maurice Ravel (zho-SEHF moh-REES rah-VEHL) was born in the small town of Ciboure in the Basque region of France, near the Spanish border. His mother was of Basque origin, and his father was a civil engineer of Swiss origin. Ravel's family moved to Paris when he was three months old, and he lived in and around the French capital for the rest of his life. Ravel studied intermittently at the Paris Conservatory for several years, attempting multiple times to win the prestigious Prix de Rome scholarship. He always failed because his compositions were judged too controversial by the traditionalist board. This error in judgment regarding Ravel's talent led to an administrative reorganization of the Paris Conservatory under the leadership of another great French composer and friend of Ravel, Gabriel Fauré.

In 1901 Ravel formed an artistic partnership called Les Apaches with pianist Ricardo Viñes and other friends. They were adamant in defending the merits of Claude Debussy's controversial opera *Pelléas et Mélisande* (1902) against critics of the work. Ravel's most productive years as a composer were from 1905 to 1914, during which time he benefited from a contract and an annuity from the publisher Durand. He began a series of concert tours in 1909 (the first one being to London) which broadened his fame outside France. By the advent of World War I, he was considered one of France's great composers.

In March, 1916, Ravel joined the war effort, driving a supply truck, and he was near the front lines at the Battle of Verdun. Ravel's poor health during this time (as a result of his military service) plus the death of his mother in 1917 resulted in three years of compositional inactivity. In 1921 Ravel bought a villa in Montfort l'Amaury, a small village west of Paris, and he lived there until his death.

In the 1920's and 1930's he concertized all over Europe, but his compositional output had lessened to approximately one piece a year. In 1928 he embarked on a successful twenty-five-city tour of North America, where he was promoted as the greatest living French composer. In 1933 he began suffering from the effects of apraxia and aphasia, which caused mental fatigue, memory loss, and difficulty with motor skills and with speech. By 1937 his health greatly deteriorated to the point where a brain operation was required. Shortly after the operation, he lapsed into a coma, and he died on December 28, 1937.

The Music

Ravel's distinctive compositional voice emerged early in his career. Like the slow unfolding of the theme in his *Boléro*, he gradually developed the contours and dimensions of his style throughout the rest of his life. Unlike other twentieth century European composers, such as Igor Stravinsky and Arnold Schoenberg, Ravel did not make any sharp turns or radical departures in his musical style.

Some essential elements of his compositional style include Impressionism, the contrast between modality and tonality, the use of dance rhythms,

Maurice Ravel. (Library of Congress)

the influence of Spanish dance music, and a fascination with the exotic. Ravel was essentially a miniaturist. His large-scale works (the ballets and operas) were assemblages of smaller sections, yet unified by melodic transformation.

Ravel regarded the piano as his primary medium of expression and an essential element in his compositional process. He treated orchestration as a separate task from composition, thus many of his orchestral works were arrangements of his previously composed piano works. He spent a lot of time arranging and reshaping his works to the extent that nearly half of his oeuvre exists in more than one form. He arranged other composers' works as well, the most popular being his orchestration of Modest Mussorgsky's piano suite *Pictures at an Exhibition* (1886).

Periodically throughout his life, Ravel would return to his birthplace, drawn by memories of his mother's Spanish folk songs and the Basque countryside. Thus, much of his music reflects a distinctive Spanish influence and a yearning for the past, most clearly felt in the *Rapsodie espagnole* and *Boléro*.

Ravel's fascination with the exotic began with the Paris Exhibition in 1889 when he was fourteen. He was interested in Chinese and Japanese art, American jazz, and Javanese gamelan music. He

was often drawn to ancient myths as a basis for his musical ideas, and his fascination with mechanical devices is evident in his meticulously crafted compositions.

Jeux d'eau. Although *Pavane for a Dead Infanta* is one of Ravel's most recognizable pieces for piano, *Jeux d'eau* was his first masterpiece for the instrument, opening up a new avenue of expression. This piece was among the first Impressionistic character pieces written for piano. Influenced by Franz Liszt's *Les Jeux d'Eaux à la Villa d'Este* from his *Années de Pèlerinage* (1883), the title translates to playing water or fountains. Many of Ravel's compositional trademarks are at work in this piece, including the use of modal harmony, pentatonic scales, and polytonality.

Miroirs. *Miroirs* builds upon the pianistic innovations of *Jeux d'eau*. These five Impressionistic pieces conjure up vivid images of animal life, the ocean, Spain, and pastoral landscapes. The first, *Noctuelles* (*Night Moths*), uses polyrhythms, shifting meters and melodic fragments to portray flittering moths. The second, *Oiseaux tristes* (*Sad Birds*), sounds like an improvisation, and it has an elegiac and melancholy tone. The third, *Une barque sur l'océan* (*A Boat on the Ocean*), shows Ravel's skill in depicting water scenes. The fourth, *Alborada del gracioso* (*Aubade of the Jester*), portrays a fool trying to serenade a lady with a lugubrious song. The fifth, *La vallée des cloches* (*The Valley of Bells*), evokes church bells with its use of modal scales. Ravel later orchestrated the third and fourth pieces of this set.

Daphnis et Chloé. Ravel was commissioned to compose this ballet by Sergei Diaghilev, the Russian impresario and leader of the Ballets Russes. Based on a Greek pastoral romance about the love between a goatherd and a shepherdess, the ballet is considered by most musicologists to be Ravel's greatest orchestral work. It is heard in concert halls most often in the form of two suites that Ravel created from extracting accessible sections of the score.

Piano Concerto for the Left Hand in D. Ravel began work on this piece in 1929 after meeting Austrian pianist Paul Wittgenstein, who lost his arm in combat in World War I on the Russian front and who was the brother of the philosopher Ludwig Wittgenstein. This piece is among the several compositions created later in Ravel's life that were influenced by jazz rhythms and harmony. Ravel gave the piano part a thick texture and a wide range in order to disguise the fact that only the left hand of the pianist is playing. The concerto is in one movement, yet it encompasses the several moods, keys, and tempi associated with a multimovement work.

Boléro. This is easily Ravel's most well-known work. Although it was written as a ballet, it is almost exclusively performed as an orchestral piece. It earned immediate success, and it has been a staple of the concert repertoire since it first premiered. The piece consists solely of one melody in two sections repeated and developed into an ornate orchestral tapestry of sound over an unchanging rhythm played on two snare drums. Remarkably, although it has a rigid and machinelike rhythm, the melody never sounds constrained or confined. There is no piece like it in the orchestral repertoire, and it remains a prime example of Ravel's ability to write compelling music within a tightly constructed framework.

Musical Legacy

Ravel's oeuvre, comprising approximately sixty works in all, is small compared to that of most composers, yet he is considered to be among the greatest of French composers, alongside Josquin des Prez, François Couperin, Jean-Philippe Rameau, Hector Berlioz, and Debussy. Ravel's music was not of one school, be it Impressionism, Expressionism, or modernism, but it drew from a combination of these and other influences.

Ravel's legacy has suffered from an almost constant association with Debussy. Ravel greatly admired Debussy and his music, yet he strove to compose music that was more grounded in form than Debussy's. In fact, Ravel was often referred to as a classicist by other composers, and he even called himself one, because he frequently placed his musical ideas into familiar structures rather than creating his own. Ravel has been influential in demonstrating that fresh ideas can be cast into already existing forms, such as the waltz (Noble and Sentimental Waltzes illustrate this).

Ravel's influence can be observed to some degree in the works of Stravinsky, Debussy, and many other French composers (such as Arthur Honegger, Francis Poulenc, Olivier Messiaen, and Pierre Boulez). Ravel's *Boléro* was an influence on the American minimalist composers Terry Riley, Steve Reich, and others. It is largely the result of Ravel's orchestration of Mussorgsky's *Pictures at an Exhibition* that this work has maintained its popularity. Synthesizing the forms and styles of the past with an innovative harmonic language, Ravel enriched the possibilities of modern musical expression.

Tim J. Smolko and Joanna R. Smolko

Further Reading

Larner, Gerald. *Maurice Ravel.* London: Phaidon Press, 1996. Ravel was a notoriously secretive and enigmatic man, so attempts to explore his psychological disposition are difficult. Larner's book is a thorough biography, and it is also insightful in showing how Ravel's life, thoughts, and feelings manifested themselves in his music.

Mawer, Deborah, ed. *The Cambridge Companion to Ravel.* Cambridge, England: Cambridge University Press, 2000. This book contains eleven articles by leading authorities on Ravel's music, arranged in three sections: culture and aesthetic, musical exploration, performance and reception.

Orenstein, Arbie. *Ravel: Man and Musician.* New York: Dover Publications, 1991. This book contains a biography, an analysis of Ravel's compositions, and three excellent essays on the most important aspects of Ravel's music. It also has a discography of the earliest recordings made of his works.

_____. *A Ravel Reader: Correspondence, Articles, Interviews.* New York: Columbia University Press, 2003. Consisting of letters, articles, and lectures written by Ravel, this is an excellent collection of source material on the composer. It also includes interviews of Ravel and an appendix containing various documents related to his life and work.

Zank, Stephen. *Ravel: A Guide to Research.* New York: Routledge, 2005. This volume includes a historical chronology and an extensive annotated bibliography of books and articles on

Ravel, including editions of his music. This source is useful for in-depth research and writing on Ravel.

See also: Anastasio, Trey; Argerich, Martha; Boulanger, Nadia; Burton, Gary; Copland, Aaron; Debussy, Claude; Evans, Bill; Fiedler, Arthur; Grappelli, Stéphane; Hancock, Herbie; Heifetz, Jascha; Holst, Gustav; Honegger, Arthur; Korngold, Erich Wolfgang; Koussevitzky, Serge; Lutosławski, Witold; Ma, Yo-Yo; Messiaen, Olivier; Norman, Jessye; Piazzolla, Astor; Poulenc, Francis; Reinhardt, Django; Respighi, Ottorino; Rubinstein, Artur; Satie, Erik; Schoenberg, Arnold; Shaw, Artie; Sousa, John Philip; Stravinsky, Igor; Strayhorn, Billy; Szigeti, Joseph; Tavener, Sir John; Tiomkin, Dimitri; Vaughan Williams, Ralph; Villa-Lobos, Heitor; Watts, André.

Otis Redding

American soul singer and guitarist

One of the most revered soul singers of all time, Redding was famous for his raspy, bluesy, vocal delivery and emotionally charged, intense performances.

Born: September 9, 1941; Dawson, Georgia
Died: December 10, 1967; Lake Monona, Wisconsin
Member of: The Bar-Kays

Principal recordings

ALBUMS: *Pain in My Heart*, 1964; *The Great Otis Redding Sings Soul Ballads*, 1965; *Otis Blue: Otis Redding Sings Soul*, 1965; *Complete and Unbelievable: The Otis Redding Dictionary of Soul*, 1966; *Remembering*, 1966; *The Soul Album*, 1966; *King and Queen*, 1967 (with Carla Thomas); *The Dock of the Bay*, 1968; *History of Otis Redding*, 1968; *The Immortal Otis Redding*, 1968; *In Person at the Whiskey A Go Go*, 1968; *Love Man*, 1969; *Monterey International Pop Festival: Otis Redding/ The Jimi Hendrix Experience*, 1970; *Tell the Truth*, 1970; *Remember Me*, 1992.

The Life

Otis Redding was born on September 9, 1941, the son of Otis Redding, Sr., a sharecropper, and Fannie Mae Redding. He was born in Dawson, Georgia, but the family soon relocated to Macon, Georgia, at the height of segregation in the South. Otis, Sr., a Baptist minister, introduced his son to gospel music at an early age, and soon the boy was performing at church. Before graduating from high school, Redding decided to pursue a career as a professional singer, initially to lessen the financial burden on his family. After a brief time working as a backup singer, Redding began recording under his own name, was signed to Stax Records, and had an exceptional run of soul hits.

Redding was a lifelong family man, first providing for his parents and siblings, and then building a family of his own. He married Zelma Atwood in 1961, and they had four children: Dexter, Karla, Otis III, and Demetria. Redding's life and career were tragically cut short on December 10, 1967, when, just months after turning twenty-six, his plane crashed in Wisconsin, killing him and four members of his backing band, the Bar-Kays.

The Music

In October, 1962, Redding was in Stax Studios in Memphis, Tennessee, recording a session as a backup singer for Johnny Jenkins and the Pinetoppers. The session did not go well, and there was extra time at the end of the day. Redding stepped up to the microphone and recorded "These Arms of Mine," among others. Even though Redding had already recorded as a leader in 1960 ("She's Alright" and "Shout Bamalama"), it was this session that catapulted Redding into the role of leader of the Stax hit machine of the 1960's.

Pain in My Heart. Redding's debut album, *Pain in My Heart*, already exhibited many of the characteristics that would secure his legendary reputation: a balance of powerful, expressive ballads and grooving upbeat numbers. These featured an assortment of interesting cover choices (Sam Cooke's "You Send Me," Ben E. King's "Stand by Me," Little Richard's "Lucille") interspersed with Redding-penned originals ("These Arms of Mine," "Security," "That's What My Heart Needs," "Heh Heh Baby"). Many of Redding's original tunes were cowritten by Steve Cropper, guitarist of the Stax house band, Booker T. and the M.G.'s.

Otis Blue. Redding's second release, *The Great Otis Redding Sings Soul Ballads*, is best known for the signature Redding tune "Mr. Pitiful." However, it was Redding's third release, *Otis Blue*, that contained some of Redding and Cropper's finest compositions, famous cover choices, and classic vocal performances. The first half of the record is dominated by Redding originals, including "Ole Man Trouble," "Respect" (which would later be famously rerecorded by Aretha Franklin), and "I've Been Loving You Too Long," the biggest hit of Redding's career up until this point at number two on the rhythm-and-blues charts and number twenty-one on the pop charts. The first half of the record also features the bold cover choice of the Sam Cooke classic, "A Change Is Gonna Come," which was the first of three Cooke covers on *Otis Blue* ("Shake" and "Wonderful World" being the other two). The remainder of *Otis Blue* is filled with interesting cover choices, from B. B. King's "Rock Me Baby" to Mick Jagger and Keith Richards's "(I Can't Get No) Satisfaction." *Otis Blue* contained every aspect of Redding's musical vocabulary—powerful soul ballads; gospel-influenced, energetic, up-tempo numbers; and harder edged, rock-and-blues-influenced leanings.

Later Releases. After *Otis Blue*, Redding released several albums over the next two years, including *The Soul Album, Complete and Unbelievable, King and Queen* (with Carla Thomas), and *Live in Europe. Complete and Unbelievable: The Otis Redding Dictionary of Soul*, contained some of Redding's strongest original material ("Fa-Fa-Fa-Fa-Fa Sad Song," "I'm Sick Y'All," "She Put the Hurt on Me"), a version of the Beatles' "Day Tripper," and another one of his biggest hit singles, "Try a Little Tenderness," complete with the famous climaxing conclusion that landed it at number twenty-five on the U.S. pop charts.

Posthumous Releases. On December 10, 1967, at the height of his musical popularity and at just twenty-six years of age, Redding was in a plane crash that killed him and four members of his backing band, the Bar-Kays. Just three days before his death, Redding recorded "(Sittin' on) The Dock of the Bay," a song slightly more influenced by pop than his usual gospel-and-blues-flavored

Otis Redding. (AP/Wide World Photos)

soul. When the song was posthumously released in January, 1968, it soared to number one on the charts and sold more than one million copies, both firsts for Redding's career. *The Immortal Otis Redding*, featuring "Hard to Handle" and "The Happy Song (Dum-Dum)," and *In Person at the Whiskey A Go Go* (a live release with many of Redding's greatest hits) were also both released in the year after Redding's death. In September, 1970, *Monterey International Pop Festival: Otis Redding/The Jimi Hendrix Experience* was released—paying homage to two musical giants who had died after their performances at the festival.

Musical Legacy

Redding, along with his two musical idols, Cooke and James Brown, revolutionized soul music in the 1960's. While Cooke brought his gospel roots to the pop arena and Brown transformed the rhythmic foundation of early soul into funk music, Redding's famous Stax Records recordings remained consistent and true to the gospel-blues roots of soul music. Combined with Redding's songwriting and vocal abilities, this authenticism made him one of the most influential soul singers of all time.

Once Redding became a solo success, his fine business sense materialized, and he formed his own record label (Jotis Records) and music publishing company (Redwal Music, Inc.). He was inducted into the Rock and Roll Hall of Fame in 1989, received a Grammy Lifetime Achievement Award in 1999, and was ranked number twenty-one on *Rolling Stone*'s "100 Greatest Artists of All Time."

Eric Novod

Further Reading

Bowman, Rob. *Soulsville, U.S.A.: The History of Stax Records*. New York: Schirmer Books, 2003. A comprehensive history of Stax Records, with many references to Redding and interviews with essential Stax role players.

Brown, Geoff. *Otis Redding: Try a Little Tenderness*. Edinburgh: Canongate Books, 2001. In-depth discussions with Stax musicians, including firsthand accounts of interaction with Redding.

Freeman, Scott. *Otis! The Otis Redding Story*. New York: St. Martin's Press, 2002. Comprehensive biography of the singer.

Guralnick, Peter. *Sweet Soul Music: Rhythm and Blues and the Southern Dream of Freedom*. New York: HarperCollins, 1986. A chapter dedicated to Redding places him within the context of soul music in the American South.

Mayes, Elaine. *It Happened in Monterey: Modern Rock's Defining Moment*. Culver City, Calif.: Britannia Press, 2002. A book on the 1967 Monterey Pop Festival written by a reporter who covered it. Includes discussions of Redding, reflecting other musicians' interest in seeing him perform.

See also: Brown, James; Burke, Solomon; Cooke, Sam; Domino, Fats; Franklin, Aretha; Gibb, Barry, Maurice, and Robin; Jagger, Sir Mick; King, B. B.; Little Richard; Pickett, Wilson; Seger, Bob.

Jimmy Reed

American blues singer-songwriter

Reed was one of the leaders of the post-World War II electric blues movement.

Born: September 6, 1925; Dunleith, Mississippi
Died: August 29, 1976; Oakland, California
Also known as: Mathis James Reed (full name)

Principal recordings

ALBUMS: *I'm Jimmy Reed*, 1958; *Found Love*, 1959; *Rockin' with Reed*, 1959; *Now Appearing*, 1960; *Jimmy Reed at Carnegie Hall*, 1961; *Just Jimmy Reed*, 1962; *Wailin' the Blues*, 1962; *Jimmy Reed Plays Twelve String Guitar Blues*, 1963; *Jimmy Reed Sings the Best of the Blues*, 1963; *T'Ain't No Big Thing but He Is . . . Jimmy Reed*, 1963; *Jimmy Reed at Soul City*, 1964; *I'm the Man (Down There)*, 1965; *The Legend: The Man*, 1965; *The New Jimmy Reed Album*, 1967; *Soulin'*, 1967; *I Ain't from Chicago*, 1973; *Down in Virginia*, 1974; *Something Else*, 1974; *Blues Is My Business*, 1976; *Let the Bossman Speak*, 1976; *As Jimmy Is*, 1977; *Speak the Lyrics to Me, Mama Reed*, 1993; *Funky Funky Soul*, 2001.

The Life

Jimmy Reed was born Mathis James Reed on September 6, 1925, in Dunleith, Mississippi, in the state's northwestern cotton belt. Reed was the youngest of ten children of Joseph and Virginia Reed, African American sharecroppers who later moved to Shaw. Reed learned to play the guitar from his older brother, Buddy, and Reed began playing after working in the fields with Eddie Taylor, later a member of his band. Reed also took up the harmonica, learning to imitate Sonny Boy Williamson's "Good Morning, Little School Girl."

Looking for more opportunities, seventeen-year-old Reed moved to Chicago, working as a laborer in a coal factory until he was drafted into the armed services in 1943. After basic training with the Navy, Reed contracted the measles, so he could not be shipped overseas. When he was discharged from the service, Reed married Mary Lee Davis, from Lambert, Mississippi, on May 26, 1945.

While working at a steel mill and at an iron foundry, Reed played on street corners before becoming a backup guitarist at Club Jamboree, where he was reunited with Taylor. Rejected by Chess Records, he was signed by Vivian Carter and Jimmy Bracken of Vee-Jay Records in Gary, Indiana, in 1953. With backing by guitar great Albert King on drums, "High and Lonesome" and "Roll and Rhumba" were released as a single, but the record did not sell well. Vee-Jay gave Reed one more chance, and the result, "You Don't Have to Go," entered the *Billboard* rhythm-and-blues Top 10 chart. More hits, including "Ain't That Loving You, Baby," followed. From 1955 to 1962, Reed had more songs on the charts than any other blues musician.

Life on the road meant neglecting his family, and his drinking increased. What was initially diagnosed as delirium tremens was eventually discovered to be epilepsy. Because his drinking affected his memory, his wife began attending recording sessions to remind her husband of the lyrics. She can be heard singing in the background on many recordings.

Until Vee-Jay filed for bankruptcy in 1966, Reed continued turning out hits, including "Baby, What You Want Me to Do," "Big Boss Man," and "Bright Lights, Big City." His subsequent work for ABC-Bluesway was less successful. He entered a veterans' hospital in Downey, Illinois, in 1969, but he returned to recording in the 1970's. On August 29, 1976, in Oakland, California, after performing in San Francisco the night before, he experienced an epileptic seizure in his sleep, and he died of respiratory failure. At his funeral in Worth, Illinois, the honorary pallbearers included Muhammad Ali, Bobby "Blue" Bland, John Lee Hooker, B. B. King, and Muddy Waters.

The Music

Lyrics. Like most traditional blues performers, Reed kept his lyrics simple and concise. The repetitiveness of the lyrics is mirrored in the steady rhythm of the melody, with guitars and drums playing softly. Taylor played lead guitar on most Reed recordings, with Reed providing rhythm on both electric and acoustic guitars. The style is often referred to as walking blues, with a strong backbeat that makes the music highly accessible.

Voice. This basic smoothness of the song is often broken by the high-pitched squeal of Reed's harmonica and vocals. Reed sings in a whining, nasal voice, but he frequently varies the tone with a yelp or a shout, seemingly in imitation of the pitch and the range of the harmonica. His singing has also been described as lazy and slurred, with many lines ending in an almost indecipherable mumble. Although most of his music sounds much the same, with the tempo increased or slowed, there are often odd variations or embellishments. For example, in "Little Rain" he taps his feet to mimic the sound of raindrops hitting pavement.

Adult Themes. In the 1950's—when most popular tunes dealt with teenagers, cars, and dancing—Reed addressed adult concerns, mainly the pains of love and the consequences of adultery. In "Honest I Do," one of his most mournful songs, he asks for forgiveness without ever explaining what he has done wrong. The speakers in his songs are constantly tormented by romantic alienation, as he relates in one of his most tender ballads, "Blue, Blue Water." At their best, Reed's lyrics express an agonized sincerity.

Albums. Reed's most significant album is *Jimmy Reed at Carnegie Hall*. Not actually a live recording, it re-creates the eleven songs, most previously recorded, he performed at the legendary theater on May 13, 1961, sharing the stage with Waters and other blues musicians. This album and *The Best of Jimmy Reed* feature all of his best-known songs. His most unusual recording is *Jimmy Reed Sings the Best of the Blues*. Though Reed disliked performing songs written by others, partly because of his difficulty in remembering lyrics, Vee-Jay pressured him into recording eleven blues standards. Though some Reed purists dislike the result, the singer bends such classics as "St. Louis Blues" and "Outskirts of Town" into his distinctive style. "Trouble in Mind" was noted for its plaintive sound.

Musical Legacy

Reed's music was likely the first blues experienced by many white Americans in the 1950's and 1960's, and he reached more white listeners than any other blues performer. Some have argued that Reed's popularity helped make some Southern whites more receptive to the changes brought about during the civil rights era. His style influenced numerous white performers, including Elvis Presley, Bob Dylan, Van Morrison, and Neil Young.

Reed's songs have been recorded by such diverse performers as Aerosmith, Count Basie, Eric Clapton, Dion, the Everly Brothers, Bryan Ferry, Aretha Franklin, the Grateful Dead, John Hammond, Etta James, Jerry Lee Lewis, Taj Mahal, Delbert McClinton, Clyde McPhatter, Tom Petty, the Righteous Brothers, the Steve Miller Band, and Koko Taylor. Presley performed "Big Boss Man" and "Baby, What You Want Me to Do" on his 1968 comeback television special.

Reed's influence even extends to literature and film. Austrian novelist Peter Handke's *Die linkshändige Frau* (1976; *The Left-Handed Woman*) takes its title from a Reed song, as does Jay McInerney's book *Bright Lights, Big City* (1984). Reed's tunes can be heard in the 1988 film adapation of McInerney's book, as well as in such films as *Diner* (1982), *The Year of Living Dangerously* (1982), *Gross Pointe Blank* (1997), *Divine Secrets of the Ya-Ya Sisterhood* (2002), *Sweet Home Alabama* (2002), *All the King's Men* (2006), and *The Pursuit of Happyness* (2006).

Michael Adams

Further Reading

Forte, Dan. "Jimmy Reed." In *Blues Guitar: The Men Who Made the Music*. Edited by Jas Obrecht. San Francisco: GPI, 1990. In an interview done two months before his death, Reed gives an overview of his life and his career. His details conflict with reports from other sources.

O'Neal, Jim, and Amy van Singel. "Jimmy Reed." In *The Voice of the Blues: Classic Interviews from Living Blues Magazine*, edited by Jim O'Neal and Amy van Singel. New York: Routledge, 2002. This extensive interview was conducted in 1975, and it offers details about Reed's songs and recording sessions and difficulties he faced in collecting royalties.

Patoski, Joe Nick. "Jimmy Reed: Emancipation of the South—an Oral History." *Blues Access* 24 (Summer, 2000): 42-51. Five white musicians share their memories of Reed's impact on music in the 1950's.

Romano, Will. *Big Boss Man: The Life and Music of Bluesman Jimmy Reed*. San Francisco: Backbeat, 2006. This complete source includes an analysis

of Reed's music combined with a biography drawn from recollections of family members and fellow musicians.

See also: Dylan, Bob; Hooker, John Lee; Jagger, Sir Mick; James, Etta; King, Albert; Morrison, Van; Presley, Elvis; Waters, Muddy; Williamson, Sonny Boy, I; Young, Neil.

Lou Reed
American rock singer, guitarist, and songwriter

An early punk-rock pioneer, singer-songwriter Reed is recognized as a major influence on alternative music. He is known for focusing on the seamier aspects of life, highlighting such counterculture subjects as drug addiction and marginal lifestyles, and introducing innovative guitar techniques such as distortion and feedback.

Born: March 2, 1942; Brooklyn, New York
Also known as: Louis Alan Reed (full name); Lewis Allan Rabinowitz (birth name)
Member of: The Velvet Underground

Principal recordings

ALBUMS (solo): *Lou Reed*, 1972; *Berlin*, 1973; *Transformer*, 1973; *Sally Can't Dance*, 1974; *Metal Machine Music*, 1975; *Coney Island Baby*, 1976; *Rock and Roll Heart*, 1976; *Street Hassle*, 1978; *The Bells*, 1979; *Growing Up in Public*, 1980; *Rock and Roll Diary, 1967-1980*, 1980; *The Blue Mask*, 1982; *Legendary Hearts*, 1983; *New Sensations*, 1984; *Mistrial*, 1986; *New York*, 1989; *Songs for Drella*, 1990 (with John Cale); *Magic and Loss*, 1992; *Set the Twilight Reeling*, 1996; *Ecstasy*, 2000; *The Raven*, 2003; *Hudson River Wind Meditations*, 2007.

ALBUMS (with the Velvet Underground): *The Velvet Underground and Nico*, 1967 (with Nico); *White Light/White Heat*, 1967; *VU*, recorded 1968-1969, released 1985; *Another View*, recorded 1968-1969, released 1986; *The Velvet Underground*, 1969; *Loaded*, 1970.

The Life

Louis Alan Reed was born into a middle-class Jewish family as Lewis Allan Rabinowitz on March 2, 1942, in Brooklyn, New York, the only child of accountant Sidney Joseph and Toby (Futterman) Rabinowitz. A rebel who adopted unconventional attitudes and displayed sexual ambiguity from an early age, Reed in his teens was forced to undergo electroshock therapy in a mental institution, aimed at curing him of homosexual tendencies.

Influenced by rhythm and blues and rock and roll, Reed played with a number of bands as a teen. After high school, he attended Syracuse University. There, his mentor, the poet Delmore Schwartz, persuaded Reed to write in the vernacular. Following graduation in 1965, Reed returned to New York City, becoming a songwriter for Pickwick Records, where he joined fellow employee John Cale and other musicians to form an experimental band. Operating under a variety of names—Warlocks, Primitives, and Falling Spikes—the group eventually coalesced as the Velvet Underground. While performing dark, unconventional music at local clubs, the band was noticed by artist Andy Warhol, who became the group's manager. Reed was with the Velvet Underground from 1965 to 1970. During that time they released several albums, which gained the group a cult following but little commercial success, before Reed left to create a solo career.

Reed, who was briefly married in the early 1970's, fared better as a soloist. *Transformer* and *New York* were certified gold albums, and he had several hits, but much of Reed's recorded work (nearly thirty studio and live albums), though critically lauded, received mixed commercial notice because of the artist's mercurial personality and the unconventional nature of his music. Reed married for a second time to Sylvia Morales; they divorced in 1994. In 1995 he settled down with alternative musician and performance artist Laurie Anderson, and they were married in 2008.

The Music

The Velvet Underground. Formed in New York in 1965, Lou Reed and his Velvet Underground became countercultural icons after Warhol made them part of his Exploding Plastic Inevitable multimedia performance. The group's debut album, *The Velvet Underground and Nico*, a critical success but a commercial failure, is credited with spawning such musical subgenres as punk, noise rock, heavy metal, gothic, and alternative rock. The album featured Reed's controversial, drug-related songs ("Heroin," "I'm Waiting for the Man") and explored other taboo topics in songs such as "Venus in Furs" (sadomasochism).

The Velvet Underground's *White Light/White Heat* was notable for distorted guitar solos and feedback on such experimental cuts as "I Heard Her Call My Name," "Lady Godiva's Operation," and the title track. The album *The Velvet Underground* signaled a radical departure from previous material, with a more pop-oriented sound, characterized by "Pale Blue Eyes" and "After Hours." Reed last performed with the Velvet Underground on *Loaded*, which produced the hits "Sweet Jane" and "Rock & Roll."

Lou Reed. (AP/Wide World Photos)

Solo Albums. Reed left the Velvet Underground in 1970 (the band continued until 1973). In 1972 he released his first solo album, *Lou Reed*, containing mostly new versions of unreleased Velvet Underground material, but it sold poorly. However, his next album, *Transformer*, yielded several hits: "Perfect Day," "Satellite of Love," and especially "Walk on the Wild Side," Reed's best-known song, that would establish him as a glam-rock star.

The concept album *Berlin* provided a stark contrast: a downbeat series of songs concerning a pair of love-struck German junkies. To match the flavor of his music, Reed adopted black leather and spiked collars, makeup and dyed hair, and gave his aggressive, hostile personality—exacerbated by extensive drug abuse—free rein. Despite his off-putting behavior, Reed's next album, the rhythm-and-blues-flavored *Sally Can't Dance*, became his most commercially successful solo release, reaching the Top 10 in the United States, with such popular tracks as "Ride Sally Ride." Continuing the up-and-down theme that would characterize his entire career, Reed's double album *Metal Machine Music* consisted solely of guitar feedback and was dismissed as noise (though later critics dubbed it a progenitor of punk and industrial rock).

Middle Period. Reed's *Coney Island Baby* returned to early Velvet Underground territory, with simple arrangements and songs dealing with street life. *Street Hassle* was Reed's contribution to the punk movement then current. *The Bells* featured a hodgepodge of diverse styles—metal, jazz, disco, rhythm and blues, and experimental. *Growing Up in Public*, *The Blue Mask*, and *Legendary Hearts* all failed to crack the Top 150 yet produced such memorable tunes as "How Do You Speak to an Angel," "The Power of Positive Drinking," and "Heavenly Arms." *New Sensations*, featuring upbeat, positive songs such as "Turn to Me," made it to number fifty-four on American charts, and the next two albums, *Mistrial* and *New York*—which was certified gold—charted even higher.

Later Works. *Set the Twilight Reeling* produced such upbeat numbers as "NYC Man" and the title track. *Ecstasy* illustrated the singer's considerable energy across a range of styles, from the sarcastic "Future Farmers of America" to the distortion-laden "Big Sky." *Hudson River Wind Meditations* was a surprise from an artist who has made a career of doing the unexpected: a collection of soothing electronic sounds intended to relax the listener.

Musical Legacy

Singer, songwriter, poet, and photographer, Reed has wielded considerable influence upon rock music since the mid-1960's. An inspiration to a variety of alternative genres, Reed, both as a member of Velvet Underground and as a soloist, is considered a pioneer in several key aspects of contemporary music. As a lyricist, he was one of the first to write about subjects that had seldom been explored—including drug abuse and alternative sexuality. As a musician, he was an early experimenter with nonstandard tunings, feedback, high volume, and other technical innovations, and he continues to be an inventive composer, mingling diverse threads from various musical traditions—rock, folk, soul, and classical—to create new and different sounds. As a performer, he was an early advocate of the use of makeup, nail polish, and other accoutrements intended to enhance his visual stage presence.

Though not to everyone's taste, Reed achieved a measure of critical acclaim, in the form of gold records, Grammy Awards, induction into the Rock and Roll Hall of Fame, the Hero Award from the National Academy of Recording Arts and Sciences, and other honors.

Jack Ewing

Further Reading

Bockris, Victor. *Transformer: The Lou Reed Story*. New York: Da Capo Press, 1997. The biographer of Warhol and other controversial figures provides an intimate portrait of Lou Reed.

Johnstone, Nick. *Lou Reed Talking*. London: Omnibus Press, 2006. A chronicle of Reed's life and career, in his own words.

Reed, Lou. *Lou Reed's New York*. New York: Steidl/Edition 71, 2006. A collection of photographic images demonstrating Reed's later incarnation as a visual artist.

Roberts, Chris, and Lou Reed. *Walk on the Wild Side: The Stories Behind the Songs*. Milwaukee, Wis.: Hal Leonard, 2004. This book examines the lyrics and the inspirations to Reed's songs.

Witts, Richard. *The Velvet Underground*. Bloomington: Indiana University Press, 2006. Written by a university lecturer, this book deals with the milieu and the lasting influence of the ultimate New York band.

See also: Anderson, Laurie; Blades, Rubén; Bowie, David; Springsteen, Bruce; Vega, Suzanne.

Steve Reich

American classical composer

One of the first composers associated with minimalism, Reich paved a new road in musical experimentation, bridging the acoustic and electronic worlds and Western and non-Western music.

Born: October 3, 1936; New York, New York
Also known as: Stephen Michael Reich (full name)

Principal works

CHORAL WORKS: *Tehillim*, 1981, revised 1982 (for voices and ensemble); *The Desert Music*, 1984, revised 1986 (text by William Carlos Williams; for chorus and orchestra); *The Cave*, 1993 (with Beryl Korot; for four voices, ensemble, and video); *Three Tales*, 2002 (with Korot; for video projector, five voices, and ensemble); *You Are*, 2004 (for voices and chamber orchestra).

EXPERIMENTAL WORKS: *Pitch Charts*, 1963; *The Plastic Haircut*, 1963 (sound track; for tape); *Livelihood*, 1964 (for tape); *It's Gonna Rain*, 1965 (for tape); *Come Out*, 1966 (for tape); *Violin Phase*, 1967 (for violin and tape); *Vermont Counterpoint*, 1982; *New York Counterpoint*, 1985; *Electric Counterpoint*, 1987; *Different Trains*, 1988 (for string quartet and tape).

ORCHESTRAL WORKS: *Drumming*, 1971 (for nine percussions and two female voices); *Music for Eighteen Musicians*, 1976; *Octet*, 1979 (revised as *Eight Lines*, 1983); *Variations for Winds, Strings, and Keyboards*, 1980.

PIANO WORKS: *Piano Phase*, 1967 (for two pianos and two marimbas); *Six Pianos*, 1973 (revised as *Six Marimbas*, 1986).

The Life

Stephen Michael Reich (rik) was born in New York City to relatively wealthy parents Leonard and June (Carroll) Reich. June was a Broadway singer and lyricist noted for "Love Is a Simple Thing." His parents divorced as Reich neared his first birthday, and for the next several years, he shuttled between his father's apartment in Manhattan and his mother's house in Los Angeles. The cross-country train rides, spent in the company of his governess Virginia Mitchell, would later inspire his *Different Trains*.

Reich began piano lessons at age seven, but he felt that he was being indoctrinated in "middle-class favorites" such as Ludwig van Beethoven, Franz Schubert, and Richard Wagner, and his ultimate disinterest led him to quit lessons at age ten.

Reich found most of his musical inspiration in jazz and in the works of Johann Sebastian Bach and Igor Stravinsky. Intrigued by the rhythmic aspects he found in these, he began percussion lessons at age fourteen.

Reich entered Cornell University in 1953, where he majored in philosophy; his thesis focused on the work of Ludwig Wittgenstein. While at Cornell, Reich attended music history classes with musicologist William Austin, who shared musical interests with Reich. After graduating from Cornell, Reich studied at the Juilliard School with William Bergsma and Vincent Persichetti; among his classmates was fellow minimalist Philip Glass, though the two did not interact significantly.

Reich aborted a last-minute a plan to pursue a graduate degree in philosophy at Harvard University, choosing instead to move to California to further his study of composition. He nearly became a classmate of La Monte Young and Terry Riley at the University of California at Berkeley, but he ultimately chose to attend Mills College in Oakland to study with Luciano Berio and, for a short time, Darius Milhaud. Like many academics around the country, Berio espoused the twelve-tone system, and he used it as the basis for many lessons. The rebellious Reich decided to take a new approach to serialism by writing twelve-tone pieces without using the variations of inversions, retrogrades, and transpositions; this lack of alterations was an early indicator of the repetition to come in Reich's future works.

In 1961 Reich married Joyce Barkett, and they had a child who died in infancy. They divorced in 1963. In 1976 Reich married Beryl Korot, a visual artist who specializes in multichannel video, and they had a son, Ezra, born in 1978.

The Music

Reich's music is noted for, among other characteristics, explorations of gradual processes within music, primarily through the use of phasing techniques and, to a lesser degree, additive rhythms. Like Riley, Reich worked for a time at the San Francisco Tape Music Center, and he began his own experiments with tape loops, writing such works as *Livelihood* and scoring filmmaker Robert Nelson's *The Plastic Haircut* (1963). Though fascinated by the options that tape presented, he still desired to offer live performances, and he believed that a composer should play in his ensemble. During his last months at Mills College, Reich formed an improvisational group, consisting of violin, cello, saxophone, piano, and himself on drums. Unfortunately, improvisation was not the group's strong point, and Reich quickly realized that he had to offer them something more controlled. He wrote *Pitch Charts*, which specifies the pitches the performers are to use but not the rhythms. Reich's ensemble continued to perform his music at San Francisco Mime Troupe shows. During one of these shows, in autumn of 1964, Riley was in the audience, and he got up and left, claiming Reich's music was "too self-indulgent." Aware that Riley had left the show before it ended, Reich went to Riley's home the next day to confront him. In the course of the conversation, Riley showed Reich the score to *In C*, and Reich was instantly impressed, even offering Riley the use of his performing ensemble to help premiere the piece. Reich's belief that a clear tonal center and consistent pulse could be used as the cornerstone for new music was reinforced, and he was also made aware of what could be done through the use of compositional loops. Especially interesting to Reich was the aspect of phasing, where members of the ensemble would begin together but slip out of sync as the piece progressed.

It's Gonna Rain. Wanting to combine the use of loops with electronic tape, Reich recorded a young black preacher in San Francisco, Brother Walter, making two identical loops of a portion of his

Steve Reich. (AP/Wide World Photos)

speech. He played them back on separate machines, the two loops persistently repeating the same phrase but gradually falling out of phase. The resulting piece was *It's Gonna Rain*, which ultimately encompassed eight layers of the same portion of the speech.

Piano Phase. Invigorated by the techniques he discovered while writing *It's Gonna Rain* and the similarly constructed *Come Out*, Reich extended the phasing possibilities of tape loops to live performance. *Piano Phase* was the first of these endeavors. Written for piano duet, the piece begins with both players in unison. At specified points, the second pianist gradually increases his tempo until he realigns rhythmically with the first pianist, though now the two are out of sync pitchwise. This phasing and realigning continues in a cyclical fashion until the two players have returned to a true unison. Out of this juxtaposition of identical lines comes what Reich has termed resulting patterns, hidden material that appears as a result of the phasing process. Different listeners may identify different resulting patterns, giving pieces such as *Piano Phase* and *Violin Phase* a rather subjective quality.

Drumming. Reich's combined interest in percussion and non-Western music led him to spend several weeks studying African drumming at the University of Ghana in Accra. *Drumming* reflects the techniques Reich absorbed there, and it also represents a turning point in his musical style. It is the last piece to use phasing, and the first to explore differences of timbre within a work. Its score includes four pairs of tuned bongos, three marimbas, three glockenspiels, two female voices, whistling, and piccolo. The voices perform textless material and are treated more as instruments, supplementing the tone color of the marimbas and glockenspiels.

Tehillim. In the late 1970's, Reich felt a compulsion to reconnect with his Jewish heritage, and he began to study Hebrew, the Torah, and Hebraic cantillation. Fascinated by the melodic nature of Hebrew, Reich travelled to Israel to hear cantors steeped in the centuries-old tradition. Upon his return, he began settings of Psalms 18, 19, 34, and 150, collected under the title *Tehillim*. Completed and first performed in 1981, *Tehillim* builds on the increased instrumentation introduced in *Drumming*: clarinets, strings, mallet percussion, female voices, electric organ, and other percussive sounds called for in the scripture (tambourines without jingles, maracas, hand-clapping, and miniature cymbals). *Tehillim* exhibits Reich's interest in counterpoint, and it points toward his series of pieces using this technique: *Vermont Counterpoint*, *New York Counterpoint*, and *Electric Counterpoint*.

Different Trains. Another outgrowth of his study of Judaism led Reich to reflect on his childhood train journeys during the late 1930's and early 1940's. He recognized that train rides for European Jews during this same time had different results, and he was inspired to compose *Different Trains*, scored for string quartet and tape. The voices on the tapes include his governess, a retired train porter, and a handful of Holocaust survivors; and train noises, such as whistles, are also present. The three sections of the piece depict the different natures of rail travel: "America: Before the War"; "Europe: During the War"; and "America: After the War."

Musical Legacy

Reich's music made its mark on his minimalist contemporaries, Riley, Young, and Glass, just as their music impacted Reich. Though the four had different approaches to the broad concept of minimalism, their paths crossed in such a way that they absorbed one another's ideas. Reich's transference of concepts initially associated with electronic media to live performance broadened the vocabulary of composers writing for traditional instruments, and it influenced the practice of sampling, where electronic and live media come together. Later performers, such as Brian Eno, Mike Oldfield, and David Bowie, have made use of techniques developed by Reich. In addition, Reich's use of speech as melodic material (such as in *Different Trains*) has been used in some form by composers such as Scott Johnson and John Adams.

The incorporation of non-Western musics cannot be underestimated, and though Reich was not alone in this juxtaposition of cultures, scholars such as Keith Potter credit Reich as having more influence in this manner than his contemporaries. Likely, this is because of Reich's ability to blend non-Western techniques in such a way that the resulting product works within the Western aesthetic while expanding those aesthetic limits.

Phillip J. Klepacki

Further Reading

Duckworth, William. *Talking Music: Conversations with John Cage, Philip Glass, Laurie Anderson, and Five Generations of American Experimental Composers*. New York: Schirmer Books, 1995. Duckworth interviews Reich (and others) about his influences, his inspirations, and his compositional processes.

Hoek, D. J. *Steve Reich: A Bio-Bibliography*. Westport, Conn.: Greenwood Press, 2002. Hoek provides a periodized biography, a listing of works with premiere dates, and an extensive discography and bibliography.

Mertens, Wim. *American Minimal Music: La Monte Young, Terry Riley, Steve Reich, Philip Glass*. London: Kahn & Averill, 1983. This book opens with discussion of the life and works of the composers, and it devotes significant space to the development of minimalism and its aesthetic and ideological implications.

Potter, Keith. *Four Musical Minimalists: La Monte Young, Terry Riley, Steve Reich, Philip Glass.* Cambridge, England: Cambridge University Press, 2000. Potter gives a detailed account of the lives and works of the four stalwarts of minimalism and how they interacted. Includes a selective discography and bibliography of the works presented within the text.

Reich, Steve. *Writings on Music: 1965-2000.* Oxford, England: Oxford University Press, 2002. A collection of Reich's program notes and thoughts on his works and creative process, laid out chronologically, help trace the evolution of his style.

Schwarz, K. Robert. *Minimalists.* London: Phaidon Press, 1996. Schwarz gives a detailed discussion of the life and works of prominent minimalist composers, and he traces the development of the style in postminimalist composers such as John Adams and Arvo Pärt. Includes a categorized works list, selective discography, and suggestions for further reading.

Strickland, Edward. *American Composers: Dialogues on Contemporary Music.* Bloomington: Indiana University Press, 1991. Strickland's volume presents interviews with eleven contemporary composers (including all four of the pioneering minimalist composers). Includes index and brief bibliography.

White, Robin. *Steve Reich.* Oakland, Calif.: Crown Point Press, 1978. An interview with Reich focuses primarily on his early musical study and influences, as well as a discussion of some of his early-period works.

See also: Adams, John; Berio, Luciano; Bowie, David; Eno, Brian; Glass, Philip; Ligeti, György; Metheny, Pat; Milhaud, Darius; Oliveros, Pauline; Ravel, Maurice; Stravinsky, Igor; Thomas, Michael Tilson; Wolfe, Julia.

Django Reinhardt
Belgian jazz and film-score composer and guitarist

Known for his dazzling guitar playing, Reinhardt popularized Gypsy swing, usually played by a small ensemble of lead guitar, violin, several strong percussive rhythm guitars, and a stand-up acoustic bass.

Born: January 23, 1910; Liberchies, Belgium
Died: May 16, 1953; Fontainebleau, France
Also known as: Django Jean Baptiste Reinhardt (full name)
Member of: Quintet of the Hot Club of France

Principal works
FILM SCORE: *Le Village de la colère,* 1946 (with André Hodeir).

Principal recordings
ALBUMS (solo): *Paris 1945,* 1945; *Swing de Paris,* 1947; *At Club Saint Germain,* 1951; *Django Reinhardt and Stéphane Grappelli,* recorded 1953, released 1990; *Django Reinhardt et ses rythmes,* 1953; *The Great Artistry of Django Reinhardt,* 1954; *Django's Guitar,* 1955; *Django Reinhardt and His Rhythm,* 1959.

ALBUMS (with Quintet of the Hot Club of France): *Lady Be Good,* 1934; *Djangology,* 1935; *The Sheik of Araby,* 1937; *Tears,* 1937; *Nuages,* 1940; *Django Reinhardt and the Hot Club Quintet,* 1951.

The Life
Django Jean Baptiste Reinhardt (JAN-goh RIN-hahrt) was born in a Gypsy caravan that was wintering outside a small Belgian village in 1910. His father, Jean-Eugène, was a basket maker, an acrobat, and a musician. His mother, La Belle Laurence "Négros," was a jeweler and a dancer. Like many itinerant Gypsies, they were also entertainers.

Jean-Eugène and Négros were Manouche (French-speaking) Romany Gypsies, a stateless people who had roamed Western Europe and the Mediterranean area, traveling in clan-centered troupes for hundreds of years. Though given the name Jean by a Belgian official—because Gypsies needed a Christian name for registration—Reinhardt was most proud of his Gypsy moniker Django (meaning "I awake"). In spite of all his later international fame and success, Reinhardt remained a Gypsy at heart, maintaining Romany values and practices until he died.

Reinhardt showed great musical talent as a child, and he played banjo in Gypsy groups performing in cafés, bars, and dance halls in central France and Paris when he was twelve. By the time he was eighteen, he was a noted banjo virtuoso, and he was composing (recording at least four of his waltzes). Around 1928, Reinhardt discovered an exotic sound: African American jazz, which was being played in Paris nightclubs, a legacy of American soldiers who had come to France during World War I. Reinhardt decided this would be his music and the guitar would be his instrument.

Tragedy soon struck. When he entered his caravan trailer after finishing a show, a fire started, and Reinhardt was almost killed. Though he eventually recovered, his left hand was paralyzed by the burns. On his nineteenth birthday, he underwent an operation to save his hand, although it was only a partial success. Reinhardt retained the complete use of only his first two fingers. He had painstakingly to relearn to play the guitar, accommodating for his handicap.

Nevertheless, Reinhardt continued to perfect his version of jazz. He did this with the help of some talented collaborators, especially violinist Stéphane Grappelli, with whom he played from 1934 until the start of World War II. Though popular in the Parisian nightclubs and cabarets, Reinhardt and Grappelli were superstars in Great Britain. They were on their second English tour when World War II broke out in September, 1939. Grappelli remained in England for the war's duration, while Reinhardt went back to France, enjoying tremendous popularity on the Continent.

After the war, Reinhardt's international fame continued to rise as he moved toward the typical big band sounds of the day, and he began playing with American musicians. After a productive recording period in 1947, he became withdrawn and sullen.

He retired with his family in 1951. On the morning of May 16, 1953, Reinhardt died while having a cup of tea with friends.

The Music

Reinhardt recorded one thousand songs in a career that spanned from 1928 to 1953. More than for his instrumental virtuosity, however, he is best known for blending several musical styles—American jazz, French popular and musette dance music, and Gypsy melodies and ornamentation—into a new art form: Gypsy swing.

"Boléro." In 1934 Reinhardt and Grappelli formed the defining Gypsy jazz group of the prewar era, the Quintet of the Hot Club of France. Named for a Paris jazz nightclub, the group was unusual for its day because it was basically a string band. At a time when American jazz ensembles were dominated by horns, winds, pianos, and drums, this was a jazz group of relative simplicity: guitars, violin, and bass. Reinhardt's solos on his

Django Reinhardt. (Hulton Archive/Getty Images)

loud Selmer Maccaferri guitar were marked by sweet, lyrical melodies and by sporadic flamboyant improvisations. The intermixing of Grappelli's and Reinhardt's leads were flawless, and the bold rhythm section of two pulsating guitars gave the quintet as much swing as anything heard in Europe until that time.

In 1937 Reinhardt and Grappelli recorded "Boléro," an ambitious composition inspired by the Duke Ellington big band and Maurice Ravel's famous classical piece of the same name. It has been called a jazz concerto in miniature, and it was one of the most complex jazz tunes of its day. Reinhardt's flamencolike guitar riffs display his Gypsy roots and his deep expression of the jazz idiom.

"Nuages." Though branded as decadent by Germany's Nazi Party, jazz continued to be played in various places in occupied Europe during World War II. This was especially true in the entertainment districts of Paris. In spite of possible persecution because of his Gypsy roots, Reinhardt remained in France throughout the war, and he even opened his own club. At the height of his popularity, Reinhardt was never bothered by the German authorities. He recorded some forty records in spite of wartime shortages. In December, 1940, he recorded "Nuages" (clouds), probably his masterpiece and most well-known song. A beautiful, Impressionistic, and tranquil song—different from the frenzied, almost martial, flavor of much of hot jazz in occupied Europe—it became an immediate hit.

"Minor Swing." After the war, in October, 1946, Reinhardt traveled to the United States, where he toured with Ellington and played in New York's Carnegie Hall. Suffering from disenchantment with America and extreme homesickness, he returned to France in February, 1947. However, he absorbed much of modern American jazz and bebop, making these part of his repertoire.

In 1947 and 1949, Reinhardt took all these influences and recorded "Minor Swing," perhaps second only to "Nuages" as a Gypsy jazz signature song. Originally written and recorded with Grappelli and the Quintet of the Hot Club of France in 1937, it is an almost themeless sixteen-bar blues progression, and the soloist has a chance to improvise on the interlocking lines of all the stringed instruments, creating exciting harmonies and rhythms.

Musical Legacy

Reinhardt composed more than one hundred songs, some of which have now become part of the jazz canon. He was one of the first guitarists to demonstrate that the instrument could be a solo voice in a jazz band, rather than just a rhythm accompaniment. He also showed that Europeans could play jazz—and as creatively as Americans, bringing their own influences and sensibilities. In this way, he helped make jazz a truly international music. Indeed, the highest awards given to a European jazz musician—the Golden Django and Eurodjango—are named in his honor. Reinhardt will perhaps best be known for creating a new kind of jazz: Gypsy swing, a tradition that thrives on both sides of the Atlantic.

James Stanlaw

Further Reading

Charupakorn, Joe. *The Best of Django Reinhardt: A Step-by-Step Breakdown of the Guitar Styles and Techniques of a Jazz Giant.* Milwaukee, Wis.: Hal Leonard, 2003. The resource has one hundred pages of transcriptions and musical analyses of Reinhardt songs. It is mostly for musicians, but it also contains materials and photographs of general interest.

Delaunay, Charles. *Django Reinhardt.* Milwaukee, Wis.: Hal Leonard, 1993. A translation of the original standard biography from the 1960's by one of the men who discovered and managed Reinhardt and the Hot Club of France in the 1930's.

Dregni, Michael. *Django: The Life and Music of a Gypsy Legend.* New York: Oxford University Press, 2004. A thorough and reliable biography by an authoritative Reinhardt scholar.

_____. *Gypsy Jazz: In Search of Django Reinhardt and the Soul of Gypsy Swing.* New York: Oxford University Press, 2008. A revealing history of Reinhardt's style of jazz as played on both sides of the Atlantic, focusing on Gypsy music, history, and culture.

Dregni, Michael, Alain Antonietto, and Anne Legrand. *Django Reinhardt and the Illustrated History of Gypsy Jazz.* Denver, Colo.: Speck Press, 2006. More than two hundred illustrations chronicle the history of Gypsy jazz and Reinhardt's contributions to the genre.

Vernon, Paul. *"Django" Reinhardt: A Contextual Bio-Discography 1910-1953*. Burlington, Vt.: Ashgate, 2003. A complete source of information on Reinhardt recordings, including excerpts from letters, reviews, and newspaper articles.

See also: Christian, Charlie; Ellington, Duke; Grappelli, Stéphane; Hawkins, Coleman; Johnson, Lonnie; Lewis, John; Ravel, Maurice.

Ottorino Respighi

Italian classical composer

The most successful Italian composer of his day, Respighi was noted for his orchestral writing and use of tone color. His compositions ranged from short songs and chamber pieces to lengthy operas, ballets, and orchestral works.

Born: July 9, 1879; Bologna, Italy
Died: April 18, 1936; Rome, Italy

Principal works

BALLETS (music): *La boutique fantasque*, 1918 (choreographed by Léonide Massine); *Sèvres de la vieille France*, 1920 (choreographed by Illeana Leonidova); *La pentola magica*, 1920 (choreographed by Leonidova); *La pirrica*, 1920 (choreographed by Leonidova); *Fantasia indiana*, 1920 (choreographed by Leonidova); *Canzoni arabe*, 1920 (choreographed by Leonidova); *L'autunno*, 1920 (choreographed by Leonidova); *Fiori di mandorlo*, 1920 (choreographed by Leonidova); *Belkis, regina di Saba*, 1932 (choreographed by Massine).

CHAMBER WORKS: *Sei pezzi*, 1905; *Cinque pezzi*, 1906; Violin Sonata in B Minor, 1917.

OPERAS (music): *Re Enzo*, 1905 (libretto by Alberto Donini); *Semirâma*, 1910 (libretto by Alessandro Cerè); *La bella dormente nel bosco*, 1922 (libretto by Gian Bistolfi); *Belfagor*, 1923 (libretto by Claudio Guastalla); *La campana sommersa*, 1927 (libretto by Guastalla); *Maria egiziaca*, 1932 (libretto by Guastalla); *La fiamma*, 1934 (libretto by Guastalla); *Lucrezia*, 1937 (libretto by Guastalla); *Marie Victoire*, 2004 (libretto by Edmond Guiraud).

ORCHESTRAL WORKS: *Burlesca*, 1906; *Antiche danze et arie per liuto, Suite No. 1*, 1917; *Fontane di Roma, Suite No. 1*, 1917; *Adagio don variazoni*, 1921; *Concerto gregoriano*, 1921; *Antiche danze et arie per liuto, Suite No. 2*, 1923; *Fontane di Roma, Suite No. 2*, 1924; *I pini de Roma*, 1924; *Poema autunnale*, 1925; *Vetrate di chiesa*, 1926; *Fontane di Roma, Suite No. 3*, 1928; *Gli uccelli*, 1928 (*The Birds*); *Antiche danze et arie per liuto, Suite No. 3*, 1931; *Concerto a cinque*, 1933.

PIANO WORKS: Piano Concerto in A Minor, 1901; *Fantasia slava* in G Major, 1903; *Concerto in modo misolidio*, 1925; *Toccata*, 1928.

The Life

Born in 1869 to a piano teacher, Ottorino Respighi (aht-toh-REE-nee rehs-PEE-gee) was destined for a musical life. He studied violin and piano as a boy, and from 1891 to 1901 he was a student at the Liceo Musicale in Bologna. At the Liceo Musicale, his studies included violin and viola with Federico Sarti and composition with Luigi Torchi. Other famous teachers of Respighi were Nikolay Rimsky-Korsakov and Max Bruch. He met Rimsky-Korsakov in the winters of 1900-1901 and 1902-1903, when he worked as an orchestral violist at the St. Petersburg Imperial Opera. Between 1903 and 1908, Respighi earned his living as an orchestral musician in Bologna, where he began to gain local recognition as a composer. In January of 1913, Respighi accepted a professorship at the Liceo Musicale di Santa Cecilia in Rome. He held the post for ten years, after which he was appointed director. Respighi soon resigned from this position because it left him little time to compose. However, Respighi continued to teach advanced composition at the school until 1935.

Toward the end of his life Respighi traveled widely, appearing as guest conductor and piano soloist and often accompanying singers in the performance of his works. His favorite female vocalist was his wife Elsa, whom he married on January 11, 1919. Weakened by a heart condition, Respighi died in 1936.

The Music

Respighi's musical output includes almost every genre from short vocal works to ballets, chamber music, operas, symphonic poems, and other or-

Ottorino Respighi. (© Bettmann/CORBIS)

chestral works. Although steeped in classical forms and the stylistic tendencies of Giuseppe Verdi and Richard Strauss, Respighi's music does reflect modern orchestration and colors, most likely a result of his study with Rimsky-Korsakov. His most famous compositions are the symphonic poems written after his move to Rome, which was a great center of orchestral writing at the time.

Fontane di Roma. Composed between 1914 and 1916, *Fontane di Roma* (the fountains of Rome) is a symphonic poem in four sections. Each section of the composition recalls a specific fountain: Vale Giulia at dawn, Tritone at morning, Trevi at noon, and Villa Medici at sunset. Respighi's music includes rich orchestral writing reminiscent of Maurice Ravel and Strauss, and it presents a pictorial soundscape of each Roman fountain. The work premiered in Rome on March 11, 1917, under the direction of Antonio Guarnieri and had its American debut in New York in 1919. Although it was not an immediate success in Rome, Arturo Toscanini's

performance of the work in Milan led to its international acclaim.

Concerto gregoriano. Written in 1921, the *Concerto gregoriano* is a clear example of Respighi's use of musical elements from the past. Allusions to plainchant and modal writing are heard throughout the work, and the second movement features the Easter sequence *Victimae paschali*. Its first performance in Rome met with little enthusiasm, but violinist Alexander Schmuller's performance of the work in Amsterdam and several other European cities elicited critical acclaim and audience approval. During World War I, the concerto was destroyed in the bombing of Vienna, where it had been deposited in the warehouses of Universal Edition. The firm has since reprinted the work.

I pini di Roma. Planned as a sequel to *Fontane di Roma*, *I pini di Roma* (the pines of Rome) is an orchestral showpiece with similar use of color and rich orchestral writing. Although written in the twentieth century, both works exhibit elements of Romantic orchestration and harmony. Respighi began composition of *I pini di Roma* in 1923, and the work premiered in Rome in 1924. It, too, comprises four sections: "Villa Borghese," "A Catacomb," "Janiculum," and "Appian Way."

La fiamma. Respighi's frequently performed large-scale opera, *La fiamma* (the flame), is set in Ravenna when it was an outpost of the Byzantine Empire. The heroine, Silvana, is unhappy in her marriage and falls in love with her stepson Donello. When she learns that her marriage was brought about by her mother's witchcraft, she believes that she, too, might have magical powers. Silvana bewitches Donello, and when the pair is found together, her husband Basilio drops dead. Silvana is then tried for witchcraft and murder. Based on Hans Wiers-Jenssen's play *Anne Pedersdotter* (1917), the opera premiered in Rome on January 23, 1934. Respighi's compositional style shows elements of past musical traditions. The opera is often referred to by the Romantic term melodrama, and the orchestral writing is generally subordinate to the Verdian-style vocal writing. However, Respighi does return to his usual compositional practices with the use of archaic and exotic elements that evoke the Byzantine setting.

La campana sommersa. *La campana sommersa* (the sunken bell) is an opera in four acts after

Gerhart Hauptmann's play *Die versunkene Glocke* (1900), and it was performed for the first time in Hamburg on November 18, 1927. In Hauptmann's fantasy-drama, the mortal Enrico attempts to desert his human life after he falls in love with the elf Rautendelein. However, after his wife's suicide, Enrico is consumed by guilt and rejects Rautendelein. Enrico finds that he cannot live without her, and she returns to comfort him as he dies. Respighi's use of tone color is particularly significant in this work as he depicts the fantasy world of fairies, Enrico's magic workshop on the mountain, and the toll of the sunken bell. The orchestral writing in these fantastic settings rivals that of his programmatic compositions.

Musical Legacy

Although Respighi was the most successful Italian composer of his generation, which was due in part to his relationship with Toscanini and other famous conductors, he was by no means the most original or progressive composer of his time. He often composed in the styles of his predecessors, and after the success of *Fontane di Roma*, he turned to Gregorian chant and arrangements of earlier music. In December of 1932, he signed a manifesto that attacked the prevailing modernist trends in music. Nevertheless, Respighi was an amazing orchestrator and tone poet who broke free of Italian tradition when he composed in genres other than opera. His symphonic poems became part of the standard symphonic repertoire and illustrated Respighi's gift for creating visual images of the beauty of Rome through sound.

Sandra J. Fallon

Further Reading

Barrow, Lee G. *Ottorino Respighi, 1879-1936: An Annotated Bibliography*. Lanham, Md.: Scarecrow Press, 2004. This reference work provides a list and description of all books, articles, and other published references to Respighi. The majority of items are in Italian, but the work does contain a few English-language books and a number of English-language concert reviews. Includes a discography and an index of compositions.

Hess, Nathan Andrew. *Eclecticism in the Piano Works of Ottorino Respighi*. Ann Arbor, Mich.: University Microfilms International, 2005. Hess discusses Respighi's significant solo piano works, his two periods of piano composition, his attraction to the music of the past, and the influence of other composers on his works. Includes musical examples.

Pierluigi, Alverà, and Arturo Rietti. *Portraits of Greatness: Respighi*. Translated by Raymond Rosenthal. New York: Treves, 1986. This short biography contains historical information and illustrations.

Respighi, Elsa. *Fifty Years of a Life in Music, 1905-1955*. Translated by Giovanni Fontecchio and Roger Johnson. Lewiston, N.Y.: Edwin Mellen Press, 1993. Respighi's wife provides a biography of her life with Respighi and discusses his travels, his compositions, and his relationships with other musicians. Includes illustrations.

Sachs, Harvey. *Music in Fascist Italy*. New York: W. W. Norton, 1988. In his discussion of the musical climate in Fascist Italy, Sachs makes numerous references to Respighi and helps the reader understand the environment in which he composed.

See also: Chung, Kyung-Wha; Ravel, Maurice; Rota, Nino; Strauss, Richard.

Silvestre Revueltas

Mexican classical composer

A volatile musical force, Revueltas composed music that is polytonal, highly rhythmic, and influenced by popular music idioms as well as indigenous folkloric elements.

Born: December 31, 1899; Santiago Papasquiaro, Durango, Mexico
Died: October 5, 1940; Mexico City, Mexico

Principal works

BALLET: *El renacuajo paseador*, 1940.
CHAMBER WORKS: String Quartet No. 1, 1930; String Quartet No. 2, 1931; String Quartet No. 3, 1931; String Quartet No. 4, 1932 (*Música de feria*); *Planos*, 1934; *Homenaje a Federico García Lorca*, 1936.

FILM SCORES: *El indio*, 1936 (*The Indian*); *Redes*, 1936 (*The Fishermen's Nets*); *Vámonos con Pancho Villa*, 1936 (*Let's Go with Pancho Villa*); *El signo de la muerte*, 1939 (*The Sign of Death*); *La noche de los Mayas*, 1939 (*The Night of the Mayas*); *Mala yerba*, 1940; *¡Que viene mi marido!*, 1940.

ORCHESTRAL WORKS: *Cuanáhuac*, 1930 (revised 1932); *Colorines*, 1932; *Ranas*, 1932 (*Frogs*); *Janitzio*, 1933 (revised 1936); *Itinerarios*, 1938; *Sensemayá*, 1938.

The Life

Silvestre Revueltas (sihl-VEHS-truh reh-VWEHL-tahs) was a Mexican composer whose writings constituted a small but significant body of music. He was born in the mountainous state of Durango, but he spent most of his years in Mexico City until his death in 1940 from pneumonia brought on by alcoholism. A child prodigy on the violin, Revueltas gave his first recital at age eleven, and at seventeen he traveled to Austin, Texas, to study at St. Edward's College before completing his musical training at Chicago Musical College. Upon returning to Mexico City in 1929, Revueltas taught violin and composition at the conservatory, and he served as assistant conductor of Orquesta Sinfónica de México under Carlos Chavez.

The Music

The music of Revueltas reflects the influence of his culture. His music is best described as highly rhythmic, raw, and sensual, yet it is refined in a manner set apart from the European musical tradition. There is also a folkloric quality to his music, though it is rare for Revueltas to quote melodies or rhythms directly. He weaves folklike melodies into his music, and he infuses them with rhythmic ostinatos, dissonant drones, and countermelodies. During his short lifetime, Revueltas composed nearly forty works before his untimely death, including six works for full orchestra and eight works for film.

Sensemayá. Composed in 1938, *Sensemayá* is a musical setting of a poem of the same title by Nicolas Guillen that describes the ritual sacrifice of a snake. There are two main themes in this composition, which are set in opposition. The first is introduced by the tuba and continued by the brass section while the strings initiate the second. These themes are representative of the two elements at odds in this composition—the snake and the ceremonial leaders—and their struggle is exacerbated by a relentless ostinato of syncopated rhythms. It begins with a slow trill in the bass clarinet that gives way to a rhythmic ostinato played by a solo bassoon. This is all accompanied by the percussion section, which drives the music forward with its syncopated rhythms. The first theme is introduced by the tuba and is joined by other members of the brass section. After a series of horn calls and clarinet trills, the strings begin with the second theme, which is ultimately overtaken by the brass. Following the climax, the two themes play in opposition, pitted against each other, all while being thrown tumultuously forward by the unrelenting rhythms into a riotous state.

The Night of the Mayas. Revueltas wrote the music for the 1939 film *La noche de los Mayas* and it was later arranged in a four-movement suite by José Ives Limantour. It is the largest in scale of all of

Silvestre Revueltas. (© CORBIS)

his works, and it is scored for orchestra with an immense percussion battery of twelve players. The opening movement shares the same title as the complete work, and it sets the mood of the piece. It is descriptive in nature, evoking an untamed and primitive locale. The second movement, titled *Noche de Jaranas* (*Night of Revelry*), is a play on words. Jaranas can mean revelry, but it also refers to a folkloric dance form. The movement is noted for its polymetric composition and unique timbral colors. The third movement, *Noche de Yucatán* (*Night of the Yucatan*) serves as the slow movement of the composition, and it is written in the form of a nocturne. Here he quotes a Mayan folk song, which for Revueltas is rare. The suite comes to an end with the finale, titled *Noche de Encantamiento* (*Night of Enchantment*). Composed as a theme and variations, it takes on a frenzied pace as the percussion section drives persistently forward, repeating melodic material from earlier movements before bringing itself to a vociferous end.

Homenaje a Federico García Lorca. Paying homage to the late Andalusian poet, this work is a three-movement composition scored for a small chamber orchestra, and it is considered by many critics to be the most advanced composition of Revueltas. The lively disposition of the two outer movements seems to contradict idea of a lament, but in Mexican and Spanish cultures it is customary to regard death as a celebration of life. The first movement, *Baile* (dance), is a fast, energetic movement that begins with a quasi-recitative trumpet solo accompanied by a dissonant chord in the piano. Following the poignant character of the solo, the movement proceeds with an energetic dance section in 4/16 time. The lamentlike second movement, *Duelo* (sorrow), is best described as a trumpet solo with orchestral ostinato-like accompaniment. The work concludes with a movement titled *Son*, incorrectly translated as *Sound* in published scores. Son has no English equivalent, but it can be best described as a traditional musical form of Mexico, and here it serves as the loudest, most complex movement of the work. Beginning with fortissimo septuplets in the piano and strings and following with multiple glissandi and driving staccato sections, the movement advances through multiple metric changes and variations in timbre and sonority.

This work illustrates the unique timbral elements of Revueltas's compositional style; he gives the tuba prominence as a solo instrument with high and fast melodies, often doubling the piccolo line. Interesting instrumental treatment is also exhibited in the doubling of the clarinet and piccolo and the use of extended parallel thirds. The latter is analogous to mariachi music popular in Mexican culture. Revueltas also writes many of his melodic lines a half-step apart, favoring piercing, dissonant sonorities.

Musical Legacy

Revueltas's music is known for its complex rhythmic organization, a unique harmonic language of melodic and harmonic dissonance, and experimentation with polytonal composition. He is also noted for his ability to absorb the contemporary Mexican folk and popular sources around him and mold them into a unique mixture of highly chromatic and occasionally abrasive-sounding material infused with his signature driving, ostinato-like rhythms. Though he prefers not to be called a nationalist composer, his work is most often described as Mestizo realism. Through his synthesis of folkloric elements with his own unique style, Revueltas captured the essence and rawness of his culture, exposing the soul of his people.

Rachel E. Mitchell

Further Reading

Béhague, Gerard. *Music in Latin America: An Introduction.* Englewood Cliffs, N.J.: Prentice Hall 1979. This is an excellent survey of Latin American music and composers, including Revueltas.

Garland, Peter. *In Search of Silvestre Revueltas: Essays, 1978-1990.* Santa Fe, N.Mex.: Soundings Press, 1991. One of the few resources in English about Revueltas, this covers the significant details of the composer's life and works.

Hess, Carol A. "Silvestre Revueltas in Republican Spain: Music as Political Utterance." *Latin American Music Review* 18, no. 2 (Fall/Winter, 1997): 278-296. This article chronicles Revueltas' time spent in Spain during the civil war as a member of the group League of Revolutionary Artists and Writers (LEAR).

Malmström, Dan. *Introduction to Twentieth Century Mexican Music.* Uppsala, Sweden: Institute of

Musicology, Uppsala University, 1974. The first two chapters of this book discuss Revueltas and other contemporary Mexican composers.

Mayer-Serra, Otto. "Silvestre Revueltas and Musical Nationalism in Mexico." *The Musical Quarterly* 27, no. 2 (April, 1941): 123-45. Written within a year of Revueltas's death, this article examines the effect of nationalism on the composer's unique compositional style.

See also: Chávez, Carlos; Crumb, George; Golijov, Osvaldo; Nancarrow, Conlon; Salonen, Esa-Pekka.

Sir Tim Rice

English musical-theater lyricist and librettist

Working with Andrew Lloyd Webber and Elton John, Rice is noted for developing a new form of musical theater: rock opera.

Born: November 10, 1944; Amersham, Buckinghamshire, England

Also known as: Timothy Miles Bindon Rice (full name)

Member of: The Aardvarks

Principal works

FILM SCORES (lyrics): *Aladdin*, 1992 (music by Alan Menken; also lyrics by Howard Ashman); *The Road to El Dorado*, 2000 (music by Elton John).

MUSICAL THEATER (lyrics and libretto): *Cricket*, 1986 (music by Andrew Lloyd Webber); *Jesus Christ Superstar*, 1971 (music by Webber); *Evita*, 1978 (music by Webber); *Joseph and the Amazing Technicolor Dreamcoat*, 1982 (music by Webber); *Chess*, 1986 (music by Benny Andersson; libretto by Richard Nelson); *Beauty and the Beast*, 1994 (music by Alan Menken; libretto by Linda Woolverton; lyrics with Howard Ashman); *King David*, 1997 (music by Alan Menken); *The Lion King*, 1997 (music by Elton John; libretto by Roger Allers and Irene Mecchi); *Aida*, 2000 (music by Elton John; libretto by Woolverton, Robert Falls, and David Henry Hwang).

The Life

Educated at Lancing College on the south coast of England and at the Sorbonne in Paris, Timothy Miles Bindon Rice worked in a law office before he became the lead singer for the Aardvarks, a group with whom he appeared from 1961 to 1963. In 1965 Rice met his famous collaborator, Andrew Lloyd Webber, and by 1968 Webber and Rice had created *Joseph and the Amazing Technicolor Dreamcoat*, a twenty-minute show for London's Colet Court School. In 1970 came their first major hit, *Jesus Christ Superstar*, which was initially released as a concept album. Rice married Jane McIntosh in 1974, and their marriage lasted until the 1980's. Their daughter, Eva, is a best-selling novelist. In 1978 came Rice and Webber's biggest hit, *Evita*, which won seven Tony Awards in New York and later was made into a highly successful film. Rice's partnership with Webber severed in 1981, and Rice worked with ABBA and briefly rejoined with Webber in 1986 for *Cricket*, a twenty-five-minute comedy to celebrate Queen Elizabeth's 60th birthday. Summoned in 1992 by Walt Disney Studios, Rice teamed with Elton John on a number of hit films and stage productions. In 1994 he was knighted. He has won many Tony Awards and Academy Awards.

The Music

Rice and his colleague Webber are credited with creating the musical form known as rock opera. Rice is also successful as a composer of popular songs and as a lyricist for film and traditional stage musicals.

Early Works. In 1965 Rice published his first hit song, "That's My Story." In that same year, he met Webber, and the two men began a sixteen-year partnership, with Webber as composer and Rice as lyricist. Together they wrote a number of popular songs, including "It's Easy for You," recorded in 1976 by Elvis Presley.

Jesus Christ Superstar. In 1970 Rice and Webber created a concept album for the first rock opera, *Jesus Christ Superstar*. In 1971 it was presented in a highly successful London stage production, and by 1972 it had become the longest-running show in London theater history. In 1973 there followed a film of *Jesus Christ Superstar*.

Evita. In 1976 *Evita* was released as a concept album. Its featured song, "Don't Cry for Me, Argentina," reached the top of the singles chart in England in 1978. That year *Evita* opened on the London stage, and it ran for 2,900 performances. The New York production of *Evita* ran for more than fifteen hundred performances, and it won seven Tony Awards. In 1993 *Evita* was released as a major film, winning an Academy Award for Rice and Webber and making the song "Don't Cry for Me, Argentina" a hit throughout the world. Another song from *Evita*, "Oh, What a Circus," was used by Rice as the title of his 1999 autobiography. In 1996 *Evita* was released as a film, and in 2006 it was presented in revival in London.

Chess. In 1981 Rice's partnership with Andrew Lloyd Webber dissolved in a disagreement over the lyrics for the show *Cats*. In the 1980's, Rice worked with ABBA on the musical *Chess*, which opened with great success in London in 1986, although it was less well received on Broadway. Later, Rice worked on several popular songs with Marvin Hamlich, John Barry, Paul McCartney, and others.

Broadway and Hollywood. Rice created the lyrics for Disney's Broadway production of *Beauty and the Beast*. Lyrics were also written for the 1992 film *Aladdin*. In 1994 Rice teamed with Elton John for the film *The Lion King*, which was converted to a hit Broadway show in 1997. In 2000 he worked with John on the Broadway production of *Aida*, and in the same year, he contributed lyrics to the DreamWorks film *The Road to El Dorado*.

Musical Legacy

Rice's work with Webber yielded several major stage and film hits. Together they created the modern rock opera. Rice has fashioned lyrics for thirteen major theatrical productions and five major films. In 1999 he was inducted into the Songwriters Hall of Fame, and in 2002 Rice was named a Disney Legend.

August W. Staub

Further Reading

Gantz, Kurt. *The Encyclopedia of Musical Theatre.* New York: Schirmer Books, 2001. This resource has information on Rice's contributions to the development of contemporary musical theater, especially the rock opera form.

Kershaw, Baz, ed. *The Cambridge History of the British Theatre: Volume III: Since 1895.* Cambridge, England: The University Press, 2002. Rice's contribution to English theater is discussed in several entries.

Rice, Tim. *Oh, What a Circus.* London: Hodder and Stoughton, 1999. This detailed and witty autobiography covers Rice's work until 1999, with a focus on his collaborations with Webber and John. Special attention is given to the issue of marrying words with music.

Snelson, John. *Andrew Lloyd Webber.* New York: Yale University Press, 2004. A biography of Webber outlines Rice and Webber's contributions to British, American, and international music.

See also: Hamlisch, Marvin; Lloyd Webber, Sir Andrew; McCartney, Sir Paul.

Keith Richards

English rock guitarist, singer, and songwriter

Richards's innovative guitar stylings, his work as a songwriter, and his outlaw persona helped to propel the Rolling Stones to enduring success.

Born: December 18, 1943; Dartford, Kent, England
Member of: The Rolling Stones; the X-Pensive Winos

Principal recordings

ALBUMS (solo): *Talk Is Cheap*, 1988; *Main Offender*, 1992.

ALBUMS (with the Rolling Stones): *The Rolling Stones (England's Newest Hitmakers)*, 1964; *12 × 5*, 1964; *December's Children (and Everybody's)*, 1965; *Out of Our Heads*, 1965; *The Rolling Stones No. 2*, 1965; *The Rolling Stones Now*, 1965; *Aftermath*, 1966; *Between the Buttons*, 1967; *Flowers*, 1967; *Their Satanic Majesties Request*, 1967; *Beggar's Banquet*, 1968; *Let It Bleed*, 1969; *Sticky Fingers*, 1971; *Exile on Main Street*, 1972; *Jamming with Edward*, 1972; *Goats' Head Soup*, 1973; *It's Only Rock 'n' Roll*, 1974; *Black and Blue*, 1976; *Some Girls*, 1978; *Emotional Rescue*, 1980; *Tattoo You*, 1981; *Undercover*, 1983; *Dirty Work*,

1986; *Steel Wheels*, 1989; *Voodoo Lounge*, 1994; *Bridges to Babylon*, 1997; *A Bigger Bang*, 2005.

The Life

Keith Richards was born in Dartford, Kent, in England on December 18, 1943, the only child of Bert Richards and Doris Dupree. When he was an infant, he and his mother were evacuated from their home to escape German bombing attacks. Their home was damaged in one of the attacks, after Richards and his mother had departed. His father, a member of the British army, was wounded at Normandy. After the war, the family moved back to Dartford, and his father worked in a factory while his mother kept the house. His paternal grandparents were Socialists and involved in politics. His maternal grandmother introduced him to jazz, and his maternal grandfather, Augustus Theodore Dupree, led the British big band Gus Dupree and His Boys. It was through his maternal grandparents that Richards developed his desire to be a musician. Richards sang in the Westminster Abbey choir as a soprano until his voice changed, and he even performed for the queen. As a teenager, he played guitar in various skiffle groups, and he identified himself with the teddy-boy subculture.

When he attended Sidcup Art College, near Kent, he spent more time honing his guitar skills than studying. He was eventually expelled from the school. Around the same time, his parents divorced, and he met Brian Jones. In addition, Richards reconnected with Mick Jagger, a former schoolmate. He moved into an apartment with Jones and Jagger in 1962. The three played music separately and together in various loosely formed groups, and they would occasionally jam at a blues club run by British bluesman Alexis Korner. Not long afterward, they formed the Rolling Stones.

Richards became famous for his guitar playing and his outlaw persona. He often ran afoul of the law, usually because of his use of illegal substances. In 1967 he and Jagger were arrested at Richards's Sussex home. The arrests and trial made headlines, and the notoriety of the defendants led the usually staid *London Times* to editorialize against the prosecution and conviction. Because of the public outcry, Richards was released after only two days in prison. He was watched by the police in every country he visited, and he was arrested several

more times for minor offenses that were often drug-related.

Sometime in the late 1960's, Richards began using heroin, and rumors abounded about the parties and drug sessions held at this home and in hotel rooms when the Rolling Stones were on tour. In 1977 he was arrested in Canada and charged with importing twenty-two grams of heroin. Although he faced a minimum of seven years in prison, Richards was put on probation with the stipulation that he undergo treatment for his heroin addiction. In addition, Richards and the Rolling Stones performed two benefit concerts for the Canadian National Institute for the Blind at Oshawa Civic Auditorium on April 22, 1979. The concerts were opened by fellow Stones guitarist Ron Wood and his band the New Barbarians, which also featured Richards. Besides his work with the Rolling Stones, Richards did solo work with the New Barbarians in the late 1970's. In 1988 he formed the band the X-Pensive Winos with drummer Steve Jordan, bassist Charley Drayton, singer Sarah Dash, guitarist Waddy Wachtel, and keyboardist Ivan Neville, with Bernie Worrell playing in later versions of the band. They released three albums between 1988 and 1992.

Richards was romantically involved with German model and actress Anita Pallenberg throughout much of the 1960's and 1970's. Pallenberg was originally involved with Jones, but their tempestuous relationship ended in 1967 after a fight in Marrakech, Morocco. Although they never married, Richards and Pallenberg had three children. Richards met Patti Hansen in 1979, and they married in 1983. They have two children. Richards remained close to his mother throughout his life, and after years of estrangement, he reconciled with his father in 1982. In 1986 he appeared in and helped organize a concert and film tribute to Chuck Berry titled *Hail! Hail! Rock 'n' Roll*. He appeared as the pirate Jack Sparrow's father in the third installment of the incredibly popular film series *Pirates of the Caribbean* in 2006.

The Music

Out of Our Heads. This Rolling Stones album contained seven songs written by Richards and Jagger, including "(I Can't Get) No Satisfaction," a clear departure from the band's previous work, which consisted primarily of blues and rock-and-roll covers. "(I Can't Get) No Satisfaction" features Richards on acoustic guitar. Both Richards and Jagger said that this period of songwriting was an apprenticeship for them, and their songs show both pop and blues influences. This represents some of Richards's earliest recorded work as a songwriter. His guitar work here is reminiscent of Berry's, but it shows flashes of American blues rhythmic stylings.

Beggar's Banquet. This album was heavily influenced by Richards's collection of blues albums. Although some of the songs were lifted directly (and eventually acknowledged), Richards primarily used these old blues as inspiration for the music he wrote. His acoustic guitar work on "No Expectations" and his electric-slide-guitar work on "Jigsaw Puzzle" are heartbreakingly beautiful. The percussive beats of "Sympathy for the Devil" make this Richards song a great rock song. Richards sings the opening verse to the album's final song, "Salt of the Earth." Most of the guitar on the album is played by Richards.

Let It Bleed. This Rolling Stones album followed the creative and commercial success of *Beggar's Banquet*. Richards is featured singing on "You Got the Silver." Rock critic Robert Palmer noted that Richards should join the list of greatest rock guitarists based solely on his work on *Let It Bleed*. His opening licks on the album's first song, "Gimme Shelter" provide the aura of menace the lyrics demand. His acoustic work on "Country Honk" makes the song sound like a lazy jam in the American South. The fact that Jones had died and Mick Taylor had taken his place may partially explain Richards's incredible playing on this record. Despite Taylor's presence, Richards plays most of the guitars on the album, thanks to overdubbing of tracks.

Talk Is Cheap. On Richards's first solo album (backed by the members of the X-Pensive Winos), he seems more intent on establishing and sustaining movable grooves than catchy melody lines, as in his other work. Richards also manages, perhaps for first time since "You Got the Silver" on *Let It*

Keith Richards. (AP/Wide World Photos)

Bleed, to create memorably striking vocals. He proves that he can be a bandleader, even if his vocals are uneven.

Live at Hollywood Palladium. Featuring the X-Pensive Winos, this album presents Richards at his best: performing live. The sound is good, and it highlights Richards's live guitar playing and his rhythm-friendly arrangements. (An added bonus on the DVD of the concert is the chance to see Richards's friendly manner with the band and the audience.)

Musical Legacy

Richards's role in forming the Rolling Stones and his continuing role in the band's success is his most lasting legacy. In addition, the hundreds of songs he wrote (mostly with Jagger) include some of popular music's most recognizable tunes. Richards's guitar stylings helped blur the differences between lead and rhythm guitar. He did this by substituting a technique by which melodic riffs are grafted onto a rigorous rhythm consisting of chords, partial chords, and low-register lines. Furthermore, his discovery and use of open tunings popular among early twentieth century blues musicians popularized these tunings among other rock and country rock guitarists. Always understated, Richards's guitar playing is a prime example of how restraint and a few notes can create more interesting music than flashy long riffs and scale repetition.

Ron Jacobs

Further Reading

Beaumont, Marc. "Interview with Keith Richards." *New Musical Express* (April 4, 2007). In this interview with the British pop music magazine, Richards speaks seriously about his music, he jokes about his life, and he gives his opinions about rock music of the past and the present. He discusses his earlier addiction to heroin, his love of early rock and roll, and his favorite actors and musicians.

Bockris, Victor. *Keith Richards: The Biography*. New York: DaCapo Press, 2003. Bockris's biography examines Richards's career and his importance to the Rolling Stones. It a bit gossipy but overall balanced biography. It relies primarily on interviews with people who knew Richards and other secondhand sources, but it does a good job of presenting Richards as an essentially amiable music lover.

Booth, Stanley. *Keith: Standing in the Shadows*. New York: St. Martin's Press, 1995. Booth first met Richards in the mid-1960's and the two became friends. This is essentially an oral history of the Rolling Stones as seen through Richards's eyes. Includes Richards's views on his music, his relationship with Jones, and his life as a rock star. Surprisingly forthright, the tone is rarely gossipy or angry.

Needs, Chris. *Keith Richards: Before They Make Me Run*. Medford, N.J.: Plexus, 2004. Titled after Richards's song of the same name, this book draws on archives, interviews, and Needs's knowledge of the Rolling Stones' discography. Richards is portrayed as a blues-infatuated working-class kid who became a world-famous musician able to constantly reinvent himself while remaining true to his music. Includes photographs and interviews.

Sandford, Christopher. *Keith Richards: Satisfaction*. New York: Carroll & Graf, 2004. This biography looks beyond the sensationalist aspects to examine Richards's life and music in a more subtle manner. The writing style is accessible, and Sandford's musical knowledge is helpful.

See also: Berry, Chuck; Burke, Solomon; Carter, Maybelle; Diddley, Bo; Everly, Don and Phil; Jagger, Sir Mick; James, Etta; Johnson, Robert; Neville, Aaron; Parsons, Gram; Paul, Les; Redding, Otis; Tosh, Peter; Webb, Jimmy.

Jean Ritchie

American folksinger, guitarist, dulcimer player, and songwriter

An influential singer-songwriter in the folk-music revival of the 1950's and 1960's, Ritchie performed and recorded music of the southern Appalachian Mountains based on her family's vast musical repertoire of British folk ballads, Old Regular Baptist hymns, and children's songs. She is credited with introducing the mountain dulcimer to an international audience.

Born: December 8, 1922; Viper, Kentucky
Also known as: Mother of Folk; Than Hall

Principal recordings

ALBUMS: *Traditional Songs of Her Kentucky Mountain Home*, 1952; *Courting Songs*, 1954; *Field Trip*, 1954; *Kentucky Mountain Songs*, 1954; *Shivaree*, 1955; *The Singing Family of the Cumberlands*, 1955; *American Folk Tales and Songs*, 1956; *Children's Songs and Games from the Southern Mountains*, 1956; *Saturday Night and Sunday Too*, 1956; *Songs from Kentucky*, 1956; *The Ritchie Family of Kentucky*, 1958; *Carols for All Seasons*, 1959; *Riddle Me This*, 1959 (with Oscar Brand); *Ballads from Her Appalachian Family Tradition*, 1961; *British Traditional Ballads, Vol. 1*, 1961; *British Traditional Ballads, Vol. 2*, 1961; *Precious Memories*, 1962; *Jean Ritchie and Doc Watson at Folk City*, 1963; *Time for Singing,*

1966; *Marching Across the Green Grass and Other American Children's Game Songs*, 1968; *Clear Waters Remembered*, 1971; *Jean Ritchie at Home*, 1971; *None but One*, 1977; *High Hills and Mountains*, 1979; *Christmas Revels: Wassail! Wassail!*, 1982; *The Most Dulcimer*, 1984; *O Love Is Teasin'*, 1985; *Kentucky Christmas, Old and New*, 1987; *Mountain Born*, 1995; *High Hills and Mountains*, 1996; *Childhood Songs*, 1997.

WRITINGS OF INTEREST: *Singing Family of the Cumberlands*, 1955 (autobiography); *The Dulcimer Book*, 1963.

The Life

Jean Ritchie was the fourteenth child of Abigail and Balis Ritchie, of Viper, Kentucky, a Cumberland Mountain community in the region of coal mines, farms, and the post-Civil War railroad industry. Her large family descended from early English settlers, and like many Appalachian families, they retained and preserved the ancient ballads and folk songs of England. In 1936 Alan Lomax met Ritchie when he recorded her family's music for the Library of Congress, creating a lasting archive for the traditional songs collected over the years by Ritchie's father and her uncle.

After graduating from the University of Kentucky in 1946 with a degree in social work, Ritchie moved to New York City to work with underprivileged children at the Henry Street Settlement House. Her performances singing the traditional Appalachian music of her home in the Cumberland Mountains led to national and international recognition as the Mother of Folk.

Ritchie married photographer George Pickow 1950, and along with his uncle Morris Pickow, they manufactured and sold dulcimers, a stringed musical instrument, in Brooklyn, New York. She was awarded a Fulbright scholarship in 1952 to research Appalachian ballads in England, Scotland, and Ireland. Pickow and Ritchie had two sons: Peter, born in 1954, and Jonathan, born in 1958. Her performing and recording career progressed as the dulcimer business and international interest in the instrument grew as well.

The Music

Starting with performances for schoolchildren and friends in the late 1940's, Ritchie sang the ballads and songs her name would later come to represent. At the settlement house, she introduced children to the singing games and folk music of her youth, and she performed for folk-music gatherings and radio programs. She accepted invitations to appear on radio and television programs, such as *Rainbow Quest*, hosted by Pete Seeger. Her public-performing career continued for more than sixty years.

Dulcimer Music. As Ritchie became known through her performances and affiliations with musicians and folklorists such as Seeger, Leadbelly, Cisco Houtston, Woody Guthrie, and Lomax, she often accompanied her voice with the mountain or lap dulcimer, a family instrument from Kentucky. She became associated with dulcimer music, and in 1963 she wrote *The Dulcimer Book*. Her first published collection of songs in *Jean Ritchie's Swapping Song Book* (1964) was well received. All five of Ritchie's books were reprinted during her later years, indicating a renewal of interest in her work.

Appalachian Traditions. Along with her playing the dulcimer, her simple singing style and her unaffected narrations established Ritchie as an authentic folksinger, at a time when folk music was becoming commercialized through the concerts and the recordings of popular music groups. In addition to the publication of song collections and an autobiography, she signed a contract with Elektra Records, for which she made albums between 1952 and 1962. In the meantime, Lomax continued to record her ballads for the Library of Congress. She participated in planning and performing at the first Newport Folk Festival in 1959, and she served as a festival trustee for many years afterward. Though her performance repertoire and style were based on her own heritage as an Appalachian traditional musician, she recognized the need to include commercially successful musicians to appeal to the broad age span of folk music lovers.

Protest Songs. Ritchie's interest in the power of musical messages led her to compose several songs protesting the strip-mining coal industry. She published many of these songs under the pseudonym Than Hall, in order to protect her identity as a woman and to shield her mother from political problems associated with those who wrote and performed protest songs in the 1960's. Although Ritchie's political interests were focused primarily on the issue of coal mining, she was once listed in a publication called *Marxist Minstrels*, which warned readers about her communistic ideas. Her songs "Blackwaters" and "The L&N Don't Stop Here Anymore" told of the difficulties of people living in communities affected by the coal-mining industry, and they were recorded by other artists.

Recordings. Ritchie's pure soprano vocals were recorded on thirty-two albums, beginning in 1952. Though most of her performances were solo appearances, she collaborated several times with other musicians and family members in her recordings. Early in her career, Ritchie met and performed with North Carolina traditional guitarist Doc Watson, at the Ash Grove Coffeehouse in Hollywood, California. The pair recorded a live album called *Jean Ritchie and Doc Watson at Folk City* at Folk City in New York City's Greenwich Village in 1963. In 1977 *None but One* earned for Ritchie the *Rolling Stone* Critics Award. Ritchie involved several members of her family in the seasonal album *Kentucky Christmas, Old and New*.

Musical Legacy

Ritchie committed her life to fostering traditional music, starting with that of her own family history and repertoire in the mountains of eastern Kentucky. Her influence as a traditional folksinger and dulcimer player, along with her contribution to the scholarship of Appalachian music traditions, led to prestigious performances at the Royal Albert Concert Hall in London and at Carnegie Hall in New York City. To celebrate fifty years of performing, Ritchie recorded the album *Mountain Born*, featuring the instrumental and vocal music of her sons. The same title was used for a biographical PBS documentary in 1995. Ritchie's songs were recorded by several well-known country musicians, including Johnny Cash, Dolly Parton, Emmylou Harris, Lester Flatt, Earl Scruggs, Linda Ronstadt, and Kathy Mattea. Ritchie was recognized by President Ronald Reagan in 1986 for her contributions to folk music, and she received the Folk Alliance Lifetime Achievement Award in 1998. In 2002 Ritchie was given a National Heritage Fellowship, which is awarded by the National Endowment for the Arts. In 2007 she was invited to submit recordings to the Library of Congress Folk Music Archives.

Susan W. Mills

Further Reading

Briscoe, James, ed. *Contemporary Anthology of Music by Women*. Bloomington: Indiana University Press, 1997. Musical scores, recordings, and essays on women composers and songwriters. This source offers a brief introductory essay about Ritchie.

Metcalfe, Jean. "A Dulcimer Heritage: Jean Ritchie." *Dulcimer Players News* 22, no. 1 (February-April, 1996): 24-29. The article contains an interview with Ritchie about the roots of the dulcimer and how the instrument is produced.

Ritchie, Jean. *Folk Songs of the Southern Appalachians*. 2d ed. Lexington: University Press of Kentucky, 1997. With a foreword to the original edition by Lomax, this volume contains information about song origins and variants from the British Isles.

_____. *Singing Family of the Cumberlands*. Lexington: University Press of Kentucky, 1955. Ritchie introduces her family's life through stories from childhood.

See also: Cash, Johnny; Flatt, Lester; Guthrie, Woody; Harris, Emmylou; Leadbelly; Lomax, Alan; Parton, Dolly; Scruggs, Earl; Seeger, Pete; Watson, Doc.

Tex Ritter

American country singer, guitarist, and songwriter

Ritter was instrumental in transforming hillbilly music to country and western. In addition, with his trademark white clothes and white horse, Ritter helped establish the stereotyped Western hero.

Born: January 12, 1905; Murvaul, Texas
Died: January 2, 1974; Nashville, Tennessee
Also known as: Maurice Woodward Ritter (full name)

Principal recordings

ALBUMS: *Songs from the Western Screen*, 1957; *Psalms*, 1958; *Blood on the Saddle*, 1960; *Hillbilly Heaven*, 1961; *The Lincoln Hymns*, 1961; *Stan Kenton and Tex Ritter*, 1962; *Border Affair*, 1963;

The Friendly Voice of Tex Ritter, 1964; *Sweet Land of Liberty*, 1966; *Just Beyond the Moon*, 1967; *Bump Tiddle Dee Bum Bum!*, 1968; *Tennessee Blues*, 1968; *Tex Ritter's Wild West*, 1968; *Chuck Wagon Days*, 1969; *Love You Big as Texas*, 1969; *Green, Green Valley*, 1970; *Jamboree, Nashville Style*, 1970; *Tex*, 1971; *Fall Away*, 1975; *Comin' After Jinny*, 1976.

SINGLES: "Goodbye Ole Paint," 1933; "Rye Whiskey," 1933; "Get Along Little Dogie," 1935; "Sam Hall," 1935; "Jingle, Jangle, Jingle," 1942; "I'm Wastin' My Tears on You," 1944; "There's a New Moon over My Shoulder," 1944; "You Two Timed Me One Time Too Often," 1945; "Deck of Cards," 1948; "Pecos Bill," 1948; "Rye Whiskey," 1948; "Daddy's Last Letter (Private First Class John H. McCormick)," 1950; "High Noon: Do Not Forsake Me Oh My Darlin'," 1952.

The Life

Maurice Woodward "Tex" Ritter, the son of James Everett Ritter and Martha Elizabeth Matthews, grew up on the family ranch in Panola County, Texas. He attended grade school in Carthage, Texas, and he graduated with honors from South Park High School in Beaumont. In high school, Ritter played for the basketball, baseball, and football teams, and he was on the debate team, he starred in the junior-class play, and he was elected president of the senior class. After graduation he majored in prelaw, taking courses in government, political science, and economics at the University of Texas in Austin, where he also sang in the Glee Club and the Oratorio Society. His interests, however, changed from law (although he needed just one more course to finish his law degree) to entertainment, and in 1928 he sang cowboy songs on the KPRC radio station in Houston. After attending several performances, he joined the male chorus of the Schuberts' traveling entertainment company, and he left with the troupe when it went back to New York City. When the show closed, he returned to Texas, and he got a job as the choir director for the Third Presbyterian Church in Houston, where he also had a radio program. He then went back to New York, where he appeared in the Broadway show *The New Moon* (1928). Not having lost sight of his legal ambitions, he went to Chicago,

where he enrolled in Northwestern University's School of Law, although he did not finish his law degree. He returned to New York, where he got parts in stage productions and made some recordings and appearances on radio. In 1936 he moved to Los Angeles to star in Western films for Grand National Pictures. Five years later, on June 14, 1941, he married Dorothy Fay, with whom he had appeared in so-called B Westerns. The couple had two sons, John, who went on to be a television and film star, and Thomas, who had cerebral palsy but went on to become a successful producer of television shows and of documentaries. After Ritter discovered that Thomas was affected by cerebral palsy, he helped found the United Cerebral Palsy Association, and he campaigned on its behalf. Since Ritter was too old to be drafted for World War II, he served his country by entertaining at military bases throughout the war.

Ritter moved to Nashville, Tennessee, the home of country music, in 1965, where he worked with the Grand Ole Opry. The rest of his family stayed in California until John finished high school, at which time they joined him in Nashville. A staunch conservative, he was persuaded by friends to enter politics. He ran against William Brock in the primary for the Republican nomination for the U.S. Senate in 1970. Despite his name recognition, Ritter was soundly defeated.

Ritter had his last recording session for Capitol Records in 1973, and in 1974, while he was in Nashville trying to arrange bail for one of his band members, he died of a heart attack.

The Music

The Singing Cowboy. Ritter's musical career began with his appearances singing cowboy songs on radio station KPRC in Houston, but when he moved to New York City in 1928, his career developed quickly. After singing in the men's chorus in the Broadway show *The New Moon*, he was cast as the cowboy in another Broadway show, *Green Grow the Lilacs* (1931), the forerunner of the smash hit *Oklahoma!* (1943), and in it he sang four songs and he served as the understudy for the lead, Franchot Tone. His cowboy persona was enhanced when he played Sagebrush Charlie in *The Round Up* (1932) and in *Mother Lode* (1934). In addition to his dramatic roles, he played cowboys on radio shows. He was the star, singing cowboy songs and telling tales of the Old West, of WOR's *The Lone Star Rangers*, and he wrote and starred in WINS's *Cowboy Tom's Roundup*, a show that was carried on three East Coast radio stations from 1933 to 1936. Other radio appearances were on WHN's *Barndance* and on NBC radio, both of which involved singing. In *Bobby Benson's Adventures* and *Death Valley Days* he was cast in dramatic roles on the radio.

Recording Career. In 1933 his career took another turn: He signed with the America Record Company (Columbia Records), and he made his first recordings: "Goodbye Ole Paint" and "Rye Whiskey." Two years later he switched studios, joining Decca Records, where he made his first original recordings, among them "Get Along Little Dogie." (He recorded twenty-nine songs for Decca Records, the last one in 1939.)

Film Appearances. In 1936 Ritter moved to Los Angeles, where he signed a contract with Grand National Pictures, and he made twelve films with the company. Among the B Western films he starred in were *Headin' for the Rio Grande* (1937) and

Tex Ritter. (AP/Wide World Photos)

Trouble in Texas (1937), a film in which his costar was Rita Cansino, who later changed her name to Rita Hayworth. When Grand National Pictures had financial problems, Ritter moved to Monogram Pictures, where he made an additional twenty singing-cowboy films, many costarring Fay, whom he later married. In 1941 he switched from Monogram Pictures to Columbia Pictures, and then he moved to Universal Studios and PRC Studios. His character in Western films was dressed in white and riding a white horse, the white symbolizing his innocence and goodness. White Flash was Ritter's horse. By 1945, with the film *Flaming Bullets*, his film career was effectively over, although he made a few Westerns during the 1950's. After that he made some cameo appearances, and he narrated some documentaries, notably the nostalgic *The Cowboy* (1954).

Country Hits. Capitol Records lured Ritter away from Decca Records, and he recorded his first session on June 11, 1942. With its first Western singer, Capitol had a string of hits during the 1940's. "Jingle, Jangle, Jingle" was one of Ritter's most popular songs. "I'm Wastin' My Tears on You" was number one on the country charts and number eleven on the pop charts. On the *Billboard* Most Played Jukebox Folk Records Poll in 1945, his records ranked one, two, and three; in 1945 and 1946, he had seven consecutive Top 5 hits, including "Blood on the Saddle" and "You Two Timed Me One Time Too Often," which held the number-one spot. When he redid "Rye Whiskey" in 1948, it made the Top 10. Many of his songs were associated with Texas, which remained his lifelong focus, and other songs were religious and patriotic.

To add to his laurels, he recorded the song that won the award for Best Song at the first televised Academy Awards in 1952. At the ceremony he sang "High Noon: Do Not Forsake Me Oh My Darlin'" from the award-winning Western *High Noon* (1952), which featured a sheriff's conflict between love and duty. After touring Europe in 1952, he appeared on *Town Hall Party* on radio and on television in Los Angeles.

Music Publishing and Production. In 1955, with Johnny Bond, Ritter established Vidor Publications, a company specializing in publishing music. Two years later, he produced his first album, *Songs from the Western Screen*, and he starred in *Ranch Party*, a television series featuring Western music, which ran until 1959. In 1961 he recorded "Hillbilly Heaven," which he had revised and updated, and it reached the Top 5 on the country charts and the Top 20 on the pop charts. One of the founding members of the Country Music Association in Nashville and its president in 1963, Ritter was the fifth person and the first singing cowboy to be inducted into the Country Music Hall of Fame in 1964. He moved to Nashville, which had become the center for Western and country music, and he worked for WSM radio and the Grand Ole Opry, of which he became a lifetime member.

Musical Legacy

Ritter defined cowboy music for a generation enchanted with the Old West as depicted in film and dime novels. His ballads displayed the gentler side of the cowboy icon, expressing an ideal image of honesty, honor, endurance, and love of the American frontier. After Ritter's death, a number of his albums were rereleased, and his "Blood on the Saddle" emanated from an animated grizzly bear at Disney World and Disneyland. Many of his old films are available on video. His life and career are memorialized at the Country Music Association Hall of Fame, at the Tex Ritter Museum in Carthage, Texas, near his hometown, and at the Grand Ole Opry. He has also received a star on the Hollywood Walk of Fame, and he was inducted into the Western Performance Hall of Fame at the National Cowboy and Western Heritage Museum in Oklahoma City, Oklahoma.

Thomas L. Erskine

Further Reading

Bond, Johnny. *The Tex Ritter Story*. New York: Chappell, 1976. This early biography written by a friend contains many anecdotes about Ritter from his associates and his family members. Includes family photographs, a filmography of Ritter's films (and his wife's), a list with credits of his Broadway plays, a discography (including the names of the songs in his record albums), a chronology, and the lyrics from his most popular recordings.

Cooper, Texas Jim. *Tex Ritter, the Inside Story*. Carrollton, Tex.: Longhorn Productions, 1979. By a fan, this biography is highly complimentary to Ritter.

O'Neal, Bill. *Tex Ritter: America's Most Beloved Cowboy*. Austin, Tex.: Eakin Press, 1998. Well-researched and thorough biography of Ritter. It contains many photographs, a filmography, a discography, and a comprehensive bibliography (including magazine and newspaper articles).

See also: Acuff, Roy; Arnold, Eddy; Axton, Hoyt; Blackwell, Otis; Brooks, Garth; Haggard, Merle; Nelson, Willie; Tiomkin, Dimitri; Travis, Merle; Watson, Doc; Williams, Hank; Wynette, Tammy.

Max Roach

American jazz drummer and composer

Roach was one of the leaders of the bebop and bop movement of the 1940's. He was an innovator in the field of jazz, exploring new ideas in drumming and in improvisation.

Born: January 10, 1924; New Land, North Carolina

Died: August 16, 2007; New York, New York

Also known as: Maxwell Lemuel Roach (full name)

Member of: The Max Roach Quartet; the Max Roach Four; M'Boom; the Clifford Brown-Max Roach Quintet

Principal recordings

ALBUMS (solo): *Daahound*, 1954 (with Clifford Brown); *Max Roach and Clifford Brown, Vol. 1*, 1954; *Max Roach and Clifford Brown, Vol. 2*, 1954; *Standard Time*, 1954; *Clifford Brown and Max Roach at Basin Street*, 1956; *Jazz in 3/4 Time*, 1956; *Drummin' the Blues*, 1957; *Percussion Discussion*, 1957; *Deeds, Not Words*, 1958; *The Hardbop Academy*, 1958; *Max*, 1958; *Max Roach with the Boston Percussion Ensemble*, 1958; *Award Winning Drummer*, 1959; *The Many Sides of Max*, 1959; *Max Roach*, 1959; *Drum Conversation*, 1960; *Jazz in Paris: Parisian Sketches*, 1960; *Long as You're Living*, 1960; *Moon-Faced and Starry-Eyed*,

1960; *We Insist! Max Roach's Freedom Now Suite*, 1960 (with others); *Percussion Bitter Sweet*, 1961; *It's Time*, 1962; *The Max Roach Trio, Featuring the Legendary Hasaan*, 1964 (with Hasaan Ibn Ali); *Drums Unlimited*, 1965; *Lift Every Voice and Sing*, 1971 (with the J. C. White Singers); *Force: Sweet Mao—Suid Africa '76*, 1976; *The Loadstar*, 1977; *Streams of Consciousness*, 1977 (with Abdullah Ibrahim); *Birth and Rebirth*, 1978 (with Anthony Braxton); *Pictures in a Frame*, 1979; *Again*, 1980; *Swish*, 1982 (with Connie Crothers); *It's Christmas Again*, 1984; *Survivors*, 1984; *Easy Winners*, 1985 (with the Double Quartet); *Bright Moments*, 1986; *Max and Dizzy: Paris 1989*, 1989 (with Dizzy Gillespie); *To the Max!*, 1990; *Max Roach with the New Orchestra of Boston and the So What Brass Quintet*, 1993; *Explorations . . . To the Mth Degree*, 1995 (with Mal Waldron); *Festival Journey*, 1996 (with the Orchestra of Boston).

ALBUMS (with the Max Roach Four): *Max Roach Plus Four*, 1956; *Max Roach Four Plays Charlie Parker*, 1957; *Max Roach Plus Four on the Chicago Scene*, 1958; *Quiet as It's Kept*, 1960.

ALBUMS (with the Max Roach Quartet): *The Max Roach Quartet, Featuring Hank Mobley*, 1953; *Speak, Brother, Speak!*, 1962; *Chattahoochee Red*, 1981; *In the Light*, 1982; *Scott Free*, 1984.

ALBUMS (with M'Boom): *M'Boom*, 1979; *M'Boom Re: Percussion*, 1980.

The Life

Maxwell Lemuel Roach was born in 1924 in New Land, North Carolina, and he moved with his family to Brooklyn at age four. His early musical influences came from his family and from the church: His mother was a gospel singer, and his aunt taught him the fundamentals of piano. After receiving his first drum set at age twelve, Roach began avidly listening to jazz, and he was especially influenced by drummers Sid Catlett and Jo Jones. Upon leaving high school in 1942, Roach worked briefly with Duke Ellington's orchestra, and he appeared with Charlie Parker at Monroe's Uptown House in Harlem, where he took part in jam sessions that helped lay the groundwork for bebop. By the mid-1940's, he was appearing regularly on Fifty-second Street with Parker, Dizzy Gillespie, and others, and he made his first recording with Coleman Hawkins in

December, 1943. In the late 1940's, Roach was one of the most sought-after drummers in modern jazz, and he appeared most often with Parker's quintet. He also participated in such landmark recordings as Miles Davis's *Birth of the Cool* sessions in 1949 and 1950 and the quintet's *Jazz at Massey Hall* in 1953.

In 1954 Roach formed his own quintet, which he led with the outstanding young trumpet player, Clifford Brown. During the next two years, the Clifford Brown-Max Roach Quintet was one of the hottest in jazz, pioneering elements of the new hard-bop style while imbuing their tunes with hard-driving swing and virtuosic improvisation. Tragically, the quintet ended with the deaths of Brown and pianist Richie Powell (as well as Powell's wife) in an automobile accident in June, 1956. The blow was devastating to Roach both personally and professionally: He had lost two close friends and colleagues at the height of their group's critical and commercial success. Later in the 1950's, Roach re-formed his quintet with the additions of Booker Little, trumpet, and Ray Draper, tuba.

While established as one of jazz's leading drummers, Roach continued to transcend musical boundaries for the remainder of his life. He worked closely with singer Abbey Lincoln (his wife from 1962 to 1968), combining solo voices and chorus with jazz ensemble and composing and performing many works addressing African American civil rights. In 1970 he organized M'Boom, an ensemble of eight percussionists who played more than a hundred instruments. Later in the 1970's, Roach organized another quartet, and he continued to perform with two of its members, saxophonist Odean Pope and trumpeter Cecil Bridgewater, for more than two decades. Beginning in the 1970's, Roach played and composed for various ensembles and contexts, including theater, dance, film, and television, and he also appeared with hip-hop artists, kodo drummers of Japan, and avant-garde jazz artists such as Cecil Taylor and Anthony Braxton. He also formed the Max Roach Double Quartet, a combination of his quartet with the Uptown String Quartet (whose violist was his daughter Maxine), and he appeared in spoken-word concerts with writers Toni Morrison and Amiri Baraka. In 1972 Roach was hired as professor at the University of Massachusetts at Amherst, a position that allowed him the flexibility to travel to Africa and explore more fully African drumming and culture. Roach died after a long illness at the age of eighty-three.

The Music

In the 1940's and 1950's, Roach pioneered a new style of jazz drumming. His imaginative style, based on subtlety and polyrhythm, paid as much attention to a song's melody as to its beat, and it elevated the drums to a front-line instrument in jazz. His new concept of musical time played the pulse on the cymbal rather than on the bass drum, resulting in a more flexible, flowing rhythmic conception, that would then be disturbed by dramatic accents (known as "bombs"). Other characteristics of Roach's style included sensitive, strong, and swinging playing; careful interaction of pitch and timbre; subtleties of sound

Max Roach. (AP/Wide World Photos)

and silence; and rhythmic and metrical variety. While a fabulous leader, Roach was also one of the most sought-after band members of the 1950's, known for his clear articulation and accuracy at any tempo, as well as for his sensitivity and subtlety in matching each tune, ensemble, and soloist.

Charlie Parker: Bird on 52nd Street. These 1948 recordings document Parker and his quintet at the height of their musical imagination. In addition to Parker on alto saxophone and Roach on drums, the quintet includes Miles Davis, trumpet; Duke Jordan, piano; and Tommy Potter, bass. Despite the poor sound quality (the recordings were made on a home tape recorder), the tracks are dazzling in their virtuosity and inventiveness. The quintet performs a lineup of bop standards at lightning-fast speeds, including "Fifty-second Street Theme," "Hot House," "A Night in Tunisia," and "Chasin' the Bird." The takes are primarily short ones, with improvisations by Parker and Davis. However, Roach's clear, articulate phrasing, his melodic and rhythmic inventiveness, and his accuracy at any speed are evident throughout. While a challenge to listen to because of the poor sound quality, the disc is well worth the effort.

The Quintet: Jazz at Massey Hall. *Jazz at Massey Hall* is a live recording that took place in Toronto,

featuring the all-star lineup of Dizzy Gillespie, trumpet; Parker, alto saxophone; Bud Powell, piano; Charles Mingus, bass; and Roach, drums. The album features primarily up-tempo bop standards performed with intensity and imagination, with most of the tracks lasting seven to nine minutes: "Perdido," "Salt Peanuts," "Wee," "Hot House," and "A Night in Tunisia," as well as the ballad "All the Things You Are." While it is impossible to single out individual tracks for acclaim, one particular highlight of the album is "Salt Peanuts," which opens with Roach's intense drumming before the entire group joins in the theme. Roach's four-chorus solo is a masterpiece of bop drumming, as he explores the theme in various timbres and textures while exhibiting the masterful independence of his four limbs.

Clifford Brown and Max Roach at Basin Street. This final recording of the Clifford Brown-Max Roach Quintet exhibits the fabulous heights the group had attained before the tragic deaths of Brown and pianist Richie Powell. Recorded January and February, 1956, in New York City, the quintet features Brown, trumpet, and Roach, drums; with Sonny Rollins, tenor saxophone; Powell, piano; and George Morrow, bass. Roach is spectacular throughout as a leader and supporter, as he works flawlessly with the rhythm section and the front line. Roach's drumming and Powell's arranging are remarkable on "I'll Remember April," which begins with mid-tempo rhythmic and melodic explorations of the theme before launching into a rapid series of solos (Brown, Rollins, Powell, Roach). Roach's solo exhibits his mastery of timbre and texture in a masterful feat of polyrhythm. Noteworthy is Powell's "Gertrude's Bounce," with a popular hard-bop feel that serves as the backdrop for joyous and inventive solos by Brown, Rollins, Powell, and Roach.

Deeds, Not Words. The opening track of *Deeds, Not Words*, "You Stepped Out of a Dream," could not be further from the ebullient optimism of "Gertrude's Bounce" two years earlier. Having established himself as one of the most important drummers and bandleaders in jazz, Roach continually sought new realms of musical expression. The sparse and open sound of "You Stepped Out of a Dream" reflects Roach's new conception: The group includes no pianist, and it features Roach on drums, Booker Little on trumpet, George Coleman on tenor saxophone, Ray Draper on tuba, and Art Davis on bass. Harmonies are implied throughout this album, which presents a linear conception of jazz melody that allows both the soloists and Roach to shine. The album also features tunes by a number of young jazz composers, including Little ("Larry-Larue"), Draper ("Filidé"), and Chicago bassist Bill Lee ("Jodie's Cha-Cha" and "Deeds, Not Words"), as well as Roach's own "Conversation."

We Insist! Max Roach's Freedom Now Suite. In this collaboration with singer Lincoln (to whom Roach was married for a few years) and lyricist Oscar Brown, Jr., Roach created a large-scale composition in response to the active liberation movements in the United States and Africa. While the recorded version represents only a portion of Roach's original conception, it is powerful in its portrayal of slavery, freedom, and continuing oppression. In "Driver Man," Lincoln is accompanied by only Roach on tambourine in the opening vocal statement, before the rest of the ensemble enters, backing Hawkins's plaintive and intense solo. This representation of slavery is followed by the hopeful, but doubting, "Freedom Day," celebrating the Emancipation Proclamation. The tentative hope of "Freedom Day" contrasts with "Triptych: Prayer, Protest, Peace," and its realization of the ongoing denial of equal opportunity for African Americans. Lincoln's textless vocalizations are accompanied by only Roach on drums throughout. The suite shifts to Africa for the two final numbers, "All Africa" and "Tears for Johannesburg."

Drums Unlimited. This album features one standard, W. C. Handy's "St. Louis Blues," together with four compositions by Roach and one by bassist Jymie Merritt. The album returns somewhat to a more aggressive, and sometimes joyful, nature, and it features Roach on drums joined by James Spaulding on alto saxophone, Freddie Hubbard on trumpet, Ronnie Mathews on piano, and Merritt on bass. The opening tune, "The Drum Also Waltzes," features Roach solo, exhibiting his proclivity for exploring rhythmic innovations, and particularly waltz time, as evidenced by his earlier album, *Jazz in 3/4 Time*. The percussive and innovative nature of the album is notable in two other tracks on which Roach plays unaccompanied (both his own compositions): "Drums Unlimited" and "For Big Sid."

Musical Legacy

For more than sixty years, Roach was one of the leading drummers in jazz, demanding respect for his clear, articulate, and imaginative style. Throughout his life, Roach explored new sounds both within and beyond the world of jazz, ranging from his playing with Parker in the 1940's to his appearances later in his life with performers as varied as hip-hop artists and a classical string quartet. He also contributed many important compositions, many of them addressing racial and political issues, such as his *We Insist! Max Roach's Freedom Suite Now*. Roach was recognized for his accomplishments, being named top drummer in the *Down Beat* Readers Poll, the *Down Beat* Critics Poll, and the Metronome Readers Poll. In 1980 he was inducted into the *Down Beat* Critics Hall of Fame. Roach twice received the French Grand Prix du Disque, the top award for recordings, and he was the recipient of eight honorary degrees. He held an important role as a jazz educator at the School of Jazz at Lenox, Massachusetts, and the University of Massachusetts at Amherst. His immense discography continues to inspire young players throughout the world of jazz.

Mark A. Peters

Further Reading

Fox, Charles. "Sit Down and Listen: The Story of Max Roach." In *Repercussions: A Celebration of African-American Music*, edited by Geoffrey Haydon and Dennis Marks. London: Century, 1985. An accessible overview of Roach's life and music from his early years through the 1970's.

Horricks, Raymond. "Max Roach and Art Blakey: The Role of the Drummer-Leader." In *These Jazzmen of Our Time*. London: Victor Gollancz, 1959. Overview of Roach's early career, with detailed musical analysis of his style (particularly in relation to Blakey's).

Korall, Burt. *Drummin' Men: The Heartbeat of Jazz—The Bebop Years*. Oxford, England: Oxford University Press, 2002. Detailed story of Roach's life and music punctuated by quotes about Roach from numerous interviews conducted by the author and enlivened by the author's own experience as a jazz drummer.

Roach, Max. "Beyond Categories." In *Keeping Time: Readings in Jazz History*, edited by Robert Walser. Oxford, England: Oxford University Press, 1999. A short but intense statement by Roach on jazz, civil rights, and American racism.

Weinstein, Norman C. "Max Roach: Drumming the Tales of African and African-American Liberation." In *A Night in Tunisia: Imaginings of Africa in Jazz*. Metuchen, N.J.: Scarecrow Press, 1992. Exploration of Roach's lifelong quest for African American and African liberation in his music, with particular attention to his *We Insist! Max Roach's Freedom Now Suite*.

See also: Belafonte, Harry; Brown, Clifford; Carter, Benny; Davis, Miles; Dolphy, Eric; Ellington, Duke; Gillespie, Dizzy; Handy, W. C.; Hawkins, Coleman; Mingus, Charles; Monk, Thelonious; Parker, Charlie; Powell, Bud; Rollins, Sonny; Taylor, Cecil.

Robbie Robertson

Canadian rock singer, guitarist, and songwriter

The leader, guitarist, and primary songwriter for the Band, Robertson forged an authentically North American musical response—that fused folk, pop, country, and rock and roll—to the British invasion-inspired pop music that dominated the musical scene in the late 1960's.

Born: July 5, 1943; Toronto, Ontario, Canada
Also known as: Jaime Robert Robertson (full name)
Member of: The Band

Principal recordings

ALBUMS (solo): *So Many Roads*, 1965 (guitar; with John Hammond, Jr.); *I Can Tell*, 1967 (guitar; with Hammond); *Robbie Robertson*, 1987; *Storyville*, 1991; *Music for the Native Americans*, 1994; *Contact from the Underworld of RedBoy*, 1998.

ALBUMS (with the Band): *Music from Big Pink*, 1968; *The Band*, 1969; *Stage Fright*, 1970; *Cahoots*, 1971; *Moondog Matinee*, 1973; *The Basement Tapes*, 1975; *Northern Lights—Southern Cross*, 1975; *Islands*, 1977; *The Last Waltz*, 1978 (with others).

The Life

Jaime Robert Robertson was born in Toronto to a mother of Mohawk descent and a Jewish father who died when Robertson was in his infancy. He was raised on the Six Nations Reservation, ran away with a carnival in his teens (providing experiences he later drew upon for the film *Carny*), and by sixteen was a professional musician and songwriter.

Fame came with his association with Bob Dylan, and by 1969 the Band had become the first rock group featured on the cover of *Time*. He costarred with Jodie Foster and Gary Busey in the film *Carny* in 1980, and became one of the first rock musicians to become a major sound-track composer, producing music for films by Martin Scorsese and others. Among awards, he earned Grammy nominations for Best Rock Vocal for both of his first two solo albums, was inducted into the Rock and Roll Hall of Fame with the Band, and received the Lifetime Achievement Award from the National Academy of Songwriters.

Working widely as a record producer and executive, Robertson also became guiding force behind the Native American Music Association, and his lyrics were used as captions for Myron Zabol's *People of the Dancing Sky*, a collection of photographs and profiles of Iroquois people and artifacts.

The Music

Robertson began writing songs for rockabilly legend Ronnie Hawkins when he was fifteen years old and playing guitar for his band, the Hawks, when he was sixteen. Robertson was a phenomenally proficient guitarist, and within a few years the Hawks had been transformed into the Band: Robertson, Levon Helm, Rick Danko, Richard Manuel, and Garth Hudson. After leaving Hawkins, they became Dylan's backing group when he shifted from folk to electric rock at the peak of his fame. Robertson was immediately recognized as a brilliant songwriter in his own right when the Band emerged from Dylan's shadow. Dissolving the Band after eight albums, Robertson released four solo albums (two of rock music, two rooted in Native American music) and several film sound tracks, as well as producing albums for other artists.

Music from Big Pink. The Band's first album, *Music from Big Pink*, sounded unlike anything else in the popular music of the time. A decade of touring had given them a seemingly telepathic ability to interweave their voices and instruments into subtle patterns that demanded repeated listening to appreciate how the parts formed into a whole. Eschewing slick production and accessible themes, they offered a set of songs with a rough-edged and rural feel, melodically and rhythmically halting and uncertain, with deceptively simple but ultimately opaque lyrics, often steeped in Old Testament imagery. Songs such as "The Weight" sounded like old standards from the moment they were released, saturated in a rich mixture of American musical styles, especially in those identified with the Deep South, including blues, country, soul, rockabilly, and gospel.

The Band. While the first album had included songs by Dylan, Danko and Manuel, Robertson wrote or cowrote every song on the second album, *The Band*, as well as serving as engineer and primary producer. He seldom sang, preferring to assign the vocal parts to Helm, Danko, and Manuel, who blended and alternated their distinctive voices like a gospel choir. Every member of the group was a talented multi-instrumentalist, enabling them to switch their instrumentation to suit the material rather than play every song with the same fixed lineup, as had almost every rock band preceding them. Even though everyone except Helm was Canadian, the album was even more deeply rooted in traditional American music than *Music from Big Pink*, and Robertson claimed at one point that he could have called the concept album *America*. His portrait of a bygone era was also an implicit commentary on the contemporary American scene, and even a song set in a seemingly distant past, such as "The Night They Drove Old Dixie Down," which presented Civil War vignettes from the point of view of a Confederate soldier, could also be covered by Joan Baez for its relevance to the Civil Rights movement.

The Last Waltz. In this album Robertson combined his musical and cinematic interests for the Band's farewell concert after sixteen years together on Thanksgiving Day, 1976, which featured guest appearances by Hawkins, Dylan, and several other stars, including Muddy Waters, Van Morrison, Eric Clapton, Joni Mitchell, and Neil Young. The documentary film of the event, directed by Scorsese, was ranked by *Rolling Stone* in 2007 as the Top Music DVD of All Time.

Robbie Robertson. His first solo album revealed Robertson to be a surprisingly effective vocalist, with much greater range than his rare vocals with the Band might have suggested, and a still-inspired songwriter and guitarist. While the sounds often recalled the Band, and Danko and Hudson made guest appearances (Manuel had committed suicide, and Helm, who blamed Robertson for breaking up the Band, stayed away), Robertson added new tones and complexity to the familiar musical palette with numerous other guest musicians who had long admired his work, including Peter Gabriel, U2, the BoDeans, Ivan Neville, and jazz legend Gil Evans.

Musical Legacy

At the dawn of the era of psychedelic music, heavy metal, and stadium rock, Robertson was determined that the louder and flashier everyone else got, the quieter and more thoughtful he would get, a direction quickly followed by most of his musical peers. A short list of the artists he influenced as leader of the Band would include the Beatles, the Rolling Stones, Morrison, Clapton, and Bruce Springsteen. Both of the Band's first two albums—*Music from the Big Pink* and *The Band*—were still ranked in the Top 50 of the 2003 list of *Rolling Stone's* 500 Greatest Albums of All Time, nearly thirty-five years after their release, a testimony to their timeless value, and "The Weight" was also in the Top 50 of the same magazine's Greatest Songs of All Time.

William Nelles

Further Reading

Fetherling, Douglas. *Some Day Soon: Essays on Canadian Songwriters*. Kingston, Ont.: Quarry Press, 1991. Provides an overview of Robertson's work with the Band, but devotes only a paragraph to his solo work.

Helm, Levon, with Stephen Davis. *This Wheel's on Fire: Levon Helm and the Story of the Band*. Rev. ed. Chicago: A Capella, 2000. Though colored by Helm's bitterness over the breakup of the Band, for which he never forgave Robertson, there is a wealth of colorful anecdotes from their sixteen years of playing together.

Hoskyns, Barney. *Across the Great Divide: The Band and America*. Rev. ed. Milwaukee, Wis.: Hal Leonard, 2006. Complete study of the Band, balanced and thoroughly researched.

Kubernik, Harvey. *Hollywood Shack Job: Rock Music in Film and on Your Screen*. Albuquerque: University of New Mexico Press, 2006. Includes a chapter on Robertson in a 2002 interview.

See also: Baez, Joan; Clapton, Eric; Diamond, Neil; Dylan, Bob; Mitchell, Joni; Morrison, Van; Young, Neil.

Paul Robeson

American classical and musical-theater singer

With his powerful and elegant voice, Robeson revived interest in traditional African American music, especially the spiritual.

Born: April 9, 1898; Princeton, New Jersey
Died: January 23, 1976; Philadelphia, Pennsylvania
Also known as: Paul LeRoy Bustill Robeson (full name)

Principal works

MUSICAL THEATER ROLES: *Show Boat*, 1932 (libretto by Oscar Hammerstein II; based on the play by Edna Ferber; lyrics by Hammerstein; music by Jerome Kern); *John Henry*, 1940 (libretto and lyrics by Roark Bradford; music by Jacques Wolfe).

Principal recordings

ALBUMS: *A Lonesome Road: Paul Robeson Sings Spirituals and Songs*, 1927; *Big Fella*, 1928; *The Inimitable Paul Robeson*, 1931; *Carry Me Back to Green Pastures*, 1933; *Great Voices, Vol. I*, 1933; *Great Voices, Vol. II*, 1933; *Paul Robeson Sings "Ol' Man River,"* 1933; *The Voice of Mississippi*, 1933; *Ballad for Americans*, 1939; *For Free Men*, 1944; *The Political Years*, 1944; *The Power and the Glory*, 1945; *Peace Arch Concerts*, 1953; *Freedom Train*, 1957; *Paul Robeson Live at Carnegie Hall, May 9, 1958*, 1958; *The Historic Paul Robeson*, 1961; *The Odyssey of Paul Robeson*, 1961.
WRITINGS OF INTEREST: *Here I Stand*, 1958; *Paul Robeson Speaks: Writings, Speeches, and Interviews, 1918-1974*, 1978 (edited by Philip Sheldon Foner).

The Life

Paul LeRoy Bustill Robeson (ROHB-suhn) was born the eighth and youngest child of schoolteacher Maria Louisa Bustill and William Drew Robeson, a former slave who had escaped from North Carolina on the Underground Railroad, studied at Lincoln University, and became a minister. Robeson's mother died in 1904 from burns received in an accident involving a coal-fueled stove, and in 1910 his father became pastor at St. Thomas A.M.E. Zion Church in Somerville, New Jersey. Robeson graduated from Somerville High School in 1915, and he went on to study at Rutgers University. From 1915 to 1919, as the university's only African American student, he endured abuse; nevertheless, he was a member of the College Football All-America Teams in 1917 and 1918; a sports letterman in baseball, basketball, and track and field; a member of Phi Beta Kappa and the Cap and Skull Society; and class valedictorian. He entered Columbia University Law School in 1920, receiving his juris doctor degree in 1923, partially supporting himself by acting and singing. His legal career at the firm of Stotesbury and Miner did not last for long—he resigned in disgust over an issue of racial discrimination. In 1920 he began his acting career, performing the title role in Ridgely Torrence's play *Simon the Cyrenian* (1917). His professional singing debut took place in 1921, when Robeson was part of the chorus in the musical *Shuffle Along* (1921).

On August 7, 1921, he married Eslanda Cardozo Goode. The couple had a lasting though troubled marriage, which ended upon Eslanda's death in 1965. Their only child, a son named Paul Robeson, Jr., was born on November 2, 1927. In 1922 Robeson went to England to appear in the London stage production of *Voodoo* (1922).

During the 1920's Robeson starred in Eugene O'Neill's *All God's Chillun Got Wings* (1924) and *The Emperor Jones* (1920). However, it was his rendition of the part of Joe in *Show Boat* (1927) that established his fame. His most highly acclaimed acting roles were two major productions of *Othello* (1930 and 1942-1945).

Robeson enjoyed a lengthy cinematic career, making his debut in a silent film called *Body and Soul* (1928). He later starred in *Borderline* (1930), *The Emperor Jones* (1933), *Sanders of the River* (1935), *Song of Freedom* (1936), *King Solomon's Mines* (1937), *Jericho* (1937), *Big Fella* (1937), *Proud Valley* (1939), and *Tales of Manhattan* (1942).

Robeson's outspoken denunciation of racial discrimination in the United States coupled with his advocacy of Marxist ideology and the Soviet Union and his support for the radical labor movement brought him widespread criticism. A violent backlash culminated in the Peekskill Riots of August 28

and September 4, 1949, when clashes between pro- and anti-Robeson crowds forced the cancellation of his concert at Peekskill, New York. In 1950 the U.S. State Department revoked his passport. Undaunted, Robeson in 1958 wrote *Here I Stand*, to denounce his persecutors and justify his stance. That same year a Supreme Court decision reversed his passport ban.

The Civil Rights movement brought about a rehabilitation of Robeson's reputation. He was seen as an early martyr to the cause of racial equality. By this time his health had begun to fail, and he died, after being hospitalized for a stroke, on January 23, 1976.

The Music

Though Robeson had been noted for the power of his singing voice from his college days, it was on a sudden impulse to earn some money to pay for law school that he participated in the chorus of the musical *Shuffle Along* at Harlem's Cotton Club in 1921. Although his professional singing debut was in a small part, it brought him instant notice. When he was in London a year later, on the set of *Voodoo*, he met Lawrence "Larry" Brown, a black musician who became Robeson's leading performing partner. From 1925 to 1948, Brown provided the musical accompaniment for Robeson's international singing tours and traveling concerts.

Show Boat. As Joe in *Show Boat*, Robeson attained almost iconic status. Even though it was Jules Bledsoe who first sang the musical's major song, "Ol' Man River," in the New York stage production, it became indelibly identified with Robeson, who sang it in London. "Ol' Man River" was Robeson's signature song, and he changed the lyrics to more militantly defiant.

"Ballad for Americans." Robeson was further noted for the choral portions in his cinematic productions. His musical interpretation of the patriotic poem "Ballad for Americans" was one of the most popular songs in the United States in the years preceding America's entry into World War II.

Musical Legacy

Robeson's masterful baritone voice and imposing presence made him one of the first internationally renowned African American celebrities, and he was a trailblazer for later African American male vocalists. In his collaboration with Brown, Robeson promoted the black spiritual in his performances and in his recordings, elevating a forgotten genre into a respected art form. His renditions of "The Battle of Jericho," "Swing Low, Sweet Chariot," "Go Down Moses," and "Every Time I Feel the Spirit" have become enduring classics.

Raymond Pierre Hylton

Further Reading

Duberman, Martin Bauml. *Paul Robeson*. New York: Alfred A. Knopf, 1988. Richly detailed and illustrated and meticulously researched, this scholarly biography of Robeson is genuinely sympathetic to its subject.

Freedomways. *Paul Robeson: The Great Forerunner*. New York: Dodd, Mead, 1978. An intriguing collection of essays, tributes, and selections from Robeson's speeches and articles, emphasizing his versatility and his role as a man ahead of his time.

Hine, Darlene Clark, William C. Hine, and Stanley Harrold. *The African-American Odyssey*. Upper Saddle River, N.J.: Prentice Hall, 2000. This is a general work that is useful in placing Robeson within the greater context of twentieth century African American history.

Larsen, Rebecca. *Paul Robeson: Hero Before His Time*. New York: Franklin Watts, 1989. This succinct and elegant biography equates Robeson to an epic hero. It describes the social and historical events of the time, condemning the effects of the Jim Crow system.

Robeson, Paul. *Here I Stand*. Boston: Beacon Press, 1971. Some assert that this book prefigured the Civil Rights movement of the 1960's. It consists of Robeson's strident reply to official attempts to muzzle him, and he equates these attempts to "massive resistance" efforts against racial equality.

Robeson, Paul, Jr. *The Undiscovered Paul Robeson: An Artist's Journey, 1898-1939*. New York: J. Wiley, 2001. Written by the artist's son, this book has an intimacy and intensity lacking in more conventional biographies. The younger Robeson focuses on the formational influences in his father's career.

Robeson, Susie. *The Whole World in His Hands: A Pictorial Biography of Paul Robeson*. Seacaucus, N.J.: Citadel Press, 1981. This biography by the singer's granddaughter is probably the best starting point for understanding Robeson as a man.

See also: Belafonte, Harry; Blake, Eubie; Hammerstein, Oscar, II; Hunter, Alberta; Kern, Jerome; Odetta; Seeger, Pete.

Smokey Robinson
American rhythm-and-blues/soul singer and songwriter

As a singer, Robinson helped define the Motown sound with his smooth vocal presentations and soulful songs. As a songwriter, he created a public-pleasing combination of rhythm and blues, soul, and pop that resulted in hit singles for himself and other artists.

Born: February 19, 1940; Detroit, Michigan
Also known as: William Robinson, Jr. (full name)
Member of: The Miracles; Smokey Robinson and the Miracles

Principal works

ALBUMS (solo): *Smokey*, 1973; *A Quiet Storm*, 1975; *Smokey's Family Robinson*, 1976; *Deep in My Soul*, 1977; *Big Time*, 1977; *Love Breeze*, 1978; *Smokin'*, 1978; *Where There's Smoke*, 1979; *Warm Thoughts*, 1980; *Being with You*, 1981; *Yes It's You Lady*, 1982; *Touch the Sky*, 1983; *Essar*, 1984; *Smoke Signals*, 1986; *One Heartbeat*, 1987; *Love, Smokey*, 1990; *Double Good Everything*, 1991; *Intimate*, 1999; *Food for the Spirit*, 2004; *Timeless Love*, 2006.

ALBUMS (with the Miracles): *Hi, We're the Miracles*, 1961; *Cookin' with the Miracles*, 1962; *I'll Try Something New*, 1962; *Shop Around*, 1962; *Christmas with the Miracles*, 1963; *Doin' Mickey's Monkey*, 1963; *The Fabulous Miracles*, 1963; *The Miracles Live on Stage*, 1963; *I Like It Like That*, 1964; *Renaissance*, 1973; *Do It Baby*, 1974; *City of Angels*, 1975; *Don't Cha Love It*, 1975; *The Power of Music*, 1976; *Love Crazy*, 1977; *The Miracles*, 1977.

ALBUMS (with Smokey Robinson and the Miracles): *Going to a Go-Go*, 1965; *Greatest Hits from the Beginning*, 1965; *Away We Go-Go*, 1966; *Make It Happen*, 1967; *Special Occasion*, 1968; *Time out for Smokey Robinson and the Miracles*, 1969; *Four in Blue*, 1969; *What Love Has . . . Joined Together*, 1970; *Season for Miracles*, 1970; *The Tears of a Clown*, 1970; *A Pocket Full of Miracles*, 1970; *From the Beginning*, 1971; *One Dozen Roses*, 1971; *Smokey and the Miracles*, 1971; *Flying High Together*, 1972.

WRITINGS OF INTEREST: *Smokey: Inside My Life*, 1989.

The Life

William Robinson, Jr., was born on February 19, 1940, and grew up in the North End section of Detroit, Michigan (the city that would later produce Motown Records). His affinity for cowboy films during his youth resulted in the nickname Smokey Joe, which was simplified to Smokey by the time he became a teenager. Music as well as movies interested the youngster, who was immediately attracted to the musical side of town (which featured a burgeoning soul, doo-wop, and rhythm-and-blues scene).

In 1955 Robinson started the vocal group Five Chimes, which shifted members and names by 1957 to Matadors. The lineup continued to change, eventually incorporating Robinson's future wife Claudette Rogers, and the group caught the ear of local songwriter Berry Gordy. The relationship started when Gordy cowrote a simple song called "Got a Job," and it helped the young group gain a more professional sound.

Eventually the group changed its name to the Miracles, and Robinson coaxed Gordy into starting his own label. It started as Tamla Records, and later it was rebranded Motown Records. Gordy signed the Miracles as Motown's first act, and he made Robinson vice president and songwriter for other artists. In 1959, with their professional careers launched, Robinson married Claudette, although the group's constant touring made a stable life hard to achieve.

During the 1960's, the couple tried to start a family, but the strain of touring resulted in seven miscarriages. Claudette remained a background singer with the group through 1972. Later, the couple had a son, Berry William Robinson, and a daughter, Tamla Claudette Robinson. However, the music business eventually pulled Robinson and Claudette apart, resulting in a 1986 divorce.

In 1989 Robinson published a tell-all autobiography, *Smokey: Inside My Life*, in which he admitted to having extramarital affairs and using cocaine, which catalyzed his divorce from Claudette. Even with his personal difficulties, Robinson maintained a prominent career. Later, in an attempt to rebuild his life, he reclaimed the Christian faith of his upbringing (traced later on 2004's *Food for the Spirit*) and explored projects outside of the music industry. He went into the food business, with Smokey Robinson's Soul in the Bowl gumbo and red beans and rice products sold in supermarkets across the country.

The Music

Early Works. With the Miracles as his main mouthpiece, Robinson's vocals were introduced to

Smokey Robinson. (AP/Wide World Photos)

the world in 1961's *Hi, We're the Miracles*. The album was primarily noted for the doo-wop and soul-flavored single "Shop Around," which became the group's and Motown's first million-selling hit. It topped the *Billboard* rhythm-and-blues charts and placed second as a pop single. *Cookin' with the Miracles* did not earn those ratings, but it did have some success with the singles "Ain't It Baby" and "Everybody's Gotta Pay Some Dues" as singles. The title cut from *I'll Try Something New* also made the charts.

The Fabulous Miracles. The grouped proved its initial chart run was not a fluke with this cohesive collection of doo-wop sing-alongs and romantic ballads. "You Really Got a Hold on Me" became a million-selling single, gaining additional prominence for the group and record label as a whole. In fact, the success of the project paved the way for 1963's *The Miracles Recorded Live on Stage*, chronicling the group's hits up until that point in a concert setting.

Doin' Mickey's Monkey. The Miracles modulated their sound on this album to highlight the dance crazes of the day, with the title track of *Doin' Mickey's Monkey* getting tremendous play on the radio and in clubs. The collection also included covers of the "The Twist," "Land of 1000 Dances," and "Twist and Shout." The group took a break from the studio the following year, but in 1965 it produced a double-album compilation, *Greatest Hits from the Beginning*.

Going to a Go-Go *and* Make It Happen. Under the new name Smokey Robinson and the Miracles, *Going to a Go-Go* peaked at number eight on the *Billboard* Top 200 albums chart and spawned four Top 20 singles: "Ooo Baby Baby," "The Tracks of My Tears," "Going to a Go-Go," and "My Girl Has Gone." These tracks featured increased vocal prominence from Robinson, who by that time was also a highly regarded songwriter. *Make It Happen* found Robinson similarly in the spotlight, in the easygoing concert favorite "More Love" and the vibrant "The Tears of a Clown" (which featured cowriting from Stevie Wonder).

Time out for Smokey Robinson and the Miracles. Though 1968's *Special Occasion* was responsible for the hits "If You Can Want," "Yester Love," and "Special Occasion," it was soon overshadowed by the success of 1969's *Time out for Smokey Robinson*

and the Miracles. Aside from the stormy single "Baby, Baby Don't Cry," the collection was regarded for a group interpretation of "My Girl," penned by Robinson, although it was originally made famous by the Temptations. Though Smokey Robinson and the Miracles continued recording for the remainder of the decade, its last major single came in 1970 (with the rerelease of "The Tears of a Clown"), and Robinson soon set out on a solo career.

Smokey. Robinson recorded for the last time with the Miracles on 1972's *Flying High Together*, which scored only one Top 40 pop hit, "We've Gone Too Far to End It Now." Despite the title, he went solo the following year with *Smokey*, which earned a bit of publicity, but it failed to match the group's peak period. The project found Robinson exploring a warm soul sound, which was perhaps out of step with the burgeoning funk and dance movements that presaged disco by the end of the decade.

Where There's Smoke. Robinson flirted with the disco craze on 1979's *Where There's Smoke*, but the public gravitated to the track "Cruisin'," a sultry ballad. It became the singer's biggest single since "The Tears of a Clown" with the Miracles. The comeback of sorts led to *Warm Thoughts*, with the slow and seductive "Let Me Be the Clock," a formula reprised on 1981's *Being with You*, known for the breezy title cut that followed pop patterns.

One Heartbeat. Despite the surge at the start of the 1980's, Robinson's streak did not last long. His personal life spiraled out of control with drugs and a divorce. By 1987, however, he was back to form, producing *One Heartbeat*, with the tender title track and the potent pop single "Just to See Her" (which earned a Grammy Award for Best Rhythm and Blues Vocal Performance). This success put Robinson back on the concert circuit, which he continued through the 1990's.

Later Works. In 2004 the gospel-flavored *Food for the Spirit* highlighted Robinson's spiritual beliefs, and *Timeless Love* covered a series of classics originally performed by Frank Sinatra, Ella Fitzgerald, Sarah Vaughan, Billie Holiday, and others. No matter the stature of those legends, Robinson interpreted each track in his subtle but skillful personal style.

Robinson offered a diverse list of specialty albums in the 2000's. These included a holiday collection, a gospel record, and reinterpretations of standards, all marked with Robinson's distinctive vocal stamp.

Musical Legacy

Starting with his rise to recognition in the Miracles, Robinson helped shape the Motown sound from its beginning. Combining doo-wop elements with rhythm and blues, soul, and pop, the singer-songwriter was among the first to introduce the melded sound to the public, which swooned over his romantic lyrics and smooth crooning abilities.

Besides being part of the Miracles' remarkable string of hit singles, Robinson branched out as a Motown executive, and he composed memorable material for other artists. His writing contributions for the Temptations, Mary Wells, Marvin Gaye, and the Marvelettes, to name a few, solidified their success. In fact, artists spanning all genres showed their appreciation. Folk troubadour Bob Dylan called Robinson "America's greatest living poet." Former Beatle George Harrison wrote a musical tribute called "Pure Smokey." The new wave band ABC paid homage to Robinson with the song "When Smokey Sings."

Andy Argyrakis

Further Reading

Christian, Margena A. "Smokey Robinson, the 'Poet Laureate of Soul,' Celebrates Fifty Years of Music." *Jet* (April 2, 2007). A cover-story interview recalls the singer's storied career in commemoration of his fiftieth anniversary in the music business.

Gordy, Berry. *Berry Gordy: To Be Loved, the Music, the Magic, the Memories of Motown.* New York: Warner Books, 1994. Motown's founder tells his side of the story on several artists' rise to fame, including numerous accounts of working with Robinson as an artist and executive. Robinson championed this book, supporting its accuracy.

Posner, Gerald. *Motown: Music, Money, Sex, and Power.* New York: Random House, 2002. An exhaustive investigation of the legendary record label, including references to Robinson as a singer for the Miracles, songwriter for the group, and solo artist in later years.

Pruter, Robert, ed. *The Blackwell Guide to Soul Recordings.* Oxford, England: Blackwell, 1993. A

breakdown of soul music's different eras and geographic locations, including several entries on Robinson, solo and with the Miracles.

Robinson, Smokey, with David Ritz. *Smokey: Inside My Life.* New York: McGraw-Hill, 1989. Robinson offers his life story, with his insights about Motown, his solo career, working with other artists, and life behind the scenes.

See also: Cooke, Sam; Dylan, Bob; Gaye, Marvin; Harrison, George; Jamerson, James; Kirk, Rahsaan Roland; Sinatra, Frank; Wonder, Stevie.

Jimmie Rodgers

American country singer, guitarist, and songwriter

Through his recordings and performances, Rodgers made Southern and rural music popular, laying the foundation for country music.

Born: September 8, 1897; Meridian, Mississippi
Died: May 26, 1933; New York, New York
Also known as: James Charles Rodgers (full name); Singing Brakeman

Principal recordings

SINGLES: "Away out on the Mountain," 1927; "Ben Dewberry's Final Run," 1927; "Blue Yodel No. 1," 1927; "Mother Was a Lady (If Brother Jack Were Here)," 1927; "Sleep, Baby, Sleep," 1927; "The Soldier's Sweetheart," 1927; "Blue Yodel No. 2," 1928; "Blue Yodel No. 3," 1928; "The Brakeman's Blues," 1928; "Daddy and Home," 1928; "Dear Old Sunny South by the Sea," 1928; "I'm Lonely and Blue," 1928; "In the Jailhouse Now," 1928; "Lullaby Yodel," 1928; "Memphis Yodel," 1928; "My Carolina Sunshine Girl," 1928; "My Little Lady," 1928; "My Little Old Home down in New Orleans,"1928; "My Old Pal," 1928; "Never No Mo' Blues," 1928; "The Sailor's Plea," 1928; "Treasures Untold," 1928; "Waiting for a Train," 1928; "You and My Old Guitar," 1928; "Anniversary Blue Yodel (Blue Yodel No. 7),"

1929; "Any Old Time," 1929; "Blue Yodel No. 5," 1929; "Blue Yodel No. 6," 1929; "Blue Yodel No. 11," 1929; "Desert Blues," 1929; "Everybody Does It in Hawaii," 1929; "Frankie and Johnnie," 1929; "High Powered Mama," 1929; "Hobo Bill's Last Ride," 1929; "I'm Sorry We Met," 1929; "I've Ranged, I've Roamed, and I've Traveled," 1929; "Jimmie's Texas Blues," 1929; "The Land of My Boyhood Dreams," 1929; "Mississippi River Blues,"1929; "My Rough and Rowdy Ways," 1929; "Nobody Knows But Me," 1929; "She Was Happy Till She Met You," 1929; "That's Why I'm Blue," 1929; "Train Whistle Blues," 1929; "Tuck Away My Lonesome Blues," 1929; "Whisper Your Mother's Name," 1929; "Why Did You Give Me Your Love?," 1929; "Yodeling Cowboy," 1929; "Blue Yodel No. 8 (Mule Skinner Blues)," 1930; "Blue Yodel No. 9," 1930; "For the Sake of Days Gone By," 1930; "I'm Lonesome Too," 1930; "In the Jailhouse Now, No. 2," 1930; "Jimmie's Mean Mama Blues," 1930; "Moonlight and Skies," 1930; "My Blue-Eyed Jane," 1930; "The Mystery of Number Five," 1930; "The One Rose (That's Left in My Heart)," 1930; "Pistol Packin' Papa," 1930; "Take Me Back Again," 1930; "Those Gambler's Blues," 1930; "Why Should I Be Lonely?," 1930; "The Carter Family and Jimmie Rodgers in Texas," 1931; "Gambling Polka Dot Blues," 1931; "Jimmie Rodgers Visits the Carter Family," 1931; "Jimmie the Kid," 1931; "Let Me Be Your Sidetrack," 1931; "Looking for a New Mama," 1931; "My Good Gal's Gone Blues," 1931; "Southern Cannon-Ball," 1931; "T.B. Blues," 1931; "Travelin' Blues," 1931; "What's It?," 1931; "When the Cactus Is in Bloom," 1931; "Why There's a Tear in My Eye," 1931; "The Wonderful City," 1931; "Blue Yodel No. 10," 1932; "Down the Old Road to Home," 1932; "Gambling Barroom Blues," 1932; "Hobo's Meditation," 1932; "Home Call," 1932; "In the Hills of Tennessee," 1932; "I've Only Loved Three Women," 1932; "Long Tall Mama Blues," 1932; "Miss the Mississippi and You," 1932; "Mississippi Moon," 1932; "Mother, the Queen of My Heart," 1932; "My Time Ain't Long," 1932; "Ninety-nine Years Blues," 1932; "No Hard Times," 1932; "Peach-Pickin' Time

down in Georgia," 1932; "Prairie Lullaby," 1932; "Rock All Our Babies to Sleep," 1932; "Roll Along, Kentucky Moon," 1932; "Sweet Mama Hurry Home (or I'll Be Gone)," 1932; "Whippin' That Old T.B.," 1932; "Blue Yodel No. 12," 1933; "The Cowhand's Last Ride," 1933; "Dreaming with Tears in My Eyes," 1933; "I'm Free (From the Chain Gang Now)," 1933; "Jimmie Rodgers' Last Blue Yodel," 1933; "Mississippi Delta Blues," 1933; "Old Love Letters," 1933; "Old Pal of My Heart," 1933; "Somewhere down Below the Dixon Line," 1933; "Years Ago," 1933; "Yodeling My Way Back Home," 1933; "The Yodeling Ranger," 1933.

The Life

Jimmie Rodgers was born James Charles Rodgers in 1897 in Meridian, Mississippi. Rodgers admired his father Aaron, who was a railroad section foreman, and Rodgers used his father as the source of his songs, including "Daddy and Home." His mother died when he was only six years old, forcing Rodgers to live with various relatives and instilling in him a perennial wanderlust. Though never really the destitute orphan depicted in his songs or in his publicity stories, Rodgers never had another permanent home until he bought a mansion just before he died.

Meridian, the largest city in Mississippi, hosted entertainers of all kinds. Rodgers was starstruck, and he decided early on that he wanted to be a performer. The first hint of success came with his winning a small talent contest when he was twelve, singing the parlor-song hits "(Won't You Come Home) Bill Bailey" and "Steamboat Bill" (also known as "Casey Jones"). After some time on the medicine-show circuit with only modest success, he settled down at home, working with his father on the New Orleans and Northeastern Railroad as a brakeman. These wages allowed Rodgers to enjoy his favorite pastimes: girls, records, and music concerts. Rodgers married a local beauty, Stella Kelly, in 1917, but the marriage ended in a few months because of money problems.

Rodgers eloped with his second wife, Carrie Williamson, in 1920 against her family's wishes (financial security again being an issue). It was not a good time to marry: The post-World War I economic slump made times hard, and Rodgers lost his railroad job. The birth of their daughters in 1921 and 1923 compounded their difficulties. In addition, in the fall of 1924, Rodgers was diagnosed with tuberculosis. Largely ignoring his ill health, Rodgers began to take his amateur music career more seriously, playing in dance bands, in medicine shows, in blackface minstrel shows, and in a Hawaiian carnival. He also went back to work on the railroad. However, in 1927, for reasons that are still unclear, Rodgers went to Asheville, North Carolina, where he played a number of part-time gigs before going on the road and stopping off to see a couple of musician friends in Bristol, Tennessee, where he made some recordings for Victor Records.

He had a brief success, but even though people were willing to spend seventy-five cents for one of his records (almost twice the price of a good steak at that time, one observer noted), the Great Depression took its toll. By 1932 record sales plummeted, and it was hard for Rodgers to find work; he had to resort to touring with small tent shows. His health was failing fast, too, causing him to cut back on those few personal appearances he could find. A large cash settlement in 1932 with his first wife over child support for a daughter (who may or may not have been his) added to his financial burdens. In 1933, against his doctor's advice, Rodgers traveled from Texas to New York for a week-long, thirteen-song recording session to provide money for his family after his death. Two days after finishing, Rodgers died.

The Music

When Rodgers began his career just after World War I, country music had not yet been defined. Songs based on Southern rural-oriented dance tunes and folk ballads were just beginning to be noticed as a genre, although they were often dismissed as hillbilly music. At that time, commercial popular music, mostly confined to the Northern cities, consisted of live music hall and vaudeville shows outside the home and various family parlor

Jimmie Rodgers. (Hulton Archive/Getty Images)

musical instruments (with their sheet music) inside the home.

Soon, radio and records began to introduce new musical styles to different audiences, offering Southern musicians new opportunities to perform as professionals and allowing many to make a living playing the tunes they grew hearing. Southern radio stations found that broadcasting live local talent was an inexpensive way to fill airtime, attract listeners, and gain sponsors. Artists found radio to be a good way to increase attendance at their personal appearances (where they made most of their money). With the advent of the automobile, local talent could appear at a greater number of venues, and the latest city stars and songs could come out to the farms. In the South, square dance songs, rural white mountain folk ballads, and African American Delta blues mixed easily with the latest urban show tunes, rags, and Tin Pan Alley novelty hits from the North. By the 1920's hillbilly music was becoming commercialized, and many artists from the South, including Rodgers, dreamed of national fame and fortune.

Recording Country Music. New York record company executives discovered that Northerners, too, were interested in hillbilly music, believing it to be reflective of simpler, pastoral times. Ralph Peer, a producer and talent scout for the Victor record label, was one of the first to realize there was a national audience for authentic (or songs that sounded authentic), old-time Southern songs, and he made some of the first country-music recordings in the early 1920's. In 1927 he visited the Appalachian town of Bristol (Tennessee or Virginia, the state line runs down the main street) on a field trip in search of local rural musicians and traditional songs he might be able to copyright. He recorded nineteen artists, who performed seventy-six songs over a ten-day period. Six songs were by the Carter Family, a group that helped to define country music. Two others were by a scrawny kid who looked younger than his twenty-nine years: Rodgers.

Yodeler. At that time, Rodgers was a bandleader without a band, because he and his musicians had split up over an argument about money. Calling themselves the Tenneva Ramblers, the others decided to audition without him. Peer was dubious about a Rodgers solo audition, but he was impressed by Rodgers's yodel. Rodgers's two numbers were a Spanish-American World War I ballad called "The Soldier's Sweetheart" and a country lullaby called "Sleep, Baby, Sleep."

In spite of apocryphal tales to the contrary, Peer did not immediately recognize Rodgers's genius nor did these songs become instant hits. Though they sold moderately well, considering Rodgers was unknown, they did not make Rodgers an immediate star. However, typical of his optimism or perhaps his denial of unpleasant news, Rodgers traveled to New York and persuaded Peer to record him again. One of the records made then, "Blue Yodel No. 1," became Rodgers's breakthrough hit and his trademark tune. Finally seeing Rodgers's great commercial potential, Peer became the singer's manager, working with him until his death in 1933. Within months Rodgers's name spread all over the country, and soon he was making radio appearances and traveling the concert circuit.

The Singing Brakeman. Rodgers's career would only last another five years, but his unique yodel and choice of material struck the heartstrings of listeners, both Northern and Southern. His fame spread with each new record and personal appearance. He worked with some of the most famous entertainers of the day, including jazz trumpeter Louis Armstrong and humorist Will Rogers. In 1929 Rodgers made what was probably the first country-music video, *The Singing Brakeman*, a ten-minute film short of Rodgers in a brakeman's outfit outside a railroad café singing three songs to an elderly lady and young waitress. This was one of the early "talkies" and the first Hollywood feature to depict a country artist.

Musical Legacy

Rodgers helped commercialize country music, giving it national attention by taking it out of its regional and rural roots. He sold more than twelve million records in his lifetime. He could play railroad songs, cowboy laments, Mississippi blues, mountain ballads, and vaudeville pop tunes, and he never adopted the hillbilly persona that other Southern artists were using as their stage presence. Though publicity stills often showed him in railroad overalls or a cowboy hat, his live performances always had him in fashionable suits and ties.

Rodgers provided the vocal model that the first generation of country stars emulated—from cowboy troubadours such as Gene Autry to bluegrass artists such as Bill Monroe to Western swingers such as Bob Wills. The singer-songwriter genre, whether folk or rock, is a direct offshoot of his style, a kind of music that Rodgers often said was "just me and my old guitar."

Peer reissued Rodgers's records through the 1960's, probably to keep his royalties coming. Regardless of Peer's motivation, this exposed new generations to Rodgers's music. Critical recognition began to come some three decades after his death. He was inducted as a first charter member into the Country Music Hall of Fame in 1961, the Nashville Songwriters Hall of Fame in 1970, and the Rock and Roll Hall of Fame (Early Influence) in 1986. He was inducted into the National Academy of Popular Music Songwriters Hall of Fame in 1986. Rodgers was the first person of European descent to receive the W. C. Handy Blues Award for contributions to blues. The Smithsonian Institution's two-record set of Rodgers's songs was nominated for two Grammy Awards in 1987, and his song "Blue Yodel No. 9" entered the Grammy Hall of Fame in 2007. The image of Rodgers appeared on a U.S. Postal Service first-class stamp in 1978.

James Stanlaw

Further Reading

Comber, Chris, and Mike Paris. "Jimmie Rodgers." In *Stars of Country Music*, edited by Bill Malone and Judith McCulloh. New York: Da Capo Press, 1975. This brief reference gives new information on Rodgers's musical styles.

Ellison, Curtis. *Country Music Culture: From Hard Times to Heaven*. Jackson: University of Mississippi Press, 1995. This book examines the development of country music as social history.

Hagan, Chet. "Jimmie Rodgers." In *Country Music Legends in the Hall of Fame*. Nashville, Tenn.: Thomas Nelson, 1982. This resource provides biographies of twenty-six country-music artists, among them Rodgers. Includes illustrations.

Lilly, John. "Jimmie Rodgers and the Bristol Sessions." In *The Bristol Sessions: Writings About the Big Bang of Country Music*, edited by Charles Wolfe and Ted Olson. Jefferson, N.C.: McFarland, 2005. The book describes the discovery of Rodgers at the historic sessions in Bristol that started country music. Includes an excerpt from Rodgers's widow's biography and an article comparing the careers of Rodgers with that of Alfred G. Karnes, a harp-guitar playing gospel singer and preacher, explaining why one artist at these sessions fell into obscurity while the other achieved superstardom.

Malone, Bill. "The First Country Singing Star: Jimmie Rodgers." In *Country Music USA*. Austin: University of Texas Press, 1985. This book is an excellent single-volume history of the country-music genre through the 1970's, with good information on Rodgers.

Peterson, Richard. "Renewable Tradition: The Carter Family and Jimmie Rodgers." In *Creating Country Music*. Chicago: University of Chicago Press, 1997. This resource discusses the institutionalization of country music: how fans, musicians, and promoters negotiated what would be authentic and popular country music.

Porterfield, Nolan. *Jimmie Rodgers: The Life and Times of America's Blue Yodeler*. Urbana: University of Illinois Press, 1992. A well-researched and thorough biography of Rodgers, addressing rumors and myths that have shrouded his personal and professional life.

Rodgers, Carrie. *My Husband Jimmie Rodgers*. Nashville, Tenn.: Vanderbilt University Press, 1995. This was the first book-length biography written about a country musician (originally published in 1935, a few years after this death). This edition includes photographs and a critical introduction by Rodgers scholar Nolan Porterfield.

See also: Armstrong, Louis; Carter, Maybelle; Frizzell, Lefty; Guthrie, Woody; Lewis, Jerry Lee; Monroe, Bill; Tubb, Ernest; Watson, Doc.

Richard Rodgers
American musical-theater composer

Rodgers, an innovator in the world of the Broadway musical, composed musical plays in which the songs were integral to character development, reflecting emotions and personality. His music thus provided the link that tied elements of the play together and advanced plot.

Born: June 28, 1902; New York, New York
Died: December 30, 1979; New York, New York
Also known as: Richard Charles Rodgers (full name)

Principal works

MUSICAL THEATER (music): *Poor Little Ritz Girl*, 1920 (with Sigmund Romberg; lyrics by Alex Gerber; libretto by Lew M. Fields and George Campbell); *No Strings*, 1962 (lyrics by Rodgers; libretto by Samuel Taylor); *Do I Hear a Waltz?*, 1965 (lyrics by Stephen Sondheim; libretto by Arthur Laurents); *Two by Two*, 1970 (lyrics by Martin Charnin; libretto by Peter Stone); *I Remember Mama*, 1976 (lyrics by Charnin; libretto by Thomas Meehan; based on Kathryn Forbes's novel *Mama's Bank Account*); *Rex*, 1976 (lyrics by Sheldon Harnick; libretto by Sherman Yellen).

MUSICAL THEATER (music; lyrics by Oscar
    Hammerstein II): *Oklahoma!*, 1943 (libretto by
    Hammerstein; based on Lynn Riggs's play
    Green Grow the Lilacs); *Carousel*, 1945 (libretto
    by Hammerstein; based on Ferenc Molnár's
    play *Liliom*); *Allegro*, 1947 (libretto by
    Hammerstein); *South Pacific*, 1949 (libretto by
    Hammerstein and Joshua Logan; based on
    James A. Michener's novel *Tales of the South
    Pacific*); *The King and I*, 1951 (libretto by
    Hammerstein); *Me and Juliet*, 1953 (libretto by
    Hammerstein); *Pipe Dream*, 1955 (libretto by
    Hammerstein); *Cinderella*, 1957 (libretto by
    Hammerstein); *Flower Drum Song*, 1958
    (libretto by Hammerstein and Joseph Fields;
    based on C. Y. Lee's novel); *The Sound of Music*,
    1959 (libretto by Howard Lindsay and Russel
    Crouse; based on Maria von Trapp's novel *The
    Story of the Trapp Family Singers*).
MUSICAL THEATER (music; lyrics by Lorenz Hart):
    The Melody Man, 1924 (libretto by Herbert
    Fields); *Dearest Enemy*, 1925 (libretto by Fields);
    Betsy, 1926 (libretto by Irving Caesar, David
    Freedman, and Anthony McGuire); *The Garrick
    Gaieties*, 1926 (revue); *The Girl Friend*, 1926
    (libretto by Fields); *Lido Lady*, 1926 (libretto by
    Ronald Jeans); *Peggy-Ann*, 1926 (libretto by
    Fields); *A Connecticut Yankee*, 1927 (libretto by
    Fields); *One Dam Thing After Another*, 1927
    (revue; libretto by Jeans); *Chee-Chee*, 1928
    (libretto by Fields); *Present Arms*, 1928 (libretto
    by Fields); *She's My Baby*, 1928 (libretto by Bert
    Kalmar and Harry Ruby); *Heads Up!*, 1929
    (libretto by Paul Gerard Smith); *Spring Is Here*,
    1929 (libretto by Owen Davis); *Evergreen*, 1930
    (libretto by Benn W. Levy); *Simple Simon*, 1930
    (libretto by Guy Bolton and Ed Wynn);
    America's Sweetheart, 1931 (libretto by Fields);
    Jumbo, 1935 (libretto by Ben Hecht and Charles
    MacArthur); *On Your Toes*, 1936 (libretto by
    Rodgers, George Abbott, and Lorenz Hart);
    Babes in Arms, 1937 (libretto by Rodgers and
    Lorenz Hart); *I'd Rather Be Right*, 1937 (libretto
    by George S. Kaufman and Moss Hart); *The
    Boys from Syracuse*, 1938 (libretto by Abbott;
    based on William Shakespeare's play *The
    Comedy of Errors*); *I Married an Angel*, 1938
    (libretto by Rodgers and Lorenz Hart); *Too
    Many Girls*, 1939 (libretto by George Marion,

Jr.); *Higher and Higher*, 1940 (libretto by Gladys
    Hurlbut and Joshua Logan); *Pal Joey*, 1940
    (libretto by John O'Hara); *By Jupiter*, 1942
    (libretto by Rodgers and Lorenz Hart).
TELEVISION SCORES: *Victory at Sea*, 1952; *The
    Valiant Years*, 1960.
WRITINGS OF INTEREST: *Musical Stages*, 1975
    (autobiography).

The Life

Richard Charles Rodgers was born to William
Abraham Rodgers, a physician, and Mamie Levy, a
homemaker. An accomplished pianist, his mother
often played and his father sang songs from Broadway musicals and operettas. Rodgers became used
to the sounds of melody and, as he states in his autobiography, developed a "lifelong love affair with
music." By age four he played the piano by ear. At
age six he had taught himself to play with both
hands, making up and playing his own tunes.
Rodgers's first song, written at summer camp when
he was fourteen, was "Camp Fire Days." Rodgers
also loved musical theater. Of the many musicals
he saw, Jerome Kern's *Very Good Eddie* (1915) made
a lasting impression with its simplicity and the
American "feel" of the music.

In 1917, at age fifteen, Rodgers wrote his first
score for a musical comedy. The show *One Minute
Please*, an amateur effort to raise money to purchase
tobacco for American troops serving in Europe,
was a success. In 1919 Rodgers conducted an orchestra for the first time and wrote music for twenty
songs for a second amateur production, *Up Stage
and Down*. However, Rodgers needed a lyricist, and
a friend introduced him to Lorenz Hart. Their first
success came with Columbia University's annual
variety show. At age seventeen Rodgers had enrolled at Columbia University just so he would be
eligible to write the Varsity Show. Although
Rodgers and Hart were competing with four other
entrants, the judges selected their *Fly with Me* as the
Columbia Varsity Show of 1920. At the end of his
sophomore year, Rodgers left Columbia to enroll in
a two-year course at the Institute of Musical Art
(later renamed Juilliard), studying musical theory
and harmony. In 1923 he left to devote himself to
composing, struggling for recognition. Discouraged, he considered taking a job in the garment industry. However, when he and Hart were offered a

chance to write a musical revue, Rodgers never again considered leaving the music business.

Rodgers married Dorothy Feiner on March 5, 1930, and they had two children. In 1931 Rodgers and Hart relocated to Hollywood to write for the movies but later returned to New York to compose some of their best musicals. After Hart became increasingly undependable and ill from alcoholism, Rodgers began working with Oscar Hammerstein II. That second partnership produced a series of classic Broadway musicals. Following Hammerstein's death in 1960, Rodgers continued composing with other lyricists. After a spate of health problems, Rodgers died in New York City in 1979.

The Music

Rodgers had two distinctive musical careers. With Hart he wrote songs that could stand independent of the musical. With Hammerstein his music was more dramatic, tied closely to the plot of the story.

Early Works. Rodgers and Hart developed a method of working together. After studying the requirements of the plot, Rodgers wrote the music, and then Hart then supplied the lyrics. *The Garrick Gaieties* was their first success and included their first hit song, "Manhattan." During the 1920's they wrote fourteen shows, including *Dearest Enemy*. In his autobiography Rodgers recalls this show as the occasion he became aware of the "multiple possibilities" of varying the love duet, which should be "fresh both musically and lyrically," fitting different situations and becoming a "part of what is happening onstage." Rodgers saw the necessity of making the relationship between lovers more meaningful through music. *A Connecticut Yankee*, for example, included the hit songs "My Heart Stood Still" and "Thou Swell." Always looking for innovation, Rodgers in *Chee-Chee* interwove short musical numbers through the story, complementing the stage action.

After their time in Hollywood, Rodgers and Hart returned to New York and wrote their greatest hits, including *Babes in Arms*, *The Boys from Syracuse*, and *By Jupiter*. For their shows the term "musical comedy" was replaced by "musical play," reflecting a developing seriousness in the subject matter. The music was no longer a "number" to interrupt the action of the plot; it contributed to the action, em-

phasizing emotion and dramatic conflict. Rodgers and Hart viewed their works as dramatic entities, and, with each show, they added something new in form and content, such as using the chorus and dance as elements basic to the plot.

On Your Toes. This was the first musical for which Rodgers and Hart helped write the book, continuing to work toward a fusion between text and music. It was also the first musical play in which dancing was an integral part of the action: Without the ballet "Slaughter on Tenth Avenue," there was no conclusion to the story. The music for the ballet, with its distinctive lament and jazzy secondary theme, was Rodgers's first sustained piece of orchestral writing. The ballet is often performed as a solo piece.

Pal Joey. Based on a series of pieces John O'Hara had written for *The New Yorker*, *Pal Joey* has a nontraditional hero, a conniver and braggart who would do anything and sleep with anyone to get ahead. Rodgers and Hart were adamant that each song would adhere to the hard-edged nature of the story. They enjoyed writing songs satirizing the tacky na-

Richard Rodgers. (Library of Congress)

ture of the nightclub in which it is set, and the hit song "Bewitched, Bothered, and Bewildered" contrasted Rodgers's flowing, sentimental melody with Hart's unsentimental, self-mocking lyrics.

Oklahoma! Writing with Hammerstein was completely different from writing with Hart. Hammerstein, a disciplined hard worker, wrote the lyrics before Rodgers wrote the music. Whereas Hammerstein agonized over the words, Rodgers was inspired by the words and often wrote the music quickly. Hammerstein took three weeks to write the lyrics to "Oh, What a Beautiful Mornin'," and Rodgers stated, "When you're given words like 'the corn is as high as an elephant's eye,' you get something to say musically." He composed the music in less than ten minutes.

Appearing in 1943, *Oklahoma!* was a different show from the beginning. Traditionally a musical started with an overture, introducing several melodies and maybe a waltz, but not this time. The overture was a brief run-through of melodies, as if they had been thrown together (and they had). The curtain rose to silence—without the traditional chorus or upbeat, jazzy song—to reveal an old lady churning butter. Offstage, a male voice began singing a ballad. Before *Oklahoma!*, songs tended to stop the action; here songs popped out of the script, almost like dialogue. One song, "Surrey with the Fringe on Top," incorporates singing and speaking. Also distinctive was the way the musical themes wove in and out of the story, sometimes under dialogue, similar to opera composer Richard Wagner's leitmotifs, contributing to the unity of the story. Rodgers was careful in writing the score to make the songs sound natural when sung by cowboys, ranchers, and farm girls of that time and place. With its American-sounding music, *Oklahoma!* has been called a folk opera, and most historians of musical theater agree that it reinvented the musical as an art form.

Carousel. Of all his musicals, Rodgers's favorite was his 1945 version of Ferenc Molnár's play *Liliom* because "it tries to say the most and says it best." Rodgers again had the opportunity to write American music from a distinctive region, this time Maine. Because of the almost operatic theme of the story and the score, the orchestra used more instruments than in previous Broadway musicals. Quickly establishing the mood of the play, the mu-

sical begins with hurdy-gurdy sounds that eventually become a waltz. Notable is the eight-minute "Soliloquy," which Rodgers wrote after hearing John Raitt audition. Rodgers knew his voice was right for an aria, expressing the character of the hero, Billy Bigelow.

Along with the successes, Rodgers had some failures with Hammerstein. The film *State Fair* had an Academy Award-winning song, "It Might as Well Be Spring." In *Allegro* they attempted a unified musical: words, music, dance, and the physical production as well. However, with its lack of major songs and its recitative of a Greek chorus developing the story, *Allegro* was not a success.

South Pacific. For *South Pacific*, they approached racial issues through music with the song "You've Got to Be Carefully Taught." Again capitalizing on the singing talent of a lead player, Rodgers wrote operatic songs for the Metropolitan Opera basso Ezio Pinza, and he astounded everyone by composing "Bali Ha'i" in five minutes. In "Twin Soliloquies" Émile and Nellie express their thoughts about each other through the music, at first hesitatingly and finally with assurance as the orchestra swells to reflect their certainty.

The King and I. For *The King and I*, Rodgers determined not to attempt Oriental-style music and had to write his songs with a range comfortable for the star Gertrude Lawrence. Rodgers wished to bring his ideas of what a Broadway musical should be to a wider audience, and *Cinderella*, starring Julie Andrews, had a television audience of 107 million. The last musical Rodgers wrote with Hammerstein was *The Sound of Music*.

Victory at Sea. Although primarily a composer of show music, Rodgers composed *Ghost Town*, an American folk ballet, commissioned by the Ballet Russe de Monte Carlo. His most famous nontheater composition was *Victory at Sea*, a thirteen-hour-long symphonic score that accompanied twenty-six half-hour television programs. One million feet of film from ten different countries detailed the naval war in the Pacific theater during World War II, and to support the action on the film, Rodgers created a number of musical themes, marches, and ballads. His "Guadalcanal March" is a favorite with marching bands, and the tango "Beneath the Southern Cross" was incorporated into his musical *Me and Juliet* as "No Other Love."

Musical Legacy

Rodgers wrote more than one thousand songs. Of these, at least two hundred have been hits, and more than one hundred are popular music classics. With his collaborators, Rodgers also created something new in the world of musicals. As Rodgers wrote in an article for *Opera News* in 1961, "The musical comedies of the twenties, with few exceptions, were devoted purely and simply to entertainment." The plot was basically boy finds girl, boy loses girl, boy gets girl. There were no major obstacles to overcome, and the subject matter was not deep. The shows consisted of fast songs, ballads, dance numbers, and the big finish. Rodgers and Hart changed the formula, creating scores that reflected a situation in the plot and enhanced character development, seeing themselves as dramatists, not simply songwriters. With Hammerstein, Rodgers continued to develop musical shows that had American themes and reflected American issues, such as racial prejudice in *South Pacific*. The shows were still entertainment, but the subject matter went beyond the boy-meets-girl formula. Perhaps because of the popular film versions of his musicals with Hammerstein, these shows are more frequently revived and known by contemporary audiences.

Taking a chance on controversial settings and subjects, such as in *Pal Joey* and *Pipe Dream*, Rodgers and his lyricists paved the way for musicals that dealt with political revolution, Americans in Vietnam, and psychologically damaged characters. Rodgers with Hart and Hammerstein created the bridge from the simple, happy musicals of the 1920's to the street gangs of *West Side Story*, the serial murderer of *Sweeney Todd*, and the tormented musical genius of *The Phantom of the Opera*.

Marcia B. Dinneen

Further Reading

Block, Geoffrey. *Richard Rodgers*. New Haven: Yale University Press, 2003. General background on Rodgers's life and his composition methods are supplemented by in-depth coverage of a number of musicals.

Ewen, David. *Richard Rodgers*. New York: Henry Holt, 1957. A comprehensive discussion of the works of Rodgers, including his methods of creating songs and scores.

Green, Stanley. *The Rodgers and Hammerstein Story*. New York: Day, 1963. Includes background on each man as well as discussion of their collaborative works. Appendix lists all the songs they wrote as well as the singer who introduced each song.

Mordden, Ethan. *Beautiful Mornin': The Broadway Musical in the 1940's*. New York: Oxford University Press, 1999. The coverage of Rodgers and Hammerstein includes material on *Oklahoma!*, *Carousel*, and *Allegro*.

Rodgers, Richard. "How to Write Music in No Easy Lessons." *Theatre Arts*, October, 1939, 741-746. The composer's inside view of how he writes.

_____. *Musical Stages: An Autobiography*. New York: Random House, 1975. Rodgers details the events in his life, particularly his collaborations with Hart and Hammerstein. Pictures are included.

Taylor, Deems. *Some Enchanted Evenings: The Story of Rodgers and Hammerstein*. New York: Harper, 1953. This biography from a renowned music critic provides factual and insider information on Rodgers, focusing on his collaborations with Hart and Hammerstein.

See also: Andrews, Dame Julie; Berlin, Irving; Chevalier, Maurice; Cohan, George M.; Coward, Sir Noël; Fiedler, Arthur; Fields, Dorothy; Goodman, Benny; Hamlisch, Marvin; Hammerstein, Oscar, II; Hart, Lorenz; Horne, Lena; Kern, Jerome; Lee, Peggy; Loewe, Frederick; McPartland, Marian; Mercer, Johnny; Newman, Alfred; Romberg, Sigmund; Simone, Nina; Sondheim, Stephen; Tormé, Mel; Van Heusen, Jimmy.

Sonny Rollins

American jazz saxophone player and composer

A noted tenor saxophonist, Rollins is known for his aggressive sound, his commitment to swing, his prodigious harmonic imagination, and his innovative and inventive approaches to improvisation and composition.

Born: September 7, 1930; New York, New York
Also known as: Theodore Walter Rollins (full name)
Member of: The Clifford Brown-Max Roach Quintet; the Sonny Rollins Quartet; the Sonny Rollins Quintet

Principal recordings

ALBUMS: *Sonny and the Stars*, 1951; *Sonny Rollins and the Modern Jazz Quartet*, 1951 (with the Modern Jazz Quartet); *Sonny Rollins Quartet*, 1951 (with the Sonny Rollins Quartet); *Moving Out*, 1954; *Sonny Rollins Plays Jazz Classics*, 1954; *Sonny Rollins Quintet*, 1954 (with the Sonny Rollins Quintet); *Saxophone Colossus*, 1956; *Sonny Rollins Plus Four*, 1956; *Sonny Rollins, Vol. 1*, 1956; *Tenor Madness*, 1956; *Newk's Time*, 1957; *Sonny Rollins, Vol. 2*, 1957; *The Sound of Sonny*, 1957; *Way Out West*, 1957; *Brass and Trio*, 1958; *Freedom Suite*, 1958; *Quartet*, 1958 (with Sonny Rollins Quartet); *Sonny Rollins and the Big Brass*, 1958 (with the Big Brass); *The Bridge*, 1962; *What's New?*, 1962; *All the Things You Are*, 1963; *Sonny Meets Hawk*, 1963 (with Coleman Hawkins); *Stuttgart*, 1963 (with Sonny Rollins Quartet); *Now's the Time*, 1964; *Sonny Rollins and Co., 1964*, 1964; *Three in Jazz*, 1964; *East Broadway Rundown*, 1966; *Sonny Rollins's Next Album*, 1972; *Horn Culture*, 1973; *Nucleus*, 1975; *Easy Living*, 1977; *Don't Ask*, 1979; *Love at First Sight*, 1980; *No Problem*, 1981; *Sunny Days, Starry Nights*, 1984; *Dancing in the Dark*, 1987; *Sonny Rollins/Thad Jones*, 1988 (with Thad Jones); *Here's to the People*, 1991; *Old Flames*, 1993; *The Meeting*, 1994; *Sonny Rollins Plus Three*, 1996; *Global Warming*, 1998; *This Is What I Do*, 2000; *Portrait*, 2003; *Sonny, Please*, 2006; *Soneymoon*, 2007.

The Life

Theodore Walter "Sonny" Rollins (RAWL-lihnz) was born in New York City in 1930 to parents from the Virgin Islands. After piano lessons at a young age, Rollins's interest in music shifted to the alto saxophone, which he took up at about age eleven. His choice of instrument was influenced not only by the beauty of the alto saxophone's appearance but also by the playing of jump saxophonist Louis Jordan. Rollins soon switched to tenor saxophone because of his admiration for Coleman Hawkins. Rollins was working already as a professional jazz musician upon his graduation from high school, rehearsing with Thelonious Monk and appearing with Miles Davis, Art Blakey, and others. However, his early career was erratic because of his addiction to heroin. On one hand, Rollins was recognized as one of the hottest young tenor saxophone players in jazz, recording frequently with Miles Davis. A high point was his appearance on *Bags' Groove* (1954) with Davis, Horace Silver, and Milt Jackson, a recording date that featured three Rollins compositions: "Oleo," "Doxy," and "Airegin." On the other hand, Rollins spent time in prison for armed robbery and for violating his parole.

In 1954 Rollins enrolled a drug treatment program in Lexington, Kentucky, and he overcame his addiction. Wary of returning immediately to the temptations of the jazz scene, he instead worked menial jobs in Chicago for a time before his triumphant return with the Clifford Brown-Max Roach Quintet in November, 1955. With the influence of Brown's spectacular virtuosity and with Rollins's determination to stay off drugs, he transformed his life and career. He quickly became a vital member of the group, which was already one of the hottest in jazz. After Brown's tragic death in a car accident (with the quintet's pianist, Richie Powell, and Powell's wife) on June 26, 1956, Rollins continued with Roach for a time before moving out on his own as a leader. The years 1956 to 1958 were some of the most spectacular of Rollins's career, as he toured extensively and recorded tirelessly, producing such masterpieces as *Saxophone Colossus*, *Way Out West*, *Newk's Time*, and *Freedom Suite*. In 1959, at the height of his critical and commercial success, Rollins suddenly withdrew from the jazz scene. Apparently concerned he was not playing at the level to which he aspired, Rollins took two years off

Sonny Rollins. (AP/Wide World Photos)

to practice and to explore all the possibilities of the tenor saxophone. After a successful return in 1962, Rollins took a second and longer sabbatical, from 1966 to 1972, this time to study Eastern religion and refocus his energy on his music. When he returned in 1972, Rollins continued with a scaled-back performance schedule, and he records an album every year or two on the Milestone label, produced first by Orrin Keepnews and then by his wife, Lucille Rollins.

The Music

Rollins entered the jazz world at the height of the bebop era, and he quickly established himself as a composer and improviser at the level of Parker. Although he played extensively in the bebop and hard-bop styles, Rollins formed a distinctive voice in jazz that remained faithful to swing and improvisation, while constantly exploring innovative approaches to the art. He has been lauded for his masterful conception of structure in his improvisations, as well as for his use of thematic repetition and alteration (which led to Gunther Schuller's description of Rollins's "thematic improvisation"). Rollins

is also distinguished by the strength and individuality of his sound, his dynamic speechlike phrasing, and his great variety of articulation and color. His playing is intense, while remaining grounded in the blues and in swinging, complex rhythms. Rollins began composing his own tunes early in his career, and has contributed jazz standards such as "Oleo," "Doxy," "Airegin," "St. Thomas," and "Blue Seven." In addition to his own compositions, Rollins is known for his wide-ranging tune choices, including calypso (reflecting his West Indian heritage) and popular song.

Sonny Rollins Plus Four. This is one of Rollins's early dates as a leader, and he was joined for this March 22, 1956, recording by the other members of the Clifford Brown-Max Roach Quintet: Brown on trumpet, Richie Powell on piano, George Morrow on bass, and Max Roach on drums. The album features outstanding interchanges between Brown and Rollins on the front line, all supported by a fabulous rhythm section. The improvisations are stunning in their virtuosity and in their extroverted, and even joyful, enthusiasm. The tunes swing hard, from hard-bop classics "Kiss and Run" and "I Feel a Song Coming On" to Rollins's own compositions "Valse Hot" and "Pent-Up House." "Valse Hot" demonstrates an early Rollins experiment with time, with its 3/4 time signature as opposed to the standard 4/4. It anticipates Roach's album, on which Rollins appeared, *Jazz in 3/4 Time* (1956). Rollins's other composition, "Pent-Up House," is one of the highlights of the album, an extended exploration of masterfully swinging improvisation by one of the most exciting groups in jazz's history.

Saxophone Colossus. Considered by many to be Rollins's masterpiece, *Saxophone Colossus* confirmed his reputation as one of the hottest players in jazz and one of its most inventive composers and improvisers. He appears with an all-star cast of Tommy Flanagan on piano, Doug Watkins on bass, and Roach on drums, performing both standards and original compositions. Particularly noteworthy is the opening track, "St. Thomas," an upbeat and fun calypso that became one of Rollins's trademark tunes (although "St. Thomas" has been attributed to Rollins, he states that it is a traditional tune from the Virgin Islands). Another highlight of the album is Rollins's "Strode Rode," particularly his exciting improvisation that begins accompanied by Watkins on bass. In addition to a final Rollins composition, "Blue 7" (the improvisation of which served as the basis for Schuller's famous analysis of Rollins's "thematic improvisation"), the quartet presents masterful versions of "You Don't Know What Love Is" and "Moritat" ("Mack the Knife").

Newk's Time. Rollins appears with an outstanding rhythm section of Wynton Kelly on piano, Watkins on bass, and Philly Joe Jones on drums. The album opens with two intense bop tunes, Davis's "Tune Up" and Kenny Dorham's "Asiatic Raes." The latter tune especially exhibits Rollins's mastery of rhythmic innovation, with its constantly shifting sense of time. Perhaps the most innovative number on the album is the popular "The Surrey with the Fringe on Top," performed entirely as a duet between Rollins on tenor saxophone and Jones on drums. In the absence of the harmonic structure provided by piano and bass, Rollins makes an extensive exploration of the theme while supported masterfully by Jones on drums. The album also includes one Rollins composition, "Blues for Philly Joe," a blues tune in the tradition of his earlier "Blue 7."

The Bridge. A famous photograph taken during Rollins's sabbatical of 1959 to 1961 shows the lone saxophonist practicing high on the Williamsburg Bridge (between Manhattan and Brooklyn). Appropriately, his first album upon his return was entitled *The Bridge,* featuring a Rollins composition of that name. While some fans and critics were disappointed that Rollins had not returned with a new musical style, his playing on this recording gives evidence of his hard work and of his extensive exploration of the saxophone during his sabbatical. Rollins is commanding both as a leader and as an improviser, demonstrated on his two compositions, "John S." (a tribute to his friend and colleague John Coltrane) and "The Bridge." These lightning-fast tunes contrast with Rollins's gripping and emotional version of the Billie Holiday classic "God Bless the Child," which honors the memory of Holiday after her death in 1959. A final noteworthy aspect of this album is its instrumentation, as Rollins included guitarist Jim Hall in place of a pianist, resulting in a more open, linear sound for the quartet.

Sonny Rollins's Next Album. This album marked Rollins's return after his longest sabbatical, from 1966 to 1972. During his time away, the jazz scene had changed substantially: Coltrane had died in 1967, the free jazz movement increasingly ignored audiences and established jazz as an elite music, and the rise of rock and roll was pushing jazz out of the mainstream. Rollins returned to jazz on his own terms, not as a savior but as a master musician dedicated to the ideals of swing and improvisation. Those listeners who had hoped Rollins would avoid the popular jazz-rock fusion were disappointed: The opening tune is a spirited and funky Rollins original, "Playin' in the Yard," featuring electric piano and electric bass. Another innovation appears with the second track, with Rollins performing on soprano saxophone in tribute to his deceased friend Coltrane. The album is rounded out by two Rollins compositions, "The Everywhere Calypso" and "Keep Hold of Yourself," and the Hoagy Carmichael tune "Skylark," which opens and closes with Rollins playing extensive unaccompanied improvisations.

Sonny Rollins Plus Three. This album is representative of the best of Rollins's playing in the later decades of his career. Like his earlier albums, this includes a mix of original compositions and standards. The two Rollins compositions, "Biji" and "H.S.," are full of energy and funk, particularly the latter, a fitting tribute to hard-bop pianist Silver. Other highlights of the album include the opening "What a Difference a Day Made" as well as Rollins's renditions of "They Say It's Wonderful" and "Mona Lisa."

Musical Legacy

Despite early immersion in bebop and hard bop, Rollins is remarkable for his individual approach to sound conception. His constant negotiation between tradition and innovation has led to an intensely personal style. Rollins's contributions to the world of jazz include live performances and recordings spanning the decades since the late 1940's. Although many saxophonists have imitated his style, Rollins encourages admirers to find their own voice. In addition to his monumental discography and his many tunes that have become jazz standards, Rollins has won two Grammy Awards (in 2000 and 2004) as well as a Lifetime Achievement Award from the National Academy of Recording Arts and Sciences (in 2004).

Mark A. Peters

Further Reading

Blanq, Charles. *Sonny Rollins: The Journey of a Jazzman.* Boston: Twayne, 1983. After a brief overview of Rollins's life, Blanq focuses on a technical musical analysis of Rollins's playing. Includes extensive musical examples.

Goldberg, Joe. "Sonny Rollins." In *Jazz Masters of the Fifties.* New York: Da Capo, 1965. An accessible introduction to Rollins's early career up to the early 1960's, based on an interview with the saxophonist. Includes numerous quotations from Rollins and others.

Nisenson, Eric. *Open Sky: Sonny Rollins and His World of Improvisation.* New York: St. Martin's Press, 2000. This detailed biography of Rollins is based on extensive interviews by the author with Rollins and with others. This provides a readable commentary on Rollins's life and music, punctuated by frequent quotations from the saxophonist.

Palmer, Richard. *Sonny Rollins: The Cutting Edge.* New York: Continuum, 2004. An exploration of Rollins's life and music by a fan, this book provides good basic information and includes three transcriptions of Rollins solos with commentary by Ken Rattenbury.

Stern, Chip. "Sonny Rollins: The Cross and the Rose." In *The Jazz Musician,* edited by Mark Rowland and Tony Scherman. New York: St. Martin's Press, 1994. The chapter about Rollins is an interview, in which the saxophonist talks about his life, his career, and his views on music and musicians.

Wilson, Peter N. *Sonny Rollins: The Definitive Musical Guide.* Berkeley, Calif.: Berkeley Hills Books, 2001. Interesting background material on Rollins's life, personality, and style provides a backdrop for the extensive discography, which makes up the bulk of the volume. Includes detailed annotated entries on all of Rollins's recordings as a leader and many of his important ones as a sideman.

See also: Blakey, Art; Brown, Clifford; Coltrane, John; Gillespie, Dizzy; Hancock, Herbie; Hawkins, Coleman; Holiday, Billie; Jones, Elvin; Jordan, Louis; Kirk, Rahsaan Roland; Lewis, John; Metheny, Pat; Monk, Thelonious; Navarro, Fats; Roach, Max; Sanders, Pharoah; Tormé, Mel; Young, Lester.

Sigmund Romberg

Hungarian musical-theater songwriter and lyricist

With his nostalgic waltzes and rousing marches, Romberg was a leading composer of American operetta in the 1910's and 1920's.

Born: July 29, 1887; Nagykanizsa, Austria-Hungary (now Hungary)
Died: November 9, 1951; New York, New York
Also known as: Sigismund Romberg; Siegmund Romberg; Siegmund Rosenberg

Principal works

MUSICAL THEATER (music): *The Whirl of the World*, 1914 (lyrics and libretto by Harold Atteridge); *The Passing Show of 1916*, 1916 (with Otto Motzan; lyrics and libretto by Atteridge); *Robinson Crusoe, Jr.*, 1916 (with James Hanley; lyrics by Atteridge; libretto by Edgar Smith); *Maytime*, 1917 (lyrics and libretto by Rida Johnson Young); *The Passing Show of 1917*, 1917 (with Motzan; lyrics and libretto by Atteridge); *Monte Cristo, Jr.*, 1919 (lyrics and libretto by Atteridge); *The Passing Show of 1918*, 1918 (with Jean Schwartz; lyrics and libretto by Atteridge); *Sinbad*, 1918 (with Al Jolson; lyrics and libretto by Atteridge); *The Passing Show of 1919*, 1919 (with Schwartz; lyrics and libretto by Atteridge); *Blossom Time*, 1921 (with Franz Schubert; lyrics and libretto by Dorothy Donnelly); *The Blushing Bride*, 1922 (lyrics by Cyrus Wood; libretto by Edward Clark); *The Passing Show of 1923*, 1923 (with Schwartz; lyrics and libretto by Atteridge); *Artists and Models*, 1924 (with J. Fred Coots; lyrics by Clifford Grey and Sam Coslow; libretto by

Harry Wagstaff Gribble); *The Passing Show of 1924*, 1924 (with Schwartz; lyrics and libretto by Atteridge); *The Student Prince*, 1924 (lyrics and libretto by Donnelly); *Louie the 14th*, 1925 (lyrics and libretto by Arthur Wimperis; based on a play by Paul Frank and Julius Wilhelm); *The Desert Song*, 1926 (lyrics and libretto by Oscar Hammerstein II and Harbach); *The New Moon*, 1928 (lyrics and libretto by Hammerstein); *Rosalie*, 1928 (with George Gershwin; lyrics by P. G. Wodehouse and Ira Gershwin; libretto by William Anthony McGuire and Guy Bolton); *May Wine*, 1935 (lyrics by Hammerstein; libretto by Frank Mandel); *Up in Central Park*, 1945 (lyrics by Dorothy Fields; libretto by Dorothy Fields and Herbert Fields).

The Life

Born in Hungary to an upper-middle-class Jewish family, Sigmund Romberg (SIHG-muhnd RAHM-burg) spent his early adulthood in Vienna, where he was a rehearsal accompanist at the Theater an der Wien, a house known for its operetta productions. He arrived in New York City in 1909, and he soon found employment as a pianist and orchestra leader in restaurants. His music came to the attention of theater impresario J. J. Shubert, who engaged Romberg as a staff composer in 1914. During the 1910's Romberg contributed music to numerous Shubert productions, including revues, musical comedies, and adaptations of Central European operettas.

Romberg created a string of successful operettas for the Shuberts, including *Maytime*, *Blossom Time*, and *The Student Prince*, works that were unashamedly sentimental in their bittersweet endings and that had scores revolving around a recurring waltz duet. Eventually, Romberg left the Shuberts, embarking on a new approach to operetta with works such as *The Desert Song* and *The New Moon*. They had happy endings and, in addition to waltzes, prominent songs in popular American idioms.

In the 1930's Romberg moved to Hollywood and worked in the film industry. In the 1940's he toured the United States with an orchestra, chorus, and soloists, giving concerts titled An Evening with Sigmund Romberg. He also made numerous radio and television appearances and recorded studio ver-sions of his most popular works. Throughout his life, he continued to write for Broadway. Many of these shows had innovative features: For example, *May Wine* treated songs as internal soliloquies, and *Up in Central Park* employed dance to do much of the storytelling.

The Music

Romberg began his Broadway career writing individual songs for revues, musical comedies, and adaptations of European operettas. These interpolations were almost always in the conventional verse-refrain form typical of American popular music at the time. His first acclaimed song, the nostalgic waltz "Auf Wiedersehen," was the recurring musical number in *The Blue Paradise*, an adaptation of a Viennese operetta that included music by both its original creator, Edmund Eysler, and Romberg.

Maytime. When the Shuberts decided to adapt Walter Kollo's Berlin operetta *Wie einst im Mai* (as once in May) for Broadway, the anti-German sentiment at the time inspired them to move the multigenerational love story, in which a couple's romance is realized by their grandchildren, from Berlin to New York. Additionally, the Shuberts chose not to include any of Kollo's songs in the score (going against the norm for adaptations) and asked Romberg to create entirely new music. The waltz duet "Will You Remember?" (also known as "Sweetheart, Sweetheart") appears in each of the four acts and is the score's centerpiece. Jeannette MacDonald and Nelson Eddy starred in the heavily altered 1937 film version.

Blossom Time. Based on a fictional story about the nineteenth century composer Franz Schubert, *Blossom Time* has a score unified by a recurring waltz duet, "Song of Love," the principal melody of which is derived from a theme in Schubert's *Unfinished Symphony*.

The Student Prince. The longest-running Broadway musical of the 1920's, with 604 performances, *The Student Prince* was extremely influential in the rehabilitation of German culture following World War I. The tale of a prince whose love with a commoner cannot be realized takes place in idyllic nineteenth century Heidelberg, a nostalgic re-creation of a politically benign Germany. Musical highlights include the recurring waltz duet "Deep in My Heart" and songs for the energetic male chorus, especially "Drinking Song" and "Students Marching Song." Noteworthy is the moving "Serenade," scored for the title character, male trio, and male chorus.

The Desert Song. Capitalizing on the fame of actor Rudolf Valentino, of the adventurer Lawrence of Arabia, and of the general American fascination with Orientalism during the 1920's, Romberg and his collaborators Oscar Hammerstein II and Otto Harbach created *The Desert Song*, a work set in contemporary Morocco about a milquetoast Frenchman who, in disguise, helps the oppressed Riffs. Romberg employed a basic though effective means for distinguishing between the French and the Moroccans: The former sang in major keys and the latter in minor keys. In addition to the glorious title waltz, the score's highlights include the boisterous "Riff Song," the effervescent "Romance," and the sweeping "One Alone." Warner Bros. released three full-length film versions of the operetta, in 1929, 1944, and 1954.

The New Moon. Two jazz standards, "Softly, as in a Morning Sunrise" and "Lover, Come Back to Me," are among the musical highlights of *The New Moon*, a tale set in Louisiana and the Caribbean around the time of the French Revolution. True love and freedom from tyranny both emerge victorious at the final curtain with the reprise of the rousing march "Stouthearted Men." Other musical highlights include the rapturous duet "Wanting You" and the graceful waltz "One Kiss." Opera stars Lawrence Tibbett and Grace Moore starred in the 1930 film version, and Jeannette MacDonald and Nelson Eddy appeared in the 1940 version.

Up in Central Park. In 1945 Romberg proved that he could create a musical in the style of Richard Rodgers and Hammerstein with *Up in Central Park*. The story deals with government corruption in the days of Boss Tweed, and the score includes the soaring ballad "Close as Pages in a Book."

Musical Legacy

Waltzes feature prominently in Romberg's works, often with nostalgia-tinged lyrics. Such Romberg songs as "Will You Remember?" led to the association of the musical-theater waltz with nostalgia, seen much later in "Try to Remember" from 1960's *The Fantasticks*. Romberg championed

the male chorus, often creating for it assertive marches, such as "Stouthearted Men." He collaborated with such notable wordsmiths as Rida Johnson Young, Dorothy Donnelly, Dorothy Fields, and Hammerstein. Romberg had a keen desire to please audiences interested in what he called "middlebrow music—too highbrow for jazz conductors and too lowbrow for symphony ones."

William A. Everett

Further Reading

Arnold, Elliott. *Deep in My Heart: A Story Based on the Life of Sigmund Romberg*. New York: Duell, Sloan, and Pearce, 1949. The novelized popular biography was the basis for Metro-Goldwyn-Mayer's 1954 film about Romberg's life. Includes a valuable chronology and works list.

Everett, William A. "American and British Operetta in the 1920's: Romance, Nostalgia, and Adventure." In *The Cambridge Companion to the Musical*, edited by William A. Everett and Paul R. Laird. New York: Cambridge University Press, 2008. Chapter surveys the work of prominent operetta composers, including Romberg, and discusses the distinguishing features of the genre.

_____. *Sigmund Romberg*. New Haven, Conn.: Yale University Press, 2006. Romberg's work for Broadway is the focus of this study, which includes material on the film adaptations of Romberg's stage works and his original music for Hollywood.

Green, Stanley. "Sigmund Romberg." In *The World of Musical Comedy*. New York: Da Capo Press, 1984. Overview of Romberg's career is amply illustrated with production stills and other photographs.

Romberg, Sigmund. "A Peep into the Workshop of a Composer." *Theatre Magazine* 48, no. 6 (December, 1928): 27, 72, 74. Shortly after *The New Moon* opened, Romberg offered insights into his working methods and aesthetic approach to operetta.

See also: Fields, Dorothy; Gershwin, George; Gershwin, Ira; Hammerstein, Oscar, II; Hart, Lorenz; Loewe, Frederick; Rodgers, Richard; Steiner, Max.

Linda Ronstadt

American folksinger

With her powerful, expressive voice, Ronstadt moved from her first success as a folksinger to alternative country, rock, big band, and traditional Mexican music.

Born: July 15, 1946; Tucson, Arizona
Also known as: Linda Maria Ronstadt (full name); First Lady of Rock; the Queen of Rock
Member of: The Stone Poneys

Principal recordings

ALBUMS (solo): *Hand Sown . . . Home Grown*, 1969; *Silk Purse*, 1970; *Linda Ronstadt*, 1971; *Don't Cry Now*, 1973; *Heart Like a Wheel*, 1974; *Prisoner in Disguise*, 1975; *Hasten down the Wind*, 1976; *Simple Dreams*, 1977; *Mad Love*, 1980; *What's New*, 1983 (with the Nelson Riddle Orchestra); *Lush Life*, 1984 (with the Nelson Riddle Orchestra); *For Sentimental Reasons*, 1986 (with the Nelson Riddle Orchestra); *Trio*, 1987 (with Emmylou Harris and Dolly Parton); *Canciones de Mi Padre*, 1987; *Cry Like a Rainstorm, Howl Like the Wind*, 1989; *Mas Conciones*, 1991; *Winter Light*, 1993; *Feels Like Home*, 1995; *Dedicated to the One I Love*, 1993; *Western Wall—The Tucson Sessions*, 1999 (with Harris); *A Merry Little Christmas*, 2000; *Adieu False Heart*, 2006 (with Ann Savoy).

ALBUMS (with the Stone Poneys): *Evergreen, Vol. 2*, 1967; *The Stone Poneys Featuring Linda Rondstadt*, 1967; *Linda Ronstadt, Stone Poneys, and Friends, Vol. III*, 1968.

The Life

Linda Maria Ronstadt (RAWN-stat) was born in Tucson, Arizona, to Gilbert Ronstadt and Ruthmary Copeman. She was raised with two brothers and a sister on the family's ten-acre ranch. Her father, who descended from prominent Mexican ranchers, played the guitar and sang Mexican songs. Her mother, of German descent, played the ukulele and favored the operetta songs of W. S. Gilbert and Arthur Sullivan. At the age of fourteen, Ronstadt formed a trio with her sister Suzy and her brother Peter. Under the names Union City Ramblers and the Three Ronstadts, they sang at coffeehouses and on college campuses with a mixed repertoire of folk, bluegrass, country, and Mexican songs.

While attending college, Ronstadt met Bob Kimmel, a guitarist, and he persuaded her to move to Los Angeles in 1964. There they were joined by guitarist Kenny Edwards, who wrote some songs with Kimmel, and together they formed the Stone Poneys. In 1967 their first album, *The Stone Poneys*, was released, but it was not until their second album, *Evergreen, Vol. 2*, that the group got noticed. The album's hit single, "Different Drum," peaked at number thirteen on the *Billboard* Hot 100 chart. The Stone Poneys produced one more album, and by that time Ronstadt had gone solo.

Hand Sown . . . Home Grown, Ronstadt's initial solo effort, was described as the first alternative country album recorded by a woman. Several albums followed, and the singer embarked on years of touring to support them, which exacted an emotional and physical toll. Nevertheless, the singer was gaining popularity for her brand of country-rock songs. In 1973 Ronstadt met Peter Asher, who became her producer, a fruitful relationship that resulted in her first solo hit, *Heart Like a Wheel*. With its combination of rock and country-roots songs, it reached number one on the *Billboard* album and country charts, with Ronstadt winning the Grammy Award for Best Country Vocal Performance.

Ronstadt's first commercial success was followed by a series of chart-topping albums that also earned Grammy Award nominations. Listeners were captivated by the singer's warm, expressive voice that could croon a country tune and punch out a rock song as well as glide through a folk harmony. Her ease in crossing genres led to a surprise career move in 1980 when she agreed to star as Mabel in Joseph Papp's New York production of Gilbert and Sullivan's *Pirates of Penzance* with Kevin Kline and Rex Smith. This version of the operetta opened in Central Park and moved to Broadway for a run of 787 performances. Ronstadt was nominated for a Tony Award for her portrayal of the Major General's daughter, a role that showcased her glorious soprano voice. Later Ronstadt starred in the film version.

In 1983, to the initial dismay of her label, Elektra Records, Ronstadt veered in another musical direction, when she began a collaboration with Nelson Riddle, the arranger and orchestra leader. The album *What's New*, with his lush orchestrations and her versatile voice, was a tribute to the Great American Songbook, bringing popular songs of an earlier era to a new audience. Again Ronstadt's musical instincts proved to be right on key: *What's New* was followed by *Lush Life* and *Sentimental Reasons*, and the trilogy had combined sales of eight million copies.

In 1987 Ronstadt joined Emmylou Harris and Dolly Parton for the album *Trio*, a collection of traditional, country, gospel, and soft rock songs that highlighted their individual voices as well as their smooth harmony. Returning to her roots, Ronstadt released in the same year *Canciones de Mi Padre*, an album of Mexican mariachi music, for which the singer won a Grammy Award for Best Mexican-American Performance.

While charting her success in the music business, Ronstadt also achieved notoriety in her personal life. In the 1970's she famously dated the governor of California, Jerry Brown, and in the 1980's she became engaged to the director of *Star Wars*, George Lucas. Unmarried, the singer adopted two children, Mary and Carlos.

The Music

Heart Like a Wheel. In 1974 Ronstadt owed Capitol Records one more album to fulfill her contract. She did it—to immense success—with *Heart Like a Wheel*. The contribution made by Asher as producer was major, especially because he helped the singer to realize her ambitions to expand her sound. In this album, she moves away from a strictly folk style to add country and rock elements, in songs that were old and new. "You're No Good" was the hit single, reaching number one on the *Billboard* Hot 100. "Willing" was a mellow folk-rock ballad, and Ronstadt produced a soulful "When Will I Be Loved," the Everly Brothers' signature song. This album established Ronstadt as a commercially viable singer, and it was followed by a string of hits. *Rolling Stone* placed it at number 164 on its list of the 500 Greatest Albums of All Time.

Linda Ronstadt. (Hulton Archive/Getty Images)

What's New. In 1983 Ronstadt approached arranger Riddle with her idea of making an album of popular standards. She knew about Riddle from his work with Frank Sinatra, Nat King Cole, Judy Garland, and Peggy Lee. Riddle, who had little interest in rock music, did not even know who Ronstadt was. Nevertheless, the collaboration was a huge success, beginning with the album *What's New*, the first in a trilogy. Riddle arranged such songs as George and Ira Gershwin's "I've Got a Crush on You" and "Someone to Watch over Me" and Irving Berlin's "What'll I Do?" to emphasize Ronstadt's rich voice, which expressed the romantic lyrics so effectively that, along with the Gershwins and Berlin, Jule Styne, Sammy Cahn, and Johnny Burke found legions of new fans.

Canciones de Mi Padre. In this album, Ronstadt embraced her Mexican heritage, singing fluently in Spanish the songs of her father, as the title translates. The singer took the title from a booklet written by her aunt, Luisa Espinel, and published by the University of Arizona in 1946 in which she preserved the songs her father (Ronstadt's grandfather) had brought from Sonora, Mexico. They include rancheras (folk dances), ballads, corridos (story songs), and mariachis (band music). Accompanied by guitars, violins, and trumpets, Ronstadt the singer offered bold and colorful renditions of the songs she heard sung in her childhood home. When it was released, *Canciones de Mi Padre* became the top-selling non-English-language album in U.S. history.

Musical Legacy

In her long career, Ronstadt has sung in a wide variety of genres, fearlessly moving from folk, country, and rock to big band and traditional Mexican music. With each stylistic change, she attracted new listeners and created more hit albums. Her more than thirty solo albums have earned eleven Grammy Awards and seventeen nominations, and she was the first woman to have four consecutive platinum albums. After the success of *Canciones de Mi Padre*, Ronstadt made a tour with several Mexican singers and dancers centered on the songs on the album, continuing the work of her aunt, who sought to preserve the culture of Mexican song. In 2008 she was chosen by the National Council of La Raza, a Latino civil rights and advocacy organization, to receive an ALMA Award, which honors those who have presented a fair and accurate portrayal of Latinos in the entertainment industry.

Constance Pollock

Further Reading

Berman, Connie. *Linda Ronstadt: An Illustrated Biography*. Carson City, Nev.: Proteus, 1980. This is a brief biographical sketch with many photographs, and it is especially revealing in the behind-the-scenes views on concert tours.

Hirshey, Gerri. *We Gotta Get Out of This Place: The True, Tough Story of Women in Rock*. New York: Grove Press, 2001. In this history of women in rock, Hirshey, a writer for Rolling Stone, has references to Ronstadt, calling her the first "arena-class rock diva."

Leach, Anita Mabante. "Linda Ronstadt." *AARP Segunda Juventud* (August, 2007). In this interview, Ronstadt talks about the music that filled her childhood home, how she was drawn to the music of big bands and Gilbert and Sullivan, and why she has made her home in San Francisco.

See also: Axton, Hoyt; Berlin, Irving; Cole, Nat King; Garland, Judy; Gershwin, George; Gershwin, Ira; Harris, Emmylou; Lee, Peggy; Parton, Dolly; Sinatra, Frank; Styne, Jule.

Diana Ross
American soul/pop singer

Whether singing with the Supremes or solo, Ross is a soulful pop artist, whose versatile voice and innovative recordings helped to build Motown Records and to create the Motown sound.

Born: March 26, 1944; Detroit, Michigan
Also known as: Diane Ernestine Earle (birth name)
Member of: The Supremes; Diana Ross and the Supremes

Principal recordings

ALBUMS (solo): *Diana Ross*, 1970; *I'm Still Waiting*, 1971; *Lady Sings the Blues*, 1972; *Diana and Marvin*, 1973 (with Marvin Gaye); *Touch Me in the Morning*, 1973; *Baby It's Me*, 1977; *The Boss*, 1979; *Diana*, 1980; *Why Do Fools Fall in Love?*, 1981; *Silk Electric*, 1982; *Swept Away*, 1984; *Eaten Alive*, 1985; *Red Hot Rhythm and Blues*, 1987; *Workin' Overtime*, 1989; *The Force Behind the Power*, 1991 (with others); *Christmas in Vienna*, 1993 (with Plácido Domingo and José Carreras); *Forever, Diana*, 1993; *Stolen Moments: The Lady Sings . . . Jazz and Blues*, 1993; *Take Me Higher*, 1995; *Gift of Love*, 1996; *Every Day Is a New Day*, 1999; *Blue*, 2006; *I Love You*, 2007.

ALBUMS (with Diana Ross and the Supremes): *Supremes Sing Rodgers and Hart*, 1967; *Diana Ross and the Supremes Join the Temptations*, 1968; *Diana Ross and the Supremes Sing and Perform "Funny Girl,"* 1968; *Love Child*, 1968; *Reflections*, 1968; *TCB*, 1968 (with the Temptations); *Cream of the Crop*, 1969; *Let the Sunshine In*, 1969; *On Broadway*, 1969 (with the Temptations); *Together*, 1969 (with the Temptations).

ALBUMS (with the Supremes): *Meet the Supremes*, 1963; *A Bit of Liverpool*, 1964; *Where Did Our Love Go*, 1964; *Merry Christmas*, 1965; *More Hits by the Supremes*, 1965; *Supremes Sing Country, Western, and Pop*, 1965; *We Remember Sam Cooke*, 1965; *I Hear a Symphony*, 1966; *Supremes a Go Go*, 1966; *Supremes Sing Holland, Dozier, Holland*, 1967.

WRITINGS OF INTEREST: *Secrets of a Sparrow: Memoirs*, 1993.

The Life

Diane Ernestine Earle was born in the relatively poor surroundings of inner-city Detroit. She was the second of six children, and her parents, Fred Ross and Ernestine Moten, instilled in their children a positive attitude and an adherence to the Baptist faith. Her father changed jobs often, and her mother was frequently ill. When her mother was diagnosed with breast cancer, the family moved briefly to Bessemer, Alabama, for her medical treatment.

When Ross was fourteen, the family moved back to Detroit's Brewster housing project. She began to be interested in music, and she befriended Mary Wilson, Florence Ballard, and Betty McGlown. Throughout their teenage years, the foursome participated in the doo-wop group the Primettes, refining their skills on the local scene. In 1961 Motown Records offered the girls a contract (and Ross a secretarial position), at which time McGlown was replaced by Barbara Martin. They changed the group's name to the Supremes.

The Supremes toured and recorded extensively, and in 1971 Ross married her manager, Robert Ellis Silberstein. In addition, her daughter Rhonda Suzanne Silberstein was born that year. The child took the name of Ross's husband, although she was conceived with Motown Records' head Berry Gordy. In 1972 Ross and Silberstein had a daughter, Tracee Joy Silberstein. Three years later, the couple had Chudney Lane Silberstein; Ross and Silberstein divorced in 1977. Ross married Norwegian businessman Arne Næss in 1985. The pair had two sons, Ross Arne Næss and Evan Olaf Næss; Ross and Næss divorced in 2000.

The Music

The Supremes. After signing a contract with Motown Records and changing its name from the Primettes to the Supremes, the group became a trio, consisting of Ross, Wilson, and Ballard. During the first few years, they switched lead vocal parts. In late 1963, however, Gordy named Ross lead singer of the Supremes. The group's chart-topping single "Where Did Our Love Go" was written by Lamont Dozier and Brian and Eddie Holland, the team known as Holland-Dozier-Holland, who also wrote the Supremes' next four hit singles: "Baby Love," "Stop! In the Name of Love," "Come See About Me," and "Back in My Arms Again."

Solo Career. Ross became more of a central figure to the Supremes, and the other two members, Wilson and newcomer Cindy Birdsong, became little more than backup singers, making only small contributions to "Love Child" and "Someday We'll Be Together." Because of increasing tensions, Ross left the group in 1969, and she was replaced by Jean Terrell. Although the Supremes continued with a variety of lineups through 1977, their prominence was overshadowed by Ross's successful solo career. From the outset, Ross worked with songwriters-producers Nickolas Ashford and Valerie Simpson, and her self-titled debut album yielded the number-one single "Ain't No Mountain High Enough."

Film Acting. Two years later, Ross starred in the film *Lady Sings the Blues* (1972), paying tribute to Billie Holiday. Despite controversy surrounding the vocal differences between Ross and Holiday, Ross's performance earned favorable reviews and an Academy Award nomination for Best Actress. Throughout the 1970's, she balanced work in films with work in recording. In 1973 Ross sang the chart-topping ballad "Touch Me in the Morning," and in 1975 she appeared in the film *Mahogany*, which featured the successful single "Theme from *Mahogany* (Do You Know Where You're Going To)." In 1978 Ross joined the cast of the film *The Wiz*, which was based on a 1975 Broadway musical that reworked *The Wizard of Oz* (1939) with an entirely African American cast. In *The Wiz*, Ross was reunited with Michael Jackson, whom she had mentored during his early Jackson Five days.

Disco Era. In the 1980's, Ross recruited producers Bernard Edwards and Nile Rodgers (of Chic) to create a disco sound for her album *Diana* and for a series of club singles, such as "I'm Coming Out" and "Upside Down." Her duet with Lionel Richie on "Endless Love" showed she was still capable of producing a power ballad.

RCA Recordings. Despite her two decades with the company and her close relationship with its owner, Ross left Motown Records and signed a contract with RCA in a reported twenty-million-dollar deal. Her self-produced 1981 album for the label, *Why Do Fools Fall in Love?*, featured a cover of the title track (originally by Frankie Lymon and the Teenagers), along with a solo version of "Endless Love," and it sold more than a million copies. The following year's *Silk Electric* was a mostly self-produced project that featured another reunion with Jackson, who produced the hit "Muscles." Ross's next (and final) hit album for RCA was *Swept Away*, which featured the soulful ballad "Missing You."

Back to Motown. Because of shifting musical trends that resulted in disappointing sales, Ross dissolved her partnership with RCA in 1989, and she returned to Motown Records, with the hope of reviving her career and the label's faltering fortunes. *Stolen Moments: The Lady Sings . . . Jazz and Blues* helped reestablish the star as a vocal force, and it stimulated publicity for her autobiography, *Secrets of a Sparrow: Memoirs*. In 1993 Motown released the box set *Forever Diana: Musical Memoirs*, a compilation of Ross's career hits.

In 1995 Ross released *Take Me Higher*, which was designed for club play, and another album with dance tracks, *Until We Meet Again*, appeared in 1999, when Ross starred in the ABC television film *Double Platinum* (alongside rhythm-and-blues singer Brandy).

New Record Label. In 2006 Motown rereleased *Blue* (a previously shelved album of jazz standards originally meant to follow *Lady Sings the Blues*) and *The Definitive Collection* (a collection of songs from Ross's Motown and RCA eras). Ross signed a contract with the EMI label to produce the studio album *I Love You*. Featuring her signature combination of classic rock songs and love ballads, the

Diana Ross. (AP/Wide World Photos)

album debuted at number thirty-two on the *Billboard* 200.

Musical Legacy

Ross and the Supremes helped make Motown Records a significant record label, and, with their soaring harmonies, coordinated dance steps, glamorous outfits, and classy demeanor, they paved the way for girl groups of all genres. As a solo performer, Ross showed her versatility by expanding her repertoire to include jazz, disco, and dance works, along with her blues and pop standards. While advancing her career, Ross also helped other artists, such as Jackson and Lionel Richie.

The entertainer crossed musical and racial boundaries on a number of occasions, with her film roles and her public appearances across the globe. In group and in solo contexts, Ross's recording catalog is among the most extensive in history, and she is one of few artists to have singles and albums land on the charts for a span of five decades.

In 2007 Ross played a mentor role for *American Idol* contestants. That same year she received a Lifetime Achievement Award from Black Entertainment Television and the Kennedy Center Honors for cultural influence throughout her career.

Andy Argyrakis

Further Reading

Adrahtas, Thomas. *Diana Ross, the American Dreamgirl: A Lifetime to Get Here.* Bloomington, Ind.: AuthorHouse, 2006. Although unauthorized, the book provides an exhaustive account of Ross's solo and Supremes career, which spans more than forty years.

Posner, Gerald. *Motown: Music, Money, Sex, and Power.* New York: Random House, 2002. Somewhat sensational although still factual, this history of Ross's longtime record label includes numerous references to the Supremes, to Ross's working relationships with other artists, and to her solo career. The text traces her involvement in the building of the label and her personal contributions to its success.

Ross, Diana. *Secrets of a Sparrow: Memoirs.* New York: Villard Books, 1993. This poignant autobiography addresses everything from Ross's start in show business to the early days of Motown, leading the Supremes, and embarking on solo stardom. It provides a revealing look at her personal life, tracing her various marriages and the lives of her children.

Smith, Suzanne E. *Dancing in the Street: Motown and the Cultural Politics of Detroit.* Cambridge, Mass.: Harvard University Press, 1999. The early Motown groups are featured in this extensive account of the record label, which features several references to the Supremes and Ross's success outside the group. It also recounts behind-the-scenes details of her relationship with Gordy and her collaborations with such artists as Marvin Gaye and Smokey Robinson and the Miracles.

Taraborrelli, J. Randy. *Diana Ross: A Biography.* Yucca Valley, Calif.: Citadel, 2007. This text updates 1989's *Call Her Miss Ross*, with additional information on Ross and her career in the intervening years. The updated account includes more references to the Supremes and Ross's experience later working with Wilson.

Wilson, Mary. *Dreamgirl and Supreme Faith, Updated Edition: My Life as a Supreme.* New York: Cooper Square Press, 2000. Wilson offers her side of the Supremes story, providing an intimate portrait of the group's beginnings, details on her relationship with Ross both on and off the stage, and a chronicle of the group's demise.

See also: Domingo, Plácido; Dozier, Lamont; Gaye, Marvin; Gibb, Barry, Maurice, and Robin; Goffin, Gerry; Holiday, Billie; Holland, Eddie and Brian; Horne, Lena; Iglesias, Julio; Jackson, Michael; Jamerson, James; Legrand, Michel; Notorious B.I.G.; Summer, Donna; Wilson, Brian.

Mstislav Rostropovich

Russian classical cellist and conductor

Rostropovich's mastery of the cello expanded the cello repertoire, which reached new levels of complexity under his influence. His relationships with composers and artists and his staunch support for Russian cultural identity in the face of Soviet opposition had a significant impact on music and Russian culture.

Born: March 27, 1927; Baku, Soviet Union (now in Azerbaijan)
Died: April 27, 2007; Moscow, Russia
Also known as: Mstislav Leopoldovich Rostropovich (full name); Slava

Principal recordings

ALBUMS (as cellist): *Britten: Cello Suites Nos. 1 and 2*, 1989; *Brahms: The Cello Sonatas*, 1990; *Dinner Classics: The Viennese Album*, 1990; *Haydn Concertos*, 1991; *Bach: Cello Suites Nos 1-6*, 1995; *Slava 75: The Official 75th Birthday Edition*, 2002; *Artist Portrait: Mstislav Rostropovich*, 2005; *The Glory of Rostropovich: 80th Birthday Tribute*, 2007; *Mstislav Rostropovich: Cello Concertos*, 2007; *Mstislav Rostropovich Plays Cello Works*, 2008.

ALBUMS (as conductor): *Eugene Onegin*, 1970; *Tchaikovsky Ballet Suites*, 1979; *Shostakovich: Lady Macbeth of Mtensk*, 1990; *Shostakovich: Symphony No. 5*, 1990; *Boris Gudounov*, 1991; *Tchaikovsky: Symphony No. 1; Rococo Variations*, 1991; *Shostakovich: Symphony No. 8*, 1992; *Shostakovich: Symphony No. 11*, 1993; *Prokofiev: Symphonies*, 2002; *Rostropovich Conducts Shostakovich*, 2004; *Prokofiev: Violin Concertos Nos. 1 and 2; Glazunov: Violin Concerto*, 2006.

The Life

Mstislav Leopoldovich Rostropovich (MIH-stih-slahv rohs-troh-POH-vihch) developed a passion for music that was ignited early in life at his boyhood home in Baku as he listened to the sounds of his father's cello and his mother's piano. In 1931 Rostropovich's father moved the family to Moscow, where the boy could obtain a complete musical education. Three years later, Rostropovich made his debut. From 1939 to 1941, Rostropovich studied cello with his father at the Central Music School in Moscow. Through the intervention of Mikhail Ivanovich Chulaki and Vissarion Yakovlevich Shebalin, Rostropovich entered the Moscow Conservatory in 1943, where he studied cello with Semyon Mateievich Kozolupov, composition with Shebalin, and orchestration with composer Dmitri Shostakovich. This period marked the beginning of a lifelong friendship between Rostropovich and Shostakovich, resulting in the Cello Concerto No. 1 in E-Flat (1959) as well as several smaller works for cello written toward the end of the composer's life.

Rostropovich received first prize in cello in the 1945 All-Union Performers' Competition, one of several awards he would receive. This was followed by success at the International Youth Festival in Prague and at the Budapest Youth Festival International Competition in 1949, where he shared first place with Daniel Shafran. He placed first again in the 1950 Vihan International Cello Competition, a position he shared with Shafran. That same year, and at only twenty-three years of age, Rostropovich was awarded the Stalin Prize, the highest honor available in the arts in Russia.

Rostropovich debuted in the West in 1951 with a performance in Florence, Italy. Amid his hectic schedule, Rostropovich married the first lady of the Bolshoi Theater, Galina (Galya) Pavlovna Vishnevskaya, in 1955. The following year Rostropovich made his American debut at Carnegie Hall.

Throughout these performing years, Rostropovich continued his relationship with the Moscow Conservatory, and as an assistant to Kozolupov, Rostropovich began teaching there in 1948. In 1959 Rostropovich became a full professor, succeeding Svyatoslav Nikolayevich Knushevitsky in 1961 as head of the cello department. He continued to teach at the Moscow Conservatory and in St. Petersburg until 1967.

The 1960's marked the beginning of Rostropovich's conducting career. In November, 1962, Rostropovich premiered as a conductor with the first public performance of Shostakovich's orchestration of Modest Mussorgsky's *Songs and Dances of Death* (1877). In 1968 Rostropovich was invited to conduct at the Bolshoi Theater in Moscow.

Rostropovich's activities led to life long friendships with many Russian composers and literary figures. In 1948 Sergei Prokofiev attended one of Rostropovich's recitals. Their ensuing friendship and intellectual collaboration led to the composition of many challenging works for cello, including Sonata in C for Cello (1949) and the Cello Concerto in G Minor (1952), which was completed by Rostropovich and Dmitri Kabalevsky.

In 1969 Rostropovich opened his home to Aleksandr Solzhenitsyn, who was under government censure at the time. Reacting to continued government persecution of the author, Rostropovich wrote an open letter to *Pravda*, the leading Soviet newspaper, in 1970. The letter, which received wide notice abroad but was never published in

Mstislav Rostropovich. (Library of Congress)

Russia, strongly criticized the Soviet government for bringing Russian cultural development to a halt. A short time later, the Soviet government banned both Rostropovich and Galina from the Bolshoi Theater, canceled performances without notice, and prohibited the couple from traveling abroad, performing, and recording. In 1974 the Rostropovich family was granted a travel visa for the first time in five years. Their travels brought them to Washington, D.C., where, in March, 1975, Rostropovich was invited to guest-conduct the National Symphony Orchestra. Rostropovich was appointed director of the National Symphony Orchestra in 1977, thus beginning a long-term relationship with the orchestra during which Rostropovich brought it to international prominence. The following year and with little warning, the Soviet Union revoked both Rostropovich's and Galina's citizenship.

Rostropovich continued to champion Russian culture and democracy while he was in exile. When the news of the imminent collapse of the Soviet Union broke in 1989, Rostropovich traveled to Berlin to perform Johann Sebastian Bach's Six Suites for Unaccompanied Cello (1717-1723) as the Berlin Wall fell. Russian President Mikhail Gorbachev reinstated Rostropovich's citizenship in 1990, and in 1991 Rostropovich went to the aid of President Boris Yeltsin and Russian democracy during an attempted military coup.

Rostropovich's humanitarian services are numerous. In 1988, he and Galina held a benefit concert for Armenian earthquake survivors. In 1991 he founded the Vishnevskaya-Rostropovich Foundation (VRF), and in April, 2006, Rostropovich was appointed UNAIDS Special Representative, to raise awareness on AIDS. He died on April 27, 2007, of intestinal cancer.

The Music

Rostropovich's performing career was long and varied. Often divided between the Russian and post-Russian years, his recordings reflect an ongoing relationship with his homeland. Recordings during Rostropovich's self-identified "Russian years" often include new works by young Russian composers as well as numerous transcriptions of French works. His move to Eastern Europe allowed him the freedom to revitalize the works of the great Russian composers Mussorgsky, Prokofiev, and Shostakovich. Not content with the politically acceptable versions of many works, Rostropovich was a pioneer in recording Russian operas with their original scoring and librettos. Among his numerous recordings of Russian operas and new commissions, listeners will also find Rostropovich's complete recordings of Prokofiev's symphonies.

The Russian Years, 1950-1974. This thirteen-album compilation edition consists of more than forty works most representative of Rostropovich's career as a cellist in Russia. Hand-selected by the performer, recordings presented here include Rostropovich's own transcriptions for cello of smaller works, various works dedicated to the cellist, and world premiere performances. A small sampling of works included in the collection are Rostropovich's transcriptions of Igor Stravinsky's "Russian Song" from *Marva* (1922), the world premiere recording of Benjamin Britten's Symphony for Cello and Orchestra, Op. 68 (1963), and Shostakovich's Cello Concerto No. 2, Op. 126 (1966). The accompanying booklet provides Rostropovich's commentary and recollections regarding selected performances.

Eugene Onegin. Captured in Paris with the Bolshoi Theater Opera, *Eugene Onegin* (1879) represents Rostropovich's first Western appearance as a conductor. Performing the opera in the evenings and recording in the mornings, Rostropovich and Russian opera rose to prominence on the Western European stage with *Eugene Onegin*. Singing lead under Rostropovich's baton were Galina Vishnevskaya (Tatiana), Yuri Mazurok (Onegin), Vladimir Atlantov (Lensy), Tatiana Tugarinova (Larina), Tamara Sinyavskaya (Olga), Larissa Avdeyeva (Filievna), and Alexander Ognivtsev (Gremin).

Lady Macbeth of Mtensk. This recording bears historical significance for Shostakovich's *Lady Macbeth of Mtesnk* (1932). Following a 1936 newspaper blitz and Stalin's repression of the opera, Shostakovich heavily edited the music and libretto, presenting the work again in 1958 under the new title *Katerina Ismailova*. Much of the original musical concept and political import of the libretto were compromised, however, and Rostropovich took it upon himself to return the piece to its original form. Owing to his great friendship with the composer, Rostropovich was able to resurrect the original score and give the opera its first Western European performance in 1979, captured in this recording.

The Symphonies. Shortly after being granted a travel visa in 1974, Rostropovich began conducting a full season of Prokofiev's work. This "Prokofiev cycle" remained a recurring theme in Rostropovich's conducting career, and it certainly enhanced the Prokofiev Festival, which Rostropovich helped organize in 1991. A four-compact-disc set, this recording is a testament to Rostropovich's dedicated efforts to vindicate Prokofiev's music in the light of the crushing reaction against the composer by the Soviet Culture Bureau. Informing these performances is Rostropovich's long friendship with the composer.

Boris Gudounov. With the definitive version completed in 1872, Mussorgsky had to wait two more years for the first full performance of his opera, subjected as it was to cuts. Successive editing and rewriting of the opera follow the evolution of Russian and Soviet politics, producing no less than five different versions, including one by Nikolay Rimsky-Korsakov. This 1972 version, edited by Rimsky-Korsakov, is commonly accepted as the definitive version, although it enjoyed only a few performances in Russia. Recorded with the National Symphony Orchestra, Rostropovich resurrects Mussorgsky's 1972 version for the first time for Western audiences.

Bach: Cello Suites Nos. 1-6. Although he had a long relationship with Bach's cello suites, this marks Rostropovich's first recording of all six suites. Rostropovich began studying the work at the age of fifteen, and he never abandoned it. Attesting to his long relationship with these suites, Rostropovich hurriedly flew to Berlin and performed the works in the open air as the Berlin Wall was being torn down. The cellist had played Bach's cello suites for fifty-three years, and this recording captures a lifetime of study and development.

Musical Legacy

Rostropovich's wide-ranging influence is felt in cello technique, cello and orchestral repertoire, and humanitarian aid. His capacity for learning new works and easily conquering technical challenges is credited with opening the realm of compositional possibilities for the cello and for vastly expanding the repertoire. Inspired by Rostropovich's mastery of the cello and his understanding of complex musical ideas, many composers wrote new and increasingly difficult works for the cello, among them Prokofiev (*Sinfonia Concertante*, 1952) and Benjamin Britten (Symphony for Cello and Orchestra, 1964).

As a conductor, Rostropovich played a significant role in restoring many Russian operas to their original scoring and librettos. Subjected to the censure of the Soviet Culture Bureau, many of the major operatic works of Prokofiev, Shostakovich, and Mussorgsky underwent dramatic editing. Such severe rewriting often undermined the stylistic development of many composers and subverted the intended cultural representation. Rostropovich made it his mission to restore these works to their original scoring in defense of Russian cultural identity. Among these works are Prokofiev's *War and Peace* (1945), Mussorgsky's *Boris Gudounov*, Shostakovich's *Lady Macbeth of Mtensk*, and Tchaikovsky's *Eugene Onegin*.

Rostropovich's defense of Russian democracy and human rights continued offstage as well. Through the Vishnevskaya-Rostropovich Foundation, created in 1991 by the cellist and his wife, Rostropovich made significant contributions to the Russian health-care infrastructure. Among the major accomplishments of the organization were the donation of millions of hepatitis B vaccinations for Russian children and health-care workers as well as dozens of state-of-the-art maternity wards built in remote rural regions.

Lisa Hooper

Further Reading

Barnes, Bart. "Cellist-Conductor Mstislav Rostropovich Dies at 80." *The Washington Post*, April 27, 2007. Commemorating the musician, this article provides a brief synopsis of the major events in Rostropovich's life.

Ivashkin, Alexander, and Josef Oehrlein. *On the Life and Achievement of Msistlav Rostropovich*. Schweinfurth, Germany: Reimund Maier Verlag, 1997. This German-English biography explores the life and works of Rostropovich, and it is supplemented with numerous illustrations and with commentary by various friends.

Samuel, Claude. *Mstislav Rostropovich and Galina Vishnevskaya: Russia, Music, and Liberty, Conversations with Claude Samuel*. Translated by E.

Thomas Glasow. Portland, Oreg.: Amadeus Press, 1995. Wide-ranging conversations offer insights into Rostropovich's views on life, politics, art, music, and teaching.

Vishnevskaya, Galina. *Galina: A Russian Story*. Translated by Guy Daniels. San Diego, Calif.: Harcourt Brace, 1984. Rostropovich's wife describes her life with the cellist. She relates the challenges they faced living in the repressive Soviet Union.

See also: Casals, Pablo; du Pré, Jacqueline; Gubaidulina, Sofia; Mutter, Anne-Sophie; Oistrakh, David; Prokofiev, Sergei; Rampal, Jean-Pierre; Serkin, Rudolf; Shostakovich, Dmitri; Stern, Isaac.

Nino Rota

Italian classical and film-score composer

Rota was revered in Italy and the rest of the world for his compositions for film. In addition, he composed numerous works for theater, orchestra, and chamber ensemble in a style strikingly similar to the one he adopted for film music. An incredibly talented melodist, Rota remained faithful to his neoclassical tonal style.

Born: December 3, 1911; Milan, Italy
Died: April 10, 1979; Rome, Italy

Principal works

BALLETS: *La rappresentazione di Adamo ed Eva*, 1957 (scenario by Aurelio M. Milloss); *Aci e Galatea*, 1971 (scenario by Marcella Otinelli; based on Ovid's *Metamorfosi*); *Le Molière imaginaire*, 1976 (comedic ballet); *Amore di poeta*, 1978 (*A Poet's Love*; scenario by Maurice Béjart; based on Robert Schumann and Heinrich Heine's song cycle *Dichterliebe*).

CHAMBER WORKS: *Invenzioni*, 1933 (for string quartet); Viola Sonata, 1934; *Canzona for Eleven Instruments*, 1935; Quintet, 1935 (for flute, oboe, viola, cello, and harp); *Sonata for Flute and Harp*, 1937; Violin Sonata, 1937; String Quartet, 1954; Trio for Flute, Violin, and Piano, 1958; *Elegy*, 1959 (for oboe and piano); *Nonet*, 1959; Sonata for Organ and Brass, 1968; Trio for Clarinet, Cello, and Piano, 1973.

CHORAL WORKS: *L'infanzia di San Giovanni Battista*, 1922 (*The Childhood of Saint John the Baptist*; oratorio for solo voices, chorus, orchestra, and organ); *Il martirio di San Giovanni Battista*, 1924 (oratorio for solo voices, chorus, and organ); *Allegro concertante*, 1953 (for chorus and orchestra); *Meditazione*, 1954 (for chorus and orchestra); *Mysterium catholicum*, 1962 (oratorio for voices, chorus, children's chorus, and orchestra); *Il natale degli innocenti*, 1970 (oratorio); *La vita di Maria*, 1970 (oratorio for solo voices, chorus, and orchestra); *Roma capomunni*, 1971 (cantata for baritone, chorus, and orchestra).

FILM SCORES: *Treno popolare*, 1933; *Il birichino di papà*, 1943; *Le miserie del signor Travet*, 1946; *The Glass Mountain*, 1949; *Lo sceicco bianco*, 1952 (*The White Sheik*); *Filumena marturano*, 1951; *I vitelloni*, 1953; *La strada*, 1954; *Il bidone*, 1955; *War and Peace*, 1956; *Le notti bianche*, 1957; *Le notti di Cabiria*, 1957; *La dolce vita*, 1959; *Plein soleil*, 1959; *Rocco e i suoi fratelli*, 1960; *Le tentazioni del dottor Antonio*, 1962; *The Taming of the Shrew*, 1967; *Romeo e Giulietta*, 1968 (*Romeo and Juliet*); *Toby Dammit*, 1968; *Satyricon*, 1969; *I clowns*, 1970 (*The Clowns*); *Waterloo*, 1970; *The Godfather*, 1972; *Roma*, 1972; *Amarcord*, 1973; *Film d'amore e d'anarchia*, 1973 (*Love and Anarchy*); *The Godfather, Part II*, 1974; *Il Casanova*, 1976; *Caro Michele*, 1978; *Death on the Nile*, 1978; *Prova d'orchestra*, 1979.

OPERAS (music): *Il principe porcaro*, written 1926, premiered 2003 (*The Swineherd Prince*; based on Hans Christian Andersen's fairy tale); *Ariodante*, 1942 (libretto by Ernesto Trucchi); *Torquemada*, 1943 (libretto by Trucchi; based on Victor Hugo's poem); *I due timidi*, 1950 (radio opera; libretto by Suso Cecchi d'Amico); *Il cappello di paglia di Firenzi*, 1955 (musical farce; libretto by Ernesta Rota and N. Rota; based on Eugène Labiche and Marc-Michel's comedy *Un Chapeau de paille d'Italie*); *La scuola di guida*, 1959 (for voices and orchestra; libretto by Mario Soldati); *La notte di un nevrastenico*, 1959 (opera buffa; libretto by Riccardo Bacchelli); *Lo scoiattolo in gamba*, 1959 (libretto by Eduardo De Filippo); *Aladino e la lampada magica*, 1968 (based on the *Arabian Nights* stories); *La visita meravigliosa*, 1970 (based on H. G. Wells's *The Wonderful Visit*); *Napoli milionaria*, 1977 (*The Millions of Naples*; based on De Filippo's play).

ORCHESTRAL WORKS: Cello Concerto, 1925; *Balli*, 1932; *Serenata*, 1932; Symphony No. 1 in G, 1939; Symphony No. 2 in F, 1941 (*Anni di pellegrinaggio: Tarantina*); *Sinfonia sopra una canzone d'amore*, composed 1947, first performed 1972; Harp Concerto, 1948; *Variazioni e fuga sul nome B-A-C-H*, 1950; *Variazioni sopra un tema gioviale*, 1954; Symphony No. 3 in C, 1957; *Fantasia sopra dodici note del di W. A. Mozart*, 1960; *Two Piano Concertos*, 1960; Concerto in F, 1961 (*Festivo*); *Fantasia sopra*, 1961; Concerto in C, 1962 (formerly Partita); *Concerto soirée*, 1962 (for piano and orchestra); Fifteen Preludes, 1964; Concerto for Strings, 1965; Sonata for Organ, 1965; Trombone Concerto, 1968; *Divertimento concertante*, 1969 (for double bass and orchestra); Cello Concerto No. 1, 1972; Cello Concerto No. 2, 1973; *Castel del Monte*, 1976 (for horn and orchestra); Bassoon Concerto, 1977; Piano Concerto in E, 1978 (*Piccolo mondo antico*).

VOCAL WORKS: *Die Maus*, 1925 (for voice and small orchestra); *Messa "Mariae dicata,"* 1960 (for solo voices and orchestra); *Rabelaisiana*, 1977 (three songs for solo voice and orchestra).

The Life

Nino Rota (NEE-noh ROH-tuh) was born into a family of musicians: His grandfather, Giovanni Rinaldi, was a composer, and his mother, Ernesta Rinaldi, was a pianist. Rota played the piano by the age of four, and he composed by the age of eight. His oratorio *L'infanzia di San Giovanni Battista* was successfully performed under his direction when he was twelve. Despite being a child prodigy—or perhaps because of it—he had difficulty finding a suitable teacher. During his brief time at the Milan Conservatory he studied with Giacomo Orefice and Ildebrando Pizzetti, who hindered the production of Rota's first opera, *Il principe porcaro*. In 1926 Rota moved to Rome to study with Alessandro Casella. After receiving a diploma in composizione from Rome Conservatory in 1929, with barely passing grades, he studied for three years, from 1930 to

1932, at the Curtis Institute in Philadelphia with Rosario Scalero (composition) and Fritz Reiner (conducting). While in the United States he befriended Aaron Copland and Samuel Barber, and he became acquainted with the music of Leonard Bernstein and George Gershwin, as well as with American films, musicals, and popular songs.

Returning to Italy, Rota earned a degree in Italian literature from Milan University in 1938. He began his teaching career at Taranto Conservatory before transferring to Bari Conservatory in 1939. Rota found a stimulating and friendly environment in Bari, where his talents and gregarious personality were fully appreciated. He composed much of his instrumental music for his friends, who were musicians in Puglia, the region where Bari is located. He served as the director of Bari Conservatory for nearly three decades, from 1950 to 1979, declining the position of director of the more prestigious Rome Conservatory.

Rota's career as film music composer began early with Raffaello Matarazzo's *Treno popolare*, but it was after World War II that his fame grew. After 1942 he worked frequently for the Lux Film Company in Rome and acquired international renown with Henry Cass's *The Glass Mountain*. Rota's body of work includes 150 film scores for directors such as Renato Castellani, Mario Soldati, Alberto Lattuada, Eduardo De Filippo, Luchino Visconti, René Clement, King Vidor, Sergei Bondarchuk, and Francis Ford Coppola. However, his name is particularly associated with Federico Fellini, with whom he collaborated on sixteen films from *Lo sceicco bianco* to *Prova d'orchestra*. Fellini described Rota as a funny, naive, gentle little man, perhaps underestimating the composer's remarkable inventiveness, flexibility, and problem-solving ability. Throughout his career, he composed symphonic, chamber, and theater music. However, while his fame as film composer increased, his serious music was prejudicially deemed mediocre and popular.

The Music

Both the film scores and the concert music by Rota demonstrate his ability to parody different styles as well as his predilection for rhythms, textures, and orchestrations that enhance lyricism and intelligibility. Though fundamentally an eclectic composer, Rota selectively absorbed only those elements that he found germane to his inspiration and taste. At the beginning of his career Rota was influenced by the generation of Italian composers born in the 1870's and 1880's (Ottorino Respighi, Gian Francesco Malipiero, Alfredo Casella); then, in America, he learned (from Copland and Gershwin) to exploit popular idioms and (from Antonín Dvořák, Nikolay Rimsky-Korsakov, and Modest Mussorgsky) East European symphonic styles that appealed to him. Finally, like many composers of his time, he was fascinated by the phenomenon of Igor Stravinsky; Rota's oratorio *Mysterium catholicum* resembles Stravinsky's *Symphony of Psalms* (1930). When the jagged melodic leaps and spare orchestration typical of Anton von Webern became predominant, Rota's tuneful tonal music was the object of harsh criticism. However, the composer avoided ideological debates and never took up serial techniques. Significantly, in Rota's *Fantasia sopra dodici note del di W. A. Mozart* for piano and orchestra, the twelve-tone theme is presented as parody of Webern's pointillist orchestration (each note has a different timbre), but the theme is treated tonally.

Il cappello di paglia di Firenze. Rota and his mother derived the libretto of this *farsa musicale* from Eugène Labiche and Marc Michel's vaudeville play *Un Chapeau de paille d'Italie* (1851). The protagonist of this farce, Ferdinand, must find a straw hat during his wedding in Paris to replace one accidentally eaten by his horse. If he fails, the woman who owned the rare hat risks the retaliation of her violent and jealous husband. Ferdinand and his wedding guests pass through an endless sequence of ridiculous situations before discovering that, fortunately, an identical hat has been delivered as a wedding gift. Without any commission, Rota composed *Il cappello di paglia di Firenze* during the summers of 1945 and 1946. Sometimes he set new words to melodies he had previously composed for films. *Il cappello di paglia di Firenze* was performed for the first time at Palermo Teatro Massimo in 1955 and repeated with similar success for two years at Milan Theater Piccola Scala under the direction of Giorgio Strehler. In time it became the most performed Italian twentieth century opera after Giacomo Puccini's works. This comic opera has many characteristics of vaudeville, including bright orchestration, fast pace, snapshot puns, and

Nino Rota. (Hulton Archive/Getty Images)

brilliant portrayals of people, places, and situations. Moreover, there are frequent references to opera buffa and operetta. Rota wittily mocked a variety of musical styles ranging from that of Gioacchino Rossini to that of Jacques Offenbach.

La strada. The Fellini-Rota relationship is a favorite subject of film scholars. In Fellini's films Rota's music sometimes seems disconnected from the visual content, adding a supplementary layer of meaning. Perhaps this disconnection exists because Fellini often added Rota's music only at a late stage of the editing and because Rota frequently adapted music from other compositions. The result of this accidental combination was an enchanting marriage of music and images that became part of the so-called collective imagination. In the case of *La strada*, the most vivid sound-image association is Gelsomina's solo trumpet theme, with her image as a bittersweet clown. Gelsomina is a poor, ugly girl sold by her mother to a homeless circus artist, Zampanò. Though she finds a true vocation in entertaining people and taking care of her brutal mate, tragedy seems to be their destiny. Besides the trumpet theme that she keeps playing, a kindred gloomy sentimentality broods in the entire sound track: in Zampanò's wandering theme for strings as well as in the procession music for marching band that accompanies the scenes of the little town festival.

In 1966 *La strada* became a ballet for Milan La Scala (choreography by Mario Pistoni). Carla Fracci performed it to great popular and critical acclaim. Though the ballet, which uses pantomime extensively, closely follows the story line of the film, Rota rearranged the film score, borrowing more than forty minutes of music from his other works. The twenty-minute suite from the ballet *La strada* is one of Rota's symphonic works that is often performed and recorded.

The Godfather. When Coppola asked him to write the sound track for his Mafia film *The Godfather*, Rota was already a world-famous film composer. Coppola showed Rota an early version of the film and suggested music not strictly bound to the ethnicity of the characters. Also, Coppola wanted a recurring dancelike motif to be played in association with the chain of murders. Rota provided three main themes, which were freely edited without his supervision: the godfather theme (a waltz introduced at the beginning by a trumpet solo), the son theme (not used), and the love theme (for the scenes in Sicily). The third one became the most popular, and it is sometimes erroneously called "*The Godfather* theme." The love theme was an elaboration of a march Rota had composed for De Filippo's film *Fortunella* (1958). This self-borrowing prevented Rota from being nominated for an Academy Award, but he did win an Academy Award in 1974 for the sound track of the sequel, *The Godfather, Part II*.

Nonet. Rota's chamber music is distinctively neoclassical. He never included extended techniques, electronics, aleatory passages (sounds chosen by the performer or left to chance), or other typical twentieth century innovations; rather, he scored for nineteenth century classical instruments and ensembles (string quartet, wind quintet, piano trios, piano and solo instrument sonatas). The *Nonet* for flute, oboe, clarinet, bassoon, horn, violin, viola, cello, and double bass was composed in 1959

for the ensemble Solisti Dauni, led by bassoonist Domenico Losavio. Rota revised the piece from 1974 to 1977 for publication. Considered Rota's chamber masterpiece, the *Nonet* is remarkably long (about thirty minutes) compared with the rest of his works. The closest model seems to be Stravinsky's neoclassical style of the 1920's, although Rota's style is simpler harmonically and rhythmically, and it does not feature Baroque forms. Instead, the *Nonet* is shaped in five classical movements: sonata-allegro (*Allegro*), slow movement (*Andante*), scherzo (*Allegro con spirito*), theme and variations (*Canzone con variazioni*), and rondo (*Vivacissimo*).

Musical Legacy

After the late 1950's, Rota's concert music was considered out of date by prestigious Italian critics. Rota was accused of pleasing popular taste and using an inappropriate film-music style for serious music. However, for Rota any difference between popular music and cultivated music was spurious. "The only thing that changes," he wrote, "is technical domain." Rota preferred not to experiment with more fashionable compositional techniques and, alluding to the omnipresent Webernism, he was not afraid to state that most contemporaneous serious music *rompe le palle* (stinks).

Even though Rota was likely remembered for scoring Coppola's *The Godfather* and the best of Fellini's films, a burgeoning group of scholars argued that it was time to remove the unfair discrimination imposed on Rota's concert and theater music. With the advent of postmodern ideology and aesthetics, according to which it is no longer possible to invent anything absolutely new, Rota's derivative attitude could be wholly appreciated. In retrospect, the main characteristics of Rota's nonfilm music—his eclecticism, his self-indulgent irony, his pervasive borrowing, his parodies, his pastiches, and his refurbished use of uncomplicated harmony and appealing tuneful idioms—identified him as a postmodern composer.

Francesco Dalla Vecchia

Further Reading

Dyer, Richard. "The Talented Mr. Rota." *Sight and Sound* 14, no. 9 (2004): 42-45. An evaluation of Rota's originality and his ability to compose musical scores for comedies.

Sciannameo, Franco. *Nino Rota, Federico Fellini, and the Making of an Italian Cinematic Folk Opera "Amarcord."* Lewiston, N.Y.: Edwin Mellen Press, 2005. Case study on the Rota-Fellini relationship, with biographical information and many photographs.

Simon, John. "The Other Rota." *The New Criterion* 19, no. 1 (2000): 53-39. Includes a discography of Rota's nonfilm work.

See also: Barber, Samuel; Bernstein, Leonard; Copland, Aaron; Elfman, Danny; Gershwin, George; Mancini, Henry; Stravinsky, Igor.

Miklós Rózsa

Hungarian classical and film-score composer

A giant in the field of American film composition, Rózsa created memorable music, from intimate melodramas to sweeping epics.

Born: April 18, 1907; Budapest, Hungary, Austro-Hungarian Empire (now in Hungary)
Died: July 27, 1995; Los Angeles, California

Principal works

CELLO WORK: *Toccata Capricciosa for Cello*, Op. 36, 1977.

CHAMBER WORK: *Duo*, Op. 7, 1931 (for cello and piano).

FILM SCORES: *The Divorce of Lady X*, 1937; *Knight Without Armour*, 1937; *The Squeaker*, 1937 (*Murder on Diamond Row*); *Thunder in the City*, 1937; *The Four Feathers*, 1939; *On the Night of the Fire*, 1939 (*The Fugitive*); *The Spy in Black*, 1939 (*U-Boat 29*); *Ten Days in Paris*, 1939 (*Missing Ten Days; Spy in the Pantry*); *Four Dark Hours*, 1940 (*The Green Cockatoo; Race Gang*); *The Thief of Bagdad*, 1940; *Lydia*, 1941; *Sundown*, 1941; *That Hamilton Woman*, 1941 (*Lady Hamilton*); *The Jungle Book*, 1942; *Five Graves to Cairo*, 1943; *Sahara*, 1943; *So Proudly We Hail*, 1943; *The Woman of the Town*, 1943; *Dark Waters*, 1944; *Double Indemnity*, 1944; *The Hour Before Dawn*, 1944; *The Man in Half Moon Street*, 1944; *Blood on the Sun*, 1945; *Lady on a Train*, 1945; *The Lost Weekend*, 1945; *A Song to Remember*, 1945; *Because of Him*, 1946; *The Killers*, 1946; *Spellbound*, 1946; *The Strange Love of Martha Ivers*, 1946; *Brute Force*, 1947; *Desert Fury*, 1947; *A Double Life*, 1947; *The Other Love*, 1947; *The Red House*, 1947; *Song of Scheherazade*, 1947; *Criss Cross*, 1948; *Kiss the Blood off My Hands*, 1948 (*Blood on My Hands*); *The Naked City*, 1948; *The Secret Beyond the Door*, 1948; *A Woman's Vengeance*, 1948 (*The Gioconda Smile*); *Adam's Rib*, 1949; *The Bribe*, 1949; *Command Decision*, 1949; *East Side, West Side*, 1949; *Madame Bovary*, 1949; *The Red Danube*, 1949; *The Asphalt Jungle*, 1950; *Crisis*, 1950; *The Miniver Story*, 1950 (with Herbert Stothart); *Ivanhoe*, 1951; *The Light Touch*, 1951; *Quo Vadis?*, 1951; *Plymouth Adventure*, 1952; *All the Brothers Were Valiant*, 1953; *Julius Caesar*, 1953; *Knights of the Round Table*, 1953; *Young Bess*, 1953; *Green Fire*, 1954; *Men of the Fighting Lady*, 1954 (*Panther Squadron*); *Seagulls over Sorrento*, 1954 (*Crest of the Wave*); *Valley of the Kings*, 1954; *Diane*, 1955; *The King's Thief*, 1955; *Moonfleet*, 1955; *Bhowani Junction*, 1956; *Lust for Life*, 1956; *Tribute to a Badman*, 1956; *The Seventh Sin*, 1957; *Something of Value*, 1957; *Tip on a Dead Jockey*, 1957; *A Time to Love and a Time to Die*, 1958; *Ben-Hur*, 1959; *The World, the Flesh, and the Devil*, 1959; *El Cid*, 1961; *King of Kings*, 1961; *Sodom and Gomorrah*, 1962; *The V.I.P.s*, 1963; *The Green Berets*, 1968; *The Power*, 1968; *The Private Life of Sherlock Holmes*, 1970; *The Golden Voyage of Sinbad*, 1973; *Providence*, 1977; *Fedora*, 1978; *The Private Files of J. Edgar Hoover*, 1978; *The Last Embrace*, 1979; *Time After Time*, 1979; *Eye of the Needle*, 1980; *Dead Men Don't Wear Plaid*, 1981.

ORCHESTRAL WORKS: *Theme, Variations, and Finale*, Op. 13, 1933; Violin Concerto, Op. 24, 1956 (for violin and orchestra); *Notturno ungherese*, Op. 28, 1964; *Sinfonia concertante*, 1966 (for violin, cello, and orchestra); Piano Concerto, Op. 31, 1967 (for piano and orchestra); Viola Concerto, Op. 37, 1984 (for viola and orchestra).

WRITINGS OF INTEREST: *Double Life*, 1982 (autobiography).

The Life

Miklós Rózsa (MEEK-lohsh ROH-zah) was born April 18, 1907, in Budapest, Hungary. His father,

Gyula, was a successful industrialist and landowner, and his mother, Regina, had been a piano student at the Budapest Academy of Music. Rózsa began playing the violin when he was five and later studied the viola and the piano. When he was seven, Rózsa conducted a children's orchestra in a performance of Leopold Mozart's Toy Symphony. He was influenced by the music of the Palóc peasants on his father's estate and began writing down their folk songs.

In high school Rózsa angered the administration by championing the modern composers Béla Bartók and Zoltán Kodály. Enrolling at the University of Leipzig in 1925, Rózsa studied chemistry until one of the music professors, Hermann Grabner, told the senior Rózsa that his son should become a composer. After graduating cum laude in 1929, Rózsa worked as Grabner's assistant until he moved to Paris in 1931.

Rózsa returned to Budapest for a performance of his orchestral work *Serenade* and received encouragement from Richard Strauss. Rózsa's breakthrough came in 1934 when the Duisberg Symphony Orchestra performed his *Theme, Variations, and Finale*, inspired by Hungarian folk music. In 1937 the twenty-minute piece became his first composition played, by the Chicago Symphony Orchestra, in the United States. Because his concert music, however, earned him little money, Rózsa supported himself by composing popular tunes under the pseudonym Nic Tomay.

Rózsa's career changed when he saw the French film *Les Misérables* (1934) and noticed how it was enhanced by the score of his friend Arthur Honegger. Rózsa was then approached by Jacques Feyder to write the score for the director's *Knight Without Armour* (1937), and the composer began working for Alexander Korda's London Films.

His film scores were merely a sideline to more serious work as Rózsa won Hungary's highest musical award, the Franz Josef Prize, in both 1937 and 1938. However, when he scored *The Thief of Bagdad* in 1940, everything changed. Because of the outbreak of World War II, Korda moved the production to Hollywood, where his composer then settled permanently. Rózsa was nominated for an Academy Award, and his immensely popular score was released as a recording in an era when sound tracks were not distributed.

At a party given by June Duprez, one of the stars of *The Thief of Bagdad*, Rózsa met British actress Margaret Finlason, whom he married in 1943. The couple had a son, Nicholas, and a daughter, Juliet.

After Korda shut down his production company, Rózsa began a relationship with Billy Wilder, scoring the director's *Five Graves to Cairo*, *Double Indemnity*, and *The Lost Weekend*. He won Oscars for Alfred Hitchcock's *Spellbound* and George Cukor's *A Double Life*.

In 1945 Rózsa joined the faculty of the University of Southern California; he taught there until 1965. Working freelance after Korda, he signed with Metro-Goldwyn-Mayer in 1949 for financial security and after being granted approval of the editing of his scores. In the early 1950's, Rózsa's concert music began to attract the attention of recording companies, especially his *Duo* for cello and piano and his *Theme, Variations, and Finale*.

With *Quo Vadis?*, Rózsa began specializing in historical epics. He won his third and final Academy Award for one of these, *Ben-Hur*, and was nominated for eleven other films. After *Ben-Hur*, Metro-Goldwyn-Mayer did not know what to do with Rózsa and loaned him to producer Samuel Bronston for *King of Kings* and *El Cid*. Although Rózsa composed for several more films, he considered *El Cid* his last major score. Ironically, as demands for Rózsa's services declined, new recordings of his music, much of it never before recorded, began to appear, often with the composer as conductor.

In 1974 the composer returned to Hungary for the first time in forty years to conduct a concert of his music in Budapest. A stroke in 1982 left him partially paralyzed, and he suffered from a back ailment and the neuromuscular disorder myasthenia gravis. Despite his declining health, Rózsa produced eight new works, including chamber music, during the 1980's. In honor of Rózsa's eightieth birthday, he was given a Golden Sound Track Award by the American Society of Composers, Authors, and Publishers. Los Angeles Mayor Tom Bradley declared April 18, 1987, Miklós Rózsa Day, with the ceremonies including a performance of his *Toccata Capricciosa for Cello* by cellist Timothy Landau. Failing eyesight forced him to abandon composing in 1988. Three weeks following another stroke, Rózsa died in Los Angeles on July 27, 1995.

The Music

The influence of Hungarian folk songs can be heard in the sharp rhythms and strong modal coloration in Rózsa's concert and film music. In his autobiography *Double Life*, he writes that the music of Hungary is imprinted on every bar of his music. Rózsa added the influences of Bartók, who also collected folk songs, and Igor Stravinsky to create vibrant, rhythmic scores with longer melodic lines than usual in film music.

Korda Films. With their mixture of Middle Eastern and Oriental influences, the exotic melodies of *The Thief of Bagdad* complemented the depiction of genies and wizards. For *The Jungle Book*, Rózsa created music to approximate the personalities of the animal characters. Rózsa rerecorded the score, with narration by the film's star Sabu, with the NBC Symphony Orchestra, and the RCA recording became the first to feature a complete film orchestral score.

The Theremin. Hitchcock asked for a new sound to convey paranoia in *Spellbound*, the first Hollywood film to feature the theremin, an electronic instrument. Because of production delays, however, *Spellbound* was released after *The Lost Weekend*, which used the theremin to suggest the alcoholic hero's loss of equilibrium. Hitchcock and producer David O. Selznick were supposedly outraged that Rózsa had betrayed them. The composer used the instrument one more time for *The Red House*.

Crime Films. For *Double Indemnity*, a tale of deception and murder, Wilder wanted Rózsa's score to reflect the film's cynicism, so the theme conveyed the image of a march to the gallows. Paramount executives were shocked by the dissonant score, but the director stood by his composer. This success led to work for Rózsa on several other examples of the moody, brooding genre that would become known as film noir. Such scores often featured jolting chords to underline the psychological anguish of the characters. Sharp accents and bitonal harmonies were prominent in *The Killers* and *Brute Force*. In *A Double Life* Rózsa provided a nervous, repetitive score to stress the protagonist's mania. When he places his hands over his ears to shut out a cacophony of voices, it is almost as if he is trying to stop the music that spells out his mental state.

Madame Bovary. For *Madame Bovary*, Rózsa wrote a waltz for the scene in which Emma Bovary is swept off her feet by Rodolphe Boulanger. With the couple oblivious to the other dancers, the music becomes more symphonic to emphasize the evolution of their feelings and then more frantic to reflect their passion. Rózsa scholars consider it one of his greatest achievements.

Epics. While earlier composers such as Max Steiner, Erich Wolfgang Korngold, and Franz Waxman created thundering scores for adventure films, Rózsa's similar work seems both more muscular, full of cymbals and trumpets, and more tender, with frequent interludes of intimate music. Weaving dances, fanfares, and marches, his epic scores continued the exoticism of his early film work.

Quo Vadis? employed three musical styles. For the scenes involving Romans, Rózsa had replicas made of ancient instruments based on their depictions in statues. He then imagined how the instruments would have sounded. Because the hymns of early Christians are also not extant, Rózsa based this music on Greek and Jewish liturgical music and on a Gregorian anthem. The slaves were Babylonians, Egyptians, Persians, and Syrians, so he used ancient Asian music as the basis for their scenes.

For *Ben-Hur* Rózsa used an organ, a vibraphone, and a harp in the opening strains to establish a religious impression. This theme is repeated whenever the hero undergoes moments of spirituality. The composer created a Jewish theme (grave tones, elegiac expressiveness) with woodwinds to indicate Ben-Hur's longings for his homeland. Marches appear throughout, becoming more prominent during the film's most famous scene, the chariot race.

El Cid was typical of Rózsa's approach in the epics of alternating heroic music with more intimate melodies underscoring the melancholy side of the hero's nature. For the finale, following the protagonist's death, Rózsa began with a solo organ before adding fiery battle music.

Later Concert Music. One of his most personal orchestral works was *Notturno ungherese*, which he described as an attempt to recapture the beauty of his family's estate. Rózsa enjoyed composing for musicians he knew and admired, as with his *Sinfonia concertante* for violin, cello, and chamber orchestra, written for the cellist Gregor Piatigorsky. Other new pieces included a piano concerto composed for Leonard Pennario. His Viola Concerto received its world premiere in 1984, with Pinchas Zukerman performing with the Pittsburgh Symphony conducted by André Previn.

Later Scores. Rózsa combined the two sides of his double life when he used his Violin Concerto, commissioned by Jascha Heifetz and considered by many to be his greatest concert piece, as the basis of his score for *The Private Life of Sherlock Holmes*. The music for the time-travel romance *Time After Time* is among the best of the composer's lush, romantic scores. The score for the World War II spy thriller *Eye of the Needle* is reminiscent of music from his Korda period, particularly *The Spy in Black*. When Carl Reiner and Steve Martin paid loving tribute to film noir in *Dead Men Don't Wear Plaid*, Rózsa was hired to provide his distinctive touch. Rózsa particularly enjoyed collaborating with director Alain Resnais on *Providence*. This personal drama about a dying writer included *Valse Crépusculaire*, a poignant piano piece evoking Rózsa's nostalgia for his youth.

Musical Legacy

Along with Bernard Herrmann, Rózsa helped lead a musical revolution during a time when most Hollywood scores sounded alike, moving sound tracks toward a more modern idiom. Echoes of Rózsa can be heard in Jerry Goldsmith's driving rhythms for *Chinatown* (1974). His distinctive mixture of heroic and intimate melodies inspired Maurice Jarre's work on *Lawrence of Arabia* (1962). Rózsa's use of choral music and unusual instruments found a follower in Ennio Morricone, in such films as *The Mission* (1986). For such scores as *Out of Africa* (1985), John Barry borrowed Rózsa's soaring romanticism. With the possible exception of Herrmann, no film composer has been more imitated.

In his autobiography, *Double Life*, Rózsa reveals that he never cared for films. Although he composed scores primarily as a source of income, however, he never lost sight of his profession. His film music closely resembles his concert music and was clearly as personal.

Michael Adams

Further Reading

Brown, Royal S. *Overtones and Undertones: Reading Film Music*. Berkeley: University of California Press, 1994. Analysis of *Double Indemnity* explains how Rózsa broke from the traditional Hollywood score epitomized by the work of Steiner. Includes a lengthy interview.

Evans, Mark. *Soundtrack: The Music of the Movies*. New York: Hopkinson and Blake, 1975. Offers concise analysis of major scores. Introduction by Rózsa.

Karlin, Fred. *Listening to Movies: The Film Lover's Guide to Film Music*. New York: Schirmer Books, 1994. This excellent introduction to film music includes lengthy analysis of *Spellbound*.

Palmer, Christopher. *The Composer in Hollywood*. London: Marion Boyars, 1990. Chapter on Rózsa offers excellent analysis of many scores.

_____. *Miklós Rózsa: A Sketch of His Life and Work*. London: Breitkopf & Hartel, 1975. The composer's former assistant gives a brief overview of his life and a perceptive analysis of the major scores.

Prendergast, Roy M. *Film Music, a Neglected Art: A Critical Study of Music in Films*. 2d ed. New York: Norton, 1992. Analyzes Rózsa's scores for *Julius Caesar*, *Quo Vadis?*, and *Spellbound*.

Rózsa, Miklós. *Double Life: The Autobiography of Miklós Rózsa*. New York: Hippocrene Books, 1982. Title refers to his two lives as composer of concert and film music. Describes working with directors, producers, and actors. Heavily illustrated.

Thomas, Tony. *Film Score: The Art and Craft of Movie Music*. Burbank, Calif.: Riverwood Press, 1991. Includes a brief essay in which Rózsa discusses how film composers overcome problems that confront them in their field.

_____. *Music for the Movies*. 2d ed. Los Angeles: Silman-James Press, 1997. Chapter on Rózsa includes commentary on *Quo Vadis?* by the composer.

See also: Bartók, Béla; Goldsmith, Jerry; Heifetz, Jascha; Honegger, Arthur; Previn, Sir André; Strauss, Richard; Theremin, Léon.

Artur Rubinstein

Polish American pianist

Rubinstein was one of the most highly regarded pianists in the world over the last forty years of his very long career, playing a wide-ranging repertoire of solo pieces, concertos, and chamber music. After his death, he faded somewhat from view but remained famous for his distinctive tone and ability to bring out the particular qualities of whatever work he was playing.

Born: January 28, 1887; Łódź, Poland
Died: December 20, 1982; Geneza, Switzerland
Also known as: Arthur Rubinstein; Arturo Rubinstein

Principal recordings

ALBUMS: *Schumann: Symphony No. 1—Spring*, 1929; *Chopin: Scherzos*, 1934; *Bach: Toccata in C Major*, 1936; *Chopin: Nocturnes for Piano*, 1937; *Mozart: Concerto in A Major*, 1940; *Ravel: Trio in A Minor*, 1950; *Tchaikovsky: Trio for Piano and Strings in A Minor, Op. 50*, 1950; *Chopin: Complete Waltzes*, 1955; *Chopin: Ballades for Piano*, 1959; *Beethoven: Sonatas No. 21 in C and No. 18 in E-Flat*, 1960; *Mozart: Piano Concertos*, 1961; *Schubert: Impromptus*, 1961; *Schumann: Quartet for Piano and Strings in E-flat Major, Op. 44*, 1966; *Brahms: Three Piano Quartets*, 1969; *Johannes Brahms*, 1971; *Mozart: Quartet for Piano and Strings, No. 1 and No. 2*, 1971; *Saint-Saëns: Concerto No. 2: En sol mineur, Op. 22*, 1971; *Brahms: Trios/Schumann: Trio No. 1 in D Minor*, 1975; *Chopin: Études for Piano*, 1975; *Brahms: Piano Concerto No. 1 in D Major, Op. 15*, 1976; *Schubert: Trios Nos. 1 and 2*, 1976; *Beethoven: Piano Sonata No. 18 in E-Flat*, 1978; *Beethoven: Sonata No. 2 in G Minor, Op. 5*, 1978.

WRITINGS OF INTEREST: *My Young Years*, 1973; *My Many Years*, 1980.

The Life

Artur Rubinstein (AHR-tur REW-bihn-stin) was a child prodigy, teaching himself piano at the age of two or three by listening in on his sisters' piano lessons. He was born into an upper-middle-class Jewish family in the Polish city of Łódź, but at the age of ten he was sent to Berlin to study music under the supervision of the renowned violinist Joseph Joachim, with whom his family had a connection. His piano instruction at this time was provided by Karl Heinrich Barth, who taught him for six years. He also received coaching from the famous Polish pianist Ignace Paderewski and had his official professional debut with the Berlin Philharmonic at the age of thirteen.

Feeling limited by Barth, Rubinstein left him and moved to Paris at the age of seventeen, in February, 1904, after which he had no further formal instruction. Over the next three decades he became a popular performer, especially in Spain and South America, but was less well regarded in the United States. He himself said that he was not as good as he could have been at this time; without a teacher to guide him, he lacked discipline, would practice as little as possible, and would surmount the difficulties he encountered in works by changing notes or just dropping them. During this period he led a nomadic life, traveling widely through Europe and the Americas, spending much of his time moving in high society, entertaining at private parties, and engaging in numerous love affairs. In 1908, at a low point in his career, he made a halfhearted attempt at suicide; he took the failure of his attempt as a sign that he should persevere.

In 1910 Rubinstein won an honorary first prize in the Russian piano competition named for the nineteenth century pianist Anton Rubinstein (no relation). This led to a tour of Russia with the conductor Serge Koussevitzky. Rubinstein met and performed with such notable figures as the cellist Pablo Casals and the violinist Jascha Heifetz. He also befriended the composers Igor Stravinsky and Heitor Villa-Lobos, both of whom composed works for him, and associated with numerous celebrities, from actor Cary Grant to novelist Thomas Mann.

In 1932 Rubinstein married Aniela (Nela) Młynarska, the daughter of a Polish conductor. The marriage is generally seen as the turning point in his career. Rubinstein himself said that he did not want his children to think of him as second-rate, so in 1934 he went on a retreat in Switzerland, during which he practiced and restudied the many works in his repertoire.

After his retreat, Rubinstein for the first time became a success in the United States, and he maintained a high reputation there and in the rest of the world for the next forty years. He moved to the United States at the beginning of World War II and became an American citizen in 1946. He also saw himself as a Polish patriot, a strong supporter of the state of Israel, and a citizen of the world.

In 1977 Rubinstein left his wife for Annabelle Whitestone, a young woman almost sixty years his junior. He performed until he was almost ninety, stopping only because of failing eyesight.

The Music

Through his main teacher, Barth, Rubinstein learned the Germanic approach to the piano, a calm, correct attitude with an emphasis on sitting up straight, producing a full but not harsh sound, and being direct and straightforward rather than adding showy effects. However, Rubinstein eventually broke with Barth and in his early career was known for his showmanship, which he often introduced to cover up technical difficulties. At the same time, however, he rejected the romantic approach to the music itself (which characterized the playing of Paderewski, among others) and spurned the notion of taking liberties with the music as written.

Over the years critics saw different things in Rubinstein, some calling him romantic and passionate, others regarding him as austere and intellectual. Some saw him as best with the works of his compatriot, the Polish composer Frédéric Chopin, while to others he was best with the Germanic works of Ludwig van Beethoven and Johannes Brahms. Still others preferred his performances of early twentieth century works, such as those of the French composers Claude Debussy and Maurice Ravel. Because Rubinstein had such a long career, with a midcareer change of direction from showy performer to serious musician, these different views of his accomplishments may be the result of changes in his interpretations and his emphases; they

may also be the result of his immersion in each individual work in order to bring out its special character.

Berlin, December 1, 1900. Despite complaints that his teacher, Barth, limited his repertoire, in his professional debut while still under Barth's tutelage Rubinstein played a wide-ranging concert, including Wolfgang Amadeus Mozart's Piano Concerto in A Major and the second piano concerto of Camille Saint-Saëns, two works he would perform frequently in the early part of his career. He also played solo pieces by Chopin and Robert Schumann, and his performance was highly praised by the critics, who saw him as more than an ordinary child performer, someone who already demonstrated maturity and brilliant technique.

Buenos Aires, Argentina, July 2, 1917. During World War I, unable to continue touring in central Europe and so distressed by reports of German atrocities that he never again performed in Germany, Rubinstein sought out alternative venues, including Spain and South America. He had come to feel an affinity for Spanish music and added some to his program, notably works by Isaac Albéniz and Manuel de Falla. He had great success

Artur Rubinstein. (Hulton Archive/Getty Images)

with these works, especially with de Falla's spectacular "Ritual Fire Dance" (from his 1915 *El amor brujo*), but later said that this was tragic in a way because, although this music was popular and helped him create a powerful connection with his audiences, especially in Spanish-speaking countries, in fact his heart really belonged to the classics from nineteenth century Germany, along with the works of Chopin, Debussy, and Ravel.

In fact, Rubinstein did play the classics in South America. His July 2, 1917, debut concert in Buenos Aires, a highly successful solo recital, included works by Beethoven, Chopin, and Franz Liszt as well as "Navarra" (1912), by Albéniz. Rubinstein mounted a similar concert in Montevideo, Uruguay, and went on to perform concertos by Beethoven, Brahms, and Peter Ilich Tchaikovsky at later Buenos Aires concerts. In 1918, he had another series of successful solo recitals in Brazil, including works by Beethoven, Ravel, Chopin, and Liszt as well as Albéniz.

New York City, Carnegie Hall, January 7, 1938. Rubinstein appeared at New York's Carnegie Hall as early as 1906 and toured the United States several times in that decade and the next, but with only mixed success, so in the late 1920's he vowed never to return. However, after the transformation of his career in the mid-1930's, he returned triumphantly with a concert tour that began with a performance with the New York Philharmonic on November 17, 1937, at which he played Brahms's Second Piano Concerto. This performance was overshadowed by another work on the program, a premiere of a new American symphony, but later performances on the tour won an enthusiastic response from both critics and the general public.

One of the high points was the January 7, 1938, Carnegie Hall solo recital, including works by César Franck, Frances Poulenc, Debussy, Ravel, Stravinsky, and Chopin. The critics praised Rubinstein for his verve, power, imagination, and great dynamic range, and the audience cheered excitedly.

Chopin's Mazurkas, 1939. Although Rubinstein left Poland at the age of ten, he returned frequently to perform and considered himself a Polish patriot. He felt especially attracted to the Polish spirit of the music of Chopin and wanted to convey to the world what Chopin's music meant to the Polish people.

He especially felt this way about Chopin's fifty-one mazurkas, and he recorded all of them during sessions that ended in May, 1939, not long before Poland was invaded by Germany at the beginning of World War II.

Music Marathon, London and Paris, November, 1955. In 1955 Rubinstein showed off his wide-ranging repertoire and the stamina he still had at the age of sixty-eight by performing a series of concerts in London and Paris in the course of one month, during which he played all of Beethoven's piano concertos, along with concertos by Brahms, Chopin, Mozart, Tchaikovsky, Liszt, Schumann, Edvard Grieg, and Sergei Rachmaninoff. He repeated the feat at Carnegie Hall in New York in February, 1956, marking the fiftieth anniversary of his Carnegie Hall debut. In 1961, he reprised his marathon performance by playing ninety different pieces by seventeen different composers during ten solo recitals spread over six weeks at Carnegie Hall.

Musical Legacy

At his farewell concerts, first at New York's Carnegie Hall in March, 1976, and then in London in May of that year, Rubinstein played to rapturous audiences. His career had lasted more than seventy-five years, for the last forty of which he had been regarded as one of the foremost pianists of his time. Critics praised his verve, power, and imagination, and he was awarded the Medal of Freedom in the United States, membership in the French Legion of Honor, and knighthood in England.

In 1996, fourteen years after his death, one critic said that Rubinstein had vanished from the public consciousness owing to his lack of a distinctive personality as a pianist; it had been his stage presence rather than his music that had won applause. On the other hand, three years later, in 1999, a ninety-four-disc set of all of Rubinstein's recordings was released to much acclaim for his lyricism, elegance, and full, round tone. One commentator singled out his distinctive tone, at the same time noting that one of Rubinstein's greatest accomplishments was to make Spanish music sound Spanish, French music French, and so on. His greatest legacy may thus have been the respect he paid to the music he played rather than imposing his own personality.

Sheldon Goldfarb

Further Reading

Gillespie, John, and Anna Gillespie. "Artur Rubinstein." In *Notable Twentieth-Century Pianists: A Bio-Critical Sourcebook*. 2 vols. Westport, Conn.: Greenwood Press, 1995. Brief biography, along with excerpts from critics and analysis of recordings. Bibliography, discography.

Kaiser, Joachim. "Artur Rubinstein." In *Great Pianists of Our Time*. Translated by David Woolridge and George Unwin. London: Allen & Unwin, 1971. Analyzes specific performances by Rubinstein. Includes excerpts from musical scores and a discography.

Rubinstein, Artur. *My Young Years*. New York: Knopf, 1973. The first volume of Rubinstein's autobiography is the only source for much of the information about Rubinstein's early life.

_____. *My Many Years*. New York: Knopf, 1980. The second volume of Rubinstein's autobiography is at times a catalog of romances and concerts, along with self-justifications.

Sachs, Harvey. *Rubinstein: A Life*. New York: Grove Press, 1995. A detailed biography, correcting the inaccuracies of earlier accounts and providing information about Rubinstein's love affairs and other personal relationships. Includes commentary on selected recordings and a discography compiled by Donald Manildi. Illustrations, bibliography.

Schönberg, Harold C. "Arthur Rubinstein: Joie de Vivre." In *The Glorious Ones: Classical Music's Legendary Performers*. New York: Times Books, 1985. Analyzes Rubinstein's style of playing. Illustrations.

Teachout, Terry. "Whatever Happened to Arthur Rubinstein?" *Commentary* 101, no. 2 (February, 1996): 48-51. Suggests that Rubinstein has been forgotten because of his lack of a distinctive performance style.

See also: Heifetz, Jascha; Szymanowski, Karol; Villa-Lobos, Heitor.

Otis Rush

American blues singer, songwriter, and guitarist

Rush is a gifted blues guitarist whose innovative guitar technique strongly influenced bands of the British Invasion that infused 1960's and 1970's rock with Rush's distinctive Chicago blues sound.

Born: April 29, 1934; Philadelphia, Mississippi
Also known as: Little Otis

Principal recordings

ALBUMS: *This One's a Good Un*, 1968; *Mourning in the Morning*, 1969; *Door to Door*, 1970 (with Albert King); *Screamin' and Cryin'*, 1974; *Right Place, Wrong Time*, 1976; *Cold Day in Hell*, 1975; *Live in Europe*, 1977; *Lost in the Blues*, 1977; *So Many Roads: Live in Concert*, 1978; *Troubles, Troubles*, 1978; *Groaning the Blues*, 1980; *Tops*, 1985; *Live at the Chicago Blues Festival*, 1993; *Ain't Enough Comin' In*, 1994; *Live in Japan 1986*, 1994; *Live and Awesome*, 1996; *Any Place I'm Going*, 1998; *Live and in Concert from San Francisco*, 2004; *All Your Love (I Miss Loving): Live at the Wise Fools Pub, Chicago*, 2005; *Otis Rush and Friends: Live at Montreux 1986*, 2006 (with Eric Clapton and Luther Allison).

SINGLES: "I Can't Quit You Baby," 1956; "All Your Love (I Miss Loving)," 1958; "Double Trouble," 1958.

The Life

Left-handed blues guitarist and singer Otis Rush was born in Philadelphia, Mississippi. He taught himself to play guitar while growing up on the family farm, developing a technique on an inverted guitar that left the bass strings closest to the floor and that gave his playing a distinctive wailing quality. At age fourteen, he moved to Chicago, where he absorbed the sounds of Muddy Waters's amplified urban blues over the radio and worked as a truck driver and meatpacker in the stockyards. Promoting himself as Little Otis, Rush played clubs on the city's west side, and he became a key creator of the west side guitar style. By 1958 he had released three of his best-known songs—"I Can't Quit You

Baby," "All Your Love," and "Double Trouble"—on Cobra Records before that company's bankruptcy in 1959. He subsequently recorded with both Chess Records and Duke Records, though his previous successes eluded him. His recording career further deteriorated into the 1970's when Capitol Records chose not to release the virtuosic *Right Place, Wrong Time* album; critics expressed their frustration in 1975 by awarding Rush the *Down Beat* magazine International Critics Award for Rock-Pop-Blues Group Deserving Wider Recognition. Rush toured nationally and internationally for the next two decades, and he enjoyed belated career success with the 1994 Mercury Records album *Ain't Enough Comin' In* and 1998's *Any Place I'm Going*, for which he received the Grammy Award for Best Traditional Blues Album. The bluesman suffered a minor stroke in 2004 that prohibited further public performances.

The Music

Rush's music represents a convergence of gospel singing and urban and country blues music with the wide-scale developments in amplification and recording technologies after World War II. Inspired by B. B. King, Rush embraced a blues that was more urbanized and seamless than its Delta counterpart, developing a fluid, distinctively voicelike guitar technique. His sound is influenced by Albert King and T-Bone Walker, particularly in his ability to bend full chords and to create the rapid vibrato characteristic of slide guitarists. Despite his gifts and technical superiority, however, Rush's recording history reflects a musical unevenness that was righted only late in his career.

"I Can't Quit You Baby." Originally written by bluesman Willie Dixon, this tune became Rush's first hit for Cobra Records when it landed at number six on the rhythm-and-blues charts in 1956. The session also included harmonica virtuoso Walter Horton, guitarist Wayne Bennett, pianist Lafayette Leak, and Dixon himself. "I Can't Quit You Baby" is notable for its powerful vocals rather than expert guitar playing, as Rush had yet to develop the distinctive timing and clean technique that would mark his later recordings. The direct simplicity of Rush's singing secured the recording's popularity and heralded the talented young bluesman's professional arrival. The song was

later popularized by the British rock band Led Zeppelin.

"So Many Roads, So Many Trains." This is Rush's only successful recording with Chess Records. Released in 1960, it shows a mature, confident guitarist with a clear sense of phrasing and dramatic timing. Unlike "I Can't Quit You Baby," Rush shines here in an extended solo passage that wails with mourning and loss and forecasts the advent of 1960's blues-steeped soul ballads. The song's mystical nature is heightened by characteristic Chess echo and reverb elements and Rush's edgy high vocals.

Right Place, Wrong Time. The prescient nature of this album's title foretold its fate: Although Rush recorded it for Capitol Records in 1971, it was not released until the independent label Bullfrog Records acquired the rights in 1976. The recording is widely regarded as Rush's best work. His solos on "Easy Go" and "Take a Look Behind" offer a clear representation of his mature musicianship.

Ain't Enough Comin' In. Disillusioned by the Capitol debacle, Rush performed and recorded on a limited basis for the next fifteen years. *Ain't Enough Comin' In* became his first studio album in more than fifteen years. The 1994 album showcases Rush's instrumental and vocal prowess in equal measure as he covers songs associated with B. B. King, Ray Charles, and Sam Cooke. The title track, the album's sole original composition, was composed by Rush.

Any Place I'm Going. Produced in Memphis with the guidance of producer Willie Smith, *Any Place I'm Going* offers a blending of soul with Chicago blues, and it sheds light on the degree to which guitarists such as Eric Clapton were influenced by Rush's playing. Like its immediate predecessor, this album is enhanced with saxophone, keyboards, and trumpet. It earned Rush his first Grammy Award for Best Traditional Blues Album in 1999.

Musical Legacy

Along with Buddy Guy and Luther Allison, Rush shaped the electric, jazz-influenced Chicago west side guitar sound. His vibrato-laden, string-bending playing style and gospel-inspired vocal delivery greatly influenced musicians such as Clapton, Stevie Ray Vaughan, and Jeff Beck. He achieved widespread recognition during the last two decades of his career as one of the most influential and distinctive blues artists.

Margaret R. Jackson

Further Reading

Harris, Sheldon. *Blues Who's Who: A Biographical Dictionary of Blues Singers*. New Rochelle, N.Y.: Arlington House, 1979. This source, with 571 concise biographies of blues singers, has a valuable listing of Rush performances from the 1950's to the late 1970's.

Kienzle, Richard. *Great Guitarists*. New York: Facts On File, 1985. Musicologist Kienzle provides a biographical portrait of Rush and a musical analysis of his playing technique and music.

Obrecht, Jas. *Blues Guitar: The Men Who Made the Music, from the Pages of Guitar Player Magazine*. San Francisco: GPI Books, 1993. This resource includes interviews from 1987 and 1993 with Rush by Obrecht, the senior editor of *Guitar Player* magazine, in which the bluesman discusses his early years in Mississippi and Chicago, his personal playing style, and the album *Ain't Enough Comin' In*.

_____. *Rollin' and Tumblin': The Postwar Blues Guitarists*. San Francisco: Miller Freeman Books, 2000. Obrecht contextualizes Rush's music and stature within blues history and the extended blues community.

Palmer, Robert. *Deep Blues*. New York: Penguin, 1981. Palmer's blues primer traces the social, musical, and cultural histories of the blues from their Mississippi Delta origins to the clubs of Chicago. Rush is discussed as a distinctive talent among contemporary blues guitarists.

See also: Beck, Jeff; Charles, Ray; Clapton, Eric; Cooke, Sam; Dixon, Willie; Guy, Buddy; King, Albert; King, B. B.; Plant, Robert; Vaughan, Stevie Ray; Walker, T-Bone; Waters, Muddy.

Tom Rush

American folksinger, guitarist, and songwriter

Rush has enjoyed three periods of acclaim: first as a 1960's folksinger, then in an early 1970's folk-rock electric band, and again in an annual radio folk concert aired on public radio.

Born: February 8, 1941; Portsmouth, New Hampshire

Principal recordings

ALBUMS: *At the Unicorn*, 1962; *Blues, Songs, and Ballads*, 1963; *Got a Mind to Ramble*, 1963; *Tom Rush*, 1965; *Take a Little Walk with Me*, 1966; *The Circle Game*, 1968; *Wrong End of the Rainbow*, 1970; *Merrimack County*, 1972; *Ladies Love Outlaws*, 1974; *New Year*, 1982; *Late Night Radio*, 1984; *Live at Symphony Hall, Boston*, 2001; *Trolling for Owls*, 2006.

The Life

Tom Rush was born in Portsmouth, New Hampshire, and grew up in Concord, New Hampshire, where his father was a teacher at the prestigious St. Paul's School, from which Rush graduated. He attended Harvard University, where as an undergraduate he launched his solo career as a folksinger at Club 47, Club Passim, and the Unicorn. His first album, *At the Unicorn*, was issued by a small label while he was still a senior at Harvard.

Prestige Records signed Rush to a two-record contract, and with *Got a Mind to Ramble* and *Blues, Songs, and Ballads*, he established a regional and eclectic following within the North American folk-music community. Rush moved to Elektra Records for a wider distribution network, and the albums that followed defined folk and singer-songwriter expectations for the industry: *Tom Rush*, *Take a Little Walk with Me*, *The Circle Game*, and *Classic Rush*. In the early 1970's Rush continued to write his own songs and to record the songs of his folk peers—notably Jackson Browne, James Taylor, and Joni Mitchell. He usually recorded and performed on electric guitar, with an accompanying four- or five-piece combo, and produced some of his most commercially successful work, including *Wrong End of the Rainbow, Merrimack County*, and *Ladies Love Outlaws*.

In the mid-1970's, Rush, who had bought a farm in south-central New Hampshire, stopped touring and built a recording studio at the farm both to record his own music and to record, produce, and promote aspiring folksinger-songwriters. In the early 1980's Rush organized the annual Club 47 concert series (an homage to the Cambridge coffeehouse that was seminal to the development of his career). It began at Symphony Hall in Boston and continues in venues large (Carnegie) and small (Harvard Yard) across the country, bringing together traditional acoustic stars with emerging talent. Although Rush relocated to California, he would remain associated with the Boston and New England, British-influenced branch of American folk music.

The Music

Rush is in many ways a paradigmatic figure of the folk and folk-rock movements in American popular music. He began his career playing acoustic guitar and covering Appalachian and Lowland Scots folk songs, placing himself in the vanguard of the folk movement. However, after Bob Dylan went electric at the Newport Folk Festival in 1965, a disharmony developed between folksingers who remained committed to the acoustic guitar and washtub bass and those drawn to the electric guitar and synthesizer. Rush was singular in his ability to maintain enduring credibility in the folk community, although he went electric and toured extensively in the early 1970's as the lead figure in what could be characterized as a rock-and-roll band.

At the Unicorn. Accompanied by Fritz Richmond on washtub bass, Rush played acoustic guitar and performed all vocals on this critically and commercially successful live album, recorded at the classic Boston folk venue. Rush covered a number of folk classics, including "Walkin' Blues" and "Pretty Boy Floyd," while also recording some original compositions, most notably "Julie's Blues."

Take a Little Walk with Me. With the continuing tutelage of producer Paul Rothchild, with whom Rush worked for his recordings on Prestige Records and Elektra Records, Rush in this 1966 release redirected himself toward rock rather than

folk, taking the blues standard "Statesboro Blues" and arranging it as a hard-driving rock-and-roll song, five years before the Allman Brothers did the same. He covered "Joshua Gone Barbados," a haunting folk tune written by his friend Eric von Schmidt, and performed rock arrangements for such rhythm-and-blues classics as "Who Do You Love?" and "You Can't Tell a Book by the Cover."

The Circle Game. First released in 1968, this has been a consistent best seller for Rush, as it adeptly combines his best original compositions ("Rockport Sunday" and "No Regrets") with memorable covers of the Mitchell title track and her "Urge for Going." Always interested in promoting the work of other singer-songwriters, Rush included distinctive versions of Taylor's "Something in the Way She Moves" and Browne's "Shadow Dream Song."

Merrimack County. Perhaps Rush's best foray into the rock-band genre, this album included an ironic Rush composition that received significant radio play, "Kids These Days," along with other notable compositions such as the title track and "Seems the Songs." Browne's "Jamaica Say You Will" was covered well in Rush's sensitive folk-rock arrangement.

Live at Symphony Hall, Boston. Continuing a tradition that began on New Year's Eve, 1981, when Rush organized famous and emerging folk musicians for a Boston Symphony Hall concert, this 2001 release utilized the full-stage approach to addressing old folk audiences and identifying new audiences to perpetuate folk traditions in music. This release included several of Rush's signature songs ("Merrimack County") as well as his standard covers of fellow folksingers Mitchell ("Urge for Going") and Browne ("Jamaica Say You Will").

Musical Legacy

Rush's legacy is threefold: as an acoustic folksinger-songwriter; as an avatar of the folk-rock movement; and as a promoter of young folk talent, interested in educating as well as entertaining the public.

Richard Sax

Further Reading

Cantwell, Robert S. *When We Were Good: The Folk Revival.* Cambridge, Mass.: Harvard University Press, 1997. Traces the folk revival from minstrel shows through Paul Robeson, Woody Guthrie, and Pete Seeger to the contemporary folk scene.

Cohen, Ronald D. *Rainbow Quest: The Folk Music Revival and American Society, 1940-1970.* Amherst: University of Massachusetts Press, 2002. Focuses on the political activist dimensions of folk music, from World War II-era Greenwich Village through the British invasion and the development of folk rock.

Filene, Benjamin. *Romancing the Folk: Public Memory and American Roots Music.* Chapel Hill: University of North Carolina Press, 2000. Authoritative study of the collection of folktales by musicologists in Britain and America, followed by a well-documented discussion of the intersection of European peasant music with Negro spirituals and cowboy songs.

Lankford, Ronald D. *Folk Music USA: The Changing Voice of Protest.* New York: Schirmer Books, 2005. Well-written introduction to the continuing multiple traditions of folk music in America.

Unterberger, Richie. *Turn! Turn! Turn! The Sixties Folk-Rock Revolution.* San Francisco: Backbeat Books, 2002. Describes origins of folk in the blues, the intersection of folk and rock, and the use of folk rock as a vehicle of social change.

Weissman, Dick. *Which Side Are You On? An Inside History of the Folk Music Revival in America.* London: Continuum, 2006. Informed discussion of American folk music, especially sections on folk songs as protest and the business and marketing of folk music.

See also: Browne, Jackson; Dylan, Bob; Mitchell, Joni; Patton, Charley; Taylor, James.

John Rutter

English classical composer and conductor

A prominent composer of hymns and Christian choral works, Rutter is virtually synonymous with sacred vocal music.

Born: September 24, 1945; London, England
Also known as: John Milford Rutter (full name)

Principal works

CHAMBER WORK: *Suite Antique*, 1979 (for flute, harpsichord, and strings).

CHORAL WORKS: *The Falcon*, 1969 (for chorus and orchestra); *Fancies*, 1972 (for chorus and piano or chamber orchestra); *Gloria*, 1974 (for chorus, brass ensemble, percussion, and organ); *Canticles of America*, 1976 (for chorus and orchestra); *The Reluctant Dragon*, 1978 (for chorus and chamber orchestra); *The Wind in the Willows*, 1981 (for chorus and chamber orchestra); *Requiem*, 1985 (for soprano, chorus, and chamber orchestra); *Te Deum*, 1988 (for chorus and various accompaniments); *Magnificat*, 1990 (for soprano, chorus, and ensemble); *Psalmfest*, 1993 (for soloists, chorus, and orchestra); *Birthday Madrigals*, 1995 (for chorus, string bass, and piano); *Come Down, O Love Divine*, 1998 (for double chorus); *Psalm 150*, 2002.

OPERAS (music): *Bang!*, 1975 (children's opera; libretto by David Grant); *The Piper of Hamelin*, 1980 (children's opera; libretto by Jeremy James Taylor).

ORCHESTRAL WORKS: *Partita*, 1973; *Beatles' Concerto*, 1977 (for two pianos and orchestra); *Reflections*, 1979 (for piano and orchestra).

Principal recordings

ALBUMS: *Olde English Madrigals and Folk Songs at Ely Cathedral*, 1984; *Brother Sun, Sister Moon*, 1988; *Carols from Clare College*, 1988; *Three Musical Fables*, 1991; *Requiem*, 1997; *Magic of Christmas*, 1998; *Feel the Spirit*, 2001; *Music for Christmas*, 2001; *John Rutter Christmas Album*, 2002.

The Life

John Milford Rutter was born into a family inclined not to music but to science and engineering. Rutter's grandmother lived on Baker Street in central London, where he was born, but Rutter grew up in Cambridge. Rutter did not receive standard musical instruction until his early teenage years. In interviews he has said that he often spontaneously played improvised compositions on the family piano, thus developing a personal musical idiom that was not filtered through existing models. Rutter's parents recognized his talent and sent him to the

John Rutter. (Ian West/PA Photos/Landov)

matriculated at the less-storied Clare. There, at eighteen, he composed his first major work, "Shepherd's Pipe Carol." This drew the attention of the man most associated with King's College's musical reputation, David Willcocks, with whom Rutter studied harmony and counterpoint. Willcocks had spearheaded the revival of the boys' choir as a vehicle for sacred music, and he became a major supporter of Rutter. They co-edited several collections of historic carols, and with Willcocks's encouragement Rutter published his music with Oxford University Press.

In 1980 Rutter married Joanne Redden, and the couple had two children and as well as a daughter from Redden's previous marriage. Rutter stepped down as musical director of Clare College, a position he had held since 1975, and worked as a freelance composer. In 1981 Rutter founded and directed the Cambridge Singers, an a capella choir that has sung and recorded his compositions. In 1983 he founded a music label, Collegium, on which these recordings were often released. Rutter toured frequently and assumed various guest-conducting positions throughout the 1980's and 1990's as his work became increasingly popular in church services, Christmas concerts, and major public ceremonies such as the hundredth-birthday celebration of the Queen Mother in 2000. Rutter's compositions became particularly popular in the United States, where he appeared often.

Rutter often received criticism for what some considered the oversentimentality of his compositions. While some of this may have been motivated by envy, other critics have been offended by Rutter's statements that he is not religious.

In 2001 Rutter suffered a personal setback when his son Christopher, a singer and a member of the Clare College Chapel Choir, was killed in an automobile accident. Rutter's *Mass of the Children* was widely understood to be his emotional response to his son's untimely death.

As he passed the age of sixty, Rutter vowed to slow down his traveling schedule and cut back on the number of commissions he accepted. In 2007 he was named Commander of the British Empire by Queen Elizabeth II in her New Year Honours List.

Highgate School in London. His primary teacher was Edward Chapman, the school's choirmaster. Rutter concentrated on learning composition and became proficient at piano and organ. Among his classmates was John Tavener, who became known as a Christian composer, and Nicholas Snowman, who became a prominent musical director of British orchestras and festivals. The pianist Howard Shelley, younger than Rutter by five years, also attended the school at the same time. Rutter credits his interest in sacred music to the spirituality emphasized at Highgate School, in the tradition of the Edwardian-era Anglo-Irish composer Charles Villiers Stanford. Highgate had unusual access to such musical legends as Benjamin Britten, who conducted his *War Requiem* (1962) at the school, in which Rutter sang.

Not wanting to be swamped by the horde of musical aspirants at King's College, Cambridge, Rutter

The Music

Rutter's first serious composition, "Shepherd's Pipe Carol," heralded his entire career, with its polyphonic voice, insouciant instrumental background, and combination of modern compositional techniques with choral traditions stretching back to the Renaissance. The busy instrumental background, featuring piano as well as the piping of the recorder, adds to the clamorous joy of Rutter's musical representation of a shepherd's celebration of Jesus' birth.

"The Star Carol." This rousing Nativity anthem uses variation in voice level, choral response, and flute and other instrumental background to bestow a sense of exuberance and associate the joy of Christmas with Mary, the mother of God.

"For the Beauty of the Earth." Rutter's most famous composition epitomizes the Christian attitude toward nature: reverence but not worship. The song begins with a series of repeated soft organ chords, followed by rising voices. Just as certain organ phrases are repeated, the fourth line of each stanza is repeated, giving focus to how all the elements of the cosmos stand in praise of God. As the song ascends in seriousness, the organ goes lower and deeper, miming the notes sung by the choir, acknowledging and confirming their words.

"The Lord Bless You and Keep You." Written for the funeral of Chapman, Rutter's choir director at the Highgate School, the song begins mournfully, the boy chorister's voice isolated and ethereal. Other voices begin to infiltrate, and the polyphonic buildup mirrors the joy that can be found even in death as God accepts the soul of the deceased into his care.

"What Sweeter Music." Set to a text by the seventeenth century poet Robert Herrick, "What Sweeter Music" is vocally demanding in the high tones and places unusual stress on the lyrics. This piece rebuts the argument that Rutter's choral work is overly sentimental and sugary.

Requiem. The most popular of Rutter's more extended works, this is one of the few where the orchestra is as important as the choir, with memorable solos for oboe, cello, and flute. The *Requiem*, like many in the Christian tradition, does not follow a set liturgical text but incorporates various psalms and hymns in a patchwork of lament and affirmation. The interplay of darkness and light is reflected in the alternating dirge and rally conveyed by the music.

Magnificat. This setting of Mary's song of celebration is introspective, with the mellifluous plucking of the harp interspersed with voices emphasizing the gravity of the auspicious occasion. Blending English folk melodies with classical traditions, Rutter's treatment is fresh as well as stately.

Psalm 150. Rutter's setting of the last of the biblical Psalms, performed at Queen Elizabeth II's Golden Jubilee in 2002, is majestic, with dramatic use of cymbals, harp, and psaltery. The instruments are characters in this Rutter song, not just background to the voices. The culminating "Alleluia," suspenseful as well as climactic, ends the song on an uplifting note.

Musical Legacy

Rutter's approach is not simply a recapitulation of existing musical traditions. He has embraced innovative techniques in his compositions, such as quartal harmony. His music is associated with the joy of holiday celebrations and the more somber occasions of general mourning. His *Requiem* was one of the most frequently performed pieces at memorial services honoring victims of the September 11, 2001, terrorist attacks.

Nicholas Birns

Further Reading

Banfield, Stephen, ed. *Music in Britain: The Twentieth Century*. Oxford, England: Blackwell, 1995. Places Rutter's work in the context of such twentieth century composers as Benjamin Britten, Michael Tippett, and Peter Warlock; also discusses his use of irregular rhythm and quartal harmony.

Church, Michael. "The Choir Master." *The Independent (London)*, December 13, 2005, p. 46. Extended newspaper profile discusses the interrelation of Rutter's life and work, especially his long acquaintance with John Tavener and the influence the heritage conveyed. Also discusses the composer's daily routine.

Reel, James. "A Conversation with John Rutter." *Fanfare* 22 (November/December, 1998): 131-135. Perhaps the most technical of Rutter's widely available interviews; particularly useful for the musician or scholar of music who wants to understand Rutter's compositional techniques.

White, Michael. "The Carol Singer's Shining Star" *The Sunday Telegraph*, December 9, 2001, p. 7. Efficient overview of Rutter's life and work, particularly his association with Christmas music.

Wilson, John Christian. *Jesus and the Pleasures*. Minneapolis: Augsburg Fortress, 2003. Puts Rutter's music in the context of contemporary celebrations of the Christian message.

See also: Britten, Benjamin; Tavener, Sir John; Tippett, Sir Michael.

Frederic Rzewski

American classical composer and pianist

Rzewski's works employ improvisation, political theater, lavish virtuosity, and musical quotations.

Born: April 13, 1938; Westfield, Massachusetts
Also known as: Frederic Anthony Rzewski (full name)
Member of: Musica Elettronica Viva

Principal works

CHAMBER WORKS: *Les Moutons de Panurge*, 1968; *Spots*, 1986; *Piano Sonata*, 1991; *The Road*, 1998.

ORCHESTRAL WORKS: *What Is Freedom?*, 1974; *The People United Will Never Be Defeated*, 1975; *The Price of Oil*, 1980; *Lost Melody*, 1989; *De Profundis*, 1992.

PIANO WORK: *Winnsboro Cotton Mill Blues*, 1980.

VOCAL WORKS: *Jefferson*, 1970 (text from the *Declaration of Independence*); *Attica*, 1972 (text by Sam Melville); *Coming Together*, 1972 (text by Melville); *Apolitical Intellectuals*, 1973 (text by Otto René Castillo); *Lullaby: God to a Hungry Child*, 1974 (text by Langston Hughes); *No Progress Without Struggle*, 1974 (text by Frederic Douglass); *Antigone-Legend*, 1982 (text by Bertolt Brecht); *The Persians*, 1985 (text by Aeschylus); *The Triumph of Death*, 1988 (text by Peter Weiss).

The Life

Born in Westfield, Massachusetts, Frederic Anthony Rzewski (ZHEHV-skee) began his musical training as a pianist with Charles Mackey. Later, he studied at Harvard University, with Walter Piston and Randall Thompson serving as his principal professors, and he earned a bachelor of arts degree in music. Next, he attended Princeton University, where he studied with Roger Sessions and Milton Babbitt, and he earned a master of arts degree in musical composition. Throughout his education, he took keen interest in Greek language and literature. After a sojourn to Italy where he studied with Luigi Dallapiccola, he embarked on a career as a composer and pianist.

His work during the 1960's fused virtuosity and improvisation. This led him to cofound the ensemble Musica Elettronica Viva with Alvin Curran and Richard Teitelbaum. Together these three honed their talents as improvisers of live electronic music. The ensemble worked from 1966 to 1971, producing performances of aggressively challenging and often politically charged music.

In the 1970's, Rzewski produced several major works for piano, noted for their astonishing complexity, duration, technical difficulty, and political themes reflecting a Marxist thirst for social change. In 1977 Rzewski joined the faculty of the Conservatoire Royal de Musique in Liège, Belgium. He retired from this post in 2003. He has continued to compose and perform, with extensive engagements in the United States and other countries.

The Music

Les Moutons de Panurge. Typical of Rzewski's passion for classic literature, this work's title is derived from François Rabelais's novels covering *The Life of Gargantua and Pantagruel* (1552-1555). The composition, written while associated with Musica Elettronica Viva, calls for an unspecified number of players on melodic instruments. The piece unfolds at a rapid pace, as all performers begin together, playing a melody comprising sixty-five notes. However, each player must play the first note; then the first and second notes; then the first, second, and third notes; and so forth, through all the notes. Upon playing the entire melody, the process continues as players drop notes from the beginning of the melody one at a time. The magic of the work appears when a player makes a mistake, as Rzewski instructs players never to compensate for their errors by dropping notes and rejoining the group. The resulting work changes on each performance, as, one by one, players begin falling away from the group. Often a dense, contrapuntal work results, but with practice and repetition, flawless performances have also been reported, especially by Musica Elettronica Viva toward the end of the ensemble's time together. This work established Rzewski's credentials as an important contributor to experimental music by fusing the improvisational spirit of the larger movement with the musical intensity of a virtuoso.

Coming Together. The second part of this two-part work for speaker and ensemble demonstrates Rzewski's political sympathies. The text for the work is a letter written by an inmate at Attica prison who was killed during the violent restoration of government control after the prisoners rioted. The repression of the prisoners offended many Americans who found the state and local governments' recourse to violence reprehensible. The text ends with the speaker's impassioned shout of the letter's closing line, "feeling for the inevitable direction of my life." The fact that the author of the text was killed, possibly in retribution after the National Guard quelled the prison unrest, lends the work much of its impact.

The People United Will Never Be Defeated. This masterful collection of thirty-six variations on a Chilean Marxist protest song, "El pueble unido jamás sera vencido" by Sergio Ortega and Quila-payùn, reveals Rzewski's virtuosic composing. The collection links Rzewski's contemporary musical sensibility with such earlier traditions as Franz Liszt's pianistic virtuosity. Composed not long after the overthrow of Chile's popularly elected left-wing president, Salvador Allende, by military forces backed by the United States, the piece serves to support and to inspire Chile's progressive movement that Rzewski and others hoped would never be defeated.

Winnsboro Cotton Mill Blues. This attractive work of minimalist cant exists in two versions, one for solo piano and the other for two pianos. With its mechanistic figures descriptive of the titular locale, Rzewski achieves a celebration of the American working class. He evokes the working-class milieu in a context where harmonic and melodic figures derived from soulful blues intertwine with Rzewski's trademark heroic virtuosity. Rzewski tells a story using descriptive figures such as the machinery of the cotton mill to paint a vivid and specific narrative picture.

Musical Legacy

Rzewski provides an important contrast to his fellow experimentalists. While his friend and fellow Harvard graduate Christian Wolff preferred to express himself through applications of game theory to musical composition, resulting in works that often prescribe no particular pitches, Rzewski mostly produced scores with particular pitches indicated, and ones that place extraordinary technical demands on players. The two men share a common interest in improvisation, radical rethinking of formal methods, and presentation of political texts advocating social change along progressive lines. However, Rzewski's music demonstrates the importance of pianistic traditions and techniques in his writing. Wolff and other experimentalists exemplify little interest in such historical connections. Rzewski's voice can be heard in chorus with the experimental movement, but it also sounds a solo note for emphasizing profound links to past musical practices.

Michael Lee

Further Reading

Asplund, Christian. "Frederic Rzewski and Spontaneous Political Music." *Perspectives on New Music* (Winter-Summer, 1995). Asplund, who teaches theory and composition at Brigham Young University, provides an interesting and detailed discussion of the proximity of improvisation and political texts in selected Rzewski works.

Pollack, Howard. *Harvard Composers: Walter Piston and His Students, from Elliott Carter to Frederic Rzewski*. Metuchen, N.J.: Scarecrow Press, 1992. This book provides a substantial discussion of Rzewski's music in the light of his studies with Piston by an influential scholar of American music. The author contrasts Rzewski with others artists, revealing him to provide a unique voice. No work of Rzewski is analyzed in depth, but melodic, harmonic, and rhythmic elements of his primary works are discussed.

Rockwell, John. "The Romantic Revival and the Dilemma of the Political Composer." In *All American Music: Composition in the Late Twentieth Century*. New York: Da Capo Press, 1997. This collection of essays includes one that focuses on Rzewski's proximity to neo-Romanticism, his virtuosic and heroic methods, and his political sensibilities.

Zimmerman, Walter. *Desert Plants: Conversations with Twenty-three American Musicians*. Vancouver, B.C.: Aesthetic Research Center Publications, 1976. Zimmerman's interview with Rzewski includes lucid and penetrating questions, asked not long after the premiere of Rzewski's *The People United Will Never Be Defeated*.

See also: Babbitt, Milton; Berio, Luciano; Stockhausen, Karlheinz.

S

Buffy Sainte-Marie

Canadian folksinger, guitarist, and songwriter

Sainte-Marie is regarded as one of the first activist Native American popular musicians. She is known for her powerful protest songs, but she also composed romantic ballads and brought her distinctive vocal style and musical ideas to folksinging, rock, country, and electronic music.

Born: February 20, 1942; Piapot Reserve, Saskatchewan, Canada
Also known as: Beverly Sainte-Marie (full name)

Principal recordings

ALBUMS: *It's My Way*, 1964; *Many a Mile*, 1965; *Little Wheel Spin and Spin*, 1966; *Fire and Fleet and Candlelight*, 1967; *I'm Gonna Be a Country Girl Again*, 1968; *Illuminations*, 1969; *She Used to Wanna Be a Ballerina*, 1971; *Moonshot*, 1972; *Native North American Child*, 1973; *Quiet Places*, 1973; *Buffy*, 1974; *Changing Woman*, 1975; *Sweet America*, 1976; *Coincidence and Likely Stories*, 1992; *Up Where We Belong*, 1996.

The Life

Beverly Sainte-Marie (saynt muh-REE) was born on the Piapot Cree reservation in Saskatchewan, Canada. Soon orphaned, she was adopted by American relatives partially of Native American descent and raised in Massachusetts. In her teenage years she reconnected with the Cree tribe and learned its traditions, ceremonies, and teachings. Although her 1962 degree from the University of Massachusetts was in philosophy and teaching, by the end of 1963 her performances in the coffeehouses of Greenwich Village established her as a major folksinger and songwriter.

Sainte-Marie moved to Hawaii in the late 1960's and in 1974 married Hawaiian surfing teacher Dewain Bugbee. When that marriage failed, she married Sheldon Wolfchild, with whom she had

a son, Dakota Starblanket Wolfchild. From 1976 to 1981 she and her son Cody appeared on the children's television show *Sesame Street*. During this time she earned a Ph.D. in fine arts and became active in the Baha'i faith. In 1983 she married musician-composer Jack Nitzsche, and in 1993 she settled down with the man who would become her husband some years later, Hawaiian Chuck Wilson.

Sainte-Marie remained active within the Native American community; in 1996 she founded the Cradleboard Teaching Project, a curriculum based on Native American cultural perspectives. In her later years she exhibited her digital art in museums and galleries, served as an adjunct professor at various educational institutions, and lectured on a number of subjects in the United States and Canada. Her music has received numerous awards, especially in Canada.

The Music

Sainte-Marie began her musical career in the early 1960's, singing folk and jazz favorites as well as her original compositions. By 1965 her exotic beauty, musical originality, and distinctive voice brought her both a national and an international following. Sainte-Marie's performances were distinguished by her unmistakable voice, with its broad vibrato and a timbre that ranged seamlessly from the harsh to the tender. Also distinctive was Sainte-Marie's use of the mouth-bow, a traditional Native American instrument, which became a signature part of her sound, along with her original, self-taught guitar style.

It's My Way. One of the few female singer-songwriters on the contemporary music scene, Sainte-Marie was also the only musical artist who introduced a Native American perspective into her work; her trademark song "Now That the Buffalo's Gone" is widely considered to be the first Native American protest song. This song was recorded in 1964 on Sainte-Marie's first album, *It's My Way*, which also included "Universal Soldier." Inspired by wounded soldiers returning from Vietnam,

"Universal Soldier" became an anthem of the antiwar movement. This album featured "Cod'ine," based on Sainte-Marie's own experience with the drug and placing her ahead of her generation in addressing the issue of drug addiction. *It's My Way* was more musically adventurous than the average folk album, and several of its songs were covered by other performers with great commercial success.

Many a Mile. Although Sainte-Marie is generally associated with protest music, her second album, *Many a Mile*, featured her gentle love song "Until It's Time for You to Go." This song was covered by many popular singers of the time, including Elvis Presley, Cher, Neil Diamond, Barbra Streisand, and Carmen McRae. "Sometimes When I Get to Thinkin'" and "Soulful Shade of Blue" further established her reputation as a writer of romantic ballads.

Buffy Sainte-Marie. (AP/Wide World Photos)

"My Country 'Tis of Thy People You're Dying." Sainte-Marie's subsequent albums also included original ballads and protest music as well as traditional folk songs. Her powerful song about the betrayal of Native Americans, "My Country 'Tis of Thy People You're Dying," generated considerable controversy and is a good example of the passion and sense of contained fury associated with her performance of her protest songs. "Starwalker," written in the early 1970's, became an anthem of the American Indian Movement (AIM). Sainte-Marie also explored other types of music, such as country, rock, and art songs; her experimental album *Illuminations* was avant-garde in its deployment of the Buchla synthesizer and, while speaking to the 1960's interest in the psychedelic, also evoked a sense of timeless mysticism.

Coincidence and Likely Stories. By 1977 Sainte-Marie had stopped recording as a result of the waning of the folk music scene and an unofficial government blacklisting of artists associated with criticism of the Vietnam War. She found renewed musical recognition in 1982, when she received an Academy Award, along with cowriters Will Jennings and Jack Nitzsche, for the song "Up Where We Belong," written for the film *An Officer and a Gentleman* (1982). In 1992, after a sixteen-year break from recording, Sainte-Marie employed her computer to produce the album *Coincidence and Likely Stories* in her home studio in Hawaii. While her lyrics continued her idiom of protest and love songs, her music featured the synthesized sounds of electronic music instead of the acoustic guitar and mouth-bow of her early records. Throughout her musical career Sainte-Marie's work has demonstrated sustained creativity as well as considerable versatility. The warmth, power, and striking timbre of her voice remained unchanged, as did her social and political concerns, especially those involving Native American rights and Native American culture.

Musical Legacy

Buffy Sainte-Marie was a major force in folk and popular music in the 1960's. An innovative artist, she explored folk, rock, country, and art songs and was an early adopter of electronic music and the personal computer as a means of musical expression. While her unusual voice made it difficult for her to succeed as a commercial singer, her songs became hits when recorded by other artists; her much-recorded ballad "Until It's Time for You to Go" has become a standard. She has a legacy of protest songs, especially concerning Native Americans, and is regarded as the one of few Native Americans to have enjoyed worldwide popularity in the field of popular music. She has received many awards, especially for songs that demonstrate her support for Native American culture and for social justice. Her protest song "Universal Soldier" was inducted into the Canadian Songwriters Hall of Fame in 2005.

Margaret Boe Birns

Further Reading

Hunter, Shaun. *Visual and Performing Artists*. New York: Crabtree, 1999. Featuring Sainte-Marie on the cover, this book covers her in a series of six in-depth profiles of contemporary women artists of varied races and nationalities.

Malinowski, Sharon, and Simon Glickman. *Native North American Biography*. New York: UXL, 1996. Includes Sainte-Marie in profiles of notable Native Americans.

Sainte-Marie, Buffy. *The Buffy Sainte-Marie Songbook*. New York: Grosset and Dunlap, 1972. Self-illustrated songbook of early songs, including "Universal Soldier" and "Now That the Buffalo's Gone."

Thompson, Christian, ed. *Saskatchewan First Nations: Lives Past and Present*. Regina, Sask.: Canadian Plains Research Center, 2004. Includes a three-page entry on Sainte-Marie.

Wishart, David, ed. *Encyclopedia of the Great Plains Indians*. Lincoln, Nebr.: Bison Books, 2007. Discusses Sainte-Marie within the context of Plains Indians and in the context of other important North American figures such as Russell Means and Leonard Peltier, activists in Native American causes.

See also: Diamond, Neil; Odetta; Presley, Elvis; Streisand, Barbra.

Esa-Pekka Salonen

Finnish classical composer and conductor

Salonen is renowned for his role in championing the cause of contemporary music. A conducting prodigy, he is also a versatile composer of evocative works that feature unusual textures, contrasts, and sound effects.

Born: June 30, 1958; Helsinki, Finland
Member of: Toimii

Principal works

CHAMBER WORKS: *Floof*, 1982 (revised in 1990); *Meeting*, 1982; *Yta I*, 1982 (*Surface I*; for flute); *Yta III*, 1987 (*Surface III*; for cello); *Second Meeting*, 1992; *Five Images After Sappho*, 1999.

ORCHESTRAL WORKS: Concerto for Alto Saxophone and Orchestra, 1981; *Mimo II*, 1992; *Giro*, 1997; *L.A. Variations*, 1997; *Gambit*, 1998; *Mania*, 2000; *Foreign Bodies*, 2001; *Insomnia*, 2002; *Wing on Wing*, 2004.

PIANO WORKS: *Yta II*, 1985 (*Surface II*); *Dichotomie*, 1998; Piano Concerto, 2007.

RADIOPHONIC WORK: *Baalal*, 1982 (for tape).

Principal recordings

ALBUMS (solo; as conductor): *Lutosławski: Symphony No. 3*, 1985; *Messiaen: Turangalila*, 1986; *Mahler: Symphony No. 4*, 1992; *Bartók: The Three Piano Concertos*, 1995; *Bartók: Concerto for Orchestra—Music for Strings, Percussion, and Celesta*, 1996; *Anton Bruckner: Symphony No. 4—Esa-Pekka Salonen*, 1998; *Mahler: Symphony No. 3 in D Minor*, 1998; *Sensemayá: Music of Silvestre Revueltas*, 1999; *The Triumph of the Piano*, 2000.

ALBUMS (with Toimii): *Magnus Lindberg, Action-Situation-Signification*, 1982; *Magnus Lindberg: Kraft*, 1985.

The Life

Esa-Pekka Salonen (EH-sah PEHK-kah SAH-lah-nehn) was born in Helsinki, Finland, on June 30, 1958. Salonen received his early education at the Sibelius Academy in Finland, where he concentrated on the French horn, composition, and conducting. At the Sibelius Academy, he and his fellow composers formed an informal ensemble, Korvat Auki! (Ears Open!), that arranged concerts featuring contemporary music.

Salonen furthered his studies in Italy, with private teachers Franco Donatoni and Niccolò Castiglioni. In 1979 he made his conducting debut with the Finnish Radio Symphony Orchestra. Guest engagements followed, including a last-minute opportunity to conduct the Philharmonia Orchestra of London in Gustav Mahler's Symphony No. 3 (1902). This opportunity led to an American debut with the Los Angeles Philharmonic in November, 1984.

The following year, Salonen was named principal guest conductor of the Philharmonia Orchestra and principal conductor of the Swedish Radio Symphony Orchestra, positions that he occupied until 1994 and 1995, respectively. In 1992 he accepted an engagement as music director and conductor of the Los Angeles Philharmonic. In 2008 he became principal conductor and artistic adviser to the London Philharmonia Orchestra. Salonen's conducting career has also included performances with the Orchestre de Paris, New York Philharmonic, and Chicago Symphony Orchestra.

Salonen has composed more than thirty solo and orchestral works, many of which were commissioned or premiered by major performers or orchestras. He is also an active promoter of music in the community. From 1995 to 1996, he served as artistic director of the Helsinki Festival. In 1999 and 2001, he directed the Ojai Music Festival in California, and in 2003 he cofounded the Baltic Sea Festival and has since served as its artistic director.

Recognition of Salonen's achievements include the Accademia Chigiana's Siena Prize in 1993, as the first conductor ever to receive this award, and the Opera Award (1995) and Conductor of the Year Award (1997) from the Royal Philharmonic Society. He was named an Officier de l'Ordre des Arts et des Lettres by the French government in 1998, was awarded a Helsinki Medal in 2005, and was named Musician of the Year by *Musical America* in 2006. In addition, he holds an honorary doctorate from the

Esa-Pekka Salonen. (AP/Wide World Photos)

Sibelius Academy, a Literis et Artibus award from the King of Sweden, and a Pro Finlandia award from the Finnish government.

Salonen and his wife, Jane, formerly a violinist with the Philharmonia Orchestra, have three children: Ella, Anja, and Oliver.

The Music

Salonen is celebrated for his compositional creativity and his capacity for eliciting unconventional effects, textures, colors, and contrasts. Frequently virtuosic, his music is often built around central evocations, such as poetry, nature, geometric figures, machinery, or chorale texture.

Concerto for Alto Saxophone and Orchestra. This early work of Salonen was inspired by Franz Kafka's novel *The Trial* (1925). The work is often known by the original title of the second movement (removed in the 1983 revision): *Auf den ersten Blick und ohne zu wissen* (at first sight and without knowing). Each of the work's three movements is characterized by a different orchestration and texture, although a light and almost tentative quality prevails throughout.

Surface. Salonen published the first piece of his three-part *Surface* series in 1982. *Surface I* is composed for alto flute, *Surface II* for piano, and *Surface III* for cello. A revised version of *Surface II*, *Surface IIb*, was transcribed for harpsichord in 1987. Each piece is virtuosic and subtly nuanced. *Surface I* incorporates audible breaths by the flutist to communicate the impression of breathlessness. *Surface II* and *Surface IIb*, inspired by snow and ice crystals, feature five musical concepts that peak in successive climaxes: trill, arpeggio, cluster, note C, and scale. *Surface III*, Salonen's first programmatic instrumental work, portrays the death of a moth (inspired by Aleksandr Scriabin's *Vers a flamme*, 1914), resulting from contact with the fire of a lamp.

L.A. Variations. This orchestral work was commissioned by the Los Angeles Philharmonic in 1996, and it premiered the following year. Based on two hexachords that make up a twelve-tone sonority, the work is structured around sections featuring canon, chorale, hexachord reinterpretation, and other forms of variation.

Mania. Salonen originally composed *Mania* for his friend Anssi Karttunen, a cellist, in 2000. An ensemble version was published in the same year, and it was premiered by Ensemble Avanti! in Porvoo, Finland. *Mania* is composed around the key concepts of metamorphosis, extremity, and incessant movement, marked by displays of virtuosity and constant yet smooth transitions.

Wing on Wing. Salonen composed this work to honor the completion of architect Frank Gehry's Walt Disney Concert Hall in Los Angeles. Written for two sopranos and orchestra, the piece is dedicated to the Los Angeles Philharmonic. Through a range of musical and other sound effects, Salonen portrays a synthesis of water and wind, as well as of humans and machines.

Piano Concerto. Commissioned by the New York Philharmonic and dedicated to Yefim Bronfman, this work premiered in 2007. Modeled after the nineteenth century Romantic concerto genre, Salonen's concerto is characteristically virtuosic, featuring double octaves, large chords, and complex syncopation.

Other major works of Salonen include *Giro, Floof, Gambit, Five Images After Sappho, Dichotomie, Foreign Bodies*, and *Insomnia*.

Musical Legacy

Salonen garnered an international reputation as a champion of contemporary music, an inclination that has materialized substantially in the repertoire of the Los Angeles Philharmonic. As a conductor,

he has led premieres of works by John Adams, Bernard Rands, Rodion Shchedrin, and Steven Stucky.

Salonen's discography comprises more than eighty recordings, a number of which feature his own compositions. Although he has recorded primarily for Sony Classical and Deutsche Grammophon, he has also been featured under labels such as Phono Suecia, Ondine, Finlandia, Musidisc, BIS, Warner Classics, Philips Classics, Jive USA, Daphne, and Musica Sveciae. He also collaborated with composer John Corigliano, conducting his musical score for the 1999 film *The Red Violin*.

Siu-Yin Mak

Further Reading

Fleischmann, Ernest, and Alex Cline. *Oral History with Ernest Fleischmann*. Los Angeles: University of California, Los Angeles, Oral History Program, 2001. Transcription of an interview conducted with Fleischmann, managing director of the Los Angeles Philharmonic during the early years of Salonen's tenure. He discusses the orchestra, its directors, and its conductors, including Salonen.

Henken, John. "L.A. Philharmonic's Esa-Pekka Salonen Hits Town . . . Running." *Los Angeles Times*, November 28, 1989: p. F1. Article about Salonen's visit during negotiations with the Los Angeles Philharmonic.

Ross, Alex. "The Anti-Maestro: How Esa-Pekka Salonen Transformed the Los Angeles Philharmonic." *The New Yorker* (April 20, 2007): 60. Lengthy article about Salonen's involvement with the Los Angeles Philharmonic.

Salonen, Esa-Pekka. "Variations and Traditions: Classical Music in the Twenty-first Century." In *Symphony: Frank Gehry's Walt Disney Concert Hall*, edited by Garrett White and Gloria Gerace. New York: Harry N. Abrams, in association with the Los Angeles Philharmonic, 2003. Article by Salonen describes how the soaring design of the concert hall complements his choice of repertoire. Includes full-color photographs of the structure.

Sharpe, Roderick, and Jeanne Stierman. *Maestros in America: Conductors in the Twenty-first Century*. Lanham, Md.: Scarecrow Press, 2008. Contains a brief biography of Salonen.

See also: Beach, Amy; Ligeti, György; Scriabin, Aleksandr.

Salt and Pepa

American rap singer-songwriters

As part of Salt-n-Pepa, James and Denton were trailblazers, breaking into a musical genre dominated by men and largely misogynistic in its lyrical content.

Pepa

Born: November 9, 1961; Kingston, Jamaica
Also known as: Sandra Denton (birth name)

Salt

Born: March 28, 1964; Brooklyn, New York
Also known as: Cheryl James (birth name);
  Cheryl Wray (married name)
Members of: Salt-n-Pepa

Principal recordings

ALBUMS (with Salt-n-Pepa): *Hot, Cool, and Vicious*, 1986; *A Salt with a Deadly Pepa*, 1988; *A Blitz of Salt-n-Pepa*, 1989; *Blacks' Magic*, 1990; *Very Necessary*, 1993; *Brand New*, 1997.

The Lives

Sandy Denton was born in Kingston, Jamaica, in 1961, and as a child moved with her family to Queens, New York. Cheryl "Salt" James was born in Brooklyn, New York, in 1964. In 1985 Denton was working in a Sears store when she met James, a fellow employee. The duo's coworker, Hurby "Luv Bug" Azor (who was dating James at the time), asked them to rap on a project for his audio production class at New York City's Center for Media Arts.

Together, Azor, Denton, and James wrote "The Show Stopper" in response to Doug E. Fresh and Slick Rick's "The Show." The song was an underground hit in the summer of 1985—going to number forty-six on the rhythm-and-blues charts—and it led the duo to sign a contract with Azor to be their manager. Now called Salt-n-Pepa, the duo signed a contract with Next Plateau Records, a label that focused on the emerging New York hip-hop scene. Denton took the name "Pepa" from a line in "The Show Stopper." Salt and Pepa would add a third to the group, Deidra "Dee Dee" Roper (DJ Spinderella).

In 1998 Denton and rapper Anthony Criss had a daughter named Egypt; the next year they were wed in what *Ebony* called "the hip-hop wedding of the decade." The extravagant wedding was presided over by the Reverend Run of Run-DMC. After eight years of dating and two years of marriage, the couple divorced in 2001.

In 2002 James abruptly quit Salt-n-Pepa. Denton said she was devastated by the news, which she received in a phone call from James. James became a born-again Christian and made a home with her husband and two children, a son and a daughter, on Long Island, under the married name Cheryl Wray.

Denton moved on with her acting career. From 2000 to 2003, she had a recurring role on the HBO series *Oz* as Officer Andrea Phelan. In 2005 Denton was featured on *The Surreal Life*, a reality television show that placed celebrities who were out of the spotlight in a Hollywood mansion together for two weeks.

In October, 2007, Denton worked on *The Salt-n-Pepa Show* for cable network VH1, in which James also starred. The idea originally started with a sitcom pilot in 1994, but development of this show began in 2004. The show chronicled Salt and Pepa's efforts to reunite and make a comeback after more than five years out of the musical spotlight.

The Music

Hot, Cool and Vicious. Salt-n-Pepa's first album, which also featured deejay Pamela Green as Spinderella, was entitled *Hot, Cool, and Vicious*. Throughout 1987, "My Mike Sounds Nice," "Tramp," and "Chick on the Side" were all modest hits, but it was not until a deejay in San Francisco remixed the single "Push It" that Salt-n-Pepa had their first hit. The single became the first Grammy Award-nominated rap song in 1989. Around this time, Green left the group, and teenage rapper Deidra Roper took over for her as Spinderella.

A Salt with a Deadly Pepa. In 1988 the group released *A Salt with a Deadly Pepa*. This album included a remix of the Isley Brothers' song "It's Your Thing" titled "Shake Your Thang," which became a Top 10 rhythm-and-blues hit. *A Blitz of Salt-n-Pepa*, a remix album, was released in 1989 while the group began production of *Blacks' Magic*, one of the first rap albums to cross over to the pop charts, where it peaked at number twenty-six. In 1992 the single "Let's Talk About Sex" reached number eleven on the charts, was nominated for a Grammy

Award, and became a signature hit of the hip-hop genre.

Very Necessary. *Very Necessary* marked the height of the group's popularity in the 1990's. Denton, James, and Roper produced the album after splitting from Azor. The album reached number one on the rhythm-and-blues and rap charts and number four on the *Billboard* Top 200. It featured such hits as "Shoop," "None of Your Business," and "Whatta Man," a remake of Linda Lyndell's 1968 song. *Very Necessary* proved that women rappers could be just as successful as their male counterparts.

While the group took a break between *Very Necessary* and its next album, Denton opened an Atlanta clothing store called Hollyhood, and Salt-n-Pepa sang a single titled "Champagne" for the film *Bulletproof* (1996). The group was also featured on *The Songs of West Side Story* (1996). Denton began her acting career in 1993 with her role as Teesha Braxton in the comedy *Who's the Man?*, which featured her longtime boyfriend Criss as well as rapper Dr. Dre.

Brand New. It took about four years for the group to release its next album, *Brand New. Rolling Stone* described the album as a "richer piano-, guitar- and vocal-filled sound, emphasizing gritty soul and sweet, unadulterated funk." However, the album did not perform well in the marketplace.

Musical Legacy

Although some considered Salt-n-Pepa a novelty act, the group earned three platinum albums by the mid-1990's. The group also has taken well-publicized advocacy stances that set it apart from other hip-hop acts. *Very Necessary* ends with a group of young Boston actors making a public service announcement about AIDS. In another case, the group recorded a safe-sex awareness rap, "Let's Talk About AIDS," which corrects common misinformation about AIDS. All the proceeds benefited the National Minority AIDS Council and the T. J. Martel Foundation for AIDS Research. As a pioneer in the rap industry, Denton helped create more opportunities for female rappers while showing her own style and personality as an artist. After almost twenty years in the spotlight, Denton is still pursuing her careers in music and acting.

Louis R. Carlozo and Laura Burns

Further Reading

Brady, Lois Smith. "Vows: Sandra Denton and Anthony Criss." *The New York Times*, August 1, 1999. This article describes Denton and Criss as the "royal couple of rap," detailing Denton's contribution to the genre and her "ghetto fabulous" wedding.

George-Warren, Holly, ed. "Salt-n-Pepa." In *The New Rolling Stone Encyclopedia of Rock and Roll*. New York: Fireside, 1995. The entry on Salt-n-Pepa chronicles the rise of the duo and the group's contribution to the field of rap and hip-hop.

Watrous, Peter. "Three Women Rap Out Their Independence." *The New York Times*, May 30, 1994. In a review of a concert by Salt-n-Pepa, the writer describes the singers as women in control.

See also: Dr. Dre.

Carl Sandburg
American folksinger, guitarist, and songwriter

Sandburg was a champion of American music, labor, and history through his work as a folk musician, poet, biographer, and journalist. Often referred to as the Poet of the People, Sandburg inspired Americans to cherish their culture.

Born: January 6, 1878; Galesburg, Illinois
Died: July 22, 1967; Flat Rock, North Carolina
Also known as: Carl August Sandburg (full name); Poet of the People

Principal works

ALBUM: *The Great Carl Sandburg: Songs of America*, 1999.

WRITINGS OF INTEREST: *The American Songbag*, 1927; *New American Songbag*, 1950.

The Life

Carl August Sandburg was the second of seven children born to Swedish immigrants August and Clara Anderson Sandburg. He dropped out of school after the eighth grade to help support his family. At age eighteen he traveled throughout the Midwest, befriending hobos and workers from whom he learned a variety of folk songs. Then, after a brief stint in the Army during the Spanish-American War, Sandburg enrolled at Lombard College in 1898.

With the encouragement of one of his professors, Sandburg began to write poetry and to express his liberal political views. Motivated to improve conditions for American workers, Sandburg took a job as a labor organizer for the Wisconsin Social Democrats in 1907, through which he met Lilian Steichen, whom he married in 1908. The newlyweds soon moved to the Chicago area, where Sandburg began a career as a writer. Sandburg's critically acclaimed collection of poetry, *Chicago Poems*, was published in 1916. Written in free verse and full of colloquial language, the poems revealed his commitment to the American worker—a commitment that would continue throughout his career and which can be seen in such works as *Cornhuskers* (1918), *The People, Yes* (1936), and *Remembrance Rock* (1948).

In 1919 Sandburg became a staff member of the *Chicago Daily News*, a position he held for thirteen years, but he continued to write poetry and to give lecture-recitals across the country. While traveling, Sandburg added to his growing collection of American folk songs, which he eventually published in *The American Songbag* and the *New American Songbag*. Sandburg also gained fame for his six-volume biography of Abraham Lincoln, which was published in two installments: The first two volumes were published as *Abraham Lincoln: The Prairie Years* and the remaining four as *Abraham Lincoln: The War Years*, for which he won the Pulitzer Prize in 1940. Sandburg maintained this multifaceted career as biographer, poet, and troubadour until his death in 1967.

The Music

Throughout his career, Sandburg frequently traveled across the country giving lectures, readings, and recitals. His recitals typically consisted of his singing folk songs while accompanying himself on the guitar. While Sandburg was not a trained musician, he had been passionate about music of the people since childhood, and many listeners found his clear baritone voice moving. He loved

Carl Sandburg. (Library of Congress)

learning new folk songs and traditions from those ordinary people he met during his travels. *The American Songbag* and the *New American Songbag*—Sandburg's published collections of folk songs from across the nation—served as significant documents of American folklore as well as practical songbooks for amateur musicians. In addition, Sandburg was close to several classical musicians, and his poetry was frequently set to music by American composers, including Ruth Crawford Seeger, Roy Harris, and Lukas Foss. Sandburg was also featured as the narrator in Aaron Copland's *Lincoln Portrait* (1942).

"Boll Weevil Song." Sandburg first heard "Boll Weevil Song" from John Lomax. It is included in *The American Songbag* with a piano accompaniment arranged by Chicago composer Hazel Felman. The song humorously conveys the damage that so many cotton farmers experienced from the insect commonly known as the boll weevil. Although the song is lighthearted, the lyrics express the harsh realities of cotton farming in America. The lyrics also provide an example of the regional dialects that Sandburg could so expertly reproduce.

"I Ride an Old Paint." This song comes from the American Southwest, and Sandburg first heard it from Margaret Larkin and Linn Riggs. "I Ride an Old Paint" is likewise included in *The American Songbag* with piano accompaniment by Felman. The song is upbeat, and it conveys a tender relationship between a cowboy and his horse.

"Frankie and Her Man." In *The American Songbag*, Sandburg includes six variants of this popular ballad. The heroine, sometimes called Josie or Sadie, upon discovering the infidelity of her man (typically named Johnny or Albert), murders him and is subsequently sentenced to execution. In addition to the protagonists' names, the music is different in each version, but each variant has the same basic structure: each stanza ends with a refrain about how Johnny (or Albert) had "done her [Frankie] wrong." Chicago composers Edward Collins and Alfred G. Wathall arranged the accompaniments for these variants.

"Hallelujah, I'm a Bum!" Sandburg first heard this song during his early sojourn with the vagabonds along the railroads in Kansas. The song gained popularity through its adoption by the International Workers of the World union (with altered lyrics). This humorous song, full of irony, was one of Sandburg's favorites, and he regularly performed it at gatherings and recitals. It is included in *The American Songbag* with a piano accompaniment arranged by New York composer Henry Joslyn.

"Lincoln Campaign Song." It is fitting that the great Abraham Lincoln biographer would collect and sing songs about his favorite president. In *The American Songbag* and the *New American Songbag*, Sandburg presents three songs about Lincoln. The "Lincoln Campaign Song" appears in the *New American Songbag*, and, unlike the majority of the other songs, it is published with only the melody. Chords are indicated above the melody, which a

guitarist or keyboardist may use to amplify the accompaniment. According to Sandburg, Lincoln heard this song from a glee club supporting him in the election of 1860, and he immediately adopted it for his campaign.

Musical Legacy

Sandburg's work as a collector and performer of American folk songs, along with that of John and Alan Lomax, laid the foundation for the folk music revival of the 1950's. Groups such as the Kingston Trio and the Limeliters performed and recorded many of the folk songs included in *The American Songbag*, making them widely available and popular with the American public. Several recordings of Sandburg singing his collection of songs while accompanying himself on guitar are also available. Through these recordings, generations of Americans can experience his simple yet heartfelt performances of these national musical treasures.

Jennifer Smull

Further Reading

Dodson, Kenneth. *The Poet and the Sailor: The Story of My Friendship with Carl Sandburg*. Edited by Richard Dodson. Urbana: University of Illinois Press, 2007. Contains the correspondence between Sandburg and Dodson, a lieutenant in the U.S. Navy to whom Sandburg began writing in 1944. Offers insight into Sandburg's writing method and the last twenty years of his life.

Niven, Penelope. *Carl Sandburg: A Biography*. New York: Charles Scribner's Sons, 1991. An extremely thorough biography covering Sandburg's life and career.

Sandburg, Carl. *The American Songbag*. New York: Harcourt, Brace, 1927. A collection of 280 American folk songs with piano accompaniments, compiled by Sandburg.

_____. *New American Songbag*. New York: Broadcast Music, 1950. This later collection includes fifty-nine songs, some of which also appeared in the original *The American Songbag*.

See also: Copland, Aaron; Lomax, Alan; Seeger, Ruth Crawford.

Pharoah Sanders

American jazz and world fusion composer and saxophone

A vibrant saxophone voice of the free jazz explosion of the early 1960's, Sanders has matured into a respected master of his instrument.

Born: October 13, 1940; Little Rock, Arkansas
Also known as: Ferrell Sanders (full name)

Principal recordings

ALBUMS (solo): *Pharoah's First*, 1965; *Tauhid*, 1966; *Izipho Zam*, 1969; *Jewels of Thought*, 1969; *Karma*, 1969; *Deaf Dumb Blind (Summun Bukmun Umyun)*, 1970; *Thembi*, 1970; *Live at the East*, 1971; *Village of the Pharoahs*, 1971; *Wisdom Through Music*, 1972; *Elevation*, 1973; *Love in Us All*, 1973; *Voyage to Uranus*, 1974; *Pharoah*, 1976; *Love Will Find a Way*, 1977; *Beyond a Dream*, 1978; *Journey to the One*, 1980; *Rejoice*, 1981; *Shukuru*, 1985; *Africa*, 1987; *A Prayer Before Dawn*, 1987; *Oh Lord, Let Me Do No Wrong*, 1987; *Moon Child*, 1989; *Welcome to Love*, 1990; *Crescent with Love*, 1992; *Message from Home*, 1996; *Save Our Children*, 1999; *Spirits*, 2000; *The Creator Has a Master Plan*, 2003; *With a Heartbeat*, 2003.

ALBUMS (with John Coltrane): *Ascension*, 1965; *Kulu Sé Mama*, 1965; *Live in Seattle*, 1965; *Meditations*, 1965; *Om*, 1965; *Expression*, 1967; *The Olatunji Concert: The Last Live Recording*, 1967.

The Life

Born in Little Rock, Arkansas, to parents who were music teachers, Ferrell Sanders was encouraged in music at an early age, and he studied clarinet as a youth. In high school, he switched to tenor saxophone; under the guidance of his music teacher, Jimmy Cannon, he began to listen to modern jazz saxophone players such as Sonny Rollins, Charlie Parker, and Harold Land. Sanders also began to play gigs while in high school with touring musicians such as Bobby Bland and Junior Parker.

Upon graduation, Sanders traveled to Oakland,

California, where he played in both conventional and new styles. In 1961 he went to New York, and he began to perform in free jazz sounds. At this time, he worked briefly with Sun Ra, who modified his first name into Pharoah. By 1964 he had been heard by his longtime musical idol John Coltrane, who was impressed by Sanders's sound. That year Sanders recorded his first session as a bandleader, and in 1965 he was invited to join Coltrane in recording as a guest, then touring as a regular band member. The pairing of these two free jazz tenor saxophone giants was impressive, as each one fed the other's explorations of the music, showing stylistic sympathy yet remaining distinctive in their two sounds.

In July, 1967, Coltrane died of liver cancer, and Sanders was left to become a band and session leader for their sympathetic record label, Impulse, and producer, Bob Thiel. From then through the mid-1970's, Sanders recorded a series of albums for Impulse in which he explored the combination of his modal jazz style and African, Asian, and Latin American music and instruments, thus presaging the worldwide interest in similar musical fusions.

For the rest of the century, Sanders pursued his musical vision in collaboration with trusted longtime sidemen and in new adventures, such as a 1994 recording session with Moroccan music master Maleem Mahmoud Ghania. Sanders continues to appear in jazz festivals around the world.

The Music

When Sanders reached New York in 1961, he learned his art from jazz masters so quickly that, within a few years, he had joined jazz music titan Coltrane as an equal on tenor saxophone. Sanders did not attempt to be Coltrane's musical heir upon the latter's untimely death, but instead he developed a new and distinct style, utilizing modal jazz improvisation over propulsive and simpler chord progressions, often over a musical pattern derived from and made with instruments from around the world. Through his use of non-Western instruments and musical precepts, Sanders was a pioneer of Western interest in world music.

"The Father and the Son and the Holy Ghost." Recorded early in 1966 with Coltrane, this piece is an extended session in which Coltrane's quartet is enlarged by Sanders and a second drummer. The four-piece rhythm section provides a foundation for the free-form improvisations made by the two tenor saxophone players. Because of the common ideas and technical abilities shared by Coltrane and Sanders, differentiation can be tricky when the two are not playing simultaneously, but with careful attention, their respective musical personalities can be discerned. This performance is both powerful and challenging.

Upper Egypt and Lower Egypt. From Sanders's first album on Impulse in 1966, *Tauhid*, this is a seventeen-minute piece, in a scale that would become customary for Sanders. The work begins quietly, with assorted bells and percussion establishing the sound. Sanders assists in the percussion and occasional piccolo, and roughly halfway through the piece, the pianist begins a pleasant four-note riff that increases the musical tension. When, at long last, Sanders enters on tenor saxophone, the effect is one of climactic excitement and glorious consummation.

"The Creator Has a Master Plan." From Sanders's 1969 album *Karma*, this piece is around twenty minutes in length. The entire band is heard from the beginning, as the piano plays a pretty two-chord accompaniment over various percussion. Jazz singer Leon Thomas adds lyrics meditating upon the piece's title, appearing near the beginning and at the end. The piece varies from pleasantly easy sounds to more challenging sections, wherein Sanders imposes tenor saxophone cries over the rhythm section, then relaxes, letting the singer and lighter instrumentalists have their turn as well.

"Kazuko (Peace Child)." From Sanders's 1980 album *Journey to the One*, this is a meditative piece for tenor sax, harmonium, and koto, an ancient Chinese stringed instrument. The harmonium establishes a drone, over which the koto applies its bright, brief plucked notes. Then Sanders enters, playing with restraint and compassion. His performance is melodic and tuneful, occasionally incorporating some modern playing effects, yet done with sensitivity and gentility.

Musical Legacy

Sanders is acclaimed as a tenor saxophonist invited to play alongside the legendary Coltrane as a regular member of his combo. Sanders's Impulse albums of the late 1960's and early 1970's remain beautiful and emotive listening experiences. Since the 1980's, Sanders has seen interest in his music dwindle, then resurge. His inclusion of non-Western musical concepts and instruments into his early albums constitutes for many the first introduction for Western listeners to such musical ideas. Sanders was one of the first to teach Westerners that there are fascinating musics other than what is derived from European models.

Jeffrey Daniel Jones

Further Reading

Crouch, Stanley. *Considering Genius*. New York: Basic Civitas Books, 2006. In this book's lengthy epilogue, Crouch discusses Coltrane's late years and Sanders's intense involvement in the former's sound.

Jenkins, Todd S. *Free Jazz and Free Improvisation: An Encyclopedia*. Westport, Conn.: Greenwood Press, 2004. This resource includes an article on Sanders, giving detail on his sidemen and his stylistic changes.

Ratliff, Ben. *Coltrane: The Story of a Sound*. New York: Farrar, Straus and Giroux, 2007. This biography of Coltrane makes frequent mention of Sanders in the context of Coltrane's 1966-1967 work.

Terrell, Tom. "Moonchild: Pharoah Sanders." *JazzTimes* 30, no. 8 (October, 2000): 54-57. This is an interview with Sanders, who is described as an "avant-garde jazz pioneer."

Williams, Martin. *Jazz Changes*. New York: Oxford University Press, 1992. This book has an interesting chapter on Sanders, describing in detail his musical maturity in the 1960's free jazz environment.

See also: Coltrane, John; McFerrin, Bobby; Parker, Charlie; Rollins, Sonny; Sun Ra.

Carlos Santana

Mexican Latin rock songwriter and guitarist

Santana and his eponymously titled band introduced the fusion of Latin music with rock and roll in the late 1960's and redefined both genres.

Born: July 20, 1947; Autlán de Navarro, Jalisco, Mexico
Also known as: Carlos Augusto Alves Santana (full name); Devadip
Member of: Santana

Principal recordings

ALBUMS (solo): *Love Devotion Surrender*, 1973 (with John McLaughlin); *Illuminations*, 1974 (with Alice Coltrane); *Oneness: Silver Dreams, Golden Reality*, 1979; *The Swing of Delight*, 1980; *Havana Moon*, 1983 (with Booker T. and the MGs, Willie Nelson, and the Fabulous Thunderbirds); *Blues for Salvador*, 1987; *Santana Brothers*, 1994 (with Jorge Santana and Carlos Hernandez).

ALBUMS (with Santana): *Santana*, 1969; *Abraxas*, 1970; *Santana III*, 1971; *Caravanserai*, 1972; *Welcome*, 1973; *Borboletta*, 1974; *Lotus*, 1975; *Amigos*, 1976; *Festival*, 1977; *Moonflower*, 1977; *Inner Secrets*, 1978; *Marathon*, 1979; *Zebop!*, 1981; *Shango*, 1982; *Beyond Appearances*, 1985; *Freedom*, 1987; *Spirits Dancing in the Flesh*, 1990; *Milagro*, 1992; *Supernatural*, 1999; *Shaman*, 2002; *All That I Am*, 2005.

SINGLES (with Santana): "Evil Ways," 1970; "Black Magic Woman," 1971; "Oye como va," 1971.

The Life

Carlos Augusto Alves Santana (san-TAN-ah) was born on July 20, 1947, in Autlán de Navarro, Jalisco, Mexico, the son of a world-class mariachi violinist. At age five, Santana took up the violin, though he transitioned to guitar by age eight, which he continued practicing throughout his youth and teen years. When the family moved to Tijuana, Santana played on the local club circuit, which expanded his genre base toward rock, blues, and rhythm and blues.

When his parents announced that the family was moving to San Francisco, Santana wanted to stay, since he and his music were getting attention in the Tijuana clubs. Eventually he was persuaded to move to the United States, and he worked on his music and education at Mission High School in San Francisco.

Upon graduation in 1965, Santana found musical zeal was unquenchable, and he often attended concerts at the legendary Fillmore Auditorium in San Francisco. He formed the Santana Blues Band in 1966, and he dreamed of performing on the big stage. Three years later, under the single name Santana, the band signed with music mogul Clive Davis at Columbia Records, soon winning fame after the release of the albums *Santana* and *Abraxas*. In 1972 Santana turned inward for a spiritual awakening that involved East Indian philosophies and meditation. He became a devout follower of spiritual teacher Sri Chinmoy and adopted the surname Devadip, which symbolizes God's eye and light. The following year Santana married Deborah King, and they would have three children: Salvador, Stella, and Angelica. In addition to raising a family, the couple performed charity work, supporting such causes as Greenpeace, Amnesty International, the Hispanic Education and Media Group, Doctors Without Borders, and Rainforest Action Network. In 1998 the couple cofounded the Milagro Foundation, which promoted health, general education, and artistry among underprivileged youth. In 2003 they joined Artists for New South Africa, a collective that sought to combat the AIDS pandemic. All proceeds from a concert tour that year went to the program, which created more public awareness. Deborah filed for divorce in 2007, and Santana continued to make public appearances, collaborating with other artists and working on new material.

The Music

Early Works. Just prior to his first recording with Santana the band, the guitarist appeared on *Live Adventures of Mike Bloomfield and Al Kooper*, recorded in 1968 at the Fillmore in San Francisco and released the following year. Concert promoter Bill Graham heard about Santana's revolutionary guitar style, and he helped Santana and his backing musicians Gregg Rolie (keyboards and vocals), David Brown (bass), Michael Shrieve (drums), José

"Chepito" Areas (percussion), and Michael Carabello (percussion) get a slot at 1969's historic Woodstock Music and Art Festival. Woodstock happened before the band's official debut album appeared in stores, but Santana was such a hit onstage and on the Woodstock video and sound track that the band found immediate fame. In fact, public attention was so high that when the group released its self-titled project later that year, the lead single, "Evil Ways," shot up to number nine on the *Billboard* Hot 100.

Abraxas. In the wake of the psychedelic rock movement, 1970's *Abraxas* was a refreshing change of pace, with its Latin rock rhythms incorporating jazz, blues, and jam-oriented elements. The project featured an eclectic reworking of the salsa song "Oye como va" (originally cut by Tito Puente) and the radio favorite "Black Magic Woman" (first recorded by the Peter Green-led Fleetwood Mac).

Santana III. That same lineup (with the addition of second guitarist Neal Schon) reprised its success on 1971's *Santana III*. The collection is noted for its thick layering of grinding guitars and a live instrumental feel, especially on the radio singles "Everybody's Everything" and "No One to Depend On." Though the album hit the top spot, it would be the last time this lineup would record together, because Rolie and Schon left to form Journey. At this point in the band's history, the backing musicians and

vocalists regularly rotated, but they were anchored consistently by Santana's familiar guitar styles.

Moonflower *and* Havana Moon. Santana spent much of the 1970's on the road, and despite the revolving door of players, he maintained the band's unique sound. The double album *Moonflower* chronicled a live show, including extended versions of previous hits (such as "Black Magic Woman") and new additions to its repertoire (including a cover of the Zombies' "She's Not There"). Though the players would continue to record and tour at regular intervals, Santana's popularity declined outside his core fans because of his jazzier direction. In the 1980's the band attempted to return to its radio roots, and at the same time Santana worked on a solo project, calling upon Willie Nelson, Booker T. and the MGs, and the Fabulous Thunderbirds to appear on *Havana Moon*.

Supernatural. The bulk of the 1980's through most of the 1990's found Santana and his band a staple on the live circuit, performing previous hits with sprinklings of new tunes. Santana and the troupe experienced a career resurgence on *Supernatural*, marking the band's debut on Arista Records (again under the direction of Davis) and a return to collaboration. The lead single, "Smooth," included vocals from Rob Thomas (leader of alternative rock band Matchbox Twenty) and earned the top slot on the *Billboard* Hot 100 for an astounding twelve weeks, thanks to its relevant and fresh direction. Others on the album included Eric Clapton, Dave Matthews, Everlast, and Wyclef Jean. *Supernatural* introduced Santana to a new generation of listeners, and it received nine Grammy Awards (including Album of the Year) and sold more than twenty-five million copies.

Shaman. Enjoying more attention was the similarly themed *Shaman*, which featured Matthews and Clapton along with other new and classic acts. Relative newcomer Michelle Branch provided her buoyant vocals on "The Game of Love" (which also scored a Grammy Award for Best

Carlos Santana. (AP/Wide World Photos)

Pop Collaboration with Vocals), and other fresh faces included heavy rockers P.O.D. and Nickelback front man Chad Kroeger. The double-platinum-selling album was even more diverse than *Supernatural*, including Latin rockers Ozomatli, deejay-singer Citizen Cope, soul crooner Macy Gray, and opera star Plácido Domingo.

All That I Am. Adapting the same concept, *All That I Am* went gold, though it was not as widely sold as its similarly packaged predecessors. "I'm Feeling You" was a radio favorite, backed by reprised vocals from Branch. Aerosmith's Steven Tyler made an appearance for "Just Feel Better," while the album also utilized *American Idol* alumnus Bo Bice on "Brown Skin Girl" and Latin rockers Los Lonely Boys on "I Don't Wanna Lose Your Love" (who also backed Santana on a tour in support of the project).

Ultimate Santana. *Ultimate Santana* (2007) was the band's first compilation to span its entire career. Singles such as "Evil Ways," "Oye como va," and "Black Magic Woman" were taken from the Santana lineup, and many collaborations from the 1990's and 2000's were included (such as "Smooth" and "The Game of Love"). The project earned publicity for introducing previously unreleased versions of familiar songs (such as Tina Turner offering lead vocals on "The Game of Love"), and it featured a new collaboration with Jennifer Lopez and Baby Bash called "This Boy's Fire." Though not an exhaustive retrospective, *Ultimate Santana* served as an apt summary of Santana's pioneering past.

Musical Legacy

Santana's legacy can be traced to his band's groundbreaking debut at the Woodstock Music and Art Festival. In keeping with that event's historic tradition, Santana and his backing band delivered a brand-new sound that fused Latin influences with rock and roll, igniting a craze that transferred to their self-titled debut. From there, the guitarist constantly reinvented the group's sound, shifting from lengthy jam sessions to radio-friendly hybrids of pop, rock, and Latin, accented with artistic experimentation.

After his initial surge to fame in the late 1960's and early 1970's, Santana maintained a fan base with constant touring, showcasing his unique guitar sounds and influencing a younger generation of players. Though his public profile tapered during the 1980's and much of the 1990's, he rebounded with another sonic reinvention when he collaborated with pop artists.

Playing with Thomas, Clapton, Matthews, and soul star Lauryn Hill, Santana expanded his listener base. He continued a similar tradition into the early twenty-first century, inviting other stars to participate (such as Kroeger from Nickelback and Branch). With a career going in such unpredictable directions, Santana demonstrated his evolutionary musical prowess.

Andy Argyrakis

Further Reading

Leng, Simon. *Soul Sacrifice: The Santana Story*. Atlanta, Ga.: Firefly, 2000. The onetime editor of Santana's fan magazine presents Santana's life, from his early days through major fame in the 1970's and his resurgence in the late 1990's.

Santana, Deborah. *Space Between the Stars: My Journey to an Open Heart*. New York: Ballantine, 2005. Santana's ex-wife chronicles their thirty-plus-year marriage, her role as manager of his band, and the couple's spiritual beliefs.

Shapiro, Marc. *Carlos Santana: Back on Top*. New York: St. Martin's Griffin, 2002. Written during Santana's career comeback, the biography emphasizes Santana's creative rebirth with several pop-rock collaborations in the late 1990's and early 2000's.

Slavicek, Louise Chipley. *Carlos Santana: The Great Hispanic Heritage*. New York: Chelsea House, 2006. Geared toward students, this educational text specifically addresses Santana's role as a Hispanic figure who gained fame across all culture lines.

Woog, Adam. *Carlos Santana: Legendary Guitarist*. San Diego: Lucent Books, 2006. Santana's seminal artistry seen through the eyes of his nationality and cultural customs.

See also: Clapton, Eric; Domingo, Plácido; Hancock, Herbie; Hooker, John Lee; Puente, Tito; Shorter, Wayne; Turner, Tina; Valens, Ritchie.

Erik Satie

French classical composer

Satie was an innovator in the French avant-garde. His involvement with parallel artistic movements, such as Cubism, Dadaism, and Surrealism, and his commitment to the French ideals of simplicity, clarity, and economy were embodied in his musical compositions.

Born: May 17, 1866; Honfleur, France
Died: July 1, 1925; Paris, France
Also known as: Alfred Éric Leslie Satie (full name)

Principal works

BALLETS (music): *Le fils des étoiles*, 1892 (*Son of the Stars*; libretto by Joséphin Péladan); *Parade*, 1917 (revised 1919; libretto by Jean Cocteau); *Mercure*, 1924 (libretto by Leonide Massine); *Relâche*, 1924 (libretto by Francis Picabia); *Jack in the Box*, 1926 (revised as a play in 1937; libretto by George Balanchine); *Uspud*, 1979 (libretto by J. P. Contamine de Latour).

CHORAL WORKS: *Messe des pauvres*, 1895 (*Mass for the Poor*); *La Diva de l'empire*, 1904 (*The Star of the Empire*); *Je te veux*, 1909 (*I Want You*).

FILM SCORE: *Cinéma*, 1924.

MUSICAL THEATER (music and libretto): *Le Piège de Méduse*, 1913 (*Medusa's Trap*); *La Belle Eccentrique (Fantaisie sérieuse)*, 1920.

OPERA (music and libretto): *Socrate*, 1920 (based on Plato's works).

ORCHESTRAL WORKS: *Tendrement*, 1902; *Danse*, 1903; *En habitat de cheval*, 1912.

PIANO WORKS: *Ogives*, 1886; *Trois sarabandes*, 1887 (revised 1911); *Trois gnosiennes*, 1893; *Trois gymnopédies*, 1888; *Vexations*, 1893; *Prélude de la porte héroïque du ciel*, 1894 (*Prelude to the Heroic Gate of Heaven*); *Pièces froides*, 1897 (*Cold Pieces*); *Trois morceaus en forme de poire*, 1903 (*Three Pieces in the Form of a Pear*); *Passacaille*, 1906; *Préludes flasques (pour un chien)*, 1912 (*Flabby Preludes [for a Dog]*); *Descriptions automatiques*, 1913; *Embryons desséchés*, 1913 (*Dried Up Embryos*); *Gnossiennes*, 1913; *Heures séculaires et instantanées*, 1914 (*Age Old Instantaneous Hours*);

Sports et divertissements, 1914 (*Sports and Diversions*); *Avant-dernières pensées*, 1915 (*Next to Last Thoughts*); *Sonatine bureaucratique*, 1918 (*Bureaucratic Sonatina*); Five Nocturnes, 1920.

The Life

Alfred Éric Leslie Satie (sah-TEE) was born to Alfred Satie and Jane Leslie Anton in the harbor town of Honfleur. The family moved to Paris at the end of the Franco-Prussian War, but after Jane's death in 1872, Satie and his younger brother Conrad returned to Honfleur to be raised by Alfred's parents. Satie received his earliest music education from the local organist, who piqued Satie's interest in medieval chant. Satie and his brother rejoined their father in Paris after the death of their grandmother in 1878. Much to Satie's dismay, his father married piano teacher and salon composer Eugénie Barnetche in 1879. She sent Satie to study piano at the Paris Conservatory, where he was deemed talented but lazy. According to his friend Contamine de Latour, Satie continued to study at the Paris Conservatory only to reduce his military service time. Once inducted into the military, he purposely contracted bronchitis to ensure an even earlier dismissal.

In 1887 Satie left home for the bohemian district of Montmartre, introducing himself as "Erik Satie, gymnopédiste." He performed as pianist for the cabarets Le Chat Noir and Auberge du Clou, where he met composer Claude Debussy. He became affiliated with Joséphin Péladan's Rose + Croix society in 1891, but he soon became disillusioned, leaving to found the Metropolitan Church of Art of Jesus the Leader. As chapel master and sole member, Satie presided from his apartment and published tracts excommunicating his critics. He made three failed attempts to be admitted to the Académie des Beaux-Arts, and his tempestuous affair with trapeze-artist-turned-painter Suzanne Valadon (his only known intimate relationship) ended in 1893 after only six months. In 1895 he used a small inheritance to purchase seven identical suits, replacing his priestly cassock with the garb of the Velvet Gentleman. Struggling financially by 1898, he moved to Arcueil and earned income by accompanying singer Vincent Hyspa in the café concerts of Montmartre.

Satie enrolled at the Schola Cantorum in 1905, resolved to improve his technique by studying counterpoint with Albert Roussel and composition with Vincent d'Indy. He was a diligent student, though his sarcastic wit was still evident in homework assignments, entitled *Agreeable Despair* and *Unfortunate Example*. In 1911 Maurice Ravel rediscovered Satie as the harmonic predecessor of Impressionism, and performances of Satie's works increased demand for his humorous piano pieces. He complied with works such as *Flabby Preludes (for a Dog)* and *Dried Up Embryos*.

A performance of *Three Pieces in the Form of a Pear* caught the attention of Jean Cocteau, and thanks to Cocteau's advocacy, Satie was brought into contact with the leading Parisian artists. After his ballet *Parade* became notorious for the scandals it created at its premiere, Satie earned his income primarily from commissions, and he was able to devote more time to writing articles. His involvement with the Dada movement culminated in the ballets *Mercure* and *Relâche*, both of which provoked audience riots.

Beset with cirrhosis of the liver and pleurisy, Satie could be energized for only so long by the momentum of *Relâche*'s scandalous premiere. He was hospitalized the following February, and he died July 1, 1925.

The Music

Satie's musical style did not develop in a conventional sense; rather, his diverse output reflects continual self-renewal and experimentation. Popular music, along with the French qualities of wit and precision, pervade nearly all of his works. In a 1917 statement of his compositional aesthetic, Satie wrote, "Do not forget that the melody is the Idea . . . the harmony is an illumination." He insisted that ideas, not craftsmanship, elevated artists to greatness.

Early Works. Satie's first significant compositions—*Ogives, Trois sarabandes, Trois gymnopédies*, and *Trois gnossiennes*—all reflect his interest in the distant past. His fascination with the Gothic architecture of Notre Dame Cathedral gave rise to *Ogives*, in which modal melodies, absence of bar lines, and parallel voice leading mimic medieval chant and organum. *Trois sarabandes* infuse a Baroque dance form with unresolved seventh and ninth chords, while *Trois gymnopédies* evoke ancient Greek dance through modal melodies and a slow,

waltzlike accompaniment. The gnossiennes (a style of composition for which Satie coined the name gnoisienne) share common harmonic language with *Trois Gymnopédies*, while introducing exotic scales from the Romanian music that Satie heard at the 1889 Exposition Universelle in Paris. The title of the gnossiennes is a neologism: Satie may have been referring the ancient world of Knossos or to religious Gnosticism. The gnossiennes also marked the first instance of Satie's puzzling performance instructions, such as "very shiny" or "with the tip of your thought."

Vexations. Following the traumatic end of his relationship with Valadon, Satie wrote *Vexation*, a thirteen-bar cantus firmus with two harmonizations and instructions for 840 repetitions after a preparatory period of meditation. The funereally slow tempo, seemingly endless repetition, confusing enharmonic note spellings, and jarringly atonal harmonies make this piece vexing indeed for the performer. *Vexations* is often cited as the first minimalist work, though this is perhaps an anachronistic distortion of Satie's intentions. No evidence indicates that Satie meant this piece for public, or even complete, performance: It was most likely a study in boredom and frustration.

Three Pieces in the Form of a Pear. Reputedly an irreverent response to Debussy's complaint that Satie's music lacked form, *Three Pieces in the Form of a Pear* is in fact a set of seven pieces for piano duet. Satie claimed that the work marked a turning point in his life. Rather than displaying any new stylistic features, *Three Pieces in the Form of a Pear* was instead an anthology of Satie's accomplishments to date, with references to cabaret songs. Included in this compendium are a gnossienne from Satie's incidental music for Péladan's play *The Son of the Stars* (1891); the song "The Widower," written with Hyspa; *Danse*, Satie's first work for orchestra; and *The Angora Ox*, a piano piece inspired by a tale of Lord Cheminot (Contamine de Latour). *Three Pieces in the Form of a Pear* is notable for its eclectic self-borrowing and fluid blending of popular and art music. As musical autobiography, this work also reflects Satie's collaborations with three important figures in his life: the Rosicrucian Péladan, the cabaret singer Hyspa, and the poet Latour.

Sports and Diversions. The solo piano work *Sports and Diversions* paired Charles Martin's

Erik Satie. (Hulton Archive/Getty Images)

graphic designs and illustrations with Satie's music and prose in twenty vignettes depicting various recreations, including tennis, golf, yachting, flirting, and dancing the tango. The absence of bar lines allows the music to freely unfold, and text painting abounds both in the musical content and in Satie's calligraphic notation. Prefacing the work is Satie's *Unappetizing Chorale*, dedicated to his detractors and serving as an ironic foil of mock solemnity to the lighthearted musical portraits that follow.

Parade. The ballet *Parade* was born of a historic collaboration among some of Paris's most prominent modernist artists: Satie created the music, Cocteau the scenario, Léonide Massine the choreography, and Pablo Picasso the set and costume design. Sergei Diaghilev's Ballets Russes danced to a score that included elements of popular music and even such noisemaking instruments as a typewriter, a revolver, and a lottery wheel. These were analogous to the found objects of Marcel Duchamp, just as the juxtaposed blocks of seemingly unre-

lated musical material paralleled Cubist art. The synthesis of the everyday with the artistic marked *Parade* as the ultimate embodiment of the French modernist vanguard.

Socrate. Widely considered Satie's masterpiece, the unusually serious symphonic drama *Socrate* for female voices and orchestra set selections from Victor Cousin's French translation of Plato's dialogues. Satie's vocal writing is simple and linear, accommodating the natural inflections of the text. Transparent orchestration, ostinato-like accompaniments, and limited dynamic range make *Socrate* a work that epitomizes the French admiration for classical restraint. Satie sought to capture the pristine purity of classical antiquity, and he claimed to prepare for this task by consuming only white foods such as eggs, sugar, grated bones, animal fat, coconut, turnips, and cotton salad.

Relâche *and* Cinéma. Satie's final work was his collaboration with Francis Picabia on the Dadaist ballet *Relâche*, ironically titled because relâche was the term used for a canceled performance. Though the stage action was nonsensical, Satie's score was an organized work with a carefully balanced form and tonal plan. In between acts of the ballet, Satie's *Cinéma* score accompanied René Clair's Surrealist film *Entr'acte* (1924). *Cinéma* was one of the earliest examples of music synchronized to film, as well as an application of Satie's revolutionary furniture music—music that functioned only as background. At the end of the ballet, Picabia and Satie drove onstage in a tiny Citröen, waving to the infuriated audience.

Musical Legacy

Satie was an influential composer of the French avant-garde, not influenced by the dominating aesthetic of nineteenth century German Romantic composer Richard Wagner. Satie despised discipleship of any kind, especially those who followed Wagner and Debussy, and he discouraged any of his would-be followers. Nevertheless, the young composers of Les Six—including Darius Milhaud and Francis Poulenc—and the less-celebrated Arcueil School considered Satie their musical forefather. The older generation of Debussy and Ravel also claimed Satie as their antecedent.

However, Satie's influence extended beyond the work of his contemporaries: Most of the significant movements in twentieth century classical music are prefigured in his oeuvre. Igor Stravinsky is often credited as the first proponent of neoclassicism, but it was Satie who initiated this trend with the use of classical forms and smaller instrumentations in *Medusa's Trap*, *Socrate*, and especially his *Bureaucratic Sonatina*, an adaptation of Muzio Clementi's Sonatina, Op. 36, No. 1. The use of noisemaking instruments in *Parade* corresponded to the practices of Italian Futurists; minimalists of the 1960's adopted *Vexations* and the short, repeated phrases of *Cinéma* as part of their aesthetic heritage; and furniture music is acknowledged as the precursor to Muzak and the ambient music of Brian Eno.

In his lifetime, Satie was considered "worthless" by the Paris Conservatory and a "lunatic" by the Académie des Beaux-Arts, regarded as a "gentle medieval musician lost in this century" by Debussy, and hailed as the ideal embodiment of the French "new spirit" by Cocteau and poet Gustave Apollinaire. After his death, he was dismissed as a mere practical joker by his critics, but he was lauded by John Cage as indispensable to twentieth century music. His *Trois gymnopédies* have become background music of elevators and grocery stores, and his *Vexations* have become the fodder for twenty-hour-long avant-garde concerts.

Helena Kopchick

Further Reading

Davis, Mary E. *Erik Satie*. London: Reaktion Books, 2007. In a unique consideration of Satie's life and works through the lens of fashion, Davis proposes that Satie's changes in personal appearance were calculated to mirror changes in his artistic output.

Gillmor, Alan M. *Erik Satie*. New York: Norton, 1992. Comprehensive biography of Satie, with excellent analysis of his works.

Orledge, Robert. *Satie the Composer*. Cambridge, England: Cambridge University Press, 1990. Neither a traditional biography nor a pure analysis of Satie's works, this is an exploration of Satie's compositional aesthetic and the diverse influences that shaped it.

_____, ed. *Satie Remembered*. Portland, Oreg.: Amadeus Press, 1995. Impressions and accounts of Satie by his contemporaries.

Perloff, Nancy. *Art and the Everyday: Popular Entertainment and the Circle of Erik Satie*. Oxford, England: Oxford University Press, 1993. Focuses on *Parade*, with its mix of popular and art elements, as the departure point for French modernism.

Shattuck, Roger. *The Banquet Years: The Origins of the Avant-Garde in France, 1885 to World War I*. New York: Vintage Books, 1968. Shattuck's seminal work groups Satie, Henri Rousseau, Apollinaire, and Alfred Jarry as the avatars of French modernist art.

Volta, Ornella, ed. *A Mammal's Notebook: Collected Writings of Erik Satie*. Translated by Anthony Melville. London: Atlas Press, 1996. A diverse collection of Satie's published and private writings, with photographs and illustrations.

_____. *Satie Seen Through His Letters*. Translated by Michael Bullock and introduced by Cage. New York: Marion Boyars, 1989. This collection of Satie's correspondence gives vivid insight to his life, works, and cultural environment.

Whiting, Steven Moore. *Satie the Bohemian: From Cabaret to Concert Hall*. New York: Oxford University Press, 1999. Interprets Satie's involvement with Parisian popular music as a constant influence on his career, enabling him to dissolve the barrier between popular and art music.

See also: Cage, John; Debussy, Claude; Eno, Brian; Glass, Philip; Koussevitzky, Serge; Milhaud, Darius; Poulenc, Francis; Ravel, Maurice; Thomson, Virgil; Walton, Sir William.

Pierre Schaeffer

French classical music and film-score composer

Schaeffer was a major figure in French radio broadcasting, and he was the inventor of musique concrète, which highlights the musical potential in sounds recorded from the everyday world. Schaeffer expanded the concept of music to include sounds of all types, even those usually considered noises.

Born: August 14, 1910; Nancy, France
Died: August 19, 1995; Les Milles, Aix-en-Provence, France

Also known as: Pierre Henri Marie Schaeffer (full name)

Principal works

FILM SCORES: *Masquerage*, 1952; *Sahara d'aujourd'hui*, 1957 (with Pierre Henry); *Garabatos*, 1964; *Les Montréalistes*, 1965.

TAPE RECORDINGS: *Concertino-Diapason*, 1948 (with J. J. Grünewald); *Étude de bruits*, 1948; *Suite pour quatorze instruments*, 1949; *Variations sur une flûte mexicaine*, 1949; *Bidule en ut*, 1950 (with Pierre Henry); *La Course au kilocycle*, 1950 (with Henry); *Symphonie pour un homme seul*, 1950 (with Henry); *Toute la lyre*, 1951 (with Henry); *Orphée 53*, 1953 (with Henry); *Continuo*, 1958 (with Luc Ferrari); *Étude aux allures*, 1958; *Étude aux sons animés*, 1958; *Exposition française à Londres*, 1958 (with Ferrari); *Étude aux objets*, 1959; *Nocturne aux chemins de fer*, 1959; *Phèdre*, 1959; *Simultané camerounais*, 1959; *Le Trièdre fertile*, 1975 (with Bernard Durr); *Diapason Concertino*, 1971; *Bilude*, 1979.

WRITINGS OF INTEREST: *Traité des objets musicaux*, 1966 (treatise on musical objects).

The Life

Although Pierre Henri Marie Schaeffer (pyehr SHAY-fehr) was born into a musical family, he was captivated by telecommunications. A graduate of the École Polytechnique, he worked as a technician for various radio stations until 1941, when he became a cofounder of Studio d'Essai. It was the primary broadcasting station for the French Resistance during World War II, and it was Schaeffer's first laboratory for musique concrète.

Musique concrète is constructed from the inherent properties of mechanically recorded sounds. Schaeffer used radio equipment to pioneer this groundbreaking style of composition in such works as *Études de bruits*. In 1951 Schaeffer established what would become the Groupe de Recherches Musicales, with whom he explored the musical potential of every kind of sound and developed original strategies for composing. His research drew from physics and philosophy as well as his knowledge of music. In fact, by 1960 Schaeffer had abandoned composition to devote himself to theoretical work on *objets sonores*, or sound objects, and music perception. He documented his theories in his *Traité des objets musicaux* (1966; treatise on musical objects).

In 1968 Schaeffer returned to practical composing, joining the Paris Conservatory as a professor of electroacoustic composition. He was the force behind several influential projects in the French artistic community. Before his death in 1995, he established a foundation to continue his research and to make his archives available to scholars worldwide.

The Music

As an electroacoustic composer, Schaeffer worked with acoustic signals collected by electrical equipment, usually a tape recorder, and emblazoned them on a fixed medium such as magnetic tape. Musique concrète was his term for music consisting of recorded sounds spliced together in such a way that reveals the musicality innate to the sounds. The rhythms, melodies, and formal structure of an ideal musique concrète work derived from the properties of the sounds heard in the piece.

Though he did not always succeed, Schaeffer sought to turn from traditional abstract schemes, such as classical forms, to concrete sound as the structural foundation of his music. He wanted to demonstrate that all sounds were inherently musical, even everyday sounds, such as locomotive noises. He believed that listeners could train themselves to hear and think beyond the parameters of traditional music and come to enjoy the music of their surroundings.

A first step in this direction would be to mentally isolate sounds from the sources that produce them, in what Schaeffer called the acousmatic reduction. Achieving this reduction would enable the listener to concentrate on the inherent characteristics of sounds, as opposed to their relationships to objects and situations.

Études des bruits. One of the earliest known works of musique concrète, Schaeffer's *Études des bruits* premiered on French radio in 1948. The original version comprises five "Studies in Noise" (including *Étude au piano*, *Étude aux chemins de fer*, *Étude aux tourniquets*, *Étude pathétique*, and *Étude violette*). Each study consists of recorded, or sampled, sounds collected on disc and tape and subjected to various manipulations. Schaeffer's methods included fading the sounds in and out, altering the speeds and volumes of the recordings, playing sounds backward, and superimposing multiple sounds. In contrast to these cutting-edge techniques, with which Schaeffer compiled the material for the études, the forms of the pieces remember traditional styles. For instance, *Étude aux chemins de fer* (railroad study) seems to be a set of variations on locomotive noises, in an overall binary form (two parts plus a coda). Schaeffer revised this piece in 1971, condensing five pieces into four.

Diapason Concertino. Also known as the *Tuning-Fork Concertino*, this work originated as one of Schaeffer's *Études des bruits*. In this piece, samples of an orchestra tuning up interact with piano improvisations. As such the concertino refers to classical concerto form, in which an orchestra interacts with a soloist. In a notable twist, Schaeffer captures both orchestra and soloist engaging in spontaneous activities, tuning and improvising, rather than the scripted dialogue of the traditional concerto. He revised the *Diapason Concertino* in 1971 into a four-movement version with traditional titles and ordering. As in a classical concerto, an Allegro serves as the opening movement, followed by an Andante and an Intermezzo. An Andantino concludes the work.

Symphonie pour un homme seul. The symphony for a man alone marks the beginning of the collaboration between Schaeffer and Pierre Henry, and it premiered in Paris in 1950. In 1955 Maurice Béjart set the *Symphonie pour un homme seul* to modern-dance choreography in the first musique concrète ballet. The *Symphonie pour un homme seul*'s final version consists of twelve movements with vaguely descriptive titles, such as "Erotica," "Cadence," and "Apostrophe." The piece attempts to highlight the rhythmic and melodic aspects of human noises such as breathing and laughter, blending them with noiselike sounds produced by traditional musical instruments. Schaeffer and Henry wished their audiences to appreciate every sound in the piece for its own sake, and not for the meaning that might arise from the connection between a sound and the instrument that produced it. Thus, *Symphonie pour un homme seul* attempts to put Schaeffer's acousmatic thesis into practice.

Musical Legacy

Musique concrète quickly won the curiosity of other artists. Schaeffer invited many composers, among them Pierre Henry, Luciano Berio, and Olivier Messiaen, to create their own musique concrète compositions at his studio. John Cage, who also worked with recorded sounds, was intrigued by Schaeffer's work, but he was not wholly convinced by it. Schaeffer himself harbored some doubts about musique concrète, particularly as it pertained to the acousmatic thesis. He found that it was basically impossible for listeners not to think of the sources of sounds upon hearing them. He therefore dispensed with the term musique concrète in 1958, preferring simply to call his work experimental music.

Schaeffer's *Traité des objets musicaux* inspired new research in electroacoustics, aesthetics, and music perception. The idea that sound, as opposed to the strategy for organizing sound, is the defining aspect of music inspired the work of several composers, including Morton Feldman and Christian Wolff.

Mandy Suzanne Wong

Further Reading

Dack, John. "Pierre Schaeffer and the Significance of Radiophonic Art." *Contemporary Music Review* 10, no. 2 (1994): 3-11. Describes the influence of Schaeffer's work with radio on his compositions and the relationship that he perceived between music and machines. Clarifies the meaning of acousmatic.

Palombini, Carlos. "Pierre Schaeffer: From Research into Noises to Experimental Music." *Computer Music Journal* 17, no. 3 (1993): 14-19. An overview of Schaeffer's career, including his transition from technician to composer. Comments briefly on several of his early works and on a few of his theories, such as the pseudo-instrument.

See also: Berio, Luciano; Cage, John; Feldman, Morton; Messiaen, Olivier; Stockhausen, Karlheinz; Zappa, Frank.

Artur Schnabel

Austrian American classical composer and pianist

Renowned for his pioneering and sensitive interpretations of the piano music of Ludwig van Beethoven, Franz Schubert, and Wolfgang Amadeus Mozart, Schnabel bequeathed his musical approaches to generations of students. His legendary interpretations have been documented through his recordings and his editions of the Beethoven piano sonatas.

Born: April 17, 1882; Kunzendorf, Moravia, Austro-Hungarian Empire (now Lipnik, Poland)

Died: August 15, 1951; Axenstein, Switzerland

Principal works

CHORAL WORKS: *Dance and Secret*, 1944 (for chorus and orchestra); *Joy and Peace*, 1944 (for chorus and orchestra).

ORCHESTRAL WORKS: Symphony No. 1, 1938; Symphony No. 2, 1943; Symphony No. 3, 1949.

PIANO WORKS: *Dance Suite*, 1921; *Stück*, 1936 (*Piece*; composed of seven movements).

Principal recordings

ALBUMS: *Beethoven: Complete Piano Sonatas*, 1933-1935 (released on some two hundred sides of 78-rpm records).

WRITINGS OF INTEREST: *Reflections on Music*, 1933; *Music and the Line of Most Resistance*, 1942; *My Life and Music*, 1988.

The Life

Artur Schnabel (AHR-tur SHNAH-behl) was born to Jewish parents of Austrian descent. When Schnabel was seven years old, his family moved to Vienna, where he commenced performance studies with Hans Schmitt at the Vienna Conservatory and later with Theodor Leschetizky. During the same period, he engaged in theory studies with Eusebius Mandyczewski, a mentor who permitted Schnabel access to important musical manuscripts in Vienna's archives, thus laying the groundwork for Schnabel's future editorial endeavors.

Schnabel moved to Berlin in 1900, and in 1905 he married the singer Therese Behr. The couple had two sons: Karl Ulrich Schnabel (a pianist who would later perform in a duo with his father) and Stefan Schnabel (a television and film actor). Behr and Schnabel were frequent musical collaborators in recital—a pairing that reached its height with a series of all-Schubert recitals given in Berlin in 1928. He published his editions of the Beethoven piano sonatas from 1924 to 1927 and gave his first complete cycle of all the Beethoven sonatas in Berlin on seven consecutive Sundays in 1927. He taught at the Berlin Hochschule für Musik from 1925 until 1933, when the rise of the Nazi regime prompted him to move for a time to Switzerland.

In the 1930's Schnabel made extensive performance tours of the United States and Europe, gaining an international reputation as a recitalist and an ever-growing group of devotees. In the same decade he was contracted by the HMV (His Master's Voice) recording label in London and became the first person to record all the Beethoven piano sonatas on gramophone.

In 1939 he left Switzerland for the United States, where he taught a performance class at the University of Michigan from 1940 to 1945. He became a naturalized citizen of the United States in 1944. At the University of Chicago in 1945 he gave a famous series of lectures, the transcripts of which are reproduced in the book *My Life and Music*. Although he continued to concertize regularly in his late years, poor health drove him to return to Switzerland in 1951. A bout of uremia exacerbated an existing heart condition, and he died in the Grand Hotel in Axenstein on August 15, 1951.

The Music

Schnabel's musical career is notably varied: He is remembered foremost as the pianist who intellectualized the piano recital. By concentrating on the repertoire of Beethoven, Mozart, and Schubert, he challenged audiences with abstract and lengthy programs. Beyond his pianistic achievements, Schnabel edited a number of performing editions of the works of Beethoven, Mozart, and Johannes Brahms. Although he was a composer for most of his life, his considerable corpus of original compositions remains undiscovered by most listeners today.

Early Years. Schnabel's youthful studies with Schmitt and Leschetizky formed the basis of his technical and interpretive approach to piano playing. As was customary for students of Leschetizky, Schnabel first studied with Annette Essipoff (Leschetizky's wife) and with Malwine Brée (his assistant) to lay technical groundwork. When Schnabel eventually took lessons directly from the master, Leschetizky forewent the usually curriculum of virtuoso concert pieces and instead encouraged Schnabel to seek out the neglected piano sonatas of Schubert. Schnabel was a frequent fixture in the Leschetizky master classes, where he was called upon at most of the gatherings to demonstrate the correct manner in which to play. Schnabel gave his Viennese debut recital on February 12, 1897. The program, which included works by Johann Sebastian Bach and Beethoven, also included virtuoso pieces by Moritz Moszkowski and Leschetizky himself, in accordance with Viennese taste.

Artur Schnabel. (AP/Wide World Photos)

The Berlin Years. Schnabel's years in Berlin were some of his most musically fruitful. During this time Schnabel collaborated with such musical luminaries as composer and conductor Richard Strauss, pianist and composer Ferruccio Busoni, and violinist Carl Flesch, with whom Schnabel prepared editions of the violin sonatas of Mozart and Brahms. He formed a piano trio with violinist Alfred Wittenberg and cellist Anton Hekking. Although the members of the group changed over the years, Schnabel's chamber music concerts remained popular events in Berlin.

Schnabel made serious efforts in composition during this time, producing a number of works for piano solo and his first string quartets. Schnabel's compositional style was decidedly modern, inspired by the atonal trends being championed by such composers as Arnold Schoenberg. Interestingly, although Schnabel played the new musical works of his contemporaries, he did not promote his own compositions in performance, nor did he record his works.

Beethoven. Schnabel's serious study of Beethoven began in the 1920's, when he was approached to produce a new edition of the piano sonatas. For this project, Schnabel had access to the scholarly complete edition of Beethoven's works, as well as the manuscripts housed in the Prussian State Library in Berlin. Originally published separately from 1924 to 1927, Schnabel's edition of the sonatas was reissued in two volumes by Simon & Schuster in the United States, Oxford University Press in England, and Edizioni Curci in Italy. Schnabel's editorial work was aimed directly at the performer. His copious instructions to the pianist (including fingerings, tempo indications, pedaling instructions, musical analysis, and explanatory footnotes) were attempts to clarify the essence of Beethoven's music. While Schnabel never advocated strict adherence to his own editorial markings, he intended them as a guide for others who sought a thoughtful and musical approach to the performance of these works.

The publishing project ended in 1927, the centenary year of the death of Beethoven. To mark the occasion, Schnabel presented in Berlin his first complete cycle of all thirty-two Beethoven sonatas. Schnabel did not perform the sonatas chronologically but rather in an order that made aesthetic sense—and one that he repeated in his cycles of concerts in New York and London. Schnabel's all-Beethoven events were a notable artistic undertaking at the time, given that concerts tended to showcase variety and virtuosity.

In the 1930's, Schnabel made his landmark recordings of all thirty-two Beethoven piano sonatas and the five concerti for the HMV label in London. Schnabel found this an arduous process. In the days prior to splicing and editing, a mistake meant rerecording an entire movement (or approving the recording with errors), and Schnabel doubted that the electronic process could truly capture his musical intentions. Despite Schnabel's initial misgivings, at the time of their release these landmark recordings sold at a rapid pace. Offering them to the public on a subscription basis, HMV had sold more than $500,000 worth of the records by 1939. With their recent reissue on compact disc, they remain pioneering and iconic interpretations.

Teaching and Composition. Increasingly, Schnabel turned to teaching in his later years. He taught classes on Lake Como in Italy during the summers. While living in New York, he kept a small studio. As a teacher in the grand master-class tradition, Schnabel rarely gave private lessons—it was common for two or three students to observe a typical two-hour lesson. His courses at the University of Michigan included only a handful of students but a large number of observers. His teaching focused on interpretive and musical issues; technique was addressed only if it served a particular musical aim. Among his students were Leonard Shure, Leon Fleischer, Clifford Curzon, and Claude Frank. Schnabel's students have become internationally renowned pedagogues themselves, ensuring that Schnabel's teachings live on through his musical lineage.

In composition Schnabel turned to larger musical structures even as he maintained his abstract compositional style. His first symphony was written in the late 1930's, but it did not receive a premiere until 1947 in Minneapolis, Minnesota. Notably, Schnabel completed two other symphonies, a rhapsody for orchestra, and works for piano solo and chamber ensembles in the last decade of his life. Composer Roger Sessions referred to Schnabel's act of composition as "a vital avocation, one into which, to be sure, he was able to pour all the re-

sources of his tremendous gift of expression, his unsurpassed musicality, his inexhaustibly live imagination."

Musical Legacy

By eschewing standard virtuoso fare and programming the music of composers such as Beethoven and Schubert, Schnabel advanced the notion of the piano recital as an artistic and intellectual event. Schnabel was fond of saying that he performed only music that was better than it could be played. Critics of his playing pointed to his inaccuracies in performance and claimed that he lacked sufficient technical apparatus; proponents of his playing praised his consummate lyricism and his rhythmic verve. His legion of pupils continued teaching in the tradition of Schnabel, keeping his musical legacy alive today.

Although his compositional output goes nearly unnoticed today, Schnabel remained a serious composer throughout his life, leaving a sizable body of work. His career as a composer was complemented by his activities as a musical editor. Over the years, his editorial work has been criticized for distorting the original compositions and overromanticizing the classic musical tradition; however, his editions of the Beethoven sonatas remain a crystallization of his individual approach to interpretation and are still in wide circulation among musicians today.

Schnabel's extensive recorded legacy is unique among pianists of his generation. His complete Beethoven cycles (in recital and on record) were marvels of their time. Since the time of Schnabel, numerous artists have duplicated his feat of recording all of Beethoven's piano sonatas. While the newer recordings can attest flawless accuracy and digitally enhanced sound, Schnabel's recordings from the 1930's remain important historic performances and artifacts of revered status.

Joseph A. Bognar

Further Reading

Beethoven, Ludwig van. *Thirty-two Sonatas for the Pianoforte.* 2 vols. Edited by Artur Schnabel. New York: Simon & Schuster, 1935. Schnabel's views as a performer and interpreter of Beethoven are encapsulated in his edition of Beethoven's sonatas for solo piano.
Saerchinger, César. *Artur Schnabel: A Biography.*

New York: Dodd, Mead, 1957. The most complete biography of Schnabel in English, with lists of Schnabel's recital programs and his compositions and discography.

Schnabel, Artur. *My Life and Music.* New York: Dover, 1988. Fascinating and engaging transcripts from the autobiographical talks Schnabel gave at the University of Chicago in 1945. Reproduced in this edition is the speech given by Schnabel in Manchester, England, on the occasion of receiving his honorary doctorate from that institution. Includes twenty black-and-white photographs.

Schonberg, Harold C. "The Man Who Invented Beethoven." In *The Great Pianists: From Mozart to the Present.* New York: Simon & Schuster, 1987. The long-standing music critic of *The New York Times* offers his opinions on Schnabel's Beethoven recitals and recordings.

Teachout, Terry. "The Great Schnabel." *Commentary* (May, 2007): 61-64. The music critic for *The Wall Street Journal* discusses Schnabel's recorded output and its legacy.

Wolff, Konrad. *Schnabel's Interpretation of Piano Music.* 2d ed. New York: W. W. Norton, 1972. A Schnabel student recounts his teacher's specific technical and interpretive teachings. Includes an account of Schnabel's lessons and a foreword by pianist Alfred Brendel.

See also: Anderson, Leroy; Busoni, Ferruccio; Gould, Glenn; Schoenberg, Arnold; Schreker, Franz; Strauss, Richard.

Alfred Schnittke

Russian classical composer

Schnittke was among the first Russian composers to experiment with serial, aleatoric, and improvisational techniques and with musical styles from all genres and historical periods. This polystylistic music was wholly at odds with the Soviet establishment.

Born: November 24, 1934; Engels, Volga German Autonomous S.S.R. (now in Saratov Oblast, Russia)

Died: August 3, 1998; Hamburg, Germany
Also known as: Alfred Garyevich Schnittke (full name)

Principal works

BALLETS (music): *Labrynths*, 1978 (libretto by Vladimir Vasilyev); *Sketches*, 1985 (libretto by Andrei Petrov; based on a theme by Nikolai Gogol); *Peer Gynt*, 1989 (libretto by John Neumeier; based on the play by Henrik Ibsen).

CHAMBER WORKS: Sonata No. 1, 1964 (for violin and piano); String Quartet No. 1, 1967; Sonata No. 2, 1969 (for violin and piano; revised for cello and piano, 1994); *Suite in the Old Style*, 1972 (for violin and piano or harpsichord); Quintet for Piano and Strings, 1976; String Quartet No. 2, 1980; String Quartet No. 3, 1984; String Trio, 1985; String Quartet No. 4, 1989; Sonata No. 3, 1994 (for violin and piano).

CHORAL WORKS: *Redeyet oblakov letuchaya gryada*, 1953 (*The Passing Line of Clouds Grows Thinner*; lyrics based on a poem by Alexander Pushkin); *Beryozka*, 1955 (*Birch Tree*; lyrics by Stephan Shchiparev); *Nagasaki*, 1959; *Songs of War and Peace*, 1960 (lyrics by Anatoly Lechtyev and Andrei Pokrovsky); *Voices of Nature*, 1975; *Requiem*, 1977; *Minnesang*, 1981.

OPERAS (music): *Life with an Idiot*, 1992 (libretto by Viktor Yerofeyev); *Gesualdo*, 1995 (libretto by Richard Bletschacher); *Historia von D. Johann Fausten*, 1995 (libretto by Jörg Morgener and Schnittke).

ORCHESTRAL WORKS: Poème, 1953; Poem About Space, 1961; Concerto No. 1, 1963 (for violin and orchestra); Concerto No. 2, 1966 (for violin and chamber orchestra); Symphony No. 1, 1972; Concerto Grosso No. 1, 1977; Concerto No. 3, 1978 (for violin and chamber orchestra); Symphony No. 2, 1979; Symphony No. 3, 1981; Concerto Grosso No. 2, 1982; Concerto No. 4, 1984 (for violin and orchestra); Symphony No. 4, 1984; Concerto Grosso No. 3, 1985; Concerto No. 1, 1986 (for cello and orchestra); Concerto Grosso No. 4, 1988 (also known as Symphony No. 5); Concerto No. 2, 1990 (for cello and orchestra); Concerto Grosso No. 5, 1991; Symphony No. 6, 1993; Concerto Grosso No. 6, 1994; Symphony No. 7, 1994; Symphony No. 8, 1994.

PIANO WORKS: Concerto for Piano and Strings, 1979; Piano Sonata No. 1, 1988; Piano Sonata No. 2, 1991; Piano Sonata No. 3, 1996.

The Life

Alfred Garyevich Schnittke (SHNIHT-kee) was in many ways a composer without a home: His father was Jewish, his mother was German, and he was born in the town of Engels in the Volga-German Republic of the Soviet Union. To complicate matters further, the family moved to Vienna, Austria, in 1946, where Schnittke's father worked for a Soviet newspaper. Schnittke began his musical studies at this point, playing an old accordion and taking piano and theory lessons from Charlotte Ruber, who lived in the same building as the Schnittke family. After two years, the Schnittkes moved back to the Soviet Union, settling on the outskirts of Moscow in 1948. This constant moving had two powerful effects on Schnittke's musical career: First, though he had some talent as a pianist, he was already fourteen years old and did not have enough technique to pursue a career as a performer. Second, when Schnittke turned to composition instead, the upheavals of his childhood played an important role in determining his mature style.

In the year after his return to Russia, Schnittke was admitted to study at the Choirmasters' Department at the October Revolution Music College in Moscow, and at the same time he began private theory and analysis lessons with Iosif Ryzhkin. At the age of eighteen, Schnittke was admitted to the Moscow Conservatory, where he studied composition with Evgeny Golubev from 1953 to 1958. Schnittke remained at the conservatory for postgraduate work until 1961, at which point he was accepted into the Composers' Union. This official acceptance of Schnittke's work was short-lived: Soon he was blacklisted by the union for writing music that was too modern. Unfazed by this official reprimand, Schnittke accepted a post at the Moscow Conservatory, where he taught composition, orchestration, counterpoint, and harmony until 1971.

Schnittke composed a series of important chamber works in the 1960's, including Sonata No. 1 and Sonata No. 2 for violin and String Quartet No. 1. At the same time, because Soviet leader Nikita Khrushchev had eased restrictions, Schnittke was allowed to study the music of the European avant-garde, which had been forbidden under the rule of Joseph Stalin. Schnittke soon published articles on the music of Béla Bartók, Luciano Berio, György Ligeti, Igor Stravinsky, and Anton von Webern. Equally important to his development, Schnittke began to compose music for films in 1962, which he continued part-time for more than twenty years. In his film scores, Schnittke borrowed from and quoted different styles of music, resulting in what he called polystylism. These experiments migrated into his concert music, until he finally seized upon the idea of a massive polystylistic work, Symphony No. 1. Its first performance was highly controversial, and the head of the Composers' Union, Tikhon Khrennikov, effectively banned the work.

Schnittke's growing reputation resulted in numerous performances abroad, although the Composers' Union rarely permitted him to leave the Soviet Union. This situation changed in the mid-1980's with Mikhail Gorbachev's support of perestroika, which encouraged creative endeavors. By that time, however, Schnittke was suffering from poor health. During the period of 1985 to 1994, Schnittke suffered three severe strokes, yet he still managed to compose three operas and many other major works. In 1990 Schnittke immigrated to Hamburg, Germany, where he remained until his death in 1998.

The Music

Schnittke's music was extremely important in the Soviet Union because it was shocking and powerful, incorporating the forbidden concepts and techniques of the European avant-garde. Many of Schnittke's works from the late 1960's and early 1970's were violently polystylstic; his refinements to the technique culminated in his most famous work, Concerto Grosso No. 1.

Schnittke was baptized a Catholic in 1980, though he remained curious about other religious and philosophical systems. His works of the 1980's often contain religious symbolism, and, in particular, they display his lifelong fascination with the Faustian myth. As a result, he began to compose in a more cohesive style—polystylistic elements are often present, but they are quickly subsumed into larger compositional structures. As he suffered through repeated strokes, Schnittke simplified his musical language in the late works, favoring dark and brooding textures and a direct mode of expression, with only faint echoes of the polystylistic methods for which he is famous.

Early Works. As a student at the Moscow Conservatory, Schnittke composed a wide variety of chamber music, songs, choral music, and a symphony. Like most young composers in Russia, he was heavily influenced by the music of Dmitri Shostakovich. An intelligent and curious student, Schnittke had no desire merely to imitate, but rather he sought to discover the inner workings of Shostakovich's music. His graduation piece, the oratorio *Nagasaki,* contained the required subject matter (a political poem written by an official Soviet poet); however, his music was already too modern, and he was criticized for formalism. During his postgraduate studies, Schnittke became interested in folk music, and he composed a cantata based on Russian folk songs called *Songs of War and Peace,* his first published work. At one point, it appeared that Schnittke might be reformed, and he was admitted to the Composers' Union based on the orchestral work *Poem About Space,* his first work to use electronic instruments. Schnittke was quickly commissioned to write two official operas, *The Eleventh Commandment* and *African Ballad,* which were neither completed nor performed. After finishing the piano score of *The Eleventh Commandment,* he was again attacked for modernist tendencies. When Schnittke refused to revise the score, he was blacklisted by the Composers' Union. In order to make a living, he began composing film music for the Mosfilm studio in Moscow, a career choice with extraordinary implications.

Sonata No. 2. Schnittke's first polystylistic score was the music for the animated film *The Glass Accordion* (1968). In the same year, he took the unconventional step of using this film score as the basis for Sonata No. 2 for violin, his most explosive composition of the 1960's. Several aspects of this piece permeated Schnittke's music for the next two decades. One of the building blocks of the composition is the musical monogram "B-A-C-H" (corresponding to the pitches B-flat, A, C, B). A musical quotation also appears in the sonata, but not from Ludwig van Beethoven's piano sonata to which Schnittke's subtitle refers (Op. 27, No. 2, *Quasi una fantasia*). Instead, Schnittke uses a passage from Beethoven's *15 Variations and Fugue on an Original Theme,* Op. 35

(1802), also known as the *Eroica Variations.* The ingenuity of this choice is typical of Schnittke's working methods: With only a minor modification, the Beethoven quote is transformed into the B-A-C-H monogram, a clever sleight of hand. The overall structure of the work is unusual for a sonata. It is cast in one long movement, with emphasis on formal ruptures and violent collisions. Though he had written earlier sonatas, concerti, and a symphony, with the Sonata No. 2 Schnittke began a lifelong journey of reexamining these forms in a modern context. In this case, the subtitle suggests that Schnittke is asking a question: Is it still a sonata? This kind of question, fundamental to the music of Schnittke, reappears in different guises in subsequent works.

Symphony No. 1. Schnittke composed Symphony No. 1 during the time that he worked on the music for the film *The World Today,* a documentary on the social and military upheavals of the twentieth century. Not coincidentally, in Symphony No. 1 Schnittke attempts to document the entire history of Western music, both classical and popular. The work is as much a theater piece as a symphony. Only one performer sits on the stage at the beginning, with the orchestra members appearing one by one, improvising and tuning up as they arrive. Quotations of classical music gradually pile up into massive climaxes, with intervening episodes of jazz improvisation, Baroque dances, and grotesque marches. Finally, after a polystylistic recapitulation of epic proportions, the musicians leave the stage as they arrived. Only two violinists remain, repeating the final measures of Franz Joseph Haydn's *Farewell Symphony* (1772), another example of Schnittke's predilection for multilayered quotation (Haydn's work also ends with the musicians gradually leaving the stage).

Concerto Grosso No. 1. Schnittke's growing international reputation was solidified by Concerto Grosso No. 1. In it, Schnittke masterfully weaves together a variety of musical styles, which he identified as fragments from his animated film music, a children's chorus, an atonal serenade in the style of Webern, a piece in the style of the Baroque composer Arcangelo Corelli, and his grandmother's favorite tango. It is a mark of Schnittke's brilliance that from this motley collection he was able to create a unified work.

Musical Legacy

Along with his contemporaries Edison Denisov, Sofia Gubaidulina, and Andrey Volkonsky, Schnittke was instrumental in bringing Russian composition up to date. It had languished since the innovations of the 1950's European avant-garde were forbidden and therefore virtually unknown in the Soviet Union. Schnittke's polystylistic technique has not been adopted by a substantial number of composers; like those of Charles Ives, Schnittke's methods are too idiosyncratic to support a school of composition. Nevertheless, Schnittke's compositional experiments of the 1960's and 1970's were revolutionary, and his lasting influence in Russia is represented by his scholarly activities. In his teaching at the Moscow Conservatory, he emphasized the study of European composers; he was among the first in the Soviet Union to publish articles on contemporary music; and he was noted for his extensive score library and his impromptu study sessions with young composers.

Tim Sullivan

Further Reading

Adamenko, Victoria. *Neo-Mythologism in Music: From Scriabin and Schoenberg to Schnittke and Crumb*. Hillsdale, N.Y.: Pendragon Press, 2007. A wide-ranging study of the relationship between composers and mythology in the twentieth century, this book features several interesting sections on Schnittke's music. Included are analyses of portions of Symphony No. 1 and an examination of Schnittke's obsession with the Faust myth.

Bauer, Svetlana. "Modalities and Intonation in Musical Analysis: Some Observations on the Fourth Symphony of Alfred Schnittke." In *Musical Semiotics in Growth*, edited by Eero Tarasti. Bloomington: Indiana University Press, 1996. A somewhat esoteric study of the semiotic (pertaining to signs) aspects of Schnittke's Symphony No. 4. Although this is not easy reading, there are interesting observations about symbolism in Schnittke's music.

Ivashkin, Alexander. *Alfred Schnittke*. London: Phaedon Press, 1996. This book provides an excellent overview of the composer's life and works. Includes illustrations, list of works, discography, and bibliography.

Odam, George, comp. *Seeking the Soul: The Music of Alfred Schnittke*. London: Guildhall School of Music and Drama, 2002. A short collection of scholarly writings on Schnittke's music, accompanied by a compact disc featuring recordings of three of the discussed works. Includes bibliography and discography.

Schnittke, Alfred. *A Schnittke Reader*. Translated by John Goodliffe, edited by Alexander Ivashkin. Bloomington: Indiana University Press, 2002. A collection of English translations of Schnittke's writings: interviews, notes on his compositions, and, most important, his articles on twentieth century music. Includes a chronology of Schnittke's life.

See also: Bartók, Béla; Berio, Luciano; Gubaidulina, Sofia; Ives, Charles; Ligeti, György; Nono, Luigi; Pärt, Arvo; Shostakovich, Dmitri; Stravinsky, Igor; Theremin, Léon; Webern, Anton von.

Arnold Schoenberg

Austrian American classical composer

Schoenberg is noted for breaking from tonal harmony and for inventing the twelve-tone, or serial, method of composition.

Born: September 13, 1874; Vienna, Austro-Hungarian Empire (now in Austria)
Died: July 13, 1951; Los Angeles, California
Also known as: Arnold Franz Walter Schönberg (birth name)

Principal works

CHAMBER WORKS: Scherzo in F Major, 1897; String Quartet in D Major, 1897; Trio in A Minor, 1897 (for string quartet); *Verklärte Nacht*, Op. 4, 1899 (*Transfigured Night*; for string sextet); String Quartet No. 1 in D Minor, Op. 7, 1905; *Die eiserne Brigade*, 1916 (*The Iron Brigade*; for piano quintet); *Weihnachtsmusik*, 1921 (*Christmas Music*; for piano quartet); *Serenade for Nine Players*, Op. 24, 1923; Wind Quintet, Op. 26, 1924; Suite, Op. 29, 1925 (for three clarinets, violin, viola, cello, and piano); String Quartet No. 3, Op. 30, 1927; String Quartet No. 4, Op. 37, 1936; Piano Concerto, 1942; *Fanfare on Motifs of "Die Gurrelieder,"* 1945 (for eleven brass instruments and percussion); String Trio, Op. 45, 1946; *Phantasy for Violin and Piano*, Op. 47, 1949.

CHORAL WORKS: *Friede auf Erden*, Op. 13, 1907 (*Peace on Earth*); *Drei Satiren*, Op. 28, 1926 (*Three Satires*; for mixed chorus); *Secht Stücke*, Op. 35, 1930 (*Six Pieces*; for male chorus); *Kol nidre*, Op. 39, 1938 (for chorus and orchestra); *Prelude to "Genesis,"* Op. 44, 1945 (for chorus and orchestra); *A Survivor from Warsaw*, Op. 46, 1947 (for narrator, men's chorus, and orchestra); *Three Folksongs*, Op. 49, 1948 (for mixed chorus); *Dreimal tausend Jahre*, Op. 50a, 1949 (*Three Times a Thousand Years*); *Psalm 130: "De profundis,"* Op. 50b, 1950 (for mixed chorus a cappella).

OPERAS (music): *Die glückliche Hand*, Op. 18, 1913 (*The Hand of Fate*; libretto by Schoenberg); *Erwartung*, Op. 17, composed 1909, first performed 1924 (*Expectation*; libretto by Marie Pappenheim); *Von Heute auf Morgen*, Op. 32, 1930 (*From Today to Tomorrow*; comedy opera; libretto by Max Blonda); *Moses und Aron*, Op. 3, 1957 (libretto by Schoenberg).

ORCHESTRAL WORKS: *Pelleas und Melisande*, 1903 (based on the play by Maurice Maeterlinck); *Five Pieces for Orchestra*, Op. 16, 1909; *Pierrot lunaire*, Op. 21, 1912; Cello Concerto, 1933; Concerto, 1933 (based on George Frideric Handel's Concerto Grosso in B-flat Major, Op. 6, No. 7); Suite in G Major for String Orchestra, 1934; Violin Concerto, 1936.

PIANO WORKS: *Three Piano Pieces*, Op. 11, 1909; Suite for Piano, Op. 25, 1923.

VOCAL WORKS: String Quartet No. 2 in F-sharp Minor, Op. 10, 1908 (for soprano and strings; based on Stefan George's poetry); *Gurrelieder*, 1913 (based on poems by Jens Peter Jacobsen).

WRITINGS OF INTEREST: *Harmonielehre*, 1911 (*Structural Functions of Harmony*, 1954); *Models for Beginners in Composition*, 1943; *Style and Idea*, 1950; *Preliminary Exercises in Counterpoint*, 1963; *Fundamentals of Musical Composition*, 1967.

The Life

Born and raised in Vienna, Arnold Schoenberg (AHR-nuld SHURN-behrg) was deeply interested in music from an early age. His first compositions were modeled on the duets he studied in violin lessons, yet more formal training was beyond his family's means. At age sixteen, his father died, and he was forced him to go to work as a bank clerk. During this period, he relied on friends for his musical education, and although during the middle 1890's he studied composition with Alexander von Zemlinsky, an accomplished musician three years his senior, he was primarily self-taught.

By the late 1890's, Schoenberg was supporting himself and his family by conducting amateur working-class choruses and arranging operettas. He continued his work as an arranger in Berlin, where he lived from 1901 to 1903. Returning to Vienna, he drew widening notice as a composer, he gained the patronage of the conductor and composer Gustav Mahler and the architect Adolf Loos, and he began attracting students. These included Anton von Webern and Alban Berg, who became his close associates.

The ensuing years were tumultuous. He endured a crisis in his marriage (to Zemlinsky's sister Mathilde) in 1908, and his compositions encountered virulent hostility. Largely in response to this hostility, he began a lifelong habit of writing as a way to explain himself. During these years, and especially in 1910, he was also a prolific painter. Throughout this period, his compositions showed a steady evolution, and by 1909 (spurred on by the innovations of his student Webern), he broke with tonality. Following a second period in Berlin (1912-1915), Schoenberg contributed to the Austrian war effort by twice joining the army and twice being medically discharged.

After the war, Schoenberg turned to performance, founding and directing a Society for Private Musical Performances that was dedicated to high-quality, open-minded performances of contemporary music and traveling to various European cities to conduct his works. By the early 1920's, Schoenberg had arrived at his twelve-tone method, which led to a prolonged fertile period of composition. His wife Mathilde died in 1923, and he remarried in 1924. Recognized as a leading figure in the musical world, he moved to Berlin for a third time in 1926 to take the chair in composition at the Prussian Academy of the Arts.

Schoenberg experienced increasing anti-Semitic attacks from the early 1920's, and in 1933, following the ascent of Adolf Hitler in Germany, he reconverted to Judaism (having been baptized a Lutheran in 1898) and moved with his wife and young daughter to America. From 1936 to 1944, he taught at the University of California, Los Angeles, and he lived in Los Angeles with his wife and their children until his death in 1951.

The Music

Early Works. Schoenberg's earliest mature work, *Transfigured Night*, with its atmospheric blend of the familiar styles of Johannes Brahms and Richard Wagner, already reveals Schoenberg's harmonically and melodically adventuresome voice. Between 1899 and 1909, he pursued this adventuresomeness in a variety of genres, including string quartets, songs, the enormous oratorio *Gurrelieder*, and the symphonic poem *Pelleas und Melisande*. By 1909 his harmonic style had passed beyond tonality, the system that has served as the "grammar" for Western music since the late seventeenth century. In tonality, all pitches are heard in relation to consonant chords and to the key of the piece (such as C major or E-flat minor), and dissonances, while plentiful, are carefully controlled. Because dissonance is "emancipated" (Schoenberg's word) from such control, and because the chords and keys of tonality are not present, Schoenberg's music from 1909 on is generally called atonal. Schoenberg disliked the term because he believed his music encompassed tonality and more. Others have called the music expressionist, a term borrowed from parallel early twentieth century trends in art and film.

Schoenberg's earliest atonal works are intuitively composed musical representations of flashes of consciousness. They may sound brooding and disoriented, as in the one-act, one-character psychological opera *Erwartung*; alternately anxious and placid, as in the *Five Pieces for Orchestra*, Op. 16; or witty and impulsive, as in *Pierrot lunaire*.

Three Piano Pieces, Op. 11. Schoenberg arrived at his intuitive aesthetic while composing the *Three Piano Pieces*, Op. 11. The first two of these pieces make up for the absence of tonality through coherence provided by a fabric of melodies and interwoven motives (short, recognizable musical ideas that recur often). In the third piece, Schoenberg jettisons even this mode of coherence, abandoning himself to completely intuitive and highly virtuosic music.

Pierrot lunaire. German actors at the start of the twentieth century often performed recitations of poems with musical accompaniment. The accompaniments were typically nondescript, but one actress commissioned Schoenberg to compose accompaniments to a set of poems by Albert Guiraud about the puppet-show character Pierrot (also the title character of Igor Stravinsky's 1911 ballet *Petrouchka*). Inspired by the poems' mixture of comic and violent imagery, Schoenberg composed a sparkling score for flute, clarinet, violin, cello, and piano, and a vocal part in which he specified the pitches on which the reciter was to speak. This was one of the earliest uses of a technique called Sprechstimme (speaking voice).

The Twelve-Tone Method. By 1912 Schoenberg was finding it difficult to compose works longer

Arnold Schoenberg. (Library of Congress)

than a few measures, as it had been tonality that enabled composers to organize large sections of music and to relate the material in one section of a piece with material in the others. For the next several years, Schoenberg, Webern, and Berg groped toward strategies for large-scale musical organization that Schoenberg systematized in the twelve-tone method by about 1921. A composition using this method is based on a twelve-tone row developed specifically for it, which guarantees that all the pitches in the piece are related to each other. For example, the tone row of Schoenberg's Suite for Piano, Op. 25 is E, F, G, C-sharp, F-sharp, D-sharp, G-sharp, D, B, C, A, B-flat; that of *Moses und Aron* is A, B-flat, E, D, E-flat, D-flat, G, F, F-sharp, G-sharp, B, C. A piece will cycle through the row many times, but rather than causing repetitiousness, the row offers a plethora of creative possibilities. For example, when the row is repeated, different notes may be chosen for the melody and the accompaniment. In addition, to create large-scale contrasts, the composer may transpose the entire row up or down, cycle through it in reverse order, or invert it (replacing rising pitch relationships with falling). Whereas the most basic compositional decisions had been constant matters of concern in intuitive atonal composition, the twelve-tone method brought on years of creativity by freeing Schoenberg from these concerns.

Suite for Piano. Schoenberg's first fully twelve-tone work, the Suite for Piano, shows the composer far removed from his prewar expressionist style. In a nod to the neoclassical movement of the 1920's, the movements of the suite make reference to the lively rhythms of eighteenth century dance types. Still, the suite does not exhibit any return to actual eighteenth century style, such as heard in the neoclassical works of Stravinsky and others.

Moses und Aron. Schoenberg considered his Jewish heritage in several works. *Moses und Aron*, his only full-scale opera, is an imaginative retelling of the biblical account in which Moses and his brother Aaron led the Jewish people out of Egypt. The opera reflects Schoenberg's inner struggle between his sense of a call to compose progressive, prophetic music and his desire to reach a large audience. Thus the stern Moses, singing only in Sprechstimme, is unable to lead the people without the assistance of his brother, whose charisma is apparent in his lyric tenor voice but who is too permissive with the people.

Later Works. Schoenberg was passionately concerned about the plight of European Jews, even before Hitler gained power in Germany. After World War II, when Schoenberg began learning details of what had happened in the Holocaust, he composed *A Survivor from Warsaw*, a short but stirring work for Sprechstimme narrator, chorus, and orchestra, which culminates as the chorus sings a Hebrew prayer, Shema Yisroel, to a twelve-tone melody. One of the composer's last instrumental works, String Trio, expressionistically portrays Schoenberg's delirium following a nearly fatal heart attack in August, 1946. The work may be heard as an example of Schoenberg's mastery of twelve-tone composition, but, as with many of Schoenberg's compositions, a musical image is created. Certain chords represent the doctor's needle penetrating Schoenberg's heart, which saved his life.

Musical Legacy

Schoenberg thought the twelve-tone method would be his legacy, and from the 1950's to the 1970's, many agreed that the twelve-tone system would be the musical grammar of the future. In this view, Schoenberg was the single greatest composer of the twentieth century, although avant-garde composers modeled their work more on Webern's crystalline twelve-tone constructions than on Schoenberg's or Berg's relatively melodic works.

Although at this time few compose twelve-tone music, Schoenberg is recognized as a composer of the first rank. Composers continue to develop musical techniques made known by Schoenberg, such as Sprechstimme and Klangfarbenmelodie (or tone-color melody, a somewhat vague term he coined to denote melodies using timbre the way ordinary melodies use pitch). The vast range and consistent creativity of his large compositional output still entices musicians and audiences, and works such as *Transfigured Night* and *Pierrot lunaire* are staples of the repertory. Schoenberg's roots in the fascinating culture of Vienna before World War I excite interest, as does his later effort to express his Jewish identity through music.

Schoenberg was also an extraordinary composition teacher and the author of several music-theory textbooks. His students composed in a wide range of styles, and they included not only Webern and Berg, who composed in a Schoenbergian style, but also Henry Cowell, John Cage, Lou Harrison, and Alfred Newman.

Alfred W. Cramer

Further Reading

Auner, Joseph Henry. *A Schoenberg Reader: Documents of a Life*. New Haven, Conn.: Yale University Press, 2003. This book collects many of Schoenberg's writings to tell the composer's life story in his own words.

Bailey, Walter B., ed. *Schoenberg, Berg, and Webern: A Companion to the Second Viennese School*. Westport, Conn.: Greenwood Press, 1999. In this volume, several noted experts provide chapters on Schoenberg, focusing on issues such as his biography, his influence, and how he composed atonal and twelve-tone music. The book is intended for general readers, although at times it becomes fairly technical. Includes discography.

Haimo, Ethan. *Schoenberg's Transformation of Musical Language*. Cambridge, England: Cambridge University Press, 2006. Tracing Schoenberg's development from 1899 to 1909, this book offers insight into the process by which Schoenberg established himself as a young composer. The musical analyses are somewhat technical but clearly explained.

Schoenberg, Arnold. *Style and Idea: Selected Writings of Arnold Schoenberg*. Translated by Leo Black, edited by Leonard Stein. New York: St. Martin's Press, 1975. This large anthology of essays, lectures, and other writings by Schoenberg is full of compelling and provocative commentary on subjects from music to culture to politics. In some of the lectures, Schoenberg explains his own compositional approach to a general audience.

Shawn, Allen. *Arnold Schoenberg's Journey*. New York: Farrar, Straus and Giroux, 2002. This introduction to Schoenberg's music is lively and accessible, although at times Shawn asks his readers to read music. Emphasizes Schoenberg's expressive aims and compositional methods in the context of his biography.

Smith, Joan Allen. *Schoenberg and His Circle: A Viennese Portrait*. New York: Schirmer Books, 1986. Smith interviewed many people who knew Schoenberg, and their words and Smith's helpful historical commentary create a vivid portrait of Schoenberg, the musical life that revolved around him, and his relationship to Viennese art, architecture, and culture.

Stuckenschmidt, Hans Heinz. *Schoenberg: His Life, World, and Work*. Translated by Humphrey Searle. New York: Schirmer Books, 1978. Although many additional facts have been uncovered since this book was published, it remains a valuable reference biography.

See also: Adams, John; Babbitt, Milton; Barber, Samuel; Beach, Amy; Beecham, Sir Thomas; Berg, Alban; Berio, Luciano; Boulanger, Nadia; Boulez, Pierre; Britten, Benjamin; Cage, John; Chávez, Carlos; Cowell, Henry; Crumb, George; Gershwin, George; Gould, Glenn; Harnoncourt, Nikolaus; Harrison, Lou; Hindemith, Paul; Holst, Gustav; Ives, Charles; Karajan, Herbert von; Klemperer, Otto; Mahler, Gustav; Martin, Frank; Mingus, Charles; Newman, Alfred; Nielsen, Carl; Nono, Luigi; Norman, Jessye; Poulenc, Francis; Previn, Sir André; Puccini, Giacomo; Ravel, Maurice; Schnabel, Artur; Schreker, Franz; Scriabin, Aleksandr; Serkin, Rudolf; Sibelius, Jean; Solti, Sir Georg; Stokowski, Leopold; Stravinsky, Igor; Takemitsu, Tōru; Walton, Sir William; Webern, Anton von; Weill, Kurt.

Franz Schreker

Austria classical composer

A successful opera composer, Schreker broke new ground by exploring Freudian subject matter with a richly sensuous musical language. A celebrated teacher, he made the Berlin Musikhochschule a conservatory of international renown.

Born: March 23, 1878; Monaco
Died: March 21, 1934; Berlin, Germany
Also known as: Franz August Julius Schreker (full name)

Principal works

BALLET (music and libretto): *Der Geburtstag der Infantin*, 1908 (*The Birthday of the Infanta*; based on Oscar Wilde's novella).

OPERAS (music and libretto): *Der ferne Klang*, 1912 (*The Distant Chiming*); *Das Spielwerk und die Prinzessin*, 1913 (*The Music Box and the Princess*; revised as *Das Spielwerk*, 1915); *Die Gezeichneten*, 1918 (*The Stigmatized*); *Der Schatzgräber*, 1920 (*The Treasure Digger*); *Irrelohe*, 1920; *Der singende Teufel*, 1928; *Der Schmied von Gent*, 1932 (based on a folk take by Charles de Coster); *Christophorus: Oder, Die Vision einer Oper*, 1978.

ORCHESTRAL WORKS: Intermezzo, 1900; Scherzo, 1900; *Romantische Suite, Op. 14*, 1903; *Festwalzer und Walzerintermezzo*, 1908; *Valse lente*, 1908; *Vorspiel zu einem Drama*, 1913 (*Prelude to Drama*); Chamber Symphony, 1917 (for twenty-three instruments); *Kleine Suite für Kammerorchester*, 1928 (*Short Suite for Chamber Orchestra*); *Vier kleine Stücke für grosse Orchester*, 1930 (*Four Short Pieces for a Large Orchestra*).

SONGS: *Des Knaben Wunderhorn*, 1894 (*The Youth's Magic Horn*; based on children's folktales); *Des Meeres und der liebe Wellen*, 1894 (*The Sea and the Sweet Waves*; based on the writings of Richard Weitbrecht); *Die Rosen und der Flieder*, 1894 (*The Roses and Lilacs*; based on the writings of Otto Gruppe); *Zwei Lieder auf den Tod eines Kindes, Op. 5*, 1898 (*Two Songs on a Child's Death*; based on Mia Holm's poem *Mutterliedern* [*Mother's Love*]; contains *O Glocken, böse Glocken* [*O Bells, Evil Bells*] and *Dass er ganz ein Engel werde* [*He Becomes an Angel*]); *Fünf Lieder Op. 3*, 1900 (based on the poetry of Paul Heyse; contains *In alten Tagen* [*In Olden Days*] and *Es kommen Blätter* [*Leaves Are Coming*]); *Fünf Lieder Op. 4*, 1900; *Fünf Gesänge*, 1922.

The Life

Franz August Julius Schreker (SHREH-kur) was the oldest of four surviving children born to a Jewish father, Ignaz Schrecker, a noted portrait photographer, and a Catholic mother, Eleonore von Clossmann, a member of the minor aristocracy. The family settled in Linz in 1881, but it moved to Vienna after Ignaz's death in 1888. Schreker graduated from the Vienna Conservatory in 1900, and that year he changed the spelling of his surname.

Schreker's compositional breakthrough came with the pantomime *The Birthday of the Infanta*, commissioned for the 1908 Kunstschau (art exhibition) organized by Gustav Klimt and his circle. However, it was the Frankfurt premiere of his opera *The Distant Chiming* in 1912 that established his international fame. That same year he was appointed to the Vienna Academy (the renamed Vienna Conservatory), where he became renowned as one of the leading composition teachers of his generation (his students include Ernst Krenek, Alois Hába, and Berthold Goldschmidt). Schreker was also a noted conductor, and with his Philharmonic Chorus, founded in 1907, he led many notable premieres, including Arnold Schoenberg's *Gurrelieder* (1913).

The premieres of two operas, *The Stigmatized* in 1918 and *The Treasure Digger* in 1920, catapulted Schreker to the front ranks of contemporary composers. In 1920 he was appointed director of the Berlin Musikhochschule (High School for Music), which he helped transform into Europe's leading conservatory (his appointments included Artur Schnabel, Emanuel Feuermann, and Paul Hindemith). Schreker's greatest triumphs came during the early 1920's (at which time his wife, Maria Binder, whom he married in 1909, became a leading interpreter of his music). In the course of the decade, however, musical tastes changed and two later operas, *Irrelohe* and *Der singende Teufel*, had little success.

In June, 1932, under political pressure, Schreker resigned his post at the Musikhochschule, and in October, 1932, the premiere of his opera *Der Schmied von Gent* was marred by Nazi demonstrations. Soon after Adolf Hitler's ascent to power in January, 1933, Jews were purged from public office, and Schreker was dismissed from his position at the Prussian Academy of the Arts. In December, 1933, in the midst of planning his emigration, Schreker suffered a stroke, and he died on March 21, 1934.

The Music

During his studies with Robert Fuchs at the Vienna Conservatory, Schreker absorbed lessons from both Johannes Brahms, the classroom model, and Richard Wagner, an extracurricular passion. However, his distinctive idiom, which emphasizes structures built upon the juxtaposition of varied textures and harmonies, is more akin to techniques found in the music of Franz Schubert and Anton Bruckner. Schreker's propensity for abrupt chordal and modal shifts evolved into a harmonic language of mixed and even bitonal sonorities, and he exhibits a fascination with color and timbre. Such qualities suggest an affinity with contemporary French music, with which, however, Schreker had little contact. Schreker's vocal writing is characterized by pliant expressivity, flexible rhythm, and sensitivity to declamatory nuance. His later compositions, influenced by his work in recording, film, and broadcasting, are more angular and acerbic, and they frequently employ strict contrapuntal forms.

The Distant Chiming. In this seminal work, begun around 1904 and completed in 1910, a composer abandons the girl he loves to search for a distant sound he hears, only to realize, too late, that it was her presence that inspired the sound. The opera's mixture of realist, Symbolist, and Expressionist elements (the libretto, as in all subsequent operas, is by the composer) is mirrored in a radical plurality of musical styles and aesthetic sensibilities that call to mind the collage techniques of Charles Ives and a scenic dramaturgy that anticipates innovations to come in cinema. *The Distant Chiming* had a major influence upon Alban Berg, who prepared the opera's piano vocal score.

The Stigmatized. This libretto, originally written for the composer Alexander Zemlinsky in 1911, is set in Renaissance Italy. A hunchbacked nobleman, Alviano Salvago, seeks to deed an artificial paradise, the island Elysium, to the people of Genoa, but the sensual passions unleashed by the island's allure prove fatal for the woman Alviano loves, the painter Carlotta Nardi, and drive him into madness. Many consider this dark, brooding opera, composed between 1913 and 1915, to be Schreker's masterpiece. Its overture is the epitome of Schreker's dazzling command of orchestral color and sonority.

Chamber Symphony. Premiered in 1917, this work offers many parallels to Schoenberg's Chamber Symphony of 1907, including a four-movements-in-one structure. Scored for twenty-three solo instruments, Schreker's work is a transparent distillation of his preoccupation with timbre.

The Treasure. Schreker's most successful opera, written between 1915 and 1919, is set in a timeless Middle Ages. A young minstrel, Elis, whose magic lute leads him to hidden treasure, sets about finding the queen's stolen jewels (which impart youth and beauty) only to discover that it is Els, the mysterious woman he loves, who instigated the theft. This is Schreker's most lyrical and tonally centered opera, with a supremely balanced and translucent orchestral texture.

Christophorus: Oder, Die Vision einer Oper. Written between 1925 and 1929, the opera tells the story of a young composer's attempt to write a modern opera about St. Christopher; only through failure does he learn the true moral of the legend. At once a satire of contemporary fashion and a profound meditation on the creative process, this opera is one of most innovative works of the 1920's. Its layered dramaturgy, reminiscent of contemporary Expressionist films in which vision and reality are entwined, is reflected in a diaphanous score juxtaposing at its extremes modal stasis and anguished atonality, lyric cantilena, and spoken dialogue. Political pressure forced cancellation of the scheduled premiere in 1933, and the work was not heard until 1978.

Musical Legacy

Schreker's operas (championed by the powerful critic Paul Bekker, who likened them to those of Wagner) were attacked by conservatives for their sexual subject matter and sensual "un-German" musical style. Dogmatic modernists, on the other hand, dismissed Schreker as a naive late Romantic.

The revival of Schreker's operas, which began in the 1970's, has restored his reputation as a pioneer of modernism. Today he is regarded as an important transitional figure whose stylistic pluralism, extensions of tonality, experiments with timbre, and innovative dramaturgy opened paths to some of the most advanced music of the second half of the twentieth century, including the works of Witold Lutosławski and György Ligeti. Moreover, Schreker's music has significantly broadened our understanding of Viennese musical modernism, and it has revealed the artificiality of the divide between tonality and atonality.

Christopher Hailey

Further Reading

Haas, Michael, and Christopher Hailey, eds. *Franz Schreker: Granzgänge/Grenzklänge* (*Franz Schreker:*

Border Crossings/Musical Frontiers). Vienna: Jewish Museum Vienna, 2004. An exhibition catalog with English- and German-language essays on Schreker's life and works as well as two compact discs of excerpts from his operas.

Hailey, Christopher. *Franz Schreker (1878-1934): A Cultural Biography*. Cambridge, England: Cambridge University Press, 1993. The first major biography places Schreker within the cultural context of Vienna and Berlin. Contains an extensive bibliography and works list.

See also: Berg, Alban; Hindemith, Paul; Ligeti, György; Lutosławski, Witold; Schnabel, Artur; Schoenberg, Arnold.

Albert Schweitzer

German organist

A man of diverse talents, Schweitzer was a renowned organist, a musicologist, a theologian, a philosopher, a physician, and a humanitarian. Schweitzer's research on Johann Sebastian Bach and on organ building was a catalyst for the Orgelbewegung *movement in the 1920's.*

Born: January 14, 1875; Kaysersberg, Upper Alsace, Germany (now in France)
Died: September 4, 1965; Lambaréné, Gabon

Principal recordings

ALBUMS: *Albert Schweitzer Plays Bach, Vol. I*, 1936; *Albert Schweitzer Plays Bach, Vol. II*, 1936.

WRITINGS OF INTEREST: *J. S. Bach: Musicien-Poète*, 1905 (*J. S. Bach: The Musician Poet*, 1911); *Aus meinem Leben und Denken*, 1931 (*Out of My Life and Thought*, 1933).

The Life

Albert Schweitzer (SHVIT-zur) was raised in Alsace, which was under German control at the time. His father, a Lutheran pastor, began his son's music education, and Schweitzer took courses in theology and philosophy at Strasbourg University from 1893 to 1898. After earning his doctorate in philosophy, he was appointed assistant vicar of the Church of

St. Nicholai in 1899, and he was promoted to vicar upon receiving his theology degree the following year.

Schweitzer joined the theological faculty at Strasbourg in 1902, and four years later his eschatological book *The Quest of the Historical Jesus* was published. He was spiritually compelled to become a missionary doctor in equatorial Africa, and in 1911 he completed his medical degree dissertation on "The Psychiatric Study of Jesus." One year after their marriage in 1912, he departed with his wife Helen Bresslau to start a hospital in Lambaréné, Gabon. During World War I they were detained as enemy aliens because of their German citizenship. Schweitzer's beliefs, culminating in his Reverence for Life ethic, evolved during this time, later earning him the 1952 Nobel Peace Prize.

When Alsace was ceded to France after 1918, Schweitzer was given French nationality, which he retained for the remainder of his life. He continued to travel back and forth between Lambaréné and Europe, where he gave lectures and performed in fund-raising concerts. He received awards for his humanitarian efforts and earned honorary degrees in music, theology, and philosophy, topics on which he continued to publish writings until his death in 1965.

The Music

Schweitzer was a notable organist, and he was also an exceptional music scholar and historian. He began piano and improvisation lessons with his father at age five. He continued with organ studies at Mülhausen with Eugène Münch, who acquainted Schweitzer with the music of Johann Sebastian Bach, an introduction that shaped much of his future musical endeavors.

In 1893 he secured a spot in Charles-Marie Widor's studio in Paris, usually reserved for members of the master's organ class at the conservatory. Schweitzer impressed the teacher with his extensive knowledge of Bach and with his application of historical performance practice ideals to Bach's works. He continued to hone his expertise by accompanying Bach cantatas and passions in the Bach Society under the direction of Ernest Münch, music director at the Church of St. Wilhelm's in Strasbourg. Schweitzer performed in countless benefit concerts to raise funds for the African mission, and he recorded Bach's organ music for Columbia Records between 1935 and 1937 and once more in 1951.

J. S. Bach: The Musician Poet. Schweitzer published his famous work on Bach in French in 1905, the same year he cofounded the Paris Bach Society. What began as a modest request from Widor became the first literature on Bach in French that ventured beyond pure biographical information. The book introduced Bach's identity as tone poet, discussing how it affected the nature of his music and how it should affect its interpretation, thus representing one of the earliest inquiries into a historical performance practice of early music.

Albert Schweitzer. (Hulton Archive/Getty Images)

Shortly after the completion of the French version, Schweitzer resolved to undertake a German adaptation, transforming the old text into a new work. It was released in 1908 with 389 more pages than its French counterpart, and Ernest Newman used this version for his English translation, which was published in 1911.

"The Art of Organ-Building and Organ-Playing in Germany and France." Schweitzer's first book on Bach served as impetus for his 1906 essay "The Art of Organ-Building and Organ-Playing in Germany and France." His interest in organ building was inspired at a young age by his maternal grandfather, an enthusiast on the subject. Schweitzer's essay acknowledged the merits of the French style of organ building over the German; the former continued the traditions of the craft and focused on sound quality, while the latter was more geared toward technological advances at the expense of the sounds produced.

Schweitzer pushed for a reform in organ building, a call that was heeded in 1909 at the Congress of the International Music Society held in Vienna. He headed the first section on organ building in drafting the *Internationales Regulativ für Orgelbau*. These international regulations for organ building effectively framed the basis for the *Orgelbewegung*, or the organ revival, of the early twentieth century.

J. S. Bach's Complete Organ Works. In 1910 the New York publishing house of G. Schirmer asked Schweitzer and Widor to collaborate on a critical edition of Bach's complete organ works. Despite complications brought about by Schweitzer's missionary duties at Lambaréné, five of the eight volumes, including the preludes, fugues, sonatas, and concerti, were completed before progress was halted by World War I.

Following the war, circumstances did not favor continued work on the Bach edition: A series of miscommunications with the publishing firm and Widor's death in 1937 seemed to pose insurmountable obstacles. Eventually, with the assistance of fellow Alsatian organist Edouard Nies-Berger, Schweitzer completed the editions, with the sixth volume prepared by 1954 and the remaining two published posthumously.

Musical Legacy

Schweitzer's legacy is most prominent in the field of music scholarship, particularly pertaining to organ musicology and J. S. Bach. His seminal biography on the esteemed church musician marked a turning point in the treatment of Bach and sparked the modern Bach revival. His detailed explanations on performing Bach's works were based on extensive research on Baroque performance practices, especially ornamentation. His critical edition, somewhat a novelty during his time, served as a template for later musicologists, and his writings on the organ and organ-building led to a movement with more impetus than he had anticipated, culminating in the *Orgelbewegung* of the twentieth century. Living and working in an era of rapid changes in music worldwide, it is clear that Schweitzer played an integral part in that change.

Julie H. Huang

Further Reading

Murray, Michael. *Albert Schweitzer, Musician.* Brookfield, Vt.: Ashgate, 1994. Focuses on Schweitzer as a musician, discussing his musical experiences as a performer, editor, biographer, student, teacher, and more.

Nies-Berger, Edouard. *Albert Schweitzer as I Knew Him.* Hillsdale, N.Y.: Pendragon Press, 2003. Nies-Berger describes his collaboration with Schweitzer on the latter volumes of the Bach edition, giving insight into Schweitzer's academic approach and his complex life.

Schweitzer, Albert. *J. S. Bach.* Translated by Ernest Newman. 2 vols. New York: Dover, 1966. Schweitzer's biography of Bach and his survey of Bach's works reflect the author's quality and style of scholarship and his devotion to the comprehension of Bach and his compositions.

_____. *Out of My Life and Thought: An Autobiography.* Translated by C. T. Campion. New York: Henry Holt, 1949. Schweitzer's autobiography tracks his basic musical, theological, humanitarian, and medical journeys, and it includes the development of his famous life philosophies.

Seaver, George. *Albert Schweitzer: The Man and His Mind.* New York: Harper & Brothers, 1947. Biographical sketch followed by an inquiry into Schweitzer's thoughts. Includes photographs.

See also: Denver, John; Hogwood, Christopher.

Gil Scott-Heron

American rapper, pianist, and songwriter

Though not technically a rapper, Scott-Heron descends from the 1940's and 1950's tradition of Beat poets, who recited their social commentary to the accompaniment of music. The ideas of social change reflected in his lyrics have influenced rap groups such as Public Enemy.

Born: April 1, 1949; Chicago, Illinois
Member of: The Midnight Band

Principal recordings

ALBUMS: *Small Talk at 125th and Lenox,* 1970; *Pieces of a Man,* 1971; *Free Will,* 1972; *Winter in America,* 1973 (with Brian Jackson); *The First Minute of a New Day,* 1975 (with Jackson); *From South Africa to South Carolina,* 1976 (with Jackson); *Bridges,* 1977; *Secrets,* 1978; *1980,* 1979; *Real Eyes,* 1980; *Reflections,* 1981; *Moving Target,* 1982; *Spirits,* 1994.

WRITINGS OF INTEREST: *The Last Holiday,* 2003.

The Life

Gil Scott-Heron was born in Chicago, the son of a Jamaican professional soccer player and a librarian. His early years were spent in Lincoln, Tennessee, with his maternal grandmother, who taught him about music and how to read, instilling in the child a deep love for music and literature. At the age of fourteen, Scott-Heron was one of three African American children in his school selected to integrate an all-white elementary school in nearby Jackson. The racial prejudice and abuse that he experienced proved overwhelming, and he was sent to live with his mother in New York. These experiences were the genesis of his later writings. As a teenager, Scott-Heron was strongly attracted to literature, especially modern black poetry. He was particularly influenced by the poetry of Langston Hughes and Amiri Baraka (LeRoi Jones). In 1970, when he was twenty, Scott-Heron published his first novel, *The Vulture.* This was soon followed by the publication of a book of poetry, *Small Talk at 125th and Lenox.*

He enrolled in Lincoln University in Oxford, Pennsylvania, where he met Brian Jackson, Charlie

Saunders, and Eddie Knowles; the four would later become collaborators on Scott-Heron's recordings as the Midnight Band. In 1974 Scott-Heron signed a contract with Arista Records, and it immediately released the album *The First Minute of a New Day* with the Midnight Band. This was followed by *From South Africa to South Carolina*, which included the Top 20 rhythm-and-bluest hit "Johannesburg," an antiapartheid song. Several other releases followed in the 1970's and into the 1980's. He records his poetry raps and songs, and he tours extensively around the world. He is an outspoken critic of the powers in Washington, and he has commented unfavorably about the administrations of President Ronald Reagan and Presidents George H. W. and George W. Bush.

The Music

Scott-Heron has a deep bass voice with a limited melodic range. His keyboard playing consists mostly of chords and arpeggios behind his recitations and singing, leaving other members of his bands to supply the intricate melodic lines. His musical style has been described as a jazz-based urban funk sound behind highly literate black-consciousness lyrics. Scott-Heron and his college friends considered themselves members of the Black Arts movement in the early 1970's, along with radical poets such as Baraka, Sonia Sanchez, Stanley Crouch, the Watts Prophets, and the Last Poets. These artists took part in performances of poetry recited to the accompaniment of percussion and flutes, a spare, dynamic environment for politically charged recitations. As his music grew out of the works of politically oriented jazz musicians who combined elements of rhythm and blues, funk, blues, free jazz, lyrics, and poetry, Scott-Heron helped create a distinct aesthetic in the Black Arts movement. The result was a deeply funky and sophisticated style of music, dramatic and often dissonant, but easily accessible to a wide audience.

Jazz and Funk. Scott-Heron's first recordings, on the Flying Dutchman label, were accompanied recitations of the poetry in *Small Talk at 125th and Lenox*. Of special significance for Scott-Heron's career was the recitation of "The Revolution Will Not Be Televised" on his second album, *Pieces of a Man*. After signing with Arista Records and working with the Midnight Band, he created works that featured more singing and less recitation. Surrounding himself with talented jazz musicians, Scott-Heron found his music taking on more aspects of jazz and of funk. Several of his studio recordings were improvised both musically and lyrically, with Scott-Heron extemporizing his recitations and keeping the rap on track by using note cards to remind him of issues.

Social Comment. Several of Scott-Heron's songs from the mid-to-late 1970's dealt with the problems of substance abuse in the black community, particularly "Angel Dust" from *Secrets* and "The Bottle" from *Winter in America*. Others are concerned with the problems facing the world's environment, especially the dangers of nuclear accidents. In this vein, Scott-Heron recorded "Shut 'Em Down," a call to shut down nuclear reactors, on the album *1980* and "We Almost Lost Detroit," a song that recounts the nuclear accidents at Three-Mile Island in Pennsylvania and Chernobyl in Russia and a core meltdown at a breeder reactor near Detroit. The latter was recorded on the live *MUSE* (Musicians United for a Safe Environment) *Concerts for a Non-Nuclear Future* (1979).

A champion of his fellow man, particularly the downtrodden, Scott-Heron has composed songs that draw attention to problems of illegal aliens, such as "Aliens (Hold on to Your Dreams)" on *1980*, and to dangerous conditions in prisons, such as "Angola, Louisiana" on *Secrets*. Some critics consider him to be "the poetic conscience of America."

Political Statements. In 1978 Scott-Heron denounced the administration of Richard Nixon in works such as "H2O Gate Blues" from *The Mind of Gil Scott-Heron*. Continuing through the 1980's and 1990's, Scott-Heron commented on the powers in Washington, D.C., in strongly worded political statements. Several songs and recitations speak out against the era of Reagan. A good example is the recitation "B Movie" from *Reflections*, in which he mentions by name members of Reagan's administration: George Bush, Alexander Haig, Casper Weinberger, and more. Scott-Heron continues to be an outspoken and highly literate critic of the political establishment.

Musical Legacy

Scott-Heron's musical legacy lies in his politically charged poetry and songs, with angry lyrics and dissonant musical accompaniment. While he denies a characterization as the Godfather of Rap, he has been highly influential in the creation of urban political poetry accompanied by music. His poetry and song lyrics have been a huge influence on rap groups such as Public Enemy, who also have helped to raise consciousness toward the problems in black inner-city communities.

Stephen Valdez

Further Reading

Clifford, Mike. *The Illustrated Encyclopedia of Rock.* New York: Harmony Books, 1976. The encyclopedia contains a brief entry on Scott-Heron, and it provides a short discography of his albums to 1975.

Light, Alan, ed. *The Vibe History of Hip-Hop.* New York: Three Rivers Press, 1999. This book of essays contains a few references to Scott-Heron's influence on the development of rap.

Rose, Tricia. *Black Noise.* Hanover, N.H.: Wesleyan University Press, 1994. This source has a few sentences on Scott-Heron and the development of rap.

Scott-Heron, Gil. *Small Talk at 125th and Lenox.* New York: World Publishing, 1970. This book of poetry is the source of the songs and recitations on Scott-Heron's first album, of the same title, and his second album, *Pieces of a Man*.

See also: Chuck D; Combs, Sean; Dr. Dre; Jay-Z.

Aleksandr Scriabin

Russian classical composer

Scriabin was an iconic figure in Russian music, composing for piano and orchestra. Through the innovative use of Western tonality, he created his own harmonic language, which was neither tonal nor atonal.

Born: January 6, 1872; Moscow, Russia
Died: April 27, 1915; Moscow, Russia
Also known as: Aleksandr Nikolayevich Scriabin (full name); Aleksandr Scryabin

Principal works

ORCHESTRAL WORKS: Piano Concerto, Op. 20, 1896; *Mechti/Rêverie*, 1898; *Fantaziya*, 1889; Symphony No. 1 in E Major, Op. 26, 1900; Symphony No. 2 in C Minor/Major, Op. 29, 1901; Symphony No. 3 in C Minor, Op. 43, 1904; Symphony No. 4 in C Major, Op. 54, 1908; *Prométhée*, 1911; Symphony No. 5 in F-sharp Major, Op. 60, 1911.

PIANO WORKS: Twenty-four Preludes, Op. 11, 1888-1896; Étude in C-sharp Minor, Op. 2/1, 1889; Ten Mazurkas, Op. 3, 1889; Three Pieces, Op. 2, 1889; Five Preludes, Op. 16, 1894-1895; Twelve Études, Op. 8, 1894; Two Pieces, Op. 9, 1894; Six Preludes, Op. 13, 1895; Piano Sonata No. 2 in G-sharp Minor, Op. 19, 1897; Piano Sonata No. 3 in F-sharp Minor, Op. 23, 1897; *Fantaisie in B Minor*, Op. 28, 1900; Eight Études, Op. 42, 1903; Piano Sonata No. 4 in F-sharp Major, Op. 30, 1903; Two Mazurkas, Op. 40, 1903; Two Poèmes, Op. 32, 1903; Piano Preludes, Op. 48, 1905; Four Pieces, Op. 51, 1906; Piano Sonata No. 5 in F-sharp Major, Op. 53, 1907; Two Pieces, Op. 57, 1908; Piano Sonata No. 7 in F-sharp Major, Op. 64, 1912; Piano Sonata No. 9, Op. 68, 1913; Piano Sonata No. 10, Op. 70, 1913; Piano Preludes, Op. 74, 1914; *Vers la flamme, poème*, Op. 72, 1914.

The Life

Aleksandr Nikolayevich Scriabin (skree-AH-bihn) was born to Nikolai Aleksandrovich, a lawyer, and Lyubov Petrovna Shchetinina, a famous Russian female composer and pianist. While Scriabin most likely inherited his mother's musical gifts, her untimely death while he was still in his infancy and his father's subsequent remarriage ultimately left him in the care of his devoted maternal aunt, Lyubov Aleksandrovna. She encouraged and orchestrated his early studies, including piano lessons at the age of eleven with Georgy Conus and at sixteen with Nikolai Zverev. Scriabin undertook the study of music theory with Sergei Taneyev in 1885 and continued these lessons after entering the Moscow Conservatory in 1888. At the conservatory he began piano lessons with Vasili Safonov.

Scriabin had a pronounced competitive spirit and a tendency toward nervousness, particularly with regard to his compositions. This combination led to difficulties for the young man. He practiced incessantly, at times leading to his own physical distress.

Scriabin graduated from the conservatory in 1892, earning a Small Gold Medal, as opposed to his classmate, Sergei Rachmaninoff, who won the Great Gold Medal that year. This was largely because of Scriabin's many disagreements with his teacher, Anton Arensky, who found the young man's stubbornness difficult to mitigate.

After leaving the conservatory, Scriabin began concertizing as a pianist, which led to an introduction to Pyotr Jürgenson, who published fourteen of his pieces in 1893. It was through Safonov that Scriabin's work was introduced to Mitrofan Belyayev, who became the composer's publisher in 1894 and funded his trip to Europe in 1895. Scriabin wrote a number of pieces during this trip, including many of the Op. 11 preludes. His well-received European debut took place in Paris at the Salle Erard in January of 1896. During this same year he composed and premiered the Piano Concerto, Op. 20.

Scriabin married the pianist Vera Isakovich in 1897. In 1898 they gave a joint recital of Scriabin's works in Paris. Safonov and Belyayev arranged for a teaching position at the Moscow Conservatory, in which Scriabin served from 1898 to 1902, using the summers to compose. During these years several of his pieces premiered, including his orchestral works *Mechti/Rêverie*, Symphony No. 1, and Symphony No. 2.

In 1903 he began a long-standing affair with Tatiana Schloezer, the sister of his friend, music critic Boris de Schloezer. Scriabin moved to Switzerland with her in 1904, where he completed his Symphony No. 3. In 1906 he traveled to America at the invitation of Modest Altschuler, and he made his debut with the Russian Symphony and performed in solo recital. Altschuler continued to champion Scriabin's works after the composer's return to Paris.

Scriabin met Serge Koussevitzky in the spring of 1908. The latter, a conductor and publisher, became one of Scriabin's most enthusiastic supporters, signing him to a five-year contract with the newly established Éditions Russes and providing him with a stipend of five thousand rubles a year. Koussevitzky arranged a solo tour for Scriabin to all the major cities and towns along the Volga River in the

Aleksandr Scriabin. (Hulton Archive/Getty Images)

summer of 1910. In return, Scriabin composed *Prométhée*, an ambitious work with a substantial piano part, which premiered in March, 1911. Not long after, Koussevitzky and Scriabin parted ways with a clash of mighty egos and an argument over money. The rift between them caused Scriabin to leave Koussevitzky's publishing firm and in 1912 sign a contract once again with Jürgenson.

In 1913 and 1914 Scriabin toured successfully in performances of his own works in London. He gave a number of concerts after his return to Russia in 1915, the last of which took place in St. Petersburg on April 2, 1915. Scriabin developed a boil on his upper lip, which caused blood poisoning and ultimately led to his death.

The Music

Interestingly Scriabin's early works reflected the influence of notable nineteenth century composers, particularly Frédéric Chopin, Franz Liszt, and Richard Wagner. It is little wonder that he would be influenced by such men, especially considering the fame and cult of personality that surrounded the last, Wagner. It was not long, however, before Scriabin broke away from the confines of late Romantic style and forged his own.

Piano Preludes, Op. 48. The piano preludes of 1905 illustrate Scriabin's use of the octatonic scale in place of the traditional key system. While not strictly atonal, these pieces are not tonal either. It seems apparent that Scriabin intends for there to be a reflection of tonality without the actual use of tonic. In Prelude No. 1, for instance, he moves through three octatonic scales in order to simulate tonal motion. However, he does not start on a tonic. These preludes encompassed the seeds of his harmonic style, which would come to full fruition in the Piano Preludes, Op. 74 of 1914.

Prométhée (Poème du feu). Premiered in Moscow in 1911 with the composer at the piano, Scriabin first conceived of this piece as a portion of a larger *Mysteriya* that would lead the listener through sensory input on a journey to a heightened plane of spiritual existence. He had communicated with both Rachmaninoff and Nikolay Rimsky-Korsakov in 1907 about his interest in the concept of synaesthesia, or the relationship between music and color. What eventually arose from these discussions was Scriabin's assignation of colors to specific chords in this work, which correlated to the colors of the wordless vowel sounds being sung by the choir. In addition to this, Scriabin wrote a rather large piano part within the piece that was to be played on a color keyboard (*clavier à lumière* or *tastiera per luce*). Unfortunately, the construction of a functional color keyboard was not possible, and the premiere was given without the benefit of this effect.

It is important to note that even though he eventually abandoned the idea of including *Prométhée* in a larger work, he continued to work on the ideas he developed in this piece for the rest of his life. Indeed, at his death there was a copy of the manuscript for *Mysteriya* open on his piano. The colossal concept of universality is echoed in the forces required to perform the work. Even compared to the contemporary orchestra sizes called for by Richard Strauss and Arnold Schoenberg, the instrument and player requirements for this piece are enormous. His orchestration has a uniquely Russian identity, including polyphonic layering overarching timbral ideas and contrasting hierarchies that drive the music forward in the absence of traditional tonal structures.

Piano Preludes, Op. 74. These preludes of 1914 are of particular importance because they represent the culmination of Scriabin's original harmonic style. The beginnings of these harmonic procedures were seen as early as the Op. 48 preludes. However, the experimentation with construction and harmony that Scriabin carried out in his piano compositions from Op. 58 through Op. 73 were finalized in Op. 74. Instead of using several octatonic scales to simulate tonal motion, as he did in the Op. 48 preludes, Scriabin allows for frozen moments within the music or the progression of related chords over a long period of time, which leads to resolution. He had first introduced this idea in Op. 59, No. 2, and continued to refine the technique. Demonstrated here also is his penchant for the elevation of the tritone to a harmonic tool instead of relegating it to its traditional role of dissonance. In the No. 3 prelude from Op. 74, Scriabin employs only one octatonic scale, and he utilizes sequences with transpositions at the tritone and minor third in order to achieve his resolution.

Musical Legacy

Scriabin's music drew ardent admirers and severe critics, in part because of his larger-than-life persona, seen as saintly by his friends and megalomaniacal by his enemies. While some of his contemporaries disagreed with Scriabin's musical doctrine, no one disputed his complete allegiance to it in composing his music. He sought to express the divine through his musical compositions, music being the means to immortality and heightened expression.

He was an ardent fan of philosophy, literature, art, and architecture, but only insofar as they reflected his ideals. While the synaesthetic and Theosophist movements were important to him, they were molded to his ideas, not vice versa. This was not an unusual situation within music at the time. While there was an abundance of synaesthetic composers, none truly agreed on how to apply color to sound; it was an individual creation.

Scriabin's individuality, his dynamism, his charismatic character, and his unceasing pursuit of his

ideals through music were a lasting influence on the music. His frozen moments and long progressions through related chords, as well as his interest in mysticism, could be cited as the evolutionary spark for Olivier Messiaen's music in the decades following Scriabin's death. Certainly his influence would be seen in the works of Russian composers. Elements of Scriabin's style were apparent in the early works of Sergei Prokofiev and Igor Stravinsky, as well as the compositions of Nikolai Myaskovsky, Yuri Shaporin, and Dmitri Shostakovich, who absorbed one or more aspects of Scriabin's style. It is the shift between the mature styles of Scriabin and Shostakovich that defined twentieth century Russian music.

Teri A. Herron

Further Reading

Bowers, Faubion. *Scriabin: A Biography*. Mineola, N.Y.: Dover, 1996. The information about the composer's life is laid out chronologically, with numerous first-person accounts. Includes drawings and sketches by Scriabin, photographs, and a catalog of his works.

Rimm, Robert. "Feinberg and Scriabin: Humanity and Mysticism." In *The Composer-Pianists: Hamelin and the Eight*. Portland, Oreg.: Amadeus Press, 2002. The chapter includes information regarding the composer's emotional and mental states, as well as his pursuit of the spiritual through music. Includes numerous photographs of the composer at various stages in his life, as well as quotations about him from critics, friends, and fellow composers.

Roberts, Peter Deane. *Modernism in Russian Piano Music: Skriabin, Prokofiev, and Their Russian Contemporaries*. Bloomington: Indiana University Press, 1993. Discusses the harmonic innovations of Scriabin and his contemporaries in Russia, as well as the influence they had on subsequent composers. Includes musical examples and a selected bibliography.

See also: Ashkenazy, Vladimir; Gould, Glenn; Horowitz, Vladimir; Koussevitzky, Serge; Messiaen, Olivier; Prokofiev, Sergei; Salonen, Esa-Pekka; Schoenberg, Arnold; Seeger, Ruth Crawford; Shostakovich, Dmitri; Strauss, Richard; Stravinsky, Igor; Szymanowski, Karol.

Earl Scruggs

American country singer, songwriter, guitarist, and banjo player

Propagating the three-finger rolling style of playing, Scruggs established the technique that almost every banjo player uses. He also invented the Scruggs peg, a device that allows the retuning of the banjo while playing, which greatly expanded the versatility of the instrument.

Born: January 6, 1924; Flint Hill, North Carolina
Also known as: Earl Eugene Scruggs (full name)
Member of: The Foggy Mountain Boys; Flatt and Scruggs; the Earl Scruggs Revue

Principal recordings

ALBUMS (solo): *Earl Scruggs: His Family and Friends*, 1972; *I Saw the Light with Some Help from My Friends*, 1972; *Dueling Banjos*, 1973; *Rockin' 'Cross the Country*, 1973; *The Earl Scruggs Revue*, 1973; *Family Portrait*, 1976; *The Earl Scruggs Revue 2*, 1976; *Strike Anywhere*, 1977; *Bold and New*, 1978; *Today and Forever*, 1979; *Storyteller and the Banjo Man*, 1982 (with Tom T. Hall); *Top of the World*, 1983; *Superjammin'*, 1984; *Earl Scruggs and Friends*, 2001 (with others).

ALBUMS (with Flatt): *Foggy Mountain Jamboree*, 1957; *Country Music*, 1958; *Lester Flatt and Earl Scruggs*, 1959; *Flatt and Scruggs with the Foggy Mountain Boys*, 1960; *Songs of Glory*, 1960; *Foggy Mountain Banjo*, 1961; *Songs of the Famous Carter Family*, 1961; *Folk Songs of Our Land*, 1962; *The Ballad of Jed Clampett*, 1963; *The Original Sound of Flatt and Scruggs*, 1963; *The Fabulous Sound of Flatt and Scruggs*, 1964; *Beverly Hillbillies*, 1965; *Town and Country*, 1965; *The Versatile Flatt and Scruggs*, 1965; *Stars of the Grand Ole Opry*, 1966; *When the Saints Go Marching In*, 1966; *Changin' Times*, 1967; *Hear the Whistles Blow*, 1967; *Sacred Songs*, 1967; *Strictly Instrumental*, 1967; *Nashville Airplane*, 1968; *The Original Foggy Mountain Breakdown*, 1968; *Original Theme from "Bonnie and Clyde,"* 1968; *Songs to Cherish*, 1968; *The Story of Bonnie and Clyde*, 1968; *Detroit City*, 1969; *Breaking Out*, 1970; *Final Fling*, 1970; *Flatt and Scruggs*, 1970; *Foggy Mountain Chimes*, 1970; *Country Boy*, 1972; *A Boy Named Sue*, 1973; *Blue Ridge Cabin Home*, 1979; *You Can Feel It in Your Soul*, 1988; *Father's Table Grace*, 2002; *Foggy Mountain Special*, 2003.

The Life

Earl Eugene Scruggs was born into a musical farming family in the Piedmont section of North Carolina. He starting playing the banjo when he was four years old, around the time his father died, and he basically taught himself the complex three-finger picking style that some old-time players in the area used. Spending every spare minute playing the banjo, Scruggs soon extended this technique, emphasizing melodic lines and complicated syncopated rhythms in original ways. Scruggs got his first professional job in 1939 when he was fifteen, but it was not until after World War II ended that the fledgling musician had more opportunities to play. When the group Scruggs was playing with disbanded, Lester Flatt, the guitar player with the Bill Monroe band who was impressed by Scruggs's dynamic and unique style, pushed for him to join the group. Monroe, after hearing Scruggs on a Saturday, told him to be ready to tour Monday.

The Music

Early Works. Scruggs's early work included twenty-one cuts with Bill Monroe and Blue Grass Boys in 1946 and 1947. These tracks created by this band are considered by many to be a defining moment in bluegrass history. When Flatt and Scruggs left in 1948 to form their own group, the Foggy Mountain Boys, they established a solid reputation with such standards as "Rollin' in My Sweet Baby's Arms," "Salty Dog Blues," and "'Tis Sweet to Be Remembered" (which became a Top 10 country hit in 1952). The 1959 gospel hit "Cabin on the Hill" stayed on the *Billboard* chart for almost thirty weeks. Two songs that became synonymous with Flatt and Scruggs and the Scruggs banjo sound are "The Ballad of Jed Clampett" and "Foggy Mountain Breakdown."

"The Ballad of Jed Clampett." During the 1950's, Flatt and Scruggs were a major presence on the country and bluegrass music scene in the Southeast of the United States, although their major audience was still rural. Their live radio programs and appearances on television variety shows brought them many fans. With the urban folk music revival in the 1960's, they found new listeners on college campuses and at the outdoor music festivals that hosted a new generation of folksingers, such as Bob Dylan and Joan Baez. The music of Flatt and Scruggs made thousands of new bluegrass fans; performances at Carnegie Hall and Vanderbilt University made bluegrass music mainstream. After seeing Flatt and Scruggs at the Newport Folk Festival, a *New York Times* music critic called Scruggs the Paganini of the banjo. This attracted the notice of the producer of a new television program, *The Beverly Hillbillies*, and the show's theme song—"The Ballad of Jed Clampett," which provided the backstory for the series—became a number-one country hit single in 1962, and it reached number forty-four on the pop charts.

"Foggy Mountain Breakdown." Another signature piece, this song may be the most widely recognized bluegrass song in the world. Recorded in 1949 (and later again in 1965), this was the first instrumental to clearly showcase the three-finger Scruggs style of banjo picking. While it did not rise on the charts in the 1950's, it was often used for radio-show openings and closings because of its exciting rhythm and technical musical virtuosity. It was supposedly handpicked by producer-star Warren Beatty to be the theme for the 1967 film *Bonnie and Clyde*. Riding on the film's success, Flatt and Scruggs recorded it a third time, and that rendition reached number fifty-five on the *Billboard* pop charts.

Will the Circle Be Unbroken. Flatt and Scruggs split in 1969 over musical differences (Flatt wanted to remain more traditional; Scruggs wanted to become more pop-oriented). Scruggs formed a new group—the Earl Scruggs Revue—with his sons Randy and Gary, designed to appeal to younger listeners and to take the banjo in new directions. Around this time, in search of its musical roots, the country-rock group the Nitty Gritty Dirt Band started a project with established (though sometimes forgotten) country superstars such as Maybelle Carter and Roy Acuff. Scruggs was critical in uniting the members of the Nitty Gritty Dirt Band with the older country musicians, and eventually three *Will the Circle Be Unbroken* albums were released to much critical acclaim (in 1972, 1989, and

2002). One of Scruggs's contributions, "Earl's Breakdown," demonstrated how rock and bluegrass might meet. It was a new version of a classic Flatt and Scruggs song from the 1950's. It also featured one of Scruggs's detuning tricks, whereby he would change the pitch on the B or G strings of the banjo with a special cam on the headstock, giving it a different kind of gliding twang sound.

Musical Legacy

In 1985 Flatt and Scruggs were inducted into the Country Music Hall of Fame as well as into the Society for the Preservation of Bluegrass Music's Preservation Hall of Greats. Scruggs has been nominated for Grammy Awards more than a dozen times, with "Foggy Mountain Breakdown" winning in 1968 for Best Country Instrumental Performance and a rerecorded version of the song winning again in 2001. In 1999 "Foggy Mountain Breakdown" was placed in the Grammy Hall of Fame for songs of historical significance. Scruggs won a Grammy Award for Best Country Collaboration with Vocals for "Same Old Train" in 1998. With the Nitty Gritty Dirty Band, he took the Grammy Award for Best Country Instrumental Performance for "Earl's Breakdown" in 2004. Scruggs received a Grammy Lifetime Achievement Award in 2008. Scruggs was made a National Endowment for the Arts National Heritage Fellow in 1989, and he received the President's National Medal of Arts. He got a star on the Hollywood Walk of Fame in 2003 (the first banjo player so honored). He was given an honorary doctorate from the Berklee College of Music in 2005. In 2007 Flatt and Scruggs were inducted into the Nashville Songwriters Hall of Fame, and the North Carolina House and Senate passed a joint resolution honoring Scruggs.

James Stanlaw

Further Reading

Goldsmith, Thomas, ed. *The Bluegrass Reader*. Urbana: University of Illinois Press, 2004. This is a collection of journalism on and criticism of bluegrass music. Country singer Marty Stuart's reminiscences of Flatt and Scruggs are entertaining.

Kingsbury, Paul, and Alanna Nash, eds. *Will the Circle Be Unbroken: Country Music in America*. New York: DK, 2006. This beautifully written and lavishly illustrated history offers a chapter

on bluegrass music that includes a wealth of material on Flatt and Scruggs.

Malone, Bill, and Judith McCulloh, eds. *Stars of Country Music*. New York: Da Capo Press, 1975. An early collection of essays on twenty country musicians, including Flatt and Scruggs, by two country-music scholars.

Rosenberg, Neil. *Bluegrass: A History*. Urbana: University of Illinois Press, 2005. This new edition of a well-researched and thorough history of bluegrass includes material on Scruggs and his banjo found nowhere else.

Scruggs, Earl. *Earl Scruggs and the Five-String Banjo: Revised and Enhanced Edition*. Milwaukee, Wis.: Hal Leonard, 2005. This standard method book includes material on banjo history and Scruggs's life, chronicling the artist's love affair with his instrument.

See also: Acuff, Roy; Baez, Joan; Carter, Maybelle; Dylan, Bob; Flatt, Lester; Fleck, Béla; Monroe, Bill; Ritchie, Jean; Stanley, Ralph; Watson, Doc.

Charles Seeger
American ethnomusicologist

Seeger helped to establish the disciplines of musicology and ethnomusicology in the United States, and as a music theorist and educator, he influenced the development of modern composition; as a scholar, he raised fundamental questions about the relationship between music and language.

Born: December 14, 1886; Mexico City, Mexico
Died: February 7, 1979; Bridgewater, Connecticut
Also known as: Charles Louis Seeger (full name)

Principal works

WRITINGS OF INTEREST: *An Outline of a Course in Harmonic Structure and Simple Musical Invention*, 1913 (with Edward Griffith Stricklen); *Systematic and Historical Orientations in Musicology*, 1939; *Folk Song U.S.A.: The 111 Best American Ballads*, 1947 (with John A. Lomax and Alan Lomax); *Studies in Musicology, 1935-1975*, 1975.

The Life

The son of a merchant who had offices in the United States and Mexico, Charles Louis Seeger studied music composition at Harvard. After graduating in 1908, he went to Germany, where he studied conducting, and he conducted for the Cologne municipal opera. After a period in Europe, he returned to the United States and, in 1911, married violinist Constance de Clyver Edson. They gave concerts together, and soon they moved to Berkeley, where Seeger had been invited to help start the music department at the University of California. Along with developing a systematic study of music, he immersed himself in academic life, learning from his colleagues in other disciplines. The outspoken Seeger disagreed with powerful figures over American involvement in World War I, in which his brother had been killed, and chose not to return after a sabbatical.

The Seegers moved to the New York area in 1919. In the 1920's Seeger began teaching music theory at the Institute of Musical Art, which later became the Juilliard School. In the early 1930's, he lectured at the New School for Social Research. Before Seeger and Constance separated, they had three children, among them Pete, who became a famous folksinger and political activist.

Seeger's egalitarian political views led to his involvement with like-minded intellectuals, including modern composers such as his former student Ruth Crawford, who became his second wife in 1932. By 1935 the political climate had shifted in response to the Great Depression, and Seeger joined the government as an expert on music. He became part of the Resettlement Administration, which moved struggling families into planned communities. He and his family moved to Washington, D.C. In 1937 Seeger became deputy director of the Federal Music Project, which employed musicians for performances, teaching, and, in what became especially important for the Seegers, the research and documentation of American folk music. Together with their friends John Lomax and his son Alan Lomax, Charles and Ruth Crawford Seeger worked on the Archive of Folk Culture for the Library of Congress, which resulted in the publication in 1947 of *Folk Song U.S.A.: The 111 Best American Ballads*, for which the Seegers served as music editors. The Seegers had four children.

Seeger's next government position was chief of the Music and Visual Arts Division of the Pan American Union and director of its Inter-American Music Center. In this office, which he held from 1941 to 1953, he worked with his staff to give music educators access to Latin American material, arranged for an exchange of musicians throughout the Americas, and improved the conditions for Latin American composers, whose work had sometimes been pirated by publishers in the United States.

Ruth Crawford Seeger died suddenly in 1953 from an illness, and Seeger, who was the subject of a an investigation by the Federal Bureau of Investigation (FBI) into his activist past, resigned from his government position. He stayed active in scholarly circles and helped to found the Society for Ethnomusicology in 1956. In his seventies, in response to an invitation from ethnomusicologist Mantle Hood, Seeger returned to a full-time academic career, becoming a research professor at the Institute for Ethnomusicology at the University of California, Los Angeles, from 1961 to 1971 and contributing to the legendary interdisciplinary Wednesday seminars that influenced future leaders in the field of ethnomusicology. He spent his last decade in Connecticut, lecturing occasionally at nearby institutions.

The Music

Dissonant Counterpoint. As a composer, performer, and teacher of twentieth century classical music, Seeger believed in the importance of developing a modern approach to the study of counterpoint. He devised a method of preparing and resolving consonances (into dissonances), a dialectical inversion of the traditional species counterpoint that had changed little since the Renaissance. Seeger made a formal presentation of these ideas in his article "On Dissonant Counterpoint," published in *Modern Music* in 1930. He was also interested in the concept of rhythmic dissonance and phrase structure, and he included rigorous training in rhythm as part of his music-theory curriculum at the University of California, Berkeley, and the Institute of Musical Art. The composer Henry Cowell, who attended music classes at Berkeley, as a special underage student, was among the early recipients of Seeger's ideas about dissonance.

Music and Society. In the early 1930's, Seeger was a member of the Composer's Collective, a branch of the leftist Workers Music League. At this point in his career, he and his colleagues, such as Ruth Crawford Seeger, Elie Siegmeister, and Aaron Copland, associated their own personal modernist artistic styles with their dreams of liberation for the masses. However, they soon discovered that the workers they wished to help did not necessarily appreciate the heavily dissonant, intellectually intense pieces that were intended to inspire them. Gradually, the Seegers became more interested in the musical traditions enjoyed and cultivated by the laborers. Together, the Seegers made a transition in interest from modernist composition to direct involvement with American folk music.

Seeger expanded his theoretical work to encompass not only musical structure but also social significance, reflecting to some extent the shift in his professional responsibilities. In the late 1930's, Seeger identified a difference in emphasis between earlier musical folklorists (who emphasized the preservation of folk music as a kind of historical artifact) and the newer scholars, especially those involved in government-sponsored folk-music programs (who saw folk traditions as fulfilling an ongoing social need). Seeger once attempted to implement the use of music to strengthen a faltering relocation program for farmers. In later years, as the field of ethnomusicology matured, Seeger developed a more observational approach to music as a social function, asserting the need to encompass music in all of its forms, as practiced and utilized by all groups and all economic classes.

Music and Speech. Seeger was well read in philosophy, and he was a great admirer of the field of linguistics, which he considered to be decades ahead of musicology. As one of the first musicologists in the United States, he was conscious of musicology's dependence on writing, which Seeger regarded as a form of speech, to discuss music: the use of one mode of communication to examine another. Although Seeger was aware of and fascinated by their similarities, he was skeptical of simplistic analogies between the two modes and regarded their juncture as one of the essential challenges of musicology.

Objective Music Transcription and the Melograph. In his quest for objectivity, Seeger

turned to the possibilities of using mechanical devices to transcribe melody. Although he had once spent years helping Ruth Crawford Seeger transcribe American folk songs, he found that staff notation, with its built-in cultural assumptions and other flaws, was inadequate for capturing the melodic subtleties and possibly unrecognized structural features of the increasingly diverse music he was analyzing. He followed developments in the sciences related to phono-photography and worked with his eldest son, Charles, an astronomer, on developing prototypes for what he would call the melograph. The first, model A, was built at his own expense in 1956, and in 1958 Hood, director of a graduate program in ethnomusicology at the University of California, Los Angeles, secured funding to build model B. After 1968, model C, which used computer circuits to display pitch, spectrum, and volume, gave graduate students and other researchers a radical new view of sound, stimulating new dimensions of analysis.

Music as Logic. One of Seeger's most philosophical and challenging articles, "On the Moods of a

Charles Seeger. (AP/Wide World Photos)

Music Logic," brought together concepts on which he had worked in his early years as a composer and music theorist with his efforts to bring the precision of linguistics to the discussion of music. He first wrote the piece in 1956, and he revised it in 1976. By outlining and categorizing the essential elements of the compositional process, and extending these into all levels and dimensions, Seeger tried to ensure that music could be presented in its own terms. Ultimately, he viewed this as an important goal for both musicology and ethnomusicology, which he believed should not exist as separate disciplines. His emphasis on process (as synthesis) rather than design (as analysis) revealed a dynamic approach that balanced the more familiar static, text-dependent methods.

Musical Legacy

Considering the length, intensity, and diversity of his lifetime of teaching, it is difficult to overestimate Seeger's impact on several generations of students in the areas of composition, music theory, music history, ethnomusicology, and related disciplines, extending from the classrooms of the World War I era to the graduate seminars of the 1960's. His seminal publications and ideas continued to stimulate scholarship in music. Three of his children were influenced deeply by Seeger's immersion in American folk music and became professional performers in traditional styles: Pete Seeger, a famous folksinger, songwriter, banjoist, and activist; Peggy Seeger, a singer, songwriter, and multi-instrumentalist; and Mike Seeger, a founding member of the New Lost City Ramblers. Seeger's grandson Anthony became a prominent scholar and administrator who, like his grandfather, served as president of the Society for Ethnomusicology.

As a government administrator during the 1930's and 1940's, Seeger contributed to the development of institutions and policies that asserted the value and ongoing viability of American musical traditions. Some of the scholarly societies that Seeger helped to found, including the Society for Ethnomusicology, the American Musicological Society, and the College Music Society, grew over the years. They held annual conferences, published a steady flow of publications, and continued the lively dialogues that Seeger enjoyed.

John Myers

Further Reading

Dunaway, David King. *How Can I Keep from Singing: Pete Seeger*. New York: McGraw-Hill, 1981. Comprehensive biography, with coverage of Pete's early years in the Seeger family, including his exposure to folk music and activism during the 1930's. Includes discography, references, illustrations, and index.

Filene, Benjamin. *Romancing the Folk: Public Memory and American Roots Music*. Chapel Hill: University of North Carolina Press, 2000. Detailed account of the expansion of interest in American folk music, including government sponsorship, scholarly work, and public performances, primarily from the 1930's through the 1960's, with attention to the prominent role of Seeger as an activist, administrator, and scholar. Includes photographs.

Hisama, Ellie M. *Gendering Musical Modernism: The Music of Ruth Crawford, Marion Bauer, and Miriam Gideon*. Cambridge, England: Cambridge University Press, 2006. Focuses on connections between musical structure and political expression and identity in Ruth Crawford Seeger's compositions.

Perlis, Vivian, and Libby Van Cleve. *Composer's Voices from Ives to Ellington: An Oral History of American Music*. New Haven, Conn.: Yale University Press, 2005. Includes biographical material, commentary, photographs, and an eleven-page transcription of interviews with Seeger recorded in 1970 and 1977.

Pescatello, Ann M. *Charles Seeger: A Life in American Music*. Pittsburgh, Pa.: University of Pittsburgh Press, 1992. Definitive biography includes analysis of Seeger's theories as well as an account of his diverse activities and accomplishments. Includes photographs, bibliography, and index.

Seeger, Charles. *Studies in Musicology, 1935-1975*. Berkeley: University of California Press, 1977. Assembled and edited by Seeger, this collection of eighteen essays explores both the systematic and historical approaches to the field. Includes music examples, illustrations, maps, bibliography, and index.

_____. *Studies in Musicology II, 1929-1979*. Edited by Ann M. Pescatello. Berkeley: University of California Press, 1994. This anthology embraces a wider period of time than the first volume of *Studies in Musicology*, and it includes Seeger's treatise on composition and his manual on dissonant counterpoint as well as seminal works exploring the relationship between speech and music as modes of communication.

Tick, Judith. *Ruth Crawford Seeger: A Composer's Search for American Music.* New York: Oxford University Press, 2000. Includes details of the composer's professional collaborations and musical relationship with Charles Seeger as well as their mutual quest to reconcile the written and oral traditions in music. Includes a reprint of "On the Moods of a Music Logic" and references and index.

See also: Copland, Aaron; Cowell, Henry; Lomax, Alan; Seeger, Mike; Seeger, Peggy; Seeger, Pete; Seeger, Ruth Crawford.

Mike Seeger

American folk and country singer, songwriter, and banjo player

Seeger's prowess as a multi-instrumentalist and his mining of a deep vein of obscure yet striking song material made him a charismatic figure on the folk music revival scene.

Born: August 15, 1933; New York, New York
Member of: The New Lost City Ramblers

Principal recordings

ALBUMS (solo): *Solo: Old Time Music*, 1962; *Tipple, Look, and Rail*, 1965; *Strange Creek Singers*, 1968 (with Strange Creek Singers); *Music from True Vine*, 1972; *American Folk Songs for Children*, 1977 (with Peggy Seeger); *Fresh Oldtime String Band*, 1988; *American Folk Songs for Christmas*, 1989 (with Peggy Seeger and Penny Seeger); *Animal Folk Songs for Children*, 1992 (with Peggy Seeger, Penny Seeger, and Barbara Seeger); *Third Annual Farewell Reunion*, 1994 (with others); *Way Down in North Carolina*, 1996 (with Paul Brown); *Southern Banjo Sounds*, 1998; *True Vine*, 2003; *Early Southern Guitar Sounds*, 2007.

ALBUMS (with the New Lost City Ramblers): *The New Lost City Ramblers, Vol. 1*, 1958; *The New Lost City Ramblers, Vol. 2*, 1959; *Old-Timey Songs for Children*, 1959; *Songs from the Depression*,

1959; *Earth Is Earth Sung by the New Lost City Bang Boys*, 1961; *The New Lost City Ramblers, Vol. 3*, 1961; *The New Lost City Ramblers, Vol. 4*, 1961; *American Moonshine and Prohibition*, 1962; *The New Lost City Ramblers, Vol. 5*, 1963; *Radio Special No. 1*, 1963; *String Band Instrumentals*, 1964; *Rural Delivery No. 1*, 1965; *Remembrance of Things to Come*, 1966; *Modern Times*, 1968; *The New Lost City Ramblers with Cousin Emmy*, 1968; *On the Great Divide*, 1973; *Old Time Music*, 1994; *There Ain't No Way Out*, 1997.

The Life

Mike Seeger is the son of ethnomusicologist Charles Seeger and musicologist-composer Ruth Crawford Seeger. Pete Seeger is his half brother; Peggy Seeger is his sister. The Seeger children heard Library of Congress field recordings and other original source material at impressionable ages. Largely self-taught on a wide variety of instruments, Seeger was the one who excelled as an instrumentalist and who adopted a performance aesthetic grounded in the grittier string band and related traditions of the 1920's. While learning to play, he was also recording still-active exponents of those traditions in the Washington, D.C., area, where he grew up.

In 1958 he joined forces with like-minded musicians and singers Tom Paley and John Cohen to form the New Lost City Ramblers. Through performance and recordings, the New Lost City Ramblers exerted an influence far exceeding the group's limited commercial success. They epitomized the traditionalist side of the folk music revival, in marked contrast to such pop-oriented folk groups as the Kingston Trio.

In 1962 Seeger released his first solo album on the Folkways label. Over the next decade, he recorded and toured extensively, both as a soloist and with the New Lost City Ramblers and with similar groups such as the Strange Creek Singers. All the while he continued to do extensive field recording and to rediscover musicians such as singer-banjoist Dock Boggs, one of many remarkable old-timey artists Seeger brought to the Newport Folk Festival and other urban concert venues. By the mid-1970's, the New Lost City Ramblers were only occasionally performing (Tracy Schwartz replaced Paley in 1962), but Seeger continued as a veritable one-man band, performing what he dubbed "music from the true vine" on an impressive array of instruments. Seeger is a vital exponent of musical styles that appeared all but extinct when he embraced them in the 1950's.

The Music

A typical Seeger performance finds him playing no fewer than eight instruments: banjo, fiddle, guitar, harmonica, autoharp, Jew's harp, quills (panpipes), and a homemade "shaker" (percussion instrument). In this way he produces an impressive range of sounds and styles that supports his vintage songs.

Some of those sounds originated on 1920's vintage "hillbilly" records, while others came from older musicians Seeger discovered and from whom he learned firsthand. In both cases, he distilled his source material to produce his individual sound. The songs he sings may be comic ("Tennessee Dog") or tragic ("Wind and Rain"), but rarely are they interpreted precisely in the manner of Seeger's source.

"Don't Let Your Deal Go Down." The source for this song is a 1927 recording by Fiddlin' John Carson and His Virginia Reelers. Seeger first recorded his arrangement on the album *Music from True Vine*. He had then only recently experimented with playing the fiddle and harmonica (held in a rack) at the same time. Thirty years later, Seeger rerecorded the song for a Smithsonian Folkways album entitled *True Vine*.

It was the sole song to appear on both those albums. The eerie sound Seeger coaxes from the fiddle and harmonica accentuates the darker implications of Carson's original. Seeger makes the tune plainer, even more archaic-sounding than his source. This has long been a standout of Seeger's performance repertoire.

"Down South Blues." Dock Boggs recorded this song with banjo in 1927. Seeger learned it from him when they toured together in the 1960's. Seeger's right hand picking is faithful to Boggs's original, while Seeger's left hand uses a slide to fret the banjo, something Boggs never did. Nevertheless, Seeger's instinct for musically appropriate revision is flawless. This performance appears on the ambitious album *Southern Banjo Sounds*, an audio guide to a wide range of banjo styles performed on a vari-

ety of mostly vintage instruments. Seeger created a series of three instructional DVDs, which teach the twenty-six tunes on the album.

"Gold Watch and Chain." Recorded at the Newport Folk Festival around 1963, this performance of a Carter family standard with Seeger on lead vocal and autoharp captures the reverence the New Lost City Ramblers show their sources and the audience's admiration for the group's authenticity. This and other live performances of Seeger, the New Lost City Ramblers, and such legends as Maybelle Carter appear on the album *Old Time Music*.

Musical Legacy

Seeger performs a diverse repertoire otherwise destined to be known only to a handful of folklorists and record collectors. His combination of musical scholarship, performance flair, and interpretive acuity inspired others to take up the "old-timey" music cause. Along with his own recordings, his legacy includes extensive field recordings he has made through the years of musicians both famous and obscure.

Mark Humphrey

Further Reading

Cantwell, Robert. *When We Were Good: The Folk Revival*. Cambridge, England: Harvard University Press, 1996. Cantwell's well-written meditation on the roots and flowering of the folk music revival includes an appreciation of Seeger and his unique role in it.

Dylan, Bob. *Chronicles*. New York: Simon & Schuster, 2004. Dylan's recollection of Seeger's impact on him in his early days is stunning. Dylan had such adulation for Seeger that Dylan realized he could never perform traditional folk music half as well. That realization led Dylan to write his own songs.

Goldsmith, Peter D. *Making People's Music: Moe Asch and Folkways Records*. Washington, D.C.: Smithsonian Institution Press, 1998. This fascinating portrait of the development of the premier folk music label and the man behind it includes details of Seeger's early recording career and that of the New Lost City Ramblers.

See also: Dylan, Bob; Seeger, Charles; Seeger, Peggy; Seeger, Pete; Seeger, Ruth Crawford.

Peggy Seeger

American folksinger, songwriter, and banjoist

Seeger became a central figure in the British folk revival movement, along with husband Ewan MacColl. She also became a well-known feminist.

Born: June 17, 1935; New York, New York
Also known as: Margaret Seeger (full name)
Member of: No Spring Chickens; the Critics Group

Principal recordings

ALBUMS (solo): *Folk Songs of Courting and Complaint*, 1955; *Animal Folk Songs for Children*, 1957; *Two Way Trip*, 1961; *The Female Frolic*, 1967 (with the Critics Group); *Peggy Alone*, 1967; *At the Present Moment*, 1973; *Penelope Isn't Waiting Anymore*, 1977; *Saturday Night at the Bull and Mouth*, 1977 (with Ewan MacColl); *Different Therefore Equal*, 1980; *Peggy Seeger*, 1990; *Almost Commercially Viable*, 1992 (with No Spring Chickens); *The Folkways Years, 1955-1992: Songs of Love and Politics*, 1992; *Familiar Faces*, 1993; *Songs of Love and Politics*, 1994; *Love Will Linger On*, 1995; *Classic Peggy Seeger*, 1996; *An Odd Collection*, 1996; *Period Pieces: Women's Songs for Men and Women*, 1998; *Heading for Home*, 2003 (with Calum and Neill MacColl); *Love Call Me Home*, 2005; *Bring Me Home*, 2008.

ALBUMS (with Mike Seeger): *American Folk Songs for Children*, 1955; *American Folk Songs Sung by the Seegers*, 1957; *Peggy 'n' Mike*, 1967; *American Folk Songs for Christmas*, 1990.

WRITINGS OF INTEREST: *Folk Songs of Peggy Seeger*, 1964; *Peggy Seeger Songbook: Warts and All*, 1998.

The Life

Margaret Seeger was born into a family of gifted musicians, and the work of her parents, Ruth and Charles, in compiling traditional American folk songs would have a profound influence on all of their children. Ruth's sudden death in 1953 would persuade Seeger, armed with her banjo and guitar, to leave Radcliffe College to travel widely throughout Europe, Russia, and China. McCarthyism in 1950's America—the deep fear, suspicion, and social persecution of those who exhibited sympathies for socialism, communism, or even vaguely leftist progressivism—would deter her from returning permanently to the United States until 1994.

Settling in the United Kingdom, Seeger began work with her husband, Ewan MacColl, mostly as a singer and musical arranger. Their first project together was a radio commission from the British Broadcasting Corporation (BBC) that would result in the development of an important new genre, the "radio ballad." The pair would also lead the British folk revival and created the Critics Group (1964-1971) to formalize good performance practices. During this time, Seeger also ran the *New City Songster* (1968-1985), a periodical that published more than five hundred newly composed songs in twenty-one volumes. Seeger and MacColl also began their own recording label, Blackthorne Records.

By the late 1970's, Seeger had begun to emerge as a songwriter in her own right, and her first two solo albums contained many influential feminist songs. Seeger originally fell into the feminist movement accidentally but embraced it after penning the famous "I'm Gonna Be an Engineer." In the 1980's, she became actively involved with nuclear issues and performed with her group Jade, which consisted of five singers, including Irish folksinger Irene Pyper-Scott, who would become Seeger's partner after the death of MacColl in 1989.

In 1994, after living abroad for nearly four decades, Seeger moved back to the United States, settling first in Asheville, North Carolina, then, in 2006, in Boston to take up a teaching position at Northeastern University.

The Music

Although Seeger's music helped define the feminist movement, music about women constitutes only a part of Seeger's vast output and does not define her overall style. Seeger first embraced the North American and then later the traditional British folk repertoire, which would remain the backbone of her influences. Her work with MacColl during the British folk revival spans more than thirty-three albums and includes their revolutionary "radio ballads" and *The Long Harvest* (1966-1975), a twelve-album set (two unreleased) of traditional British and North American ballads.

With her two solo albums at the end of the 1970's, Seeger had become an advocate for women's rights. In the 1980's, Seeger concentrated her songwriting on environmental causes, especially nuclear issues, and developed the all-female group Jade, which would often fill in for MacColl when he was too sick to perform. In the 2000's, Seeger began her Home series, a group of albums in which she is supported by her three children in mostly traditional North American songs, and the self-produced Timely series, which addresses contemporary political issues.

The Radio Ballads. First broadcast by the BBC between 1958 and 1964, the recordings of this series of radio programs was reissued by Topic Records in eight volumes in 1999. They consist of eight radio broadcasts, devised by MacColl, Charles Parker, and Seeger, that combined words and music to document the various unheralded working-class groups. The series was revolutionary because, rather than use the voices of radio actors, it used the field recordings of the interviewees while incorporating newly composed music and sound effects. Seeger contributed to the musical arrangements, played, sang, collected and transcribed the interviews, and worked on the scripts. The first ballad, "The Ballad of John Axon," about a heroic train driver, won accolades and a renewed contract from the BBC for seven other radio-ballad programs, all about one hour in length.

Different Therefore Equal. This album from 1980 is an important collection of songs compiled through a series of interviews about the main issues of women at the time. Nine out of ten are written by Seeger (and represent the most original content that Seeger had recorded to this time). Among these songs is the rallying cry of the feminist movement, "I'm Gonna Be an Engineer." The amusingly acerbic "Lady, What Do You Do All Day?" is about gaining equality for housewives, and "Reclaim the Night," about rape, creates intimacy and intensity with an indignant, unaccompanied vocal line. Other issues Seeger addresses in these songs include domestic violence and contraception.

The Folkways Years, 1955-1992. This retrospective album of songs chosen by Seeger contains pieces from both her traditional and new repertoires, from her earliest recordings through 1992. It includes a feisty live performance of "Lady, What

Do You Do All Day?"; the poignant "Thoughts of Time," about her future with MacColl; two songs written for her sons, "My Son" and "Song for Culum"; and the MacColl song about Seeger that was made immensely popular by Roberta Flack, "The First Time Ever (I Saw Your Face)." The collection displays Seeger's immense range of subjects and creative instrumental arrangements.

An Odd Collection. This appropriately named album is a set of songs covering a wide range of topics, including the environment, old friends, love, and women's issues. Some songs in the collection also exhibit a distinct change in style, however, displaying a warmer and more humorous side of Seeger. The album also ushered in a period of newfound love, which is celebrated in the beautiful, unaccompanied "Love Unbidden" and the meditative "So Long Since I Have Been Home." The latter makes use of the infrequently heard piano as a part of the accompaniment. "For a Job" is a blues song with saxophone that mimics the slides in Seeger's voice. "If You Want a Better Life," about unionization, is a communal barn dance with hand clappers.

Musical Legacy

On the occasion of Seeger's seventieth birthday in 2005, it was duly noted that Seeger's pivotal role in folk music has not yet received the full credit it deserves, primarily because the focus has always been on her many other talented family members including mother Ruth, brother Mike, and half brother Pete. Certainly her seminal work with MacColl as a part of the British folk revival has been acknowledged for its wide influence, especially through the couple's live performances. Seeger's songs about women's issues, however, have not yet received their full measure of recognition for documenting women's experiences and advancing the feminist movement.

A respected composer, Seeger remained active in the first decade of the 2000's, continuing to perform and give workshops on songwriting, performance practices, and singing. She will also be remembered as a talented arranger—due in part to her abilities on the guitar, five-string banjo, Appalachian dulcimer, autoharp, English concertina, and piano.

Sonya Mason

Further Reading

Cassingham, Barbee J., and Sally M. O'Neil. "Peggy, Age Sixty-Three." Chapter 2 in *And Then I Met This Woman: Previously Married Women's Journeys into Lesbian Relationships*. 2d enlarged ed. Freeland, Wash.: Soaring Eagle, 1999. Seeger shares her journey of self-rediscovery.

Cox, Peter. *Set into Song: Ewan MacColl, Charles Parker, Peggy Seeger, and the Radio Ballads*. London: Labatie Books, 2008. Outlines Seeger's pivotal role in the radio ballads.

Hamessley, Lydia. "Peggy Seeger: From Traditional Folksinger to Contemporary Songwriter." In *Ruth Crawford Seeger's Worlds*, edited by Ray Allen and Ellie M. Hisama. Rochester, N.Y.: University of Rochester, 2007. This chapter shows Seeger's extensive knowledge of both classical and folk idioms.

Hunt, Ken. "Peggy 'n' All." *fRoots* 266/267 (August/September, 2005): 50-53. An illuminating interview, discussing Seeger's life through six autobiographical songs.

Seeger, Peggy. *The Peggy Seeger Songbook: Warts and All, Forty Years of Songmaking*. New York: Oak Productions, 1998. This astounding collection of more than one hundred songs includes a short autobiography, detailed compositional methodologies, historical background for every song, a discography, and extensive indexes.

See also: Seeger, Charles; Seeger, Mike; Seeger, Ruth Crawford.

Pete Seeger

American folksinger, banjoist, and songwriter

Legendary folksinger, composer, and activist, Seeger used his music as a means of instigating social change. Spanning generations, Seeger wrote union-organizing songs, provided the musical backdrop of the Civil Rights movement, and gave voice to the antiwar movement.

Born: May 3, 1919; Patterson, New York
Also known as: Peter R. Seeger
Member of: The Almanac Singers; the Weavers

Principal recordings

ALBUMS (solo): *Gazette*, 1958; *Song and Play Time with Pete Seeger*, 1958; *American Playparties*, 1959; *Folk Songs for Young People*, 1959; *Abiyoyo and Other Story Songs for Children*, 1960; *Champlain Valley Songs*, 1960; *Song and Play Time*, 1960; *American Folk, Game, and Activity Songs for Children*, 1962; *Little Boxes and Other Broadsides*, 1965; *Pete Seeger Sings Woody Guthrie*, 1967; *Traditional Christmas Carols*, 1967; *Pete Seeger Sings Leadbelly*, 1968; *Rainbow Race*, 1973; *Banks of Marble*, 1974; *The World of Pete Seeger*, 1974; *Precious Friend*, 1982 (with Arlo Guthrie); *Link in the Chain*, 1996; *Pete*, 1996.

ALBUMS (with the Almanac Singers): *Deep Sea Chanteys*, 1941; *Songs for John Doe*, 1941; *Talking Union*, 1941; *Whaling Ballads and Sod Buster Ballads*, 1941; *Dear Mr. President*, 1942; *American Folk Songs for Children*, 1953; *Goofing-Off Suite*, 1954; *Pete Seeger Sampler*, 1954; *Birds, Beasts, Bugs, and Fishes Little and Big: Animal Folk Songs*, 1955; *With Voices We Sing Together*, 1956; *American Favorite Ballads, Vol. 1*, 1957; *American Industrial Ballads*, 1957; *American Favorite Ballads, Vol. 2*, 1959; *Dangerous Songs!?*, 1966; *Darling Corey*, 1981.

ALBUMS (with the Weavers): *Folk Songs of America and Other Lands*, 1951; *It's Almost Day*, 1951; *Around the Corner*, 1952; *Clementine*, 1952; *Go Tell It on the Mountain*, 1952; *Hard Ain't It Hard*, 1952; *We Wish You a Merry Christmas*, 1952; *Wimoweh*, 1952; *Benoni*, 1953; *Quilting Bee*, 1953; *Sylvie*, 1953; *Battle of New Orleans*, 1958; *Done Laid Around*, 1958; *Folk Songs Around the World*, 1959; *One Day as I Rambled*, 1959; *Little Boxes*, 1963; *The Weavers' Almanac*, 1963; *Waist Deep in the Big Muddy and Other Love Songs*, 1967; *The Weavers Songbag*, 1968.

WRITINGS OF INTEREST: *How to Play the Five-String Banjo*, 1948; *The Incompleat Folksinger*, 1972; *Where Have All the Flowers Gone: A Musical Autobiography*, 1993.

The Life

Pete Seeger (some sources list Peter R. Seeger) was born on May 3, 1919, to Charles and Constance Seeger. His father was a famous musicologist. Seeger attended Harvard University, where he took classes in sociology and belonged to the tenor banjo society. An intelligent, quiet young man, Seeger left Harvard in 1938 and took a job with the Archive of American Folk Music at the Library of Congress in Washington, D.C., working with musicologist Alan Lomax. As a part of his work, Seeger traveled throughout the country, finding and recording legendary folk artists and traditional blues singers.

In 1940 Seeger formed the Almanac Singers, joined in 1941 by Woody Guthrie. With the onset of World War II, Seeger was drafted in 1942. During the same year, he joined the Communist Party. He also married Toshi Ohta, and the couple had three children.

After the war, Seeger continued his activism for left-wing politicians and causes. He helped form the singing group the Weavers in 1948. In 1949, at a concert in Peekskill, New York, Seeger appeared with the great African American singer Paul Robeson, whose political views had led to his being banned from many American concert halls. On this occasion members of the Ku Klux Klan attacked Seeger and Robeson while police looked on. Seeger later became deeply involved in the Civil Rights movement.

In the 1950's the Weavers found themselves the target of red-baiting and blacklisting, making it difficult for them to find work. Seeger was called to testify before the House Committee on Un-American Activities to provide information about Communists in the entertainment industry. Seeger refused to testify, stating:

> I am not going to answer any questions as to my association, my philosophical or religious beliefs or my political beliefs, or how I voted in any election, or any of these private affairs. I think these are very improper questions for any American to be asked, especially under such compulsion as this.

He was charged with contempt of Congress and in 1961 convicted. The conviction was overturned on appeal, and Seeger continued to work for social justice and peace. In spite of Seeger's popularity, he was largely banned from television and radio until his famous appearance on *The Smothers Brothers Comedy Hour* in 1967.

Seeger continued his social activism through music by writing and performing antiwar and civil rights songs throughout the 1970's. In addition he was a well-known advocate for the environment. In

Pete Seeger. (AP/Wide World Photos)

1969 he launched the sloop *Clearwater*, using the boat as a platform to initiate a major environmental campaign designed to clean up the Hudson River. During the 1970's, Seeger actively protested against the Vietnam War. His appearance on *The Smothers Brothers Comedy Hour* marked the end of his blacklisting on network television.

Through the rest of the twentieth century, Seeger actively worked against pollution and war. In 1994 he received the Presidential Medal of Arts at the Kennedy Center in Washington, D.C., and in 1996 he was inducted into the Rock and Roll Hall of Fame. Arlo Guthrie and Harry Belafonte presented his award. Seeger won a Grammy Award for the Best Traditional Folk Album of 1996 for *Pete*.

In 2004 Seeger led more than a thousand voices in New York City during the Global March for Peace. A documentary of Seeger's life and career, *Pete Seeger: The Power of Song*, was released in 2007.

The Music

Born into a musical family, Seeger found himself living a life with music at its center. He began playing the banjo while still in his teens and took a job when he was only nineteen years old working with the legendary Lomax. Traveling throughout the country with Lomax, making recordings of traditional music, Seeger found himself entranced by such artists as Huddie Ledbetter (known as Leadbelly) and labor militant Aunt Molly Jackson. As a result of this experience, Seeger became committed to not only performing traditional music but also to the preservation of it. In addition he discovered the power of music to move people to social change.

Woody Guthrie and the Almanac Singers. In 1940 Seeger founded the singing group the Almanac Singers. On March 3, 1940, he met singer and composer Woody Guthrie at a migrant workers' concert, and the two began a long-term musical collaboration, with Guthrie becoming a part of the Almanac Singers. The Almanac Singers performed and recorded union-organizing songs such as "The Talking Union Blues." Their album *Songs for John Doe* was released in 1941, as the United States was entering World War II. Many of the songs on the album, including "Ballad of October 16," were songs calling for peace.

"Good Night, Irene." Seeger formed another musical group, the Weavers, in 1948, with Lee Hays, Ronnie Gilbert, and Fred Hellerman. In 1950 the group recorded and released the song "Good Night, Irene," a tune earlier recorded by Leadbelly. The song was a surprise hit, cutting across social and cultural barriers, and made the Weavers one of the most popular and best-known singing groups in the United States. The Weavers, however, soon found themselves targeted by the McCarthy-era Communist witch hunts, and they were blacklisted, leading to cancellations of many of their concerts. The group disbanded briefly but reunited in 1955 to play to a sold-out house in a now-legendary concert at Carnegie Hall. During the 1950's, however, Seeger concentrated more on his solo career and eventually left the group in 1959.

"Turn, Turn, Turn." Seeger used the words of Ecclesiastes 3:1-8 for his 1950's composition "Turn, Turn, Turn." Recorded by Seeger in 1962, the song became a major hit for Roger McGuinn and the Byrds in 1965. During the Vietnam War era, "Turn, Turn, Turn" was one of the best-known war protest songs and was recorded by nearly every folk artist of the day.

"If I Had a Hammer." Originally called "The Hammer Song," "If I Had a Hammer" was written by Seeger and Lee Hayes in 1949 in order to support the Progressive movement. The song was recorded by the Weavers but did not achieve much success. In 1962, in the midst of the Civil Rights movement and the folk revival, Peter, Paul, and Mary released a cover of "If I Had a Hammer" that became a Top 10 hit. In addition, Trini Lopez recorded the song to tremendous success. The song became immensely popular and was sung at nearly every civil rights gathering during the 1960's, as well as becoming a standard sing-along tune at summer camps and on college campuses. It has been recorded by a host of other groups and singers since 1962 and continues to be one of the best-known songs among the American people. "If I Had a Hammer" and "We Shall Overcome" (a traditional song first recorded by Seeger) became the anthems of the American Civil Rights movement.

"Where Have All the Flowers Gone?" Another major song of the antiwar movement of the 1960's and early 1970's was "Where Have All the Flowers Gone?," penned by Seeger some time during the 1950's with verses added later by Joe Hickerson. In 1961 the Kingston Trio recorded this song, claiming that it was their work. When contacted by Seeger, the Kingston Trio immediately withdrew this claim and credited Seeger. Many groups recorded this song during the era, and Bruce Springsteen recorded a well-received version. Like many of Seeger's songs, the lyrics and tune of "Where Have All the Flowers Gone?" is a standard sing-along number at concerts, camps, and campuses.

"Waist Deep in the Big Muddy." Tom and Dick Smothers insisted that Seeger, who had been blacklisted from network television for many years, be featured on their popular comedy variety show in 1967. Seeger performed a segment of songs sung by and about soldiers from the Revolutionary War to the Vietnam War, including his own composition, "Waist Deep in the Big Muddy." This song took a 1942 event involving a group of soldiers in training in Louisiana and made it into an allegory of the morass of the Vietnam War. When the episode aired, however, CBS censors had clipped this song. The Smothers Brothers threatened to break their contract, and CBS finally relented, allowing Seeger to perform the song in January, 1968.

Musical Legacy

It is impossible to emphasize enough Seeger's major role in the preservation and popularization of American folk music. During the 1930's, he was instrumental in finding and recording important folk songs that would have vanished but for the intervention of Seeger and others. In addition, in the 1930's and 1940's, along with his friend Woody Guthrie, he demonstrated the great power of song to organize and unify people. His songs are part of the history of the labor movement in the United States.

In 1948 Seeger wrote the first version of his classic text, *How to Play the Five-String Banjo*. This book taught generations of young folk musicians how to play and perform this traditional American instrument. Through it, Seeger was able to preserve the techniques and rhythms of traditional musicians, and he nearly single-handedly returned the banjo to the forefront of popular music. During the 1950's Seeger demonstrated his commitment to his political and ethical beliefs, maintaining his integrity while under pressure from powerful political forces. His stalwart defense of his rights, in the face of financial hardship and even jail, demonstrated what one person could do to change an injustice.

Throughout the 1960's and early 1970's, Seeger and his music touched the hearts and minds of the nation. His songs became the sound track for the Civil Rights and antiwar movements. In later years his influence extended to such young performers as Bob Dylan, Springsteen, Ani DiFranco and the Indigo Girls.

From his earliest years, Seeger's ability to effect social change through music was legendary. He supplied the words and music for generations of protesters, and his ability to move people to sing set him apart from other performers. Seeger gave back to the American people their traditional music and songs, and he taught his fellow citizens how to sing out for justice.

Diane Andrews Henningfeld

Further Reading

Dunaway, David King. *How Can I Keep from Singing: Pete Seeger*. New York: McGraw-Hill, 1981. The standard biography of Seeger.

Filene, Benjamin. "Performing the Folk: Pete Seeger and Bob Dylan." In *Romancing the Folk: Public Memory and American Roots Music*. Chapel Hill: University of North Carolina Press, 2000. In telling the stories of the musicologists who collected and preserved American folk music, Filene devotes a chapter to the contributions Dylan and Seeger made to popularizing the American folk heritage.

Hadju, David. "Pete Seeger's Last War: The Grand Old Lion of the American Left Sings to Fight Another Day." *Mother Jones* (September/October, 2004): 74-79. Using biographical and interview materials, Hadju writes about Seeger's protest of the war in Iraq.

Hatch, Robert, and William Hatch. "Pete Seeger." In *The Hero Project: Two Teens, One Notebook, Thirteen Extraordinary Interviews*. New York: McGraw Hill, 2006. When the authors were eleven and thirteen years old, they set out to interview their heroes and write a book. Seeger talks about performing with Paul Robeson and the attack by the Ku Klux Klan that followed.

Seeger, Pete. *Where Have All the Flowers Gone? A Musical Autobiography*. Bethlehem, Pa.: Sing Out Books, 1993. An autobiographical account of Seeger's life, including many photographs and texts of his songs.

Terkel, Studs. "The Discovery of Power: Mike Gecan, Linda Stout, Pete Seeger, and Frances Moore Lappe." In *Hope Dies Last: Keeping the Faith in Difficult Times*. New York: New Press, 2003. In this book of interviews, Terkel tries to make sense of the world after September 11, 2001. He interviews a group of activists, including Seeger, who have taken a stand against tyranny.

Wilkinson, Alec. "The Protest Singer: Pete Seeger and American Folk Music." *The New Yorker*, April 17, 2006: 44-53. A retrospective of Seeger's life and career, identifying Seeger's influence on contemporary artists, including Springsteen.

See also: Belafonte, Harry; Diamond, Neil; Dylan, Bob; Guthrie, Arlo; Guthrie, Woody; Hopkins, Lightnin'; Leadbelly; Lomax, Alan; Odetta; Paxton, Tom; Ritchie, Jean; Seeger, Charles; Seeger, Mike; Seeger, Ruth Crawford; Springsteen, Bruce; Travis, Merle.

Ruth Crawford Seeger

American classical composer

Crawford is known for her modernist musical compositions, which established her as a leading figure in the history of music by women. Through her arrangements, her teaching, and her family, she also exerted a pivotal influence on the American folk-music revival of the middle twentieth century.

Born: July 3, 1901; East Liverpool, Ohio
Died: November 18, 1953; Chevy Chase, Maryland
Also known as: Ruth Porter Crawford (birth name)

Principal works

CHAMBER WORKS: *Music for Small Orchestra*, 1926; Sonata for Violin and Piano, 1926; Suite, 1927 (for five wind instruments and piano); *Diaphonic Suite No. 1*, 1930 (for solo oboe or flute); *Diaphonic Suite No. 2*, 1930 (for two clarinets); *Diaphonic Suite No. 3*, 1930 (for flute); *Diaphonic Suite No. 4*, 1930 (for oboe or viola and cello); *Rat Riddles*, 1930; Suite No. 2, 1930 (for strings and piano); *In Tall Grass*, 1932; *Prayers of Steel*, 1933; String Quartet, 1933 (*1931*); Suite for Wind Quintet, 1952.

CHORAL WORKS: *Chant No. 1: To an Unkind God*, 1930 (for female chorus); *Chant No. 2: To an Angel*, 1930 (for soprano and chorus); *Chant No. 3*, 1930 (for female chorus).

ORCHESTRAL WORK: *Rissolty Rossolty*, 1939.

PIANO WORKS: Five Preludes, 1925; Four Preludes, 1928; Nine Preludes for Piano, 1928; *Piano Study in Mixed Accents*, 1930.

VOCAL WORKS: *Adventures of Tom Thumb*, 1925 (for voice and piano; based on the story by J. L. Grimm and W. C. Grimm); *Five Songs: Home Thoughts; White Moon; Joy; Loam; Sunsets*, 1929 (for voice and piano; based on Carl Sandburg's poetry); *Three Songs*, 1932 (for voice, oboe, percussion, and strings; based on Sandburg's poetry); *Two Ricercari No. 1: Sacco, Vanzetti*, 1932 (for voice and piano; based on H. T. Tsiang's poetry); *Two Ricercari No. 2: Chinaman,*

Laundryman, 1932 (for voice and piano; based on Tsiang's poetry).

WRITINGS OF INTEREST: *American Folk Songs for Children in Home, School, and Nursery School*, 1948; *Animal Folk Songs for Children*, 1950; *American Folk Songs for Christmas*, 1953; *Let's Build a Railroad*, 1954.

The Life

The child of a Methodist minister, Ruth Crawford lived in several Midwestern cities, moving to Jacksonville, Florida, in 1912. At the time of her high school graduation, Crawford took up the conventional occupation of children's piano teacher. Her first works were modest responses to the compositions she found for her young students, although she remained focused on a career in piano performance. She moved to Chicago in 1921 to study piano at the American Conservatory of Music. By 1923 she was studying composition; by 1926 she had become part of a circle of ultramodernist composers, including Henry Cowell, Dane Rudhyar, and the poet Carl Sandburg.

Through Cowell's influence, in 1929 she moved to New York to study composition with Charles Seeger. In 1930 she became the first woman to receive a Guggenheim Fellowship, which enabled her to spend a year in Berlin and Paris. Returning to New York, she began living with Seeger in 1931, and she married him in 1932. The years in New York were heady: Seeger and Crawford's patron Blanche Walton were forming the first American musicological organizations (from whose meetings Crawford and even Walton, as women, were excluded). Crawford helped Seeger complete his theoretical treatise on dissonant counterpoint, probably contributing ideas to it. In the midst of the ongoing economic depression, the couple saw a chance for composition to regain social relevance through use in the workers' movement.

Crawford abruptly stopped composing in 1933. The reasons are many. Never confident of her voice as a composer, she was disappointed with her opportunities following the Guggenheim Fellowship. The first of her four children was born in August, 1933. The family encountered economic hardship and moved in 1936 to Washington, D.C., a city that gave little attention to modern music. The failure of their composed music to move the proletariat led

Crawford and Seeger to shift their musical interests toward folk music. Crawford remained musically active, transcribing and arranging folk songs for a number of publications, teaching folk music at nursery schools, and privately teaching piano to children. In the last years before her untimely death from intestinal cancer, she briefly resumed original composition.

The Music

Crawford's career as a composer was short, and she tended to be modest in her estimation of her own abilities. Perhaps partly for the latter reason, nearly all of her works are for solo instruments, small chamber ensembles, or voice accompanied by piano or chamber ensemble. Her mature music tends strongly toward polyphony, taking the form of several melodic lines operating at once (rather than melody with chordal accompaniment). Coherence arises through the constant transformation of motives: initial notes will often open up a space of pitches that are later filled in with all the available notes of the chromatic scale, using related motives whose shapes grow to fit whatever musical room is available. Crawford avoids repeating pitches until at least five or six notes have passed, usually more, and this partly accounts for the absence of a pitch center such as one finds in tonal music. In addition, Crawford and Charles Seeger embraced the notion that dissonance could be the norm of modern music with occasional consonances treated as incidental, thus reversing a basic principle of tonality.

1922-1924. After a year of piano study in Chicago, Crawford's hopes for a career as a pianist dimmed, and she resolved to broaden her abilities as a musician, receiving technical grounding in composition from Adolf Weidig at the American Conservatory. Crawford's early work as a composition student is in a post-Romantic style, with chords used coloristically and pressing the bounds of tonality (that is, the familiar organization of musical works in major and minor keys).

1925-1929. Crawford's piano studies from 1925 with Djane Lavoie Herz proved decisive in her compositional development. Herz introduced her to the music of Aleksandr Scriabin, and he brought her into the ultramodernist circle of composers— Rudhyar, Cowell, Edgard Varèse, and others—

who helped shape her aesthetic outlook and who promoted her career. In opposition to such neoclassical composers as Aaron Copland, Roger Sessions, and Virgil Thomson, the ultramodernists sought to create truly indigenous American music by eschewing such putatively old-fashioned features as tonality, consonance, and repetition. However, their modernism was not a cerebral rationalism; inspired by Scriabin, they championed Theosophy and other forms of mysticism. Crawford's music from from this period shows the influence of Scriabin in its chord structures, although, unlike Scriabin, by this time Crawford was no longer writing tonal music.

Crawford established herself as a mature, cutting-edge composer quickly. Her 1926 Sonata for Violin and Piano was performed at the first Chicago concert of the International Society for Contemporary Music in 1928, and her Piano Preludes, nos. 6-9, were published in the ultramodernist journal *New Music Quarterly*. During the same year her first two preludes were performed at one of the important Copland-Sessions Concerts in New York. Works that received less notice during this period include *Music for Small Orchestra*, suites for wind quintet and piano and for string quartet and piano, and five songs to texts by Sandburg.

1929-1936. While Crawford's compositional style did not change enormously after her move to New York, certain of its features became more prominent as she studied with Charles Seeger and collaborated in his theoretical work. The melodic lines are shaped according to a basic distinction between line (in which several notes continue changing in the same direction) and twist (in which their direction changes). For example, a passage in which pitch rises throughout a series of notes is a line neume; a passage alternating between rising and falling is a twist neume. Lines and twists operate not only in the realm of pitch but also in dynamics, timbre, tempo, and other domains. (Such parallel organization of multiple musical domains is one way in which her work anticipates that of the post-World War II avant-garde.) Much of the music is organized in verse form (to use Seeger's term), which is to say that the works consist of several sections of similar length (often set apart by double bars in the scores) that are conceived to rhyme with each other.

String Quartet. The four-movement String Quartet exhibits a dissonant counterpoint of melodic lines and twists, and it makes much of dynamic and timbral twists and lines (most notably in passages in which the instruments play long notes, each getting louder and softer at different times). Ellie Hisama has claimed that the way the first violin is set apart from the rest of the quartet and the way the twist lines undercut the third movement's climax both reflect Crawford's consciousness of herself as an outsider in a man's world.

Two Ricercari No. 1 and No. 2. At the height of the Great Depression, Crawford became enthusiastically involved in radical politics. *Two Ricercari No. 1: Sacco, Vanzetti* and *Two Ricercari No. 2: Chinaman, Laundryman* are unique in her oeuvre in their piercing expression of moral outrage, expressed in the language of ultramodernist music. These works were performed at a Workers' Olympiad in May, 1933. Crawford and other ultramodernists thought their music might contribute to proletarian power through its avoidance of the kind of musical stability that they associated with bourgeois culture. However, Crawford and Seeger soon concluded that neoclassicism had carried the day in composition, and that the way toward the proletarian music of the future was through engagement with folk music.

1936-1953. Between 1933 and 1952, Crawford completed only one original composition, *Rissolty, Rossolty*, a brief work for orchestra that sounds more like a hoedown than an ultramodernist composition. During the late 1930's and early 1940's, Crawford transcribed numerous American folk songs for the publications of John and Alan Lomax, an activity she continued in her own published collections starting in 1948. In Crawford's folk-song settings, her personal compositional inclinations are evident in piano accompaniments carefully written to imitate the figurations of folk instruments, such as the guitar or banjo, as well as in the settings' emphasis on harmonic and metrical irregularities found in the originals. This work may appear to be fully removed from Crawford's earlier activity as a composer, but it seems less so when one considerts that Crawford and the Seeger family had developed a notion that folk music was a form of ongoing collective composition. In the introduction to *American Folk Songs for Children*, Crawford explains how children can be part of the folk-composition process. Nevertheless, her lone late composition, the Suite for Wind Quintet, is stylistically of a piece with her compositions of more than two decades earlier.

Musical Legacy

From the first, Crawford's innovative and moving compositions impressed those who encountered them. In particular, the melodic, dynamic, and tempo processes of her String Quartet profoundly influenced composers such as Cowell, Elliott Carter, and John Cage during her lifetime. In addition, through her husband, she seems to have influenced the scale-oriented music theories developed by Joseph Schillinger, Nicolas Slonimsky, and others in New York in the 1930's. In the decades after her death, composers such as George Perle and Morton Feldman continued to be aware of her compositions, but her reputation as a composer was eclipsed by her influence in the area of folk music, as her children's collections were used in many school curricula and her well-known children (notably Mike Seeger, Peggy Seeger, and stepson Pete Seeger) brought many of her ideas about folk music to a wider public. During the 1960's, the children's collections became infrequently used in schools, thanks to changing musical and curricular tastes as well as the efforts of anti-Communist politicians. The feminist movement of the 1970's brought Crawford the composer back into prominence, as composers, performers, and music historians sought to integrate music by women into the classical canon. Crawford continues to hold the attention of scholars and musicians because of her ability to become a first-rate, cutting-edge avant-garde composer, despite restrictions on women and because of her influence within a family of prominent musical scholars and folk musicians.

Alfred W. Cramer

Further Reading

Allen, Ray, and Ellie M. Hisama, eds. *Ruth Crawford Seeger's Worlds: Innovation and Tradition in Twentieth-Century American Music*. Rochester, N.Y.: University of Rochester Press, 2007. An important volume containing chapters by several musicologists and folklorists exploring Crawford's compositional methods, her involvement in the ultramodernist and proletarian movements, her work with folk music, and her legacies in composition and folk music.

Hisama, Ellie M. *Gendering Musical Modernism: The Music of Ruth Crawford, Marion Bauer, and Miriam Gideon.* Cambridge, England: Cambridge University Press, 2001. Hisama devotes more than half of this study to Crawford's compositions, concentrating on how they can be understood in light of her experiences as a woman. The musical analyses are technical, but they are thoroughly explained and accessible to nonspecialists able to read music.

Nicholls, David. *American Experimental Music, 1890-1940.* Cambridge, England: Cambridge University Press, 1990. This source contains a valuable account of Crawford's music viewed in the context of the new music of her time.

Seeger, Ruth Crawford. *American Folk Songs for Children in Home, School, and Nursery School: A Book for Children, Parents, and Teachers.* Garden City, N.Y.: Doubleday, 1948. In the extensive introduction to this anthology, Crawford's discussion of how children learn and use songs amounts to a simple version of her own aesthetic theory.

Straus, Joseph. *The Music of Ruth Crawford Seeger.* Cambridge, England: Cambridge University Press, 1995. A valuable introduction to Crawford's compositional approach, with concise discussions of her significance as a modernist composer and as a woman composer. Much of the musical analysis is quite technical, but the rest of the book is accessible to the general reader.

Tick, Judith. *Ruth Crawford Seeger: A Composer's Search for American Music.* New York: Oxford University Press, 1997. A full-scale biography by a leading authority on Crawford.

See also: Cowell, Henry; Feldman, Morton; Lomax, Alan; Sandburg, Carl; Seeger, Charles; Seeger, Mike; Seeger, Peggy; Seeger, Pete.

Bob Seger

American rock singer, songwriter, and guitarist

With his exquisite songwriting and powerful vocal style, Seger found an enthusiastic audience with his working-class rhythm-and-blues music.

Born: May 6, 1945; Dearborn, Michigan
Also known as: Robert Clark Seger
Member of: The Silver Bullet Band; the Bob Seger System

Principal recordings

ALBUMS (solo): *Mongrel,* 1970; *Brand New Morning,* 1971; *Smokin' O. P.'s,* 1972; *Back in '72,* 1973; *Seven,* 1974; *Beautiful Loser,* 1975; *Face the Promise,* 2006.

ALBUMS (with the Bob Seger System): *Ramblin' Gamblin' Man,* 1968; *Noah,* 1969.

ALBUMS (with the Silver Bullet Band): *Night Moves,* 1976; *Stranger in Town,* 1978; *Against the Wind,* 1980; *The Distance,* 1982; *Like a Rock,* 1986; *The Fire Inside,* 1991; *It's a Mystery,* 1995.

The Life

Robert Clark Seger was born at the Henry Ford Hospital in Dearborn, Michigan, on May 6, 1945, to parents Stewart and Charlotte Seger. His older brother, George, was born in 1941. Seger grew up in the University of Michigan town of Ann Arbor, forty miles west of Detroit. In spite of that distance, Seger's childhood was enriched by the Detroit rock and rhythm-and-blues scene. As a child, he listened to Otis Redding, Little Richard, Wilson Pickett, and James Brown, especially his 1963 album *Live at the Apollo.* When Seger was ten, his father, a part-time musician, left the family to move to California and pursue his musical career. The remaining family moved to the poor and black section of Ann Arbor, where Seger was exposed to black culture and music.

Seger toured relentlessly during the 1970's and 1980's, slowing down in the early 1990's to start a family with his wife, Annette Sinclair. Seger has two children from this marriage, and he cited letting his children, Christopher Cole and Samantha

Char, "see what daddy does" as a major reason for touring for the first time in a decade in 2006.

The Music

Seger's musical career started early and never stopped, except for a brief period when his brother was serving in the military and Seger worked at a clothing store and a pizza parlor to support himself and his mother. He performed in several bands as a teenager, including the three-piece Decibels during high school. When the Decibels played at Seger's junior prom, the applause from the audience convinced Seger to pursue a career in music.

Seger's music grew from the black neighborhoods of Ann Arbor, a combination of rock, rhythm and blues, pop, and country, and until 1976 he met with only regional success, despite his electric stage show and expert songwriting. Seger has made more than fifteen studio albums, starting with several on the Detroit label Hideout Records.

Early Works. As a teenager, Seger played keyboards in a prominent Detroit band, the Underdogs. His first hit single under his own name was "East Side Story," released in August, 1966, on the Hideout label owned by Punch Andrews. The song, however, only succeeded in Detroit, climbing the local chart to number three. After this project, Andrews became Seger's lifelong manager. The single "Heavy Music," released in July, 1967, on Hideout and nationally on Cameo-Parkway Records, featured Seger's raspy and powerful voice and his solo guitar and highlighted the influence of African American rhythm and blues on his style. In September, 1967, Cameo-Parkway folded, preventing national promotion for the single. Andrews tried to sign Seger with Motown Records, but the label thought Seger's sound was too rough. At this time, Seger performed at numerous Detroit-area festivals, sharing the stage with such artists as the Stooges, Muddy Waters, MC5, and Mitch Ryder and the Detroit Wheels.

Ramblin' Gamblin' Man. *Ramblin' Gamblin' Man* was Seger's first album release on Capitol Records, and he would stay with the label for more than two decades (except for a break from 1972 to 1974 when he signed with Andrews's Warner Bros. distributed label, Palladium). The first single promoted from *Ramblin' Gamblin' Man* was a protest song against the Vietnam War called "2 + 2 = ?"

However, the title track, "Ramblin' Gamblin' Man," climbed to number seventeen nationally and hit number one in Detroit. The driving lyrics highlighted Seger's songwriting and performing strengths. "Ivory," the follow-up single, failed to chart above number ninety-seven nationally, discouraging Seger. While he continued to tour nationally, surprisingly he built strong fan bases only in Michigan and Florida.

"Turn the Page." Seger's universal appeal was displayed with the track "Turn the Page" on the album *Back in '72*. It represents the emotions felt by touring musicians—loneliness, aggression, exhaustion, and exhilaration while on stage. "Turn the Page" has been covered by several artists, including Metallica and Marshall Chapman.

Live Bullet. Success came to Seger eight years after *Ramblin' Gamblin' Man* with the release of *Live Bullet* in 1976 on Capitol Records. The two-disc live album was recorded at Detroit's Cobo Hall over two nights in 1975, which were Seger's first arena concerts. Reaching number thirty-four nationally, *Live Bullet* was Seger's first gold record, and it stayed on the national charts for three years.

Night Moves. The album *Night Moves* was released in 1976 on Capitol Records, and it built on the success generated by *Live Bullet*. The album sold more than five million copies, and it sustained a national fan base, the title track reaching number four on the song charts. "Night Moves" is semiautobiographical, describing growing up in the Midwest.

"Old Time Rock & Roll." "Old Time Rock & Roll" was featured in the Tom Cruise movie *Risky Business* (1983). Seger was excited about the project from the start, appreciating the youthful and rebellious nature of the scene in which the song is played, with Cruise dancing around the house wearing little more than his underwear, a shirt, and sunglasses. Starting in the 1980's, Seger licensed his music for use in several major movies, including *Teachers* (1984) and *Forrest Gump* (1994).

Like a Rock. One day, while Seger was meeting with manager Andrews at a diner in Michigan, an automotive worker strode up to Seger and asked why he had never done anything to give back to the motor industry that supported his childhood city. Before that time, Seger had been approached by Chevrolet to license "Like a Rock," but he declined the offer, worried that it would upset his fans, who would not approve of the commercialization of Seger's music. With the support of the auto workers, however, Seger had the motivation to proceed. The series of Chevrolet truck ads featuring "Like a Rock" ran from 1991 to 2004, building Chevrolet's brand identity for its trucks and maintaining national awareness of Seger. The song was part of the album *Like a Rock*, released on Capitol Records.

Musical Legacy

Seger was inducted into the Rock and Roll Hall of Fame on March 15, 2004. He toured in 2006, playing thirty-six shows and grossing almost thirty-one million dollars. His albums have sold tens of millions of copies, and his early recordings on Hideout and Cameo-Parkway are considered collectors' items. His later work found a country audience, especially with *Face the Promise*. With the stage presence of James Brown, the songwriting skills of Van Morrison, and his working-class background, Seger found a way to communicate with his fans in songs about the beauty and pain of living in America.

Jasmine L. Hagans

Further Reading

Carson, David A. *Grit Noise and Revolution: The Birth of Detroit Rock and Roll*. Ann Arbor: University of Michigan Press, 2005. This history of the Detroit rock scene from the early 1950's through the late 1970's includes biographical information about and several pictures of Seger within the context of his hometown.

George-Warren, Holly, and Patricia Romanowski, eds. *The Rolling Stone Encyclopedia of Rock and Roll*. New York: Fireside Books, 1983. A biographical entry on Seger also includes a discography.

White, Timothy. "The Fire This Time: Bob Seger Finally Settles a Fifteen-Year Score with Rock and Roll Success." *Rolling Stone* (May 1, 1980): 38-41. White, who has written several articles on Seger, discusses the artist's success after the release of *Live Bullet* and *Night Moves*.

See also: Brown, James; Little Richard; Morrison, Van; Pickett, Wilson; Redding, Otis; Waters, Muddy.

Andrés Segovia

Spanish classical guitarist

Promoting the guitar on the classical concert stage during the 1920's and 1930's, Segovia stimulated a revival of interest in creating new compositions for the instrument.

Born: February 21, 1893; Linares, Spain
Died: June 2, 1987; Madrid, Spain
Also known as: Andrés Torres Segovia (full name)

Principal works

GUITAR WORKS: Roussel: *Segovia*, 1924; Sor: Compositions for Guitar, 1928; Tárrega: *Danza*, 1928; Tárrega: *Étude*, 1928; Tárrega: *Serenata*, 1928; Bach: *Chaconne*, 1935; Castelnuovo-Tedesco: Concerto in D, 1939; Ponce: *Concierto del sur*, 1941; Villa-Lobos: Concerto for Guitar and Orchestra, 1956; Rodrigo: *Fantasía para un gentilhombre*, 1958.

The Life

As a child Andrés Torres Segovia (ahn-DRAYS seh-GOH-vee-yah) had violin lessons, and he was also exposed to flamenco guitar by his uncle, who enjoyed the music. After moving to Granada, Segovia heard classical music being played on the guitar. He acquired an instrument and tried to teach himself from written sources. Some of the musicians he met tried to steer him toward more conventional classical instruments, such as cello and piano. At the time, despite the efforts of earlier generations of classical guitarists such as Francisco Tárrega, the guitar was largely associated with cheap entertainment, and rigid social stratification acted as a barrier. Such traditions as flamenco were held in low regard by members of the upper economic classes. Segovia, however, never wavered from his goal of performing classical concerts on the guitar. Soon after giving his first public concert in Granada, he moved to Seville and performed concerts there and in nearby cities while still in his teens. During the 1920's, his dreams of legitimacy and the classical world's acceptance of his chosen instrument came true, and he toured internationally for most of the rest of his life.

Segovia lived outside Spain, primarily in South America, during the years of the Spanish Civil War, but after the war was over, he returned occasionally to give concerts, differing from a famous colleague, the cellist Pablo Casals, who stayed away to boycott the repressive government of Francisco Franco (1936-1939). Finally, Segovia moved back to Spain, although by this time he had become an international citizen who spent much time out of the country. His first marriage, from which he had two children, ended in divorce in 1951.

In addition to giving concerts, Segovia did a great deal of teaching. During the 1950's and 1960's, a shift in musical style brought the guitar to the forefront of popular music, and there was an explosion of interest in the instrument. However, Segovia was extremely hostile to the electric guitar, even though many of his new young fans had had their first exposure to the guitar through popular genres that featured that instrument. Although he had gained much of his own knowledge and ability through working independently, Segovia insisted that students not deviate from his own fingerings and details of technique.

In 1961 he married one of his young students, Emilia Corral Sancho. Their son, Carlos Andres, was born when Segovia was seventy-seven. Segovia continued to tour until just before his death from a heart attack at age ninety-four.

The Music

As a young man eager for any kind of resources for classical guitar, Segovia soon encountered the written music of Tárrega and earlier nineteenth century guitarists such as Fernando Sor and Mauro Giulliani. These composer-guitarists provided the bedrock of the young Segovia's repertoire. Although Segovia was largely self-taught, the influence of Tárrega was especially important, because some of Tárrega's former pupils were still active in Spain during Segovia's early years. Tárrega's quest to reestablish the legitimacy of the guitar and his compositional use of Spanish themes inspired the

young man. Segovia, who had watched many flamenco guitarists, was already using his right-hand fingernails for greater articulation and projection, and when he first heard one of Tárrega's former pupils perform without fingernails, which was part of Tárrega's style, Segovia was not impressed. He worked diligently to develop his own approach to right-hand technique, which encompassed the brighter, more percussive technique of the folk traditions as well as the softer sounds of the Tárrega school. Also, Segovia looked beyond the guitar for ideas; he developed part of his approach to left-hand technique through careful observation of his friend Laura Monserrat when she practiced the piano. During the same period, he also studied music theory.

Transcriptions. Segovia was already an accomplished soloist by the time he met Miguel Llobet, one of Tárrega's most prominent students, who was based in Barcelona. According to Segovia's autobiography, Llobet was able to share some of his repertoire by playing it directly for the younger guitarist, phrase by phrase. Like Segovia's, Llobet's right-hand strokes used a combination of fingernails with the flesh of the fingertips. Llobet had also continued Tárrega's work of playing guitar transcriptions and arrangements of masterpieces originally written for other instruments. Segovia

Andrés Segovia. (Library of Congress)

planned concert programs that included pieces by Johann Sebastian Bach, Wolfgang Amadeus Mozart, and Ludwig van Beethoven, along with somewhat less familiar gems by earlier classical guitarists, and that proved to be a valuable strategy during his years of struggle for public recognition of the guitar as a respectable instrument.

New Solo Repertoire. Before Segovia left for his first tour of Latin America in 1920, he was introduced to the composer Moreno Torroba, who wrote a solo piece, Dance in E Major, the first of his many works for guitar. As Segovia's fame and contacts grew, more Spanish composers began to participate in this trend, and Segovia was happy to oblige them, often as a collaborator who edited and adjusted their compositions to take full advantage of the guitar's potential. Manuel de Falla and Joaquín Turina soon contributed solo pieces of their own. Segovia realized that most of the previous century's composers for the guitar had been guitarists themselves, writing primarily for their own instrument, and that this new development of prominent composers writing for guitar without being performers of the instrument was a breakthrough as well as a challenge. Soon, composers from outside Spain added their own voices, most notably Mexico's Manuel Maria Ponce, Italy's Mario Castelnuovo-Tedesco, and Brazil's Heitor Villa-Lobos from Brazil. While each of these composers had a unique style, many of the pieces could be characterized as modal, with rich harmonies and colors, sometimes utilizing motifs from folk traditions.

The Chaconne. With new pieces being created for his guitar by some of the great composers of his era, Segovia no longer had to rely as heavily on transcriptions of works from other instruments. Nevertheless, he loved those pieces, and they continued to delight audiences. He was especially attracted to a famous piece that had yet to be absorbed into the guitar repertoire, the *ciaccona* (or chaconne), the last movement of Bach's Partita in D Minor for solo violin. This challenging theme-and-variations piece was played by the greatest violinists, the single movement usually taking almost fifteen minutes. Johannes Brahms once made a piano arrangement for left hand alone, and years later Ferruccio Busoni made an arrangement for piano, both hands. Soon after Leopold Stokowski's 1930

setting for full orchestra, Segovia began work on a version of this piece for solo guitar. In his own arrangement, Segovia added some doublings to thicken the harmony and kept the original key, using Tárrega's favorite *scordatura* of lowering the sixth string to D. He also modified some of the arpeggio patterns to flow smoothly on the guitar. Although later criticized in some circles for his dramatic rendering, Segovia premiered this transcription in Paris in 1935, and it was enthusiastically received, becoming a staple of his programs.

Guitar Concerti. A few orchestral pieces featuring the guitar had been written in previous centuries, notably by Antonio Vivaldi and Mauro Giuliani. In the mid-twentieth century, many new concerti were written for guitar, and most of these were premiered by Segovia. During World War II, when he was based in Montevideo, Uruguay, he gave the premiere performances of Mario Castelnuovo-Tedesco's Concerto in D and Manuel Ponce's *Concierto del sur*. In the 1950's, he premiered two more famous concerti. Villa-Lobos wrote a concerto for guitar and orchestra, and, in response to Segovia's request, before the piece was performed in 1956, Villa-Lobos added an elaborate cadenza. Joaquín Rodrigo, whose *Concierto de Aranjuez* had been premiered by guitarist Regino Sainz de la Maza in Barcelona during the war, wrote a second piece for Segovia, *Fantasía para un gentilhombre*, which Segovia premiered in 1958.

Musical Legacy

Segovia's productive relationships with major composers for the guitar, including Villa-Lobos, Rodrigo, Torroba, Ponce, and others, led to a significant expansion of the classical guitar repertoire. Having achieved his goal of bringing the guitar out of more intimate settings, he worked with luthiers (those who build and repair stringed instruments) to increase the guitar's volume and projection, so that guitarists could be more easily heard in large concert halls without resorting to amplification. His many world-famous students included John Williams, Alirio Diaz, Christopher Parkening, and Oscar Ghilia.

Ironically, with the guitar firmly established as a serious instrument, subsequent generations of guitarists started to travel back and forth across the borders, which Segovia once guarded so carefully, between classical guitar and vernacular genres. Although many guitarists still study and perform Segovia's transcriptions of Bach and other composers, there is an increase of interest in playing this and related repertoires on the Baroque lute for which it was first composed. Segovia's interpretations of music composed specifically for him were generally more highly regarded than his interpretations of older music. Many of his prolific recordings were reissued on digital media.

Segovia won many awards and honorary degrees over his lifetime, including national medals from Spain, Italy, and Japan and Grammy Awards for recording and lifetime achievements. In 1981 Spain's King Juan Carlos granted him the title of Marques de Salobreña in honor of his cultural contributions. In Linares, the town where Segovia was born, a museum in his name is maintained by the Segovia Foundation, sponsoring concerts, publications, and conferences.

John Myers

Further Reading

Morrish, John, ed. *The Classical Guitar Book: A Complete History.* San Francisco: Backbeat Books, 2002. Includes profiles of Segovia and his most prominent students and luthiers. Includes photographs, glossary, index, and bibliography.

Segovia, Andrés. *Segovia: An Autobiography of the Years 1893-1920.* New York: Macmillan, 1976. Segovia's colorful account of his life, with anecdotes about his adventures, his personal struggles, his friendships, and his encounters with others in the arts and intellectual community during his early career. Includes photographs and index.

Summerfield, Maurice. *The Classical Guitar: Its Evolution, Players, and Personalities Since 1800.* Blaydon on Tyne, England: Ashley Mark, 2003. Comprehensive work with emphasis on biographies. Includes references, photographs, discography, and index.

Wade, Graham, and Gerard Garno. *New Look at Segovia: His Life and His Music.* Pacific, Mo.: Mel Bay, 2000. A good balance to Segovia's autobiography, this work includes Segovia's mature career in the 1950's, providing a modern perspective and political issues. Presents analysis of his characteristic repertoire, with coverage of his ed-

itorial approach. Includes scores, references, and index.

See also: Busoni, Ferruccio; Casals, Pablo; Stokowski, Leopold; Villa-Lobos, Heitor; Williams, John.

Rudolf Serkin

Bohemian classical pianist

Although he had a prodigious performing schedule, pianist Serkin influenced generations of musicians as an administrator at the Curtis Institute of Music and as a cofounder of the Marlboro Music Festival, which promoted chamber music.

Born: March 28, 1903; Cheb, Bohemia (now in Czech Republic)
Died: May 8, 1991; Guilford, Vermont

Principal recordings

ALBUMS: *Bach: Sonata for Violin and Basso Continuo in G Major,* 1929; *Beethoven: Sonata for Violin and Piano No. 3 in E-flat Major, Op. 12,* 1931; *Schubert: Fantasy for Violin and Piano in C Major,* 1931; *Vivaldi: Sonata for Violin and Basso Continuo in A Major, Op. 5,* 1931; *Beethoven: Sonata for Violin and Piano No. 5 in F Major, Op. 25,* 1933; *Sonata for Violin and Piano in F Major—Mozart,* 1937; *Arioso—George Frideric Handel,* 1939; *Bach: Chromatic Fantasia and Fugue in D Minor,* 1950; *Italian Concerto—Bach,* 1950; *Robert Schumann: Trio for Piano and Strings, No. 3 in G Minor, Op. 110,* 1956; *Schumann: Quintet for Piano and Strings in E-flat Major, Op. 44,* 1956; *Bach: Capriccio in B-flat Major—On the Departure of His Most Beloved Brother,* 1957; *Three Favorite Sonatas: Moonlight, Appassionata, and Pathétique,* 1963; *Brahms: Concerto for Piano No. 2 in B-flat Major, Op. 83,* 1966; *Serkin—Bach, Reger, Beethoven,* 1973; *Bach: Goldberg Variations—Aria,* 1976; *Haydn: Sonata for Keyboard No. 59 in E-flat Major,* 1977; *Mozart: Rondo for Piano No. 3 in A Major,* 1977; *Schubert: Sonata for Piano in B-flat Major,* 1977; *Pieces for Piano—Op. 119, No. 1, Intermezzo in B Minor,* 1979; *Brahms: Sonata for*

Cello and Piano in E Minor, Op. 38, 1984 (with Mstislav Rostropovich).

The Life

Rudolf Serkin (SUR-kihn) was born the fifth of eight children to Mordko and Auguste (Schargel) Serkin. By age four, Serkin was able to read music and play piano. Although Serkin's father had declared bankruptcy, he provided his son with piano lessons, first in his hometown with Camilla Taussig and later in Vienna with Richard Robert (who, although he worked in the shadow of the preeminent teacher Theodor Leschetizky, was an important piano pedagogue). Serkin also studied composition with Joseph Marx in Vienna.

Serkin had experienced increasing acclaim by age twelve as a piano prodigy in Vienna, and after he met Adolf Busch in 1920, he became known as both a soloist and collaborator (with Busch). In 1933 Serkin performed for the first time in the United States with the Busch String Quartet. In 1935 Serkin married Busch's daughter Irene, and they later had seven children. (One of them, Peter, became a pianist who specializes in late twentieth century music, especially chamber music, which he performs in the TASHI ensemble.)

Serkin and his family emigrated to America in 1939 to escape the Nazi regime, which was persecuting Jews. He became a professor of piano at the Curtis Institute of Music in Philadelphia, and later, from 1968 to 1976, he became its director. In 1951 Serkin and Busch cofounded the Marlboro Music Festival in Vermont, which has become one of the most respected chamber music training festivals in America. Serkin received the Presidential Medal of Freedom in 1964 and a Grammy Award for Best Chamber Music Performance in 1984 for his performance with cellist Mstislav Rostropovich of Johannes Brahms's Sonata for Cello No. 1 in E Minor (1865).

In 1972 Serkin gave his one-hundredth concert appearance with the New York Philharmonic, performing Brahms's Piano Concerto No. 1 in D Minor (1859). He was made an honorary member of the New York Philharmonic's Symphony Society of New York, sharing this elite status with composers such as Aaron Copland, Igor Stravinsky, and Paul Hindemith. Serkin made his final released recording in 1986, and in 1987 he gave his final Carnegie Hall recital, performing Beethoven's last three sonatas. He died of cancer at age eighty-eight in 1991 at his home in Vermont.

The Music

Following his early lessons, Serkin studied composition from 1918 to 1920 with Arnold Schoenberg in Vienna. At this time, Schoenberg was just formulating his twelve-tone theory, and he strongly influenced his pupil toward atonality. Serkin played only modern music during these two years, often performing free concerts at Schoenberg's Society for the Private Performance of Music. Serkin made a radical and complete break with Schoenberg's style, however, in 1920 (the same year he met Busch), stating he could never love contemporary music. He became instead a champion of the German classic and Romantic composers, especially Ludwig van Beethoven. Nevertheless, Serkin and his colleagues, such as Isaac Stern, would later acknowledge that Schoenberg's complete devotion to

Rudolf Serkin. (Hulton Archive/Getty Images)

the aesthetic ideal of music provided a grounding for Serkin's sublimation of "self" to the music.

Serkin appeared as a concerto soloist in the United States for the first time in 1936 with the New York Philharmonic, conducted by Arturo Toscanini, performing Beethoven's Piano Concerto No. 4 (1808) and Wolfgang Amadeus Mozart's Piano Concerto No. 27 (1791). Reviews in New York described him as "an artist of unusual and impressive talents," combining "the most penetrating analysis with artistic enthusiasm."

His career from this point grew to the point that, at its peak, he annually performed more than sixty recitals and concerto appearances between October and May, in addition to his teaching obligations at the Curtis Institute, his recording schedule with Columbia Records, and his summer obligations at the Marlboro Music Festival. His grueling performance schedule threatened his health on several occasions.

Throughout his performing career, Serkin maintained several professional loyalties: He performed almost exclusively on Steinway pianos (in his later career, he toured with his own piano); he remained a Columbia Records label artist; he remained with Columbia Artists management throughout his career; he performed a Beethoven sonata at every one of his annual Carnegie Hall recitals for more than fifty years; he remained, in general, loyal to German composers—in his entire career it appears he performed only two American compositions: Edward MacDowell's Piano Concerto No. 2 (1890) and Samuel Barber's Piano Sonata (1949), and he recorded only a handful of compositions by composers outside the Austro-Germanic tradition, including Frédéric Chopin's Études, Op. 25 (1837) and Antonín Dvořák's chamber music.

Musical Legacy

Serkin's most important legacy rests with his role in cofounding the Marlboro Music Festival, where professionals and amateurs could engage in the serious study of chamber music. (Later, the festival began to center upon the best talents in the music field.) Serkin influenced generations of musicians with his performances and recordings—particularly of Beethoven's music—and his administrative and artistic roles at the Curtis Institute of Music in Philadelphia.

Serkin strove to apply in his own interpretations what he had once stated was the foundation of his admiration for Toscanini's interpretations, which combined "architecture with passion." Serkin was among the pioneers of the movement in twentieth century interpretation to place priority upon musical truth achieved through a careful study of the score, resulting in a deep understanding of the composer's personality that was brought to life on the stage. While some critics labeled his interpretations cold or stiff, many others shared the opinion of conductor Max Rudolf, who stated of Serkin, "When it came to artistic decisions, he knew no compromise."

Jonathan A. Sturm

Further Reading

Ewen, David. *Men and Women Who Make Music*. New York: The Reader's Press, 1945. This book covers many artists—violinists, pianists, cellists, singers, and conductors. It is an adequate first source for general information on Serkin and his life.

Horowitz, Joseph. *Artists in Exile: How Refugees from Twentieth-century War and Revolution Transformed the American Performing Arts*. New York: Harper, 2008. Well written and provocative, this thorough volume includes references to Serkin and discussions of many other musicians who left their native countries, often fleeing Nazism and Fascism, to live in the United States.

Lehman, Stephen, and Marion Faber. *Rudolf Serkin: A Life*. New York: Oxford University Press, 2003. This biography recounts Serkin's life, with details on his personal life and considerable attention devoted to his affiliation—both professional and personal—with Adolf Busch. In addition, there are interviews with his contemporaries (among them Richard Goode, Eugene Istomin, and Arnold Steinhardt) about his performances, his teaching, and his influence at the Marlboro Music Festival. Includes a listing of Serkin's Carnegie Hall recital dates and a comprehensive discography.

See also: Busch, Adolf; Copland, Aaron; Hindemith, Paul; Levine, James; Ma, Yo-Yo; Rostropovich, Mstislav; Stern, Isaac; Stravinsky, Igor; Toscanini, Arturo.

Joseph Shabalala

South African world music singer-songwriter

An ambassador of South African music, Shabalala is the leading exponent of the South African choral genre of isicathamiya *(meaning "tiptoe guys," or "to walk on one's toes lightly"). His group Ladysmith Black Mambazo has made more than fifty studio recordings, collaborated with numerous international musicians, and performed throughout South Africa and the world.*

Born: August 28, 1941; Ladysmith, South Africa
Also known as: Bhekizizwe Joseph Siphatimandla Mxoveni Mshengu Shabalala (full name)
Member of: Ladysmith Black Mambazo

Principal recordings

ALBUMS (with Ladysmith Black Mambazo): *Induku Kethy*, 1984; *Ulwandle Oluncgwele*, 1985; *Inala*, 1986; *Shaka Zulu*, 1987; *Journey of Dreams*, 1988; *Umthombo Wamanzi*, 1988; *How the Leopard Got His Spots*, 1991 (with Danny Glover); *Two Worlds, One Heart*, 1991; *Inkanyezi Nezazi*, 1992 (*The Star and the Wiseman*); *Zibuyinhlazane*, 1992; *Gift of the Tortoise*, 1994; *Liph' Iqiniso*, 1994; *Thuthukani Ngoxolo*, 1996 (*Let's Develop in Peace*); *Heavenly*, 1997; *Live at the Royal Albert Hall*, 1999; *Thandani*, 1999; *In Harmony*, 2001; *Raise Your Spirit Higher: Wenyukela*, 2003; *No Boundaries*, 2005 (with the English Chamber Orchestra); *Long Walk to Freedom*, 2006; *Ilembe: Honoring Shaka Zulu*, 2007.

The Life

Bhekizizwe Joseph Siphatimandla Mxoveni Mshengu "Bigboy" Shabalala (shah-bah-LAH-lah) was born in 1941 on a farm in Thukela, in the district of Ladysmith, which is located in South Africa's Natal Province. Like his father and grandfather, Joseph grew up as a tenant-laborer on a white man's farm, which allowed his family to occupy a small plot of land. Shabalala attended schools in Mbuzweni and Roosboom, but after his father died

in 1952, Shabalala returned to the farm, where he worked throughout his youth to help support his family.

In 1958 Shabalala joined his first men's chorus, the Durban Choir, and in 1960 he moved to Durban, where he became active in the city's musical circles. It was also at this time that he began composing his own songs. By 1961, he was the leader of an *isicathamiya* group he called Ladysmith Black Mambazo (literally "the black ax of Ladysmith"). They gained regional fame during the 1960's through concerts and radio broadcasts, then through their recording career, which began in 1973. Over the ensuing dozen years, Ladysmith Black Mambazo solidified their place as the most renowned *isicathamiya* group ever.

Thus, by 1985, Shabalala already had an impressive career. In that year, he met and collaborated with American songwriter and lyricist Paul Simon, and his career entered a new stage that would bring his music to an international audience. Ladysmith Black Mambazo was featured on Simon's *Graceland* album (1986) and in the resulting world tour in 1987. The group's next album, *Shaka Zulu*, was popular around the world and won a Grammy Award for Best Traditional World Music Album in 1987. Shabalala and his group had broken a barrier, and thereafter they would release numerous albums, tour all over the world, and continue to receive Grammy nominations. A second Grammy came in 2004, for *Raise Your Spirit Higher: Wenyukela*.

The Music

Shabalala's entire musical career has been devoted to the practice and development of *isicathamiya*, a term meaning "to walk on one's toes lightly." This South African choral genre was born out of urban working camps during the early twentieth century, where men's a cappella groups sang for entertainment, and in all-night concerts and competitions. The essential aesthetic values of the genre embrace not only skilled musical performance but also a highly polished visual performance, including precisely choreographed movements and the impeccable physical appearance of the performers.

Unlike other performers of *isicathamiya* before him, Shabalala became a full-time musician and chose to focus on the performance of original compositions. His numerous compositions reflect the various aspects of his identity: The sounds of farm animals from his youth are used as musical sound effects, his Zulu heritage is reflected in the language and in the songs and the stories they tell, and his conversion to Christianity motivates the overall message of peace, forgiveness, and praise that enlivens his songs.

Early Works. All of the fundamental musical qualities of *isicathamiya* can be found in Shabalala's early works. A call-and-response texture between Shabalala and the group dominates. Melodies are placed within Western European triadic harmonies and rely heavily on tonic, subdominant, and dominant harmonic progressions. The quintessential form of a song, such as "Nomathemba" (a girl's name), begins with a pronouncement of text in declamatory style and homophonic texture, sung by the entire group. Following this is an extended section in which the group sings a repeated phrase while Shabalala sings an elaborating lead melody.

Joseph Shabalala. (AP/Wide World Photos)

Shabalala also attempted to modernize *isicathamiya*. His stylistic reforms of the genre include developing a feel of lightness in the group's tiptoe-style choreography and the overall timbre of the voices, as well as a narrative continuity in his song texts.

"Homeless." Knowing that he wanted to collaborate with Ladysmith Black Mambazo, Paul Simon recorded a demo of "Homeless" in which he approximated the group's style. He then sent the demo to the group before he met them in London to record in 1985. While there, Shabalala and the group took Simon's original tune and transformed it into an *isicathamiya* song, adding Zulu words. "Homeless" was Ladysmith Black Mambazo's feature track on *Graceland*, and for the international community it became their hallmark song.

Shaka Zulu. This 1987 album was the group's first release after *Graceland* and was produced by Simon. Collaboration with Simon did not have the effect of radically transforming the sound of Shabalala's music. The music on this album retains all the characteristics of basic *isicathamiya*. In fact, a number of the songs on the album were in the Ladysmith Black Mambazo songbook prior to 1985. The album does, however, have a greater number of songs using the English language, and Zulu words have been translated into English, signaling the intention of the album to reach audiences outside South Africa.

Raise Your Spirit Higher: Wenyukela. In 1975, Shabalala converted to Christianity and later became an ordained minister in the Church of God. His spirituality figures prominently in his compositional themes, as can be heard in numerous songs on this album from 2003, such as "Wenyukela" (raise your spirit higher), "Uqinisil' Ubada" (Lord is the light and truth), and "Udidekil' Umhlaba" (Lord's work).

Musical Legacy

Not only is Joseph Shabalala the most famous composer of *isicathamiya*; his influence has helped shape its present sound. Ladysmith Black Mambazo is the most successful ensemble in the history of the genre and has brought the sound of this South African genre to the attention of the rest of the world. Throughout his sixty-year career, Shabalala has collaborated with numerous international musicians in various styles such as jazz, pop, and rock. His focus, however, remains on his heritage. In the late 1990's, Shabalala began the Mambazo Foundation for South African Music and Culture, with the goal of opening a music academy in his homeland. Through the academy, he made it possible to pass on the culture, traditions, and music of his homeland to new generations of South Africans.

Mark C. Samples

Further Reading

Erlmann, Veit. *Music, Modernity, and the Global Imagination: South Africa and the West.* New York: Oxford University Press, 1999. Erlmann reckons with the myriad inter-relationships of global culture, with a focus in part 2 on Ladysmith Black Mambazo and *Graceland*.

_____. *Nightsong: Performance, Power, and Practice in South Africa.* Chicago: University of Chicago Press, 1996. An ethnomusicological treatment of *isicathamiya*, including a history and discography of the genre, as well as a biography of Shabalala.

Muller, Carol Ann. *South African Music: A Century of Traditions in Transformation.* Santa Barbara, Calif.: ABC-Clio, 2004. A history of South African music in the twentieth century that provides context for Shabalala's work and describes Ladysmith Black Mambazo in concert.

Thembela, Alex J., and Edmund P. M. Radebe. *The Life and Works of Bhekizizwe Joseph Shabalala and the Ladysmith Black Mambazo.* Pietermaritzburg, South Africa: Reach Out, 1993. The first substantial biography of Shabalala, based in large part on interviews with the musician.

See also: Makeba, Miriam; Masekela, Hugh; Simon, Paul.

Tupac Shakur
American rapper

Shakur is widely regarded as one of the most important figures in gangsta rap. He created a new kind of rap focused on voicing the social, political, racial, and economic difficulties of urban African Americans. Shakur's rapping focused on the identity of urban African Americans using a raw street language combined with a rhythm-driven music that combined rhyming spoken words and borrowed sounds (samples) from earlier popular music.

Born: June 16, 1971; New York, New York
Died: September 13, 1996; Las Vegas, Nevada
Also known as: Tupac Amaru Shakur (full name); Lesane Parish Crooks (birth name); 2Pac; Makaveli
Member of: Digital Underground

Principal recordings

ALBUMS (solo): *2Pacalypse Now*, 1991; *Strictly 4 My N.I.G.G.A.Z.*, 1993; *Me Against the World*, 1995; *All Eyez on Me*, 1996; *The Don Kiluminati: The 7 Day Theory*, 1996 (under the pseudonym Makaveli); *R U Still Down?*, 1997; *Still I Rise*, 1999 (with Outlawz); *Until the End of Time*, 2001; *Better Dayz*, 2002; *Tupac: Resurrection*, 2003; *Loyal to the Game*, 2004; *Pac's Life*, 2006; *Beginnings: The Lost Tapes, 1988-1991*, 2007.

ALBUMS (with Digital Underground): *This Is an E. P. Release*, 1990; *Sons of the P.*, 1991.

The Life

Tupac Amaru Shakur (TEW-pahc shah-KEWR) was born Lesane Parish Crooks on June 16, 1971, in New York City. His mother, Afeni Shakur, was a member of the Black Panthers. Shakur's family moved to Baltimore in 1984, and he attended the Baltimore School of the Arts as a teenager. During his studies there, Shakur developed his skills in writing and acting. Before Shakur graduated, his mother moved the family to Marin County, California. Shakur eventually dropped out of high school and was hired in 1990 as a dancer and roadie for the up-and-coming rap group Digital Underground. His success with Digital Underground led to his first solo recording, *2Pacalypse Now*.

In October, 1990, Shakur filed a civil suit against the Oklahoma Police Department (OPD), alleging that OPD police officers had beaten him for jaywalking. The suit was later settled for forty-two thousand dollars. Shakur's public fame increased in 1992 with his role in the film *Juice*, which led to a lead role in *Poetic Justice* in 1993. His success in 1993 continued with the release of his second solo album, *Strictly 4 My N.I.G.G.A.Z.* While earning respect for his acting and rapping, Shakur also had legal difficulties. He was arrested in 1992 after his involvement in a fight that resulted in the accidental shooting death of a child; charges against Shakur were later dismissed. In 1993 he was charged with shooting two off-duty police officers in Atlanta, and again the charges were dismissed. In 1994 he was sentenced to fifteen days in jail for assaulting film director Allen Hughes. In 1995, he was shot during a mugging attempt as he entered a recording studio in New York City. Shakur was next sentenced to four and one-half years in prison for the sexual assault of a female fan. Shakur would serve eight months of the sentence. Marion "Suge" Knight, president of Death Row Records, posted $1.4 million for his release. After his release from prison, Shakur began work on *All Eyez on Me*, his first recording for Death Row Records.

In the mid-1990's, Shakur appeared in two films, *Bullet* (1996) and *Gridlock'd* (1997). Before the latter was released, however, he was shot four times while riding in Knight's car in Las Vegas, after attending a boxing match at the MGM Grand Hotel. Although he was hospitalized, Shakur died four days later. His murder was not solved. Six months later, rival rapper Christopher Wallace (also known as the Notorious B.I.G.) was murdered under similar circumstances.

Shakur's notoriety increased after his death, and a series of posthumous recording releases followed, among them *The Don Kiluminati: The 7 Day Theory* (issued under the alias Makaveli), *R U Still Down?*, *Still I Rise* (1999, with Outlawz), *Until the End of Time, Better Dayz, Tupac: Resurrection, Loyal to the Game, Pac's Life*, and *Beginnings: The Lost Tapes, 1988-1991*.

The Music

Shakur espoused a concept he called "thug life" in his music. Shakur used the term "thug" to de-scribe not criminals but rather individuals who had made successful lives for themselves in spite of their oppressive surroundings. While the messages in his raps were often about individual pride and civic responsibility, the events of his life seem to contradict those ideals.

In some raps, Shakur glamorized the life of the gangsta as a high-living, macho criminal boasting about wealth and status in a criminal society. In many other raps, however—often on the same albums—Shakur portrayed the gangsta life as a desperate, self-destructive existence of fear and sudden death. He depicted the gangsta life as a vicious cycle, an inevitable and self-destructive response to racism, ghetto poverty, and police brutality.

2Pacalypse Now. Shakur's first solo recording, *2Pacalypse Now*, was publicly criticized for graphic language and descriptions of violent acts against law enforcement. U.S. vice president Dan Quayle began a broad public critique of Hollywood film and popular music after a teenager listening to *2Pacalypse Now* killed a Texas state trooper. This first solo album includes the contradictory messages that typify Shakur's recordings. The album includes "Brenda's Got a Baby," a tender story of a struggling teen mother's experience, and "I Don't Give a F***," a racially charged and violent rant against law enforcement.

"Words of Wisdom" expresses the mistrust that Shakur's generation of urban African Americans felt about the historical emphasis on Dr. Martin Luther King, Jr. Shakur questions King's pacifying message and his vision of the American dream, while extolling the more militant Malcolm X and taking the American education system to task for omitting the latter in history books:

No Malcolm X in my history text
Why is that?
Cause he tried to educate and liberate all blacks
Why is Martin Luther King in my book each week?
He told blacks, if they get smacked, turn the other cheek
. . . .
The American dream, though it seems it's attainable
They're pulling your sleeve, don't believe

Strictly 4 My N.I.G.G.A.Z. "Keep Ya Head Up" is widely regarded one of Shakur's most meaningful and influential raps. Shakur's message promotes respect for African American women in general and African American mothers in particular. The works most prominently sampled in "Keep Ya Head Up" are the main rhythm parts, borrowed from "Be Alright" by Zapp, and "Ooh Child," borrowed from the group Five Stairsteps and used for the backing vocal parts in the chorus.

Me Against the World. *Me Against the World* includes "If I Die 2Nite" and "Death Around the Corner," and both express Shakur's sense of mortality and foretell his death. The final chorus of "If I Die 2Nite" ends with a morbid prophecy:

I hope they bury me and send me to my rest
Headlines readin murdered to death, my last breath
Take a look picture a crook on his last stand
don't understand, if I die tonight

All Eyez on Me. Shakur's first recording on Death Row Records was made after his release from prison. Shakur's message had changed from the earlier focus on social resistance to an expression of his own relationships. "I Ain't Mad at Cha" includes another of Shakur's prophetic statements about his own death. Here he recounts his rise to glory and his predicted demise:

He went from a nobody nigga
To the big man on the block
He's mister local celebrity
Addicted to move a key
Most hated by the enemy
Escaping the luxury
See, first you was our nigga
But you made it
So the choice is made
Now we gotta slay you

Shakur was also self-consciously determined not to be labeled a commercial sell-out who had abandoned his cultural heritage:

So many questions
And they ask me if I'm still down
I moved out of the ghetto
So I ain't real now?
They got so much to say
But I'm just laughin at ya
You niggas just don't know
But I ain't mad at cha

The piece "California Love" from this album was one of Shakur's biggest commercial hits. Featuring Dr. Dre and Zapp singer Roger Troutman,

"California Love" samples a riff from Joe Cocker's "Woman to Woman."

The Don Killuminati: The 7 Day Theory. Released after Shakur's death, this is the final album he completed. For this recording, Shakur adopted the pseudonym Makaveli, reportedly derived from the Italian political theorist Niccolò Machiavelli, whose works he read while in prison. The album produced three hits; "To Live and Die in LA," "Hail Mary," and "Toss It Up."

Musical Legacy

Shakur and other gangsta rappers asserted their independence from the pacifying influence of the recording industry by forming their own recording labels, including Knight's Death Row Records, which recorded Shakur's final albums. After the deaths of Wallace and Shakur, the formerly dominant influence of the East and West Coast gangsta rap labels dissipated. Shakur's musical influence may be heard in recordings by the rap duos Out-Kast and and Kris Kross. Shakur's music is also sampled in recordings by numerous rappers and other prominent musicians including Eminem, Nas, Toni Braxton, Beyoncé, and Jay-Z.

Shakur received numerous awards: He was inducted into the Hip-Hop Hall of Fame in 2002, he was honored as the number-one emcee by MTV in its Twenty-two Greatest MCs program in 2003, he was honored by VH1 television at its Hip Hop Honors in 2004, and he was rated as the greatest rapper of all time by *Vibe* magazine in 2004. The Tupac Amaru Shakur Foundation and the Tupac Amaru Shakur Center for the Arts in Stone Mountain, Georgia, memorialize his life.

David Steffens

Further Reading

Dyson, Michael Eric. *Holler if You Hear Me: Searching for Tupac Shakur*. New York: Basic Civitas Books, 2001. Dyson places Shakur and gangsta rap in social and historical context by exploring Shakur's life as a microcosm of black American life and culture.

Forkos, Heather. *Tupac Shakur*. Philadelphia: Chelsea House, 2001. An extensive biographical account of Shakur's life.

Joseph, Jamal. *Tupac Shakur Legacy*. New York: Atria Books, 2006. A biographical account of

Shakur's life with removable reproductions of handwritten lyrics, notebook pages, and other personal memorabilia, as well as *Tupac Shakur Speaks*, a sixty-minute compact disc featuring interviews with Shakur.

Light, Alan, ed. *The Vibe History of Hip Hop*. New York: Three Rivers Press, 1999. Danyel Smith's chapter "Tupac Shakur" is focused on Shakur's artistic output as rapper and actor.

McWhorter, John. "Something 2 Die 4?" *New Republic* 225, no. 17 (October 22, 2001): 30-36. A review of Dyson's book *Holler if You Hear Me*.

Quinn, Eithne. *Nuthin' but a "G" Thang: The Culture and Commerce of Gangsta Rap*. New York: Columbia University Press, 2005. Quinn explores the origins, development, and popularity of gangsta rap, explaining how and why this music genre emerged by focusing discussion on Ice Cube, Dr. Dre, the Geto Boys, Snoop Dogg, and Tupac Shakur. The book includes discussions of urban geography, nonconservative politics, subcultural formations, black cultural debates, and music industry conditions.

Shakur, Tupac, Jacob Hoye, and Karolyn Ali. *Tupac: Resurrection, 1971-1996*. New York: Atria Books, 2003. Entirely in Shakur's own words, this book, a companion to the documentary film of the same name, reveals much about Shakur's childhood, career, and prison time. Includes numerous photographs.

See also: Combs, Sean; Dr. Dre; Eminem; Hammer, M. C.; Notorious B.I.G.

Ravi Shankar

Indian world music composer and sitar player

A central figure in bringing together the East and the West, Shankar exposed the world to Indian classical music, dazzling audiences and other musicians with his amazing musicianship and gentle personality.

Born: April 7, 1920; Varanasi, Uttar Pradesh, India

Also known as: Pandit Ravi Shankar (full name); Robindro Shankar Chowdhury (birth name); Robu

Principal works

FILM SCORES: *Pather Panchali*, 1955; *The Sword and the Flute*, 1959; *The Psychedelics*, 1966; *Charly*, 1968; *Sex and the Animals*, 1969; *Gandhi*, 1982; *Genesis*, 1986.

Principal recordings

ALBUMS: *Three Ragas*, 1956; *Improvisations*, 1962 (with others); *India's Master Musician*, 1963; *Ragas and Talas*, 1964; *The Genius of Ravi Shankar*, 1966; *At the Monterey International Pop Festival*, 1967; *Sound of the Sitar*, 1965; *West Meets East: The Historic Shankar/Menuhin Sessions*, 1967 (with Yehudi Menuhin); *In New York*, 1968; *A Morning Raga/An Evening Raga*, 1968; *The Sounds of India*, 1968; *The Concert for Bangladesh*, 1971 (with others); *Räga-Mälä (Sitar Concerto No. 2)*, 1982; *Pandit Ravi Shankar*, 1986; *Tana Mana*, 1987; *Inside the Kremlin*, 1988; *Passages*, 1990 (with Philip Glass); *Farewell, My Friend*, 1992; *Chants of India*, 1997 (with George Harrison); *From India*, 1997 (with Ali Akbar Khan); *Raga Jogeshwari*, 1998; *Four Ragas*, 2000; *Spirit of India*, 2005.

The Life

Robindro Shankar Chowdhury was born to Brahman father Shyam Shankar Chowdhury and mother Hemangini. With an absent father, Robu, as he was nicknamed, the youngest of four sons, was raised by his mother. At the age of ten, Shankar moved with his mother to Paris, where his eldest brother, Uday, was a professional dancer with a dance and music troupe that toured throughout Europe and North America. As a result, Shankar was exposed to Western culture, and he became a talented dancer. In 1935 the troupe engaged the classical virtuoso Ustad Allaudin Khan to accompany the dancers. Immediately, Shankar's interest in music grew, and he decided to leave the dance troupe to devote his life to learning Indian classical music.

In 1938 Shankar moved to Maihar, where he became a student of Khan, entering into the traditional guru-disciple relationship, the primary

Ravi Shankar. (AP/Wide World Photos)

means for learning to master Indian classical music. For his training Shankar was required to practice for up to twelve hours a day, to meditate, to pray, and to worship not only the music but also his guru. After seven years of intense preparation, Shankar, now known as Ravi, became a virtuoso, and he began playing public concerts. In 1941 he married Khan's daughter, Annapurna, though they later divorced. Additionally, Shankar befriended Khan's son, Ali Akbar, with whom he would later collaborate and with whom he would tour.

In the 1940's, Shankar toured throughout India, and then he began composing music for films and ballets. By the end of the decade, he had become the music director for All India Radio, and he had formed the Indian National Orchestra. This continued through the early 1950's, during which time Shankar composed the music for the film *Pather*

Panchali, which garnered worldwide exposure. Following this, Shankar decided to take his music abroad, and in 1956 he made appearances in Europe and in America. In this way, Shankar exposed Western audiences, including jazz and classical musicians, to Indian classical music. Shortly after, he began collaborating with Yehudi Menuhin and André Previn, and he began instructing John Coltrane, Don Ellis, and others in the intricacies of Indian music.

The 1960's brought Shankar to an even wider audience. The Beatles' George Harrison met Shankar in 1966, and the two began a friendship that included Harrison becoming a student of Shankar. The relationship between Harrison and Shankar brought huge success to Shankar and brought new interest in Indian music to Western audiences. In 1967 Shankar appeared at the Monterey Pop Festival and then later at Woodstock in 1969. The association with Harrison also enabled Shankar to organize a benefit concert for the refugees of Bangladesh. The concert, which took place in 1971, was a success, and Shankar had the opportunity to play in front of a sold-out audience in Madison Square Garden.

Following these large events, Shankar went back to focusing on playing traditional Indian concerts, because he did want to harm the reputation of Indian music by playing to only Western audiences. So Shankar went back to India for most of the 1970's, before continuing his fusion experiments in the 1980's. He composed another concerto for sitar, he collaborated on more film projects, including the Academy Award-nominated score for *Ghandi*, and he delved into electronic music.

As the twentieth century came to a close, Shankar continued to tour internationally, introducing his daughter Anoushka to the world stage, and he also published his autobiography, *Raga Mala*. He received more than a dozen honorary doctorates and numerous awards, including three Grammy Awards. He continues to write, record, perform, and teach with the same vigor that brought him initial success.

The Music

While much of Shankar's oeuvre consists of authentic performances of Indian classical music on sitar, he also spent considerable time composing and conducting music that fused Indian classical elements with Western music aspects. His recorded catalog spans more than fifty years, and it includes numerous live-performance recordings, which showcase his spontaneous and impassioned improvisatory style. Many of these recordings appear to be aimed at Western listeners, incorporating short introductory vocal tracks explaining the elements of Indian classical music, abbreviated raga expositions, lively percussion displays, and spirited call-and-response sections. With the fusion recordings, Western musical instruments accompany Indian ones, sometimes in the format of an improvised musical dialogue between players, sometimes in fully composed orchestrated suites. Shankar also composed music for films and ballets, which brought him worldwide recognition. Throughout all of his efforts, Shankar's virtuosity, creativity, and reverence for the music is apparent.

Three Ragas. Released in 1956, this is Shankar's first recording for Western ears. Consisting of condensed performances of three different ragas, this recording serves as an important introduction to Indian classical music. Each track begins with brief, unaccompanied sitar expositions of the raga, moving on to rapid melodic and rhythmic explorations of the raga, which build to a peak before the entrance of the tabla. With the addition of percussion, Shankar dives into precomposed gats (songs), that highlight the improvisational interplay among the musicians, culminating in exhilarating peaks of musical exchange.

Improvisations. With this album, released in 1962, Shankar records some of the first examples of jazz-fusion. On the track "Fire Night," jazz flutist Bud Shank and bassist Gary Peacock accompany Shankar in what could be described as a jam session. Important on this album is Shankar's recording of a south Indian raga, "Karnataki." Being steeped in the north Indian music tradition, it was not customary or proper for a musician to borrow a raga from the Carnatic tradition, so this further exemplifies Shankar's all-inclusive view of music, which helped bridge not only East and West, but also India's north and south.

At the Monterey International Pop Festival. Recorded live on the last day of a musical festival that included the Who and Jimi Hendrix, this album shows the moment that Shankar captured the attention of Western audiences and also of several big-name musicians. Beginning each piece with a short description of the music to be played, Shankar warmly invites the audience into his world, before exciting their ears with his playing. Highlights of this record include the tabla solo by Alla Rakha, and the following dhun (instrumental), in which Shankar and Rakha bring about an exhilarating climax with their back-and-forth rhythmic and melodic dialogue.

West Meets East: The Historic Shankar/Menuhin Sessions. The Grammy Award-winning album for Best Chamber Music Performance of 1967, *West Meets East: The Historic Shankar/Menuhin Sessions* brings two of the world's greatest classical musicians together for a historic recording. Yehudi Menuhin, a Western classical violinist, who had come to appreciate the nuances of Indian classical music, collaborates with Shankar on this and two subsequent albums. The album, while neither completely Western nor completely Indian, creates a true fusion of two music traditions. Menuhin's violin work, which aims to mimic the intricacies of Indian melodic embellishment, complements Shankar's modest playing, showcasing the mutual respect the men had for each other.

The Concert for Bangladesh. Another Grammy Award-winning contribution from Shankar, the album features performances not only from Shankar but also from Harrison and other popular musicians of the time. Recorded as part of a fundraising effort for the refugees of Bangladesh, the concert was the idea of Shankar, but it was brought to fruition through the help of Harrison. For the concert, Shankar opened the show with a lively performance with sarodist Khan. The two men, accompanied by Rakha on tabla, and Kamala Chakravaty on tamboura, presented "Bangla Dhun," a light classical piece based on Bengali folk tunes. Beginning with a typical, slow exposition of the raga and continuing on to an energetic call-and-response section between the sitar and sarod, the instrumentalists brought the crowd to its feet, setting the mood for the important benefit concert.

Rāga-Mālā (Sitar Concerto No. 2). This is Shankar's second attempt at composing a Western classical-style concerto for sitar and orchestra. Recorded in 1982 and conducted by Zubin Mehta, the concerto was received well by audiences and critics. The title refers to the mixture of ragas used in the concerto, literally translated garland of ragas. Each movement of the concerto utilizes a different raga, with Shankar, accompanied by a full Western orchestra, improvising and also playing composed flourishes. The album shows Shankar's prowess not only as a musician but also as a composer.

Tana Mana. Released in 1987, this album explores Shankar's interest in fusing electronic instruments with traditional Indian instruments. Using a combination of sitar, sarod, tabla, and tamboura with synthesizers, electric bass, guitar, and also vocals, Shankar composes short but dynamic pieces. The pieces incorporate many Indian classical elements, such as odd metered rhythmic cycles, improvised melodic passages, and vocal percussion and solfège syllables.

Passages. With this album, Shankar collaborates with American minimalist composer Philip Glass. For some of the pieces the composers orchestrate each other's melodies, so the lines between East and West become somewhat blurred, creating a true amalgamation of classical styles. The combination of instruments echoes this through the use of orchestral strings, woodwinds, and brass in conjunction with Indian traditional instruments and vocals. Nevertheless, the distinct style of each composer shines through, with Glass's haunting atmospheres supporting Shankar's melodies, and Shankar's complex rhythmic structures accentuating Glass's themes.

Musical Legacy

Shankar's influence is pervasive within many genres of music. His influence on Harrison brought about the explosion of the popularity of the sitar of the 1960's, which was exemplified in the use of Indian instruments and phrasing in pop music. In the realm of jazz, his influence is still being felt through the use of atypical rhythmic cycles and long, exploratory solos, such as those found in the music of Coltrane and his successors. Within Western classical music, the use of non-Western instruments was nothing new, yet Shankar was able to bring about authentic fusion through his inspired compositions and creativity. Shankar's students, which include his own daughter, jazz musicians, classical composers, vocalists, and other instrumentalists, carry his teachings and music to a new generation, ensur-

ing that the influence of Indian music on the West continues. Additionally, Shankar is regarded in India as one of its greatest cultural ambassadors, which earned him the Bharat Ratna, the highest civilian award in India.

Gabriel Weiner

Further Reading

Farrell, Gerry. "Indian Elements in Popular Music and Jazz." In *Indian Music and the West.* New York: Oxford University Press, 1997. A brief biography of Shankar accompanies an examination of how his influence on the Beatles and on several jazz musicians came to fruition. Analyses of Western music, which incorporate Indian classical music elements, are included with musical notation.

Lavezzoli, Peter. *The Dawn of Indian Music in the West.* New York: Continuum, 2006. An excellent collection of essays and interviews that explore the influence of Indian classical music in the West. Includes photographs and an interview with Shankar.

Neuman, Daniel M. *The Life of Music in North India: The Organization of an Artistic Tradition.* Detroit, Mich.: Wayne State University Press, 1980. Supported by extensive field research, this text explores the role of musicians within the culture and society of northern India. This is an important study in the background and development of musicians, such as Shankar.

Shankar, Anoushka. *Bapi . . . The Love of My Life.* New Delhi: Roli Books, 2002. A personal and poignant biography of Shankar from the point of view of his daughter. The book is filled with rare photographs, handwritten correspondence, and humorous anecdotes.

Shankar, Ravi. *My Music, My Life.* New York: Simon & Schuster, 1968. Shankar's first autobiography includes a history of and explanation of Indian classical music, with numerous photographs of Shankar and of various musical instruments. Additionally, the text contains an introduction to learning the sitar, complete with diagrams and music notation.

_____. *Raga Mala: The Autobiography of Ravi Shankar.* New York: Welcome Rain, 1999. Another autobiography that expands on Shankar's life, including rare photographs, personal correspondence, quotes from Harrison, Menuhin, and Shankar's wife, as well as a detailed chronology of his life.

See also: Butterfield, Paul; Coltrane, John; Glass, Philip; Harrison, George; Khan, Ali Akbar; Menuhin, Sir Yehudi; Previn, Sir André; Slick, Grace.

Artie Shaw

American jazz clarinetist and composer

An accomplished clarinetist in both swing and classical music styles, Shaw shaped the course of jazz history during the big band era of the 1930's and 1940's.

Born: May 23, 1910; New York, New York
Died: December 30, 2004; Thousand Oaks, California
Also known as: Arthur Jacob Arshawsky (birth name); King of Swing

Principal recordings

ALBUMS: *For You, for Me, Forever*, 1946; *Artie Shaw Dance Program*, 1949; *Modern Music for Clarinet*, 1949; *Artie Shaw Plays Cole Porter*, 1950; *Later Artie Shaw, Vol. 1*, 1949; *Later Artie Shaw, Vol. 2*, 1950; *Later Artie Shaw, Vol. 3*, 1950; *Artie Shaw Favorites*, 1952; *Four Star Favorites*, 1952; *Later Artie Shaw, Vol. 4*, 1953; *Artie Shaw with Strings*, 1954; *I Can't Get Started*, 1954; *Later Artie Shaw, Vol. 5*, 1954; *Later Artie Shaw, Vol. 6*, 1954; *Later Artie Shaw, Vol. 7*, 1954; *Sequence in Music*, 1954; *Artie Shaw Hour*, 1955; *Back Bay Shuffle*, 1956; *Both Feet in the Groove*, 1956; *Did Someone Say Party?*, 1956; *Any Old Time*, 1957; *Dancing on the Ceiling*, 2002; *Goodnight Angel*, 2003.
SINGLES: "Any Old Time," 1938; "Begin the Beguine," 1938; "Nightmare," 1938; "Traffic Jam," 1939; "The Blues," 1940; "Concerto for Clarinet," 1940; "Frenesi," 1940; "Star Dust," 1940; "Summit Ridge Drive," 1940; "Moon Glow," 1941; "Evensong," 1942; "Suite No. 8," 1942; "Little Jazz," 1945; "September Song," 1945.

WRITINGS OF INTEREST: *The Trouble with Cinderella: An Outline of Identity*, 1952 (autobiography); *I Love You, I Hate You, Drop Dead!*, 1997 (autobiography).

The Life

Artie Shaw was born Arthur Arshawsky in New York on May 23, 1910, to Jewish parents Harry and Sarah. At age seven, the family moved to New Haven, Connecticut. After his father deserted them, Shaw supported the family as a saxophonist with the Johnny Caverello Orchestra. Soon he switched to the clarinet, and he embarked on a long career with various dance orchestras. His first bandleader appearance in 1936 at Broadway's Imperial Theatre ignited his career. The Artie Shaw Orchestra earned sixty thousand dollars a week in 1938, and, following the recording of "Begin the Beguine," Shaw was anointed the new King of Swing. Superstardom was troublesome for Shaw, compelling him to abandon the music business periodically throughout his life.

In World War II, Shaw led a Navy Service Band, and later in the 1940's he toured with symphony orchestras. In the 1950's, Shaw formed more big bands and combos, but he abandoned his clarinet permanently in 1954. He moved to Spain, Connecticut, and finally California. Shaw avoided the music business in his later years except for a few media appearances. In the 1980's, he fronted a new orchestra, but he did not perform himself. After a lifetime of musical artistry and eight wives, Shaw died from the complications of diabetes at age ninety-four.

The Music

The big band era of the 1930's produced several gifted musicians and personalities, and Shaw stood out as one of the most colorful and adventurous of them all. Although he enjoyed immense popularity and financial success, Shaw deplored the industry that made him so successful.

Early Career. Shaw began his career at age fourteen, and a year later was traveling the country with dance orchestras. His first experience with a top orchestra was with violinist Austin Wylie in Cleveland. In 1929 he joined Irving Aaronson's Commanders in Hollywood, and was listening to such composers as Béla Bartók and Igor Stravinsky, which prompted him to experiment with string instruments in jazz settings.

Big Bands. By 1934 Shaw was already disillusioned with the music industry, and he bought a farm in Pennsylvania, where he began to write. The hiatus was short, and he returned to lead a combo at Chicago's Imperial Theatre. Using a string quartet, bass, drums, and his clarinet, Shaw impressed the audience enough to receive financial support to form his own full-size orchestra. After continuing to experiment with more unusual instrument combinations, Shaw organized a conventional big band that united outstanding musicians of the day. The 1938 recording of Cole Porter's "Begin the Beguine" was a blockbuster that elevated Shaw's status to that of rival Benny Goodman.

When his grueling schedule had caused him to collapse from exhaustion onstage during a concert, Shaw moved to Mexico, seeking peace and happiness. Just two months later, Shaw was recording again with a thirty-two-piece orchestra that produced another hit, "Frenesi." This orchestra had the full complement of woodwinds, French horns, and strings, in addition to the usual big band instrumentation. A musical first, the orchestra paved the way for similar instrumental combinations a decade later. In 1942, as World War II raged, Shaw enlisted in the Navy. He was put in charge of a service band that performed in hazardous situations, and he received a medical discharge for emotional stress and physical exhaustion.

Classical Clarinet. In 1947, with the war over, Shaw's musical priorities suddenly shifted. In New York City, he focused on classical clarinet, and he toured with the Rochester Symphony Orchestra, the National Symphony, the Dayton Symphony, and New York's Little Orchestra. In Carnegie Hall, Shaw performed *Modern Music for Clarinet*, which included delightful arrangements of short compositions by Dmitri Shostakovich, Maurice Ravel, Francis Poulenc, Claude Debussy, George Gershwin, and others. There were additional chamber ensemble performances and a climactic appearance with Leonard Bernstein and the New York Philharmonic.

Always restless, Shaw returned to big band music. His 1949 big band was shaped by the influences of bebop masters Charlie Parker and Dizzy Gillespie. A third hiatus to a dairy farm in Duchess County, New York, gave Shaw the opportunity to write his autobiography, *The Trouble with Cinderella: An Outline of Identity*.

Strains of Perfectionism. The early 1950's were pivotal for Shaw. The strain of traveling, of forming, and disbanding various ensembles, and of enduring the irritations of the business of music took its toll. Shaw suffered incurably from his obsession with perfection. In 1954 he formed a new version of Gramercy 5, playing his clarinet for the last time. His roots with the Gramercy 5 dated back to 1936.

Shaw eventually relocated to Southern California, where he continued with scholarly pursuits, giving lectures and seminars on art, literature, and the big band era at numerous universities. He received honorary doctorates from California Lutheran University and the University of Arizona.

Artie Shaw. (AP/Wide World Photos)

Musical Legacy

Shaw was suave and handsome, confident with gorgeous women, a wealthy bandleader, a superb musician, and a distinguished author. His recordings reveal his ability to perform comfortably and artistically in the jazz and in the classical music idioms and in a wide variety of musical environments. His insatiable quest for perfection prompted periodic retreats from society and the eventual termination of his career. Shaw's life is portrayed in the documentary *Artie Shaw: Time Is All You've Got* (1986), a film that was awarded an Academy Award for Best Documentary Feature. He also appeared in two motion pictures, *Dancing Coed* (1939) and *Second Chorus* (1940). His books provide a unique perspective on life during the swing era, the price of popularity, and an irreverent viewpoint of marriage. In 2004 Shaw was honored with a Grammy Lifetime Achievement Award.

Douglas D. Skinner

Further Reading

Megill, David W., and Paul O. W. Tanner. *Jazz Issues: A Critical History*. Dubuque, Iowa: William C. Brown and Benchmark, 1995. An overview of jazz history, in a chronological format with listening examples; includes references to Shaw.

Shaw, Artie. *I Love You, I Hate You, Drop Dead!* Fort Lee, N.J.: Barricade Books, 1997. Married eight times, Shaw recounts details on three of his marriages and how they gradually eroded.

_____. *The Trouble with Cinderella: An Outline of Identity*. New York: Farrar, Straus and Young, 1952. Reprinted in 2001, this self-portrait of Shaw documents how his successes turned to disillusionment with himself and with the world around him.

Simosko, Vladimir. *Artie Shaw: A Musical Biography and Discography*. Lanham, Md.: Scarecrow Press, 2000. Biographical account of Shaw, covering his numerous marriages, his musical triumphs, and his rejection of fame.

Stearns, Marshall W. *The Story of Jazz*. New York: Oxford University Press, 1970. In seven parts, this book presents a definitive look at jazz history until 1970. Includes a bibliography and fifteen essays on jazz history.

White, John. *Artie Shaw: His Life and Music*. London: Continuum, 2004. Narrative description of Shaw's rise as a big band leader and his struggle to maintain his artistic identity.

See also: Bartók, Béla; Beiderbecke, Bix; Bernstein, Leonard; Carter, Benny; Debussy, Claude; Gershwin, George; Goodman, Benny; Holiday, Billie; Horne, Lena; Miller, Glenn; Porter, Cole; Poulenc, Francis; Puente, Tito; Ravel, Maurice; Shostakovich, Dmitri; Stravinsky, Igor; Tormé, Mel; Van Heusen, Jimmy.

Wayne Shorter

American jazz composer and saxophonist

Shorter introduced a new approach to saxophone playing. Never relying on established licks or riffs, his performance uses motives and melodic intervals in flexible and nonstandard ways.

Born: August 25, 1933; Newark, New Jersey
Also known as: Mr. Gone
Member of: Art Blakey and the Jazz Messengers; the Miles Davis Quintet; Weather Report

Principal recordings

ALBUMS (solo): *Blues à la Carte*, 1959; *Introducing Wayne Shorter*, 1959; *Second Genesis*, 1960; *Free Form*, 1961; *Wayning Moments*, 1962; *JuJu*, 1964; *Night Dreamer*, 1964; *Speak No Evil*, 1964; *The All Seeing Eye*, 1965; *The Collector*, 1965; *Et Cetera*, 1965; *The Soothsayer*, 1965; *Adam's Apple*, 1966; *Schizophrenia*, 1967; *Super Nova*, 1969; *Moto Grosso Feio*, 1970; *Odyssey of Iska*, 1970; *Native Dancer*, 1974; *Atlantis*, 1985; *Phantom Navigator*, 1986; *Joy Ryder*, 1988; *High Life*, 1994; *Algeria*, 2003.

ALBUMS (with Art Blakey and the Jazz Messengers): *Africaine*, 1959; *Paris Jam Session*, 1959; *The Big Beat*, 1960; *Like Someone in Love*, 1960; *A Night in Tunisia*, 1960; *Art Blakey! Jazz Messengers!*, 1961; *Buhaina's Delight*, 1961; *The Freedom Rider*, 1961; *Mosaic*, 1961; *The Witch Doctor*, 1961; *Caravan*, 1962; *Free for All*, 1964; *Kyoto*, 1964.

ALBUMS (with the Miles Davis Quintet): *E. S. P.*, 1965; *Miles Smiles*, 1966; *Nefertiti*, 1967; *Sorcerer*, 1967; *Water Babies*, 1967; *Filles de Kilimanjaro*, 1968; *Miles in the Sky*, 1968; *Bitches Brew*, 1969; *In a Silent Way*, 1969.

ALBUMS (with Weather Report): *I Sing the Body Electric*, 1971; *Weather Report*, 1971; *Sweetnighter*, 1973; *Mysterious Traveler*, 1974; *Tale Spinnin'*, 1975; *Black Market*, 1976; *Heavy Weather*, 1977; *Mr. Gone*, 1978; *Night Passage*, 1980; *Record*, 1982; *Weather Report*, 1982; *Domino Theory*, 1983; *Procession*, 1983; *Sportin' Life*, 1984; *This Is This!*, 1985; *1+1*, 1997 (with Herbie Hancock).

The Life

Wayne Shorter was born and raised in Newark, New Jersey. His parents worked in the clothing business that thrived in Newark at the time: His father, Joseph, was a welder for the Singer Sewing Machine Company; his mother, Louise, sewed for a furrier. His first creative interests as a child were in painting and in sculpture. After completing elementary school, he was accepted into the Newark Arts High School, and when he was sixteen years old, his grandmother gave him a clarinet. To placate his father, who wanted him to play an instrument, Shorter started taking music lessons from a local bandleader. His interest in music grew rapidly, and he began studying in earnest. His proximity to New York City made it easy for him to hear some of the greatest musicians of the time, including Duke Ellington, Thelonious Monk, Stan Kenton, and Charlie Parker. He purchased a tenor saxophone when he was sixteen or seventeen, and he switched his high school major to music in his last year at Newark Arts High School. He also formed a jazz combo called the Group, which played some local gigs. After graduating from high school, he attended New York University, majoring in music education. While in college, he played at various clubs and sat in with numerous musicians. Upon graduation from New York University, he was drafted into the U.S. Army.

Shorter played with the U.S. Army Band in Washington, D.C., where he was stationed for most of his three years in military service. During that period he also played with Horace Silver's quintet. When Shorter was discharged in 1958, he moved back to New York City. Soon he met John Coltrane,

and the two men began practicing and jamming together. Shorter played in trumpeter Maynard Ferguson's band for a short while, and he became acquainted with pianist Joe Zawinul, who would join Shorter in the band Weather Report a decade or so later. In 1959 Shorter joined Art Blakey and his Jazz Messengers. He became the group's musical director, and he also began recording some records of his own for Vee-Jay. Sometime during this period, he picked up the nickname Mr. Gone, which would become the title of one of Weather Report's albums.

Shorter left Blakey in 1963, and in 1964 he made his first recording for Blue Note Records as the leader of a group. In what would be a turning point in his career, he replaced the departing Coltrane in Miles Davis's group. Coltrane had suggested Shorter as his replacement in 1959 when he was considering leaving Davis's group, but the departure did not occur until 1964. After joining Davis's group, which also included Tony Williams, Ron Carter, and Herbie Hancock, Shorter began composing in earnest. This particular combo disbanded in the winter of 1967-1968 because Davis was moving in a new direction. However, Shorter continued to play with Davis through 1969. Shorter's father died in an automobile accident in 1966.

In 1970 Shorter formed Weather Report with Zawinul and Miroslav Vitous. The three had played together in 1968 and 1969, with and without Davis and his new group of musicians during the sessions that would produce the albums *In a Silent Way* and *Bitches Brew*. Weather Report would be Shorter's main musical forum for the next fifteen years. Other aspects of his performance were several collaborations with other musicians from both rock and jazz. Probably most important among these are his recording sessions with Joni Mitchell that began with her 1977 release *Don Juan's Reckless Daughter*.

In 1970 Shorter married Ana Maria, whom he had met in 1966 when she came backstage after a Miles Davis Group date at the Village Gate in Greenwich Village. After the wedding, Ana Maria briefly considered an acting career, but she decided to become Shorter's manager instead. She introduced Shorter to a branch of Buddhism known as Soka Gakkai International-USA, which he adopted. In later interviews, he stated that it was his Buddhist beliefs that helped keep him from becoming

Wayne Shorter. (AP/Wide World Photos)

depressed over a series of personal tragedies that occurred in the 1980's. They had one child, Iska Maria, who suffered from irreparable brain damage and who died of a grand mal seizure in 1985 at the age of fourteen. In the same year, his mother died, Weather Report disbanded, and Shorter started a new band. On July 17, 1996, his wife and a niece were killed in the mysterious crash of TWA Flight 800 on their way to join Shorter in Italy. A year later he released his critically acclaimed album *1+1.* In 1987 Shorter collaborated with rock-jazz guitarist Carlos Santana on a twenty-six-city concert tour that resulted in an album recorded live at the 1988 Montreux Jazz Festival. He married Carolina Dos Santos, a close friend of Ana Maria, in 1999.

The Music

Shorter's music has two elements: his playing and his composing. Never forcing itself into a group's sound, Shorter's playing anchors the song's center, from where he rarely strays. He takes his time with each melodic interval, and he never abruptly exchanges one line for another. A sense of cohesion is present at all times.

Shorter's compositions are structured so that the melody provides cohesiveness over complex harmonic progressions. During the mid- to late 1960's, his compositions started to change dramatically. His music is often structured around pentatonic melodies, and the harmonies are complex. The instrumental solos reflect the composition's melody as much as its harmony, and they include long rests as an integral part of the music. As the 1960's progressed, Shorter began to include sixteenth-note rhythms and a backbeat borrowed from funk and rock. Shorter combined these with a modal harmony and with melodies that went from being long, varying phrases to short, catchy statements. The main change in Shorter's compositions after Weather Report is the strong presence of counterpoint.

"Footprints." This song was first recorded on Shorter's album *Adam's Apple*, before the Miles Davis Group recorded it for *Miles Smiles*. A simple twelve-bar blues in C minor played in 6/4 time, this song is considered a jazz classic, and it has been recorded by musicians around the world ever since its first appearance. It is a gentle tune during which the trumpeter, then the keyboardist, and finally the saxophonist question each other, a song looking for a resolution that comes with a return to the refrain, and then just barely.

Speak No Evil. Shorter draws on black magic and folklore for the songs on this album, and he said he began each of the compositions with a picture in his mind. The album defined a new element of jazz style. Restraint and free-form contrast in each composition, with tight tenor solos and almost ethereal rhythms creating a sound that combines serenity and tension in an almost perfect flow. Belying its dark themes, this music has a lightness and playfulness about it. It is considered a landmark in jazz composition.

E.S.P. Shorter's compositions on this album are inventive, and his tenor saxophone takes the music to soulful heights. The tunes "Little One," "Iris," and "Mood" are considered jazz masterpieces.

Weather Report. This first album from the band came out of the work Shorter and Zawinul did with

Davis during the *In a Silent Way* and *Bitches Brew* sessions. Shorter wrote only two tunes for this, but his playing shows the influences of the Brazilian music he had been listening to in between bands. His solo compositions "Tears" and "Eurydice" ranged from the Impressionistic to a more traditional jazz sound.

I Sing the Body Electric. Garnering generally positive reviews, this second album from Weather Report was considered superior to the group's debut. Not straight jazz, the music is more a series of tone poems and pieces portraying images and emotions. Once again, there were only two Shorter compositions, "The Moors," featuring a wonderful guitar solo by Ralph Towner, and "Surucucu," an edited montage of imagistic tone.

High Life. The album is filled with sonic walls of keyboard and a fair amount of funk-style rhythm. Like much of Shorter's earlier work, the music defies standardization, with intricacies and references that move it beyond the traditional jazz fare of its period.

Musical Legacy

Shorter's compositions forever changed the nature of jazz. Involved with some of the genre's most innovative musicians, Shorter took the energies and capabilities of the players and the era, and he developed a music that incorporated the new while staying true to the basics of the old. His works and the bands he played in helped popularize jazz with a new audience, while his understanding and uses of earlier forms entertained the music's existing listeners. The influence of his playing is obvious in each successive generation of saxophone players.

Ron Jacobs

Further Reading

Andrews, Laura. "Shorter Navigates His Genius." *Amsterdam News*, January 30, 2001. This brief article in an African American newspaper is a delightful look at the musical philosophy of Shorter extracted from an exclusive 2001 interview.

Davis, Francis. "A Real Gone Guy." *Atlantic Monthly* (June, 2004). This is an in-depth look at Shorter and his fabled career. Davis portrays Shorter as a trailblazer who is more than just a survivor.

Martin, Mel. "Wayne Shorter: The Interview." *The Saxophone Journal* (January/February, 1992). This wide-ranging interview covers the technical aspects of Shorter's playing, the types of horns he has used, his improvisational approach, and how he composes. In addition, Shorter and the interviewer share memories of certain performances and discuss the musician's influences.

Mercer, Michelle. *Footprints*. New York: Penguin/Tarcher, 2001. In this biography of the often-elusive Shorter, Mercer, a reviewer for *The New York Times* who reviewed several of Shorter's performances and releases, effectively chronicles the man's life and music. After gaining his trust, Mercer was able to interview Shorter and many of his friends for the book, including Mitchell and Shorter's lifelong friend, the poet Amiri Baraka. The book opens with prefaces by Herbie Hancock and Shorter.

Palmer, Robert. "Wayne Shorter: Jazz Artist Makes His 'Main Move.'" *The New York Times*, November 3, 1985. Palmer talks about Shorter's legacy and musical approach. Snippets from an interview revealing Shorter's self-deprecating humor and positive outlook appear in the article.

See also: Blakey, Art; Coltrane, John; Davis, Miles; Ellington, Duke; Hancock, Herbie; Jones, Elvin; McFerrin, Bobby; Mingus, Charles; Mitchell, Joni; Monk, Thelonious; Nascimento, Milton; Parker, Charlie; Santana, Carlos; Tyner, McCoy.

Dmitri Shostakovich

Russian classical composer and pianist

Shostakovich was a polystylist, influenced by composers from several different musical eras as well as by Russian and Jewish folk music. He was a master of the Baroque fugue, and his symphonic and chamber music employed classical models. The emotional content in his music reflected Romantic tendencies, and his use of atonality, parody, and irony showed the influence of twentieth century modernism.

Born: September 12, 1906; St. Petersburg, Russia

Died: August 9, 1975; Moscow, Soviet Union
(now in Russia)

Also known as: Dmitri Dmitrievich Shostakovich
(full name)

Principal works

BALLETS: *The Bolt*, Op. 27, 1931; Ballet Suite No. 1,
Op. 84b, 1949; Ballet Suite No. 2, 1949.

CHAMBER WORKS: Sonata for Cello and Piano in D
Minor, Op. 40, 1934; String Quartet No. 1 in C,
Op. 49, 1938; Quintet for Piano and Strings in
G Minor, Op. 57, 1940; String Quartet No. 2 in
A Major, Op. 68, 1944; String Quartet No. 3 in F
Major, Op. 73, 1946; String Quartet No. 4 in D,
Op. 83, 1953; String Quartet No. 5 in B, Op. 92,
1953; String Quartet No. 6 in G, Op. 101, 1956;
Chamber Symphony in C Minor, Op. 110a,
1960; String Quartet No. 7 in F-sharp Minor,
Op. 108, 1960; String Quartet No. 8 in C Minor,
Op. 110, 1960; String Quartet No. 9 in E, Op.
117, 1964; String Quartet No. 10 in A, Op. 118,
1964; String Quartet No. 11 in F, Op. 122, 1966;
String Quartet No. 12 in D, Op. 133, 1968;
String Quartet No. 13 in B, Op. 138, 1970;
String Quartet No. 14 in F, Op. 142, 1973; String
Quartet No. 15 in E, Op. 144, 1974.

CHORAL WORKS: Symphony No. 13 in B-flat Minor,
Op. 113, 1962 (for solo voice, chorus, and
orchestra); *Antiformalisticheskiy Rayok*, 1968
(*Antiformalist Rayok*; for solo voices, chorus,
and piano).

OPERAS (music): *Boris Godunov*, Op. 58, 1874
(libretto by Modest Mussorgsky; based on
Alexander Pushkin's novel); *Nos*, Op. 15, 1930
(*The Nose*; libretto by Shostakovich, Alexander
Preiss, Georgi Ionin, and Yevgeni Zamyatin;
based on Nikolai Gogol's novel); *Lady Macbeth
of the Mtsensk District*, Op. 29, 1932 (libretto by
Preiss and Shostakovich; based on Nikolay
Leskov's short story); *Igroki*, composed 1942,
first performed 1978 (*The Gamblers*; based on
Fyodor Dostoevsky's novel); *Khovanshchina*,
Op. 106, 1959 (libretto by Mussorgsky);
Katerina Izmaylova, Op. 114, 1963 (libretto by
Shostakovich and Preiss; based on Leskov's
short story).

ORCHESTRAL WORKS: Symphony No. 1 in F Minor,
Op. 10, 1926; Symphony No. 2, Op. 14, 1927

(*Oktyabryu*); *Tahiti Trot*, Op. 16, 1928;
Symphony No. 3, Op. 20, 1930 (*Pervomayskaya*;
The First of May); Piano Concerto No. 1 in C
Minor, Op. 35, 1933; Symphony No. 4 in C, Op.
43, composed 1936, first performed 1961;
Symphony No. 5 in D Minor, Op. 47, 1937;
Suite for Jazz Orchestra, No. 2, 1938; Symphony
No. 6 in B Minor, Op. 54, 1939; Symphony No.
7 in C Major, Op. 60, 1942; Symphony No. 8 in
C Minor, Op. 65, 1943; Symphony No. 9 in E-
flat Major, Op. 70, 1945; Violin Concerto No. 1
in A Minor, Op. 77, 1948; Symphony No. 10 in
E Minor, Op. 93, 1953; *Festive Overture in A
Major*, Op. 96, 1954; *The Gadfly*, Op. 97a, 1955;
Symphony No. 11 in G Minor, Op. 103, 1957
(*The Year 1905*); Cello Concerto No. 1 in E-flat
Major, Op. 107, 1959; Symphony No. 12, Op.
112, 1961 (*The Year 1917*); Cello Concerto No. 2
in G Major, Op. 126, 1966; Symphony No. 15 in
A, Op. 141, 1972.

PIANO WORKS: *Fantastic Dances*, Op. 5, 1920 (three
pieces); Piano Sonata No. 1, Op. 12, 1926;
Prelude for Piano in C-sharp Minor, Op. 34,
1933; Piano Quintet in G, Op. 57, 1940; Piano
Sonata No. 2 in B, Op. 61, 1943; Piano Trio No.
2 in E Minor, Op. 67, 1944; *Preludes and Fugues*,
Op. 87, 1951 (twenty-four pieces).

VOCAL WORKS: *Suite of Romances*, Op. 127, 1967
(seven verses for soprano and piano);
Symphony No. 14, Op. 135, 1969 (for solo
voices, strings, and percussion).

The Life

The mother of Dmitri Dmitrievich Shostakovich
(DMEE-tree shah-stuh-KOH-vihch) was a professional pianist, and she recognized her son's prodigious talent when she started teaching him piano at
age eight. With the help of composer Alexander
Glazunov, he was admitted into the Petrograd Conservatory at age thirteen, where he excelled at both
composition and piano performance. To support
himself at school after his father died, he worked as
a cinema pianist, which partly contributed to Shostakovich composing more than thirty film scores
over the course of his career. His graduation piece
was his highly acclaimed Symphony No. 1 in F Minor, completed in 1925.

In 1932 he married the physicist Nina Varzar,
and they had a daughter Galina in 1936 and a son

Maxim in 1938. His opera *Lady Macbeth of the Mtsensk District* premiered in 1932 to great acclaim. Unexpectedly, the opera was publicly denounced by the Communist Party on January 28, 1936, in the government-controlled newspaper *Pravda*, in an article entitled "Muddle Instead of Music." This was the result of the party's aim to root out formalism (art that the Soviet government felt was influenced by the decadent tastes of the European bourgeoisie) and to champion Socialist Realism (art that could be understood by the common citizen and addressed to the Russian people as a whole).

Shostakovich capitulated to the Communist artistic doctrines, and the next several years brought him fame and success. In 1939 he was named a professor at the Leningrad (formerly Petrograd) Conservatory. His Symphony No. 7 in C Major, which raised his status to herolike proportions, was regarded as emblematic of the Soviet resistance to Nazi aggression during World War II. However, in 1948 he and other Soviet composers, such as Sergei Prokofiev and Aram Khachaturian, were sternly

rebuked for formalism by the Secretary of the Central Committee of the Communist Party Andrey Zhdanov. During these years, several of Shostakovich's friends were sent to the gulag camps in Siberia, and he lived in fear of being sent there himself.

His fortunes improved in the 1950's when he traveled broadly within Russia and to England and to the United States. After the death of Prokofiev in 1953, Shostakovich became the most internationally recognized Soviet composer. Two years after his first wife died, Shostakovich married Margarita Kainova. The marriage proved a failure, and they divorced after three years. In 1962 he married Irina Supinskaya, a marriage that lasted for the rest of his life. In 1960 Shostakovich joined the Communist Party. Some scholars view this as an act of patriotism, some see it as cowardice, and some believe Shostakovich was forced to do it. In the last fifteen years of his life, he had two heart attacks, and he lost the use of his right arm to polio. He died of lung cancer in 1975.

The Music

Although much of Shostakovich's music was rooted in tonality and used traditional forms (symphony, string quartet, song cycle), he transformed the structures of past eras through his unique modernist musical language. Shostakovich was able to compose at a rapid speed, and he amassed a large body of work, composing in all of the major genres of his time. He was as comfortable composing a program symphony or an opera as he was composing purely abstract instrumental music.

Lady Macbeth of the Mtsensk District. Based on a novel of the same name by Russian author Nikolai Leskov, this opera earned for Shostakovich some of his greatest acclaim (from the public) and greatest disapproval (from the Soviet government). The opera centers on the life of a murderous woman named Katerina, hence the allusion to Shakespeare's murderous Lady Macbeth in the title. By giving her the most beautiful music in the opera, Shostakovich fashioned her into a sympathetic character. The opera was a great success when it was first performed, and critics proclaimed it the first truly Soviet opera. In January, 1936, Soviet leader Joseph Stalin and several other officials attended a performance of the opera. Two days later an anonymous article appeared on the front page of

Dmitri Shostakovich. (Library of Congress)

Pravda (the leading Soviet newspaper and mouthpiece of the Communist Party), denouncing the opera.

Symphony No. 5 in D Minor. This symphony, completed in 1937 and influenced by the symphonies of Mahler, was a response to the criticism that Shostakovich received for his opera *Lady Macbeth of the Mtsensk District*. The exultant last movement has been regarded by some as genuinely triumphant and by others as forced jubilation. Like much of his music, this symphony is a reflection of the composer's tenuous relationship with the Soviet regime.

Piano Trio No. 2 in E Minor. Composed in 1944, this four-movement work was dedicated to Shostakovich's Jewish friend, Ivan Sollertinsky, who died in the same year. From the haunting first-movement opening, with the cello quietly soaring high above the violin and piano placed in lower ranges, to the Klezmer music—perhaps a dance of death (totentanz)—in the final movement, the trio's mournful character reinforces the commemorative nature of the work. Further, the work was composed around the same time that Russian soldiers first discovered concentration camps in Nazi Germany. The level of Shostakovich's awareness of this fact at the time has been debated, but in any case, the historical proximity of this composition to the discovery of the horrors inflicted on the Jewish people has profoundly affected the reception and interpretation of the work.

Preludes and Fugues. Shostakovich composed these preludes and fugues as an homage to Johann Sebastian Bach and his Well-Tempered Clavier. He finished the work in five months in 1950-1951 after a trip to Leipzig for the bicentenary commemoration of Bach's death. Unlike Bach's work, in which the preludes and fugues go up the scale chromatically in parallel major-minor pairs (C major, C minor, C-sharp major, C-sharp minor), Shostakovich's preludes and fugues are organized according to the circle of fifths, with each major key's prelude and fugue followed by its relative minor (C major, A minor, G major, E minor). Although the work is tonal, Shostakovich's modernist tendencies (especially the dissonance in some of the fugues) are apparent.

String Quartet No. 8 in C Minor. Composed in just three days in July, 1960, this is among the most well-known of Shostakovich's string quartets. The work employs themes from several of his previous compositions, plus themes from Ludwig van Beethoven, Richard Wagner, and Peter Ilich Tchaikovsky. Furthermore, all five of the quartet's movements contain a four-note theme based on Shostakovich's name, DSCH, which in German transliteration forms the notes D, E-flat, C, and B natural. Because of this and because of the emotional impact of the music, the quartet is one of Shostakovich's most personal statements, a musical autobiography.

Symphony No. 13 in B-flat Minor. This choral symphony (subtitled *Babi Yar*) was a cathartic work for Shostakovich. Composed and premiered in 1962, during Khrushchev Thaw, a time when the Soviet leader, Nikita Khrushchev, relaxed repressive censorship policies, it confronted issues that Shostakovich wanted to address but could not under the scrutiny of Stalin's cultural policies. Composed for orchestra, bass solo, and male chorus, this five-movement work sets five poems by Russian poet Yevgeny Yevtushenko. These poems are about the massacre at Babi Yar of Jews and others by the Nazis during World War II, censorship, the plight of women under oppression, the widespread fear during the Stalin era, and the struggle of the Russian people to maintain their integrity.

Musical Legacy

Shostakovich was unique among the great Russian composers in that all of his works were composed during the Soviet era. As a result, much of his work reflects an uneasy mixture of politics and music. The influence of the Soviet regime on Shostakovich's music has been a hotly contested area of musicological study since the death of the composer in 1975.

Although Shostakovich was widely admired by the Russian artistic community, the influence of his music in America and Europe was minor during his lifetime. He was largely regarded as an instrument of Soviet propaganda, who had little interest in where modern music was going. In the decades after his death, his reputation was elevated, and he came to be considered one of the greatest composers of the twentieth century. The influence of Shostakovich has been noted in Benjamin Britten's music and in that of some of his former pupils, such as Khachaturian, Boris Tishchenko, and Alfred Schnittke. His son, Maxim, is a respected conductor and an authoritative interpreter of his music.

Tim J. Smolko and Joanna R. Smolko

Further Reading

Bartlett, Rosamund, ed. *Shostakovich in Context.* New York: Oxford University Press, 2000. This collection of articles is a refreshing break from the bulk of Shostakovich literature that takes a heavy-handed approach to the composer's relationship with the Soviet regime and the hidden meanings in the music. While these essays do not overlook the historical context in which Shostakovich composed his works, these articles analyze the structure of the music and Shostakovich's craft as a composer.

Fay, Laurel E. *Shostakovich: A Life.* New York: Oxford University Press, 2000. Based on fifteen years of meticulous research, this book contains a detailed account of the composer's life; the author took advantage of source material that was unavailable before the fall of the Soviet regime in 1991. Factually based, the book has been criticized for offering little insight into Shostakovich's personal life.

Hulme, Derek C. *Dmitri Shostakovich: A Catalogue, Bibliography, and Discography.* Lanham, Md.: Scarecrow Press, 2002. This catalog of Shostakovich's music presents a wealth of detail for scholarly research on the composer. Every composition listed includes information on musical form, instrumentation, premieres, publication, recordings, arrangements, and location of the autographed scores.

Shostakovich, Dmitri. *Testimony: The Memoirs of Dmitri Shostakovich as Related to and Edited by Solomon Volkov.* Translated from the Russian by Antonina W. Bouis. New York: Harper and Row, 1979. Volkov purported that these memoirs were dictated to him by the composer in the early 1970's, although many scholars believe the book contains much fraudulent information. Even if the book is misleading and unreliable, it did provoke a renewed interest in and a deeper understanding of Shostakovich's life and works.

Wilson, Elizabeth. *Shostakovich: A Life Remembered.* 2d ed. Princeton, N.J.: Princeton University Press, 2006. Well rounded and insightful, this biography is based primarily on interviews with and articles by friends, family members, conductors, and musicians who knew Shostakovich intimately.

See also: Ashkenazy, Vladimir; Britten, Benjamin; Casals, Pablo; Glass, Philip; Golijov, Osvaldo; Jarrett, Keith; Khachaturian, Aram; Ligeti, György; Mahler, Gustav; Oistrakh, David; Oldfield, Mike; Prokofiev, Sergei; Rostropovich, Mstislav; Schnittke, Alfred; Scriabin, Aleksandr; Shaw, Artie; Watts, André.

Jean Sibelius

Finnish classical composer

In his music, noted for its unconventional use of form, harmony, and mood colors, Sibelius championed Finland's language and cultural traditions.

Born: December 8, 1865; Hämeenlinna, Finland
Died: September 20, 1957; Järvenpää, Finland
Also known as: Johan Julius Christian Sibelius (full name)

Principal works

CHAMBER WORKS: *Romance,* 1904; String Quartet in D Minor, Op. 56, 1909 (*Voces Intimae*); *Suite Champêtre,* Op. 98b, 1921; *Andante Festivo,* 1939.

MUSICAL THEATER (incidental music): *Kung Kristian II,* 1898 (*King Kristian II*); *Kuolema,* 1904 (*Death*; libretto by Arvid Järnefelt; includes *Valse Triste, Op. 44*); *Pelléas och Mélisande,* Op. 46, 1905 (libretto by Maurice Maeterlinck); *Belsazars gästatbud,* 1906 (*Belshazzar's Feast*); *Svanevit,* 1909 (*Swan White*; libretto by August Strindberg); *Trettondagsafton,* 1909 (*Twelfth Night*; libretto by William Shakespeare); *Ödlan,* 1910 (*The Lizard*; libretto by Mikael Lybeck); *Stormen,* 1926 (*The Tempest*; libretto by Shakespeare).

OPERA: *Jungfrun i tornet,* 1896 (*The Maiden in the Tower*; libretto by Rafael Herzberg).

ORCHESTRAL WORKS: *Kullervo,* Op. 7, 1892 (for voice and orchestra); *En saga,* Op. 9, 1893 (*A*

Fairy Tale); *Karelia Overture*, Op. 10, 1893; *Karelia Suite*, Op. 11, 1893; *Skogsrået*, Op. 15, 1895 (*The Wood Nymph*); *Lemminkäinen Suite*, Op. 22, 1896; Symphony No. 1 in E Minor, Op. 39, 1899; *Finlandia*, Op. 26, 1900; Symphony No. 2 in D Major, Op. 43, 1902; Violin Concerto in D Minor, Op. 47, 1904; *Pohjolan tytär*, Op. 49, 1906 (*Pohjola's Daughter*); Symphony No. 3 in C Major, Op. 52, 1906; *Öinen ratsastus ja auringonnousu*, Op. 55, 1909 (*Night Ride and Sunrise*); Symphony No. 4 in A Minor, Op. 63, 1911; *Rakastava*, Op. 41, 1912 (*The Beloved*); *Barden*, Op. 63, 1913 (*The Bard*); *Luonnotar*, Op. 70, 1913 (*The Spirit of Nature*); *Aallottaret*, Op. 73, 1914 (*The Oceanides*); *Six Humoresques*, 1919 (for violin and orchestra); Symphony No. 5 in E-flat Major, Op. 82, 1921; Symphony No. 6 in D Minor, Op. 104, 1923; Symphony No. 7 in C Major, Op. 105, 1924; *Tapiola*, Op. 112, 1926.

PIANO WORKS: *Six Impromptus*, Op. 5, 1893; Sonata, Op. 12, 1893; Ten Piano Pieces, Op. 24, 1904; *Three Kyllikki Lyric Pieces*, Op. 41, 1904; Ten Pieces for Piano, Op. 58, 1909; Three Sonatinas, Op. 67, 1912.

VOCAL WORKS: *Jubal*, Op. 35, No. 1, 1908 (lyrics by Ernst Josephson); *Teodora*, Op. 35, No. 2, 1908 (lyrics by Bertel Gripenberg); *Säv, säv, susa*, Op. 36, No. 4, 1909 (*Reed, Reed, Rustle*; lyrics by Gustav Fröding); *Svarta Rosor*, Op. 36, No. 1, 1917 (*Black Roses*; lyrics by Josephson).

The Life

Johan Julius Christian Sibelius (sih-BAY-lee-uhs) was the second of three children of a military physician of modest means. As a child, he showed musical interests, and he received some basic lessons and family encouragement. By age ten, he was experimenting in composition. His formal training began at age fifteen with study of the violin. Several years of intense training won him considerable proficiency, although short of that necessary for a solo performance career. He was an active player of chamber music, and as his interests turned to composition, his first efforts were in that idiom.

Late in 1885, Sibelius began four years of formal studies in violin and in composition in Helsinki. He wrote some new works, mainly in chamber forms and conservative in character, confirming his choice of pursuing a career in composition rather than in performance. Later, he joined an important cultural circle. With the young composer Ferruccio Busoni, new to the Helsinki Music Institute's piano faculty, Sibelius could discuss progressive aesthetic ideals. With the brothers Armas Järnefelt, a composer, and Eero Järnefelt, a painter, Sibelius shared interest in the "Fennicization" movement, which promoted changing Swedish names back to Finnish.

Sibelius had been born into a world of divided identities. Finland's population consisted of three groups: ethnic Swedes, ethnic Finns who had assimilated Swedish language and culture, and rural Finns who preserved the Finnish language in a provincial world. The first two groups were urbanized, comparatively cultivated, and cosmopolitan, while the last one was relatively primitive. Sibelius had been raised in the middle group, a speaker and writer of Swedish, a language he would use all his life. Only in his teens did he study the Finnish language, whose revival was the focus of nationalist rediscovery, and only in his late twenties would he master it as part of his cultural identity. His contacts with the Järnefelt brothers, meanwhile, drew him in the pro-Finnish direction, while he was attracted to their sister, Aino, his future wife.

Through a government grant, Sibelius went abroad to pursue advanced studies in composition. In Berlin (1889-1890), he found only disillusionment. In Vienna (1890-1891), he chose sides in a culture war—rejecting the academic style represented by the music of Johannes Brahms and committing to the progressive elements of the music of Franz Liszt, Richard Wagner, and Anton Bruckner. At the same time, accompanying his engagement to Aino, was his first intensive study of *The Kalevala*. The reconstructed Finnish folk epic—of grim, rustic, pagan character—had been assembled from traditional sources and published by philologist Elias Lönrott in 1849, and it provided a crucial rallying point for advocates of a revived Finnish language as the key to recovered national identity.

In his excitement, Sibelius planned his boldest composition yet, a vast five-movement symphonic poem for soloists, chorus, and orchestra, to be titled *Kullervo*, after an ill-fated character in *The Kalevala*. Back in Helsinki, he plunged into its composition, along the way introducing himself to regional Finnish folk songs. The premiere of *Kullervo* in April,

1892, created a sensation. The two movements with Finnish texts for singers provided a revolutionary model for setting the language, while the work generally established Sibelius as the new musical voice of Finland. His nationalist orientation brought him into a new circle of like-minded artists, among them the composer-conductor Robert Kajanus, the Järnefelt brothers (whose sister, Aino, Sibelius married weeks after the premiere), and painter Akseli Gallen-Kallela.

Sibelius gave a lecture in 1896 outlining his manifesto of new nationalism. He supported it with new compositions that forged ahead in the new orchestral style presaged in *Kullervo*. Chief among these were his *En Saga*, evoking rough bardic tradition, and the four symphonic poems of the later 1890's, based on stories from *The Kalevala* that became, as a group, the *Lemminkäinen Suite*.

While earning his living by teaching, Sibelius found his growing prominence winning him a generous annual pension. Its renewals and extensions sustained him as a publicly supported artist through the rest of his life. At the same time, Sibelius became a leader in political activism. Finland had been for almost a century an "autonomous" grand duchy of the Russian Empire, but during the course of the 1890's the Russian government became increasingly oppressive and hostile, provoking intensified Finnish protest. Through the decade, Sibelius contributed orchestral music to patriotic displays of "historical scenes," especially for Helsinki's Press Pension Celebrations, some of them quite inflammatory. His regional tribute, his *Karelia* music, is one example. However, their culmination was his nationalist hymn, *Finlandia*, which he incorporated into a passionate symphonic poem, and it still his most famous and beloved work.

Meanwhile, international touring was introducing his music throughout Europe, and it was at this point that he produced his Symphony No. 1 in E Minor, followed shortly by his Symphony No. 2 in D Major and by his Violin Concerto in D Minor. His international recognition was growing, but Sibelius's frenetic pace and mounting alcoholism prompted family efforts to remove him from Helsinki and settle him in a rustic villa in a woodland at nearby Järvenpää. It was named Ainola in honor of his wife, and there—with roots firmly embedded in

Jean Sibelius. (Library of Congress)

rural Finnish soil from which he drew ever deeper inspiration—he lived the rest of his life.

Fired by knowledge of Richard Strauss's music, but repelled by that of Gustav Mahler, Sibelius adapted his extension of the Lisztian symphonic poem to *Kalevala* inspiration in *Pohjola's Daughter*. Simultaneously, he abandoned the lushness of his first two symphonies for the leaner Symphony No. 3 in C Major, the spartan Symphony No. 4 in A Minor, and the sonorous Symphony No. 5 in E-flat Major. By that time, the international progress of his music had become uneven, and the challenge of modernism's musical styles (such as those of Claude Debussy, Arnold Schoenberg, and Igor Stravinsky) put him off balance. He also faced a new round of problems with his finances and his health, complicated by the upheavals of World War I, out of which Finland emerged independent at last, but caught in civil war.

Ultimately, Sibelius's creative response was music even more personal and unconventional, as summed up in his superficially pastoral Symphony

No. 6 in D Minor, his single-movement Symphony No. 7 in C Major, and his final symphonic poem, the darkly brooding forest picture, *Tapiola*. He poured his energy into a culminating Symphony No. 8, but after much toil and anguish, his nerve failed and he burned the score.

There followed only some trifles as Sibelius abandoned composing entirely by the early 1930's and slipped into what became known as "the silence from Järvenpää." There he remained, for the last quarter century of his life, fueling speculation about his withdrawal. Sibelius died of a brain hemorrhage in 1957.

The Music

Over the span of four decades, Sibelius created an enormous legacy of compositions, totaling 116 opus-number publications and many still in manuscript, written in almost every imaginable form. His single experiment with opera, the one-act Swedish-language *The Maiden in the Tower*, was a failure, but he satisfied the Nordic appetite for theater music with several fine incidental scores for *King Kristian II*, *Kuolema*, *Pelléas och Mélisande*, *Belshazzar's Feast*, and *The Tempest*, the last containing music of extraordinary originality.

Choral Music. With choral music highly popular in northern Europe, Sibelius produced a great many pieces for female, male, and mixed voices, on both Swedish and Finnish texts. The same bilingual division marks his output of songs for voice and piano, in fourteen published sets. For some, he also arranged orchestral accompaniments.

Chamber Music. Initially a violinist, Sibelius wrote much chamber music involving the violin, most of which remains unpublished. His most important venture is his idiosyncratic String Quartet in D Minor, also known as *Voces Intimae*. At the other extreme is the great Violin Concerto in D Minor, which became one of the few such works of the twentieth century to become a repertoire staple. Though not an accomplished pianist, he composed piano music throughout his life, in total twenty-seven pieces or groups of pieces, plus unpublished items. They are mostly short and easily dismissed as salon trifles, but they deserve serious evaluation.

Orchestral Works. As an orchestral composer, Sibelius honed his most characteristic stylistic features: his transformation of traditional forms into organic entities; his use of dark instrumental colorations, sometimes evoking sounds of nature, though balanced by grandiose sonorities; his use of hovering harmonies, static chordalism, but also repetitive figures. His symphonic poems range from programmatic narrative to abstract mood evocations.

His symphonies are a uniquely personal sequence. Disillusioned with his precocious *Kullervo* as a realization of his stylistic goals, he withdrew the work and forbade its publication or performance for the rest of his life. The slightly overwrought quality of his first two symphonies, reflecting the influence of the music of Peter Ilich Tchaikovsky, was discarded in favor of a new structural and coloristic self-discipline. The lean economy of Symphony No. 3, with its interlinking of movements and thematic evolution, anticipate the more triumphant fulfillment of the formula in Symphony No. 5, while Symphony No. 4 portrayed an almost frightening loneliness and desolation in its austerity. The cryptic gentleness of Symphony No. 6 returned him to classical four-movement structure, but then Symphony No. 7 he cast into a densely compressed single movement.

Musical Legacy

Despite his position as the towering founding father of Finnish national music, Sibelius during his lifetime faced a shifting international reputation. For some audiences, his music seemed fresh and bracing, exhibiting a rugged and cleansed post-Romantic neoclassicism, even primitivism. In 1905, during the first of his recurrent visits to England, he began accumulating influential admirers and supporters there, such as composer Granville Bantock, conductors Henry Wood and Thomas Beecham, critic Ernest Newman, and writer Rosa Newmarch. In 1914 he made his first visit to the United States and met such leading figures as composers Horatio Parker and George Whitefield Chadwick, conductor Walter Damrosch, and, most significantly, the critic Olin Downes, who became an ardent Sibelian.

His progress in continental Europe disappointed him, however. His music was generally ignored in Germany and Austria, and it was actively disliked in France.

Sibelius was first hailed as a modernist, as new proponents of modernism took over the international scene, Sibelius began to be regarded as a symbol of traditionalism, an alternative to the avant-garde. With even more diffidence, he was pigeonholed as a Nordic composer, though still chief among them.

After his death, there was further decline of interest in his music, though it never disappeared from concerts and recordings. When the movement of minimalism discovered him as a forerunner, general appreciation of Sibelius's music flourished anew, and his standing as a major composer is now undeniable.

John W. Barker

Further Reading

Abraham, Gerald, ed. *Sibelius: A Symposium*. London: Lindsay Drummond, 1947. These various essays by specialists reflect an early stage of the composer's reputation.

Barnett, Andrew. *Sibelius*. New Haven, Conn.: Yale University Press, 2007. A comprehensive study, this engaging biography brings to light the life of the composer, using correspondence, diaries, and interviews. Includes a chronology of Sibelius's works.

Ekman, Karl. *Jean Sibelius: His Life and Personality*. New York: Knopf, 1938. This biography is dated, and it is an example of the reverential treatment accorded to Sibelius early in his career.

Goss, Glenda Dawn. *Jean Sibelius and Olin Downes: Music, Friendship, Criticism*. Boston: Northeastern University Press, 1995. Documentation of the composer's long and significant ties with one of his most enthusiastic champions.

_____, ed. *The Sibelius Companion*. Westport, Conn.: Greenwood Press, 1995. This is an important collection of diverse essays by major scholars and experts.

Grey, Cecil. *Sibelius: The Symphonies*. London: Oxford University Press, 1975. This is a specialized study covering all aspects of Sibelius's symphonies.

James, Burnett. *The Music of Jean Sibelius*. Rutherford, N.J.: Fairleigh Dickinson University Press, 1983. The resource provides and an analytic survey of all categories of Sibelius's music.

Johnson, Harold E. *Jean Sibelius*. New York: Knopf, 1959. This study challenges some of the mythology the composer helped to create about himself.

Layton, Robert. *Sibelius*. London: Dent, 1978. A classic and concise biography of Sibelius by a leading specialist in Nordic music.

Tawaststjerna, Erik. *Jean Sibelius*. 3 vols. Translated by Robert Layton. London: Faber & Faber, 1976, 1986, 1988. An extensive critical biography by a leading Finnish Sibelius specialist.

See also: Adams, John; Anderson, Marian; Ashkenazy, Vladimir; Beecham, Sir Thomas; Björling, Jussi; Busoni, Ferruccio; Chung, Kyung-Wha; Debussy, Claude; Gould, Glenn; Heifetz, Jascha; Lutosławski, Witold; Nielsen, Carl; Previn, Sir André; Schoenberg, Arnold; Stern, Isaac; Strauss, Richard; Stravinsky, Igor; Walton, Sir William.

Beverly Sills

American classical and opera singer

Known for her superb musical technique and bel canto voice, Sills was an impressive presence on the American opera stage. At the end of her singing career, she became an important figure in promoting the arts.

Born: May 25, 1929; Brooklyn, New York
Died: July 2, 2007; New York, New York
Also known as: Belle Miriam Silverman (birth name); Bubbles

Principal works

OPERATIC ROLES: Violetta in Giuseppe Verdi's *La Traviata*, 1951; Manon in Jules Massenet's *Manon*, 1953; Baby Doe in Douglas Moore's *The Ballad of Baby Doe*, 1958; Queen of the Night in Wolfgang Amadeus Mozart's *Die Zauberflöte*, 1964; Cleopatra in George Frideric Handel's *Giulio Cesare*, 1966; Parima in Gioacchino Rossini's *L'assedio di Corinto*, 1969; Marie in Donizetti's *La Fille du Régiment*, 1970; Lucia in Donizetti's *Lucia di Lammermoor*, 1970; Elizabeth I in Donizetti's *Roberto Devereux*, 1970; Norma in Vincenzo Bellini's *Norma*, 1971; Elvira in Bellini's *I puritani*, 1972; Mary Stuart in Donizetti's *Maria Stuarda*, 1972; Anna in

Donizetti's *Anna Bolena*, 1973; Rosina in Rossini's *Il barbiere di Siviglia*, 1974; Lucrezia in Donizetti's *Lucrezia Borgia*, 1975; Norina in Donizetti's *Don Pasquale*, 1978.

The Life

Belle Miriam Silverman, who acquired the nickname Bubbles for her effervescent personality, was gifted even as a child with great musical technique and an impressive voice. Before she became known as Beverly Sills, she was featured on such radio shows as *Uncle Bob's Rainbow House* and *Major Bowes's Capital Family Hour*. She learned how to sing arias by mimicking the recordings of singers such as Amelita Galli-Curci, and as a teenager she acquired her only voice teacher, Estelle Liebling, who advised Sills until Liebling's death in 1970. Sills's early professional training ended in 1945, and she spent ten years singing in opera and nightclubs before being signed in 1955 by the New York City Opera, the opera company with which she was most strongly identified. Her cheerful stage persona masked the difficulties of her personal life, such as the severe disabilities of her two children. Never the diva offstage, she was friendly and accessible to her fans and to journalists.

She garnered early attention as the title character in Douglas Moore's opera *The Ballad of Baby Doe* in 1958, which she recorded impressively in 1959. Full national recognition came in 1966, when she triumphantly portrayed Cleopatra in the New York City Opera's production of George Frideric Handel's *Giulio Cesare*. Her exuberant singing and impressive command of Baroque technique launched a Handel revival. For many critics, her most impressive work was her portrayal of the Tudor queens in Gaetano Donizetti's three operas loosely based on English history: *Anna Bolena*, *Maria Stuarda*, and *Roberto Devereux*. Sills made her belated debut at the Metropolitan Opera in 1975, in Gioacchino Rossini's seldom-heard opera *L'assedio di Corinto*, in a role that she had sung to critical acclaim at Milan's La Scala in 1969. In a half-dozen seasons at the Met, she sang such roles as Manon, Violetta, Lucia di Lammermoor, and Rosina before her retirement from the stage in 1980, when evidence of her vocal decline became clear.

Sills promptly stepped into a series of administrative roles, including director of the New York City Opera and chairwoman of Lincoln Center of the Performing Arts and the Metropolitan Opera. She was a prominent public voice of the arts in America as a result of her administrative roles and as the host of *Live from Lincoln Center*, which brought live performances of opera, drama, music, and dance direct from the stage to public television. Sills was active in the arts until two months before her death. Although she never smoked, she died from lung cancer.

The Music

Baby Doe and Cleopatra. The role of Baby Doe Tabor in *The Ballad of Baby Doe* was tailor-made for the youthful Sills, whose mother had once imagined turning her daughter into the Jewish Shirley Temple (a child singing and movie star of the 1930's). Flirtatious and ambitious, but fundamentally innocent, the opera's heroine manages to captivate the rich silver mine operator, Horace Tabor. In her portrayal of Baby Doe, Sills brought warmth, intelligence, technical security, impressive breath control, and purity of voice. The opera's concluding aria, "Always Through the Changing," provides the climax of a great recording; Sills reveals her absolute control over the vocal line, with the same technique she applied with great effect to Italian bel canto singing. Sills achieved the greatest musical triumph of her career in 1966, with her portrayal of Cleopatra in *Giulio Cesare* at the New York City Opera. Her success in the role earned her the cover of *Newsweek* magazine.

Manon. Further success followed with regularity. In 1968 she received an enthusiastic reception for her role as the flirtatious Manon in Jules Massenet's *Manon*, a perfect combination of guile and innocence. Her rendition of Manon's aria, "Adieu, mon petite table," showed how skillful she was in walking the tightrope between understated sentiment and sentimentality.

The Queens. Sills later claimed that her most demanding roles were the three queens in Gaetano Donizetti's trilogy of Tudor operas: Anne Boleyn, Mary Stuart, and Queen Elizabeth I. In the last, Sills claimed that playing the aging and imperious Queen Elizabeth I was the single most arduous role of her career.

Parima. Sills won international recognition in 1969 when she procured the affection of the hard-

Beverly Sills. (AP/Wide World Photos)

to-please Italian audience at Milan's La Scala in *L'assedio di Corinto*. Sills's success made it impossible for Rudolf Bing, the general director of the Metropolitan Opera, to resist offering her a contract, even though Bing's antipathy to American singers was notorious. Sills repeated her triumph in *L'assedio di Corinto* in 1975 and became a mainstay of the Metropolitan Opera for the next half-dozen years, even though her vocal decline had already begun.

Extroverts. Sills charmed Metropolitan Opera audiences in such roles as Rosina in *Il barbiere di Siviglia*, Manon, Lucia in Donizetti's *Lucia di Lammermoor*, and Violetta in Verdi's *La Traviata*. Because of the warmth of her personality, cheerful extroverts such as Manon and Violetta were ideal roles. Nevertheless, she was able to illuminate the fragmentation of frail Lucia's personality with great dramatic intensity.

Musical Legacy

Perhaps because of her cheerful personality and bright stage presence, some critics did not take Sills seriously as an artist. Some lamented her ubiquitous presence, as a result of her frequent appearances on television's *The Tonight Show* and specials with the comedienne Carol Burnett. A thorough professional with a great musical technique and a strong voice, Sills deserved serious comparison with her competitors in the bel canto repertory, Maria Callas and Joan Sutherland. Her greatest singing may have been early in her operatic career, in the mid-1950's to early 1960's, before she gained the critical attention she deserved, largely because she was singing at the less prestigious New York City Opera rather than at the Metropolitan Opera. Sills left a substantial recorded legacy, but she was not recorded as much in her early years as she should have been. Her great stage roles included Cleopatra, Manon, Lucia, Violetta, and the three Donizetti queens. Sills proved that an American singer, with exclusively American training and performances mostly on American stages, could be compared favorably with the greatest European singers.

Byron Nelson

Further Reading

Bing, Rudolf. *Five Thousand Nights at the Opera*. Garden City, N.Y.: Doubleday, 1972. Gossipy memoir of the longtime general director of the Metropolitan Opera.

Sills, Beverly. *Beverly: An Autobiography*. New York: Bantam, 1987. Sills gives a frank recounting of her life, including the triumphs and the hardships.

_____. *Bubbles: A Self-Portrait*. New York: Macmillan, 1976. The earlier of Sills's two autobiographical sketches was aimed at a popular audience.

Steane, J. B. *The Grand Tradition: Seventy Years of Singing on Record*. London: Duckworth, 1974. Credits Sills for her impressive technique, dramatic presence, and distinctive voice.

See also: Callas, Maria; Sinatra, Frank; Sutherland, Dame Joan.

Joseph "Run" Simmons

American rapper

A pioneer of hip-hop music, Simmons is one of the founders of the influential hip-hop group Run-D.M.C., which is credited with creating a commercially viable form of rap and introducing the genre to mainstream music audiences.

Born: November 14, 1964; Queens, New York
Also known as: Joseph Ward Simmons (full name); Son of Kurtis Blow; Run Love; Reverend Run
Member of: Run-D. M. C.

Principal recordings

ALBUMS (solo): *Distortion*, 2005.
ALBUMS (with Run-D. M. C.): *Run-D. M. C.*, 1984; *King of Rock*, 1985; *Raising Hell*, 1986; *Tougher than Leather*, 1988; *Back from Hell*, 1990; *Down with the King*, 1993; *Crown Royal*, 1999.
WRITINGS OF INTEREST: *It's Like That*, 2000; *Words of Wisdom: Daily Affirmations of Faith*, 2006.

The Life

Joseph Ward Simmons is one of the founders of the influential hip-hop group Run-D. M. C., the founder of Rev. Run Records, and an ordained minister in Zoe Ministries. He is the younger brother of hip-hop mogul and Def Jam Records cofounder Russell Simmons. He is married to Justine Simmons, and he has six children. A seventh child was born in 2006, but she died shortly thereafter.

Simmons's music career began as a deejay for Kurtis Blow, originally calling himself Son of Kurtis Blow, before changing his name to Run Love. In the early 1980's, Simmons joined with Darryl "D. M. C." McDaniels and Jason "Jam Master Jay" Mizell to form Run-D. M. C. The group released six albums between 1984 and 1993, and it released a final album in 2001. It officially disbanded in November, 2002, after Mizell was murdered, and Simmons embarked on a solo career under the name Rev. Run, which he had been using since 1996. He released his first solo album, *Distortion*, in 2005. The same year the Simmons family began starring in MTV's reality television series *Run's*

House. In 2000 Simmons published his spiritual memoir, *It's Like That*, and in 2006 he published a book of spiritual devotions and meditations entitled *Words of Wisdom: Daily Affirmations of Faith*.

The Music

Prior to Run-D. M. C., rap was seen primarily as street music. A few performers, such as the Sugar Hill Gang and Grandmaster Flash, had begun to transform it into a viable recording genre, but it was Run-D. M. C. that convinced audiences and recording executives that rap and hip-hop would sell beyond the inner cities. It was one of the first groups to move away from using exclusively background music, or "beats," that came from sampling dance records on turntables by tapping into electronic instruments such as synthesizers and drum machines. It also introduced hard-rock guitars into a genre that was dominated by the sounds of disco. Run-D. M. C.'s forceful vocal style laid the groundwork for the hardcore rap styles that followed, forcing listeners to pay attention to the words instead of just getting caught up in the music.

"It's Like That." From the self-titled debut album, "It's Like That" was Run-D. M. C.'s first single, and it is regarded as the first song to present rap as a commercially viable style. It was one of the first hip-hop songs to use a synthesized accompaniment rather than a sampled one. The song features the two rappers trading off lines and joining together for the refrain. It is an early example of what has become known as conscious rap, or rap that focuses on social issues rather than boasting or materialism. At times, the lyrics hint at the religious sentiments expressed on the albums *Back from Hell* and *Down with the King*.

"Walk This Way." Run-D. M. C.'s album *Raising Hell* included a cover of Aerosmith's "Walk This Way," in collaboration with Aerosmith's Steven Tyler and Joe Perry. This became the first hip-hop song to break the Top 10 on the *Billboard* Hot 100, peaking at number four. As such, it is often considered to be the song that introduced rap to mainstream audiences, primarily through the video's strong presence on MTV.

The song features a combination of sampling and live music. The underlying drumbeat was played on turntables by Jam Master Jay, and so was the song's signature guitar riff. Tyler's vocals and

Perry's guitar solos, which follow each chorus, were performed live in the studio.

"Run's House." This song became an unofficial anthem for Run-D. M. C. after its release on their *Tougher than Leather* album. The song is a fairly typical rap about the artists' skills. As on some of the group's earlier releases, the two rappers alternate verses, proclaiming their hip-hop superiority and their disdain for those who think rap is just a passing fad that requires no skill. Unlike some songs of this type, neither rapper boasts about his sexual prowess, his physical toughness, or acts of violence he has committed. "Run's House" is designed for audience participation in a live setting by encouraging listeners to respond to the question "Whose house?" with the response "Run's House!"

"Can I Get a Witness." Run-D. M. C.'s albums *Back from Hell* and *Down with the King* reflected a renewed spiritual awakening for the two rappers. No song from those albums goes as far to express this religious sentiment as "Can I Get a Witness" from *Down with the King*. On the surface, the lyrics feature the same themes as "Run's House," particularly the skills of both rappers and warnings to those who are "pretenders to the throne." However, both of Run's verses feature blatant references to his Christian faith. Like many of the songs on this album, "Can I Get a Witness" features some samples of jazz and blues instrumental figures.

"Mind on the Road." "Mind on the Road" is the first single from Simmons's solo release *Distortion*. It continues in the tradition of Run-D. M. C.'s aggressive vocals, which are almost shouted. The song also features the hard-rock guitar sound that Run-D. M. C. introduced into hip-hop; in this instance it is sampled from the Joan Jette and the Blackhearts hit "I Love Rock and Roll." The song is about Reverend Run's love of touring and performing live concerts.

Musical Legacy

Simmons's legacy is tied to that of Darryl "D. M. C." McDaniels and Jason "Jam Master Jay"

Mizell. The group ushered in a period of unprecedented change in the world of hip-hop, moving from the streets of the inner city to sold-out arenas and concert halls across the country. They opened the door for a generation of rappers who followed in their footsteps, including LL Cool J., Ice-T, Will Smith, Eminem, and 50 Cent. While many rap and hip-hop acts from the 1980's have been dismissed as dated and trite, Run-D. M. C. remains among the most respected and revered groups in hip-hop history. Simmons was inducted with Run-D. M. C. into the Rock and Roll Hall of Fame in 2008.

Eric S. Strother

Further Reading

Adler, Bill. *Tougher than Leather: The Rise of Run-D. M. C.* New York: New American Library. 1987. Written by the former publicity director for Def Jam Records, this is a comprehensive biography of Simmons and the others in Run-D. M. C.

Light, Alan, ed. *The Vibe History of Hip Hop.* New York: Three Rivers Press, 1999. A collection of essays intended to trace the development of the genre, although some are commentaries rather than documentaries.

McDaniels, Darryl. *King of Rock: Respect, Responsibility, and My Life with Run-D. M. C.* New York: St. Martin's Press, 2001. This memoir by Simmons's longtime partner provides personal anecdotes about Simmons and the career of Run-D. M. C.

Ro, Ronin. *Raising Hell: The Reign, Ruin, and Redemption of Run-D. M. C. and Jam Master Jay.* New York: Amistad, 2006. This book chronicles the careers of and the scandals surrounding the members of Run-D. M. C.

Simmons, Joseph. *It's Like That.* New York: St. Martin's Press, 2000. Simmons's autobiography offers facts about his life and also personal reflections that give insight into his personal philosophy.

See also: D. M. C.; 50 Cent; Grandmaster Flash; Ice-T; LL Cool J.

Carly Simon

American rock singer, songwriter, and guitarist

With her full-throated, openhearted singing style and affecting lyrics, Simon rose to prominence as a singer-songwriter in the 1970's.

Born: June 25, 1945; New York, New York
Also known as: Carly Elisabeth Simon
Member of: The Simon Sisters

Principal works

FILM SCORES: *Heartburn*, 1986; *Postcards from the Edge*, 1990; *This Is My Life*, 1992.

Principal recordings

ALBUMS (solo): *Anticipation*, 1971; *Carly Simon*, 1971; *No Secrets*, 1972; *Hotcakes*, 1974; *Playing Possum*, 1975; *Another Passenger*, 1976; *Takin' It Easy*, 1977; *Boys in the Trees*, 1978; *Spy*, 1979; *Come Upstairs*, 1980; *Torch*, 1981; *Hello Big Man*, 1983; *Spoiled Girl*, 1985; *Coming Around Again*, 1987; *Have You Seen Me Lately*, 1990; *My Romance*, 1990; *Carly Simon's Romulus Hunt: A Family Opera*, 1993; *Bells, Bears, and Fishermen*, 1994; *Letters Never Sent*, 1994; *Film Noir*, 1997; *Bedroom Tapes*, 2000; *Christmas Is Almost Here*, 2002; *Season's Greetings from Room 139*, 2002; *Moonlight Serenade*, 2005; *Into White*, 2007; *This Kind of Love*, 2008.
ALBUMS (with the Simon Sisters): *Cuddlebug*, 1964; *The Simon Sisters Sing for Children*, 1969.

The Life

Carly Elisabeth Simon was the third and youngest daughter of Richard L. Simon, the cofounder of the Simon & Schuster publishing company, and Andrea Heinemann Simon, a singer and civil rights activist. Growing up in an affluent and highly musical family in the Riverdale section of New York City, Simon and her two sisters developed considerable musical talent. In the 1960's, Simon dropped out of Sarah Lawrence College to form a folk-singing duo with her sister Lucy. In 1971 Simon began a major solo career as a rock artist, finding both critical and popular acclaim for her confessional lyrics and for her cordial, flexible, and forthright

voice. She was also known for the striking, sometimes provocative photographs of herself on her album covers. A major success was her third album, *No Secrets*, released in November, 1972. In the same year, Simon married the equally prominent singer-songwriter James Taylor, and the celebrity couple moved to a picturesque farmhouse in Martha's Vineyard, Massachusetts, which became Simon's permanent home. Considered one of rock's royal couples, the pair collaborated musically throughout the 1970's, supported progressive political causes, and produced two children, Sally and Ben. They divorced in 1983.

Stage fright and a reluctance to leave her children led Simon to make only rare concert appearances, but she continued to record her own songs as well as popular standards and to publish children's books. In 1987 Simon married poet Jim Hart; the couple divorced in 2007. A bout with breast cancer and depression led Simon to withdraw from the music business in 1997, but she recovered to produce an album of original material in 2000. She has continued to write and to record standards and her own music.

The Music

Simon's early work was in the folk-song genre popular in the 1970's, but her material, which always contained elements of show tunes and art song, later began to connect with the traditional popular song of the prerock American songbook. Her later work exhibits the influence of contemporary New Age music.

"That's The Way I Always Heard It Should Be." This melancholy ballad was Simon's first hit, and it is considered the first antimarriage song written and sung by a woman. The lyrics also suggest that marriage in an adult world required the sacrifice of the promise of youth. Despite the skeptical lyrics written for Simon by Jacob Brackman, the underlying romanticism of Simon's work was expressed by her melody, which has been compared to the kind of French art song written by Gabriel Fauré.

"Anticipation" and "You're So Vain." The hit song "Anticipation," from the album of the same name, was an effective showcase for Simon's ardent musical persona. It also demonstrated the assured sense of rock rhythm that made her a favorite of her era. This song suggests a sense of vulnerability with regard to an anticipated romantic encounter; as with all of her work, her enunciation and phrasing brought attention to her lyrics, often perceived as confessional.

Simon's had tremendous success with "You're So Vain," on her best-selling album, *No Secrets*, and it is her signature song. Addressed to a narcissistic lover, this bold rock song was a number-one hit, consolidated her reputation as an outspoken feminist, and created decades-long speculation as to the true identity of song's subject. In the 1970's, Simon released several more albums and more hit singles, but her transition from youthful rock music into the world of adult contemporary music was announced with her 1981 album *Torch*, considered the first example of a rock star covering classic jazz standards. She recorded other such albums in the years to come.

Later Work. The 1977 film *The Spy Who Loved Me* featured Simon's version of Marvin Hamlisch and Carole Bayer Sager's "Nobody Does It Better," which became a hit song. Beginning in the 1980's, Simon herself found success as a songwriter in film.

Carly Simon. (AP/Wide World Photos)

Of special note is 1986's score for *Heartburn*, resulting in the hit song, "Coming Around Again." "Let the River Run," a feminist anthem for 1988's *Working Girl*, won the Academy Award for Best Song as well as a Golden Globe and a Grammy Award. In 2001 this song was used by the U.S. Postal Service to restore confidence after the 9/11 and anthrax attacks of 2001.

In 1993 Simon composed *Romulus Hunt: A Family Opera*, commissioned by the Metropolitan Opera Guild and the Kennedy Center in Washington, D.C. Her collaboration with New Age musician Andreas Vollenweider suggested innovative directions in Simon's music. Her album *Letters Never Sent* exhibits his influence, and it demonstrates as well her continued ability to speak to her maturing generation. Of special note in this regard is her song "Like a River," which addresses the death of her mother. After her struggle with depression and cancer, Simon self-recorded and engineered the intimate *Bedroom Tapes*, a mix of pop, rock, classical, and New Age music. In 2008 Simon explored more musical possibilities with *This Kind of Love*, a sophisticated contemporary adult album that deploys an adventurous blend of Brazilian samba, contemporary rap, jazz, and rhythm and blues.

Musical Legacy

Simon was one of the most significant female singer-songwriters of her time. Three of her songs—"That's the Way I've Always Heard It Should Be," "You're So Vain," and "Let the River Run"—have been associated with the feminist movement brought about by women who came of age in the late 1960's. Her song "You're So Vain" was voted number 216 in the Recording Industry Association of America's Songs of the Century. This song has been covered by numerous rock groups and solo artists. Her other songs have been covered by such artists as Tori Amos, Michael McDonald, Mandy Moore, Sheryl Crow, Karrin Allyson, and Chaka Khan. A multiple Grammy Award winner, Simon was inducted into the Songwriters Hall of Fame in 1994.

Margaret Boe Birns

Further Reading

Grattan, Virginia L. *American Women Songwriters: A Biographical Dictionary*. Westport, Conn.: Greenwood Press, 1993. This reference includes Simon among 184 American-born female songwriters who have contributed to American popular song.

Kors, Michael. "Carly Simon: Romance, Pain, Anticipation." *Interview* (July, 2004). Simon is interviewed by fashion designer Michael Kors, and she discusses her singing, her personal style, and her process of surviving illness.

Sherman, Dale. *Twentieth Century Rock and Roll: Women in Rock*. Burlington, Ont.: Collector's Guide Publishing, 2001. This reference includes Simon among the fifty women who have defined rock music, with a short essay and recommended discography.

Simon, Carly. *Reflections: Carly Simon's Greatest Hits*. Milwaukee, Wis.: Hal Leonard, 2004. Music and lyrics to such Simon songs as "Anticipation," "Coming Around Again," "Let the River Run," "That's the Way I've Always Heard It Should Be," and "You're So Vain."

Weller, Sheila. *Girls Like Us: Carole King, Joni Mitchell, and Carly Simon, and the Journey of a Generation*. New York: Simon & Schuster, 2008. Written with the cooperation of Simon, this book includes her in a study of the lives and songs of three major female singer-songwriters who are viewed as representative women of their generation.

See also: Hamlisch, Marvin; King, Carole; Mitchell, Joni; Stewart, Rod; Taylor, Cecil; Taylor, James.

Paul Simon

American pop-rock singer, guitarist, and songwriter

Simon epitomized the folk-rock songwriter and balladeer of the 1960's and 1970's, with his evocative and poetic lyrics and music, notably his collaborations with Art Garfunkel. Simon also became one of the most enduring and constantly evolving pop musicians to emerge from the 1960's, synthesizing a variety of international styles with American pop and remarkable for the wit and emotional spectrum he conveys in his songs.

Born: October 13, 1941; Newark, New Jersey
Also known as: Paul Frederic Simon (full name); Jerry Landis; True Taylor
Member of: Tom and Jerry; Tico and the Triumphs; Simon and Garfunkel

Principal works

MUSICAL THEATER: *The Capeman*, 1998 (music and libretto; lyrics with Derek Walcott).

Principal recordings

ALBUMS (solo): *The Paul Simon Songbook*, 1965; *Paul Simon*, 1972; *There Goes Rhymin' Simon*, 1973; *Still Crazy After All These Years*, 1975; *One Trick Pony*, 1980; *Hearts and Bones*, 1983; *Graceland*, 1986; *Negotiations and Love Songs*, 1988; *The Rhythm of the Saints*, 1990; *You're the One*, 2000; *Surprise*, 2006.

ALBUMS (with Art Garfunkel): *Wednesday Morning, 3 A.M.*, 1964; *Parsley, Sage, Rosemary, and Thyme*, 1966; *The Sounds of Silence*, 1966; *Bookends*, 1968; *The Graduate*, 1968; *Bridge over Troubled Water*, 1970.

SINGLES (as Jerry Landis): "Anna Belle," 1959; "Lipstick on Your Lips," 1961; "Play Me a Sad Song," 1961; "The Lone Teen Ranger," 1963.

SINGLES (with Tom and Jerry): "Don't Say Goodbye," 1958; "Hey Schoolgirl," 1958; "Our Song," 1958.

The Life

Paul Frederic Simon was born to Louis, a bassist, and Belle Simon, a schoolteacher. Simon grew up with his younger brother, Eddie, in Queens, New York, where he attended Forest Hills High School. During his childhood Simon met Art Garfunkel, who became his professional singing partner for more than a decade. Simon attended Queens College and graduated in 1963 with a bachelor of arts in English literature. Then, upon his mother's urging, he studied law at Brooklyn Law School for several months. In 1964-1965 Simon spent some time in England, where he shared a flat with social worker Judith Piepe, developed a romantic relationship with Kathy Chitty, and recorded *The Paul Simon Songbook*. He returned to New York in 1965 to continue recording albums with Garfunkel. Because of differences in personality and career ambitions, Simon and Garfunkel broke up in 1970 after the release of several successful albums, including *Bridge over Troubled Water*.

In 1969 Simon married Peggy Harper, and they had a son, Harper, in 1972. The couple divorced in 1975. Simon dabbled a bit in film, appearing in Woody Allen's *Annie Hall* in 1977, and went on to write and star in his own film, *One Trick Pony*, which was a commercial failure. Simon had a brief romantic relationship with actor Shelley Duvall in the late 1970's, and in 1983 he married actor Carrie Fisher, which ended in divorce soon after. In 1985 Simon traveled to Johannesburg, South Africa, where he became acquainted with South African musical styles and recorded *Graceland*. In 1990 Simon was inducted into the Rock and Roll Hall of Fame with Art

Paul Simon (left) with Art Garfunkel. (National Archives)

Garfunkel. Two years later he married musician Edie Brickell. The couple had two sons, Adrian and Gabriel, and a daughter, Lulu (who inspired Simon's song "Father and Daughter").

The Music

Influenced by the sounds of the Everly Brothers in the 1950's, Simon first achieved international fame as a member of the singing duo Simon and Garfunkel. His songs from the 1960's roughly fit into the folk-rock tradition, combining vocal counterpoint and guitar accompaniment with witty lyrics concerning political and personal issues. He embarked upon a successful solo career in 1970. His songs in the 1970's contain greater chromaticism in general while including clever lyrics that remain a hallmark of his style. Although Simon showed interest in non-Western music throughout his career, in the 1980's and 1990's he began systematically employing musicians from a variety of locales, including South Africa and Brazil, on his albums, blending international influences with American pop and rock.

Simon and Garfunkel Albums. Simon first performed with Garfunkel as part of the singing duo known as Tom and Jerry in 1957. Their musical style, geared toward a teenage audience, was influenced by the Everly Brothers and Elvis Presley. In 1964, after having signed a contract with Columbia Records, they released their first album, *Wednesday Morning, 3 A.M.*, as Simon and Garfunkel. Produced by Tom Wilson, *Wednesday Morning, 3 A.M.* features five original songs by Simon and a number of cover songs, all performed in a folk-rock hybrid style that highlights vocals in tight harmony. This album contains the acoustic version of "The Sounds of Silence," one of their best known singles. After their debut release, the pair released four more albums—*Sounds of Silence; Parsley, Sage, Rosemary, and Thyme; Bookends;* and *Bridge over Troubled Water*—before splitting up in 1970. In 1968 Simon contributed several songs for the sound track for Mike Nichols's film *The Graduate*, which included the duo's recording of "Mrs. Robinson." This sound track introduced Simon and Garfunkel to a new film audience, boosting their record sales.

Early Solo Career. After he parted ways with Garfunkel, Simon's first solo album, titled *Paul Simon*, was released by Columbia Records in 1972. He recorded it in a number of different locations, the songs reflecting the styles and settings accordingly. For example, "Mother and Child Reunion" incorporates a reggae groove, "Me and Julio Down by the Schoolyard" involves rhythm guitar played in a calypso style, and "Hobo Blues" features jazz violinist Stéphane Grappelli, in combination with Simon's typical acoustic folk style. In the following year, *There Goes Rhymin' Simon* was released. Recorded in Muscle Shoals, Alabama, this album contains upbeat songs such as "Kodachrome" and "Loves Me like a Rock." The latter involved a vocal collaboration with the Dixie Hummingbirds and recalls a gospel-influenced style. *Still Crazy After All These Years* appeared in 1975 and featured a number of mature songs including the title track as a thoughtful ballad and "Gone at Last," a gospel song recorded with Phoebe Snow and the Jesse Dixon Singers. In 1980 Simon changed recording labels from Columbia to Warner Bros. and starred in a film he wrote, *One Trick Pony*, for which he also released a sound track. This album was not as commercially successful as his earlier albums, but it does include several well-crafted songs, such as "Late in the Evening," an upbeat, high-energy effort with prominent brass and other accompaniments. In 1983 Warner Bros. released *Hearts and Bones*, which received criticism from the popular press and was commercially unsuccessful.

Graceland. In 1986 Warner Bros. released *Graceland* (titled in homage to Presley), possibly Simon's most successful, influential, and controversial solo album. Described by some scholars as an example of world beat, the album fuses South African *isiZulu*, *mbaquanga*, and *isicathamiya* musical traditions performed by Ladysmith Black Mambazo, with Zydeco and American pop styles. In light of South Africa's policy of apartheid and a United Nations cultural boycott in place, Simon received a great deal of criticism and praise for his collaboration with South African musicians at this time—views ranging from claims that he exploited these musicians unfairly to commendations that he was successful in introducing these musicians and their styles to a wider, Western audience. The title track and "Diamonds on the Soles of Her Shoes" are hallmarks of the album's hybrid styles.

The Rhythm of the Saints. Released in 1990 and produced by Hallee, *The Rhythm of the Saints* marked another significant collaboration and fusion of styles. Musicians from El Salvador and Brazil participated in the recording of this album as well as some from Louisiana, New York, South Africa, Cameroon, and Trinidad. Brazilian drumming is featured prominently in the opening track titled "The Obvious Child."

Songs from the Capeman. In the late 1990's Simon embarked upon writing and producing a full-scale Broadway musical, *The Capeman*, but it flopped. Warner Bros. released *Songs from the Capeman* in 1998, which contained the songs Simon wrote for the musical. These songs consolidate musical elements of 1950's doo-wop, Latin influences, and Simon's characteristic ballad style to tell the story of a troubled Puerto Rican youth, Salvador Agron, who brutally murdered two teenagers in 1959. Unlike his previous albums, this one featured songs sung by musicians other than Simon, including Marc Anthony, Rubén Blades, Ednita Nazario, and Frank Negron, portraying the spirit of the characters featured in the musical.

You're the One. Released in 2000, *You're the One* contains a collection of mature songs, each unfolding a captivating narrative. The album boasts a host of international performers who had appeared with Simon on previous albums, such as South African bassist Bakithi Kumalo (who played on *Graceland* and *The Rhythm of the Saints*), guitarist Vincent Nguini, and American Steve Gadd, Simon's longtime drummer. The songs on this album address weighty themes of aging, love, mortality, the passing of time, and politics, reflecting Simon's maturity and position in life.

Surprise. Produced in part with Brian Eno and released in 2006, *Surprise* offers a collection of songs that play with sound, repetition, and time. Musically, the album fuses disparate elements—drum and bass, electronica, rock, pop, and lyric-driven songwriting. Influenced in part by the American political climate post-September 11, 2001, the album projects diverse themes of compassion and prayer ("Wartime Prayers") to prejudice ("How Can You Live in the Northeast?") to the power of familial love ("Father and Daughter").

Musical Legacy

The quintessential American songwriter, Simon has interwoven themes as wide-ranging as personal love and political commentary in his songs for more than fifty years. With his uncanny ability to convey a mood or story in song, Simon has influenced countless musicians, such as songwriters Chris de Burgh and Ralph McTell, as well as pop artists Dave Matthews, Stephen Bishop, and many others.

Simon has won a number of prestigious Grammy Awards throughout his career—from several Grammy Awards for "Mrs. Robinson" as early as 1969 to multiple Grammy Awards for *Bridge over Troubled Water, Still Crazy After All These Years,* and *Graceland.* Simon has been inducted into the Rock and Roll Hall of Fame twice—first in 1990 as part of the Simon and Garfunkel singing duo and again in 2001 for his contributions as a solo artist.

Victoria Malawey

Further Reading

Erlmann, Veit. *Music, Modernity, and the Global Imagination: South Africa and the West.* New York: Oxford University Press, 1999. This source offers two chapters on Simon's impact on South Africa and South African musicians, especially Ladysmith Black Mambazo and their involvement in the making of *Graceland,* the cultural and ethical ramifications of the collaboration, and the relation of his work to globalization in general. Includes a musical analysis of "Diamonds on the Soles of Her Shoes."

Humphries, Patrick. *Paul Simon: Still Crazy After All These Years.* New York: Doubleday, 1989. Incorporating larger historical and cultural contexts, this source offers a thorough account of Simon's life and career through the release of *Graceland.* Illustrations, discography, bibliography.

Jackson, Laura. *Paul Simon: The Definitive Biography of the Legendary Singer-Songwriter.* New York: Citadel, 2002. Based largely on interviews with people who know Simon or his work intimately, this biography provides a chronological account of Simon's personal and professional endeavors through the release of *You're the One* in 2000. Illustrations.

Kingston, Victoria. *Simon and Garfunkel: The Biography.* New York: Fromm International, 1998. This text provides a detailed description of the relationship between Simon and Garfunkel and their careers through the mid-1990's. Illustrations, discography.

Luftig, Stacy, ed. *The Paul Simon Companion: Four Decades of Commentary.* London: Ominbus, 1997. This collection of essays, reviews, and interviews covers different aspects of Simon's career through the mid-1990's. Chronology, discography, filmography, bibliography.

See also: Baez, Joan; Blades, Rubén; Cliff, Jimmy; Eno, Brian; Everly, Don and Phil; Garfunkel, Art; Glass, Philip; Grappelli, Stéphane; Hancock, Herbie; Jansch, Bert; Jones, Quincy; King, Carole; Makeba, Miriam; Masekela, Hugh; Nascimento, Milton; Presley, Elvis; Shabalala, Joseph; Strummer, Joe.

Nina Simone

American jazz and rhythm-and-blues composer, singer, and pianist

Simone is noted for the depth of her musical interpretations and the sense of mystery and power in her voice and her persona. Her protest songs formed a significant aspect of her musical identity, and they added an original dimension to her versatile and adventurous blend of musical idioms.

Born: February 21, 1933; Tryson, North Carolina
Died: April 21, 2003; Carry-le-Rouet, France
Also known as: Eunice Kathleen Waymon (birth name); High Priestess of Soul

Principal recordings

ALBUMS: *Little Girl Blue,* 1957; *Nina Simone and Her Friends,* 1957; *Jazz as Played in an Exclusive Side Street Club,* 1958; *The Amazing Nina Simone,* 1959; *My Baby Just Cares for Me,* 1959; *The Original Nina Simone,* 1959; *Forbidden Fruit,* 1961; *Nina Simone Sings Ellington,* 1962; *Nina's Choice,* 1963; *Blues: Ballads,* 1964; *Broadway—Blues—Ballads,* 1964; *Folksy Nina,* 1964; *I Put a Spell on You,* 1965; *Pastel Blues,* 1965; *High Priestess of Soul,* 1966; *Let It All Out,* 1966; *Nina Simone Sings the Blues,* 1966; *Nina Simone with Strings,* 1966; *Wild Is the Wind,* 1966; *Silk and Soul,* 1967; *Black Gold,* 1969; *To Love Somebody,* 1969; *Black Soul,* 1970; *Nina Simone and Piano,* 1970; *Here Comes the Sun,* 1971; *Heart and Soul,* 1972; *Emergency Ward,* 1973; *It Is Finished,* 1974; *Baltimore,* 1978; *The Rising Sun Collection,* 1980; *Artistry of Nina Simone,* 1982; *Fodder on My Wings,* 1982; *Nina's Back,* 1985; *A Single Woman,* 1993; *Nicht mehr im Programm,* 2001; *Nina Simone Sings Billie Holiday's Blues,* 2003.

The Life

Nina Simone (sih-MOHN) was born Eunice Kathleen Waymon in a small town in North Carolina during the Great Depression. Demonstrating musical gifts at an early age, she was aided by members of the black community in her town who paid for piano lessons and eventually sent her to the Juilliard School of Music in New York. In 1954, after a music conservatory's rejection that appeared to be more about her race than about her talent, Simone took a job in a nightclub in Atlantic City, New Jersey, where she sang and played a mix of jazz, blues, and classical piano. Changing her name to Nina, Spanish for little one, and Simone, after the popular French actress Simone Signoret, she soon developed a highly successful recording and performance career. In 1961 Simone married Andy Stroud, a New York detective who became her manager, and in 1962 she gave birth to their daughter, Lisa Celeste. The marriage ended in 1970.

In the 1960's, Simone performed and spoke at many civil rights demonstrations, but, frustrated by the racial situation and the music industry, she left the United States in the 1970's, living in exile in such places as Barbados, Liberia, and Switzerland, until she settled in the South of France in 1993. Beginning in 1985, Simone returned to the United States for a series of acclaimed performances. She died in her home in France; as requested, her ashes were spread in different African countries. Two days before her death, she was given an honorary degree by the Curtis Institute, the school that had rejected her at the start of her career.

The Music

Simone is generally classified as a jazz musician, but she preferred to be associated with black classical music, which allowed for other styles of black music, such as gospel, rhythm and blues, soul, and funk. She included in her repertoire her compositions, songs from musical theater and opera, as well as cabaret, folk, rock, and pop songs. Her eclectic repertoire—which could move from a cover of Screamin' Jay Hawkins's "I Put a Spell on You" to George Harrison's "Here Comes the Sun," to Kurt Weill and Bertolt Brecht's "Pirate Jenny"—reflected her free-spirited, inventive, and un-predictable musical temperament. Her unique vocal style was distinguished by a haunting vibrato and an earthy alto, and she was capable of expressing an emotional range that included intense passion, deep anguish, playful exuberance, brooding melancholy, and cold fury. In her live performances, her commanding presence was a further confirmation of her status as the High Priestess of Soul.

Little Girl Blue. Simone's first album, *Little Girl Blue*, was released in 1958, and it became an instant success. This album included her legendary soulful performance of George Gershwin's "I Loves You, Porgy," which, as a single, became her only Top 40 hit in the United States. This album also includes her haunting, expressive interpretation of Richard Rodgers and Lorenz Hart's "Little Girl Blue," which demonstrated her signature blending of classical counterpoint, blues, and improvisational jazz. Another important track is her jaunty interpreta-

Nina Simone. (AP/Wide World Photos)

tion of Walter Donaldson and Gus Kahn's "My Baby Just Cares for Me," which, as with "Little Girl Blue," featured an inventive vocal against a Bach-style piano counterpoint. Simone's interpretation of this song would become a hit again years later in 1987, helping to relaunch her career.

"Mississippi Goddam." Written by Simone in 1964, this song was a response to the murder of civil rights leader Medgar Evers in Mississippi and the bombing of a church in Birmingham, Alabama, which killed four black children. While Simone's voice projects anger and grief, the tune is bright and up-tempo, a disarming counterpoint to the accusatory words and the bitter vocals. This song added considerably to Simone's identity as a protest singer, and it became an anthem of the Civil Rights movement in the 1960's.

"Four Women." Written in 1966 by Simone, this song made a significant contribution to the growing black feminist movement of the time. The almost novelistic song lyrics describe four black women whose personalities and situations are related to the gradations of their skin color. In exploring these women's differing backgrounds, Simone also responded to the temper of the times by introducing into her lyrics specifically African American historical references. Expressing both pain and anger, this song became a powerful expression of Simone's developing political activism and her identity as a protest singer.

"To Be Young, Gifted, and Black." Simone wrote this song in 1970 with Weldon Irvine, as a tribute to her friend, the African American playwright Lorraine Hansberry, who had an unfinished play of the same name. This song was a commercial hit, but, even more, it expressed the empowering sentiments of the growing Black Pride movement, and the song became one of its anthems. It was the most recorded song in Simone's repertoire, and it is likely her most inspiring and affirmative protest song.

Musical Legacy

Simone left a strong musical legacy of performances and recordings, and she influenced the social and political history of the United States through her involvement as a singer and songwriter in the cause of civil rights for African Americans. Her song "To Be Young, Gifted, and Black"

spoke not only to her own generation but to the black artists who came of age after the civil rights era. She has been an inspiration and a role model to such black female musical artists as Lauryn Hill, Alicia Keys, Mary J. Blige, and Meshell Ndegeocello. Her music and performance style have inspired many singers and singing groups, both black and white; her original recordings have been covered by such artists as Jeff Buckley, David Bowie, Aretha Franklin, Donny Hathaway, and Michael Bublé. Simone was the recipient of numerous music awards as well as honorary degrees in music and humanities from the University of Massachusetts and Malcolm X College.

Margaret Boe Birns

Further Reading

Acker, Kerry. *Nina Simone*. Philadelphia: Chelsea House, 2004. This biography addresses Simone's personal and professional life, and it includes a chronology, a bibliography, and suggestions for further reading.

Bratcher, Melanie E. *The Words and Songs of Bessie Smith, Billie Holiday, and Nina Simone: Sound Motion, Blues Spirit, and African Memory*. Routledge: New York, 2007. This source explores the three artists in the context of an African artistic and cultural system.

Feldstein, Ruth. "'I Don't Trust You Anymore': Nina Simone, Culture, and Black Activism in the 1960's." *The Journal of American History* (March, 2005). This is a discussion of Simone's feminism and civil rights activism as represented in her music, lyrics, and performances.

Hampton, Sylvia, and David Nathan. *Nina Simone: Break Down and Let It All Out*. London: Sanctuary Publishing, 2004. This biographical portrait includes an introduction by Simone's daughter.

Simone, Nina, and Stephen Cleary. *I Put a Spell on You*. New York: Da Capo Press, 2003. This autobiography covers Simone's childhood, rise to fame, political activism, and professional and personal life.

See also: Blige, Mary J.; Bowie, David; Brel, Jacques; Dorsey, Thomas A.; Franklin, Aretha; Gershwin, George; Gibb, Barry, Maurice, and Robin; Harrison, George; Makeba, Miriam; Newman, Randy; Weill, Kurt.

Frank Sinatra

American popular music and musical-theater singer and songwriter

Sinatra, who was noted for his relaxed, crooning style of singing, captivated audiences of all ages, especially the bobby-soxers of the 1940's, and he also became a well-known actor, first in musicals and later in dramatic films.

Born: December 12, 1915; Hoboken, New Jersey
Died: May 14, 1998; Los Angeles, California
Also known as: Francis Albert Sinatra (full name); Ol' Blue Eyes; Chairman of the Board
Member of: The Tommy Dorsey Orchestra

Principal recordings

ALBUMS (solo): *Swing and Dance with Frank Sinatra,* 1944; *The Voice of Frank Sinatra,* 1945; *Sing and Dance with Sinatra,* 1950; *In the Wee Small Hours,* 1954; *Songs for Swingin' Lovers!,* 1955; *Frank Sinatra Conducts Tone Poems of Color,* 1956; *A Jolly Christmas from Frank Sinatra,* 1957; *A Swingin' Affair,* 1957; *Close to You and More,* 1957; *Come Fly with Me,* 1957; *Where Are You?,* 1957; *Come Dance with Me,* 1958; *Only the Lonely,* 1958; *No One Cares,* 1959; *Nice 'n' Easy,* 1960; *Ring-a-Ding Ding,* 1960; *Come Swing with Me,* 1961; *I Remember Tommy,* 1961; *Point of No Return,* 1961; *Sinatra's Swingin' Session!!! And More,* 1961; *Swing Along with Me,* 1961; *All Alone,* 1962; *Sinatra and Basie,* 1962 (with Count Basie); *Sinatra and Strings,* 1962; *Softly, as I Leave You,* 1963; *It Might as Well Be Swing,* 1964; *Moonlight Sinatra,* 1965; *September of My Years,* 1965; *Sinatra at the Sands,* 1966; *Strangers in the Night,* 1966; *That's Life,* 1966; *Francis A. Sinatra and Edward K. Ellington,* 1967 (with Edward K. Ellington); *Francis Albert Sinatra and Antônio Carlos Jobim,* 1967 (with Antônio Carlos Jobim); *Frank Sinatra and Frank and Nancy,* 1967 (with Frank Sinatra, Jr. and Nancy Sinatra); *Cycles,* 1968; *The Sinatra Family Wish You a Merry Christmas,* 1968; *A Man Alone and Other Songs of Rod McKuen,* 1969; *My Way,* 1969; *Sinatra and Company,* 1969; *Watertown,* 1969; *Ol' Blue Eyes Is Back,* 1973; *Frank Sinatra Conducts the Music of*

Alec Wilder, 1976; *Trilogy,* 1979; *She Shot Me Down,* 1981; *L.A. Is My Lady,* 1984; *Duets,* 1993; *Duets II,* 1994.
SINGLES (with the Tommy Dorsey Orchestra): "I'll Never Smile Again," 1940; "Dolores," 1941; "Night and Day," 1942; "There Are Such Things," 1942; "All or Nothing at All," 1943; "In the Blue of Evening," 1943.

The Life

Francis Albert Sinatra (sih-NAH-trah) was born to Natalina Garaventa Sinatra, nicknamed Dolly, and Anthony Martin "Marty" Sinatra, a boxer. His mother, who was involved in local politics, was a crusader for voting rights for women. Sinatra grew up in a rough-and-tumble environment, and he learned how to defend himself. After his parents opened a bar and grill that catered to Hoboken's Irish American community, they began to enjoy considerable prosperity. His boxing days over, Marty became a firefighter. Dolly bought a house in the best part of town and furnished it lavishly. Sinatra, who dropped out of high school, began to sing in his parents' bar and in other local establishments.

In 1937 Sinatra won a singing contest and appeared on radio's *Major Bowes Amateur Hour,* which resulted in his being offered a six-month contract to tour the United States. Before long, he was singing regularly on radio programs. In 1939 he began singing with Harry James's band; in 1940 and 1942, he toured with Tommy Dorsey, in whose band he developed his signature crooning style that caused a generation of teenage girls to swoon. During the summer of 1939, he performed to enthusiastic audiences in the nightclub of New York City's Hotel Astor.

Sinatra quickly became one of the most celebrated singers of his day, selling out all his concerts. His rendition of "I'll Never Smile Again" enjoyed legendary success. He also became well known for his renditions of "Night and Day" and "All or Nothing at All."

From 1943 until 1945, Sinatra was a regular soloist on the weekly radio show *Your Hit Parade.* These appearances exposed him to Hollywood producers, who employed him to make musical films, such as *Anchors Aweigh* (1945) and *On the Town* (1949). In the early 1950's, his popularity as a singer waning, he took on a dramatic role in *From Here to Eternity*

1361

(1953), winning the Academy Award for Best Supporting Actor. In the next fifteen years, he appeared in several feature films.

Following a short retirement between 1971 and 1973, Sinatra returned as a vocalist, cutting more than two hundred records in two years. He toured the world, giving concerts well into the 1990's. He received such honors as the Jean Hersholt Humanitarian Award and the Presidential Medal of Freedom. In 1994 he received a Grammy Lifetime Achievement Award. His health began to fail in the 1990's, and on May 14, 1998, he suffered a fatal heart attack in Los Angeles.

The Music

Sinatra admired the singing styles of Rudy Vallee and Bing Crosby, and though Sinatra's style was not derivative, it did evoke the sound of these popular vocalists. A baritone, Sinatra exhibited a sophisticated style, marked by touches of jazz and echoes of bel canto. His singing was relaxed and intimate. He mesmerized women in the audiences, giving a sensation that he was singing directly to each individual.

Signature Tunes. Sinatra was identified with a number of songs that at various times became signature pieces for him. At the beginning of his career, "Night and Day" and "All or Nothing at All" were the songs audiences expected to hear Sinatra sing during his concerts. Although he still sang these songs decades later, he became identified with such other numbers as "My Way" and "New York, New York."

Throughout his professional life, Sinatra demonstrated a remarkable ability to appeal to a broad age spectrum. He imparted an intimacy to his songs, figuratively caressing his lyrics with his voice and paying particular attention to his phrasing.

Songwriter. Sinatra seldom contributed lyrics to the songs he sang. An exception was "This Love of Mine," a song on which he collaborated with Hank Sanicola. When Sinatra wrote this song, his marriage to Nancy Barbato, the first serious love of his life, was collapsing, and the lyrics reflect the sadness of the pair at the end of their relationship.

Later, as his personal life became increasingly complicated, Sinatra used his pain and uncertainty

Frank Sinatra. (AP/Wide World Photos)

to inform his music, giving it an emotional authenticity that captivated audiences.

Recordings. During his early years traveling with the Dorsey band, Sinatra earned little money. In 1941, when he threatened to leave, Dorsey raised his pay to $250 a week, and in January of the following year, he arranged for Sinatra to make records as a soloist. In that year, he made twenty-nine singles with Dorsey. *Billboard* designated him Male Vocalist of the Year.

During the early years of his career, many influential people connected with the world of music predicted a bright future for Sinatra. As early as 1940, Crosby stopped by the studio in which *Las Vegas Nights* (1941) was being filmed, and he heard Sinatra sing "I'll Never Smile Again." Crosby praised Sinatra's singing, little realizing that Sinatra would soon become a potent competitor.

Sinatra began to produce records at a dizzying pace. Between 1940 and 1943, twenty-three were Top 10 singles on the *Billboard* list. In 1943 he was the first nonclassical musician to be featured at the Hollywood Bowl, attracting such a large audience that the Hollywood Bowl used the proceeds from ticket sales to completely eliminate its substantial debt.

At the peak of his popularity, Sinatra performed as many as forty-five shows a week. His first concept album, *The Voice of Frank Sinatra*, was distributed in 1946 and his popularity endured for nearly five more decades.

Musical Legacy

Sinatra brought his individual style of music into venues usually reserved for classical musicians, establishing popular music as a worthwhile genre. He had no classical-music pretensions, although later in life he appeared with Beverly Sills, Luciano Pavarotti, and other opera singers. In an era in which popular music was directed largely to adults, Sinatra created a musical genre designed to appeal to and attract teenage audiences.

R. Baird Shuman

Further Reading

Carpozi, George, Jr. *Frank Sinatra: Is This Man Mafia?* New York: Manor Books, 1979. Carpozi explores Sinatra's connections with the underworld and particularly with the Mafia, providing some revealing insights.

Falcone, Vincent, and Bob Popyk. *Frankly Between Us: My Life Conducting Frank Sinatra's Music*. Milwaukee, Wis.: Hal Leonard, 2005. Falcone, who conducted Sinatra's concerts for more than fifteen years, presents many heartwarming vignettes, although the absence of an index limits this book's use.

Hamill, Pete. *Why Sinatra Matters*. Boston: Little, Brown, 1998. Hamill's study is impressively analytical, written from the vantage point of someone who knew and admired Sinatra and his work over an extended period.

Jacobs, George, and William Stadiem. *Mr. S.: My Life with Frank Sinatra*. New York: HarperEntertainment, 2003. This intimate reminiscence is by the man who for many years was Sinatra's valet.

Lahr, John. *Sinatra: The Artist and the Man*. New York: Random House, 1997. This sensitive overview of Sinatra's career is easily accessible and eminently readable.

O'Brien, Daniel. *The Frank Sinatra Film Guide*. London: Butler and Tanner, 1998. A useful and thorough overview of the many films in which Sinatra appeared.

Petkov, Steven, and Leonard Mustazza, eds. *The Frank Sinatra Reader*. New York: Oxford University Press, 1985. Although somewhat dated, this collection of essays relevant to the life and career of Sinatra is still valuable to those interested in him.

Romero, Gerry. *Sinatra's Women*. New York: Manor Books, 1976. Sinatra was a womanizer who had four marriages and many close alliances with other females. Although dated, this book presents interesting information about Sinatra's love life to 1975.

Sinatra, Tina. *Frank Sinatra: An American Legend*. New York: Reader's Digest, 1998. One of several books by Sinatra's daughter about her father, valuable for some intimate insights.

Summers, Anthony, and Robbyn Swan. *Sinatra: The Life*. New York: Alfred A. Knopf, 2005. This thorough, engaging, and comprehensive assessment of Sinatra's life and career is well written and carefully researched.

See also: Basie, Count; Belafonte, Harry; Bennett, Tony; Bergman, Alan; Bernstein, Elmer; Brel, Jacques; Brown, James; Burke, Johnny; Cahn, Sammy; Campbell, Glen; Charles, Ray; Chevalier, Maurice; Coleman, Cy; Connick, Harry, Jr.; Crosby, Bing; Davis, Sammy, Jr.; Ellington, Duke; Garland, Judy; Gilberto, João; Green, Adolph, and Betty Comden; Holiday, Billie; Jobim, Antônio Carlos; Jones, Quincy; Kern, Jerome; Leadbelly; Lee, Peggy; Mercer, Johnny; Newley, Anthony; Nichols, Red; Pavarotti, Luciano; Porter, Cole; Previn, Sir André; Robinson, Smokey; Ronstadt, Linda; Sills, Beverly; Tormé, Mel; Van Heusen, Jimmy; Walker, T-Bone; Willson, Meredith.

Grace Slick

American rock singer-songwriter

Slick was one of the first women lead singers in a major rock-and-roll group. Her work with Jefferson Airplane would open the doors for later generations of rock women, including Lita Ford, Chrissie Hynde, Joan Jett, Patti Smith, Courtney Love, and others. Her song "White Rabbit" became an emblem of the psychedelic 1960's youth culture.

Born: October 30, 1939; Evanston, Illinois
Also known as: Grace Barnett Wing (birth name)
Member of: The Great Society; Jefferson Airplane; Jefferson Starship; Starship

Principal recordings

ALBUMS (solo): *Manhole*, 1974; *Dreams*, 1980; *Welcome to the Wrecking Ball*, 1981; *Software*, 1984.

ALBUMS (with the Great Society): *Conspicuous Only in Its Absence*, 1968; *How It Was*, 1968.

ALBUMS (with Jefferson Airplane): *After Bathing at Baxter's*, 1967; *Surrealistic Pillow*, 1967; *Crown of Creation*, 1968; *Bless Its Pointed Little Head*, 1969; *Volunteers*, 1969; *Bark*, 1971; *Long John Silver*, 1972; *Thirty Seconds over Winterland*, 1973; *Jefferson Airplane*, 1989.

ALBUMS (with Jefferson Starship): *Dragon Fly*, 1974; *Red Octopus*, 1975; *Spitfire*, 1976; *Earth*, 1978; *Winds of Change*, 1982; *Nuclear Future*, 1984.

ALBUMS (with Paul Kantner): *Sunfighter*, 1971; *Baron Von Tollbooth and the Chrome Nun*, 1973.

ALBUMS (with Starship): *Knee Deep in the Hoopla*, 1985; *No Protection*, 1987; *Love Among the Cannibals*, 1989.

WRITINGS OF INTEREST: *Somebody to Love? A Rock-and-Roll Memoir*, 1999.

The Life

Grace Barnett Wing was born in Evanston, Illinois, in 1939. The family moved to California in 1942, first to Los Angeles and then to San Francisco. Wing attended Finch College in New York and the University of Miami. While in Miami, she heard of a new San Francisco phenomenon, "hippies."

Her decision to leave Miami and return to San Francisco to experience this new lifestyle proved to be pivotal.

Wing married Jerry Slick in 1961, having met him at age ten; a series of unfulfilling jobs followed, including a brief stint as a model. In 1965, with friends and family members, the couple formed a band called the Great Society (an allusion to the government welfare programs implemented by the administration of Lyndon B. Johnson during the Vietnam War era). The lifestyle of a performing artist appealed to Slick, allowing her to work minimal hours and experiment with drugs. The fledgling "psychedelic rock" subgenre was not yet widely known, but as young people flocked to San Francisco, hallucinogens such as peyote and LSD became the drugs of choice for many. The Great Society performed regularly at the Fillmore, often opening for Jefferson Airplane; Slick was invited to join that band in 1965.

After several years of separation, Slick and her husband ended their marriage in 1971. By that time she was already involved with Jefferson Airplane's guitarist, Paul Kantner; their daughter, China Wing Kantner, was born in 1971. Slick married Skip Johnson, who designed lights for Jefferson Airplane, in 1974; that marriage ended in 1994. By the end of the 1980's, Slick's music career was winding down, and she turned her attention to the visual arts, an area in which she had honed her talent since childhood.

The Music

Grace Slick and Jefferson Airplane made music that came to be known as psychedelic rock. This offshoot of rock and roll was inspired by the use of various drugs, including marijuana, LSD, and psilocybin. The essence of psychedelic rock was an emphasis on surrealism and the creation of a hypnotic musical effect, along with visual effects, such as lighting, that supported the entranced and frenetic mood of the music. Other groups who contributed to this subgenre included the Doors and the Grateful Dead, who were also working in San Francisco at the time. Intended to liberate both mind and spirit, the psychedelic movement was embodied musically by Jefferson Airplane.

Jefferson Airplane released many albums, including *After Bathing at Baxter's*, *Crown of Creation*, and *Long John Silver*. It was their 1967 album *Surre-*

alistic Pillow, however, that put Jefferson Airplane on the map and gave the group their most memorable hits: "Somebody to Love" and "White Rabbit."

"Somebody to Love." "Somebody to Love" was written by Darby Slick, Grace's brother-in-law, for the Great Society. Released in 1966 as a single, the song did not make much of an impact on the musical scene when rendered in the folk-oriented, relatively sedate style of the Great Society. After joining Jefferson Airplane, Slick took the song to the recording sessions for *Surrealistic Pillow*, where it was transformed into a more powerful rock-and-roll arrangement. This version reached number five on the *Billboard* charts.

The lyrics to "Somebody to Love" reflect a shift in values and subject matter for popular music. Unlike most pop-music love songs of its time, "Somebody to Love" was not about innocent romance or about finding or keeping love. Rather, Darby Slick's words—"Don't you. . . . Wouldn't you. . . . You'd better find somebody to love"—emphasize feelings of alienation and loneliness, focusing on the importance, even the urgency, of loving someone rather than being loved or developing intimacy. The minor key of this tune, along with its driving, insistent beat, underscores this message.

"White Rabbit." The song "White Rabbit" is Jefferson Airplane's most famous and enduring signature piece. It refers to Lewis Carroll's *Alice's Adventures in Wonderland* (1865), creating a hypnotic psychedelic atmosphere through its repetitive snare-drum pattern. Drawn to Spanish music and dance, Slick also listened repeatedly to Miles Davis and Gil Evans's *Sketches of Spain* (1959) before writing this song, which begins with a Spanish-bolero-influenced riff. The lyrics refer overtly to drugs and are cleverly entwined with references to Carroll's children's story, as in the opening: "One pill makes you larger. And one pill makes you small." Again written in a minor key, the song implicitly joins innocence with the decadence of the drug culture. The song's monotonous rhythm is offset by its rising pitch and accelerating tempo, which heighten the tension as the music crescendos to a climax in which the key modulates from minor to major. Slick ends by admonishing listeners to "remember what the dormouse said: 'Feed your head'" (a reference to the dormouse in Carroll's novel, who said nothing of the sort).

"We Built This City." Following the departure of two members of Jefferson Airplane in 1973, Slick and Paul Kantner re-formed as Jefferson Starship. When Slick was asked to leave that group in 1978 (for alcohol-related issues), she formed another offshoot, called, simply, Starship. "We Built This City" was released as Starship's debut single in 1985. It reached number one on the *Billboard* charts, making Slick the oldest female singer in *Billboard* history (she was forty-six at the time) to have a number-one single. In spite of the song's commercial success, it was not highly regarded in the years after its release, earning a spot on VH1's television show, *The Fifty Most Awesomely Bad Songs . . . Ever*. The lyrics look back, reminding listeners that "we" (Slick and her colleagues, rock musicians in general) "built this city on rock and roll."

Musical Legacy

Jefferson Airplane performed at the major, and now legendary, rock festivals of the 1960's, including Monterey in 1967 and Woodstock in 1969. Monterey's performers included many of the most notable and influential musical acts of the time: the Grateful Dead, Jimi Hendrix, Ravi Shankar, and Janis Joplin.

The Woodstock Music Festival was a seminal experience for Slick and for the musicians and youth culture of the time, a turning point in music history. Considered by many to be a generation's defining moment, Woodstock attracted half a million young people, who traveled from around the country to take part. Though poorly organized, this festival progressed without any serious negative incidents and had the effect of propelling the fame of many bands, especially Jefferson Airplane. For several years after Woodstock, Jefferson Airplane was the most highly paid touring band in the United States.

The song "White Rabbit" has been recorded by at least twenty different bands since its release. It has also figured prominently in other areas of pop culture: movies (including *Platoon*, 1986), books (including the 1971 antidrug novel *Go Ask Alice* and Hunter S. Thompson's 1971 book *Fear and Loathing in Las Vegas*), and television shows (including episodes of *The Sopranos* and *The Simpsons*).

Andrea Moore

Further Reading

Chenoweth, Lawrence. "The Rhetoric of Hope and Despair: A Study of the Jimi Hendrix Experience and the Jefferson Airplane." *American Quarterly* 23, no. 1 (Spring, 1971): 25-45. The author examines rock-and-roll culture from the perspective of the lyrics of two rock bands. Offers a historical perspective on the impact of this music on the 1960's youth culture.

Fong-Torres, Ben. "The Rolling Stone Interview: Grace Slick and Paul Kantner." In *The Rolling Stone Interviews, 1967-1980.* New York: St. Martin's Press, 1989. With background information about Jefferson Airplane's personnel and its role in the San Francisco rock-and-roll scene, this is an extensive interview by one of *Rolling Stone* magazine's top rock journalists.

Moore, Allan F. "Psychedelic Rock." In *The New Grove Dictionary of Music and Musicians,* edited by Stanley Sadie. 2d ed. New York: Grove, 2000. Offers a brief definition of the genre along with a bibliography.

Slick, Grace, with Andrea Cagan. *Somebody to Love? A Rock and Roll Memoir.* New York: Warner, 1998. Slick's conversational autobiography covers her life both as a musician and as a visual artist.

Tamarkin, Jeff. *Got a Revolution! The Turbulent Flight of Jefferson Airplane.* New York: Atria Books, 2003. A comprehensive study of Jefferson Airplane: its individual members, its role in the San Francisco music scene, and its impact.

See also: Crosby, David; Garcia, Jerry; Joplin, Janis; Morrison, Jim; Stills, Stephen; Stone, Sly.

Bessie Smith

American blues singer

One of the most popular blues singers of the 1920's and 1930's, Smith was notable for her powerful voice, her innovative style of bending notes, and her vibrant interpretation of lyrical content.

Born: April 15, 1894; Chattanooga, Tennessee
Died: September 26, 1937; Clarksdale, Mississippi

Also known as: Elizabeth Smith (full name); Empress of the Blues

Principal recordings

ALBUMS: *Lady Luck Blues,* 1923; *The World's Greatest Blues Singer,* 1923.

SINGLES: "Any Woman's Blues," 1923; "Bleeding Hearted Blues," 1923; "Downhearted Blues," 1923; "Gulf Coast Blues," 1923; "Jailhouse Blues," 1923; "Sam Jones Blues," 1923; "Tain't Nobody's Biz-ness If I Do," 1923; "Ticket Agent Ease Your Window Down," 1923; "Follow the Deal on Down," 1924; "House Rent Blues," 1924; "Pinchbacks," 1924; "Take 'Em Away," 1924; "Weeping Willow Blues," 1924; "At the Christmas Ball," 1925; "Cake Walkin' Babies (from Home)," 1925 (with Coleman Hawkins); "Careless Love Blues," 1925; "Cold in Hand Blues," 1925 (with Louis Armstrong); "I Ain't Gonna Play No Second Fiddle," 1925 (with Armstrong); "J. C. Holmes Blues," 1925 (with Armstrong); "Nashville Woman's Blues," 1925; "Reckless Blues," 1925 (with Armstrong); "Saint Louis Blues," 1925 (with Armstrong); "Sobbin' Hearted Blues," 1925 (with Armstrong); "Yellow Dog Blues," 1925 (with Hawkins); "You've Been a Good Ole Wagon," 1925 (with Armstrong); "Baby Doll," 1926; "The Gin House Blues," 1926; "Jazzbo Brown from Memphis Town," 1926; "Lost Your Head Blues," 1926; "Money Blues," 1926; "One and Two Blues," 1926; "Squeeze Me," 1926; "Young Woman's Blues," 1926; "After You've Gone," 1927 (with Hawkins); "Alexander's Ragtime Band," 1927 (with Hawkins); "Back Water Blues," 1927; "Foolish Man Blues," 1927; "A Good Man Is Hard to Find," 1927; "Mean Old Bed Bug Blues," 1927; "Muddy Water," 1927 (with Hawkins); "There'll Be a Hot Time in the Old Town Tonight," 1927 (with Hawkins); "Trombone Cholly," 1927; "Empty Bed Blues," 1928; "Me and My Gin," 1928; "Poor Man's Blues," 1928; "Nobody Knows You When You're Down and Out," 1929; "Black Mountain Blues," 1930; "New Orleans Hop Scop Blues," 1930; "I Need a Little Sugar in My Bowl," 1931; "Long Old Road/Shipwreck Blues," 1931; "Do Your Duty," 1933; "Gimme a Pigfoot," 1933 (with

Benny Goodman); "I'm Down in the Dumps," 1933; "Take Me for a Buggy Ride," 1933.

The Life

Elizabeth Smith was born into humble circumstances in 1894 in Chattanooga, Tennessee. Her father, William, a part-time Baptist preacher, died when she was a child. When Smith was nine, her mother Laura died, and her older sister Violet was left to care for Bessie and for her four siblings. Bessie and her brother Andrew performed on street corners, singing for spare change. Even at a young age, Smith possessed a raw, extraordinary voice. As a teenager, she turned to show business to make a living. In 1912, with the help of her brother Clarence, who was a comedian in the Moses Stokes Company, Smith was hired as a dancer for the traveling minstrel show. She eventually sang in the chorus, and, as her reputation grew, she gained a spot as a featured singer, impressing audiences with her full, strong voice.

Rising in popularity in the 1920's, Smith was the most highly paid African American female entertainer of her day. Her 1920 marriage to an affluent Southerner, Earl Love, ended soon after the wedding, when Love died under mysterious circumstances. In 1922 Smith met a night watchman named Jack Gee; they married in 1923. Smith signed a contract with Columbia Records, but her personal life was troubled. Her marriage was distressed by infidelities on both sides, and Smith's problem drinking resulted in physical altercations with Gee and others. When Smith discovered Gee seeing another woman, she fired a pistol at him, although the bullet did not hit him. Meanwhile, Smith became involved with Lillian Simpson, and when Gee discovered the nature of his wife's relationship with Simpson, he threatened to kill Smith.

In the 1930's, Smith's career began to decline, as her blues singing style fell out of favor with audiences. On September 26, 1937, she was riding in a car with her then-beau Richard Morgan (the uncle of future jazz vibraphonist Lionel Hampton) before dawn when their vehicle hit another one on the side of the road. Shortly after the initial crash, another car, carrying a white couple, hit the rear end of

Bessie Smith. (Library of Congress)

Morgan's vehicle. It took seven hours for Smith to gain hospital admission—either because the white woman in the accident was seen as a priority or because Smith was refused admission by one hospital because of her skin color. Record producer John Hammond speculated in the jazz magazine *Down Beat* that the latter was true. Smith reportedly bled to death, although this has never been proved. At the time of her death, Smith was forty-three years old.

The Music

When Smith's professional career began in the Moses Stokes Company, she met blues singer Ma Rainey, who became Smith's mentor. A strong vocal force, Smith used her intimidating stature to great effect on stage. In 1914 Smith began performing in Atlanta, Georgia, at Park's Big Revue in the Dixie Theater. Between 1915 and 1916, she toured with other performers, including Rainey. In 1918 Smith returned to Atlanta, where she starred in her own show, The Liberty Belles Revue. This show, which lasted about a year, featured Smith singing, dancing, and appearing in drag. She then relocated to New Jersey, where she performed with the Charles Johnson Band. In 1923 she was cast in the musical *How Come?* (1921), which was performed in Philadelphia.

Hit Recordings. It was as a recording artist that Smith made a lasting mark on popular music and cemented her reputation as a progenitor of the blues genre. In the early 1920's, she signed a contract with Columbia Records for which she recorded multiple hit songs, including "Downhearted Blues." This song sold a remarkable eight hundred thousand copies—more than any other blues record of the time.

Other hits Smith recorded during the 1920's included "Back Water Blues," "Taint Nobody's Bizness If I Do," and "Saint Louis Blues"—a song that paired her with another blues-jazz great, Louis Armstrong, and led to a role in the 1929 film of the same name. In the black-and-white film, Smith takes a belt of whiskey before singing the opening lines of the song with a mesmerizing depth of tone, raw despair, and vibrato.

Smith recorded regularly through 1928 with other important early jazz instrumentalists such as Clarence Williams (who had first sought her out to record in New York), James P. Johnson, and various members of Fletcher Henderson's band, including Armstrong, Charlie Green, Joe Smith, and Tommy Ladnier. During this period she also toured throughout the North and South, performing to large audiences.

Living the Blues. Smith did not just sing the blues—she lived them. Her personal anger and despair infused her emotional lyrical interpretations that resonated with listeners. In addition, many of Smith's fans appreciated the expression of values and ideals in her music that transcended race and gender. Although she sang about heartbreak, poverty, and struggles with substance abuse, Smith developed a dependency on alcohol that stayed with her until death.

The dissolution of her marriage to Gee inspired her to pen "Nobody Knows You When You're Down and Out," another song that became a major success (though the song is attributed to another writer, Jimmy Cox). The Great Depression had a negative effect on Smith's career, and in 1931 she recorded her last two songs for Columbia: "Safety Mama" and "I Need a Little Sugar in My

Bowl." Because of dwindling sales, Columbia Records dropped her.

Changing Tastes. Smith's waning fortunes forced her to adapt to the changing tastes of American audiences. Blues as a style was becoming less popular, and Smith had to change her performances accordingly. Although she had begun a new relationship Morgan, who was moderately wealthy, he was not rich enough to allow Smith to retire. In 1933 Smith signed with Okeh Records—a label that had rejected her in the 1920's—recording tracks with several acclaimed jazz musicians, including Buck Washington, Benny Goodman, and Jack Teagarden. Smith succeeded in staying current with her songs, performing Tin Pan Alley tunes such as "Smoke Gets in Your Eyes" and appearing at Harlem's famed Apollo Theater in 1935. In 1937, the year she died, she appeared in Winsted's Broadway Rastus Show.

Musical Legacy

Smith helped create and pass along one of the most important genres in American music: the blues. Her blues style—soulfully phrased and boldly delivered—owes a great debt to her mentor, Rainey. Unlike many other African American performers with whom she came in contact, Smith was not interested in assimilating into white culture or in modifying her musical style to meet popular tastes. Later in her career, however, she was forced to because of financial necessity At six feet tall and two hundred pounds, Smith was an impressive figure on stage, and she captivated audiences with her strong vocals.

Smith was inducted into the Rock and Roll Hall of Fame in 1989. She left behind some 160 recordings, made between 1923 and 1933. Her brash, belting vocal style influenced the blues, jazz, and rock singers that followed her, including Billie Holiday, Dinah Washington, Sarah Vaughan, Aretha Franklin, and Janis Joplin. Joplin, who imitated Smith's brassy style, paid for a headstone for Smith's unmarked grave.

Louis R. Carlozo and Judy Tsui

Further Reading

Albertson, Chris. *Bessie.* New Haven, Conn.: Yale University Press, 2003. A well-researched and thorough biography, *Bessie* traces the singer's life and tragic death. The author is a longtime contributor to *Stereo Review*, *Down Beat*, and *Saturday Review*.

Brooks, Edward. *The Bessie Smith Companion.* Cambridge, Mass.: Da Capo Press, 1983. A chronological series of listening guides to Smith's New York recordings made between 1923 and 1933, complete with discography.

Feinstein, Elaine. *Bessie Smith: Empress of the Blues.* New York: Penguin, 1985. This book explores how Smith's career mirrored the times she lived in: the Roaring Twenties brought her wealth and success, and the Great Depression of the 1930's triggered a career slide before her premature death.

Kay, Jackie. *Bessie Smith.* New York: Absolute, 1997. A Scottish-born poet, Kay profiles Smith, who inspired works in one of Kay's verse collections, *The Adoption Papers.* More a personal impression than a historical work, *Bessie Smith* interweaves poetry and prose.

Moore, Carmen. *Somebody's Angel Child: The Story of Bessie Smith.* New York: Dell, 1969. This is a largely fictionalized account of Smith's life, suitable for juvenile readers.

See also: Armstrong, Louis; Dorsey, Thomas A.; Franklin, Aretha; Goodman, Benny; Handy, W. C.; Hawkins, Coleman; Henderson, Fletcher; Holiday, Billie; Hunter, Alberta; Jackson, Mahalia; Joplin, Janis; Memphis Minnie; Rainey, Ma; Smith, Mamie; Turner, Big Joe; Vaughan, Sarah; Waller, Fats; Washington, Dinah.

Kate Smith

American popular and theater music singer

With her powerful but warm voice and friendly personality, Smith appealed to stage, radio, and television audiences. Her rendition of "God Bless America" made it an unforgettable classic.

Born: May 1, 1907; Greenville, Virginia
Died: June 17, 1986; Raleigh, North Carolina

Also known as: Kathryn Elizabeth Smith (full name)

Principal recordings

ALBUMS: *Kate Smith Sings Folk Songs*, 1958; *The Sweetest Sounds*, 1964; *How Great Thou Art*, 1965; *The Kate Smith Anniversary Album*, 1966; *The Kate Smith Christmas Album*, 1966; *Kate Smith Today*, 1966.

SINGLES: "River, Stay 'Way from My Door," 1931; "That's Why Darkies Were Born," 1931; "When the Moon Comes over the Mountain," 1931; "The Last Time I Saw Paris," 1940; "The Woodpecker Song," 1940; "Rose O'Day," 1941; "The White Cliffs of Dover," 1941; "I Don't Want to Walk Home Without You," 1942; "Don't Fence Me In," 1944; "There Goes That Song Again," 1944; "Seems Like Old Times," 1946; "Now Is the Hour," 1947; "God Bless America," 1968.

The Life

Kathryn Elizabeth Smith's parents were William H. Smith, the owner of the Capitol News Agency in Washington, D.C., and Charlotte Smith, a homemaker. Smith entertained World War I troops as a child, appeared in vaudeville by age twelve, and, despite family objections, launched a show business career. She was immediately successful as a singer and dancer, performing in New York productions of *Honeymoon Lane* (1926), *Hit the Deck* (1929), and *Flying High* (1930). She appeared in at least eight films between 1930 and 1943. In her memoirs, *Living in a Great Big Way* (1938) and *Upon My Lips a Song* (1960), however, she reveals her heartache when she realized that she was being used as a foil for stage comics who ridiculed her heavy weight, as did some reviewers and cartoonists.

She was reassured in 1930 when she met Joseph Martin ("Ted") Collins, who managed her career until his death in 1964. He realized that her weight, her traditional values, and her distaste for tobacco, alcohol, and nightclubs, while scorned on Broadway, would appeal to a general American audience, so he steered her toward radio and records. Under his guidance, she began her first regular radio series in 1931. In a few years, she became the highest-paid woman in radio. In 1938 she began a talk show, *Kate Smith "Speaking Her Mind,"* covering subjects ranging from cooking to age discrimination. This evolved into *Kate Smith Speaks,* a five-day-per-week, fifty-two-week-per-year broadcast. In 1942 she was ranked with First Lady Eleanor Roosevelt and actress Helen Hayes as the three best-known women in America. By the time her radio career ended in 1959, she had broadcast more than fifteen thousand times. Her television series, which ran from 1950 to 1954, followed by another brief series in 1960, specials, and many guest appearances, validated her belief that she could be judged by talent, not appearance.

With her warm conversational style, she was welcomed by audiences that responded generously to her appeals for charity and to her World War II bond marathons, during which she raised about $600 million for the war effort. Her many concerts began with a triumphant 1963 Carnegie Hall appearance. Her health failing, she last appeared in public in 1982, the year she received the Presidential Medal of Freedom. Smith died of complications from diabetes in 1986.

Kate Smith. (Hulton Archive/Getty Images)

The Music

Smith could not read music, but her powerful untrained contralto was flawlessly pitched and controlled. In her autobiography, she describes herself as a vehicle for the composer, refusing to add individual touches. Consequently, composers such as Irving Berlin encouraged her to introduce their music. As she describes, she first listened to a song until she understood what the composer wanted. Next, she worked on pitch, rhythm, and enunciation, finally capturing the mood of the song. Understanding her audience's mix of generations, she insisted her broadcasts and concerts mingle old songs with new.

Early Works. Although her career lasted until the 1970's, Smith was most popular during the 1930's and 1940's. Songs she introduced or simply sang generally made a profit through sheet music and record sales, even if they did not become hits. Smith's first recorded songs, hits from the successful *Honeymoon Lane,* were released in 1930. Early hits included "River, Stay 'Way from My Door," "The Last Time I Saw Paris," "The White Cliffs of Dover," and "Don't Fence Me In." Her appearances at New York's Palace and Capitol Theaters (1929-1933) were successes; she took a vaudeville production, *The Sewanee Review,* on the road in 1933-1934; and, during World War II, she toured with her cast to entertain military and industrial workers.

"When the Moon Comes over the Mountain." Adapted from a poem she had written as a girl, this became her first major hit after Collins hired Harry Woods to provide melody and Howard Johnson to add lyrics. The repetition of sustained "m" and "o" sounds emphasizes the song's dreaminess. Its wistful depiction of a dreary life redeemed by memories of past joy resonated with her Depression-era and World War II audiences. Smith sang this, her lifelong theme song, on her first series radio broadcast on March 17, 1931, and she recorded it twice in 1931. She sang it in her only feature film, *Hello, Everybody!* (1933), and she crooned a few bars in Paramount Pictures' *The Big Broadcast* (1933), where she appeared with Bing Crosby and other radio stars, and with Leopold Stokowski and the Philadelphia Orchestra.

"God Bless America." As the threat of war increased, Smith wanted a new patriotic song for her November, 1938, Armistice Day (later Veterans

Day), broadcast. She approached Irving Berlin, who had written "God Bless America" for a World War I Army show but had not used it. He revised it, she introduced it, and the song was so successful that Berlin and Smith had to oppose efforts to make it the new national anthem. Others recorded it, but Smith's version remained definitive. Her ample body and rich, powerful voice did justice to the bountiful landscape that Berlin portrays, while his personification of America as "she" preeminently suited the maternal image of Smith as singer, both strong female presences but in need of protection and guidance and both identified with home. The song can be sung as hymn, march, or ballad; Smith's version stressed optimism and determination. Berlin and Smith donated all profits from the song to the Boy and Girl Scouts of America.

Musical Legacy

In radio's early years, broadcasters sought high-culture status by presenting, with flowery, concert-stage-style introductions, operatically trained singers. Smith's simple style, which seemed like that of a friend, cut through this, opening the way for a generation of singers such as Dinah Shore and Doris Day. Smith was among the first American popular singers to disregard artificial musical boundaries, performing hymns, spirituals, jazz, blues, comedy songs, country, sentimental ballads, show music, and even opera. Her most lasting legacy, however, was her selling of "God Bless America" to the public. It created a wide demand for records and sheet music, and both the Republican and Democratic Parties adopted it as their official song for the 1940 presidential campaign. More than sixty years later, in the wake of the 2001 terrorist attacks in New York and Washington, D.C., the song was heard everywhere, its title written on placards set in lawns across America. Cementing Smith's legacy, music stores reported an increased demand for Smith's recorded version.

Betty Richardson

Further Reading

Hayes, Richard K. *Kate Smith: A Biography, with a Discography, Filmography, and List of Stage Appearances.* Jefferson, N.C.: McFarland, 1995. Lengthy biography, including broadcast information and bibliography.

Nachman, Gerald. *Raised on Radio.* New York: Pantheon Books, 1998. Overview of best-known radio series and stars, including Smith.

Pitts, Michael R. *Kate Smith: A Bio-Bibliography.* Westport, Conn.: Greenwood Press, 1988. Annotated bibliography, annotated filmography, and list of stage appearances, including comments by newspaper reviewers.

Schaden, Chuck. *Chuck Schaden's Conversations with the Stars of the Golden Age of Radio.* Morton Grove, Ill.: Nostalgia Press, 2003. A 1971 interview with Smith captures her tone.

Smith, Kate. *God Bless America: Tin Pan Alley Goes to War.* Lexington: University Press of Kentucky, 2002. Explores the government's effort to generate morale-lifting World War II songs. Smith provides an overview of popular music from the 1920's to 1945 and offers a context for Smith's popularity.

_____. *Living in a Great Big Way.* New York: Blue Ribbon Books, 1938. Smith's first autobiography.

_____. *Upon My Lips a Song.* New York: Funk & Wagnells, 1960. Smith recounts the events of her life.

See also: Berlin, Irving; Crosby, Bing; Guthrie, Woody; Stokowski, Leopold.

Mamie Smith

American blues singer and songwriter

The first black singer to record the blues, Smith reached a great popularity that enticed the record industry to record more black vocalists. These recordings spread the classical blues style, and they inspired the next generation of blues singers.

Born: May 26, 1883; Cincinnati, Ohio
Died: August 16, 1946; New York, New York
Also known as: Mamie Robinson (birth name)
Member of: Mamie Smith and Her Jazz Hounds; Mamie Smith and the Harlem Trio

Principal recordings

SINGLES (solo): "That Thing Called Love," 1920; "You Can't Keep a Good Man Down," 1920; "Do It, Mr. So-and-So," 1923; "Mistreatin'

Daddy Blues," 1923; "My Mammy's Blues," 1923; "Plain Old Blues," 1923; "You Can't Do What My Last Man Did," 1923; "Goin' Crazy with the Blues," 1926; "I Once Was Yours, I'm Somebody Else's Now," 1926; "Sweet Virginia Blues," 1926; "What Have You Done to Make Me Feel This Way?" 1926; "Don't You Advertise Your Man," 1931; "Golfing Papa," 1931; "Jenny's Ball," 1931; "Keep a Song in Your Soul," 1931.

SINGLES (with Mamie Smith and Her Jazz Hounds): "Crazy Blues," 1920; "It's Right Here for You (If You Don't Get It, 'Taint No Fault of Mine)," 1920; "Baby, You Made Me Fall for You," 1921; "Royal Garden Blues," 1921; "That Thing Called Love," 1921; "U Need Some Loving Blues," 1921; "What Have I Done?," 1921; "You Can't Keep a Good Man Down," 1921; "Carolina Blues," 1922; "The Decatur Street Blues," 1922; "I Ain't Gonna Give Nobody None o' This Jelly Roll," 1922; "I'm Gonna Get You," 1922; "Lonesome Mama Blues," 1922; "Mean Daddy Blues," 1922; "New Orleans," 1922; "You Can Have Him, I Don't Want Him, Didn't Love Him Anyhow Blues," 1922.

SINGLES (with Mamie Smith and the Harlem Trio): "Kansas City Man Blues," 1923; "Lady Luck Blues," 1923.

The Life

From an early age, Mamie Smith had an ambition to be a professional singer. At the age of ten, she joined the Four Dancing Mitchells, a minstrel group that toured Ohio and the surrounding states. Originally hired as a dancer, she gained valuable experience from the troupe. In 1912 the Four Dancing Mitchells joined Salem Tutt Whitney and Homer Tutt's show, The Smart Set. Now firmly immersed in the vaudeville circuit, Smith was confident enough to quit The Smart Set in 1913, when the show appeared in New York. Smith performed as a vaudeville, jazz, and blues singer in many of the clubs in Harlem, including Barron Wilkins' Little Savoy Club, Edmund's, Leroy's, Bank's Place, and Percy Brown's.

In 1918 she recorded "That Thing Called Love" with Victor Records, although the label decided not to make it available to the public. In 1920 Perry

Bradford, a black composer, convinced Okeh Records to record and produce some of his compositions. On February 14, 1920, Smith again recorded Bradford's "That Thing Called Love" and "You Can't Keep a Good Man Down." Although not best sellers, they did sell well in the South and in large Northern cities thanks to the *Chicago Defender*, a black weekly newspaper, pointing out its existence. In August of that year, Smith recorded two more Bradford compositions, "Crazy Blues" and "It's Right Here for You (If You Don't Get It, 'Taint No Fault of Mine)," with the backing of the Jazz Hounds, who included such musicians as Willie "the Lion" Smith and Bubber Miley. "Crazy Blues" became a huge hit, with sales reaching 75,000 records the first month of issue. In the next seven years, Smith toured the country with the Jazz Hounds, playing nightclubs and theaters. She also recorded more than one hundred songs.

During the era she was known for her vivacious lifestyle, her extravagant spending, and a procession of lovers. She was responsible for discovering the saxophonist Coleman Hawkins, and she performed with a number of the best musicians of the era. After the Wall Street crash of 1929, Smith was forced into semiretirement. On her last recording date in 1931, she recorded some of her best works, including "Jenny's Ball," her only record to be released in Britain.

In her late forties, Smith was featured in a number of short films, including *Paradise in Harlem* (1939); however, the films did not revive her career. After a short illness, she passed away at the Harlem Hospital at the age of sixty-three. She was buried in a common grave in the Frederick Douglass Memorial Park in Staten Island, N.Y.

The Music

Smith's music is solidly rooted in the minstrel tradition of the early 1900's. After settling in New York, she continued to perform the same style of songs, adding blues numbers to her repertoire for performance in Harlem. Her singing style is more refined than that of other performers of the era, mostly because of her Northern roots and the influence of popular music in New York.

"Crazy Blues." Recorded in 1920, "Crazy Blues" was the first hit record by a black blues singer. Although not a twelve-bar blues form, it epitomizes

Mamie Smith. (Hulton Archive/Getty Images)

the classic blues style of New York. Written by Bradford, the song is characterized by its combination of pop song form, Dixieland jazz, and blues lyrics. Because the song was recorded acoustically, Smith is difficult to hear over the Jazz Hounds at times.

"Don't You Advertise Your Man." Written by Jimmie Foster, this work is a cautionary tale for young women. The work, in a verse-chorus pop song form, is brought to life by the backing band. Dixieland sounds emanate from the cornets, trombones, and clarinets that support Smith. The work exhibits strong backbeats, hot rhythm, and the use of stop time. The balance between the singer and backing band is strong, and it allows Smith to use the power and ornamentation of her voice to better express the song.

"Jenny's Ball." A dressed-down pop song, "Jenny's Ball" gives a snapshot of life as a cabaret dancer in Harlem. This number exhibits a call-and-response between Smith and the Jazz Hounds. The cornet also plays an important role, commenting on the lyrics with extended solos. In this recording, the piano can be heard, unlike in "Crazy Blues." Smith repeats the first chorus, with ornamentation, for the parting advisement, accentuating the hook of the

song, increasing its popularity with the public. This was the only recording done by Smith that was released in Britain.

Musical Legacy

Smith's greatest achievement was opening the doors of white-owned recording studios to black performers. Without her pioneering work, the performances of Bessie Smith, Ma Rainey, and Blue le Burke would never have been recorded. The whole industry of race records was founded after the great success of her "Crazy Blues." The availability of recordings spread the blues out of the rural American South and the black clubs of the Northern big cities. Smith's records were released as far away as Britain, influencing new generations of musicians, both black and white, and exposing them to a style of music they might never have otherwise known.

Amanda M. Pence

Further Reading

Bourgeois, Anna Stong. *Blueswomen: Profiles and Lyrics, 1920-1945.* Jefferson, N.C.: McFarland, 1996. This work contains a brief profile of Smith and the lyrics of twelve of her recorded songs.

Jackson, Buzzy. *A Bad Woman Feeling Good: Blues and the Women Who Sing Them.* New York: W. W. Norton, 2005. This book is a study of African American women in popular music. The opening chapter contains a study of first recordings and a fair discussion of Smith's contributions.

Jones, Hettie. *Big Star Fallin' Mama: Five Women in Black Music.* New York: Viking Press, 1974. Although not one of the women studied in the book, Smith is considered as far as her contribution to the careers of others and to the recording industry.

Lieb, Sandra R. *Mother of the Blues: A Study of Ma Rainey.* Amherst: University of Massachusetts Press, 1981. Although a study of Rainey, the work provides some interesting insights in a comparison of the styles of both singers.

Stewart-Baxter, Derrick. *Ma Rainey and the Classic Blues Singers.* London: Studio Vista, 1970. This work contains an informative section on the life and career of Smith. Includes photographs.

See also: Hawkins, Coleman; Rainey, Ma; Smith, Bessie.

Michael W. Smith

American gospel singer, songwriter, and pianist

Smith's inventive songcraft and charismatic performances brought new life to congregational worship music and created an audience for contemporary Christian music.

Born: October 7, 1957; Kenova, West Virginia
Also known as: Michael Whitaker Smith (full name)

Principal recordings

ALBUMS: *Love Stories*, 1983; *Michael W. Smith Project*, 1983; *Two*, 1984; *The Big Picture*, 1986; *Christmas*, 1989; *I 2 Eye*, 1989; *Go West Young Man*, 1990; *Change Your World*, 1992; *Sing Unto Him*, 1993; *I'll Lead You Home*, 1995; *Christmastime*, 1998; *This Is Your Time*, 1999; *Freedom*, 2000; *Worship*, 2001; *Worship Again*, 2002; *Healing Rain*, 2004; *Stand*, 2006; *It's a Wonderful Christmas*, 2007.

The Life

Michael Whitaker Smith was born in Kenova, West Virginia, to Paul and Barbara Smith, an oil refinery worker and caterer respectively. Smith had one sibling, a younger sister named Kim. Although Smith's first career ambition was to play professional baseball (his father played in the minor leagues), it did not take long for his love of music to surpass his athletic aspirations. In fact, Smith wrote his first song when he was five year old.

Like many prodigious piano players, Smith learned the craft at a young age, thanks to a patient grandmother and hours of dutiful practice. That, combined with singing in the church choir, solidified Smith's love for music that communicated Gospel truths. After some college studies at nearby Marshall University, Smith was encouraged by his friend Shane Keister, a Nashville session musician, to move to Nashville in 1978 to pursue a musical career. While there, Smith took a job as a landscaper while he played the Nashville club circuit.

In Smith's early days in Nashville, the stress and excesses of trying to launch a career in music led to

what Smith has described as "a nervous breakdown." After dealing with an alcohol and a drug problem, Smith found some success. In 1979 he auditioned for keyboardist in a new Christian group, Higher Ground. Soon after landing the gig, Smith began his first stint on the road. In 1981 Smith met and married his wife, Debbie, and he signed a publishing deal with Meadowgrass Music.

Before long, Smith was making a name for himself as a songwriter for fellow artists, including Amy Grant, Sandi Patty, and Bill Gaither. He was invited to join Grant as a keyboardist on her *Age to Age* tour, but he soon realized that he was not happy being a touring musician. Since then, he has focused on composing songs and appearing as a singer. He and his wife moved to Franklin, Tennessee, and they had five children: Ryan, Whitney, Tyler, Anna, and Emily.

The Music

Smith proved that a polished pop sound and inspirational lyrics could coexist; his catalog reflects a wealth of musical influences. While many of his earlier compositions, such as "Great Is the Lord" and "Could He Be the Messiah," were designed to be sung by congregations in Sunday-morning worship services, these were accompanied with moving piano arrangements reminiscent of those of Elton John and Billy Joel. Smith's appeal is rooted in his catchy songs, whether a love song such as "I Will Be Here for You," which Smith cowrote with pop star Diane Warren, or an all-out guitar rocker, such as "Help You Find Your Way." Smith delivers the message of his songs with enticing presentations, working with respected producers and up-and-coming artists.

Early Works. "Friends," which Smith wrote in just an afternoon's time, debuted on *The Michael W. Smith Project*. Widely popular, it is played at funerals, graduations, and even the end of summer camp. The youth-group anthem is a stalwart reminder of what really lasts in life. The simple piano-driven sentiment set the pace for Smith's solo work.

The Big Picture. After delivering two successful inspirational albums, Smith produced in 1986 a decidedly rock-and-roll effort, *The Big Picture*. Mainstream producer Johnny Potoker (who has worked with Genesis and Madonna) gave *The Big Picture* an amped-up, guitar-fueled sound not typical of the

Christian music genre. Smith's songs were issues oriented, addressing such topics as self-esteem, racism, and teen sexuality.

Go West Young Man. Four years after *The Big Picture*, Smith made *Go West Young Man*. "Love Crusade" featured a spontaneous rap, and "Place in This World" became a crossover hit. Much like Grant's "Baby Baby," "Place in This World" was a hit with believers and nonbelievers alike, delivering a universal message about feeling lost. Combined with an accompanying video, the song gave Smith his first pop hit. In its wake, he was named one of *People's* Fifty Most Beautiful People, and he received an American Music Award for Favorite New Adult Contemporary Artist and other accolades from the contemporary Christian music industry.

Change Your World. On *Change Your World*, Smith teamed with Warren for the number-one adult contemporary hit, "I Will Be Here For You." In addition, Smith went on tour with a lavish set and superb backing band. The tour garnered as much praise as the songs.

This Is Your Time. This album was a response to the tragic murders of students and a teacher at Columbine High School near Denver, Colorado. Inspired by the story of Cassie Bernall, an outspoken Christian killed in the tragedy, Smith performed the title track at the memorial service in honor of the victims.

Freedom. As a longtime fan of epic motion picture sound tracks, Smith often includes at least one instrumental track on his albums. On *Freedom*, Smith's lifelong goal of recording an entire album of orchestral music was realized.

Worship. Smith had no idea that *Worship* would be released on such a tragic day in history, September 11, 2001, when terrorist attacks struck New York and Washington, D.C. The album's simple songs of praise were fitting in a time of unrest. Turning his attention back to the genre that launched his career, Smith released a follow-up project, *Worship Again*, in 2002.

Musical Legacy

Although he has appeared as an actor, serves as a pastor at his church (the New River Fellowship), owns a Christian nightclub in downtown Nashville, stays active politically, and remains an in-

volved parent, Smith always returns to his first love, music. He contributed to the success of the contemporary Christian music genre, and his music extended to the mainstream pop arena, yielding several Top 40 hits, three Grammy Awards, and international acclaim. Faith-based acts such as Switchfoot, Jars of Clay, Relient K, and the Fray flourish in the Christian and the general music markets because of Smith's significant influence.

Christa A. Banister

Further Reading

Smith, Michael W. *Old Enough to Know—Updated Edition*. Nashville, Tenn.: Tommy Nelson, 2000. Smith tells his life story in his own words, and he reveals the events that inspired his early songs.

_____. *This Is Your Time*. Nashville, Tenn.: T. Nelson, 2000. Inspired by the story of Bernall, Smith talks candidly about making your life count.

See also: Grant, Amy; Joel, Billy; John, Sir Elton.

Patti Smith

American punk-rock singer and songwriter

Smith brought an angry yet intellectual lyricism to early punk-rock music. Her raw, energetic stage performances transformed the standard punk-rock concert.

Born: December 30, 1946; Chicago, Illinois
Also known as: Patricia Lee Smith (full name)
Member of: The Patti Smith Group

Principal recordings

ALBUMS (with the Patti Smith Group): *Horses*, 1975; *Radio Ethiopia*, 1976; *Easter*, 1978; *Wave*, 1979; *Dream of Life*, 1988; *Gone Again*, 1996; *Peace and Noise*, 1997; *Gung Ho*, 2000; *Trampin'*, 2004; *Twelve*, 2007.

SINGLES (with the Patti Smith Group): "Because the Night," 1978.

The Life

Patricia Lee Smith was born in Chicago Illinois, and her family moved to Woodbury, New Jersey, when she was young. Her working-class family lived modestly, and when Smith graduated from high school in 1964, she went to work in a factory. This stint was the impetus for the first of her poems that she set to music, "Piss Factory." Smith would later tell interviewers that she spent her teenage years listening to rock music, especially the Rolling Stones and Bob Dylan. She went to New York City whenever she could to attend concerts and to experience the East Village scene. In 1967 she left Woodbury and moved to New York City. While working at the Gotham Book Mart, Smith met photographer Robert Mapplethorpe, and they remained friends until his death. In 1969 Smith and her sister traveled to Paris, France. On her return she moved into the Chelsea Hotel with Mapplethorpe, and she had a brief, heated romantic relationship with playwright Sam Shepard, appearing in his play *Cowboy Mouth* (1971). Concurrently, she wrote and read poetry, acted in other Off-Broadway productions, and wrote rock journalism for *Creem* magazine. Her first book of poetry, *Seventh Heaven*, was published in 1972 to acclaim from New York critics. She followed with two more collections in 1973 and 1978.

In 1974 Smith began playing rock music with fellow writer Lenny Kaye, Ivan Kral (guitar), Jay Dee Daugherty (drums), and Richard Sohl (piano). They released their first single, and soon after they signed a recording contract. The Patti Smith Group was an instant hit with rock critics and began a series of tours. During a show in Tampa, Florida, Smith fell fifteen feet off a stage while dancing and broke several vertebrae in her neck. She retired from touring for a while. During the hiatus, she met rock guitarist Fred "Sonic" Smith of the Detroit political rock band the MC5. They fell in love, got married, and had two children before he died in 1994. Smith released only one album during that time, *Dream of Life*. Her brother died not too long after her husband, sending her into a minor depression.

Smith and her children moved back to New York, where poet Allen Ginsberg and R.E.M.'s Michael Stipe persuaded her to return to music. In the spring of 1995, Smith toured with Bob Dylan. Smith and her band released several albums, and she toured with her band and appeared as an individual doing spoken word. In addition, Smith was ac-

tively involved in the Green Party campaign of Ralph Nader for U.S. President in 2000 and 2004. Smith appeared at numerous protests against the U.S. war in Iraq.

The Music

Horses. According to *Rolling Stone*, this is one of the fifty most influential albums in rock music. With Smith's occasionally surreal lyrics and the primal rhythms of three-chord rock progressions, the songs on *Horses* release an energy much like that experienced by musicians and audiences alike in rock's earlier days. There is nothing difficult about the music played here, but its impact is greater than its individual parts.

Radio Ethiopia. Originally dismissed by many critics and fans of Smith's first album, this work is full of loud guitar that ravages the listener's ears. Lyrically, the stories inside the songs give voice to the anger and despair symptomatic of the punk movement.

Wave. This album came out after Smith's recovery from her fall in Tampa. Musically, the songs are a mix of hard rock and beat-heavy dance tunes. The lyrics reflect Smith's ongoing interest in the dogma and nature of religion, especially Catholicism; her relationship with Fred Smith, her new lover; and her comments on U.S. politics.

Gung Ho. The third album released by Smith after her 1995 return to rock music is musically similar to the others in this period, with the exception of two tracks: "Libbie's Song," which is an old-timey ballad about the wife of General George Custer, who died at the Battle of the Little Bighorn, and "Gung Ho," which is a tribute to the Vietnamese struggle for independence from France and the United States and a celebration of that struggle's leader, Ho Chi Minh.

Musical Legacy

Smith helped create a direction for the punk genre, and she is noted for her uncompromising pursuit of fame without losing her integrity, which made her an inspiration to other rock musicians. Smith was elected to the Rock and Roll Hall of Fame in 2007, where she and her music stand with rock's most important and influential artists.

Ron Jacobs

Further Reading

Bockris, Victor, and Roberta Bayley. *Patti Smith: An Unauthorized Biography*. New York: Simon & Schuster, 1999. This biography traces Smith's life and career from her childhood through the reinvigoration of her career in the 1990's, in an informative and occasionally gossipy style.

Reynolds, Simon. "Even as a Child, I Felt Like an Alien." *Observer Music Monthly* (May 22, 2005). Lively and engaging interview with Smith. She talks a little about her life, her work, her politics, and her hopes. Much of the interview focuses on *Horses* and Smith's recollections of its recording and her reflections on its influence.

Smith, Greg. "'And All the Sinners, Saints': Patti Smith, Pioneer Musician and Poet." *The Midwest Quarterly* (Winter, 2000): 173. This interesting article uses the 1968 Rolling Stones album *Beggars Banquet* as a catalyst for a discussion of Smith's poetry and her music and its relation to her womanhood and her roles as mother and daughter.

Smith, Patti. *Patti Smith Complete, 1975-2006: Lyrics, Reflections, and Notes for the Future*. New York: Harper Perennial, 2006. This is a collection of all of Smith's poems and song lyrics, illustrated with photographs of Smith and her friends and family and artwork and sketches by Smith.

See also: Dylan, Bob; Jagger, Sir Mick; Mitchell, Joni; Morrison, Jim; Slick, Grace.

Snoop Dogg

American rapper and songwriter

Known for his smooth, relaxed vocal delivery with a slight Southern drawl, Snoop Dogg was a top rap artist during the 1990's, making his mark in the gangsta rap genre.

Born: October 20, 1972; Long Beach, California
Also known as: Cordozar Calvin Broadus, Jr. (birth name); Snoop Doggy Dogg

Principal recordings

ALBUMS: *Doggystyle*, 1993; *Tha Doggfather*, 1996; *Da Game Is to Be Sold Not to Be Told*, 1998; *No Limit Top Dogg*, 1999; *Tha Last Meal*, 2000; *Doggy Style All Stars: Welcome to tha House, Vol. 1*, 2002; *Paid tha Cost to Be da Boss*, 2002; *R & G (Rhythm and Gangsta): Tha Masterpiece*, 2004; *Me and My Homies*, 2005; *Screwed: How the West Was Screwed*, 2005; *Welcome to tha Church: Da Album*, 2005; *Tha Blue Carpet Treatment*, 2006; *Cali Iz Active*, 2006 (with Tha Dogg Pound); *Ego Trippin'*, 2008; *Revival*, 2008 (with DJ Whoo Kidd).

The Life

Born and raised in Long Beach, California, Snoop Dogg spent the three years after high school in and out of jail on drug charges. However, he changed his direction when his homemade tapes made with rapper Warren G were given to Dr. Dre, a rapper, a producer, and the co-owner of Death Row Records. Dr. Dre included Snoop, under the stage name Snoop Doggy Dogg, on the title track for the motion picture *Deep Cover* in 1991, and Snoop was also prominently featured on Dr. Dre's 1992 album *The Chronic*. Snoop released his solo album, *Doggystyle*, the following year. In August, 1993, Snoop was arrested for his alleged involvement in a drive-by shooting, and he was later acquitted of all charges in February, 1996. In 1998 Snoop shortened his stage name to Snoop Dogg after he left his original label, Death Row Records, for rapper Master P's label, No Limit Records.

Snoop Dogg has been involved in several film and television projects, including his own MTV comedy sketch show, *Doggy Fizzle Televizzle*, which ran from 2002 to 2004. He has also appeared as an actor in films such as *Soul Plane* (2004) and *Starsky & Hutch* (2004), and he has directed two pornographic films. On April 12, 2007, he was sentenced to five years of probation on charges relating to the possession of drugs and firearms.

The Music

During the 1990's, Snoop Dogg's songs helped define the genre of gangsta rap. They frequently addressed violent subject matters, perhaps reflecting his troubles with law. In the late 1990's, Snoop Dogg transitioned to tamer subject matter that promoted a lavish, misogynistic pimp lifestyle. Along with his distinctive vocal delivery and subject matter, Snoop Dogg is known for his style of slang centered on nonsensical words ending with the suffix *-izzle*.

Doggystyle. Snoop Dogg's first solo album, *Doggystyle*, cemented his position as a top gangsta rapper. The album was produced by Dr. Dre, and in many ways it is a continuation of Dr. Dre's debut album, *The Chronic*, from the previous year. *Doggystyle* utilizes the same slow, layered G-funk (or gangsta funk) beats as *The Chronic*, addressing similar street-inspired subject matter. "Murder Was the Case" describes Snoop Dogg as a drive-by shooting victim (ironically released while he was involved in a murder case). "Ain't No Fun" is about gang rape, and other songs describe gang violence, drug use, and degrading views of women.

Tha Doggfather. After the conclusion of his murder trial, Snoop released his second album, *Tha Doggfather*, on Death Row Records in November, 1996. Earlier that same year Dr. Dre had left Death Row Records, so Snoop Dogg produced many of the songs himself. The album retains bass-heavy G-funk as its musical foundation, and it reworks old funk and soul music for its beats. Lyrically, *Tha Doggfather* demonstrates Snoop's gradual evolution away from heavily gang-inspired subject matter. Nevertheless, while the lyrics are not as harsh as those found on *Doggystyle*, they still frequently address typical gangsta-rap themes. In addition to the gangsta-inspired subject matter, *Tha Doggfather*

contains party-oriented songs, for example, "Snoop Upside Your Head," and occasional attempts at social commentary, such as his remake of rapper Biz Markie's song "Vapors." Interspersed throughout the album are several skits and a "Freestyle Conversation."

R&G (Rhythm and Gangsta): The Masterpiece. On this album, released in 2004, Snoop Dogg enlists the assistance of a variety of producers and guest artists. It features collaborations with Pharrell, Lil John, 50 Cent, and even pop artist Justin Timberlake, and it demonstrates an image tamer than the one Snoop Dogg put forth on his earlier gangsta-rap works. Musically, the album draws from a variety of genres, including jazz, classic rock, and disco, and Snoop Dogg, in addition to his drawled rapping, sings on a number of songs. The result is a light, playful background for Snoop's street-inspired lyrics. The subject matter of *R&G (Rhythm and Gangsta): The Masterpiece* is not as violent as Snoop's early albums, and he generally demonstrates a less-aggressive approach toward women, though misogynistic songs ("Can U Control Yo Hoe") and songs celebrating gangsta life ("Oh No") still appear.

Musical Legacy

The career of Snoop Dogg has demonstrated that a variety of vocal deliveries can be successful in hip-hop and that all rappers do not need to adhere to a conventional norm. Snoop Dogg was instrumental in the construction of hip-hop around gangsta rap in the 1990's, and he also illustrated how a rapper can change his or her image and still remain successful. Similar to many other rappers, he has become a pop culture icon through his participation in varied entertainment mediums, and he maintains a prominent position in hip-hop culture. Snoop Dogg has assisted in the careers of many family members and friends who have become rappers, including Nate Dogg, Warren G, RBX, and Daz Dillinger.

Snoop Dogg. (AP/Wide World Photos)

He founded a film production company called Snoopadelic Films, and he runs his own record label called Doggystyle Records.

Matthew Mihalka

Further Reading

Ro, Ronin. *Have Gun Will Travel: The Spectacular Rise and Violent Fall of Death Row Records*. New York: Doubleday, 1998. During his history of Death Row Records, Ro discusses the early portion of Snoop Dogg's career with the record label.

Snoop Dogg and David Seay. *Tha Doggfather: The Times, Trials, and Hardcore Truths of Snoop Dogg*. New York: William Morrow, 1999. Snoop Dogg's autobiography illustrates his rise from poverty and the troubles he has encountered during his music career.

Snoop Dogg and David E. Talbert. *Love Don't Live Here No More: Book One of Doggy Tales*. New York: Atria Books, 2006. Written in rather simplistic language, this semiautobiographical novel follows the life of a man who desires to become a rapper, but instead he turns to dealing drugs.

Touré. "Snoop Dogg's Gentle Hip-Hop Growl." In *The Pop, Rock, and Soul Reader: Histories and Debates*, edited by David Brackett. New York: Oxford University Press, 2005. This article describes Snoop Dogg's early music and the source of his lyrics.

See also: Dr. Dre; 50 Cent.

Sir Georg Solti

Hungarian classical conductor

During a career that spanned more than six decades, Solti became one of the most famous conductors in international music circles, with a wide operatic and orchestral repertory, heightened by a serious approach to music-making that brought him great respect and admiration.

Born: October 12, 1912; Budapest, Hungary
Died: September 5, 1997; Antibes, France
Also known as: György Stern (birth name)

Principal recordings

ALBUMS: *Tchaikovsky: Symphony No. 2, Little Russian*, 1956; *Richard Strauss: Arabella*, 1957; *Wagner: Das Rheingold*, 1958; *Verdi: Aida*, 1962; *Wagner: Siegfried*, 1962; *Bartók: Piano Concerto No. 3*, 1964; *Wagner: Götterdämmerung*, 1964; *Wagner: Die Walküre*, 1965; *Strauss: Der Rosenkavalier*, 1968; *Elgar: Symphony No. 1 in A-flat Major, Op. 55*, 1972; *Elgar: Symphony No. 2 in E-flat Major, Op. 63*, 1975; *Bartók: Bluebeard's Castle*, 1979; *Tippett: Symphony No. 4*, 1979; *Beethoven: The Ninth Symphony*, 1986; *Tchaikovsky: Symphony No. 5*, 1987; *Bach: Mass in B Minor*, 1990; *Mahler: Symphony No. 5*, 1991; *Michael Tippett: Byzantium*, 1991; *Verdi: Otello*, 1991; *Haydn: The Creation*, 1992; *Strauss: Die Frau ohne Schatten*, 1992; *Mephisto Magic: Solti*, 1994; *Mozart: Don Giovanni*, 1997.

WRITINGS OF INTEREST: *Solti on Solti: A Memoir*, 1997.

The Life

Georg Solti (johrj SHOHL-tee), born György Stern, was the second child of Móricz Stern and Teréz Rosenbaum. His father, a poor businessman, worked unsuccessfully as a flour merchant, insurance salesman, and real estate broker. When World War I broke out in 1914, the family relocated temporarily to Veszprém, returning to Budapest in 1918 when Solti was six. At this time, his mother, who was musical, noticed that her son had talent and engaged a piano teacher for him. His father changed his children's last name to Solti (the name of a small Hungarian town) during the upsurge in Hungarian nationalism that followed World War I.

At age ten, Solti was admitted to the Ernö Fodor School of Music in Budapest, where he studied piano and theory with Miklós Laurisin. Two years later he entered the city's prestigious Franz Liszt Academy of Music, where he remained for six years, studying with Arnold Székely, Zoltán Kodály, Leó Weiner, Ernö Dohnányi, and, briefly, Béla Bartók. Solti later wrote that he considered his years at the Franz Liszt Academy of Music to be the most significant part of his formal musical education. He received a diploma in piano in 1930 and a diploma in composition a year later.

Solti's decision to pursue a career as a conductor

came at the age of fourteen, when he heard Erich Kleiber conduct Ludwig van Beethoven's Symphony No. 5 (1808). Upon graduation from the academy, he was engaged as a coach at the Budapest Opera House, which enabled him to develop significant knowledge of the operatic repertoire. As a Jew, Solti knew that he would not be allowed to conduct at the Budapest Opera. In October, 1932, he obtained a position as assistant to Josef Krips, who was music director of the opera house in Karlsruhe, Germany. However, Solti came back to Budapest after a few months to escape the anti-Semitism he encountered in Germany. During the summer of 1936, he attended the Salzburg Festival in Austria and returned the following year to work under the Italian conductor Arturo Toscanini.

Solti's training was as a pianist and a vocal coach, and he assisted Toscanini at the Salzburg Festivals of 1936 and 1937. Though anti-Semitism restricted his early career in his native Hungary, he did make his conducting debut there in Wolfgang Amadeus Mozart's *Le nozze di Figaro* (1786; *The Marriage of Figaro*), but it was not until after World War II that he could resume his operatic career with a performance in Munich of Beethoven's *Fidelio* (1805), which carried a message of hope to a newly liberated Europe.

While living in Zurich during the war, Solti had met Hedwig (Hedi) Oechsli; they married on October 29, 1946. The couple separated during Solti's third season at Covent Garden and eventually divorced in 1966. On November 11, 1967, he married Anne Valerie Pitts, a London journalist; they had two daughters.

Solti died of a heart attack while vacationing with his wife in Antibes, France. He is buried in Farkasreti Cemetery in Budapest, next to Bartók. At the time of his death, Solti was preparing for a London Proms concert performance of Giuseppe Verdi's *Requiem* (1874).

The Music

In 1936 and 1937, Solti assisted world-famous conductor Arturo Toscanini at the Salzburg Festival in Austria, but he did not get his first conducting job until 1938, when he led a performance of Mozart's *Le nozze di Figaro* at the Budapest State Opera. Unfortunately, his debut was overshadowed by Nazi leader Adolf Hitler's invasion of Austria;

Solti fled to Switzerland, where he remained during World War II.

War Years. While in Switzerland, Solti turned his attention to the piano, winning first prize at the Concours International piano competition in Geneva in 1942. After the war, the American forces occupying Germany began a search for musicians who could rekindle the country's musical life but who were free of Nazi associations. Solti was offered the post of music director of the Bavarian State Opera in Munich in 1946, and he served in that capacity until 1952. He also appeared at the Salzburg Festival, and he conducted in cities as diverse as Paris, Berlin, Rome, Vienna, Florence, and Buenos Aires.

Covent Garden. With his reputation on the rise and his operatic repertory increasing, Solti next accepted a position as music director of the Frankfurt City Opera; he stayed a decade. Then, from 1961 to 1971, he worked as music director at the Royal Opera House, Covent Garden, in England. His association with England and the English became a close one: He raised the visibility of both Covent Garden and British opera singers, and he made a point of programming works by native composers such as Benjamin Britten. He also conducted the British premiere of Austrian composer Arnold Schoenberg's opera *Moses und Aron* (1957), a production that won international acclaim. For his contribution to musical life in England, Solti was knighted by Queen Elizabeth II in 1972. From 1979 to 1984, he served as principal conductor and artistic director of the London Philharmonic Orchestra and later became its conductor emeritus. In 1992 he was made music director laureate at Covent Garden.

Chicago Symphony Orchestra. The pinnacle of Solti's career was probably his association with the Chicago Symphony Orchestra. He began his post with the Chicago Symphony Orchestra in 1969, and, though he resigned formally in 1991, he held the title of music director laureate until his death. Solti brought the Chicago Symphony Orchestra to international prominence, increasing its repertory and its reputation. By the mid-1970's, it had become one of the top five orchestras in North America.

Salzburg Easter Festival. In 1992 Solti began an appointment as artistic director of the Salzburg Easter Festival, and the next year he recorded the festival's production of Richard Strauss's opera *Die*

Frau ohne Schatten (1918); the recording won a Grammy Award in 1993.

In June, 1994, Solti embarked upon the Solti Orchestral Project at Carnegie Hall, a two-week workshop during which eighty instrumentalists, ranging in age from eighteen to thirty, worked with principal players from five U.S. orchestras. The purpose of the project, which was conceived by Solti and by Carnegie Hall executive director Judith Arron, was to give younger players an opportunity to perform with, and learn from, experienced orchestral musicians.

The Ring Cycle. One of Solti's biggest career undertakings was the recording of Richard Wagner's monumental cycle, *Der Ring des Nibelungen*, which includes *Das Rheingold* (1869), *Die Walküre* (1870), *Siegfried* (1871), and *Götterdämmerung* (1874), which lasted from 1958 to 1965. At the time it was released, the project was considered unsurpassed in scope, cost, and artistic and technical challenge.

Musical Legacy

During the late 1950's and 1960's, Solti dominated the international operatic scene as a conductor, and his decade of tenure at the Royal Opera House, Covent Garden, from 1961 came when he had reached the heights of an already long and varied career. When he declared his intention of making Britain's national opera house "quite simply, the best" in the world, some people thought him boastful or unrealistically ambitious, but by the end of his time there, many argued that he had succeeded in his aim, or at least made it the equal of other great houses.

Solti's conducting style was clear and direct, and many music specialists agree that Solti was at his best with German, Austrian, and Hungarian music from the late eighteenth to the early twentieth centuries, a repertory that included the works of composers Franz Joseph Haydn, Mozart, Beethoven, Franz Schubert, Robert Schumann, Johannes Brahms, Richard Wagner, Gustav Mahler, Anton Bruckner, and Strauss. In addition, Solti was renowned for his willingness to program works that fell outside of the traditional orchestral and operatic repertory. An energetic and forceful conductor, he specialized primarily in the German classical and romantic repertory, although he conducted notable performances of works by numerous twentieth century composers, including Samuel Barber, Alban Berg, Benjamin Britten, Elliott Carter, John Corigliano, David Del Tredici, Hans Werner Henze, George Rochberg, Arnold Schoenberg, Roger Sessions, and Ellen Taaffe Zwilich.

Solti left a substantial recorded legacy, with more than 250 recordings for the London Decca label (including forty-five complete operas) and thirty-two Grammy Awards (one of them a Lifetime Achievement Award). Among other numerous honors and awards, he received the National Medal of Arts from President Bill Clinton in 1993.

Martin J. Manning

Further Reading

Culshaw, John. *Ring Resounding*. New York: Viking, 1967. This resource details Solti's recording of Wagner's monumental cycle, *Der Ring des Nibelungen*, often considered a milestone in the history of the recording industry. Culshaw was the producer of the recordings.

Furlong, William B. *Season with Solti: A Year in the Life of the Chicago Symphony*. New York: Macmillan, 1974. The Chicago Symphony Orchestra was Solti's longest association as a conductor, and the book offers insights into and a frank portrayal of a master musician.

Robinson, Paul. *Solti*. Toronto: Lester and Orpen, 1979. An early biography of Solti, this focuses on his musical activities and includes a discography through February, 1979.

Solti, Georg. *Solti on Solti: A Memoir*. New York: Alfred A. Knopf, 1997. Solti's own story, published after his death, discusses his early musical studies in Budapest; his exile in Zurich during World War II; his work as music director of the Bavarian State Opera in postwar Munich and similar posts in Frankfurt and London's Covent Garden; his direction of the Chicago Symphony (1969-1991); and his freelance conducting of the world's greatest orchestras.

See also: Barber, Samuel; Bartók, Béla; Berg, Alban; Britten, Benjamin; Carter, Elliott; Kodály, Zoltán; Tippett, Sir Michael.

Stephen Sondheim

American popular music and musical-theater composer and lyricist

Sondheim's sophisticated integration of music and lyrics set a new standard for musical theater, transforming the musical from idealistic entertainment to a thought-provoking commentary on social issues.

Born: March 22, 1930; New York, New York

Also known as: Stephen Joshua Sondheim (full name)

Principal works

FILM SCORES: *Stavisky*, 1974; *Reds*, 1981 (with David Grusing).

MUSICAL THEATER (music and lyrics): *West Side Story*, 1957 (libretto by Arthur Laurents; music by Leonard Bernstein); *Gypsy*, 1959 (libretto by Laurents; music by Jule Styne); *West Side Story*, 1960 (libretto by Laurents; music by Bernstein); *A Funny Thing Happened on the Way to the Forum*, 1962 (libretto by Burt Shevelove and Larry Gelbart); *Anyone Can Whistle*, 1964 (libretto by Laurents); *Do I Hear a Waltz?*, 1965 (libretto by Laurents); *Company*, 1970 (libretto by George Furth); *Follies*, 1971 (libretto by James Goldman); *A Little Night Music*, 1973 (libretto by Hugh Wheeler); *The Frogs*, 1974 (libretto by Aristophanes; adapted by Burt Shevelove); *Pacific Overtures*, 1976 (libretto by John Weidman); *Side by Side by Sondheim*, 1977 (libretto by Sondheim); *Sweeney Todd*, 1979 (libretto by Wheeler); *Merrily We Roll Along*, 1981 (libretto by Furth); *Sunday in the Park with George*, 1984 (libretto by James Lapine); *Into the Woods*, 1987 (libretto by Lapine); *Passion*, 1994 (libretto by Lapine); *Putting It Together*, 1999 (libretto by Sondheim with Julie N. McKenzie); *Celebrating Sondheim*, 2002 (libretto by Sondheim); *Assassins*, 2004 (libretto by John Weidman).

The Life

Stephen Joshua Sondheim (SAHND-him) was the only child of Herbert and Janet "Foxy" Sond-heim. Descendants of German Jewish immigrants, Sondheim's parents prospered through their endeavors in Manhattan's garment district. They were also great patrons of the artistic opportunities offered in New York City. Sondheim began formal piano lessons around the age of seven. His mother befriended Dorothy Hammerstein, the wife of the famous Broadway lyricist Oscar Hammerstein II. Upon divorcing his father in 1940, Sondheim's mother relocated to Doylestown, Pennsylvania, with her son, staying on a large estate near the Hammerstein residence. Sondheim became a friend of the Hammersteins' son, Jimmy, developing a close relationship with the entire family. His education included George School, located in Bucks County, Pennsylvania, where he and fellow classmates wrote *By George*, a musical about campus life. He showed the manuscript to Hammerstein, thus beginning his formal training in the world of musical theater. Sondheim became a music major at Williams College, where he was influenced by faculty member Robert Barrow. Receiving the Hutchinson Prize, a two-year fellowship, Sondheim furthered his studies with composer Milton Babbitt in New York.

After graduating from college in 1950, Sondheim actively sought work as a composer-lyricist on both coasts of the United States. Jobs for a novice composer were scarce, and his initial assignments involved writing television scripts for the situation comedy *Topper*. Sondheim's interest in word games and puzzles served him well as Broadway producers, searching for proficient lyricists, discovered his talent. He gained success initially with his lyrics to Broadway blockbusters such as *West Side Story* and *Gypsy*, but his goal was to be recognized as both composer and lyricist. He teamed with Richard Rodgers, Hammerstein's previous artistic partner, in 1965 to provide lyrics for *Do I Hear a Waltz?* Because the production was a critical disaster, Sondheim resolved, from this point, to write both music and lyrics for any future shows. He had his first major success with *Company* in 1970, which helped him gain a secure footing in the Broadway arena. Simultaneously, he published a series of word puzzles in *New York* magazine. From 1973 to 1981, Sondheim served as president of the Dramatists Guild of America, the professional association of playwrights, theatrical composers, and lyricists. In 1974

Sondheim wrote *The Frogs*, a show intended to be performed in the Yale University swimming pool. He also continued to write television screenplays, finding success with the 1973 murder mystery *The Last of Sheila*. When not composing for the Broadway stage, Sondheim has occupied himself with writing numerous film scores (*Stavisky* and *Reds*) and songs for films (*The Seven Percent Solution*, 1976, and *Dick Tracy*, 1990). In 1990 Sondheim was named visiting professor of contemporary theater at Oxford University. In 2005 Sondheim's seventy-fifth birthday was celebrated with all-star tribute concerts in New York, London, and Los Angeles.

The Music

Sondheim has been instrumental in the development of a theater form that relies on the observer's intellect and sophistication. No longer merely a form of light entertainment, works for the theater by Sondheim rely on complexity of music and lyrics, humorous wordplay, hidden metaphor, and non-traditional musical form. The musical scores, particularly the later works, are a stream of continuous music instead of isolated musical numbers. The story lines of Sondheim's works are rarely frivolous, focusing on social issues, such as relationships, revenge, honor, and justice.

Early Works. Sondheim's early fame came with his admirable ability to write intricate and clever lyrics. In 1955, when Sondheim was twenty-five years old, he was hired to write the lyrics for Leonard Bernstein's *West Side Story*. This show was a critical success, and it led to another assignment: as lyricist for *Gypsy*, a musical based on the memoirs of the burlesque dancer Gypsy Rose Lee. Although Sondheim campaigned to write both music and lyrics, the musical composition for *Gypsy* was ultimately assigned to Jule Styne. The production opened in 1959 to critical acclaim.

A Funny Thing Happened on the Way to the Forum was the first show for which Sondheim was recognized as both composer and lyricist. This 1962 production was considered a financial success, with 964 performances; however, critics were divided as to Sondheim's musical score. This was followed closely by a disastrous 1964 production of *Anyone Can Whistle*, that closed after only 9 performances. *Evening Primrose*, a television musical produced for the program ABC Stage 67, aired on November 16, 1966. Adapted from John Collier's short story "Evening Primrose," Sondheim's production remained in obscurity until archival footage was revived. This record of hits and misses set the stage for Sondheim's first major success, *Company*.

Company. *Company* was one of Sondheim's early departures from the typical Broadway musical formula, and it is considered his first critical success as both a composer and lyricist. Based on a book by George Furth, *Company* opened on Broadway at the Alvin Theatre on April 26, 1970, running for 705 performances. It was Sondheim's first collaboration with director Harold Prince. The show contains an adult story line dealing with the complexity of relationships, namely an unwillingness to commit to one, in a variety of scenarios. The two-act production revolves around the main character, Bobby, on his thirty-fifth birthday. Audiences experience Bobby's inner thoughts and fears as his friends attempt to find him a companion. The fourteen musical numbers range from hilarious farce to

Stephen Sondheim. (AP/Wide World Photos)

heartbreaking musical soliloquies. The music is not complex relative to later Sondheim scores. A successful 2006 Broadway revival updated the show to attract a modern-day audience.

Sweeney Todd. This is one of Sondheim's most popular and sophisticated works. In collaboration with director Prince, and with a book by Hugh Wheeler, *Sweeney Todd* has been performed on the Broadway stage, in opera houses, and in concert versions throughout the world. The two-act show opened on Broadway at the Uris Theatre on March 1, 1979, running for 557 performances. The primary story line concerns revenge for past injustices, cannibalism, and young love. The score is complex, and it can be loosely defined as an operetta, with its nonstop music and vocal polyphony. There were two successful Broadway revivals in 1989 and 2005, and a successful film version was released in 2007.

Sunday in the Park with George. Although this show received mixed reviews and ultimately lost money, *Sunday in the Park with George* maintains a devoted fan base. This initial collaboration with playwright and director James Lapine originally opened Off-Broadway at the Playwrights Horizons in July, 1983, where it ran for twenty-five performances. The production moved to Broadway's Booth Theatre on May 2, 1984, where it ran for 604 performances. This fictional work focuses on the French painter Georges Seurat and the development of his pointillist technique in the painting *A Sunday Afternoon on the Island of La Grande Jatte* (1886). The two-act production depicts several generations of the Seurat family and their issues with relationships and artistic integrity. There is little dialogue, but the musical numbers are continuous throughout.

Into the Woods. *Into the Woods*, another collaboration with book-writer Lapine, is one of Sondheim's most popular and accessible shows. The production began in 1986 at the Old Globe Theatre in San Diego, where it ran for 50 performances. The Broadway debut was November 5, 1987, at the Martin Beck Theatre, where it ran for 764 performances. Based on classic fairy tales, *Into the Woods* deals with the darker psychology of these tales, including the dangers of wishing for more and dysfunctional maternal relationships. The first act is all in fun, and the second act deconstructs the happy world into a darker, and perhaps more realistic, place. The mu-

sical score is continuous, with little dialogue. A shorter, simpler version has been constructed for children's productions. *Into the Woods* toured nationally in 1988, and it was revived on Broadway in 2002.

Musical Legacy

Sondheim expanded the repertory of musical theater, redefining its function and its structural design, and setting a new artistic standard. Interestingly, although Sondheim has contributed more than a dozen major works to the theater repertoire, few of his vocal works are considered mainstream in the pop charts. This is primarily because of their complexity and because of the fact that few songs make sense when taken out of the show's context. Exceptions to this include "Send in the Clowns" from *A Little Night Music* and "Children Will Listen" from *Into the Woods*. The ability to sing Sondheim has become a benchmark, indicating that the artist has vocal skill and acute musical sensibility.

Critics are divided on Sondheim's musicals. Some are devoted fans; others find the scores too complex, with wordy, patter-song polyphony, and too long and dissonant. This may explain the relatively short runs and the negative reviews of several Sondheim musicals. Nevertheless, Sondheim has been lauded and recognized, with Tony Awards, Grammy Awards for *Sweeney Todd* (1979) and "Send in the Clowns" (Song of the Year, 1976), the Pulitzer Prize in Drama for *Sunday in the Park with George* (1985), an Academy Award for Best Song for "Sooner or Later" from the film *Dick Tracy* (1990), and the Award for Lifetime Achievement from the Kennedy Center Honors (1993).

P. Brent Register

Further Reading

Banfield, Stephen. *Sondheim's Broadway Musicals.* Ann Arbor: University of Michigan Press, 1993. An in-depth analysis of Sondheim's compositional process and musicals, this text examines thirteen musicals, from *West Side Story* to *Assassins*, drawing from interviews with Sondheim and access to drafts, sketches, and letters. Not for the casual reader, this book is often technical, requiring an understanding of music composition.

Gottfried, Martin. *Sondheim*. New York: Harry Abrams, 2000. An account of Sondheim's creative life based on personal interviews, with a friendly analysis of the music and lyrics, including more than one hundred photographs taken from archives and Sondheim's personal files. The text is chronological from Sondheim's birth to the production of *Passion*.

Horowitz, Mark Eden. *Sondheim on Music: Minor Details and Major Decisions*. Lanham, Md.: Scarecrow Press, 2003. Discussion and analysis of six musicals (*Passion*, *Assassins*, *Into the Woods*, *Sunday in the Park with George*, *Sweeney Todd*, and *Pacific Overtures*) based on a series of interviews with Sondheim. Includes a comprehensive song list, discography, and publishing information. A strong theoretical background in music is helpful in reading this book.

Secrest, Meryle. *Stephen Sondheim: A Life*. New York: Alfred A. Knopf, 1998. Interesting biography of Sondheim, beginning with his early childhood and stretching to the late 1990's. The biography is based on extended conversations with Sondheim as well as interviews with colleagues, friends, and family. Includes ninety-five black-and-white photographs.

Zadan, Craig. *Sondheim & Co*. New York: Da Capo Press, 1994. A record of Sondheim's creative process in the development of his musicals. The text is based on recorded interviews with Sondheim and his collaborators. Chapters include discussions on composition, lyrics, orchestrations, recording, and casting. An extensive appendix provides complete credit and cast information for Sondheim productions up to *A Little Night Music*. Includes seventy-four black-and-white photographs.

See also: Andrews, Dame Julie; Babbitt, Milton; Bernstein, Leonard; Collins, Judy; Galway, Sir James; Green, Adolph, and Betty Comden; Hamlisch, Marvin; Hammerstein, Oscar, II; Legrand, Michel; Merman, Ethel; Rodgers, Richard; Styne, Jule; Vaughan, Sarah; Weill, Kurt.

John Philip Sousa
American classical composer

Sousa was a prolific composer of marches and conductor of the internationally famous Sousa Band, which toured the United States and world for nearly four decades. His music had a worldwide influence on the development of bands and on the burgeoning recording industry.

Born: November 6, 1854; Washington, D.C.
Died: March 6, 1932; Reading, Pennsylvania
Also known as: March King

Principal works
BAND WORKS (marches): "The Gladiator," 1886; "The Rifle Regiment," 1886; "Semper Fidelis," 1888; "The Thunderer," 1889; "The Washington Post," 1889; "The High School Cadets," 1890; "The Liberty Bell," 1893; "Manhattan Beach," 1893; "King Cotton," 1895; "The Stars and Stripes Forever," 1897; "Hands Across the Sea," 1899; "The Invincible Eagle," 1901; "The Fairest of the Fair," 1908; "The Glory of the Yankee Navy," 1909; "Boy Scouts of America," 1916; "Processional (Wedding March)," 1918; "Sabre and Spurs," 1918; "Solid Men to the Front," 1918; "U.S. Field Artillery," 1918; "The Gallant Seventh," 1922; "Nobles of the Mystic Shrine," 1923; "The Pride of the Wolverines," 1926; "Golden Jubilee," 1928; "The Salvation Army," 1930.

OPERA (music): *Katherine*, 1879 (libretto by W. S. Gance and Sousa).

ORCHESTRAL WORKS: *Our Flirtation*, 1880; *The Smugglers*, 1882 (comic opera; libretto by Wilson Vance; based on Arthur Sullivan and F. C. Burnand's opera *The Contrabandista*); *Désirée*, 1884 (libretto by Edward M. Taber; based on John Maddison Morton's English comedy *Our Wife*); *The Queen of Hearts*, 1888 (libretto by E. W. Faber); *The Wolf*, 1888 (libretto by Sousa; renamed *The Bride Elect*); *El Capitan*, 1896 (lyrics by Charles Klein and Tom Frost; libretto by Klein); *The Charlatan*, 1898 (comic opera; libretto by Klein); *Chris and the Wonderful Lamp*, 1899 (libretto by Glen

MacDonough); *The Free Lance*, 1906 (military comic opera; libretto by Harry Bache Smith); *The American Maid*, 1913 (comic opera; libretto by Leonard Liebling); *The Irish Dragoon*, 1915 (libretto by Joseph Herbert; based on Charles Lever's novel *Charles O'Malley: The Irish Dragoon*); *Cubaland Suite*, 1925.

WRITINGS OF INTEREST: *The Trumpet and Drum*, 1886 (instructional); *National, Patriotic, and Typical Airs of All Lands*, 1890 (compilation); *Marching Along*, 1928 (autobiography).

The Life

John Philip Sousa (SEW-zuh) was the third of ten children born to John Antonio and Maria Elisabeth (Trinkaus) Sousa in Washington, D.C. He studied the violin and various wind instruments privately from an early age, and learned music at a local music conservatory and composition with George Felix Benkert. At age thirteen he joined the U.S. Marine Band as an apprentice musician. As a young man he performed professionally as a theater orchestra and opera violinist and conductor, and in 1880, at age twenty-five, he became the fourteenth director of the U.S. Marine Band.

During his twelve-year tenure, he served under five presidents and transformed the band into the premier American military ensemble. In 1892 Sousa resigned and formed the Sousa Band, a civilian band that rapidly became the finest performing band in the world. He hired the best musicians available and achieved tremendous success. Between 1892 and 1931 this amazing ensemble toured the United States and Canada yearly and undertook four European tours and one world tour (1910-1911). During this period the band performed an astounding 15,623 concerts, an average of more than one concert a day. In addition to the tours, the band had extended engagements at Manhattan Beach in New York, the Steel Pier in Atlantic City, and Willow Grove Park in Philadelphia. Sousa conducted more band concerts than any other composer.

Known during his lifetime as the March King, Sousa achieved early compositional success as an operetta composer. He published stage works from the early 1880's and began writing marches while still in his teens. One of the most prolific American composers of all time, Sousa composed every year of his mature life, while also transcribing and ar-

ranging a great deal of music for band. In addition to 137 marches and fifteen operettas, he composed songs, overtures, dance music, descriptive works, and fantasies. He also wrote three novels, two manuals, an autobiography, and more than 150 articles.

At age sixty-two Sousa enlisted in the U.S. Navy to help organize bands as part of the World War I effort. Composing, touring, live radio broadcasts, recording sessions, and concerts at expositions and fairs occupied Sousa's postwar years. He became active in the development of school bands and was a charter member of the American Society of Composers, Authors, and Publishers (ASCAP). By that time, Sousa was an American institution, the most famous and highest paid living musician in the world. In September, 1921, he was thrown from a horse and seriously injured his back, yet he continued to write and conduct until his death ten years later. Following a rehearsal on March 5, 1932, of the Ringgold Band in Reading, Pennsylvania, Sousa returned to his hotel room, and he died of a heart attack. He was seventy-seven years old.

The Music

There are several reasons why Sousa's music has enjoyed worldwide popularity for more than a century. He was an extraordinarily inventive composer of music for the band, resulting in marches that are national treasures. His most famous works, presented in concerts, published as sheet music, arranged for various combinations of instruments, and recorded on cylinders and discs, rapidly spread his fame. He was the symbol of his country in the decades between the Civil War and World War II when American nationalism was being recognized worldwide, and his own personal patriotism is reflected in his compositions and his performances.

An extremely skilled conductor, Sousa assembled the finest performing band in the world. By including a wide variety of transcriptions of European classics, songs and selections from the operatic stage, virtuosic solo pieces, dance and popular music, hymns and spirituals, and offering military marches as quick encores, Sousa revolutionized the way people experienced the concert performance. His music reflects the diverse influence of Sir Arthur Sullivan, Richard Strauss,

John Philip Sousa. (Library of Congress)

Jacques Offenbach, and Wolfgang Amadeus Mozart. When he introduced American ragtime during his 1900 European tour, he ignited a mania for American music that lasted for decades and influenced the compositions of Claude Debussy, Maurice Ravel, Florent Schmitt, Igor Stravinsky, and others.

"Semper Fidelis." Sketched in late 1887 during Sousa's tenure as U.S. Marine Band director, "Semper Fidelis" is widely considered to be the finest example of a regimental march by any composer. Sousa acknowledged it as one of his most effective. It was written at the suggestion of U.S. President Chester A. Arthur to replace "Hail to the Chief." The title comes from the Marine Corps motto—Always Faithful. It was played at dirge tempo by the U.S. Marine Band in 1932 as Sousa's caisson was transported to the Congressional Cemetery in Washington, D.C. Its highly regarded musical reputation stems from Sousa's inventive contrast between the bold introduction and the playful first strain, the lyrical second section, and the mesmeriz-

ing additive effect in the trio. The trio begins with the regimental drums and bugles, adds a woodwind counterpoint, and then is enhanced by a trombone countermelody. Of the brilliant final strain, Sousa said, "If you don't stand up and march then, you never will."

"The Washington Post." In 1889 the owners of the fledgling newspaper *The Washington Post* asked Sousa to compose a march for a summer ceremony on the Smithsonian Institution grounds. The march was Sousa's first big success. When it was adopted by an American dance masters' association as appropriate for the new two-step dance craze, the march, composer, and newspaper were catapulted into international fame. The march was the most requested piece on Sousa's European tours in the first years of the twentieth century and was known worldwide through twenty-two cylinder and disc recordings of the piece (recorded by the Sousa Band between 1895 and 1905). Like many of Sousa's early marches, the "Washington Post" was sold to the Harry Coleman Publishing Company for the incredibly low fee of $35.

El Capitan. Known today primarily as a march composer, Sousa wrote fifteen operettas. *El Capitan* was first produced in 1896 and quickly became his most successful and popular operetta. It holds the position of being the first successful Broadway operetta composed by an American. Sousa used some of his previously composed music for the score, but the reputation of the work rests largely on the rhythmic vitality of the music, the colorful and inventive writing for orchestra, and a fine libretto by Charles Klein. Originally scored for twelve winds, percussion, and strings, modern performances generally use a full-pit orchestra. The operetta played for more than four years in the United States, Canada, and England, and it was very successful in an excerpted version as played by the Sousa Band. The march of the same name is from the end of the first act where it is sung by the chorus. Sousa's band arrangement of it has become one of his most enduring and best-loved compositions.

"The Stars and Stripes Forever." Named "the greatest piece of music ever written by an American composer" by Harold Schonberg, esteemed music critic of *The New York Times*, "The Stars and Stripes Forever" is the official national march of the United States and has become one of the most recognizable musical symbols of America throughout the world since it premiered in 1897. It is Sousa's march masterpiece—a successful monument to his patriotic fundamentals and an extremely sophisticated composition. Close analysis reveals melodic unity among the five sections of the march and a finely crafted use of harmony and counterpoint. The trio is perhaps the most familiar march trio ever written. In it the main melody, played by the clarinet section, is enhanced by the most memorable piccolo obbligato in the repertoire, which was originally written for the Db piccolo. Following the final dogfight, a third melodic element is added as a martial counterpoint in the trombones. As performed by the Sousa Band, the cornets, massed piccolos, and trombones lined up across the stage facing the audience for the final grandioso. The effect on the audience was electrifying.

Cubaland Suite. Sousa's final suite, and one of the most popular of his thirteen, is *Cubaland Suite,* which depicts the rule of Cuba by three separate governments: Spain in 1875, the United States in 1898, and an independent Cuban government in 1925. Each of the three movements incorporates national tunes that identify the countries governing Cuba. "Under the Spanish Flag" includes excerpts from "The Spanish Constitution" and "Andalusian Dances." "Hot Time in the Old Town Tonight," "Swanee River," and selected quotations from Sousa's own "International Congress" fantasy are found in the middle movement, "Under the American Flag." The beloved traditional Cuban melody "La Bayamesa" appears in the last movement, "Under the Cuban Flag." Sousa conceived this suite during a vacation in Havana in 1924. Originally scored for band, Sousa's suites are colorful and vibrant in their scoring but difficult to play. Most were inspired by Sousa's travels around the world with his band during the first three decades of the twentieth century, and the programmatic content of his suites reflects that period of his life.

Musical Legacy

Sousa deserves credit for establishing a national audience that was as receptive to traditional classical music as it was to popular music. He standardized the concert program and the quick use of encore pieces and achieved unprecedented success with his band in small towns and large cities alike.

He has been called the greatest traveling musical entertainer. His European tours established American music for the first time as a legitimate cultural force. Sousa's compositions, the tireless performances of the Sousa Band, and his personal attention through clinics, guest-conducting appearances, and direct sponsorship had a substantial influence on the school music movement after World War I. His 1,770 commercial phonograph discs (recorded from 1897 to 1930) shaped and assured the success of the new recording industry. Sousa's patriotism was reflected in every concert, and this was another secret to his popularity. Much of his music has stood the test of time and remains enthusiastically recognized and loved.

Jerry E. Rife

Further Reading

Bierley, Paul Edmund. *The Incredible Band of John Philip Sousa.* Urbana: University of Illinois Press, 2006. A comprehensive and exhaustive history of Sousa's band, including six statistical appendixes detailing where the band played, the complete contents of the music library, membership, instrumentation, program listings, discography, and photographs.

_____. *John Philip Sousa, American Phenomenon.* Rev. ed. Miami: Warner Bros., 2001. The definitive biography of Sousa, with sections on the band, music, family, philosophy, and musical legacy.

_____. *The Works of John Philip Sousa.* Columbus, Ohio: Integrity Press, 1984. The standard and essential reference guide to every composition by Sousa. Complete background, publication, and copyright information are included.

Hansen, Richard K. *The American Wind Band: A Cultural History.* Chicago: GIA, 2006. An invaluable history of bands in America from colonial times to the big band era.

Heslip, Malcolm. *Nostalgic Happenings in the Three Bands of John Philip Sousa.* Columbus, Ohio: Integrity Press, 1982. Anecdotal insights into the day-to-day workings of bands directed by Sousa.

Newsom, John, ed. *Perspectives on John Philip Sousa.* Washington, D.C.: Library of Congress, 1983. Collection of scholarly articles by several authors on Sousa's music and his place in history.

Sousa, John Philip. *Marching Along*. Edited by Paul E. Bierley. Rev. ed. Columbus, Ohio: Integrity Press, 1994. An intriguing and colorful autobiography written by Sousa at the age of seventy-three.

See also: Debussy, Claude; Fiedler, Arthur; Horowitz, Vladimir; Ravel, Maurice; Strauss, Richard; Stravinsky, Igor; Whiteman, Paul.

Phil Spector

American rock producer

As a record producer, Spector established the multi-instrument Wall of Sound that backed the popular songs of the 1960's.

Born: December 26, 1939; New York, New York
Also known as: Harvey Philip Spector (full name)

Principal recordings

ALBUMS (as producer): *The Teddy Bears Sing*, 1959 (by the Teddy Bears); *A Christmas Gift for You from Phil Spector*, 1963; *He's a Rebel*, 1963 (by the Crystals); *Twist Uptown*, 1963 (by the Crystals); *Presenting the Fabulous Ronettes Featuring Veronica*, 1964 (by the Ronettes); *Ronettes*, 1965 (by the Ronettes); *River Deep—Mountain High*, 1966 (by Ike and Tina Turner); *All Things Must Pass*, 1970 (by George Harrison); *Let It Be*, 1970 (by the Beatles); *Plastic Ono Band*, 1970 (by John Lennon); *Imagine*, 1971 (by John Lennon); *Some Time in New York City*, 1972 (by John Lennon); *Rock 'n' Roll*, 1975 (by John Lennon); *Death of a Ladies' Man*, 1977 (by Leonard Cohen); *End of the Century*, 1980 (by the Ramones); *Silence Is Easy*, 2003 (by Starsailor).

The Life

When Harvey Philip Spector was nine years old, his father committed suicide. Four years later, his mother moved the family from the Bronx to Los Angeles. The relocation negatively affected Spector, who became insecure and withdrawn in adolescence. Later, Spector turned to music as a songwriter. His first hit, "To Know Him Is to Love Him" by the Teddy Bears, was a relatively simple, teen-themed song recorded in monophonic sound. By 1966 Spector had developed his Wall of Sound signature: recording layers of performances and blending them in monophonic sound. With this technique, he produced more than two dozen Top 40 hits (thirteen of them Top 10). In 1968 Spector married Veronica "Ronnie" Bennett, who had sung lead on Spector's productions with the Ronettes. They divorced six years later.

Shortly after the failure of *River Deep—Mountain High*, an Ike and Tina Turner production that he considered his finest, Spector retired, emerging during the next decade mainly to produce records by the Beatles (collectively and individually), Leonard Cohen, and the Ramones. Although there were a few hits among them, these albums became more notorious for being overseen by a producer who exhibited bizarre behavior, who often wielded a gun. On February 3, 2003, Spector was arrested on suspicion of murder when the body of Lana Clarkson, an actress, was discovered in his mansion. Four years later, the trial began. Spector's defense was that Clarkson had shot herself accidentally and that any statements he had made suggesting his guilt were made under the influence of medicine prescribed to combat his bipolar disorder. A mistrial was declared when the jury announced that it was deadlocked. The retrial began in October, 2008, and in April, 2009, Spector was found guilty of second-degree murder.

The Music

Spector's music is noted for his Wall of Sound, which he typically generated by recording layered performances of frequently ornate arrangements by large studio ensembles in Los Angeles's Gold Star Studios and mixing the results in monophonic sound. The core of his ensembles was a small group of studio musicians anchored by the drummer Hal Blaine and known as the Wrecking Crew. As Spector's recordings grew more ambitious, he augmented the Wrecking Crew with string sections and with multiple musicians playing the same instruments (and parts) in unison.

"To Know Him Is to Love Him." Spector took the title and refrain of his first production from the epitaph on his father's headstone, and his transformation of the line into a lover's pledge helped the song hit number one in 1958. It was performed by the Teddy Bears, a quartet that counted Spector as a member. Recorded for a mere seventy-five dollars, the song was necessarily simple in production value. Nevertheless, its effortless blending of a universal emotion with a memorable melody made the song a significant success.

"Be My Baby." This chart-topping 1963 classic is generally considered Spector's finest work. Just a year after its release, Brian Wilson was borrowing its distinctive elements (Blaine's dramatically syncopated drumbeats, lyrics about adolescent romance) to create "Don't Worry Baby" with the Beach Boys. Wilson's dreamily falsetto lead vocal, however, did not match the gritty yearning of Bennett's schoolgirl urgency, a performance so durable that many have credited the reprisal of her song's refrain on Eddie Money's 1986 "Take Me Home Tonight" (and her appearance in the accompanying video) with resuscitating Money's career.

A Christmas Gift for You from Phil Spector. Spector disliked the long-playing record format, a medium he believed shortchanged consumers by mating eight or nine lackluster songs with one or two hits. In spite of this, Spector reportedly put his finest effort into all the songs on this album. Its sales suffered initially because it appeared in stores on the day that President John F. Kennedy was assassinated. Over time, however, it has become a perennial favorite. U2 covered the album's best-known song, Darlene Love's "Christmas (Baby Please Come Home)," in 1987, paying homage to the original by following Spector's arrangement.

"You've Lost That Lovin' Feeling." Before they joined Spector in 1965, Bill Medley and Bobby Hatfield were a talented but little known blue-eyed soul duo whose biggest hit, "Little Latin Lupe Lu," did not make the *Billboard* Top 40. With this lushly produced exploration of love grown cold, however, the Righteous Brothers, as Medley and Hatfield were known, became stars, rapidly scoring three more Spector-produced hits ("Just Once in My Life," "Unchained Melody," and "Ebb Tide").

"River Deep—Mountain High." This 1966 single by Ike and Tina Turner has been cited as a watershed in Spector's career, and its failure to chart higher than eighty-eight in the United States in 1966, after all of Spector's efforts, played an important role in his decision to close Philles Records and to reevaluate his relationship with the pop-music world. In retrospect, it seems the single was simply a victim of changing tastes. The record's use of strings, for instance—which had proved so effective in dramatizing the Righteous Brothers' recordings just a year before—did not attract listeners, who seemed to prefer the electronic effects of psychedelic music.

Back to Mono, 1958-1969. Released in 1991, this boxed set comprises three discs of Spector's best-known productions until his work with the Beatles (*Let It Be*). It also includes *A Christmas Gift for You*, an elaborate booklet with analytical essays and the lyrics to all sixty songs, and a "Back to Mono" button. The set includes all but one of the singles that Spector produced for his Philles label, a generous sampling of his productions for other record companies, and the Crystals' "He Hit Me (It Felt Like a Kiss)." That single was released in

Phil Spector and the Ronettes. (Hulton Archive/Getty Images)

1962, but it was quickly withdrawn: Its lyrics are sung from a first-person point of view by a woman who regards the physical abuse she endures from her man as a sign that he loves her.

Musical Legacy

The songs that Spector wrote, cowrote, or solicited from Brill Building composers and produced with great success in the studio often expressed innocent, romantic dreams. In contrast, his wife Bennett and such artists as Cohen and Johnny Ramone have given firsthand accounts of the strange and violent behavior exhibited by Spector. Despite his eccentric persona, Spector created the innovative Wall of Sound technique that resulted in Top 10 hits in the 1960's. Although Spector enjoyed few hits after the early 1970's, his influence can be heard in the music of the Beach Boys' Wilson and Bruce Springsteen.

Arsenio Orteza

Further Reading

Brown, Mick. *Tearing Down the Wall of Sound: The Rise and Fall of Phil Spector*. New York: Alfred A. Knopf, 2007. A detailed and evenhanded account of Spector's life, covering his Wall of Sound, his withdrawal from the music world, his attempted comebacks, his increasingly bizarre behavior, and his trial for the murder of Clarkson.

Cohn, Nik. "Phil Spector." In *The Rolling Stone Illustrated History of Rock and Roll*, edited by Jim Miller. New York: Random House/Rolling Stone Press, 1980. A well-written mini-biography that grew out of interviews with Spector conducted by Cohn in the late 1960's.

Marsh, Dave. *The Heart of Rock and Soul: The 1001 Greatest Singles Ever Made*. New York: Plume, 1989. This source includes insightful discussions by the veteran rock critic Marsh of Spector-produced singles by the Ronettes, the Crystals, Lennon, Love, and Gene Pitney.

Ribowsky, Mark. *He's a Rebel: Phil Spector, Rock and Roll's Legendary Producer*. New York: Perseus, 2007. The latest edition of Ribowsky's biography includes chapters on Spector's murder trial and features well-researched information on Spector's public success and behind-the-scenes horrors.

Spector, Ronnie, and Vince Waldron. *Be My Baby: How I Survived Mascara, Miniskirts, and Madness, or My Life as a Fabulous Ronette*. New York: Harmony, 1990. The autobiography of Spector's wife, the lead singer of the Ronettes, includes harrowing descriptions of her life with Spector.

Wenner, Jann. "Phil Spector." In *The Rolling Stone Interviews*, edited by the Editors of *Rolling Stone*. New York: Warner, 1971. A lengthy, verbatim, late-1960's transcript of an interview with Spector conducted by the founder of *Rolling Stone* magazine.

Wolfe, Tom. *Kandy-Kolored Tangerine-Flake Streamline Baby*. New York: Farrar, Straus and Giroux, 1965. The chapter titled "The First Tycoon of Teen" was the first major essay published on Spector, who at the time was at the top of the pop-music business.

See also: Bono; Cohen, Leonard; Goffin, Gerry; Leiber, Jerry; Lennon, John; Orbison, Roy; Ramone, Joey; Springsteen, Bruce; Stoller, Mike; Turner, Tina; Wilson, Brian.

Bruce Springsteen
American rock singer, guitarist, and songwriter

Nearly unrivaled as a singer-songwriter and live performer, Springsteen demonstrated uncompromising artistic integrity, commitment to his craft, and belief in the redemptive, life-changing power of music.

Born: September 23, 1949; Long Branch, New Jersey

Also known as: Bruce Frederick Joseph Springsteen (full name); the Boss

Member of: Bruce Springsteen and the E Street Band

Principal recordings

ALBUMS (solo): *Nebraska*, 1982; *Human Touch*, 1992; *Lucky Town*, 1992; *The Ghost of Tom Joad*, 1995; *Devils and Dust*, 2005; *We Shall Overcome: The Seeger Sessions*, 2006.

ALBUMS (with the E Street Band): *Greetings from Asbury Park, New Jersey*, 1973; *The Wild, the Innocent, and the E Street Shuffle*, 1973; *Born to Run*, 1975; *Darkness on the Edge of Town*, 1978; *The River*, 1980; *Born in the U.S.A.*, 1984; *Tunnel of Love*, 1987; *The Rising*, 2002; *Magic*, 2007; *Working on a Dream*, 2009.

The Life

Bruce Frederick Joseph Springsteen was born into a working-class family, and he grew up in the factory town of Freehold, New Jersey, a blue-collar upbringing that stimulated his deep empathy for the tenacious underdogs who populate his lyrics. Uninterested in work or school, repressed at home, and alienated from most of his peers, Springsteen

Bruce Springsteen. (AP/Wide World Photos)

came alive when he began playing guitar at age sixteen. From that time, he dedicated himself obsessively to a career in music. After leading a series of increasingly successful bands (earning the nickname the Boss for his demands for perfectionism) and developing into a prolific songwriter, he was signed to a recording contract in 1972 by John Hammond, the executive who a decade earlier had discovered Bob Dylan. In 1985 Springsteen married model and actress Julianne Phillips, and they divorced in 1990. In 1991 he married Patty Scialfa, who had been singing backup vocals with his E Street Band since 1984. They had three children: Evan James, Jessica Rae, and Sam Ryan. Springsteen's music has been recognized with numerous Grammy and Emmy Awards, and his song for the film *Philadelphia*, "Streets of Philadelphia," which adopts the point of view of a gay man dying of AIDS, won an Academy Award in 1994.

The Music

Early Works. The connection with Hammond led to the media labeling Springsteen "the new Dylan." With few songs suitable for hit singles, his first two albums proved to be commercial disasters. However, some visionary critics, such as Steve Simels, who put the first album on his best-of-the-year list, were quick to see his talent. The influential critic Jon Landau, who became Springsteen's manager and producer, famously declared after seeing him play in 1974, "I saw rock and roll's future and its name is Bruce Springsteen." Time would justify that prediction, as several songs from those first releases became classics, staples of his live shows decades later. Many critics would now rank the second record, *The Wild, the Innocent, and the E Street Shuffle*, among his best.

Born to Run. After two commercial failures, Springsteen set out to make the greatest rock-and-roll record of all time. He succeeded with *Born to Run*, combining a guitar-driven wall of sound with passionate vocals and lyrics that reimagined the classic rock-and-roll themes of cars, romance, and dreams as adult, rather than exclusively adolescent, concerns. Even without a hit single, the record sold a million copies in the first year and became a staple of FM radio programming. Springsteen was the first musician to appear on the covers of *Newsweek* and *Time* in the same week.

Nebraska. At the peak of his popularity—*The River* was his first album to reach number one on the charts and yielded his first hit single—Springsteen astonished critics and fans with his next release, the solo acoustic *Nebraska*. Switching unexpectedly from electric to acoustic music, Springsteen produced in his listeners an intense response, similar to Dylan when he switched from acoustic to electric music in 1965. Recorded at Springsteen's home on a cassette deck, the album, with its primitive sound and bleak material (the title track is a study of a serial killer), showed the influences of country and folk music on his writing, and it revealed unsuspected depths of despair in Springsteen's generally optimistic mythology, whose protagonists were often downtrodden but seldom defeated like the isolated, psychically battered characters depicted in *Nebraska*.

Born in the U.S.A. Springsteen's seventh album was a great commercial success, producing seven Top 10 singles by combining the social realism of *Nebraska* with the epic rock-and-roll music of *Born to Run*. The opening song, "Born in the U.S.A.," was often misinterpreted as a commercial for America's superiority by listeners who ignored the lyrics (Ronald Reagan briefly used it as a theme song for his presidential campaign). Originally written for *Nebraska*, it was in fact a bitter reflection on the continuing human costs of the Vietnam War. As always, Springsteen's empathy for his characters transformed the political theme into a personal one, presenting it from the point of view of a disillusioned Vietnam veteran.

Magic. Springsteen's work continued to earn critical praise and popular success, with *Magic* debuting as the best-selling album in the world and earning unanimous critical acclaim and four Grammy Award nominations. Hailed as a return to his classic form, and featuring the full E Street Band (most of whom had been playing with him, on and off, for thirty-plus years), the album successfully combined accessible pop tunes, hard-driving rock songs, and pointed political commentary. Just as his early work had explored the impact of the Vietnam War on the lives of average Americans, this album took the war in Iraq as its primary subtext.

Musical Legacy

While many of the earlier giants of rock music had made their mark as innovators, Springsteen's trademark was his mastery of the traditional, as he worked to consolidate and extend what he saw as a valuable and distinctively American musical history. In an era when punk, new wave, and even disco were challenging the centrality of the rock tradition, Springsteen explored and revitalized the genre itself, a project that eventually took him beyond rock music into the folk and country traditions long ignored by most rock musicians. Springsteen's empathy for the problems and the everyday heroism of ordinary working people struggling to live meaningful lives in difficult times made his music important to his audience. The Beatles achieved such levels of popular and critical success, but for just a few years, while Springsteen has sustained it through four decades.

William Nelles

Further Reading

Alterman, Eric. *It Ain't No Sin to Be Glad You're Alive: The Promise of Bruce Springsteen*. Boston: Little, Brown, 1999. A concise and highly readable biography.

Graff, Gary, ed. *The Ties That Bind: Bruce Springsteen A to E to Z*. Canton, Mich.: Visible Ink, 2005. An encyclopedia with close to three hundred entries. The sixteen specialized appendixes include, for example, a listing of nearly five hundred artists who have covered his songs.

Marsh, Dave. *Bruce Springsteen: On Tour, 1968-2005*. New York: Bloomsbury, 2006. Coffee-table book by Springsteen's foremost biographer, presenting a condensed narrative of his life through a chronicle of his legendary live performances. Includes hundreds of photographs from every stage of Springsteen's career.

_____. *Bruce Springsteen: Two Hearts*. New York: Routledge, 2004. This book combines the texts of two earlier biographies by Marsh—*Born to Run* (1979) and *Glory Days* (1987)—with a new chapter to update the volume.

Rolling Stone, eds. *Bruce Springsteen: The Rolling Stone Files*. New York: Hyperion, 1996. A compendium of interviews, reviews, and articles published in the rock magazine from 1973 to 1996, mostly unavailable from other sources.

Sawyers, June Skinner, ed. *Racing in the Street: The Bruce Springsteen Reader.* New York: Penguin, 2004. An anthology of articles, reviews, poems, stories, excerpts, and interviews. Covers most of the essential shorter material not included in the *Rolling Stone* volume.

See also: Burke, Solomon; Dylan, Bob; Earle, Steve; Eddy, Duane; Harris, Emmylou; Lennon, John; McCartney, Sir Paul; Morricone, Ennio; Morrison, Van; Pickett, Wilson; Robertson, Robbie; Seeger, Pete; Spector, Phil; Sting.

Ralph Stanley

American bluegrass singer, banjoist, and songwriter

Stanley is one of the seminal artists of bluegrass music, noted for his soulful voice and his authentic performances of the traditional music of southern Appalachia.

Born: February 25, 1927; Stratton, Virginia
Also known as: Ralph Edmond Stanley (full name)
Member of: The Stanley Brothers; the Clinch Mountain Boys

Principal recordings

ALBUMS (solo): *Ralph Stanley and Raymond Fairchild,* 1989 (with Raymond Fairchild); *Saturday Night/Sunday Morning,* 1995 (with others); *Clinch Mountain Country,* 1998 (with Ralph Stanley and Friends); *Songs My Mother Taught Me and More: Clawhammer Style Banjo,* 1998; *Clinch Mountain Sweethearts,* 2001 (with Ralph Stanley and Friends); *Ralph Stanley,* 2002; *Great High Mountain,* 2004; *Shine On,* 2005.

ALBUMS (with the Clinch Mountain Boys): *Hills of Home,* 1969; *Cry from the Cross,* 1971; *Something Old, Something New, Some of Katy's Mountain Dew,* 1971; *Ralph Stanley and the Clinch Mountain Boys Play Requests,* 1972; *I Want to Preach the Gospel,* 1973; *Man and His Music,* 1974; *Let Me Rest on a Peaceful Mountain,* 1975; *Old Home Place,* 1976; *Clinch Mountain Gospel,*

1977; *Down Where the River Bends,* 1978; *I'll Wear a White Robe,* 1980; *The Stanley Sound Today,* 1981; *The Memory of Your Smile,* 1982; *Child of the King,* 1983; *Snow Covered Mound,* 1983; *I Can Tell You the Time,* 1985; *Lonesome and Blue,* 1986; *I'll Answer the Call,* 1988; *Pray for the Boys,* 1990; *Bound to Ride,* 1991; *Almost Home,* 1992; *Short Life of Trouble: The Songs of Grayson and Whitter,* 1996; *My All and All,* 1997; *While the Ages Roll On,* 2000.

ALBUMS (with the Stanley Brothers and the Clinch Mountain Boys): *Mountain Song Favorites,* 1959; *The Stanley Brothers and the Clinch Mountain Boys,* 1959; *For the Good People,* 1960; *Long Journey Home,* 1961; *Old Country Church,* 1961; *Sing the Songs They Like Best,* 1961; *The Stanley Brothers in Person,* 1961; *Good Old Camp Meeting Songs,* 1962; *Hymns of the Cross,* 1964; *Jacob's Vision,* 1966; *The Stanley Brothers Together for the Last Time,* 1972; *Banjo in the Hills,* 1976; *That Little Old Country Church House,* 1998.

The Life

Ralph Edmond Stanley was born during the Great Depression in rural Dickenson County, Virginia. Growing up on a farm in the highlands of central Appalachia, he learned the traditional mountain clawhammer banjo from his mother, Lucy. He was also a member of the Primitive Baptist church, where he learned the unique cadences and phrasings that would later define his vocal style. After serving in the U.S. Army in Europe in World War II, Stanley returned to Dickenson County in 1946. Seeking a career in music after his discharge, he joined his brother Carter to form the Clinch Mountain Boys.

The success of the duo grew steadily in the following decade. Within six years the brothers progressed from playing barn dances and school assemblies in rural Appalachia to recording albums for Columbia Records and making network television appearances. When Carter died suddenly in 1966, Stanley, though profoundly saddened, shortly re-formed the Clinch Mountain Boys, and he returned to touring and recording. Stanley would record more than one hundred albums, make thousands of live concert appearances, and remain a potent force in the world of acoustic music.

The Music

Stanley's childhood in rural Appalachia provided him with the sound, imagery, and themes that would characterize his music. As a child, Stanley was taught to play the banjo in a clawhammer style (with the melody picked downward and the hand held in the shape of a claw), just as his mother had learned. Stanley regularly attended the Primitive Baptist church, where he was exposed to a unique a cappella vocal style that he would later utilize in his performances and his recordings. Primitive Baptist worship singing includes a practice called lining, in which a song leader calls out, or "lines," a song phrase, after which the congregation repeats the line. Stanley incorporates this practice, whose origins are centuries old, into many of his gospel recordings.

The Clinch Mountain Boys. After World War II, Stanley and his brother Carter formed the Clinch Mountain Boys, performing on the regional circuit in the late 1940's. Their popularity quickly grew as bluegrass—a new, hard-driving combination of old-time traditional mountain music, tight vocal harmonies, and propulsive rhythms—became increasingly popular. Along with Bill Monroe, Lester Flatt, and Earl Scruggs, the Stanley brothers brought this music out of the hollows of central Appalachia and to national attention in the 1950's. By 1952 the Stanleys were recording albums for Columbia Records and performing to sold-out audiences.

Authentic Performances. The appearance of rock and roll created difficulties for the Clinch Mountain Boys. In the late 1950's, the concert and radio appearances began to dwindle. The growing popularity of acts such as Elvis Presley and Chuck Berry made it difficult to eke out a living performing traditional music locally. The Stanleys were forced to perform in metropolitan areas far from home, in such states as Maryland, Louisiana, Ohio, and Florida. In the late 1950's and early 1960's, the Stanleys were well regarded in many Eastern urban centers, where folk music was popular and where the Stanleys were esteemed as authentic performers.

Sparks and Skaggs. When his brother died after a brief but serious illness, Stanley hired new performers for the Clinch Mountain Boys. These included nineteen-year-old Larry Sparks on lead guitar and vocals, who had remarkable abilities as a front man, amazing audiences with his dazzling guitar work and soulful singing. Sparks left the band in 1969 to front his own group, and he would remain a successful and significant figure in modern bluegrass. Stanley later added Keith Whitley and Ricky Skaggs to his his lineup. They remained with Stanley throughout the 1970's, a period during which he gained worldwide fame as a musical purist.

O Brother, Where Art Thou? Stanley contributed several tracks to the celebrated film sound track *O Brother, Where Art Thou?* (2001), including a stunning a cappella version of his classic "O Death." The album eventually sold more than five million copies, earned several Grammy Awards, and solidified Stanley's status as a major figure in traditional American music.

Musical Legacy

Fans and music critics alike regard Stanley as an uncompromising traditionalist and an important musical innovator, remaining loyal to his roots while sharing Appalachian music with a worldwide audience. He has received three Grammy Awards, including one for Best Male Country Vocal Performance, as well as an honorary doctorate in music from Lincoln Memorial University (1976). Inducted into the International Bluegrass Hall of Honor in 1992 and the Grand Ole Opry in 2000, he received the National Medal of Arts in 2006.

Gregory D. Horn

Further Reading

Erlewine, Stephen Thomas, Vladimir Bogdanov, and Chris Woodstra. *All Music Guide to Country: The Definitive Guide to Country Music.* 2d ed. San Francisco: Backbeat Books, 2003. A concise but authoritative reference on country music's major artists, this contains an exceptional biography of Stanley.

Gates, David. "Annals of Bluegrass: Constant Sorrow—The Long Road of Ralph Stanley." In *The Bluegrass Reader*, edited by Thomas Goldsmith. Urbana: University of Illinois Press, 2004. This source documents the obstacles Stanley had to face on the long road to stardom.

Willis, Barry R. *America's Music: Bluegrass—A History of Bluegrass Music in the Words of Its Pioneers.* Franktown, Colo.: Pine Valley Music, 1997. An informative and readable study of bluegrass's major pioneers, with numerous references to the importance of Stanley, his brother Carter, and the Clinch Mountain Boys. Extensive passages explore the importance of the Stanleys to bluegrass music.

Wright, John. *Traveling the High Way Home*. Urbana: University of Illinois Press, 1993. One of the few books devoted exclusively to the life and music of Stanley, this book is scholarly but accessible.

See also: Berry, Chuck; Flatt, Lester; Monroe, Bill; Presley, Elvis; Ritchie, Jean.

Pops Staples

American gospel singer, songwriter, and guitarist

The patriarch of the gospel-singing group the Staple Singers, Staples brought gospel music into the pop mainstream with a fusion of blues guitar and gospel songwriting.

Born: December 28, 1914; Winona, Mississippi
Died: December 19, 2000; Chicago, Illinois
Also known as: Roebuck Staples (full name)
Member of: The Staple Singers

Principal recordings

ALBUMS (solo): *Peace to the Neighborhood*, 1992; *Father Father*, 1994.

ALBUMS (with the Staple Singers): *Uncloudy Day*, 1959; *Swing Low Sweet Chariot*, 1961; *Hammer and Nails*, 1962; *Swing Low*, 1962; *The 25th Day of December*, 1962; *Gamblin' Man*, 1963; *This Little Light*, 1964; *Amen!*, 1965; *Freedom Highway*, 1965; *For What It's Worth*, 1967; *Soul Folk in Action*, 1968; *Will the Circle Be Unbroken*, 1969; *Landlord*, 1970; *We'll Get Over*, 1970; *The Staple Swingers*, 1971; *Be Altitude: Respect Yourself*, 1972; *Be What You Are*, 1973; *City in the Sky*, 1974; *Let's Do It Again*, 1975; *Pass It On*, 1976; *Family Tree*, 1977; *Unlock Your Mind*, 1978; *Hold On to Your Dream*, 1981; *This Time Around*, 1981; *Turning Point*, 1984; *The Staple Singers*, 1985; *Sit Down Servant*, 1991; *Swingline*, 1991.

The Life

The youngest of fourteen children, Roebuck Staples grew up picking cotton on a plantation in Mississippi. Despite a strong church-oriented family tradition, Staples gravitated to the Delta-blues style of guitar playing after he heard legendary performers Charley Patton and Robert Johnson. In 1931 Staples joined the Golden Trumpets, a local gospel quartet, and later, once he moved his family to Chicago, he sang and played guitar for the Trumpet Jubilees.

To entertain his children, Staples began to teach them gospel songs. Soon he and his children performed at local churches throughout the Chicago area, and they even booked a weekly time slot on the radio. As they gained more fans, Staples formed the Staple Singers, which included his children on vocals and Staples on vocals and guitar.

The Staple Singers scored their first big hit with "Uncloudy Day," which combined the lyrics of the traditional hymn with Staples's blues guitar. In the 1960's, the Staples expanded their popularity. They signed a contract with the Riverside jazz label, and they recorded "For What It's Worth," a Stephen Stills composition. In 1968 they signed a contract with the Memphis, Tennessee-based label Stax, and within five years they had eight hits on the Top 40, including "I'll Take You There" and "Respect Yourself." Their appearances in films, such as *Wattstax* (1973), *Soul to Soul* (1971), and *The Last Waltz* (1978), solidified the Staple Singers' appeal across many musical genres.

Staples continued recording until the end of his life. One of his last albums, *Peace to the Neighborhood*, featuring collaborations with Ry Cooder, Bonnie Raitt, and Jackson Browne, was critically acclaimed. His final album, *Father Father*, won a Grammy Award in 1994.

The Music

Throughout his life, Staples combined gospel and blues music. With the Staple Singers, which he formed in the 1950's, he expanded his style to include folk, rhythm-and-blues, and funk music, and he often addressed social issues in his lyrics. The inclusion of Staples's guitar in gospel music often caused controversy, but the music appealed to mainstream audiences and music critics. His rough, yet gentle tenor voice was a perfect counterpoint to his daughter Mavis Staples's smoky, contralto voice.

Early Works. In the early 1960's, the Staple Singers broadened their appeal by recording protest songs by Bob Dylan ("Blowin' in the Wind") and Stills ("For What It's Worth"). In 1963, after meeting with civil rights leader Dr. Martin Luther King, Jr., Staples wanted to write songs that were socially aware. Two such songs, "March Up Freedom's Highway" and "Long Walk to D.C.," explicitly address the civil rights marches that occurred in Selma, Alabama, and Washington, D.C. The first verse and chorus of the latter song contain the quintessential Staple Singers' sound: Staples's opening guitar solo with heavy reverberation, Mavis's silky solo that increases in intensity through the first chorus, and the interjections of gospel-influenced backing harmonies provided by the family.

"Respect Yourself." In 1968 the Staple Singers signed a contract with Stax Records, which infused soul music with the sounds of rhythm and blues and funk. When this sound aligned with the Staple Singers' gospel influence and the lyrics of social activism, it was a powerful force on the rhythm-and-blues and pop music charts. "Respect Yourself" was the first such collaboration, and it immediately reached the number-two spot on the rhythm-and-blues charts and number twelve on the pop charts. Staples sings in a plaintive, yet evocative blues style that rewords the Golden Rule with references to the Ku Klux Klan.

"I'll Take You There." In 1972 the Staple Singers scored another major hit when "I'll Take You There" rose to number one on both the rhythm-and-blues and the pop charts. Embedded within the verse is a socially conscious message, and the music, modeled on a Jamaican record, is a single extended groove created by Stax producer Al Bell, his rhythm section, and Mavis Staples. The middle stanza consists of Mavis Staples vamping improvised lyrics to the accompaniment of solos from the bass, guitar, and harmonica. Despite its simple lyrical and musical structure, "I'll Take You There" occupies a high point in the history of Stax Records and the Staple Singers.

Peace to the Neighborhood *and* Father Father. In the last years of his life, Staples recorded two solo albums that received critical acclaim. The latter one, *Father Father*, received a Grammy Award in the Best Contemporary Blues group (1994). His first solo effort, *Peace to the Neighborhood*, provides a summation of his musical life: "I Shall Not Be Moved" and "This May Be My Last Time" allude to Staples's gospel upbringing; "Down in Mississippi" records the blues style on which he was raised; and "Love Is a Precious Thing" and "Miss Cocaine" continue Staples's tradition of incorporating socially conscious lyrics into his music.

Musical Legacy

Staples was responsible for popularizing contemporary gospel music. Whether in gospel quartets (the Staple Singers) or on solo albums, Staples brought a mainstream sound to his gospel performances. In addition, his socially conscious lyrics appealed to a wide audience, among them people who might not otherwise listen to gospel. The Staple Singers were inducted into the Rock and Roll Hall of Fame in 1999, and they received a Grammy Lifetime Achievement Award in 2005.

Alexander Raymond Ludwig

Further Reading

Bowman, Rob. *Soulsville, USA: The Story of Stax Records*. New York: Schirmer Books, 1997. This substantial chronicle of the dominant recording studio in the 1960's and 1970's spends a considerable time recounting the production of the Staple Singers' two major hits, "Respect Yourself" and "I'll Take You There."

Carpenter, Bil. "Staple Singers: God's Greatest Hitmakers." *Goldmine* (August 30, 1996): 19-42. Carpenter surveys the life and work of the Staple Singers in this article.

_____. *Uncloudy Days: The Gospel Music Encyclopedia*. San Francisco: Backbeat Books, 2005. In addition to a lengthy entry on the Staple Singers, this book includes an introduction written by Mavis Staples that, among other things, relates the story of how her father acquired the name Roebuck.

See also: Browne, Jackson; Dylan, Bob; Johnson, Robert; Patton, Charley; Raitt, Bonnie; Stills, Stephen.

Max Steiner

Austrian classical and
film-score composer

Steiner has been called the father of film music, having scored one of the first motion pictures using an extensive musical sound track, the original King Kong *(1933).*

Born: May 10, 1888; Vienna, Austria
Died: December 28, 1971; Hollywood, California
Also known as: Maximilian Raoul Walter Steiner (full name)

Principal works

FILM SCORES: *Rio Rita*, 1929; *Cimarron*, 1930; *A Bill of Divorcement*, 1932; *Bird of Paradise*, 1932; *The Most Dangerous Game*, 1932; *Symphony of Six Million*, 1932; *Christopher Strong*, 1933; *King Kong*, 1933; *Little Women*, 1933; *Rafter Romance*, 1933; *The Gay Divorcée*, 1934; *The Lost Patrol*, 1934; *Of Human Bondage*, 1934; *The Informer*, 1935; *The Three Musketeers*, 1935; *Top Hat*, 1935 (with Irving Berlin); *The Charge of the Light Brigade*, 1936; *The Garden of Allah*, 1936; *Little Lord Fauntleroy*, 1936; *The Life of Emile Zola*, 1937; *A Star Is Born*, 1937; *Tovarich*, 1937; *Angels with Dirty Faces*, 1938; *Jezebel*, 1938; *Confessions of a Nazi Spy*, 1939; *Dark Victory*, 1939; *Dodge City*, 1939; *Gone with the Wind*, 1939; *All This and Heaven Too*, 1940; *The Letter*, 1940; *Santa Fe Trail*, 1940; *Sergeant York*, 1941; *Shining Victory*, 1941; *They Died with Their Boots On*, 1941; *Casablanca*, 1942; *In This Our Life*, 1942; *Now, Voyager*, 1942; *The Adventures of Mark Twain*, 1944; *Arsenic and Old Lace*, 1944; *The Conspirators*, 1944; *Passage to Marseilles*, 1944; *Since You Went Away*, 1944; *The Corn Is Green*, 1945; *Mildred Pierce*, 1945; *Rhapsody in Blue*, 1945; *The Big Sleep*, 1946; *Night and Day*, 1946; *Saratoga Trunk*, 1946; *Life with Father*, 1947; *My Wild Irish Rose*, 1947; *Johnny Belinda*, 1948; *Key Largo*, 1948; *The Treasure of the Sierra Madre*, 1948; *Adventures of Don Juan*, 1949; *Beyond the Forest*, 1949; *The Fountainhead*, 1949; *The Flame and the Arrow*, 1950; *The Glass Menagerie*, 1950; *Operation Pacific*, 1951; *The Miracle of Our Lady of Fatima*, 1952; *Room for One More*, 1952; *The Charge at Feather River*, 1953; *The Jazz Singer*, 1953; *This Is Cinerama*, 1953; *The Caine Mutiny*, 1954; *King Richard and the Crusaders*, 1954; *Battle Cry*, 1955; *Come Next Spring*, 1955; *Helen of Troy*, 1956; *The Searchers*, 1956; *Band of Angels*, 1957; *The FBI Story*, 1959; *John Paul Jones*, 1959; *A Summer Place*, 1959; *The Dark at the Top of the Stairs*, 1960; *Parrish*, 1961; *The Sins of Rachel Cade*, 1961; *Lovers Must Learn (Rome Adventure)*, 1962; *Spencer's Mountain*, 1963; *Youngblood Hawke*, 1964; *Two on a Guillotine*, 1965.

The Life

Maximilian Raoul Walter Steiner (STIN-ur) was born for music, based on his ancestry and early teachers. His paternal grandfather, Maximilian Steiner, managed Vienna's Theater an der Wien. His father, Gabor Steiner, was a Viennese impresario who managed carnivals and expositions. His godfather was Richard Strauss, the German conductor who was the last of the great Romantic composers. In addition, Steiner received early piano instruction from Johannes Brahms, the German Romantic composer.

When he was only fifteen, Steiner, a child prodigy, enrolled in the Imperial Academy of Music (now the University of Music and Performing Arts) in Vienna. His instructors there included Austrian composer Gustav Mahler. He studied violin, trumpet, organ, and piano, taking only a single year to meet the requirements for the academy's four-year degree. He conducted concerts from the age of twelve, and when he was sixteen, he wrote and conducted an operetta, *The Beautiful Greek Girl*.

Steiner began working in England at age eighteen and was living in London when World War I broke out. Because of his country of origin, he found himself classified as an enemy alien. Largely through the influence of the Duke of Westminster, he obtained exit papers and sailed to the United States. When he reached New York near the end of 1914, he was carrying a little more than thirty dollars with which to begin his new life in America.

It did not take him long, however, to find work as an arranger, orchestrator, and conductor of other people's music, including that of such prominent Broadway composers as George Gershwin, Jerome

Kern, and Sigmund Romberg, in operettas and musicals. He continued these pursuits for some fifteen years. He moved to Hollywood in 1929 when he received an assignment to orchestrate *Rio Rita*, which was being adapted as a film with few changes from the original Florenz Ziegfeld play. It would become the first big hit for the young Radio-Keith-Orpheum (RKO) Pictures.

His assignment as composer for the 1933 motion picture *King Kong* established his reputation. This action-oriented, early special-effects film was one of the first sound films in the United States to be made with an extensive musical score.

Steiner moved from RKO to Warner Bros. Studios, where he did the bulk of his work, including the studio's distinctive fanfare (originally composed for *Tovarich* in 1937) opening each of its movies. He was Warner Bros. Studios's most prominent composer and produced diverse and popular scores for hundreds of its pictures. He stayed at Warner Bros. Studios through the mid-1960's, also producing music for television series. He died of congestive heart failure in 1971 after years of battling cancer.

The Music

Motion pictures had not been accompanied by sound before 1929, when Steiner scored *Rio Rita*. That was only two years after *The Jazz Singer* (1927), a mostly silent film with snatches of sound and singing, had become the first motion picture released with any sound at all. Its effect was to force studios to incorporate sound into their films. The early silent movies had, however, generally been accompanied by music, traditionally produced by a single talented organ player working in a theater who used music to illustrate the nature of the scene being shown on the screen at the moment.

It was a natural development for music to accompany sound motion pictures, highlighting the drama or comedy or action, only now it could be performed and recorded by an entire orchestra. Steiner was one of the composers who created music for all varieties of these early sound films, from dashing adventures starring actors such as Errol Flynn (*The Charge of the Light Brigade* and *They Died with Their Boots On*, for example) and sparkling musicals with singers and dancers such as the team of Fred Astaire and Ginger Rogers (*Top Hat*) to Bette

Davis dramas (*Jezebel* and *Dark Victory*, both of which received Academy Award nominations for Best Musical Score).

King Kong. This film set a trend for all beast and dinosaur epics that followed, even those with computerized special effects. It did have a silent-movie predecessor, 1925's *The Lost World*, where explorers found surviving dinosaurs on an isolated plateau. Giant ape Kong and the other creatures in the 1933 movie were animated by Willis O'Brien, who had used the same stop-motion technique—moving and filming small models a bit at a time—in the silent film eight years earlier. Both motion pictures had a similar climax, with a prehistoric beast running rampant in a city, but only *King Kong* had an advanced musical score. Steiner's music for this pioneering motion picture went from the mysterious, as during the approach to Kong's Skull Island and Kong's heard but momentarily unseen approach through the jungle, to the frenzied, as when the island's natives perform their sacrificial dance at an ever-increasing tempo, to the melancholy in Kong's death scene. The score was a trend-setting tour de force.

Gone with the Wind. Steiner's work in this 1939 epic was nominated for an Academy Award for Best Original Score, as was his *Dark Victory* in the same year, but both lost to Herbert Stothart for *The Wizard of Oz*. Nevertheless, the music from this grand-scale motion picture adapted from Margaret Mitchell's novel remains arguably Steiner's most recognized work, from the "Tara's Theme" surrounding the Southern plantation home of Scarlett O'Hara in the years before, during, and after the Civil War, to the burning of Atlanta and dramatizing the tempestuous romance between Scarlett and Rhett Butler. Recordings of it have been released many times.

Sergeant York. This account of World War I hero Alvin York, as played by Gary Cooper, also got an Academy Award nomination (Steiner was nominated eighteen times during his career and won three times). The 1941 score highlighted York's conflict: between his newly acquired religion, which told him it was wrong to kill, and the trench warfare that forced young soldiers to decide whether to kill to save other soldiers in his group. Steiner used the religious hymn "Give Me That Old Time Religion" to underpin the conflict York struggled to resolve.

The musical score added impact to the war scenes as well as the character's triumphant return for a tour followed by his arrival at his mountain home and the surprises that awaited him there.

Now, Voyager. A 1942 adaptation of Olive Prouty's novel about a shy and plain young woman blossoming through psychotherapy—with Steiner's music underscoring the transition—won an Academy Award. That is probably one of the reasons its star, Bette Davis, declared Steiner her favorite composer. Like other segments of Steiner's music, parts of the *Now, Voyager* sound track have been recorded on their own for fans of the movie or those who enjoy the music on its own merits.

Casablanca. Music plays an integral role in this World War II drama of a cynical nightclub owner (Humphrey Bogart) who comes face to face with the woman (Ingrid Bergman) he thinks abandoned him when the Nazis swarmed into Paris. Using the dueling German martial music and French national anthem in the club is not original with Steiner, but the dramatic arrangement is. "As Time Goes By" accents the doomed relationship between the former lovers, as Bogart mutters to the piano player the memorable line, "Play it, Sam." The surprises in the final scene gain dramatic tension from Steiner's music. The film has long since achieved classic status, part of which derives from the music.

The Treasure of the Sierra Madre. A different Bogart joins Walter Huston and Tim Holt as three misfits prospecting for gold in the desert who become altered by the experience as trust among them erodes and greed grows. The musical score tracks all of these moods, right up to the scene of gold dust blowing away in the desert wind.

The Searchers. In this 1956 John Ford-directed western, based on Alan LeMay's novel, Steiner's musical score evokes the atmosphere of post-Civil War Texas—the heat of battle, the quiet of a pioneer's cabin at sunset, the heartiness of a wedding dance, and the Sons of the Pioneers musical group singing a fitting closing to the story.

Spencer's Mountain. Based on a novel by Earl Hamner, Jr., and later inspiring the television series *The Waltons*, this saga of a mountain family's triumphs and tragedies is underscored effectively by Steiner. The music soars when the camera shows the majesty of the mountains.

Musical Legacy

Musical historians credit Steiner as an originator of the kind of film music movie audiences hear today, along with Erich Wolfgang Korngold, Franz Waxman, and Dimitri Tiomkin. Steiner's legacy echoes in the sweeping dramatic music by such later composers as Jerry Goldsmith and John Williams.

Besides his Oscars for *The Informer, Since You Went Away,* and *Now, Voyager,* Steiner received the King of Belgium Bronze Medal by the Cinema Exhibitors in 1936, the Golden Globe (for *Life with Father*) in 1947, the Statuette Award from the Cinema Exhibitors, Venice, Italy (for *The Treasure of Sierra Madre*) in 1948, the American Exhibitors Laurel Award in 1948, and the Italian Medal for *So This Is Paris* in 1955. A photograph of his right hand, shown writing notes on a sheet of music, was used on a U.S. commemorative postage stamp in 2003 celebrating American filmmaking. He was inducted, posthumously, into the Songwriters Hall of Fame in 1995. His work is recognized with a star on Hollywood's Walk of Fame.

His music from movies such as *Gone with the Wind* and *Now, Voyager* has been remastered for play on compact discs. Decades after his last composition, his music continues to be heard by new generations.

Paul Dellinger

Further Reading

Burt, George. *The Art of Film Music.* Boston: Northeastern University Press, 1995. Burt, a music professor who has had experience in scoring film music, provides case studies on how professionals score motion pictures.

Daubney, Kate. *Max Steiner's "Now, Voyager": A Film Score Guide.* Westport, Conn.: Greenwood Press, 2000. Although the book concentrates on a particular movie, it provides an overall look at Steiner's techniques and general contribution to filmmaking.

Davis, Richard. *Complete Guide to Film Scoring.* Boston: Berklee Press, 2000. Nineteen film-scoring professionals are interviewed in this guide to the business of and approaches to film and television music.

Morgan, David. *Knowing the Score: Film Composers Talk About the Art, Craft, Blood, Sweat, and Tears of Writing for Cinema.* New York: Harper Paperbacks, 2000. Sixteen film composers give their ideas about the process of creating a musical score for a movie.

Rona, Jeff. *The Reel World: Scoring for Pictures.* San Francisco: Miller Freeman Books, 2000. A how-to-do-it guide on the various ramifications of film scoring, with examples from specific composers.

See also: Berlin, Irving; Gershwin, George; Goldsmith, Jerry; Kern, Jerome; Korngold, Erich Wolfgang; Romberg, Sigmund; Rózsa, Miklós; Strauss, Richard; Tiomkin, Dimitri; Waxman, Franz; Williams, John.

Isaac Stern

Russian American classical violinist

A leading concert violinist, Stern performed with every major orchestra in the world during his career, which spanned six decades. He recorded extensively, he was an advocate for aspiring musicians, and he spearheaded the successful campaign to save Carnegie Hall in New York City from demolition in 1960.

Born: July 21, 1920; Kremenets, Ukrainian Socialist Republic (now in Ukraine)
Died: September 22, 2001; New York, New York

Principal recordings

ALBUMS: *Beethoven: The Complete Piano Trios*, 1960; *Debussy: Sonata in G Minor for Violin and Piano*, 1960; *Bartók and Berg: Concerto for Violin and Orchestra; Rhapsody No. 1; Rhapsody No. 2*, 1962; *Bartók: Concerto for Violin*, 1962; *Stravinsky: Concerto in D Major for Violin and Orchestra; Symphony in Three Movements*, 1962; *Mozart: Concerto No. 1 in B-flat Major for Violin and Orchestra; Concerto No. 5 in A Major for Violin and Orchestra*, 1964; *Prokofiev: Concerto No. 1 in D Major for Violin and Orchestra; Concerto No. 2 in G Minor for Violin and Orchestra*, 1964; *Barber: Concerto for Violin and Orchestra*, 1965; *Bloch: Baal Shem: Three Pictures of Chassidic Life; Sonata No. 1 for Violin and Piano*, 1965; *Hindemith: Concerto for Violin and Orchestra*, 1965;

Beethoven: Trio for Piano, Violin, and Cello, No. 6, in B-flat Major, 1966; *Dvořák: Concerto in A Minor for Violin and Orchestra; Romance*, 1966; *Bach: Concerto for Violin and String Orchestra in A Minor*, 1967; *Beethoven: Concerto for Violin and Orchestra, Op. 61, in D Major; Concerto for Violin and Orchestra, Op. 26, in G Minor*, 1967; *Brahms: The Trios for Piano, Violin, and Cello*, 1967; *Bruch: Concerto No. 1 in G Minor for Violin and Orchestra*, 1967; *Mozart: Concerto No. 3 in G Major for Violin and Orchestra; Sinfonia Concertante in E-flat Major for Violin, Viola, and Orchestra*, 1968; *Schubert: Trio in E-flat Major for Piano, Violin, and Cello*, 1970; *Sibelius: Concerto in D Minor for Violin and Orchestra; Karelia Suite*, 1970; *Bock: Fiddler on the Roof (Selections)*, 1971; *The Mozart Flute Quartets*, 1971; *Brahms: Violin Concerto*, 1972; *Mozart: Sinfonia Concertante in E-flat for Violin, Viola, and Orchestra*, 1972; *Stamitz: Sinfonia Concertante in D Major*, 1972; *Isaac Stern Plays Brahms*, 1973; *Mozart: Concerto in C Major for Two Violins and Orchestra*, 1974; *Pleyel: Sinfonie Concertante in B-flat Major*, 1974; *Mozart: Divertimento in E-flat Major for String Trio*, 1975; *Isaac Stern Plays Saint-Saëns, Chausson, Faure*, 1976; *Lalo: Symphonie espagnole*, 1976; *Brahms: Double Concerto in A Minor for Violin and Cello*, 1977; *Bartók: Sonata No. 1 for Violin and Piano*, 1978; *Bernstein: Serenade for Violin Solo, Strings, and Percussion*, 1978; *The Classic Melodies of Japan*, 1978; *Mozart: Concerto No. 4 for Violin and Orchestra in D Major; Concerto No. 5 for Violin and Orchestra in A Major*, 1978; *Mozart: Concerto No. 4 in D Major for Violin and Orchestra; Concerto No. 2 in D Major for Violin and Orchestra*, 1978; *Vivaldi: Concerto in D Minor; Concerto in C Minor*, 1978; *Vivaldi: The Four Seasons*, 1978; *Beethoven: Sonata No. 7 in C Minor for Violin and Piano*, 1979; *Frank: Sonata in A Major for Violin and Piano*, 1979; *Hindemith: Sonata for Violin and Piano*, 1979; *Mozart: Concerto in G; Concerto in D; Andante in C*, 1979; *Mozart: Sonata No. 26 in B-flat Major for Violin and Piano*, 1979; *Penderecki: Violin Concerto*, 1979; *Prokofiev: Sonata in F Minor for Violin and Piano; Sonata in D Major for Violin and Piano*, 1979; *Rochberg: Violin Concerto*, 1979; *Tchaikovsky: Concerto in D Major for Violin and Orchestra; Meditation*, 1979; *Viotti: Concerto*

No. 22 in A Minor for Violin and Orchestra, 1979; Wieniawski: Concerto No. 2 in D Minor for Violin and Orchestra, 1979; Mendelssohn and Tchaikovsky: Concerto in E Minor for Violin and Orchestra; Concerto in D Major for Violin and Orchestra, 1981; Mendelssohn: Trio No. 1 in D Minor; Trio No. 2 in C Minor, 1981; Bach and Vivaldi: Concerto in D Minor for Two Violins and String Orchestra; Concerto in C Minor for Oboe, Violin, and Orchestra; Concerto in A Minor for Two Violins and Orchestra, 1982; Haydn: "London" Trio No. 2 in G Minor; "London" Trio No. 3 in G Major; Divertissement No. 2 in G Major; Divertissement No. 6 in D Major; "London" Trio No. 4 in G Major, 1982; Bach: Trio Sonatas, 1983; Sonatas of J. S. Bach and Sons, 1983; Vivaldi, Bach, and Mozart: Le quattro stagioni; Konzert fuer zwei Violinen und Streicher; Konzert fuer fier Violinen, Streicher, und Cembalo; Sinfonia concertante fuer Violine, Viola, und Orchester, 1983; Beethoven and Kreutzer: Sonata No. 9 in A Major for Violin and Piano; Sonata No. 5 in F Major for Violin and Piano, 1984; Beethoven: The Complete Sonatas for Violin and Piano, 1985; Berg: Kammerkonzert for Piano and Violin with Thirteen Wind Instruments; Concert for Violin and Orchestra; To the Memory of an Angel, 1986; The Great Violin Concertos, 1986; Dutilleux and Sir Peter Maxwell Davies: L'Arbre des songes; Concerto pour violon et orchestre (Dutilleux); Concerto for Violin and Orchestra (Davies), 1987; Brahms: Double Concerto, Op. 102; Piano Quartet, 1988; Shostakovich: Trio No. 2 for Violin, Cello, and Piano; Sonata for Cello and Piano, 1988.

The Life

Isaac Stern was born in Ukraine, and he moved with his parents to San Francisco before he was a year old. In California he began his musical education with Robert Pollak, continuing in his teenage years with San Francisco Symphony concertmaster Naoum Blinder, whom Stern credited as being his most influential teacher. Later, he studied with Louis Persinger.

By the age of fifteen, Stern had performed with the San Francisco Symphony, although he claimed his debut was a 1936 performance of Camille Saint-Saëns's Violin Concerto No. 3 in B Minor (1880) with Pierre Monteux as the conductor. Two appear-

Isaac Stern. (AP/Wide World Photos)

ances that earned public acclaim, however, were his performance of Max Bruch's Concerto No. 1 in G Minor, Op. 26 (1866) in New York City in 1937 and his New York recital debut in 1943 at Carnegie Hall. Following his successful campaign to save Carnegie Hall from demolition in 1960, he became the chair of the Carnegie Hall Board, a post he retained for more than thirty years.

Stern was first married to ballet dancer Nora Kaye. When they divorced, Stern married Vera Lindenblit. They had three children—Shira, Michael, and David—and were married for more than forty years. Following their divorce, in 1996 he married Linda Reynolds.

Stern received many honors in his lifetime, including multiple Grammy Awards (beginning in 1961) for his numerous recordings; becoming an officer of the Legion of Honor in France in 1979; receiving a Kennedy Center Honors Award in 1984; and being named Musician of the Year by *Musical America* in 1986. He received several Emmy Awards for broadcasts on public television's *Great Performances*. In 1987 he received the Wolf Prize in Israel, the Gold Baton from the American Symphony Orchestra League, the National Music Council's American Eagle Award, and the Grammy Lifetime Achievement Award. In 1991 he was awarded the National Medal of the Arts, and in 1992 President George H. W. Bush awarded him the Presidential Medal of Freedom, America's highest civilian honor. It was followed five years later by Japan's highest honor, the Order of the Rising Sun.

Institutions of higher education that have awarded him honorary doctorates include Yale University, Bucknell Univesity, Columbia University, Harvard University, Johns Hopkins University, Oxford University, Hebrew University, the Curtis Institute of Music, and the Juilliard School.

During the 1990's, Stern collaborated with pianist Yefim Bronfman on several recordings and recital tours, and he regularly recorded and performed piano trios and quartets with pianist Emanuel Ax, cellist Yo-Yo Ma, and violist Jaime Laredo.

In his later years, Stern performed mostly in chamber settings. He died of heart failure in New York City in 2001.

The Music

In the 1950's and 1960's, under the management of impresario Sol Hurok, Stern's concert career brought him to the major concert and recital halls of the world. He increasingly included sonata recitals in his annual schedule with his long-standing collaborator, pianist Alexander Zakin.

Carnegie Hall. In 1961 Stern joined cellist Leonard Rose and pianist Eugene Istomin to create a piano trio for a benefit concert for Carnegie Hall. The performance received solid praise, and it launched the trio's further concert engagements, which lasted until Rose's death in 1984. This benefit was one of many of Stern's efforts to save Carnegie Hall from demolition in 1960. In addition, he used his considerable stature and influence and impassioned speeches to mobilize the artistic and financial communities of New York in the preservation of the cultural landmark. His success may be considered one of his finest achievements, and it added the honorific cultural statesman to his already established reputation as a violinist. In recognition of his leadership both in the 1960 preservation and in the 1986 renovation of Carnegie Hall, the main concert room was named the Isaac Stern Hall.

Musical Diplomat. Stern was a musical diplomat in several capacities: He supported the estab-

lishment of the National Endowment for the Arts in 1964 by recognizing and promoting some of the emerging talent in America and later by serving as musical ambassador from the West to China. The rise of the next generation of violin artists— including Itzhak Perlman, Pinchas Zukerman, Shlomo Mintz, Miriam Fried, and Sergiu Luca— was advanced with his energy and with the force of his powerful connections in the music world.

Concert of the Century. In 1976 Stern participated in the Concert of the Century, which recognized the eighty-fifth anniversary of Carnegie Hall. He shared the stage with conductor-composer Leonard Bernstein, cellist Mstislav Rostropovich, pianist Vladimir Horowitz, baritone Dietrich Fischer-Dieskau, violinist Yehudi Menuhin, soprano Martina Arroyo, and the New York Philharmonic. In this concert, Stern performed Johann Sebastian Bach's Concerto for Two Violins in D Minor (1731) with Menuhin and a movement from Peter Ilich Tchaikovsky's Trio in A Minor, Op. 50 (1882) with Horowitz and Rostropovich.

From Mao to Mozart. In 1979, at a time when China was just beginning to open its doors to the West, Stern took a pioneering tour of the country, serving as a cultural ambassador from the West to China. He performed several concerts, and, more importantly, he coached young Chinese musicians. Stern's experiences in China were videotaped and edited into a feature-length documentary film, *From Mao to Mozart* (1980), which opened the Western musical world's eyes to the talent and energy latent in China's musical youth that was hidden behind China's isolationist foreign policy. *From Mao to Mozart* won the Academy Award for best documentary in 1981.

Other films that featured Stern were *A Journey to Jerusalem* (1968), which arose from a concert in Israel following the Six-Day War in 1967; *Tonight We Sing* (1953), a biopic about his manager Hurok, in which he played the part of violinist Eugene Ysaÿe; *Humoreske* (1946), a dark, romantic film about a violin virtuoso and the unhappy woman who loved him, starring John Garfield; and *Fiddler on the Roof* (1971), for which Stern played the violin on the sound track.

Repertoire and Recordings. Stern's repertoire emphasized major concerti, violin sonatas, and chamber music. He was an important champion of twentieth century music, and he performed the world premieres of *Serenade* (1954) by Leonard Bernstein and of violin concerti by George Rochberg (1975), Krzysztof Penderecki (1977), Henri Dutilleux (1985), and Peter Maxwell Davies (1986).

Stern released more than one hundred recordings during his career, representing numerous composers and pieces from concerti to chamber music. His label was Sony (formerly CBS Masterworks), and he became the label's first artist laureate upon fifty years of recordings in 1985. He was highly praised for his interpretation of Johannes Brahms's Violin Concerto in D Major (1879) and Double Concerto in A Minor (1887), which Stern performed and recorded with cellist Rose. His interpretations of Henryk Wieniawski's Concerto No. 2 (1862), Felix Mendelssohn's Violin Concerto in E Minor (1845), and sonatas by César Franck, Paul Hindemith, and Sergei Prokofiev received high praise and several Grammy Awards.

Stern's violin of choice was his 1740 Guarnerius del Gésu (once thought to have belonged to violinist Ysaÿe) or his 1737 Vicomte de Panette del Gésu. He also owned at various times a 1721 Stradivarius (known as "the Kruse"), a Vuillaume (known as "the Tsar"), a Carlo Bergonzi, and two 1750's Guadagnini violins.

Critical Reception. As a concert violinist, Stern received varying reviews, dependent to some extent upon the repertoire and the time of his life. His concerto performances and recordings spanned a wide repertoire, including the concerti of Bach, Wolfgang Amadeus Mozart, Ludwig van Beethoven, Tchaikovsky, Brahms, and Jean Sibelius. His recorded repertoire was not as large as that of his contemporary Jascha Heifetz, who recorded all the Bach sonatas and partitas, commissioned several important concerti, and arranged numerous pieces originally written for other musical instruments as violin encores. Early reviews frequently mentioned the visceral tone, yet flexible interpretation that Stern produced from his violin. He was known for bringing each composer's unique personality to the fore rather than emphasizing his temperament over that of the composer's. Later in his career, however, reviews frequently mentioned imperfections in his preparation and execution, while they maintained an overall respect for his legendary stature and his contributions to the field of music.

Musical Legacy

Stern's most lasting contribution to the music world is probably his work to save Carnegie Hall. In addition, he played a significant role as a cultural ambassador in making his groundbreaking trip to China in 1979 and as a mentor in fostering the musical careers of Perlman, Zukerman, and others.

Jonathan A. Sturm

Further Reading

Applebaum, Samuel, and Sada Applebaum. *The Way They Play*. 14 vols. Neptune City, N.J.: Paganiniana, 1973. A multivolume set that describes the performing styles of great violinists from the middle twentieth century, including an entry on Stern.

Campbell, Margaret. *The Great Violinists*. New York: Doubleday, 1980. Using letters and private documents, the author looks at the lives of violin talents. She describes the artists' technique, impact on public taste, and special achievements. Includes extended references to Stern.

Cowden, Robert. *Instrumental Virtuosi: A Bibliography of Biographical Materials*. New York: Greenwood Press, 1989. A source book on virtuosi of many instruments, and Stern is among those profiled.

Creighton, James. *Discopaedia of the Violin*. Toronto: University of Toronto Press, 1974. A list of violin recordings covering nearly a century, including those made by Stern.

Roth, Henry. *Great Violinists in Performance: Critical Evaluations of over 100 Twentieth Century Virtuosi*. Los Angeles: Panjandrum Books, 1987. In this book, critic Roth makes subjective evaluations of performances and recordings, and he includes a chapter on Stern.

Stern, Isaac, and Chaim Potok. *My First Seventy-nine Years*. New York: Da Capo Press, 1999. Stern's autobiography covers his childhood and career details. In addition, he comments frankly on performances by other artists.

See also: Barenboim, Daniel; Bernstein, Leonard; Horowitz, Vladimir; Ma, Yo-Yo; Menuhin, Sir Yehudi; Perlman, Itzhak; Rampal, Jean-Pierre; Rostropovich, Mstislav; Serkin, Rudolf.

Cat Stevens

English folk and rock singer, songwriter, and guitarist

With his 1970's albums, Stevens proved that a folk music style could succeed in the era of hard rock. Further, he proved that spirituality had a place in popular lyrics, his music reflecting his spiritual journey, which culminated in his conversion to Islam in 1977.

Born: July 21, 1948; London, England
Also known as: Steven Demetre Georgiou (birth name); Yusuf Islam

Principal recordings

ALBUMS: *Matthew and Son*, 1967; *New Masters*, 1967; *Mona Bone Jakon*, 1970; *Tea for the Tillerman*, 1970; *Teaser and the Firecat*, 1971; *Catch the Bull at Four*, 1972; *Foreigner*, 1973; *Buddha and the Chocolate Box*, 1974; *Numbers*, 1975; *Izitso*, 1977; *Back to Earth*, 1978; *The Life of the Last Prophet*, 1995; *Prayers of the Last Prophet*, 1999; *I Have No Cannons That Roar*, 2000; *A Is for Allah*, 2000; *I Look, I See*, 2003; *An Other Cup*, 2006.

SINGLE: "I Love My Dog," 1966.

The Life

Yusuf Islam (YEW-suhf IHZ-lahm), formerly known as Cat Stevens, was born Steven Demetre Georgiou in the Soho area of London, near Piccadilly Circus. His father, Greek immigrant Stavros Georgiou, and his mother, Swedish immigrant Ingrid Wickman, owned a restaurant on Shaftesbury Avenue, where young Stevens was put to work as soon as he could carry dishes. By the age of twelve he was proficient on both guitar and piano, but he developed an interest in art, influenced by a maternal uncle in Sweden. At age sixteen he enrolled in Hammersmith Art School, but he was later dismissed. Undaunted, he began singing in Soho coffeehouses and pubs. Record producer Mike Hurst heard him and persuaded him to record. At the age of nineteen, the young man now calling himself Cat Stevens became a pop star. In 1977 he converted to Islam, changed his name to Yusuf Islam, turned away from recording, and devoted himself to philanthropic work.

The Music

The early Stevens hits were astonishingly good but indistinguishable from most pop songs of the 1960's. Many became hits for other artists: "Here Comes My Baby" made the charts for the Tremeloes, and Rod Stewart recorded "The First Cut Is the Deepest." Stevens, however, contracted tuberculosis after the release of his second album, and his recovery kept him away from the record industry for a few years. When he returned to recording, with *Mona Bone Jakon*, his lyrics were more introspective, and his sound was influenced by English folk. American promoters did not notice that album, but his next, *Tea for the Tillerman*, became number one on the *Billboard* chart.

Tea for the Tillerman. Selling half a million copies in six months, and finishing as the sixth best seller of 1971, *Tea for the Tillerman* boasted several songs on the Top 40 playlist in that year: "Wild World" (which peaked at number eleven on *Billboard*), "Hard-Headed Woman," and "Father and Son." Four of the songs from the album were included in the sound track of the film *Harold and Maude* (1971), receiving prominent billing in the opening credits. In 2003 *Rolling Stone* included it in its list of the top 500 albums of all time, and a book published in 2006 named it one of the *1001 Albums You Must Hear Before You Die*. "Father and Son" perfectly captured the mood of the generation gap the baby boomers felt between them and their parents. In alternating voices, Stevens sings the calm, reasonable voice of a father giving advice and the urgent, plaintive son who cannot follow it. Though certainly autobiographical, it rises from the personal to the universal with its counterpoint of both generations and avoids the sentimental and confessional excesses of the youthful-angst songs of the era.

Teaser and the Firecat. Although it did not chart as high as its predecessor, *Teaser and the Firecat* boasted several Top 40 hits: "Morning Has Broken," "Moon Shadow," and "Peace Train." "Morning Has Broken" demonstrates Stevens's folk roots by reviving an obscure Christian hymn with a traditional Scots melody, "Bun Easain." The nineteenth century lyrics were "Leanabh an Àigh"

Cat Stevens. (Hulton Archive/Getty Images)

(born in a manger). Stevens would have encountered it in his youth at St. Joseph Roman Catholic Primary School in London; the lyrics he recorded were written in 1931 by Eleanor Farjeon. Pianist Rick Wakeman of Yes performed the signature opening, though he was not credited (or paid) until 2006. "Peace Train" shows the connection between folk music and the protest song, and it became an anthem for the peace movement. Its iconic status helped Yusuf Islam build bridges between Islamic and Western culture and between his old and new identities. On December 11, 2006, Yusuf Islam performed the song at the Nobel Peace Prize Concert in Oslo.

An Other Cup. Though the pop music world hailed this album as his first recording in nearly three decades, Yusuf Islam had in fact recorded Islamic-themed material throughout the 1990's. Those recordings were minimalist in style, reflecting his respectful caution in interpreting his new faith's teachings on the role of music. Once assured of clerical approval, however, and aware that his former pop-star status could offer an important cor-

rective to the widening gap between Islam and the West in the twenty-first century, he recorded *An Other Cup* in 2006. He is billed on the album simply as Yusuf, since he felt that the familiar name (the Arabic form of Joseph) would be more personal, and that using the last name Islam might vulgarly "sloganize" the name of a great world religion.

Musical Legacy

Stevens's infusion of folk sounds that were international in flavor—he brought the Greek bouzouki into the studio, and his mandolin work was much more continental than the Appalachian sound of the folk mandolin in the 1960's—had an enduring effect on pop music. The variety of pop singers who have covered his songs ranges from hard rocker Rod Stewart to country star Dolly Parton to blues singer Sheryl Crow. Cat's early song "The First Cut Is the Deepest" scored hits for four different singers in three different countries (though not for Stevens). He was tremendously popular, selling sixty million albums, despite a hiatus from popular music of nearly thirty years (1978-2006). His return to secular music as Yusuf Islam was largely influenced by his son, Muhammad Islam, also a musician, urging his father to play again.

John R. Holmes

Further Reading

Brown, George L. *Cat Stevens: The Complete Illustrated Bibliography and Discography.* Leigh-on-Sea, England: Daddy-O Archives, 2006. A thorough treatment of Stevens, with rare photographs and personal interviews.

Dimery, Robert, ed. *1001 Albums You Must Hear Before You Die.* New York: Universe, 2006. An appreciation of fifty years of audio recording (1955-2005), naming must-hear albums, with an essay on each by a prominent music critic. *Tea for the Tillerman* is featured.

Fish, David Lee. "Cat Stevens." In *Popular Musicians.* Pasadena, Calif.: Salem Press, 1999. A concise article assessing Stevens's achievement in popular music, one of the few written after his conversion to Islam.

Luckman, Michael C. "Cat Stevens 'Sucked Up' by a Saucer." In *Alien Rock.* New York: Pocket

Books, 2005. In a book about alien abductions among rock stars, this novelty piece has an interview with Stevens on a limited subject.

Stevens, Cat. *Teaser and the Firecat*. New York: Scholastic, 1972. This children's book, with text by Stevens in English, French, and Spanish, tells the story illustrated on the cover of Stevens's album of the same name, and it includes nineteen other full-color illustrations by Stevens.

See also: Cliff, Jimmy; Parton, Dolly; Sibelius, Jean; Stewart, Rod.

Rod Stewart

English rock singer and songwriter

From his days as the lead singer of the blues-rock bands the Jeff Beck Group, and the Faces to his three decades as a performer of folk, soul, rock, disco, and Broadway-era pop, Stewart, with his distinctive raspy voice, distinguished himself as a versatile interpretive singer.

Born: January 10, 1945; London, England
Also known as: Roderick David Stewart (full name)
Member of: The Jeff Beck Group; the Faces

Principal recordings

ALBUMS (solo): *The Rod Stewart Album*, 1969; *Gasoline Alley*, 1970; *Every Picture Tells a Story*, 1971; *Never a Dull Moment*, 1972; *Smiler*, 1974; *Atlantic Crossing*, 1975; *A Night on the Town*, 1976; *Foot Loose and Fancy Free*, 1977; *Blondes Have More Fun*, 1978; *Foolish Behaviour*, 1980; *Tonight I'm Yours*, 1981; *Body Wishes*, 1983; *Camouflage*, 1984; *Every Beat of My Heart*, 1986; *Rod Stewart*, 1986; *Out of Order*, 1988; *Vagabond Heart*, 1991; *Unplugged . . . and Seated*, 1993; *Spanner in the Works*, 1995; *When We Were the New Boys*, 1998; *Human*, 2001; *It Had to Be You: The Great American Songbook, Vol. 1*, 2002; *As Time Goes By: The Great American Songbook, Vol. 2*, 2003; *Stardust: The Great American Songbook, Vol. 3*, 2004; *The Day Will Come*, 2005; *Thanks for the Memory: The Great American Songbook, Vol. 4,*

2005; *Still the Same: Great Rock Classics of Our Time*, 2006.
ALBUMS (with the Faces): *First Step*, 1970; *Long Player*, 1971; *A Nod Is as Good as a Wink . . . to a Blind Horse*, 1971; *Ooh La La*, 1973.
ALBUMS (with the Jeff Beck Group): *Truth*, 1968; *Beck-Ola*, 1969.

The Life

After trying his luck at soccer, grave digging, and street-corner singing, Roderick David Stewart became, in the mid-1960's, one of England's most sought-after lead singers, most notably with the Jeff Beck Group and, in 1970—one year after signing a solo contract with Mercury Records—the Faces.

In 1975 the Faces broke up, and Stewart left England for the United States and Mercury Records for Warner Bros. By the time his single "Tonight's the Night (Gonna Be Alright)" finished its eight-week run atop the *Billboard* charts, he was an international star. In subsequent decades, even when his sales and hits declined, he remained a first-rank concert attraction. Beginning with Alana Hamilton, to whom he was married from 1979 to 1984, Stewart was frequently seen in the company of young, attractive blondes. Two of them, Kelly Emberg and Penny Lancaster, became his second and third wives, respectively. He fathered children with all three.

In 2002 he released *It Had to Be You: The Great American Songbook, Vol. 1*, the first in what became a series of four albums of pre-rock-and-roll pop standards. The collections, all best sellers, reestablished Stewart as a formidable commercial force.

The Music

Early Works. Despite recording first as a member of Steampacket and Shotgun Express, Stewart made his best early performances on such Jeff Beck Group albums as *Truth* and *Beck-Ola* and on the Faces' albums *Long Player* and *A Nod Is as Good as a Wink . . . to a Blind Horse*. It was as a member of the Faces that Stewart recorded "Stay with Me," a long-time staple of his repertoire.

The Rod Stewart Album. The eight songs on this low-selling but critically well-regarded 1969 recording included original Stewart compositions, interpretations of the Rolling Stones' "Street Fighting Man," Ewan MacColl's "Dirty Old Town," the traditional folk song "Man of Constant Sorrow," and "Handbags and Gladrags" (written by his pianist Mike D'Abo).

Every Picture Tells a Story. Like Stewart's first two solo albums, this 1971 recording mixed Stewart originals, covers of rock, soul, folk, and traditional songs (Elvis Presley's debut single "That's All Right," the Temptations' "[I Know] I'm Losing You," Tim Hardin's "Reason to Believe," "Amazing Grace"). It was "Maggie May," however, a chart-topping, six-minute examination of a young man's soured affair with an older woman, that made the album and Stewart formidable best sellers.

A Night on the Town. Coming as it did after the coolly received albums *Smiler* and *Atlantic Crossing*, this 1976 album represented a make-or-break moment in Stewart's career. What made the album was three Top 40 singles: "The First Cut Is the Deepest" (a Cat Stevens cover), "The Killing of Georgie (Parts I and II)" (an antigay-bashing saga), and "Tonight's the Night (Gonna Be Alright)" (which spent three weeks more at number one than "Maggie May").

Storyteller: The Complete Anthology, 1964-1990. Released in 1989, this four-disc boxed set achieved double-platinum status, making it one of Stewart's two best-selling albums of the 1980's and provoking a reassessment of his first quarter-century of work. It concluded with Stewart's version of Tom Waits's "Downtown Train," which reached number three in 1990.

Unplugged . . . and Seated. This seventy-minute acoustic live album includes fifteen of the twenty-one songs that Stewart taped on February 3, 1993, for his appearance on *MTV Unplugged*. Although the greatest-hits nature of the set list made the album more a retrospective than a groundbreaking next step, *Unplugged . . . and Seated* debuted Stewart's hit version of Van Morrison's "Have I Told You Lately," and it reunited him with his fellow ex-Faces member, the guitarist Ron Wood.

It Had to Be You: The Great American Songbook, Vol. 1. Rock stars recording pop standards of the 1930's, 1940's, and 1950's was nothing new when Stewart released this album in 2002. (Carly Simon and Linda Ronstadt had released pop

Rod Stewart. (AP/Wide World Photos)

standards albums in 1981 and 1983, respectively). None of them, however, achieved the popularity of Stewart's. He recorded three more similar albums, and all four were released as a boxed set in 2007.

Musical Legacy

Stewart's complete work of more than thirty albums reveals the many facets of his talent and taste and some of the best-known folk, blues, gospel, and Broadway songs. Stewart became so identified with the songs of other composers that the fact that he had written or cowritten some of his biggest hits ("Maggie May," "You Wear It Well," "Tonight's the Night [Gonna Be Alright]," "The Killing of Georgie [Parts I and II]," "You're in My Heart [The Final Acclaim]") is often overlooked. His series of major international hits over a period of forty years is a testament to the timelessness of his appeal and of the music he helped to popularize.

Arsenio Orteza

Further Reading

Bradley, Lloyd. *Rod Stewart: Every Picture Tells a Story.* London: London Bridge, 1999. An occasionally irreverent examination of Stewart's life and music.

Ewbank, Tim, and Stafford Hildred. *Rod Stewart: The New Biography.* New York: Citadel Press, 2004. A look at Stewart's life, with a particular focus on his wives and girlfriends.

Marcus, Greil. "Rod Stewart." In *The Rolling Stone Illustrated History of Rock and Roll,* edited by Jim Miller. New York: Random House/*Rolling Stone* Press, 1980. A critical examination of Stewart's career.

Nelson, Paul, and Lester Bangs. *Rod Stewart.* New York: G. P. Putnam's Sons, 1981. Two writers for *Rolling Stone* attempt to shatter the myths surround Stewart and his successful career.

Twelker, Uli, and Roland Schmitt. *The Small Faces and Other Stories.* London: Sanctuary, 2002. A detailed account of the evolution of the Small Faces into the Faces and of Stewart's role in the latter.

See also: Beck, Jeff; Dixon, Willie; Howlin' Wolf; Jagger, Sir Mick; King, Carole; Leadbelly; Lewis, Jerry Lee; Morrison, Van; Presley, Elvis; Stevens, Cat; Sting; Waits, Tom.

William Grant Still

American classical and film composer

Composer of chamber, orchestral, and operatic works, Still incorporated the rhythms and harmonies of jazz and blues into classical compositions. Among his many groundbreaking achievements, Still was the first African American composer to have a symphony performed by a prominent orchestra, to have an opera performed by a major opera company, and to have an opera performed on network television.

Born: May 11, 1895; Woodville, Mississippi
Died: December 3, 1978; Los Angeles, California
Also known as: Billy Still; Willy M. Still (pen name)

Principal works

BALLETS: *Sahdji,* 1931 (libretto by Richard Bruce and Alain Locke); *Lenox Avenue,* 1937 (libretto by Verna Arvey).

CHAMBER WORKS: Suite for Violin and Piano, 1943; *Danzas de Panama,* 1953 (*Dances of Panama*); *Romance,* 1955 (for saxophone and piano); *The American Scene,* 1957.

CHORAL WORKS: *And They Lynched Him on a Tree,* 1940 (text by Katherine Garrison Chapin); *Songs of Separation,* 1949; *The Little Song That Wanted to be a Symphony,* 1955 (text by Arvey).

FILM SCORES: *Pennies from Heaven,* 1936; *Lost Horizon,* 1937; *Under Suspicion,* 1937; *Superman,* 1948; *South of Death Valley,* 1949.

OPERAS: *Blue Steel,* 1935 (libretto by J. Bruse Forsythe; based on the story by Carlton Moss); *Troubled Island,* 1949 (libretto by Langston Hughes and Arvey); *Costaso,* 1950 (libretto by Arvey); *Highway 1 U.S.A.,* 1963 (libretto by Arvey); *A Bayou Legend,* 1974 (libretto by Arvey).

ORCHESTRAL WORKS: *Darker America,* 1926; *From the Black Belt,* 1926; Symphony No. 1, 1931 (*Afro-American*); Symphony No. 2 in G Minor, 1937 (*Song of a New Race*); *In Memoriam: Colored Soldiers Who Died for Democracy,* 1944; *The Little Red Schoolhouse,* 1957; *Ennaga,* 1958 (for harp and orchestra); Symphony No. 3, 1958 (*Sunday Symphony*).

PIANO WORKS: *Africa,* 1930; *Seven Traceries,* 1939.

The Life

William Grant Still, Jr., was born to Carrie Fambro Still and William Grant Still, Sr., both schoolteachers, in Woodville, Mississippi. His ancestry included African American, Native American, Scottish, Irish, and Spanish heritage. His father died when he was only a few months old. Following his father's death, Still's family moved to Little Rock, Arkansas, where he lived for the next sixteen years. His mother married Charles B. Shepperson, who encouraged Still's musical interest by playing phonograph records for him, taking him to musical performances, and encouraging him in his study of the violin.

Still went to Wilberforce University in Ohio to prepare for medical school. While in college, he studied music, conducted the school band, learned to play several instruments, and composed music. He also met his first wife, Grace Bundy, whom he married after leaving Wilberforce without completing his degree.

After a stint performing in bands in Ohio, in 1916 Still began to work for the musician W. C. Handy in Memphis, Tennessee, arranging and orchestrating popular music and jazz. Still enrolled in the Oberlin Conservatory of Music in 1917. The next year he served in the U.S. Navy aboard the ship USS *Kroonland* during World War I.

After an honorable discharge, Still moved to New York City, orchestrating music for many performers, including Paul Whiteman and Eubie Blake, as well as performing in various ensembles as an oboist and a violinist. His time in New York brought him into close contact with the cultural explosion of the Harlem Renaissance. As the director of Harry Pace's Black Swan Phonograph Company, Still had contact with many African American composers and performers in the city.

William Grant Still. (Library of Congress)

Beginning in 1923, Still studied for two years under Edgard Varèse. This period of study led to numerous concert works, the first performances of which were given in 1925 by the International Composers' Guild. Over the next few years, Still arranged music for radio shows, including Whiteman's *Old Gold Hour* and *Willard Robison and His Deep River Hour*.

Still moved to Los Angeles in 1934. Within a few years, he divorced Grace and married Verna Arvey, with whom he spent the rest of his life. He worked as a composer and orchestrator for Columbia Pictures for six months in 1935. He continued composing, and many of his concert works premiered over the next decades, including a television premiere of his opera *Bayou Legend* by the Public Broadcasting System in 1974. Still died at the age of eighty-three in Los Angeles on December 3, 1978.

The Music

Still divided his work into three periods. The first (through 1925) he designated his modernist period. Studying with Varèse, he explored atonality, dissonance, and extended instrumental techniques. Disillusioned with the esotericism of musical modernism, Still later destroyed many of his compositions from this time. The second period (1925-1932) he named his racial idiom period. During this time, he overtly evoked the rhythmic, melodic, and harmonic styles of African American genres, such as blues, popular music, and jazz. Finally, during his universal idiom period (beginning in 1932), Still explored the music of different cultures, such as Caribbean music, Latin American music, and American cowboy songs, in addition to his continuing use of African American idioms.

Darker America. Still wrote this symphonic poem in 1924 during his time of study with Varèse. It received great critical acclaim at its premiere by the International Composers' Guild in 1926. Its use of orchestral colors and dissonant harmonies reflects Varèse's influence on Still's musical style. This programmatic work tells a story, through musical themes, of the "American Negro" triumphing over adversities through prayer.

Symphony No. 1. The *Afro-American* symphony is Still's best-known and most popular work. It was composed in 1930 and was premiered in 1931 by the Rochester Philharmonic, conducted by Howard

Hanson. In his notebook, Still subtitled the four movements to indicate the emotional tenor of each: "Longing," "Sorrow," "Humor," and "Aspiration." He also included an epigraph for each movement, taken from dialect poems by Paul Laurence Dunbar; these epigraphs reinforced the moods he sought to create, as well as the specific African American experience that Still represented in the movement. He created an original blues theme that weaves its way through all movements, except for the third. He added a banjo to the traditional instruments of the orchestra, instantly invoking the sound color of the blues. The symphony also uses a harmonic palette that echoes the simple patterns found in the blues.

Sahdji. This ballet is based on a short story by Richard Bruce. The plot revolves around Sahdji, wife of a chieftain in central Africa who has to choose between her husband and the man with whom she has fallen in love. When her husband is killed, she chooses to be faithful to him by committing suicide, as is the custom of her people. Still uses drums and complex rhythmic patterns to evoke the sound of African drumming throughout this work. It was premiered by the Eastman Ballet and the Rochester Civic Orchestra, conducted by Hanson.

Troubled Island. Still composed this four-act opera during the years 1937-1939. It uses a libretto by poet Langston Hughes, with the addition of lyrics by Verna Arvey for several arias. It is based on the biography of the first emperor of Haiti, Jean-Jacques Dessalines. The opening scene portrays Dessalines leading a revolt against French troops and his subsequent coronation as emperor; the opera concludes with his death through the betrayal of his friend Vuval. Still uses leitmotifs to represent various characters throughout the opera. He researched Haitian music and incorporated voodoo rhythms and dances into the opera. *Troubled Island* was first performed in its entirety by the New York City Opera Company in 1949, and it holds the distinction of being the first opera by an African American composer to be premiered by a major American opera company.

And They Lynched Him on a Tree. This choral work is based on the poem of the same name by Katherine Garrison Chapin. Composed in 1940, it was premiered in the same year by the New York Philharmonic. In this work, Still explores racial tensions and reconciliation through the use of a white chorus and an African American chorus. At the beginning of the work, the two choruses are used as oppositional forces, the white chorus dramatically portraying an angry mob, and the African American chorus portraying the victims of the mob who vehemently express an opposition to racism and hatred. At the end of the work, however, the two choruses join in a paean to the brotherhood of man and a call to tolerance.

In Memoriam: Colored Soldiers Who Died for Democracy. Commissioned by the League of Composers during World War II and premiered by the New York Philharmonic in 1944, this short, one-movement work for orchestra is Still's homage to the soldiers who had to fight for freedom both overseas and in the United States. He cited his inspiration as the fact that the first American soldier to die in World War II was African American.

The Little Song That Wanted to Be a Symphony. Composed for orchestra, three sopranos (or string soloists), and narrator, this work is an excellent example of Still's universal idiom. A musical theme is said to take a journey through the United States to visit children and is transformed to reflect the cultures and peoples of each region, including African American, Cajun, Italian, Asian, and Native American styles. The work celebrates the diversity and connectedness of the American peoples.

Musical Legacy

Christened the Dean of African American Composers, Still contributed a powerful legacy to the world of music. He wove together classical idioms with blues, jazz, spirituals, other folk music traditions, and popular music, paving the way for later generations of composers to continue these explorations. Though he was not the first to create concert works using African American idioms, he had a powerful influence on generations of composers who followed him. His work and influence were recognized through the numerous honorary degrees given to him from institutions such as Wilberforce University, Oberlin College, and the University of Southern California, among many other awards.

Best known today for his classical compositions, Still was also a prominent arranger of popular and jazz music, especially early in his career during his time in New York City. Working in New York during the Harlem Renaissance and collaborating with seminal figures such as Langston Hughes, Still can be viewed retrospectively as part of that cultural explosion.

Still's work as an African American composer of classical music was groundbreaking for generations of composers following him. Though facing obstacles from critics and others, he achieved many firsts for an African American musician, both as a composer and as a conductor. He believed that the bringing together of many cultural styles and traditions of music could serve as a model for the kind of racial reconciliation that America needed. In his music and in his words, Still sought to join diverse elements into a cohesive whole.

Joanna R. Smolko and Timothy J. Smolko

Further Reading

Arvey, Verna. *In One Lifetime*. Introduction and notes by B. A. Nugent. Fayetteville: University of Arkansas Press, 1984. Written by Still's second wife, Verna, this book is an intimate look at his life. Arvey chronicles his career and private life, using not only excerpts from his journals, personal letters, and reviews of his music but also her own reminiscences from their time together. Illuminates some of the racial prejudice, overt and subtle, that Still encountered during his lifetime.

Smith, Catherine Parsons. *William Grant Still: A Study in Contradictions*. Berkeley: University of California Press, 2000. With essays contributed by Gayle Murchison and Willard B. Gatewood, a chronology of Still's life and works by Carolyn L. Quin, and contemporary resources from the 1930's, this work is indispensable for studying Still: his life, music, and historical context. Several important essays address his place in American musical history (for example, the conjunction of his work with the Harlem Renaissance). Still's own notes on his work and life round out the volume.

Soll, Beverly. *I Dream a World: The Operas of William Grant Still*. Fayetteville: University of Arkansas Press, 2005. Soll examines Still's operas from the beginning of his compositional process through their performance history. The first part of the book examines themes and topics across the scope of his operas, including Still's compositional process, autobiographical features of the operas, character types, musical styles, and the structural aspects of the operas. In the second part of the book, Soll analyzes each of Still's eight operas in more detail.

Still, Judith Anne, Michael J. Dabrishus, and Carolyn L. Quin. *William Grant Still: A Bio-Bibliography*. Westport, Conn.: Greenwood Press, 1996. This volume consists of personal reminiscences of the composer by his daughter, a detailed biography, a catalog of works, a bibliography, and a discography. The bibliography includes the writings of Still, the writings of others about him, and Still's writings in collaboration with his wife, journalist Verna Arvey. A good starting point for research on the composer.

Still, William Grant, and R. Donald Brown. *Negro Serious Music: William Grant Still Interviewed by R. Donald Brown on November 13, 1967 and December 4, 1967*. Fullerton: California State University, Oral History Program, 1984. This interview, though sprawling in nature, is important for Still's commentary on his life, his work, and the musicians with whom he had contact. During the interview, Still comments on the direction of American music, past, present, and future. The appendix includes a comprehensive list of Still's extant compositions.

See also: Blake, Eubie; Handy, W. C.; Henderson, Fletcher; Varèse, Edgard; Whiteman, Paul.

Stephen Stills

American rock singer, songwriter, and guitarist

A versatile singer, songwriter, and guitarist, Stills was a key member of two groundbreaking folk-rock supergroups—Buffalo Springfield and Crosby, Stills, and Nash (and sometimes Young).

Born: January 3, 1945; Dallas, Texas
Member of: Buffalo Springfield; Crosby, Stills, and Nash; Crosby, Stills, Nash, and Young; Manassas
Also known as: Stephen Arthur Stills (full name)

Principal recordings

ALBUMS (solo): *Stephen Stills*, 1970; *Stephen Stills 2*, 1971; *Stills*, 1975; *Illegal Stills*, 1976; *Long May You Run*, 1976 (with Neil Young); *Thoroughfare Gap*, 1978; *Right by You*, 1984; *Stills Alone*, 1991; *Man Alive!*, 2005.

ALBUMS (with Buffalo Springfield): *Buffalo Springfield*, 1966; *Buffalo Springfield Again*, 1967; *Last Time Around*, 1968.

ALBUMS (with Crosby, Stills, and Nash): *Crosby, Stills, and Nash*, 1969; *CSN*, 1977; *Daylight Again*, 1982; *Live It Up*, 1990; *After the Storm*, 1994.

ALBUMS (with Crosby, Stills, Nash, and Young): *Déjà Vu*, 1970; *American Dream*, 1988; *Looking Forward*, 1999.

ALBUMS (with Manassas): *Manassas*, 1972; *Down the Road*, 1973.

The Life

Stephen Arthur Stills was the second child born to William and Talitha Stills. The family moved often in pursuit of Stills's father's various enterprises. Stills grew up primarily in Louisiana and in central Florida, and he also lived in Costa Rica before graduating from high school in Panama. He became interested in music at an early age, learning to play drums, piano, and guitar. During his family's travels, Stills soaked up many musical traditions, including gospel, blues, folk, jazz, country, rock, and Latin.

After graduation, Stills enrolled at the University of Florida, but he soon dropped out, moving to New York, where he sang and played folk music. He joined the folk-harmony group the Au Go Go Singers, then he formed the Company, a folk-rock band. Moving to California, Stills became a member of Buffalo Springfield. When the band broke up, he formed Crosby, Stills, and Nash, which has performed sporadically in numerous incarnations with different members, including Neil Young, since the late 1960's. Stills also founded the band Manassas and released a number of solo albums from 1970 onward.

Stills was romantically linked in the 1960's to Janis Joplin, Judy Collins, and others. Twice married and divorced, he wed Kristen Hathoway in 1996, and he became the father of five children (Chris, Justin, Henry, Jennifer, and Oliver). On his

Stephen Stills. (AP/Wide World Photos)

sixty-third birthday, Stills had successful surgery for prostate cancer.

The Music

Stills's impact on music began late in the 1960's. With singer-songwriter Ritchie Furay, bassist Bruce Palmer, drummer Dewey Martin, and singer-songwriter Neil Young, Stills formed the pioneering folk-rock band Buffalo Springfield. Though the group released only three albums between 1966 and 1968 before breaking up, the music they created greatly influenced later artists (including the Eagles, Tom Petty, Dan Fogelberg, America, Loggins and Messina, Seals and Crofts, James Taylor, and countless others).

After joining Al Kooper on 1968's gold-record *Super Session*, Stills the following year formed fortuitous friendships with ex-Byrds member David Crosby and ex-Hollies member Graham Nash. Their first album, *Crosby, Stills, and Nash*, set new standards for lyricism, vocals, and production. It also inspired a group expansion. Young was invited to join, and Crosby, Stills, Nash, and Young was formed just in time to appear at the Woodstock Music and Art Fair and at the Altamont Free Concert in 1969, where they wowed crowds with their tight harmonies.

Following several tours and the release of two highly regarded albums, Crosby, Stills, Nash, and Young broke up. Stills moved to England, where he recorded his first solo album, but he later returned to the United States, where he released more than a dozen solo albums, among them *Man Alive!* Interspersed among these are another dozen Crosby, Stills, and Nash (and sometimes Young) studio, live, and compilation recordings from a quartet of musicians who bring out the best in one another.

Buffalo Springfield. The group's highly influential debut album, released in 1966, was reissued in 1967 to include the Stills-penned antiwar hit "For What It's Worth." With its ominous opening—"There's a man with a gun over there"—the song became a counterculture anthem and propelled the album to number five on pop charts.

Crosby, Stills, and Nash. The supergroup's first release in 1969 rose to number six on U.S. pop charts and went multiplatinum, thanks to diverse musical textures, complex arrangements, and subtle lifestyle commentaries. It produced two major hits—Nash's drug-oriented "Marrakesh Express" and Stills's love paean to Judy Collins, "Suite: Judy Blue Eyes"—plus such radio standards as Crosby's "Long Time Gone," Stills's "Helplessly Hoping," and "Wooden Ships," cowritten by Crosby, Stills, and Paul Kantner of Jefferson Airplane.

Déjà Vu. The first collaboration among Crosby, Stills, Nash, and Young, this 1970 album hit number one on the pop charts and caused the group to be compared to the Beatles at their height. *Déjà Vu* produced three certified hit singles: Nash's "Teach Your Children" and "Our House," and the group's popular rendition of Joni Mitchell's "Woodstock." Ranked among the greatest albums of all time on various polls, it also included Crosby's "Almost Cut My Hair" and the title track, Stills's "Carry On," Young's "Helpless," and the Stills-Young composition "Everybody I Love You."

Stephen Stills. Stills's first solo album, released soon after *Déjà Vu*, showcased the singer-songwriter's compositional talents. *Stephen Stills* rose to number three on pop charts, thanks to strong singles such as "Love the One You're With," "Sit Your-

self Down," "Black Queen," and "We Are Not Helpless." Though dubbed a solo album, it featured many guest performances from top artists, including Ringo Starr, Jimi Hendrix, Eric Clapton, Booker T. Jones, and backup vocals by Crosby, Nash, John Sebastian, Rita Coolidge, and Cass Elliott.

CSN. Released in 1977, this album peaked at number two on the pop charts, and it featured some of the trio's strongest work since its debut. Two singles from the album—Nash's "Just a Song Before I Go" and Stills's "Fair Game"—became *Billboard* Hot 100 hits. Most of Stills's contributions, including "See the Changes," "Dark Star," and "Run from Tears," dealt creatively with the impending breakup of his first marriage. *CSN* was the first album to use string accompaniments.

Musical Legacy

A major force in the shaping of popular music since the late 1960's, Stills is recognized for his songwriting, singing, production, and guitar-playing skills. Both as a member of two highly influential folk-rock groups and as a soloist, he continued to expand his volume of quality work, whose impact on later musicians was substantial. In recognition of his unique contributions, in 1997 he was the first individual to be inducted into the Rock and Roll Hall of Fame twice on the same night: first, for his work with Buffalo Springfield, and, second, for his work with Crosby, Stills, and Nash.

Jack Ewing

Further Reading

Barbata, Johnny. *The Legendary Life of a Rock Star Drummer*. Duncanville, Tex.: DJ Blues, 2007. This is an illustrated autobiography from a drummer who worked with the Turtles, Jefferson Airplane, Crosby, Stills, Nash, and Young, and others.

Crosby, David, and Carl Gottlieb. *Since Then: How I Survived Everything and Lived to Tell About It*. New York: Putnam Adult, 2006. Revealing memoir from one of the founding members of Crosby, Stills, and Nash.

Einarson, John, and Ritchie Furay. *For What It's Worth: The Story of Buffalo Springfield*. Lantham, Md.: Cooper Square Press, 2004. Detailed and illustrated study of the rise and fall of the influential band, incorporating statements from most members.

Zimmer, Dave. *Four Way Street: The Crosby, Stills, Nash, and Young Reader.* Cambridge, Mass.: Da Capo Press, 2004. A compendium of articles and interviews, covering the lives of the members of the groundbreaking group from 1969 to 2002.

Zimmer, Dave, and Henry Diltz. *Crosby, Stills, and Nash: The Authorized Biography.* Cambridge, Mass.: Da Capo Press, 2000. Well-illustrated portrait of the three musicians and their history, together and separately.

See also: Clapton, Eric; Collins, Judy; Costello, Elvis; Crosby, David; Elliot, Cass; Hendrix, Jimi; Mitchell, Joni; Petty, Tom; Sainte-Marie, Buffy; Staples, Pops; Taylor, James; Young, Neil.

Sting

English rock singer, bassist, and songwriter

A singer, bass guitarist, and songwriter, Sting is significant for infusing rock music with literate lyrics, expressive melodies, and an eclectic blend of diverse musical styles.

Born: October 2, 1951; Wallsend, Northumberland, England
Also known as: Gordon Matthew Sumner (birth name)
Member of: The Police

Principal works

FILM SCORES: *Demolition Man*, 1993; *Living Sea*, 1995.

Principal recordings

ALBUMS (solo): *The Dream of the Blue Turtles*, 1985; *Nothing like the Sun*, 1987; *The Soul Cages*, 1991; *Ten Summoner's Tales*, 1993; *Mercury Falling*, 1996; *Brand New Day*, 1999; *Sacred Love*, 2003; *Songs from the Labyrinth*, 2006 (with Edin Karamazov).

ALBUMS (with the Police): *Outlandos d'Amour*, 1979; *Reggatta de Blanc*, 1979; *Zenyatta Mondatta*, 1980; *Ghost in the Machine*, 1981; *Synchronicity*, 1983.

WRITINGS OF INTEREST: *Broken Music: A Memoir*, 2003.

The Life

Sting was born Gordon Matthew Sumner in northeast England, the oldest of four children. His father managed a dairy farm, and as a boy Sting often helped with milk deliveries. He attended St. Cuthbert's Grammar School, a Catholic school in nearby Newcastle. After jobs as a bus conductor, a construction worker, and a tax clerk, Sting returned to school, attending Northern Counties Teacher Training College (now part of Northumbria University) from 1971 to 1974. He then worked as a teacher at St. Paul's First School in Cramlington for two years. In 1976 he married actress Frances Tomelty, and the couple had two children. The marriage ended in 1984. In 1992 Sting married actress (and later film producer) Trudie Styler, with whom he has four children.

From an early age, Sting wanted to be a musician. During the early 1970's, he played bass guitar with local jazz bands, such as the Phoenix Jazzmen, the Newcastle Big Band, and Last Exit. When he wore a striped black and yellow jersey to a performance with the Phoenix Jazzmen, the bandleader, who thought Sumner resembled a bumblebee, nicknamed him Sting.

In 1977 Sting left rural northern England for London, where he formed the trio the Police. The group was successful for several years, but it disbanded in 1984, it came back together for a short time in 1986, then it split up again. Sting went on to have a successful solo career—as a singer, a bass guitarist, and, most notably, a songwriter.

Sting has received two honorary doctoral degrees in music, in 1992 from England's Northumbria University and in 1994 from Boston's Berklee College of Music. In 2002 he was inducted into the Songwriters Hall of Fame, and he was given the honor of Commander of the Order of the British Empire. In 2003 he published his autobiography, *Broken Music*, which chronicles his early life up to his years with the Police.

Sting has also had an acting career, appearing in such films as *Dune* (1984), *Plenty* (1985), *The Bride* (1985), *Bring on the Night* (1985), *The Adventures of*

Baron Munchausen (1988), *Stormy Monday* (1988), *The Grotesque* (1995), and *Lock, Stock, and Two Smoking Barrels* (1998). In 1989 he starred as Macheath in a failed Broadway revival of *The Threepenny Opera* (1928), and he has had several guest roles on both British and American television.

The Music

Sting infused a rare level of musicianship into rock music.

Outlandos d'Amour. In early 1977, Sting formed the Police with Stewart Copeland and Henry Padovani, who was soon replaced by Andy Summers. Sting sang and played bass guitar with the band. Although the Police originated as part of the new wave scene, the group merged reggae and ska with punk and jazz, always displaying a greater level of musicianship than other punk bands of the day. As the group's principal songwriter, Sting wrote many interesting and melodic songs, such as "Roxanne," on the group's first major album, *Outlandos d'Amour*, and "Message in a Bottle," on its second album, *Regatta De Blanc*. The Police achieved global success with *Ghost in the Machine*, and it won six Grammy Awards in the early 1980's. Even more stylistically diverse than earlier albums, *Synchronicity*, the band's final album, included its most successful song, "Every Breath You Take."

The Police disbanded in 1984, but two years later reunited for a brief time before splitting up again the same year. The band came together again in the summer of 2007 for a successful thirtieth anniversary tour.

"Spread a Little Happiness." Even before the Police disbanded, Sting began to appear as a solo artist. His first live solo appearance came in 1981, when he performed on all four nights of the Secret Policeman's Other Ball, the fourth Amnesty International benefit. He sang solo versions of "Roxanne" and "Message in a Bottle," and he led a band that included Eric Clapton, Jeff Beck, Phil Collins, Bob Geldof, and Midge Ure in his own reggae-style arrangement of Bob Dylan's "I Shall Be Released." In 1982 Sting released a solo single, "Spread a Little Happiness," from the television play *Brimstone and Treacle* (1982), which became a hit in England.

The Dream of the Blue Turtles. Sting's first solo album, *The Dream of the Blue Turtles*, blended rock, reggae, jazz, and pop, and it brought together many

important jazz and fusion musicians, including pianist Kenny Kirkland, bassist Darryl Jones, drummer Omar Hakim, and saxophonist Branford Marsalis. It included the hit single "If You Love Someone, Set Them Free," and it was nominated for a Grammy Award as Album of the Year. The same year Sting led an all-star band (with some of the same members from the 1981 Amnesty International benefit) in the Live Aid Concert at London's Wembley National Stadium, and the following year he performed on Amnesty International's Conspiracy of Hope Tour of the United States.

In the later 1980's, Sting continued to explore various musical styles. In 1987 he again collaborated with jazz artists, such as Marsalis and veteran jazz arranger Gil Evans, along with former Police guitarist Andy Summers. The result was his most eclectic album to date, *Nothing like the Sun*, whose title was taken from a William Shakespeare sonnet, which begins, "My mistress's eyes are nothing like the sun." The album featured Sting's intelligent literate poetry, set to well-crafted melodies in such songs as "We'll Be Together," "Fragile," "Englishman in New York" (about the eccentric author Quentin Crisp), and "Be Still My Beating Heart" (dedicated to Sting's recently deceased mother). In February, 1988, Sting released *Nada Como el Sol*, a selection of five songs from *Nothing Like the Sun* translated into Spanish and Portuguese. Later that year he performed a solo version of the Police song "Murder by Numbers" on Frank Zappa's satirical album *Broadway the Hard Way* (1988).

"They Dance Alone." Continuing his support of various humanitarian and environmental causes, Sting joined a group of major artists, including Peter Gabriel and Bruce Springsteen, for the world Human Rights Now! Tour in 1988. The same year he released the single "They Dance Alone," which chronicled the plight of women under the Augusto Pinochet regime in Chile. Sting, along with his wife Styler and Raoni Metuktire (a Kayapó Indian leader in Brazil), founded the Rainforest Foundation.

The Soul Cages. After *Nothing Like the Sun* came the darkly introspective *The Soul Cages*, dedicated to Sting's father who had died in 1987. It included the Top 10 hit "All This Time" and the Grammy Award-winning "Soul Cages." In 1993 Sting returned to a more straightforward pop sound with *Ten Summoner's Tales*, which went triple platinum in a little over a year. The same year he joined with Bryan Adams and Rod Stewart on a recording of "All for Love," from the film *The Three Musketeers* (1993). This became the first song from Sting's post-Police career to top charts in the United States.

In 1993 Sting composed the sound track for the Sylvester Stallone and Wesley Snipes film *Demolition Man* (1993) and the sound track for the IMAX film *The Living Sea* (1995). In 1996 the album *Mercury Falling*, noted for its extensive use of synthesizer tracks and its shift away from Sting's jazz-rock style toward a smooth pop sound, was praised for its lyrics but criticized for its musical content. It failed to produce a hit single. Although his record sales slowed at this time, Sting continued to be a popular concert attraction. He spent much of the next two years recording music for a Walt Disney Studios film, *Kingdom of the Sun*, which was never used in the film but which he later reworked for another Disney film, *The Emperor's New Groove* (2000). At the same time Sting was exploring Middle Eastern and Indian musical styles for the album *Brand New Day*, which reenergized his recording career. This album features collaborations with Stevie Wonder, James Taylor, Branford Marsalis, Chris Botti, and Algerian singer Cheb Mami. The songs "Brand New Day" and "Desert Rose" won Grammy Awards, and for his performance with Mami of "Desert Rose" at the Grammy Awards ceremony, Sting received the Kahlil Gibran Spirit of Humanity Award.

The 2000's. In 2000 Sting wrote the sound track for the IMAX film *Dolphins*, and he continued to explore new musical ground and to seek innovative collaborations. In 2003 he released the album *Sacred Love*, which includes collaborations with hip-hop artist Mary J. Blige and sitarist Anoushka Shankar. Sting and Blige won a Grammy Award for their duet, "Whenever I Say Your Name."

In 2006 Sting released *Songs from the Labyrinth*, an album of lute songs by Elizabethan composer John Dowland. To prepare for this recording, Sting studied lute with Richard Levitt of the Schola Cantorum Basilensis. Sting provides the vocals and plays the archlute, but most of the accompaniment is provided by the masterful Bosnian lutenist Edin Karamazov. While some in the classical music world criticized this crossover of classical and pop, the album is another example of Sting's eclectic

musical tastes. It also brought an awareness of Dowland's music, in which Sting long had an interest, to the popular music world.

Musical Legacy

Sting has always been involved in numerous and diverse musical projects, all of which testify to his eclectic tastes. His intelligent lyrics and jazz-pop-world-classical music fusions have expanded the boundaries of popular music and have led to a richness and expressiveness that are rare in rock music. He is also among the most important musicians who have used their talent and fame to assist charitable causes.

Sting's contribution to charitable causes is legendary. He has performed on behalf of many causes, including Amnesty International. He helped found the Rainforest Foundation, which raises awareness about preserving the Brazilian rainforest and other environmental causes.

Mary A. Wischusen

Further Reading

Berryman, James. *Sting and I: The Totally Hilarious Story of Life as Sting's Best Mate*. London: John Blake, 2005. Sting's boyhood friend, Berryman, provides an entertaining account of their experiences at St. Cuthbert's Grammar School in Newcastle and afterward.

Goldsmith, Lynn. *The Police, 1978-1983*. New York: Little, Brown, 2007. Published to coincide with the group's 2007 reunion tour, this book contains remarkable and memorable photographs. It features an introduction by British music journalist Phil Sutcliffe, who, along with Goldsmith, had access to the Police during the early 1980's.

Hill, Dave. *Designer Boys and Material Girls: Manufacturing the Eighties Pop Dream*. Poole, Dorset: Blandford Press, 1986. An account of the popular music scene in the 1980's, with references to Sting.

Sandford, Christopher. *Sting: Demolition Man*. New York: Little, Brown, 1998. An unbiased critical assessment of Sting's life and musical career.

Sumner, Gordon. *Broken Music: A Memoir*. New York: Simon & Schuster, 2003. Sting's touching autobiography from his childhood to his early years with the Police.

See also: Alpert, Herb; Blades, Rubén; Clapton, Eric; Cliff, Jimmy; Cohen, Leonard; Costello, Elvis; Fleck, Béla; Hancock, Herbie; Hayes, Isaac; Iglesias, Julio; Jennings, Waylon; Legrand, Michel; Paul, Les; Pavarotti, Luciano; Taylor, James.

Karlheinz Stockhausen

German classical composer

Stockhausen was at the forefront of the post-1945 European avant-garde, with his works of serialism and his large-scale electroacoustic compositions.

Born: August 22, 1928; Mödrath, Germany
Died: December 5, 2007; Kürten-Kettenberg, Germany

Principal works

CHAMBER WORKS: *Kontra-Punkte, Nr. 1*, 1953 (*Counter-Points, No. 1*); *Zyklus, Nr. 9*, 1959; *Adieu, Nr. 21*, 1967; *Hymnen, Nr. 22 ½*, 1967; *Aus den sieben Tagen, Nr. 26*, 1969 (*From the Seven Days, No. 26*; comprises fifteen works); *Dr. K., Nr. 28*, 1969; *Für kommende Zeiten, Nr. 33*, 1970 (*For Times to Come*; comprises seventeen works); *Alphabet für Liège, Nr. 36*, 1972; *Tierkreis, Nr. 41 ½*, 1975 (*Zodiac, No. 41 ½*); *Amour, Nr. 44*, 1978; *In Freundschaft, Nr. 46*, 1978 (for clarinet); *Klang, Nr. 81*, 2004-2007 (*Sound, No. 81*; comprises twenty works, Nos. 81-101).

CHORAL WORKS: *Stimmung, Nr. 24*, 1968 (*Tuning, No. 24*; includes *Stimmung, Nr. 24 ½*); *Am Himmel wandre ich, Nr. 36 ½*, 1972 (*In the Sky I Am Walking, No. 36 ½*); *Vortrag über HU, Nr. 38 ½*, 1974; *Unsichtbare Chöre, Nr. 79*, 1979 (*Invisible Choir, No. 79*).

ELECTRONIC WORKS: *Gesang der Jünglinge, Nr. 8*, 1956; *Kontakte, Nr. 12*, 1960 (includes *Kontakte Nr. 12 ½* and *Originale, Nr. 12 ⅔*); *Hymnen, Nr. 22*, 1969; *Spiral, Nr. 27*, 1969; *Sirius, Nr. 43*, 1976 (revised 1977 to include *Aries, Nr. 43 ½*, *Libra, Nr. 43 ⅔*, and *Capricorn, Nr. 43 ¾*).

OPERAS (music and libretto): *Licht: Die sieben Tage der Woche*, 1981-2004 (*Light: The Seven Days of the Week*, includes *Donnerstag aus Licht*, 1981) (*Thursday of Light*; comprises five parts, Nos. 48, 48 ½, 49, 50, and 50 ¾); *Samstag aus Licht*, 1984 (*Saturday of Light*; comprises five parts, Nos. 51, 52, 53, 53 ½, and 54); *Montag aus Licht*, 1988 (*Monday of Light*; comprises five parts, Nos. 55-59); *Dienstag aus Licht*, 1993 (*Tuesday of Light*; comprises three parts, Nos. 60, 47, and 61); *Freitag aus Licht*, 1996 (*Friday of Light*; comprises three parts, Nos. 62-64); *Mittwoch aus Licht*, 1998 (*Wednesday of Light*; comprises six parts, Nos. 65, 66, 68, 69, 70, and 71; *Sonntag aus Licht*, 2004 (*Sunday of Light*; comprises six parts, Nos. 75-80).

ORCHESTRAL WORKS: *Gruppen, Nr. 6*, 1958; *Mixtur, Nr. 16*, 1964; *Stop, Nr. 18*, 1965; *Mixtur, Nr. 16 ½*, 1967; *Stop, Nr. 18 ½*, 1969; *Hymnen, Nr. 22 ⅔*, 1971; *Inori (Adoration), Nr. 38*, 1974; *Stop und Start, No. 18 ⅔*, 2001; *Mixtur 2003, Nr. 16 ⅔*, 2003.

PIANO WORKS: Klavierstücke I-IV, Nr. 2, 1954; Klavierstücke V-X, Nr. 4, 1954-1962; Klavierstücke XI, Nr. 7, 1957.

The Life

The parents of Karlheinz Stockhausen (KAHRL-hinz STAHK-how-zehn) died in World War II: his mother in a sanatorium in 1942 and his father on the Hungarian front in 1945. Then a teenager, Stockhausen worked in a military hospital during the conflict. He later returned to Cologne, beginning studies in piano and in composition at the Musikhochschule in 1947. In August, 1951, Stockhausen went to the Darmstadt Ferienkurse für Neue Musik, where he met, among others, Olivier Messiaen and Karel Goeyvaerts.

In January, 1952, Stockhausen left Cologne to join Messiaen's class at the Paris Conservatory, in which Pierre Boulez was also a student. While in Paris, Stockhausen was introduced to musique concrète by Pierre Schaeffer. Stockhausen's early electroacoustic compositions took inspiration from this encounter.

During the 1960's, Stockhausen's fame was at its peak. He was widely regarded as Europe's most important living composer. His music was played around the world by an ensemble that included Aloys Kontarsky and Alfred Alings. This era reached a climax at the 1970 World Fair in Osaka, where Stockhausen's entourage performed daily for six months.

After this, however, Stockhausen's fame declined. The reasons for this are multiple, but the development of his unique religious and spiritual beliefs certainly made him increasingly unpopular with younger composers. Stockhausen remained an important figure, but he never recaptured the notoriety that he had enjoyed during the 1960's.

The Music

Stockhausen often aimed to balance a mathematical type of organization with absolute aleatoricism. In his oeuvre, therefore, works of total serialism are found alongside others that are almost completely improvised. On the one hand, the influence of Messiaen's piano study *Mode de valeurs et d'intensités* (1950), which inspired total serialism, and of Stockhausen's contemporaries, such as Boulez and Goeyvaerts, is revealed. On the other hand, Stockhausen occasionally espouses aesthetics commonly associated with John Cage. Stockhausen's most memorable compositions are those in which he fused serial and aleatoric ideas. It was arguably his work with electroacoustics, the genre that eroded the barriers between noise and music, that made such an unlikely marriage possible.

Counter-Points, No. 1. *Counter-Points, No. 1* is representative of much of Stockhausen's early output, which was concerned almost exclusively with the development of total serialism. Although *Counter-Points, No. 1* had been preceded by a number of similar works, this was the first composition that Stockhausen deemed fit for publication. While *Counter-Points, No. 1* remains pointillist, it is not strictly subject to the rule of total serialism. It is composed for an ensemble of ten instruments, with the piano taking a leading role. Members of the Westdeutscher Rundfunk premiered the work in Cologne on May 26, 1953. The culmination of Stockhausen's early efforts, *Counter-Points, No. 1* was to be the last composition of its sort. A move away from techniques directly inspired by Anton von Webern came soon after.

Kontakte. This work was a major venture in electroacoustic music for Stockhausen, and it was also the first composition in which he truly removed himself from the serialism that had hitherto provided the scaffolding for his compositions. Stockhausen structured the piece around his new concept, moment form, which was concerned with the crafting of time itself. Each moment of time was to exist entirely independently. This concentration on the present was intended to act as the opening of a gateway into eternity. Scored for piano, percussion, and tape, *Kontakte* is in two parts and lasts more than thirty minutes. Pianist David Tudor and percussionist Christoph Caskel premiered *Kontakte* in Cologne, on June 11, 1960.

Klavierstücke X. Of Stockhausen's works for piano, Klavierstücke X is the most ambitious and grandiose. Like *Kontakte* before it, Klavierstücke X represents another venture into a new sound world, with Stockhausen exploring keyboard note clusters. The pianist is advised to wear woolen, fingerless gloves in order to make the note-cluster glissandi easier to play. This exploration of instrumental possibility was extremely unusual in Stockhausen's output at the time. The work is also characterized by long, interjecting periods of stillness, during which colorful sonorities are sustained with the sostenuto pedal. Frederic Rzewski premiered the work in Palermo on October 10, 1962.

Light: The Seven Days of the Week. Between 1977 and 2003, Stockhausen was absorbed with the composition of *Light: The Seven Days of the Week*, an opera cycle lasting nearly thirty hours. It is a massive cosmic-religious theatrical work, aiming to demonstrate the unity of music and religion. It revolves around three central characters, Michael, Eve, and Lucifer, and is told over the course of the seven days of the week. As one would expect in such a long project, changes made by Stockhausen to his compositional techniques are palpable throughout *Light: The Seven Days of the Week*. The work stands as a summation of Stockhausen's work, forming a catalog of his musical concerns. These include offerings of electroacoustic music, of expanded instrumental techniques, of carefully crafted microtonal scales, and so on. In addition to the musical demands posed by *Light: The Seven Days of the Week*, it would almost certainly be an extremely expensive musical project. Four helicopters are needed, for example, in the *Helikopter-Streichquartett* of *Wednesday of Light*. They fly outside the opera house, with the music being electronically transmitted to the concert hall.

Musical Legacy

Stockhausen's pioneering serial and electro-acoustic compositions opened up new avenues for exploration. From 1971 to 1977, Stockhausen held the position of composition professor at the Cologne Musikhochschule, where he had honed his own talents as a student in the 1950's. Here he directly influenced the development of young composers such as Klarenz Barlow, László Dubrovay, and Kevin Volans. In addition, his involvement with concert life shaped the careers of the significant performers of new music, such as Kontarsky. Stockhausen's electroacoustic works attracted interest from pop musicians in the 1960's, and he was even featured on the cover of the Beatles' famous album of 1967, *Sgt. Pepper's Lonely Hearts Club Band*.

Luke Berryman

Further Reading

Harvey, Jonathan. *The Music of Stockhausen*. Los Angeles: University of California Press, 1975. A thorough analytical guide to many of Stockhausen's works.

Kurtz, Michael. *Stockhausen: A Biography*. Translated by Richard Toop. London: Faber & Faber, 1992. A comprehensive account of Stockhausen's life and work up until the 1990's.

Maconie, Robin. *Other Planets: The Music of Karlheinz Stockhausen*. Lanham, Md.: Scarecrow Press, 2005. Maconie presents an assessment of Stockhausen's life and works.

_____. *The Works of Karlheinz Stockhausen*. Oxford, England: Oxford University Press, 1990. Another guide to Stockhausen's compositions, including an examination of the composer's progression through *Light: The Seven Days of the Week*.

Stockhausen, Karlheinz. *Stockhausen on Music: Lectures and Interviews*. Edited by Robin Maconie. London: Boyars, 2000. A valuable collection of Stockhausen's comments, unveiling his attitudes toward music and composition.

See also: Babbitt, Milton; Berio, Luciano; Boulez, Pierre; Cage, John; Carter, Elliott; Hancock, Herbie; Lennon, John; Ligeti, György; McCartney, Sir Paul; Messiaen, Olivier; Nono, Luigi; Schaeffer, Pierre; Webern, Anton von.

Leopold Stokowski

English classical conductor

Stokowski made Bach's organ works accessible to millions through his orchestral transcriptions, and he won both praise and criticism for the liberties he took with musical scores in an attempt to bring out the essence of the music.

Born: April 18, 1882; London, England
Died: September 13, 1977; Nether Wallop, Hampshire, England
Also known as: Leopold Bolesławowicz Stanisław Antoni Stokowski (full name); Antoni Stanlisław Bolesławowicz (birth name)

Principal recordings

ALBUMS (as conductor): *Sibelius: Symphony No. 4*, 1932; *Mozart: Sinfonia Concertante*, 1940; *Schubert: Unfinished Symphony*, 1941; *Vaughan Williams: Symphony No. 4 in F Minor*, 1943; *Beethoven: Pastoral Symphony*, 1944; *Richard Strauss: Death and Transfiguration*, 1944; *Tchaikovsky: Pathétique Symphony*, 1945; *Debussy: Children's Corner Suite*, 1949; *Haydn: Symphony No. 53, Imperial*, 1949; *Schumann: Symphony No. 2*, 1949; *Vaughan Williams: Symphony No. 6 in E Minor*, 1949; *J. Strauss II: Blue Danube Waltz*, 1950; *Sibelius: Symphony No. 1 in E Minor*, 1950; *Rimsky-Korsakov: Scheherazade*, 1951; *Bizet: Symphony in C, L'Arlesienne Suites 1 and 2*, 1952; *Sibelius: Symphony No. 2 in D Major*, 1954; *Brahms: Symphony No. 2*, 1977; *Mendelssohn: Symphony No. 4, Italian*, 1977.

The Life

Leopold Bolesławowicz Stanisław Antoni Stokowski (stoh-KAHF-skee) told fanciful stories about his origins, claiming at times that he was born in Poland, the descendant either of an aristocratic general who fought alongside Napoleon Bonaparte or of sturdy Polish peasants in the imaginary village of Stokki. At times he affected an Eastern European accent. In fact, he did have one Polish grandparent, also named Leopold Stokowski, who immigrated to England and married a Scotswoman. On his mother's side, Stokowski was half

Irish and half English, and he grew up in a lower-middle-class district in London. His mother wanted him to use the name Leo Stokes, but he did not want to Anglicize his name. Instead, Stokowski emphasized his Polish background, and he invented a more, not less, Polish-sounding name for himself—Leopold Bolesławowicz Stanisław Antoni Stokowski—according to one version.

Stokowski was a romantic who wanted to appear mysterious and exotic, and to play this role he felt it necessary to leave London, which he did in 1905 to take up a post as an organist and choirmaster for St. Bartholomew's Church in New York City. Before that, he held similar positions at St. Mary's Church and St. James's Church in London, and he acquired a degree in music from Oxford University after spending four years attending London's Royal College of Music.

Stokowski's main interest was in conducting. According to one of his stories, he was playing in a children's orchestra at the age of twelve when the conductor fell ill, and Stokowski stepped up to take his place. From that time on, he said, he knew he wanted to conduct.

Although he had minimal conducting experience, Stokowski persuaded the board of directors of the Cincinnati Symphony Orchestra to hire him to lead their orchestra in 1909. Once in the post, he flourished, winning much admiration for his musical talent and for his dashing good looks and charm.

After Stokowski quarreled with the Cincinnati Symphony Orchestra board, in 1912 he moved on to become conductor of the Philadelphia Orchestra, where he stayed for a quarter of a century, transforming the Philadelphia musicians into what some called the finest orchestra ever, notable especially for its lush "Stokowski sound." Stokowski quarreled with management in Philadelphia, too, this time over his desire to program more experimental, modern music than audiences seemed interested in hearing. Eventually, he left the position, though not before performing with the orchestra in the film *The Big Broadcast of 1937* (1936). For a while Stokowski, who appeared on the cover of *Time* magazine in 1930, contemplated a career in Hollywood. This did not materialize, though he appeared in the film *One Hundred Men and a Girl* (1938) with Deanna Durbin, and then he collaborated with

Walt Disney and Mickey Mouse on the sound and light extravaganza *Fantasia* (1940); this led to another appearance on the cover of *Time*. Stokowski had a widely publicized romance with the film star Greta Garbo, and he was married for a time to the American heiress Gloria Vanderbilt.

After leaving Philadelphia, Stokowski worked with a number of orchestras, including some he started himself. He was constantly searching for better recording technology, having been one of the first to record orchestral music, as early as 1917. In 1972 Stokowski moved back to England, where he continued conducting and recording almost until the day he died at the age of ninety-five.

The Music

Stokowski was a controversial conductor whose emphasis on conveying the spirit of the music as opposed to following strictly the notes on the music score earned him admiration and derision. Traditionalists condemned him for varying tempi and for making other alterations to what composers had written. His response was that notes were mere specks on the page; what mattered was what the composer was trying to achieve. Stokowski was at his best with the Romantic and twentieth century repertoire, which suited his emphasis on feeling and spirit. He was noted for bringing a lush full sound from his orchestras and for being able to inspire musicians to new heights. He gave up using a baton to conduct, relying on his hands and eyes instead, and he experimented with different seating arrangements for orchestra members to create a better sound. His emphasis was always on the sound, and to this end he introduced free bowing, which freed his violinists from bowing up and down in step with each other. This avoided the pauses in sound created when all the violinists in a traditional orchestra simultaneously switched from up to down, and this also allowed each musician to bring his or her own inspiration to the performance.

Mahler's Symphony No. 8. Stokowski initially won widespread popularity with his American premiere, on March 2, 1916, of Gustav Mahler's Symphony No. 8 (1911), also known as the *Symphony of a Thousand*. Long an admirer of the way Mahler could transform misery into joy in his music, and also interested in putting on a spectacle, Stokowski persuaded the Philadelphia Orchestra board to let him organize the more than one thousand performers (958 singers and 110 musicians) required for Symphony No. 8. The Philadelphia performances were such a success that he put on an additional performance at New York's Metropolitan Opera House.

J. S. Bach's Toccata and Fugue in D Minor. Besides conducting in a controversial manner, Stokowski made controversial transcriptions for orchestra of nonorchestral works by a variety of composers, most notably by Bach. Some criticized him for making Bach sound Romantic instead of Baroque, while others supported his effort to bring out the Romantic and mystical essence in Bach's works. Stokowski said that Bach wrote works for the organ that would have sounded better played by a modern orchestra. Since such an orchestra did not exist in Bach's time, Stokowski was simply producing what Bach would have produced using modern resources.

The Toccata and Fugue in D Minor (1703-1707)

Leopold Stokowski. (Library of Congress)

became famous through Stokowski's transcription, especially after he performed it in *Fantasia*. He first performed it in 1925, and he recorded it in 1927. One commentator said that as a result of the transcription, it had become the most famous organ work of all time.

Stokowski said he found cosmic attributes in the Toccata and Fugue in D Minor, and he compared its sound to thunderclouds in the Himalayas.

Stravinsky's The Rite of Spring. Although one of Stokowski's aims was to introduce millions to the standard orchestral repertoire, at the same time he sought to introduce regular concertgoers to the latest experiments in orchestral music. To this end, he programmed many American premieres, including one of Igor Stravinsky's 1913 ballet in 1930. Over the objections of management at the Philadelphia Orchestra, he made the harsh, dissonant music of Stravinsky part of a double bill with an even more experimental work, Arnold Schoenberg's 1924 opera, *Die Glückliche Hand* (*The Hand of Fate*). Despite the fears of management, the sound and light spectacle of the performance, featuring Martha Graham as the lead dancer in Stravinsky's ballet, was a popular success.

Fantasia. One of Stokowski's best-known performances is in this Walt Disney motion picture, in which he not only provides the musical background but also appears in person as the mysterious maestro who shakes hands with Mickey Mouse. Besides the Toccata and Fugue in D Minor by Bach, Stokowski performed a number of other classic works, including a menacing performance of Modest Mussorgsky's *Night on Bald Mountain* (1867); a stormy but sweet version of Ludwig van Beethoven's Symphony No. 6 (1808), also known as the *Pastoral Symphony*; and a performance of *The Sorcerer's Apprentice* (1897) by Paul Dukas. Besides these easily accessible pieces, he also played the difficult *The Rite of Spring* by Stravinsky.

Scheherazade. Stokowski recorded Nikolay Rimsky-Korsakov's 1888 work three times, the first time in 1951. It is the sort of lush romantic work he was drawn to, and it brought out his creative tendencies, producing a performance that some praised as sensual and voluptuous and others condemned as exaggerated and grotesque.

Ives's Symphony No. 4. Stokowski was drawn to the music of Charles Ives, both of them being innovators and interested in transcending everyday reality. Glenn Gould, the noted Canadian pianist, commented that Stokowski was made for such music as the Ives Symphony No. 4. Stokowski pointed to the revolutionary approach to tonality and counterpoint contained in the symphony. It is a complicated work that had remained unperformed for nearly fifty years when Stokowski put on its world premiere at New York's Carnegie Hall on April 26, 1965. He used two associate conductors to help with the complexities of the work.

Musical Legacy

"Tradition is laziness," Stokowski once said. "If something is not right, we must change it." He proceeded to change things, introducing free bowing, rearranging the seating of the musicians, discarding the baton, investigating the latest technology for recording and broadcasting, performing in motion pictures, and introducing the latest experimental music to often-resistant audiences. He also felt free to be almost a cocreator with composers, altering tempi, dynamics, and even notes. He was interested primarily in the spirit of a musical piece, in the emotions it could conjure.

In this approach he was often contrasted with his contemporary, Arturo Toscanini, who was known for his traditionalism and purism as a conductor. Some derided Stokowski for tampering with scores and especially for his transcriptions of the organ works of J. S. Bach. In those transcriptions he was closest to being a cocreator, but he believed he was bringing out what he saw as the essence of Bach's Toccata and Fugue in D Minor and other works.

Part of Stokowski's legacy is a direct result of his Bach transcriptions. Bach's organ works are much better known as a result, even if only in orchestral form. He also helped revive interest in composers such as Ives. Although his introduction of free bowing, his unusual seating rearrangements, and his discarding of the conductor's baton were not widely followed, his general emphasis on bringing out the inner feeling of a musical piece, as opposed to confining himself to tradition and the notes on the page, continues to find adherents.

Sheldon Goldfarb

Further Reading

Chasins, Abram. *Leopold Stokowski: A Profile*. New York: Hawthorn, 1979. A brief but comprehensive account of Stokowski's life, focusing on his personality. Includes illustrations, bibliography, and discography.

Daniel, Oliver. *Stokowski: A Counterpoint of View*. New York: Dodd, Mead, 1982. A massively detailed account of Stokowski's life focusing on the development of his career and on his personal relationships. Includes illustrations, bibliography, and discography.

Robinson, Paul. *Stokowski*. Toronto, Ont.: Lester & Orpen, 1977. Short study of Stokowski's musical approach, criticizing him for deviating from tradition.

Smith, Rollin. *Stokowski and the Organ*. Hillsdale N.Y.: Pendragon, 2004. A study of Stokowski's career as an organist, with a detailed chapter on his orchestral transcriptions of Bach's organ works. Includes illustrations and bibliography.

Smith, William Ander. *The Mystery of Leopold Stokowski*. Rutherford, N.J.: Fairleigh Dickinson University Press, 1990. An analytical study of Stokowski's personality and artistry, assigning him almost magical powers. Includes a detailed, annotated discography.

See also: Gould, Glenn; Ives, Charles; Segovia, Andrés; Smith, Kate; Szigeti, Joseph; Theremin, Léon; Toscanini, Arturo.

Mike Stoller

American rock songwriter and producer

With cowriter Jerry Leiber, Stoller was essential to the birth of rock and roll in the 1950's, writing influential hits for rhythm-and-blues groups and then infusing rhythm and blues into the new rock-and-roll genre. After their initial songwriting success, Leiber and Stoller became producers, further formulating the sound of the first half century of rock.

Born: March 13, 1933; Long Island, New York
Also known as: Michael Stoller (full name)

Principal works

SONGS (as producer; with Jerry Leiber): "She Cried," 1962 (recorded by Jay and the Americans); "Tell Him," 1963 (recorded by the Exciters); "Chapel of Love," 1967 (recorded by the Dixie Cups); "Leader of the Pack," 1967 (recorded by the Shangri-Las); "Stuck in the Middle with You," 1973 (recorded by Stealers Wheel).

SONGS (as songwriter; with Jerry Leiber): "Real Ugly Woman," 1950 (recorded by Jimmy Witherspoon); "Hard Time," 1952 (recorded by Charles Brown); "Hound Dog," 1952 (recorded by Willie Mae Thornton; rerecorded by Elvis Presley, 1956); "K. C. Lovin'," 1952 (also known as "Kansas City"; recorded by Little Willie Littlefield; rerecorded by Wilbert Harrison, 1959); "Black Denim Trousers and Motorcycle Boots," 1955 (recorded by the Cheers); "Riot in Cell Block #9," 1955 (recorded by the Robins); "Smokey Joe's Café," 1955 (recorded by the Robins); "Love Me," 1956 (recorded by Presley); "Ruby Baby," 1956 (recorded by the Drifters); "Jailhouse Rock," 1957 (recorded by Presley); "Loving You," 1957 (recorded by Presley); "Lucky Lips," 1957 (recorded by Ruth Brown; rerecorded by Cliff Richards and the Shadows, 1963); "Searchin'," 1957 (recorded by the Coasters); "Young Blood," 1957 (recorded by the Coasters); "Don't," 1958 (recorded by Presley); "Yakety Yak," 1958 (recorded by the Coasters); "Charlie Brown," 1959 (recorded by the Coasters); "Love Potion No. 9," 1959 (recorded by the Clovers); "Poison Ivy," 1959 (recorded by the Coasters); "There Goes My Baby," 1959 (written with Ben E. King; recorded by the Drifters); "Stand by Me," 1961 (written with and recorded by King); "I'm a Woman," 1962 (recorded by Christine Kittrell; rerecorded by Peggy Lee, 1963); "On Broadway," 1963 (written with Barry Mann and Cynthia Weil; recorded by the Drifters); "Is That All There Is?," 1969 (recorded by Lee).

The Life

Michael Stoller (STOHL-lur) was born and grew up in Long Island. As a teenager, Stoller snuck out to the jazz clubs on Fifty-second Street in New York. In 1949 his father, an engineer, moved to Los Angeles to set up a machine shop that he hoped his son could take over. However, the sixteen-year-old Stoller took after his mother, a model and a Broadway actress. His mother's signed portrait of George Gershwin hung over the piano where Stoller played his first songs.

When a would-be lyricist named Jerry Leiber approached him about writing songs together, Stoller at first was not interested, because he wanted to become a jazz pianist, and he was already playing with some Latin bands in his Mexican American neighborhood. They did began a collaboration, and by 1952 their first big hit, "Kansas City," with its authentic blues sound, was playing on radio. The same year Willie Mae (Big Mama) Thornton had the number-one rhythm-and-blues single with Leiber and Stoller's "Hound Dog." Four years later, Elvis Presley recorded "Hound Dog" and commissioned other Leiber-Stoller compositions for his films.

The Music

Stoller's musical roots were in modern jazz, classical, rhythm and blues, and the Latino rhythms of the Pachuco dances at which Stoller played. He parlayed this diversity into a distinctive sound that would, by the mid-1950's, become known as rock and roll.

"Kansas City." Stoller's ability to create an authentic blues sound is demonstrated in this classic, which blues singers assumed was a traditional blues song. Little Willie Littlefield first recorded it in 1952, changing the title to "K. C. Lovin'." It was a regional hit in Los Angeles, but it did not chart nationally. Wilbert Harrison's 1959 version, however, under the original title, did more than break into the charts: It hit the number-one spot on the *Billboard* Hot 100. Hundreds of recording artists have covered this song, including the Beatles. In 2005 Kansas City, Missouri, adopted the song as its official anthem. Major League Baseball's Kansas City Royals play the Beatles version of the song after every home win and the Harrison version after every loss.

"Jailhouse Rock." This Presley hit for the film of the same name was written by Stoller in simple verse form: There is no chorus, just verses added as needed. The form was perfect for the raw-energy, near-shouting style that Presley wanted. A single guitar chord opens the song, after which the singer crams as many notes as he can into three successive lines, followed by the invitation, "Let's rock!" The lyrics, by Leiber, combined the names of real-life criminals, such as the Purple Gang, with blues singers, such as John Willie "Shifty" Henry, a blues bass player and songwriter who died the year after the song was written.

"There Goes My Baby." This song, cowritten by Drifters lead singer Ben E. King, changed the direction of African American pop music. The first decade of rock-and-roll hits imitated the structure of the rhythm-and-blues songs from which they were derived by using a saxophone solo as a bridge in the middle eight bars between the first verse (or first two) and the last. In 1959 Stoller broke with this tradition by inserting a rich string section to highlight the richness of King's vocals. It spawned a series of imitations and a subgenre of rhythm and blues that became known as sweet soul, with heavily produced sounds and full orchestras. Stoller and King followed with another hit in the same format, with sweet strings, "Stand by Me."

"Is That All There Is?" Rock historian Robert Palmer suggests that this song marks the end of the Golden Age of rock and roll. It was certainly a change of pace for Stoller, both in rhythm and mood. As producers, Leiber and Stoller had been instrumental in altering the direction of Peggy Lee's career. Lee had covered a song Leiber and Stoller wrote for Christine Kittrell, "I'm a Woman," both as the title song of a 1963 album and as a cut on her 1964 album *In Love Again!* It did appear on the charts, but it did not rise higher than number fifty-four. In 1969 Lee asked the duo to produce an album for her, and they contributed several songs, including the title track, to the album *Is That All There Is?*, inspired by Thomas Mann's 1896 story "Disillusionment." Several of the lines in the song, an existentialist monologue, are taken verbatim from Mann's story.

Musical Legacy

Leiber and Stoller influenced nearly every songwriter of the first two decades of rock and roll. The influence was particularly acknowledged by the writers for the Aldon Music label, especially Gerry Goffin, Carole King, Barry Mann, Cynthia Weil, and Lou Adler. The Beatles, who led the British In-

vasion that temporarily stymied the success of the Leiber and Stoller style, nevertheless acknowledged the pair's influence on their own songwriting. The Beatles recorded such Leiber-Stoller tunes as "Kansas City" and "Searchin'," and the Rolling Stones recorded the Leiber-Stoller novelty "Poison Ivy." As producers, Leiber and Stoller were also influential, providing early mentoring for rock producer Phil Spector and putting their mark on the works of various recording artists, even when they performed the music of other composers. The 1995 Broadway revue *Smokey Joe's Cafe* featured Leiber and Stoller's music, and it has played in amateur and commercial productions around the world.

John R. Holmes

Further Reading

Brown, Mick. *Tearing Down the Wall of Sound: The Rise and Fall of Phil Spector*. London: Bloomsbury, 2007. This meticulously documented biography of Spector refers to Stoller throughout, but particularly in the fourth chapter.

Friedlander, Paul. *Rock and Roll: A Social History*. 2d ed. Boulder, Colo.: Westview Press, 2006. This general history of rock and roll, designed as a textbook for popular culture courses, mentions Stoller and his partner, Leiber.

Gillett, Charlie. *The Sound of the City: The Rise of Rock and Roll*. 2d ed. New York: Da Capo Press, 1996. A history of the first decade of rock music, with several references to the songs of Leiber and Stoller.

Green, Joey. *How They Met: Famous Lovers, Partners, Competitors, and Other Legendary Duos*. New York: Black Dog & Leventhal, 2003. This book describes the history-making meeting of Leiber and Stoller.

Lahr, John. *Baby, That Was Rock 'n' Roll: The Legendary Leiber and Stoller*. New York: Harcourt, Brace, Jovanovich, 1978. This is a complete collector's guide to recordings written and produced by Leiber and Stoller, with a detailed history of their collaboration by Robert Palmer.

See also: Gershwin, George; Goffin, Gerry; King, Carole; Lee, Peggy; Leiber, Jerry; McCartney, Sir Paul; Presley, Elvis; Spector, Phil.

Sly Stone

American soul/funk singer, guitarist, and songwriter

Stone pioneered the emerging funk genre during the 1960's and 1970's, and his innovations as a bandleader, composer, instrumentalist, and producer reshaped jazz, rock, and soul.

Born: March 15, 1943; Denton, Texas
Also known as: Sylvester Stewart (birth name)
Member of: Sly and the Family Stone

Principal recordings

ALBUMS (solo): *High on You*, 1975; *The Electric Spanking of War Babies*, 1981 (with Funkadelic).

ALBUMS (with Sly and the Family Stone): *A Whole New Thing*, 1967; *Dance to the Music*, 1968; *Life!*, 1968; *Stand!*, 1969; *Woodstock*, 1970 (with others); *There's a Riot Goin' On*, 1971; *Fresh!*, 1973; *Small Talk*, 1974; *Heard Ya Missed Me, Well I'm Back*, 1976; *Back on the Right Track*, 1979; *Ten Years Too Soon*, 1979; *Ain't but the One Way*, 1983.

The Life

Sly Stone, the second child of K. C. and Alpha Stewart, grew up with four siblings. The Stewart family moved from Texas to the blue-collar city of Vallejo, California, in the late 1940's. Religion and music-making unified the Stewarts, whose children sang in church and on records. A teenage prodigy, Stone sang, played various instruments, and swiftly became a notable figure in Northern California's early 1960's music scene. As a junior-college student, Stone took courses in music composition and theory. San Francisco-based Autumn Records hired Stone as a songwriter and producer when he was in his early twenties, and he oversaw sessions for numerous solo artists and groups that included future Jefferson Airplane members.

By the mid-1960's Stone was also a popular disc jockey on two San Francisco soul stations. During his off hours Stone performed in clubs with embryonic versions of the Family Stone, which led to a recording contract in 1967. Over the next four years Stone made his diverse band—featuring women

and men, African Americans, and whites—a dominant and positive musical and cultural force. By the mid-1970's, however, fame and misfortune overcame Sly and the Family Stone. Stone's problems included bankruptcy, the departure of most of the original band personnel, and incapacitating drug use. His late 1970's comeback efforts were futile, and the last album under his name appeared in the 1980's. With rare exceptions, notably his brief appearance at Sly and the Family Stone's 1993 Rock and Roll Hall of Fame induction, Stone withdrew from public life. At the 2006 Grammy Awards ceremony Stone made a controversial cameo performance, and in 2007 he appeared sporadically on tour with the Family Stone Band, an ensemble featuring several original group members. Despite these encouraging signs, Stone's notorious reputation justifies skepticism about a career resurrection.

The Music

Sly and the Family Stone's original lineup was Stone, his younger brother Freddie (guitarist and singer), his younger sister Rose (keyboardist and singer), Gregg Errico (drummer), Larry Graham (bass guitarist and singer), Jerry Martini (saxophonist), and Cynthia Robinson (trumpeter and singer).

A Whole New Thing. The assertive title of Sly and the Family Stone's first recording struck an innovative chord, but most of its songs were unadventurous compared with the group's subsequent records. Disappointed by low sales, Stone took more chances and scored more hits with *Dance to the Music* and *Life!*, both released in 1968. Still, *A Whole New Thing* displayed musical versatility and creative potential that impressed veteran musicians, notably jazz performers who embraced both Stone and Jimi Hendrix, who also debuted as a bandleader in 1967.

Stand! The fourth Sly and the Family Stone album, *Stand!*, was the ensemble's definitive, most beloved statement. In addition to its title song, *Stand!* boasted "Everyday People," "Sing a Simple Song," and the euphoric "I Want to Take You Higher," the pinnacle of the band's legendary performance at the 1969 Woodstock Festival. Although the positive urgency of these hits dominated *Stand!*, the record also featured edgier compositions that hinted at mounting personal and professional troubles for Stone and his bandmates. These difficulties eroded the Family Stone's cohesion at its wildly popular peak. As the band's focal point, Stone had a penchant for unreliability and substance abuse that was extreme by rock-world standards. Still, even if Stone was not dependable as a concert attraction—he failed to show at so many performances that promoters stopped working with him—his singles with the Family Stone were consistent hits. Whether it was the lilting sweetness of "Hot Fun," the positive pluralism of "Everybody Is a Star," or the hard funk punch of "Thank You Falettinme Be Mice Elf Agin," the top of the charts was Stone territory as the 1960's drew to a close.

There's a Riot Goin' On. Stone's long-awaited album was disturbingly different from its predecessors. Errico left the Family Stone before *There's a Riot Goin' On*'s release, and Stone replaced him with drum machines on most songs, recruited soul legends Bobby Womack and Billy Preston as session players, and took over many instrumental and vocal parts himself. Although *There's a Riot Goin' On* often sounds like an unhappily self-absorbed solo album, it went to the top of the charts and maintains stature as Stone's most complex, critically praised effort. Experimentation in subject matter, instrumentation, and arrangements is evident throughout *There's a Riot Goin' On*, which contains the hits "Runnin' Away" and "Family Affair" along with extended abstract compositions, numerous allusions to Stone's personal and professional struggles, and cryptic references to Africa in its song titles. Although he would record several more albums, some under the Family Stone's name and some as Sly Stone, *There's a Riot Goin' On* was Stone's last major commercial and critical triumph and remains a cornerstone of his career that reflects his artistic and personal strengths and weaknesses.

Musical Legacy

Stone's unrealized potential and unsettling questions about his future do not compromise his galvanic impact on multiple popular music genres. In addition to expanding and often exploding the soul and rock vocabulary, Stone redrew boundaries to include jazz and gospel traditions and ventured into funk territory. Like his similarly talented and troubled peer Jimi Hendrix, Stone was an innovator who influenced other pioneers, notably Miles Davis and other jazz leaders who responded to Stone's creative challenges. His interracial, gender-balanced band not only sounded different but also looked different, with flamboyant self-confidence and positive multicultural energy. Although Stone himself remains elusive, his impact is currently heard in hip-hop sampling of his riffs and rhythms, the swaggering rock of Lenny Kravitz, the endlessly creative genre-transcendent excursions of Prince, and so much more.

Ray Pence

Sly Stone. (AP/Wide World Photos)

Further Reading

Anthony, Dalton. "A.K.A. Sly Stone: The Rise and Fall of Sylvester Stewart." In *Rip It Up: The Black Experience in Rock 'n' Roll*, edited by Kandia Crazy Horse. New York: Palgrave Macmillan, 2004. A brief but passionate analytical reflection on Stone's career, its cultural significance, and its impact on the author.

Crouse, Timothy. "The Struggle for Sly's Soul at the Garden." In *Twenty Years of Rolling Stone: What a Long, Strange Trip It's Been*, edited by Jann S. Wenner. New York: Straight Arrow Press, 1987. Interviews with Stone and his manager illustrate Stone's personal and career problems in detail.

Henderson, David. "Sly and the Family Stone: Black Music Criticism." In *Nineteen Necromancers from Now*, edited by Ishmael Reed. Garden City, N.Y.: Doubleday, 1970. Henderson captures the delirium of Stone's live performances and celebrates their significance in African American culture.

Marcus, Greil. "Sly Stone: The Myth of Staggerlee." In *Mystery Train: Images of America in Rock and Roll*. 4th ed. London: Faber and Faber, 2000. One of the finest rock-and-roll critics investigates Stone's connections to African American oral folk traditions and situates his work in the turmoil of the early 1970's.

Selvin, Joel. *Sly and the Family Stone: An Oral History*. New York: Avon Books, 1998. Indispensable chronicle of Stone's career, based on interviews with dozens of family members, friends, business associates, and musical collaborators.

See also: Davis, Miles; Hendrix, Jimi; Prince.

George Strait

American country singer, songwriter, and guitarist

An uncompromisingly traditional country-music singer, Strait is known for his authentic Texas honky-tonk sound.

Born: May 18, 1952; Poteet, Texas
Also known as: George Harvey Strait (full name)
Member of: The Ace in the Hole Band

Principal recordings

ALBUMS: *Strait Country*, 1981; *Strait from the Heart*, 1982; *Right or Wrong*, 1983; *Does Fort Worth Ever Cross Your Mind?*, 1984; *Something Special*, 1985; *Merry Christmas Strait to You*, 1986; *Number Seven*, 1986; *Ocean Front Property*, 1987; *If You Ain't Lovin' (You Ain't Livin')*, 1988; *Beyond the Blue Neon*, 1989; *Livin' It Up*, 1990; *Chill of an Early Fall*, 1991; *Holding My Own*, 1992; *Pure Country*, 1992; *Easy Come Easy Go*, 1993; *Lead On*, 1994; *Blue Clear Sky*, 1996; *Carrying Your Love with Me*, 1997; *One Step at a Time*, 1998; *Always Never the Same*, 1999; *Merry Christmas Wherever You Are*, 1999; *George Strait*, 2000; *The Road Less Traveled*, 2001; *Honkytonkville*, 2003; *Somewhere Down in Texas*, 2005; *It Just Comes Natural*, 2006; *Troubadour*, 2008.

The Life

George Harvey Strait was born in Poteet, Texas, in 1952 and raised in nearby Pearsall. His father, a middle-school math teacher, and his mother, a homemaker, divorced when Strait was in fourth grade; his mother left her two sons—George and Buddy—to be raised by their father. Strait and his brother spent a lot of time at the family ranch, located in Big Wells, Texas. While Strait admits that his childhood was not particularly musical, he became interested in country music after hearing a Bob Wills record. After graduating from Pearsall High School, Strait married his high-school sweetheart, Norma. In 1970 Strait began attending Southwest Texas State University in San Marcos, only to drop out after three semesters to join the Army.

While stationed in Hawaii, Strait became serious about making music, and he was the lead singer with the Army base's country band. When his stint in the Army was finished, Strait chose country music over a career with the rodeo, roping cattle. With help from the GI Bill, which provided aid to veterans, he went back to college, studying agricultural science. In 1975 he started singing the lead for the Ace in the Hole Band, and he began performing in local nightclubs. The band focused on traditional honky-tonk, dance-hall numbers, and Strait perfected his smooth vocals. Even though by 1979 the country-music scene began imitating the pop sound, Strait was able to land a record deal with MCA.

He began touring and making successful albums, steadfast in respecting the traditional country sound. Although Strait was never interested in fame, after his daughter's fatal car accident in 1986, he withdrew even more from the public eye. He was, however, still touring and making albums. In

1988 Strait set a record in concert-ticket sales, and in 1989 he won the Country Music Association's Entertainer of the Year award. Even though Strait had a record-breaking decade, he forged into the 1990's with his signature singing style and continued to please his loyal fan base. He also starred in the film *Pure Country* (1992). Strait has never made a musical move to Nashville, Tennessee, remaining faithful to his Texas country roots. For relaxation, he retreats to his South Texas ranch for hunting and roping.

The Music

Influenced by Merle Haggard, George Jones, and Bob Wills and His Texas Playboys, Strait was the lead singer in a country band, Ace in the Hole. Even though this band made some records for an independent Dallas-based label, Strait and the band struggled to achieve commercial viability. In 1981, after playing old-style Western swing and honky-tonk in Texas nightclubs for years, Strait finally got his big break. With the support of Erv Woolsey, MCA allowed Strait to record and release one single. His record deal depended on the single's radio play, sales, and general success. MCA released "Unwound," and the up-tempo song was an instant favorite. Shortly thereafter, Strait released his first album, *Strait Country*. With his conservative and traditional country-music sound, he quickly became associated with the new traditionalist movement, and this label has stayed with him throughout his career. While he has never been interested in songwriting, Strait's smooth, talented vocals, cowboy good looks, and knack for selecting good songs have all helped establish his credibility and made him into a country-music superstar.

Strait Country. Recorded at Music City Music Hall in Nashville, Strait's first album, *Strait Country*, included "She's Playing Hell Trying to Get Me to Heaven," "Blame It on Mexico," "If You're Thinking You Want a Stranger (There's One Coming Home)," and "Her Goodbye Hit Me in the Heart." Because the album was varied in its song selections (ranging from ballads to up-tempo dance-hall tunes), Strait's audiences and record executives had a good look at his vocal range and musical ability.

Ocean Front Property. This 1987 album was Strait's first to debut at number one on the *Billboard* country albums chart. "Ocean Front Property," written by Dean Dillon, Hank Cochran, and Royce Porter, sarcastically describes a broken relationship. With its catchy refrain and inventive lyrics, the title track quickly hit number one. This trend continued, as two other singles, "All My Ex's Live in Texas" and "Am I Blue," both vaulted to number one as well. With these tracks exhibiting the Texas swing and the traditional dance-hall sound, the album unifies the older structures successfully with Strait's crooning vocals. This was also the first album Strait recorded with his Ace in the Hole Band, which performed on the tracks "Hot Burning Flames" and "You Can't Buy Your Way Out of the Blues."

Blue Clear Sky. This 1996 album not only reaffirmed Strait's success in the music industry but also highlighted his consistency in the country-music business. Again, the title track reached number-one status, and once more, Strait had incorporated traditional country sounds into pop-country tunes. With tracks such as "I Can Still Make Cheyenne," a slower, country ballad tracing the

George Strait. (AP/Wide World Photos)

steps of an on-the-road cowboy, and "Do the Right Thing," an up-tempo number asking a lover to make a choice, Strait created an album that caters to all aspects of his musical career. He infused these tracks with the immediately recognizable steel guitar, traditional shuffle rhythms, and Texas honky-tonk. *Blue Clear Sky* was awarded the Country Music Association's Album of the Year award.

Musical Legacy

Strait was inducted into the Country Music Hall of Fame in 2006, and this honor was preceded by other accolades. The third-biggest-selling country artist ever, Strait has proven himself to be an industry favorite. He chooses his song material meticulously, and his choices result in solid country hits that incorporate traditional country-music sounds, rhythms, and ideals with the fast-moving and ever-changing country-music industry.

April L. Prince

Further Reading

Bego, Mark. *The Story of Country's Living Legend: George Strait*. New York: Kensington Books, 1997. This biography offers a comprehensive look at Strait's life and career, and it includes a discography.

Cabal, Ron. *A Honky-Tonk Odyssey: My Eight Years with George Strait*. Austin, Tex.: M. Cabal, 2003. The original lead guitarist for the Ace in the Hole Band, Cabal offers a firsthand look at the rise of the country-music superstar.

Emery, Ralph. *Fifty Years Down a Country Road*. New York: HarperCollins, 2000. Drawing on interviews from his syndicated radio show and his television shows, Emery couples his own experiences with biographical snippets to effectively illuminate Strait's career and his position in country music.

Kingsbury, Paul. *The Grand Ole Opry History of Country Music: Seventy Years of the Songs, the Stars, and the Stories*. New York: Villard Press, 1995. This general introduction to the world of country music situates Strait within the traditional resurgence in country music, while simultaneously offering a brief biography.

Sgammato, Jo. *Keepin' It Country: The George Strait Story*. New York: Ballantine Books, 1998. This biography considers the appeal of Strait, his au-

thenticity within the industry, and his ability to balance the old country with the new.

See also: Brooks, Garth; Frizzell, Lefty; Haggard, Merle; Jones, George; Milsap, Ronnie.

Richard Strauss
German classical composer

Strauss transformed symphonic and operatic traditions, demonstrating that the mundane activities of everyday people were worthy subjects for operas and programmatic pieces.

Born: June 11, 1864; Munich, Germany
Died: September 8, 1949; Garmisch-Partenkirchen, Germany
Also known as: Richard Georg Strauss (full name)

Principal works

CHAMBER WORKS: Violin Concerto in D Minor, Op. 8, 1882; Cello Sonata in F Major, Op. 6, 1883; Horn Concerto No. 1 in E-flat Major, Op. 11, 1884; Violin Sonata in E-flat Major, Op. 18, 1888; *Hochzeitspräludium*, 1924; Horn Concerto No. 2 in E-flat Major, Op. 132, 1942; *Metamorphosen*, 1946 (for twenty-three solo strings); Oboe Concerto in D Major, Op. 144, 1946; *Allegretto in E*, 1948 (for violin and piano).

OPERAS (music): *Guntram*, 1894 (libretto by Strauss); *Feuersnot, Op. 50*, 1901 (libretto by Ernst von Wolzogen); *Salome*, Op. 54, 1905 (libretto by Strauss; based on the play by Oscar Wilde); *Elektra*, Op. 58, 1909 (libretto by Hugo von Hofmannsthal); *Der Rosenkavalier*, Op. 59, 1911 (*The Knight of the Rose*; libretto by Hofmannsthal); *Ariadne auf Naxos*, Op. 60-II, 1916 (libretto by Hofmannsthal); *Die Frau ohne Schatten*, Op. 65, 1918 (*The Woman Without a Shadow*; libretto by Hofmannsthal); *Intermezzo*, Op. 72, 1924 (libretto by Strauss); *Die Ägptische Helena*, Op. 75, 1928 (*The Egyptian Helen*; libretto by Hofmannsthal); *Arabella*, Op. 79, 1933 (libretto by Hofmannsthal); *Daphne*, Op. 82, 1938 (libretto by Joseph Gregor); *Capriccio*,

Op. 85, 1942 (libretto by Strauss and Clemens Krauss).

ORCHESTRAL WORKS: Symphony in D Minor, 1880; Serenade in E-Flat, Op. 7, 1882 (for thirteen wind instruments); Suite in B-flat Major, Op. 4, 1884 (for thirteen wind instruments); *Don Juan*, Op. 20, 1889; *Burleske in D Minor*, Op. 85, 1890 (for piano and orchestra); *Macbeth*, Op. 23, 1890; *Tod und Verklärung*, Op. 24, 1890 (*Death and Transfiguration*); *Also sprach Zarathustra*, Op. 30, 1896 (*Thus Spoke Zoroaster*; better known as *Also sprach Zarathustra*); *Till Eulenspiegels lustige Streiche*, Op. 28, 1896 (*Till Eulenspiegel's Merry Pranks*); *Don Quixote*, Op. 35, 1898 (for cello and orchestra); *Ein Heldenleben*, Op. 40, 1899 (*A Hero's Life*); *Sinfonia Domestica*, Op. 53, 1904; *Eine Alpensinfonie*, Op. 64, 1915 (*An Alpine Symphony*); *Der Bürger als Edelmann*, Op. 60-IIIa, 1920; *Tanzsuite*, Op. 107, 1923; *Divertimento*, Op. 86, 1943.

VOCAL WORKS: Six Songs, Op. 17, 1888; Four Songs, Op. 27, 1894; *Enoch Arden*, Op. 38, 1897 (for voice and piano); Five Songs, Op. 48, 1900; Six Songs, Op. 56, 1906; *Fünf kleine Lieder*, Op. 69, 1918 (*Five Little Songs*); *Acht Gedichte aus Letzte Blätter*, Op. 10, 1940 (*Eight Poems from Letzte Blätter*); *Vier letzte Lieder*, 1950 (*Four Last Songs*).

The Life

Richard Georg Strauss (strows) was born June 11, 1864, to Franz and Josepha Strauss in Munich. His father was first horn player for the Munich Court Orchestra, and he was director of the Wilde Gung'l ensemble. Strauss began piano lessons at age four and then violin lessons with Benno Walther at age seven. He entered Ludwig Grammar School in 1874. In 1875 he studied piano with Carl Niest, and he began composition studies with Friedrich Wilhelm Meyer. By age eighteen, he had already published several compositions.

Strauss attended Ludwig-Maximillian University from 1882 to 1883, but he left to focus on his musical career. When Hans von Bülow brought the Meiningen Orchestra to Munich in November, 1884, he asked Strauss conduct his Suite in B-flat Major for woodwinds, marking his debut as a conductor. In 1885 Strauss became Bülow's conducting assistant in Meiningen. Strauss later took over as head conductor of the orchestra.

At Meiningen, through his friendship with the violinist Alexander Ritter, Strauss studied the operas of Richard Wagner, the symphonic poems of Franz Liszt, and the symphonies of Johannes Brahms. These composers would have a lasting influence upon Strauss throughout his compositional career.

In 1886 he accepted the post of assistant conductor at the Court Theater of Munich under Hermann Levi and Franz Fischer. Strauss traveled throughout Italy in the summer before starting his new position. When Strauss started his assistant conducting position in Munich, however, he stagnated in the theater's rigid hierarchy, although that was somewhat relieved by his busy conducting schedule in other German cities. He frequently met with Ritter, Friedrich Rösch, Anton Seidl, and Ludwig Thuille to discuss recent music and the writings of Arthur Schopenhauer and Friedrich Nietzsche. Completely turning to programmatic music, Strauss composed his first cycle of tone poems in 1888 and 1889.

In 1889 Strauss became the music director in Weimar, working for the Grand Duke Saxe-Weimar-Eisenach. During this time, he made Weimar a center for Wagner's operas by establishing a branch of the Wagner Society. In 1891 and 1892, Strauss became ill, and he recuperated in Egypt and Greece. He debuted his first opera, *Guntram*, in 1894 in Weimar. After news of his appointment as music director of the Munich Court Opera, Strauss married the singer Pauline de Ahna in September. Starting as director of the Munich Court Opera in 1895, Strauss staged *Guntram* again, but it failed, having only one performance. His son Franz was born in Munich in April of 1897.

In 1898 Strauss completed the second cycle of tone poems. In the same year, he left Munich to direct the Berlin Court Opera. He helped to establish the German Composers' League to protect composers' copyrights in 1903. He also edited the journal *Die Musik*; he was president of the General German Music Association; and he conducted the Berliner Tonkünstler Orchestra. From 1902 to 1904, he conducted at various cities in North America.

In the twentieth century, Strauss mainly composed operas. Premiering at the Dresden Royal Op-

Richard Strauss. (Library of Congress)

man leader Adolf Hitler. Strauss discontinued his work with the writer Stephan Zweig because he was Jewish. Though Strauss complained about the Nazis, he did compose music for party rallies and events. Strauss also used his contacts in the Nazi government to protect his Jewish daughter-in-law from arrest.

In 1936 Strauss worked with young theater historian Joseph Gregor on new librettos. When war raged throughout Europe in 1944, the Nazis canceled operatic and concert performances, and Strauss withdrew to his summer home in Garmisch. The Allied armies spared his home, and the American oboist John de Lancie visited the composer.

With Germany and Austria in utter disarray, Strauss moved to Zurich, Switzerland, where he sold many of his manuscripts and sketchbooks to raise money. He finally returned to his home in Garmisch in May, 1949. His last public appearance as a conductor was at the Prinzregententheater in Munich on June 10, 1949, in which he led the orchestra in act 2 of *Der Rosenkavalier*. On August 15, 1949, he suffered a heart attack, and on September 8, 1949, he died of kidney failure.

The Music

Strauss's compositional career was long and dynamic. He focused upon metaphysical ideals derived from philosophy and literature, while at the same time he depicted mundane activity. Strauss's music is characterized by explicit and virtuosic orchestral writing, such as having instruments mimic animals or sexual activities. In his operas, he emulated the declamation of speech as close as possible, while he accompanied the voice with a large and expressive orchestra. In his music, Strauss juxtaposed unconventional writing with wonderfully lyrical melodies or banal dance tunes, and he played with conventional harmonic writing, dramatically shifting keys or superimposing tonalities. This combination of virtuosic orchestration and unconventional harmonies almost marks Strauss as part of the Expressionist movement. Nevertheless, Strauss remained firmly in the mainstream, stepping back from the musical avant-garde. While Strauss seemed to conduct and compose as a detached craftsman, churning out one work after the next, rarely revising, his tireless work as a com-

era House, *Feuersnot* was a one-act opera in which Strauss found his own voice in the operatic world. Later, Strauss made headlines throughout Europe with the 1905 premiere of his opera *Salome* in Dresden. In 1906 he began his working relationship with the playwright Hugo von Hofmannsthal on the opera *Elektra*.

After World War I, Strauss became codirector of the Vienna Opera in 1919. The following year, Strauss helped start the Salzburg Mozart Festival. After writing his own libretto to *Intermezzo*, he worked with Hofmannsthal again on two more operas. In 1924, after difficulties with his codirector, Franz Schalk, Strauss left the Vienna Opera to pursue other conducting engagements. He guest-conducted at various Strauss festivals throughout Europe. He also performed again in the United States and South America.

When the Nazi Party came to power in 1933, Strauss was appointed as the president of Reichmusikkammer (Reich Music Chamber) by the Ger-

poser and conductor did advance modern musical culture.

Early Works. Strauss began his long career as a composer under the direct supervision of his father, who detested the music of Wagner and who focused his son's attention on traditional composers such as Wolfgang Amadeus Mozart and Felix Mendelssohn. The young Strauss composed in small genres (solo piano, lieder, and chamber), so that his family members could perform them. With the help of his teacher Meyer, Strauss wrote his first large-scale works: Symphony in D Minor, Serenade in E-Flat, Op. 7, Violin concerto in D Minor, Op. 8, and Horn Concerto No. 1 in E-flat Major.

In Meiningen, when Strauss was no longer under the shadow of his father, he studied the works of Brahms and Wagner. In 1886 Strauss composed *Burleske in D Minor* for piano and orchestra, which marked the emergence of his distinctive style. He combined the idiomatic piano writing of Brahms, while quoting from the operas of Wagner. A continual theme in Strauss's music is his lighthearted mocking of current debates and even his own music.

Don Juan, Op. 20. Though his tone poem *Macbeth* was written earlier (but performed later), it was *Don Juan* that marked Strauss as a leader of the modernist movement. Strauss labeled his works tone poems to distinguish them from Liszt's work. Strauss was guided by a poetic idea (in this case, a poem by Nikolaus Lenau) that shaped and transformed the composition. He used the extreme ranges of the orchestra in a virtuosic manner, as he coupled heroic horn calls (to represent Don Juan's sexual conquest) with hurried passages for strings and woodwinds (to represent Don Juan scurrying off to the next lady).

Also sprach Zarathustra. This tone poem, part of his second cycle, is based on the philosophical work by Nietzsche, a writer Strauss studied and greatly admired. The work depicts eight episodes in the life of Nietzsche's prophet, Zarathustra, who is filled with disgust toward humanity. The opening, prominently used in the film *2001: A Space Odyssey* (1968), represents the sunrise, and Zarathustra's desire to help humanity transcends its limiting nature. Strauss used conflicting key areas (B versus C, for example) and various leitmotifs to represent Zarathustra's struggles. Another theme that runs

throughout this work is the falsity of established religions, and Strauss quotes from the Mass the "Credo in unum deum" in a cold and distant manner to represent humanity's blind faith.

The unique orchestral effects, juxtaposition of themes, and the philosophical narrative left some critics claiming the program was too hard for audience members to grasp. However, other critics praised Strauss's work, saying it was in line with the symphonic works of Ludwig van Beethoven.

Salome. Strauss's first opera, *Guntram*, was a complete failure, and *Feuersnot* received good reviews but did not travel outside of Germany. It was *Salome* that earned Strauss recognition as an opera composer and popularity throughout Europe. In *Feuersnot* and *Salome*, Strauss sidestepped the shadow of Wagner, focusing on compact, one-act operas. When Strauss worked in Berlin, he saw director Max Reinhardt's production of Oscar Wilde's play about Salome dancing for King Herod in pursuit of the head of John the Baptist. Cutting a little of the dialogue, Strauss directly set the play to music. The opera's suggestions of incest and its depiction of necrophilia (Salome kisses and dances with the severed head) along with Strauss's gritty musical setting created some notoriety. The opera premiered in Dresden in 1905, and, though banned or censored in some cities, the opera spread throughout Germany and then the rest of Europe.

Der Rosenkavalier. Hofmannsthal and Strauss began a long career as librettist and composer of operas with *Elektra*. In 1909 they started working on *Der Rosenkavalier*, and it was completed and staged at Dresden in January, 1911. Whereas *Elektra*, his first project with Strauss, was dark and tragic, Hofmannsthal crafted this libretto based on the eighteenth century plays of Molière and Pierre de Beaumarchais and on a series of paintings, *Marriage à la Mode*, by William Hogarth. In the earlier tone poems and operas, Strauss moved away from conventional musical idioms, depicting grotesque sexual or violent acts, which makes the plot and music of *Der Rosenkavalier* appear anachronistic. Strauss based his music on the operas of Mozart and the pleasant waltzes of Johann Strauss, Jr. Although Strauss and Hofmannsthal included in the opera themes of transformation and the passage of time, critics, slightly taken aback, called it "banal" and full of "low-class" humor. Nevertheless, the opera was widely popular with audience members. In 1926 Strauss and Hofmannsthal adapted the opera for a silent film version.

Intermezzo. After the failure of Hofmannsthal and Strauss's opera *Die Frau ohne Schatten* at the Vienna Opera, Strauss wrote his own libretto to the opera *Intermezzo*. This work debuted at the Dresden Opera in November,1924. Like the tone poem *Sinfonia Domestica*, Strauss based the libretto on his personal life and on conversations with his wife. Strauss had the characters declaim the text (even spoken dialogue at points) with little lyrical writing, used only when his wife flirts with other men. The small orchestra sonically represents the psychology and the feelings of each character. With its subject matter and musical setting, *Intermezzo* influenced the development of the genre of Zeitoper, a style of opera that focused on relevant, everyday subjects that would appeal to a diverse audience.

Metamorphosen. With World War II raging throughout Europe, Strauss retreated to his home in Garmisch, where he kept composing. Strauss called *Metamorphosen* a study for twenty-three solo strings, and he based it on the poem "Niemand wird sich selber kennen" ("No One Can Know Himself") by Johann Wolfgang von Goethe. The piece was designed as a variation on a lament that transforms itself to find meaning in the chaos of war. Strauss quoted the funeral march from Beethoven's 1805 Symphony No. 3 (*Eroica*) near the end to mark the death of the ideals of German culture.

Musical Legacy

Strauss created music that bridged the late Romantic movement of the nineteenth century to the modernist era of the twentieth century. Although he was viewed as an iconoclast who pushed the boundaries of classical conventions, his music was popular during his lifetime within small artistic circles as well as with large audiences. His expansion of the orchestral and harmonic language had a lasting influence on experimental composers in the twentieth century.

Eric Olds Schneeman

Further Reading

DelMar, Norman. *Richard Strauss: A Critical Commentary on His Life and Works.* Ithaca, N.Y.: Cornell University Press, 1986. This three-volume work covers both the life of the composer and an analysis of his works. Illustrations, bibliography.

Gilliam, Bryan. *The Life of Richard Strauss.* Cambridge, England: Cambridge University Press, 1999. A foremost scholar on Strauss provides a wonderfully concise yet in-depth discussion of the composer's life and his works. Illustrations, bibliography.

Potter, Pamela. "Strauss and the National Socialists: The Debate and Its Relevance." In *Richard Strauss: New Perspectives on the Composer and His Works*, edited by Bryan Gilliam. Durham, N.C.: Duke University Press, 1992. This probing essay examines the controversy still surrounding Strauss's involvement with the Third Reich. Musical examples, bibliography.

Wilhelm, Kurt. *Richard Strauss: An Intimate Portrait.* Translated by Mary Whittall. New York: Thames & Hudson, 1989. Full of photographs of the composer and his family, this books contains lighthearted anecdotes about the day-to-day activities of his life.

Youmans, Charles. *Richard Strauss's Orchestral Music and the German Intellectual Tradition: The Philosophical Roots of Musical Modernism.* Bloomington: Indiana University Press, 2005. This resource attempts to penetrate the aesthetic and philosophical background of Strauss's early tone poems and to dispel the myth of Strauss's detachment from his work. Music examples.

See also: Anderson, Marian; Bartók, Béla; Beecham, Sir Thomas; Britten, Benjamin; Carter, Elliott; Chung, Kyung-Wha; Elgar, Sir Edward; Fischer-Dieskau, Dietrich; Flagstad, Kirsten; Golijov, Osvaldo; Gould, Glenn; Heifetz, Jascha; Hindemith, Paul; Holst, Gustav; Honegger, Arthur; Ives, Charles; Karajan, Herbert von; Korngold, Erich Wolfgang; Lehmann, Lotte; Menotti, Gian Carlo; Newman, Alfred; Nielsen, Carl; Norman, Jessye; Pavarotti, Luciano; Price, Leontyne; Puccini, Giacomo; Respighi, Ottorino; Rózsa, Miklós; Schnabel, Artur; Scriabin, Aleksandr; Sibelius, Jean; Solti, Sir Georg; Sousa, John Philip; Steiner, Max; Stokowski, Leopold; Szell, George; Tiomkin, Dimitri; Toscanini, Arturo; Waxman, Franz.

Igor Stravinsky

Russian classical composer

A prolific composer who dominated the international musical scene throughout his life, Stravinsky developed a personal compositional identity, which appropriated influences ranging from nationalism to primitivism and from neoclassicism to serialism.

Born: June 17, 1882; Oranienbaum (now Lomonosov), Russia
Died: April 6, 1971; New York, New York
Also known as: Igor Fyodorovich Stravinsky (full name)

Principal works

BALLETS (music): *L'Oiseau de feu*, 1910 (*The Firebird*); *Petrushka*, 1911, revised 1947; *Le Sacre du printemps*, 1913, revised 1947 (*The Rite of Spring*); *Pulcinella*, 1920, revised 1965; *Les Noces*, 1923 (*The Wedding*); *Apollon musagète*, 1928 (revised 1947); *Le Baiser de la fée*, 1928 (*The Fairy's Kiss*); *Jeu de cartes*, 1936 (*Card Game*); *Orpheus*, 1947; *Agon*, 1953.

CHAMBER WORKS: Three Pieces, 1914, revised 1918 (for string quartet); *Ragtime*, 1918 (for eleven instruments); *Histoire du soldat*, 1918 (*A Soldier's Tale*; libretto by C. F. Ramuz); *Octet*, 1923, revised 1952 (for wind instruments); Concerto in D, 1946 (for strings); *Cantata*, 1952; *In Memoriam Dylan Thomas*, 1954.

CHORAL WORKS: *King of the Stars*, 1939; *Mass*, 1948 (for chorus and double wind quintet); *Canticum Sacrum*, 1956.

OPERAS (music): *Renard*, 1916; *Oedipus Rex*, 1927, revised 1948; *The Rake's Progress*, 1951 (libretto by W. H. Auden and Chester Kallman).

ORCHESTRAL WORKS: *Fireworks, Fantasy*, Op. 4, 1908, revised 1930; *Scherzo fantastique*, Op. 3, 1908, revised 1930; *Chant du rossignol*, 1917 (*The Song of the Nightingale*); Concerto for Piano and Wind Instruments, 1924, revised 1950; *Capriccio*, 1929, revised 1949 (for piano and orchestra); *Symphony of Psalms*, 1930, revised 1948 (for chorus and orchestra); Violin Concerto in D Major, 1931; Concerto for Chamber Orchestra in E-flat Major, 1938; Symphony in C, 1940; *Danses concertantes*, 1942 (for chamber orchestra); *Ode, Elegiacal Chant*, 1943; *Circus Polka (For a Young Elephant)*, 1944; *Ebony Concerto*, 1945 (for clarinet and jazz band); *Scherzo à la Russe*, 1945; Symphony in Three Movements, 1945.

PIANO WORKS: Five Easy Pieces for Piano, 1917; *Piano-Rag-Music*, 1919; *Tango*, 1940.

The Life

The third of four boys born to Fyodor Ignat'yevich Stravinsky (a successful operatic bass) and Anna Kholodovsky, Igor Fyodorovich Stravinsky (EE-gohr strah-VIHN-skee) grew up in St. Petersburg. After his formative years at Gurevich School, Stravinsky briefly studied law before turning exclusively to music. He had studied piano, harmony, and counterpoint since the age of nine, and by his teens he had composed short pieces for piano. In 1902 he met Nikolay Rimsky-Korsakov, who became Stravinsky's main teacher and mentor (until Rimsky-Korsakov's death in 1908) and who helped Stravinsky get his early pieces premiered. Composed for the wedding of Rimsky-Korsakov's daughter, *Fireworks, Fantasy* caught the attention of Sergei Diaghilev, impresario, founder of the Ballets Russes, and cultural ambassador of Russian art to Paris, who offered the young composer his first major commission for *The Firebird*, a ballet based on a Russian fairy tale. The success of *The Firebird* catapulted Stravinsky to notoriety, placing him in the artistic elite.

The naive Russian émigré quickly transformed into the cosmopolitan European, and soon he moved his family out of Russia. Stravinsky had married his first cousin Katerina Nossenko in 1905, and they had two sons and two daughters. In 1910 the Stravinskys moved to Switzerland, living in Clarens and Lausanne, until 1920.

Stravinsky's second ballet, *Petrushka*, was premiered by the Ballets Russes in 1911. The following summer, Stravinsky began work on *The Rite of Spring*. The premiere of *The Rite of Spring* in Paris on May 29, 1913, made history as one of the most scandalous ever. The audience riot was a reaction to the subject matter and to the choreography as much as to the music. Ultimately, the scandal did not harm the work's success; in fact, one might argue that it was the work's most potent publicity.

Stravinsky's brief trip to Russia in July, 1914, to collect folk material for his next project, *The Wedding*, was to be his last visit to his homeland for almost fifty years. The Russian border was closed shortly after, because of the outbreak of World War I. Living in Switzerland was an obvious choice for the Stravinskys at that time, although the composer had problems of income. With the assistance of his friends, such as conductors Thomas Beecham and Ernest Ansermet, Stravinsky weathered the rough economic times and managed to compose several successful works, notably *A Soldier's Tale*. During this period he also had his conducting debut in Geneva, an activity upon which he would rely for income for the rest of his life.

Following the end of the war, Stravinsky moved his family to France in 1920, where he would stay until the brink of the next world war in 1939. They moved frequently within the country until settling in Paris in 1934. After the Russian revolution, he managed to get his mother out of Russia, and she joined the Stravinskys in France. With several family members depending on him for income, he became more active in conducting and in performing his own works on the piano. The years 1938 and 1939 were devastating for the composer: His wife and daughter Ludmila died of tuberculosis, which had also infected him, and later his mother died.

Frustrated because of his failure to be elected to the French Academy, sensing the outbreak of another world war, and suffering the loss of half his family, Stravinsky decided to move to the United States, where his fame was growing. With him came Vera de Bosset, the wife of Diaghilev's collaborator Serge Sudeikin, with whom Stravinsky had been having an affair since the early 1920's. They arrived in New York on September 30, 1939, and Stravinsky presented the Norton Lectures at Harvard (later published as *Poetics of Music: In the Form of Six Lessons*) and went on a brief conducting tour before finally settling down in Hollywood. Stravinsky and Vera were married in 1940, and they became American citizens in 1945.

In the United States, Stravinsky proved to be proficient in securing commissions, notably from the Chicago Symphony for the Symphony in C (composed in part before he moved to the United States) and the New York Philharmonic for the Symphony in Three Movements. He did have some failed attempts at composing motion-picture scores. Through an exclusive publishing contract with Boosey & Hawkes, he revised many of his earlier scores. He also wrote two pieces without a commission: his *Mass* and his first opera in English, *The Rake's Progress*, on a libretto by W. H. Auden.

In 1947 Stravinsky met Robert Craft, a young conductor who became his protégé and musical assistant. They coauthored several books, and Craft conducted some works and rehearsed others while Stravinsky was busy conducting in the United States and overseas. It was through Craft that Stravinsky was exposed to serial music, which was to be the composer's next stylistic phase.

Igor Stravinsky. (Library of Congress)

In 1962 the octogenarian Stravinsky received the U.S. State Department Medal and dined in the White House with President John F. Kennedy. In addition, the composer took his first trip to Russia after fifty years to conduct his music, which was accepted favorably, a validation that was important to him. By 1969 the composer's health had declined considerably, and the Stravinskys moved to New York, where he died in April, 1971. He was buried in Venice, on the island of San Michele.

The Music

Stravinsky's output can be classified in three major stylistic categories, generally chronological, but sometimes slightly overlapping: the Russian works, the neoclassical works, and the serial works.

The Russian Works. Centered around the three ballets, this group of works includes several dramatic pieces, mostly based on Russian folk themes. There is significant stylistic growth from one work to another.

The Firebird. Rimsky-Korsakov's influence is abundant in 1910, notably in the use of Russian thematic material and the octatonic scale. However, it's also clear that Stravinsky is influenced by the French Impressionist composers in his use of orchestral color and extended instrumental techniques.

Petrushka. Stravinsky's second project is also inspired by Russian folk material. It was originally conceived for piano and orchestra, and at Diaghilev's suggestion it was transformed into a ballet. Based on the tale of a puppet that comes to life, the score is more angular, daring, and original musically than *The Firebird*, featuring extended use of bitonality.

The Rite of Spring. A definite breakthrough in music history, this depiction of pagan Russia is known for its additive rhythms, driving pulsations, dissonant polytonal harmony, and larger-than-life treatment of the orchestra. Despite the embarrassing similarities between the themes in *The Rite of Spring* and a collection of Russian folk tunes revealed by musicologist Richard Taruskin in his 1996 book, the impact and inventiveness of this masterpiece remain unblemished.

A Soldier's Tale. This was conceived in 1918 by Stravinsky and writer C. F. Ramuz as a portable chamber dramatic work for three actors, a dancer, and seven musicians that could be taken on the road on a small budget. Skillfully scored for lean forces, with constantly changing meters and references to dance forms, this work foreshadows Stravinsky's later style.

The Wedding. A 1923 vocal dramatic work depicting a Russian wedding ritual, this work is related closely to *The Rite of Spring* in its conception. The score is extremely percussive, written for the unusual combination of vocal soloists, chorus, four pianos, and percussion, and it explores the voices at the limit of their expressive power.

The Neoclassical Works. Stravinsky's fresh look into older styles is an expansion of his collage approach, in the sense that older styles are revisited as found objects and resynthesized in a different context. Along with a rethinking of classical and Baroque formal structures, smaller orchestral forces, more winds, and increased choral forces are characteristics of this style.

Pulcinella. Commissioned by Diaghilev, this ballet is Stravinsky's first intentional neoclassical work, and it is based on an eighteenth century commedia dell'arte work by Giovanni Pergolesi. Stravinsky borrows thematic and textural elements, combining them with his signature angular rhythms, harmonies, and cadences and scoring them for a modern chamber orchestra and vocal soloists.

Symphony of Psalms. Uninterested in religion in his youth, Stravinsky found himself returning to the Orthodox faith in 1926. *Symphony of Psalms* employs choral and orchestral forces to set Psalms in Latin, mostly in octatonic and (church) modal pitch formations with extended fugato sections reflecting liturgical music of the Renaissance and Baroque.

The Serial Works. Stravinsky eventually (after Arnold Schoenberg's death in 1951) found ways of appropriating serial procedures in his style without relinquishing any of his personal traits. At first he worked with less-than-twelve-tone sets, in chamber pieces such as the *Cantata*, *A Soldier's Tale*, and notably in *In Memoriam Dylan Thomas*.

Canticum Sacrum. Stravinsky's first piece to contain an entire movement based on a tone row was composed for and dedicated to the city of Venice, intended for performance in Saint Mark's Cathedral. It is scored for tenor, baritone, chorus, orchestra, and organ.

Agon. Stravinsky's third collaboration (after *Apollon Musagète* and *Orpheus*) with choreographer George Balanchine is a plotless, abstract musical contest for eight dancers. The pitch material moves gradually from diatonic passages to increasingly serially treated ones, consolidating in a single piece a catalog of the composer's devices used throughout his career.

Musical Legacy

Amid a circle of innovative artists in their own disciplines—painter Pablo Picasso, filmmaker Jean Cocteau, writers Vladimir Nabokov and Auden—Stravinsky personified the image of the twentieth century composer, not only with his music but also with his image, taste, and personality. Aware of his own legacy and adept at managing his career, he projected a cosmopolitan air, and, unlike most of his colleagues, he gained near celebrity status.

Stravinsky was a master of style in his music. His treatment of orchestral color and sonority was innovative and fresh, always contextually appropriate. His materials, whether borrowed or invented, were assembled with precision and with regard to proportion. His uses of ostinatos, polytonality, motivic permutations, additive rhythmic cells, and metric displacement were extensively imitated by composers who followed him.

His greatest accomplishment was his ability to maneuver through the external and internal stylistic influences and shifts, without losing hold of his personal voice, which remained instantly recognizable in all of his works. He remained relevant and progressive stylistically, and his music never lost popularity throughout his life.

Yiorgos Vassilandonakis

Further Reading

Andriessen, Louis, and Elmer Schoenberg. *The Apollonian Clockwork: On Stravinsky.* New York: Oxford University Press, 1989. A fresh approach to Stravinsky's music that attempts to unite his different stylistic periods and distill the composer's style. Several works are analyzed and compared.

Craft, Robert. *Down a Path of Wonder: Memoirs of Stravinsky, Schoenberg, and Other Cultural Figures.*

London: Naxos Books, 2006. From an objective and insightful writer on Stravinsky, this book concentrates on the Los Angeles years.

Stravinsky, Igor. *An Autobiography.* New York: W. W. Norton, 1998. The composer reveals facts and anecdotes about the first half of his life (originally written in 1934) with his usual flair, as they relate to music, art, and social life, giving the reader insight into Stravinsky's mind and personality.

_____. *Poetics of Music: In the Form of Six Lessons.* Cambridge, Mass.: Harvard University Press, 1993. Based on his Norton Lectures at Harvard, this book is Stravinsky's personal artistic credo, concerned with technical and philosophical matters as they relate to his music.

Taruskin, Richard. *Stravinsky and the Russian Traditions: A Biography of the Works Through Mavra.* Berkeley: University of California Press, 1996. This seminal analytical work in understanding Stravinsky and the emergence of his style offers an in-depth study of Stravinsky's style within the context of the Russian tradition in which he was nurtured. Contains a groundbreaking analysis of *The Rite of Spring* and shines a new light on Stravinsky with the author's unique perspective of Russian culture.

See also: Babbitt, Milton; Barber, Samuel; Beach, Amy; Beecham, Sir Thomas; Berg, Alban; Berio, Luciano; Boulanger, Nadia; Carter, Elliott; Chávez, Carlos; Copland, Aaron; Debussy, Claude; Holst, Gustav; Honegger, Arthur; Ives, Charles; Lucier, Alvin; Mahler, Gustav; Martin, Frank; Martinů, Bohuslav; Nancarrow, Conlon; Nielsen, Carl; Norman, Jessye; Orff, Carl; Piazzolla, Astor; Poulenc, Francis; Prokofiev, Sergei; Puccini, Giacomo; Ravel, Maurice; Reich, Steve; Rota, Nino; Rózsa, Miklós; Rubinstein, Artur; Schnittke, Alfred; Schoenberg, Arnold; Scriabin, Aleksandr; Serkin, Rudolf; Sibelius, Jean; Stokowski, Leopold; Szigeti, Joseph; Szymanowski, Karol; Tavener, Sir John; Thomas, Michael Tilson; Villa-Lobos, Heitor; Webern, Anton von.